14,000 QUIPS & QUOTES

For Speakers, Writers, Editors, Preachers, and Teachers

E. C. McKENZIE

BAKER BOOK HOUSE
Grand Rapids, Michigan 49516

Contents

Contents

Contents

Contents

Contents

Contents

Contents

Contents

A

Ability
Accidents
Accidents–Automobile
Achievement
Action
Actors
Actresses
Adolescence
Adversity
Advertising
Advice
Advice–Free

Age
Agreement
Air Age
Alarm Clocks
Alcoholics
Alibis
Alimony
Ambition
America
Americans
Ancestors
Anger

Animals
Antiques
Appearance
Applause
Appreciation
Arguments
Atheists
Attention
Authority
Autobiographies
Automation
Automobiles

Ability

Ability is what will get you to the top if the boss has no daughter.

We rate ability in men by what they finish, not by what they attempt.

Ability without ambition is like a car without a motor.

The remarkable thing about most of us is our ability to live beyond our means.

Ability is the most important tool in your life.

Many people doubt their ability, but few have any misgivings about their importance.

There is far more opportunity than there is ability.

Executive ability is a talent for deciding something quickly and getting someone else to do it.

It is better to have a little ability and use it well than to have much ability and make poor use of it.

Be big enough to admit and admire the abilities of people who are better than you are.

You can always tell luck from ability by its duration.

What lies behind us and what lies before us are tiny matters compared to what lies within us.

Executive ability is the art of getting credit for all the hard work that somebody else does.

No man is fully accomplished until he has acquired the ability to attend to his own business.

Don't envy anybody. Every person has something no other person has. Develop that one thing and make it outstanding.

We increase our ability, stability, and responsibility when we increase our sense of accountability to God.

You can do everything you ought to do.

The tragedy is that so many have ambition and so few have ability.

Ability will enable a man to get to the top, but it takes character to keep him there.

Personal magnetism is that indefinable something that enables us to get by without ability.

Accidents

Accidents happen every hunting season because both hunter and gun are loaded.

Most accidents occur in the home. Many men use this as an excuse to stay out late.

A certain gentleman in Oregon read that most accidents take place in airplanes and bathtubs — he hasn't been in either since.

The worst thing about accidents in the kitchen is that you usually have to eat them.

Politically speaking, the ideal accident would be a collision between the man seeking the office and the office seeking the man.

Anybody who thinks hit-and-run accidents aren't on the increase hasn't been in a supermarket lately.

Most accidents happen accidentally.

One way to reduce motor accidents is to build cars so they can't go any faster than the average person thinks.

A rock and roll singer had a bad accident recently. His partner slammed the car door on his hair.

Man blames most accidents on fate — but feels a more personal responsibility when he makes a hole-in-one on the golf course.

Most accidents are caused by motorists who drive in high while their minds are in neutral.

It's reported that half of all accidents occur at home. Apparently the rest happen in voting booths.

According to sales reports, automobile manufacturers had a bang-up year. According to accident reports, so did their customers.

It's not the fall that injures; it's the sudden stop.

The number of accidents in the home are rising; people aren't spending enough time there to know their way around.

It's the nut *behind* the wheel and not the nut *on* the wheel that causes traffic accidents.

1

A man in Mississippi was told that most accidents happen within twenty miles of home — so he moved to another town fifty miles away.

Fewer accidents are caused by traffic jams than by pickled drivers.

You can't get anywhere unless you start.

There are two places the jet planes have brought closer together — this world and the next.

Some hospitals are so crowded that the only way you can get in is by accident.

There are a lot of men in this world who started at the bottom — and stayed there.

A good way to get your name in the newspaper is to cross the street reading one.

"All the world is a stage," and railroad crossings furnish some of the exits.

Skiing may be a winter activity, but some think of it as a fall sport.

Accidents — Automobile

The lesson you learn in a traffic accident could be your last one.

Highway accidents will diminish when brainpower matches horsepower.

Some accidents are caused by two motorists aiming at the same pedestrian.

Auto accident statistics prove that telephone poles are getting more careless all the time.

Anybody who thinks hit-and-run accidents aren't on the increase hasn't been in a supermarket lately.

One way to reduce motor accidents is to build cars so they can't go any faster than the average person thinks.

Most accidents are caused by motorists who drive in high while their minds are in neutral.

According to sales reports, automobile manufacturers had a bang-up year. According to accident reports, so did their customers.

It's the nut *behind* the wheel and not the nut *on* the wheel that causes traffic accidents.

A man in Mississippi was told that most accidents happen within twenty miles of home — so he moved to another town fifty miles away.

Fewer accidents are caused by traffic jams than by pickled drivers.

America is a land where, thanks to its high birthrate, people are being born faster than the automobile can kill them.

Drive carefully. Uncle Sam needs every taxpayer he can get.

Nothing will add heat to an argument like rubbing car fenders together.

If you think a seat belt is uncomfortable, you've never tried a stretcher!

Automobiles did away with horses and now they're working on people.

The auto industry accounts for one out of every twenty jobs in the United States — and this does not include morticians.

The springs of the late-model cars are of such high quality that you can hardly feel the bump when you run over a pedestrian.

There are few Americans who have never seen an automobile, but plenty who have not seen one soon enough.

Automobiles are gradually doing away with absent-minded people.

In these days of high speed and crowded highways, it doesn't take much of a car to last a lifetime.

The first thing that strikes a visitor in New York City is a big car.

Our grandparents never dreamed that the steering wheel would become America's only family circle.

It's not only the cost and the upkeep of a car that worries you, but also the possible turnover.

Power brakes may stop a car on a dime, but it usually costs more than a hundred dollars to get the rear end fixed.

An automobile has been described as a four-wheeled vehicle that runs up hills and down pedestrians.

An automobile can help you see the world, but it's up to you to decide which world!

An automobile dealer in Nevada offers a big extra — he supplies two friendly witnesses for your first accident.

Thank heaven! More people get autos than autos get people.

The careful driver stops at a railroad crossing for a minute; the careless one, forever.

Cars and bars mean stars and scars.

If you must drive while drinking, drive a nail. Then the only thing you'll hit is your finger.

The difference between learning to drive a car and learning to play golf is that when you learn to play golf you don't hit anything.

The old narrow trails where two cars could barely pass without colliding are happily being replaced by splendid wide highways on which six or eight cars can collide at the same time.

After you hear two witnesses to an automobile accident testify in court, you're not so sure about history.

Quite often a motorist will knock a pedestrian down because his windshield is obscured by safety stickers.

A motorist recently admitted running over the same man twice. The time evidently has come when there aren't enough pedestrians to go around.

A good way to get your name in the newspaper is to cross the street reading one.

Recent figures show more accidents but fewer fatalities. The drivers are no more careful than usual, but pedestrians are getting tougher.

One reason why so many pedestrians don't look where they're going is because they're in an ambulance.

In the old days a man who "died with his boots on" was known as a bad man. Now he's a pedestrian.

A reckless driver is seldom reckless for very long.

Many people drive their automobile as if they were rehearsing for an accident.

Every year thousands of American motorists discover that their car lasted them a lifetime.

It takes a thousand nuts to hold an automobile together, but just one to spread it all over the landscape.

The advisability of passing a car on a curve depends on whether your widow thinks the loss will be covered by insurance.

A telephone pole never hit an automobile except in self-defense.

Sleeping at the wheel is a good way to keep from growing old.

If half of your wishes came true, your troubles would probably double.

A woman driver in Ohio hit a guy and knocked him six feet in the air. Then she sued him for leaving the scene of the accident.

Achievement

We rate ability in men by what they finish, not by what they attempt.

Ability without ambition is like a car without a motor.

Some fellows dream of worthy accomplishments, while others stay awake and do them.

You can't make a place for yourself under the sun if you keep sitting in the shade of the family tree.

It is when we forget ourselves that we do things that are most likely to be remembered.

No man is fully accomplished until he has acquired the ability to attend to his own business.

There are four steps to accomplishment: Plan purposefully. Prepare prayerfully. Proceed positively. Pursue persistently.

A man seldom knows what he can do until he tries to undo what he did.

Every accomplishment, great or small, starts with the right decision, "I'll Try."

A man's accomplishment in business depends partly on whether he keeps his mind or his feet on the desk.

Don't measure yourself by what you have accomplished, but what you should have accomplished with your ability.

It's difficult to inspire others to accomplish what you haven't been willing to try.

It is simply remarkable how the apostle Paul covered so much territory and accomplished so much without a car.

3

It is not only what you do, but also what you don't do, for which you are accountable.

The only thing in life achieved without effort is failure.

You must first be a believer if you would be an achiever.

The only thing some people can achieve on their own is dandruff.

Today's preparation determines tomorrow's achievement.

Some men achieve distinction by the kind of car they drive — others by the kind of wife that is driving them.

If you want a place in the sun, you will have to expect some blisters.

Man's maximum achievement often falls short of God's minimum demands.

The world has finally achieved perpetual commotion.

Do something. Either lead, follow, or get out of the way!

A man whose actions leave his wife speechless has really done something!

We never see the target a man aims at in life; we see only the target he hits.

Choice, not chance, determines destiny.

Some of the world's greatest deeds have been accomplished by two types of men — those who were smart enough to know it could be done, and those too dumb to know it couldn't.

Education is not received. It is *achieved.*

If it were as easy to arouse enthusiasm as it is suspicion, just think what could be accomplished!

Fear of criticism is the kiss of death in the courtship of achievement.

Having money and friends is easy. Having friends and no money is an accomplishment.

A genius shoots at something no one else sees — and hits it!

To be born a gentleman is an accident — to die one is an accomplishment.

Happiness is a by-product of achievement.

Money, achievement, fame, and success are important, but they are bought too dearly when acquired at the cost of health.

Hope sees the invisible, feels the intangible, and achieves the impossible.

Hope is the anchor of the soul, the stimulus to action, and the incentive to achievement.

One sure way for you to gain adherents to your cause is to start winning.

It's a mistake to try to judge a man's horse-power by the size of his exhaust.

Liberty is not a gift of God but a hard-won achievement with the help of God.

With many people telling lies is not a short-coming but is one of their major achievements.

You cannot control the length of your life, but you can control its breadth, depth, and height.

A mistake is proof that someone was at least trying to accomplish something.

Most of us measure our success by what others haven't done.

Action

Do something. Either lead, follow, or get out of the way!

You can't get anywhere unless you start.

Kind actions begin with kind thoughts.

Actions speak louder than words — and speak fewer lies.

The thing to try when all else fails is again.

Just over the hill is a beautiful valley, but you must climb the hill to see it.

Do it now! Today will be yesterday tomorrow.

Giving it another try is better than an alibi.

It's better to look where you're going than to see where you've been.

The best time to do the dishes is right after your wife tells you to.

People may doubt what you say, but they will always believe what you do.

We cannot do everything we want to do, but we should do everything God wants us to do.

Don't forget that people will judge you by your actions, not your intentions. You may have a heart of gold — but so does a hard-boiled egg.

Don't just stand there — do something!

It pays to keep your feet on the ground, but keep them moving.

Action is what you don't take when the other guy is bigger than you are.

Our actions are our own; their consequences are not.

Every action of our lives touches some chord that will vibrate in eternity.

Having a great aim in life is important. So is knowing when to pull the trigger.

If you're going to climb, you've got to grab the branches, not the blossoms.

The actions of men are the best interpreters of their thoughts.

It is a great deal better to do all the things you should do than to spend the rest of your life wishing you had.

Kind words can never die, but without kind deeds they can sound mighty sick.

Action speaks louder than words but not nearly as often.

It doesn't do any good to sit up and take notice if you keep on sitting.

The man who gets ahead is the man who does more than is necessary — and keeps on doing it.

"Push" will get a person almost everywhere — except through a door marked "pull."

Doing beats stewing.

God gives us the ingredients for our daily bread, but He expects us to do the baking.

The fellow who does things that count doesn't usually stop to count them.

There are three ways to get something done: do it yourself, hire someone to do it, or forbid your kids to do it.

No thoroughly occupied man has ever been known to be miserable.

Begin where you are. But don't stay where you are.

You can do everything you ought to do.

Knowing without doing is like plowing without sowing.

The best time to do something worthwhile is between yesterday and tomorrow.

You can never get much of anything done unless you go ahead and do it before you are ready.

Actions speak louder than words — and are just as apt to be misquoted or misinterpreted.

A man whose actions leave his wife speechless has really done something!

No one ever climbed a hill just by looking at it.

When you do something and don't want anybody to know it, it's either very good or very bad.

A man ordinarily has time to do all the things he really wants to do.

Don't sit back and take what comes. Go after what you want.

Our ship would come in much sooner if we'd only swim out to meet it.

The fellow who has an abundance of push gets along very well without pull.

If you don't climb the mountain, you can't see the view.

Where we go and what we do advertises what we are.

There's no sense aiming for a goal with no arrow in your bow.

Having the right aim in life doesn't mean a thing if you're loaded with blanks.

It is useless to have an aim in life unless one has ammunition to back it up.

Many people have a good aim in life, but for some reason they never pull the trigger.

Too many of us shoot blanks when aiming at our goals.

Think what others ought to be like, then start being like that yourself.

The surest way to gain respect is to earn it by conduct.

It's nice to be important, but it's more important to be nice.

None of us is responsible for all the things that happen to us, but we are responsible for the way we act when they do happen.

Many pious people would rather study the Bible than practice what it teaches.

It's not the load that breaks you down, it's the way you carry it.

Business is like a wheelbarrow — it stands still unless somebody pushes it.

A true test of a man's character is not what he does in the light, but what he does in the dark.

Think right, act right; it is what you think and do that makes you what you are.

A person is never what he ought to be until he is doing what he ought to be doing.

It isn't what you have, but what you are, that makes life worthwhile.

Cheerfulness is contagious, but don't wait to catch it from others. Be a carrier!

Christianity requires the participants to come down out of the grandstand and onto the playing field.

Christians are the light of the world, but the switch must be turned on.

The Christian who is pulling the oars doesn't have time to rock the boat.

The Christian's walk and talk must go together.

A genuine Christian is like a good watch: he has an open face, busy hands, is made of pure gold, is well-regulated, and is full of good works.

Some church members are like wheelbarrows — they go only when they are pushed.

A committee of three gets things done if two don't show up.

Common sense is the knack of seeing things as they are, and doing things as they ought to be done.

It might be more worthwhile if we stopped wringing our hands and started ringing our congressman.

A man's conscience tells him what he shouldn't do — but it does not keep him from doing it.

Those who can — do. Those who can't — criticize.

You don't have time to criticize when you harmonize, sympathize, and evangelize.

If it were not for the doers, the critics would soon be out of business.

Your creed may be interesting but your deeds are much more convincing.

Few people ever get dizzy from doing too many good turns.

The smallest good deed is better than the grandest intention.

You can't reduce by talking about it. You must keep your mouth shut.

The true object of education should be to train one to think clearly and act rightly.

We make more enemies by what we say than friends by what we do.

We won't go far without enthusiasm, but neither will we go far if that's all we have.

Experience is a form of knowledge acquired in only two ways — by doing and by being done.

Failure always overtakes those who have the power to do without the will to act.

There are a lot of ways to become a failure, but never taking a chance is the most successful.

Failure is not the worst thing in the world. The very worst is not to try.

Faith without works is like an automobile without gas.

In all relationships of life, faith is worthless unless it leads to action.

Faith with works is a force. Faith without works is a farce.

The fellow who's always leaning on his family tree never seems to get out of the woods.

No farmer ever plowed a field by turning it over in his mind.

Even if a farmer intends to loaf, he gets up in time to get an early start.

The one thing worse than a quitter is the man who is afraid to start.

The only thing we have to fear is not doing something about the fear we have.

Promises may get friends, but it is performance that keeps them.

We make our future by the best use of the present.

Genius is 1 percent inspiration and 99 percent perspiration.

People who live by the Golden Rule today never have to apologize for their actions tomorrow.

The Golden Rule is of little value unless you realize that you must make the first move.

Looking for trouble is wasted energy. All a guy has to do is to sit down and wait.

Going to heaven is like riding a bicycle — you must either go on or get off.

The hope is that some day the Christian ideal will be put into practice.

Unexpressed ideas are of no more value than kernels in a nut before it has been cracked.

Some people entertain ideas; others put them to work.

A "sensational new idea" is sometimes just an old idea with its sleeves rolled up.

Good ideas need landing gear as well as wings.

Ideas are funny things. They don't work unless you do.

Every time one man expresses an idea, he finds ten men who thought of it before — but they only thought.

An idea is more than information; it is information with legs, and — it is headed somewhere.

You can't make a hit with the bat on your shoulder.

There is nothing more terrifying than ignorance in action.

Good intentions die unless they are executed.

Never judge a man's actions until you know his motives.

A little knowledge that acts is worth infinitely more than much knowledge that is idle.

Leisure is a beautiful garment, but it will not do for constant wear.

It isn't how high you go in life that counts, but *how* you got there.

When all the affairs of life are said and done, there is more said than done.

Works, not words, are the proof of love.

Some people never make a mistake, nor do they ever make anything else.

A mistake proves somebody stopped talking long enough to do something.

Even when opportunity knocks, a man still has to get off his seat and open the door.

Never waste time reflecting on opportunities you have missed. While thus reflecting you might miss some more.

There are still a few people who believe in gittin' up and gittin', while a great many prefer sittin' down and sittin'.

After saying our prayers we ought to do something to make them come true.

The right angle to approach a difficult problem is the "try-angle."

All progress is due to those who were not satisfied to let well enough alone.

People are won to your religious beliefs less by description than by demonstration.

For success, try aspiration, inspiration, and perspiration.

If you itch for success, keep on scratching.

The man who fails while trying to do good has more honor than he who succeeds by accident.

Before proceeding with a difficult task, stop and think. Then remember to start again.

It's about time for folks to carry this do-it-yourself craze to thinking.

Acting without thinking is a lot like shooting without aiming.

A spoken word and a thrown stone cannot be recalled.

Our words may hide our thoughts, but our actions will reveal them.

Words should be used as tools of communication and not as a substitute for action.

You can't clean up this old world with soft soap; it takes grit.

The world we live in is old-fashioned. It still judges a man by what he does.

Actors

A certain Hollywood actor would really become a big star if the public liked him as much as he does.

One of the Ringling Brothers trapeze artists refuses to travel by plane — even if they put a net under it.

The lines actors like best are the ones in front of the box office.

Actors are the only honest hypocrites.

You can pick out actors by the glazed look that comes to their eyes when the conversation wanders away from themselves.

There are lots of bad actors who are not on the stage.

A Hollywood actor denies he is egotistical. He says he just deeply admires people with great talent.

An actor is a man who tries to be everything but himself.

Some actors think they are elevating the stage when they're merely depressing the audience.

Did you hear about the Hollywood actor with so little personality that he appeared on a color TV show and it came out in black and white?

There's a new alarm clock on the market for actors. It doesn't ring — it applauds.

A Hollywood star boasts he's been happily married for twenty years. Of course, it took him five marriages to do it.

It is more important to deserve the applause of people than to obtain it.

Nostalgia has really caught on in show business. Some Hollywood actors are remarrying their ex-wives.

A Hollywood celebrity recently hired two press agents to tell the world how modest he is.

The best acting job done in Hollywood is done by the man congratulating his ex-wife's husband on the choice he made.

A certain Hollywood actor carries a note in his wallet, "I am a celebrity. In case of an accident — call a reporter."

Ordinary people have sore throats. Broadway stars have laryngitis.

Actresses

A Hollywood actress is now teaching a course on educational TV — husbandry!

Someone described an aging film beauty, "Her figure was legendary — but now the legend is beginning to spread."

A young actress in a southern state insists she's not conceited, "although you understand I have every right to be."

There's an unusual actress in Hollywood — she's signed more marriage certificates than autographs.

On TV talk shows the Hollywood actresses always seem to mention either their last picture or their next husband.

The age of an actress is like the speedometer on a used car — you know it's been set back but you can't tell how far.

An actress in Hollywood described her ex-husband, "He's six feet tall in his socks and $2,000 short in his alimony payments."

Did you hear about the movie actress who was so sentimental she got divorced in the same dress her mother was wearing when she got her divorce?"

An actress in New York City has broken up so many homes that she's listed in the Yellow Pages under "Demolition Experts."

A Hollywood actress once had an hourglass figure, but the sands of time have shifted.

Many actresses won't wear a dress that's not original, but they'll take a secondhand husband.

A Chicago actress says she's been so busy planning her sixth marriage she hasn't time to cook for her fifth husband.

To some young actresses the difference between fame and farm is form.

Adolescence

Adolescence is when children start bringing up their parents.

Some adolescents become bad eggs because they have been set on too long — or not long enough.

Adolescence is the awkward age when a child is too old to say something cute and too young to say something sensible.

All anybody expects of an adolescent is that he act like an adult and be satisfied to be treated like a child.

Adolescence is something like a hitch in the army — you'd hate to have missed it, but you'd hate to repeat it.

An adolescent is a youth old enough to dress himself if he could just remember where he dropped his clothes.

Adolescence is the period when children are certain they will never be as stupid as their parents.

An adolescent is a minor who is sometimes a major problem.

Adolescence is a period of rapid change. Between the ages of twelve and seventeen, for example, a child may see his parents age twenty years.

Adversity

Adversity is the only diet that will reduce a fat head.

We learn some things from prosperity, but we learn many more from adversity.

The average man can stand adversity better than prosperity.

He who swells in prosperity will shrink in adversity.

When you're down and out something always turns up — and it's usually the noses of your friends.

Adversity is never pleasant, but sometimes it's possible to learn lessons from it that can be learned in no other way.

In adversity a man can become very well acquainted with himself because he is free from admirers.

Another thing learned in adversity is that a tire isn't the only thing you can patch.

When things get rough, remember: It's the rubbing that brings out the shine.

Your character is what you have left when you've lost everything you can lose.

The address of character is often carved on the corner of Adversity Avenue and Determination Drive.

Nearly all men can stand adversity, but if you want to test a man's character, give him power.

Character, like sweet herbs, should give off its finest fragrance when pressed.

The difficulties of life are intended to make us better — not bitter.

There are two ways of meeting difficulties: alter the difficulties, or alter yourself to meet them.

Education is an ornament in prosperity and a refuge in adversity.

All men need a faith that will not shrink when washed in the waters of affliction and adversity.

How would a person ever know whether his faith was weak or strong unless it has been tried and tested?

The friends you make in prosperity are those you lose in adversity.

A real friend will tell you your faults and follies in times of prosperity, and assist you with his hand and heart in times of adversity.

Prosperity makes friends; adversity tries them.

God often tries us with a little to see what we would do with a lot.

When you're up to your ears in trouble, try using the part that isn't submerged.

The triumphal song of life would lose its melody without its minor keys.

The ladder of life is full of splinters, but you never realize it until you begin to slide down.

Love is a fabric which never fades, no matter how often it is washed in the water of adversity and grief.

You can usually determine the caliber of a man by ascertaining the amount of opposition it takes to discourage him.

The reformers need not worry. The movies are never as wicked and vulgar as the advertisements promise.

Some people pray for a bushel, but carry a cup.

Most people who sit around waiting for their ship to come in often find it is a hardship.

In times of prosperity men ask too little of God. In times of adversity, they ask too much.

Usually it is on the detours that we pick up the tacks.

Trouble is what gives a fellow a chance to discover his strength— or lack of it.

Advertising

Sign in a florist's window: "Smoking, or forgetting your wife's birthday, can be hazardous to your health."

Where we go and what we do advertises what we are.

Advertising can be very expensive, especially if your wife can read.

Classified ad in an Oklahoma City newspaper: "Used tombstone for sale. Ideal for a family named Jones."

In good times businessmen want to advertise; in bad times they have to.

Advertising is a good deal like marriage. There may be a better way, but what is it?

One form of advertising that's a liability instead of an asset is a person blowing his own horn.

The man who stops advertising to save money is like the man who stops the clock to save time.

A loan company's advertisement: "We take the moaning and groaning out of loaning."

Nothing makes installment buying as easy as the advertising.

Advertising pays — particularly for the advertising agency.

Doing business without advertising is like winking at a girl in the dark. You know what you're doing, but she doesn't.

Advertising is the science of arresting the human intelligence long enough to get money from it.

A small town newspaper in Texas advertised, "Read your Bible to know what people ought to do. Read this paper to know what they actually do."

Advertising is the fine art of making you think you have longed for something all your life that you never heard of before.

Some resort ads don't always tell the truth. One place that promised "miles of uncrowded beaches" turned out to be a naval gunnery range.

One picture may be worth ten thousand words, but some advertisers believe in using both in the same ad.

Advertising helps raise the standard of living by raising the standard of longing.

Newspaper ad in New Orleans: "Retired trombone player will sell one dozen sport jackets with one arm longer than the other."

Advertising is what transforms a yawn into a yearn.

Sign on an antique shop in Stockton, California: "Come in and buy what your grandmother threw away."

Sign in an antique shop in Baltimore: "Our prices are firm. The management is not emotionally equipped to haggle."

A bachelor in Denver advertised for a wife in a newspaper: "Bachelor with waterbed desires to meet a nice, hard-working girl with short toenails."

Sign in a Baltimore barber shop: "Six Barbers — Panel Discussions."

Sign in a South Dakota bookstore, "Read a good novel before Hollywood ruins it."

If it's as easy to borrow money from a bank as the advertisements claim, why should anybody want to rob it?

On December 22, 1977, the following sign appeared in a Los Angeles church: "Come in and pray today. Beat the Christmas rush."

Anti-cigarette commercial: "Truth or cancerquences."

If you listen to the loan company commercials, you'll almost believe you can borrow yourself out of debt.

Advertising is what tells us which luxuries we can't do without.

Do you realize we're living in a time when almost everybody reads a newspaper, and the only thing they believe are the ads?

Advice

Any man who has to ask for advice probably isn't married.

Advice is like mushrooms. The wrong kind can prove fatal.

You sometimes profit from the advice you don't take.

When offering helpful advice, make it a small helping.

If you can separate good advice from bad advice, you really don't need any advice.

Advice is what you get when you're not going to get anything else.

Giving good advice does not qualify as charity.

A bit of advice: Say nothing often.

Never give advice before you're asked — or after!

It's a pleasure to give advice, humiliating to need it, normal to ignore it.

Advice is least heeded when most needed.

Successful men follow the same advice they prescribe for others.

Too many people are anxious to give you advice when what you really need is help.

To profit from good advice requires more wisdom than to give it.

Don't hesitate to give advice. It passes the time and nobody listens to it anyway.

Advice to the bridegroom: No matter how she treats you, always try to look a little hurt.

It's extremely difficult to take advice from some people — they need it so much themselves.

Some people never take advice from anybody; others take advice from everybody.

We might be more eager to accept good advice if it did not continually interfere with our plans.

Advice is like a laxative — easy to take but hard to predict the outcome.

What good is good advice if you don't take it?

Advice to some people: If you had your life to live over — don't do it!

The most valuable advice you can get usually comes from one who is the most reluctant to give it.

It is as easy to give advice to yourself as to others — and as useless.

The trouble with giving advice is that people want to repay you.

Advice is the only commodity on the market where the supply always exceeds the demand.

Seldom does the one who really needs advice ask for it.

The best advice is only as good as the use we make of it.

An intelligent person not only knows how to take advice, but also how to reject it.

No one gives advice with more enthusiasm than an ignorant person.

We can give advice but we can't give the wisdom to profit by it.

Advice is like snow — the softer it falls, the deeper it goes.

Never give advice — sell it!

Advice to men over fifty: Keep an open mind and a closed refrigerator.

Who needs advice? We've got a lot of it passed down from generation to generation that's never been used.

The fellow who tells you "frankly" what he would do if he were in your place probably doesn't know what to do in his own place.

Advice is never appreciated. If it turns out well, the recipient thinks it was his own idea; and if it turns out badly, he eternally blames the giver.

Advice is like medicine — the correct dosage works wonders, but an overdose can be dangerous.

An advisory capacity is the only capacity in which some people are willing to serve.

Advice is the one thing which is "more blessed to give than to receive."

The better the advice, the harder it is to take.

Be careful when you give advice — somebody might take it.

"Be yourself" is about the worst advice you can give to some people.

We naturally admire the wisdom and good judgment of those who come to us for advice.

Giving advice to the poor is not the best form of charity.

Some advice isn't worth the trouble of taking.

It takes a great man to give sound advice tactfully, but a greater man to accept it graciously.

Most of us find it impossible to take advice from people who need it more than we do.

Advice is seldom welcome. Those who need it most like it least.

Before you offer a man advice, be sure to find out what kind will suit him best.

We don't mind if someone wants to give us advice; we only object if they insist we take it.

Advice is that which the wise don't need and fools won't take.

When a man gets too old to set a bad example, he usually starts giving good advice.

Offering good advice may be noble and grand, but it's not the same as a helping hand.

Most people, when they come to you for advice, want their opinions strengthened, not corrected.

Always listen to the advice of others — it won't do you any harm, and it will make them feel better.

Advice to hunters: Don't get loaded when your gun is.

In many instances the person who gives advice to another hasn't tried it himself and wishes to see it tested so he can know whether or not it really works.

The only time to give advice is when it is asked for — and then only in small doses.

People sensible enough to give good advice are also sensible enough not to.

The best advice you'll get is from someone who made the same mistake himself.

Anybody who has to ask for advice probably doesn't have any close relatives.

A word to the wise usually starts an argument.

Most people find that running a business is no trouble at all — as long as it's the other fellow's.

Many a man's idea of charity is to give advice to others that he can't use himself.

Giving advice to the poor is about as close to charity as some people get.

No one is more confusing than the fellow who gives good advice while setting a bad example.

When a man won't listen to his conscience, it's usually because he doesn't want advice from a stranger.

A bad cold wouldn't be so annoying if it weren't for the advice of your friends.

Every father should remember that one day his son will follow his example instead of his advice.

A good example has twice the value of good advice.

What can't be done by advice can often be done by example.

What the world wants is not advice but examples. Any fool can talk.

Maybe children could keep on the straight and narrow path if they could get information from someone who's been over the route.

A pint of example is worth a gallon of advice.

People take your example far more seriously than they take your advice.

Trying to give people the benefit of your experience is one way of getting a lot more.

If you want people to notice your faults, start giving advice.

The best way to lose a friend is to tell him something for his own good.

The best thing one friend can do for another is to refrain from giving advice.

One form of generosity that can lead to trouble consists in giving others a piece of your mind.

About all some people are giving these days is advice.

Juvenile delinquency would disappear if kids followed their parent's advice instead of their examples.

A juvenile delinquent usually prefers vice to advice.

Marriage is perhaps the most expensive way to get advice for nothing.

The worst thing about growing old is having to listen to a lot of advice from one's children.

Old age is that period when a man is too old to take advice but young enough to give it.

The only way a man can attain perfection is to follow the advice he gives to others.

Commencement speaker in Michigan: "My advice to young people who are going out in the world today — don't go!"

Free advice to public speakers: When you're done pumping, let loose of the handle.

Many people would have been a tremendous success long ago if they had used the advice they gave to others.

Three cases where supply exceeds demand are: taxes, trouble, and advice.

The typical American youth is always ready to give those who are older than himself the full benefit of his inexperience.

Advice — Free

Free advice is often overpriced.

Some of the most expensive advice that most of us ever had was free.

It seems the only thing that hasn't increased in cost is free advice.

Doctors and lawyers are always giving *fee* advice.

Too many people are cheerful givers only when they get a chance to hand out free advice.

When a person starts handing you a lot of free advice, it's pretty certain it wasn't worth keeping for his personal use.

One of the most costly things anyone can acquire is free advice.

The best things in life are free — also the worst advice.

The person who gives you free advice is probably charging you too much for it.

Free advice is the kind that costs you nothing unless you act upon it.

Advice may be had for nothing and is usually worth it.

A lot of folks think they are generous because they give free advice.

Age

Age is what makes furniture worth more and people worth less.

Which do you suppose ages faster — whiskey or the man who drinks it?

Age is like love. It cannot be hidden.

Forty is the age when you begin to realize how much fun you had when you were twenty.

By the time a man finds greener pastures, he's too old to climb the fence.

A man is usually as young as he feels but seldom as important.

The time-tested method of slowing down advancing age seems to be misrepresentation.

Age is the best possible fire extinguisher for flaming youth.

Sixty-five is the age when one acquires sufficient experience to lose his job.

To be seventy years young is sometimes more cheerful and hopeful than to be forty years old.

You can judge your age by the amount of pain you feel when you come in contact with a new idea.

The awkward age is when you are too old for the Peace Corps and too young for Social Security.

People aren't really living any longer — it just seems that way.

Regardless of their age, most folks are not as old as they hope to be.

Some people think the proper age for a man to start thinking of marriage is when he's old enough to realize he shouldn't.

Life's golden age is when the children are too old to need baby sitters and too young to borrow the family car.

By all means go ahead and mellow with age. Just be wary of getting rotten.

A California woman says her husband is at the dangerous age when all females look alike to him — desirable!

Age has nothing to do with learning new ways to be stupid.

As a man gets older he suspects that nature is plotting against him for the benefit of doctors and dentists.

Hardening of the heart ages people more quickly than hardening of the arteries.

Twenty-nine is a wonderful age for a man to be — and for a woman to stay.

The dangerous age is any time between one and ninety-nine.

It is possible that a man could live twice as long if he didn't spend the first half of his life acquiring habits that shorten the other half.

Age stiffens the joints and thickens some brains.

People usually feel they reached forty prematurely.

Many of us are at the "metallic age" — gold in our teeth, silver in our hair, and lead in our pants.

Age doesn't always bring wisdom. Sometimes age comes alone.

You're getting along in years when the only urge you feel in the spring is to climb out of your long underwear.

Life not only begins at forty — it begins to show.

Youth looks ahead, old age looks back, and middle age looks tired.

Nothing ages a man faster than trying to prove he's still as young as ever.

A man begins to show his age at about the same time he begins to show pictures of his grandchildren.

It's a sign of age if you feel like the morning after the night before, and you haven't been anywhere.

The three ages of man are youth, middle age and, "My, but you are looking well."

Few women admit their age. Few men act theirs.

Our aim in life improves as we grow older, but it seems that we soon run out of ammunition.

Her birthday cake had so many candles on it she was fined for air pollution.

Cosmetics are used by teen-age girls to make them look older sooner, and by their mothers to make them look younger longer.

Some of the older generation's criticism of the younger generation is heavily tinged with envy.

A gentleman in Georgia says he's at the age where he's too old for castor oil and too young for Geritol.

Gray hair usually comes along about twenty years after you thought it would make you look distinguished.

A man in Nevada says that when he was a boy his hair was light; then it turned dark, then it turned grey, then it turned loose.

In this life the old believe everything, the middle-aged suspect everything, and the young know everything.

A fellow's mistakes always bother him, especially when he realizes he's too old to repeat them.

Everybody wants to live a long time, but nobody wants to get old.

It's so sad that people are like plants — some go to seed with age and others go to pot.

Most people like the old days best — they were younger then.

Some people grow up and spread cheer; others just grow up and spread.

Agreement

It's surprising how often people will agree with you if you just keep your mouth shut.

About the only thing people in every walk of life will agree about is that they are underpaid and overcharged.

Most of us are too fond of people who agree with us and food that doesn't.

No two people in a car can agree on which window should be open — and how much.

As soon as you observe that everybody agrees with you, you can be sure they don't mean it.

How come only the most sensible people agree with us?

Just about everybody will agree that our country is on the move, though there is plenty of argument about the direction.

It's a lot easier to nod as if you agree with someone than it is to explain why you don't.

When two men in business always agree about everything, one of them is unnecessary.

Reasonable men always agree if they understand what they're talking about.

This country needs closer agreement on what this country needs.

When you say that you agree to a thing in principle, you mean that you do not have the slightest intention of carrying it out.

It's easier to get folks to agree to do better tomorrow than to get them to do their best today.

A "gentleman's agreement" is a deal which neither party cares to put in writing.

It's a pretty safe rule that the fellow who always agrees with you is not worth talking to.

An intelligent conversationalist is one who nods his head in agreement while you're talking.

The real spirit of conversation consists in building on another man's observation, not overturning it.

A divorce is what couples agree on when they can't agree on anything else.

The man who always agrees with you lies to others also.

Air Age

There are two places the jet planes have brought closer together — this world and the next.

Airplane fares have been increased considerably. Even the cost of going up is going up.

You can't fool all the people all the time, but the airplane schedules come pretty close.

Our modern airplanes fly so fast we don't have time to get acquainted with all the stewardesses.

Our new faster-than-sound jet planes are wonderful. You can eat dinner in London and get indigestion in New York City.

Air travel is wonderful. It allows you to pass motorists at a safe distance.

The wife of a pilot is the only woman who is glad to see her husband down and out.

It's a small world, once you've made the long trip to the airport.

Alarm Clocks

One thing an alarm clock never arouses is our better nature.

Did you ever have one of those days when the only thing that goes off as planned is your alarm clock?

What most folks need is an alarm clock that will ring when it's time for them to rise to the occasion.

There's a new alarm clock on the market for actors. It doesn't ring — it applauds.

The trouble with alarm clocks is that they always go off when you're asleep.

An alarm clock is a device for awakening people who don't have small children.

When the alarm clock rings the best part of the day is over.

A fortune awaits the inventor of an alarm clock that can't go off.

Blessed is the man who can hear his alarm clock on Sunday as well as on Monday.

An alarm clock is a device that makes men rise and whine.

You can often gauge a man's ambition by whether he hates his alarm clock or considers it his dear friend.

Alcoholics

Accidents happen every hunting season because both hunter and gun are loaded.

The favorite drink of an alcoholic is the next one.

To escape alcoholism is simple. Never take the drink just before the second one.

An alcoholic can neither live with alcohol nor without it.

No alcoholic is really anonymous.

There's now an AA for midget alcoholics. It's called aa.

An alcoholic is not one who drinks too much, but one who can't drink enough.

15

The typical alcoholic insists he drinks only on special occasions, like when the sun goes down every day.

An alcoholic claims a little too much liquor is just about right.

An alcoholic from Texas says he refused a drink only once in his life and that was when he misunderstood the question.

Alcoholic joys are brief — the results are lasting.

It is useless for alcoholics to worry about the future for there will soon be no future for them to worry about.

Alcoholics Alias is a group in which they continue to drink, but under an assumed name.

A man in Colorado complains that the only thing lit up on his block after 11 P.M. is his neighbor.

With all the diets we hear and read about, it appears there are more problem eaters than problem drinkers.

A drunkard can live neither with alcohol nor without it.

There's nothing more stubborn than a drunkard trying to convince you he isn't.

Some folks drink liquor as if they want to be mentioned in "BOOZE WHO."

Some recent laws would indicate the lawmakers not only passed the bar but also stopped there.

Alibis

Giving it another try is better than an alibi.

The worst buy is an alibi.

Many a husband has learned that an ironclad alibi isn't as effective as a diamond-studded one.

An alibi is first cousin to an excuse, and they're both mighty poor relatives.

An alibi is the legal proof that a person wasn't where he was and, therefore, couldn't do what he did.

Ignorance of the law is no excuse, but it's better than no alibi at all.

What the weatherman saves for a rainy day is probably an alibi.

Alimony

An actress in Hollywood described her ex-husband, "He's six feet tall in his socks and $2,000 short in his alimony payments."

Paying alimony is like paying installments on a car after you've wrecked it.

Alimony is different from take-home pay; it's leave-home pay.

Anybody who thinks severance pay is something new probably doesn't understand alimony.

Alimony is when a fellow mails home the money instead of bringing it.

A man never realizes how short a month is until he starts paying alimony.

Alimony is a system in which one pays for the mistakes of two.

Alimony is another war debt a lot of husbands would like to see cancelled.

Alimony probably works out right after all. The less a woman deserves it, the more it's worth to be rid of her.

Alimony is payment for services not rendered.

The word *alimony* is a contraction of "all his money."

Americans have always been willing to pay and price for freedom. If you don't believe it, look at the divorce statistics!

A girl becomes a woman when she stops living on her allowance and starts living on her alimony.

Some girls get married for financial security; others get divorced for the same reason.

In Hollywood there's a group called Divorce Anonymous. If a male member feels the urge to get a divorce, they send over an accountant to talk him out of it.

Nothing makes for undying love in Hollywood like the prompt arrival of alimony checks.

A guaranteed income is nothing new in this country. We've had alimony for years.

A man doesn't know the value of a woman's love until he starts paying alimony.

In the old days a woman married a man for his money, but now she divorces him for it.

There's only one thing more expensive than a wife — an exwife!

Husbands never know what their wives are worth until a judge sets the alimony payments.

Ambition

We rate ability in men by what they finish, not by what they attempt.

Some fellows dream of worthy accomplishments, while others stay awake and do them.

Every accomplishment, great or small, starts with the right decision, "I'll Try."

Don't just stand there — do something!

Don't sit back and take what comes. Go after what you want.

The fellow who has an abundance of push gets along very well without pull.

Once it was ambition that kept people on the move. Now it's no parking signs.

The average man's modest ambition is to make his weekly paycheck last a week.

You can often gauge a man's ambition by whether he hates his alarm clock or considers it his dear friend.

One of the secret ambitions of many people is to be able to enjoy some of the evils which go with having too much money.

Ambition never gets anywhere until it forms a partnership with work.

Young men who leave home to set the world on fire usually have to come back home for more matches.

The average man's ambition is to be able to afford what he's spending.

Ambition in America is still rewarded — with high taxes.

Watch out for ambition! It can get you into a lot of hard work.

Every man has a secret ambition to outsmart horses, fish, and women.

The tragedy is that so many have ambition and so few have ability.

A man with a burning ambition is seldom fired.

The ambition of some girls is to make a man a good husband.

Ambition without determination has no destination.

There are only two kinds of failures: the man who will do nothing he is told, and the man who will do nothing else.

Abraham Lincoln was great, not because he once lived in a cabin, but because he got out of it.

The plain fact is that human beings are happy only when they are striving for something worthwhile.

If more husbands had self-starters, fewer wives would have to be cranks.

Don't wait for your ship to come in if you haven't sent one out.

Most lazy people have about as much initiative as an echo.

The average man doesn't want much and usually gets less than that.

The man with PUSH will pass the man with PULL.

Most great men come from small towns. We don't know whether it's because of ambition or gossip.

It is the secret ambition of every loyal American to discover the stream in which a president should never be changed in the middle of.

The best ammunition to fight poverty is a load of ambition fired with effort toward a definite goal.

The world has too many cranks and not enough self-starters.

America

Just about everybody will agree that our country is on the move, though there is plenty of argument about the direction.

This country needs closer agreement on what this country needs.

17

Ambition in America is still rewarded — with high taxes.

Never in the history of America have so few loused up so much for so many.

America is always a land of promise in an election year.

One reason America is great is because we have been unable to exhaust our natural resources in spite of our best efforts.

The donkey and the elephant play important roles in American politics. The bull plays a major role too.

America is a country where permanent waves are increasing and permanent wives are decreasing.

In America we'll try anything once — except criminals.

Our forefathers founded an enduring republic that has had to endure a lot more than they thought it would have to endure.

America may be the land of the free, but not the debt-free.

One quarter of America is covered with forests and the rest with beer cans.

America has drive-in theaters, drive-in supermarkets, drive-in restaurants, and drive-in banks. What it needs now are more drive-in parking places.

Foreign observers say America is no longer a young country — it's fast reaching meddle age.

America is a land of six-lane highways, one-way streets, and four-way cold tablets.

The beauty of America is that the average man always thinks he's above average.

America is a land of opportunity. Everybody can become a taxpayer.

As the IRS sees it, America is a land of untold wealth.

America has the highest standard of living in the world. Now let's raise our standard of thinking.

Naturalists who claim America's wildlife is disappearing don't stay up very late at night.

America is the only country in the world where it takes more brains to make out the income tax return than it does to make the income.

There are two things in America that are growing bigger together — garbage cans and taxes.

America is a land where, thanks to its high birthrate, people are being born faster than the automobile can kill them.

According to recent reports, America produces 92 percent of the world's natural gas — not counting the speeches of our senators and congressmen.

America is rapidly achieving a high standard of poverty.

The way to get ahead of Russia is to get behind America.

What is hurting America today is the high cost of low living.

America is a country where Groucho Marx has more followers than Karl Marx.

Much has been said about what America stands for. Let's not forget some things that America won't stand for.

You can say what you please in America — but nobody listens.

America has some fine old ruins. Many of them can be seen in our nightclubs.

Maybe this country would not be in such a mess today if the Indians had adopted more stringent immigration laws.

It's hard to believe that America was founded to avoid high taxation.

America's number one energy crisis is Monday morning.

The trouble with America today is that all the stupid people are cocksure of everything and all the intelligent people are full of doubt.

America leads the world in the highway distribution of beer cans.

What America really needs most are those things which money can't buy.

America unquestionably has the highest standard of living in the world. Too bad we can't afford it.

One thing America isn't running out of is debts.

18

In America today there is a surplus of food, a surplus of manufactured goods, and a surplus of people who think they know how to run the government.

America is rapidly proving to be a place with two cars in every garage — and none of them paid for.

America was better off when folks opened meals with a prayer instead of a can opener.

America has more transportation facilities than any other nation, but they're so crowded we can't use them.

Our country was in better condition when there were more whittlers and fewer chiselers.

America has turned out some great men, but there are others not so great that ought to be turned out.

America is the land of the spree and the home of the crave.

Americans are a religious people. You can tell they trust in God by the way they drive.

There are too many middle-of-the-roaders in America, and they all drive cars.

Our forefathers built this country with three tools: an ax, a plow, and a book. That book was the Bible.

Our beloved country recently celebrated its two-hundredth birthday, and all we've learned in that time is how to go fast, work less, waste more, and die quicker.

It's easy to believe that any American boy can become president when you observe some of them who have.

Most kids can't understand why a country that makes atomic bombs would ban firecrackers.

In some foreign countries girls dress like their mothers, but in America it's the other way around.

In America it's "Believe it or not," but in communist countries it's "Believe it or else."

Communism will be defeated in America and in all countries where Christians are more interested in being mobilized than in being tranquilized.

A Communist in the United States is a person who says everything is perfect in Russia but stays in this country because he likes to rough it.

Why did they have to admit to the Union the State of Confusion?

Anybody who thinks conversation is a lost art in America doesn't play bridge.

It's now costing Americans twice as much to live beyond their means as it did twenty years ago.

Foreign aggressors don't realize that even if they invaded the United States they couldn't afford to live here.

The crime situation is so bad in some American cities you could walk five blocks and never leave the scene of the crime.

Every person born in the United States is endowed with life, liberty, and a substantial share of the national debt.

Diplomats are frequently decorated in European countries. We'd like to crown some of ours here in this country.

If it weren't for picketing many Americans wouldn't walk at all.

The American dream is owning a British sports car, smoking a Havana cigar, and drinking Russian vodka on the French Riviera.

The way the American economy is going, we'll soon have a system of checks and bounces.

What this country needs today is fewer experts on what this country needs.

Not as many people have lost faith in America as you might think. An awful lot of them still sign up for a thirty-year mortgage.

The trouble with some American families is that they have Cadillac tastes and compact incomes.

Under the Constitution of the United States every man has the right to make a fool of himself as he sees fit.

This country is as free today as it ever was — unless you happen to be a taxpayer.

In this country you are still privileged to free speech, but that's as far as the Constitution goes. It doesn't guarantee listeners.

The young people of the United States squander over ten billion dollars a year on games of chance. This does not include weddings, starting a business, passing cars on a hill, or buying a television set.

In Africa certain of the native tribes practice the strange custom of beating the ground with clubs and uttering wild bloodcurdling yells. Anthropologists call this a form of primitive expression. In America we call it golf.

Nothing in recent years seems to have improved the health of the American people as much as the staggering cost of being sick.

There are three stages in American history: the passing of the buffalo, the passing of the Indian, and the passing of the buck.

In many ways the past two hundred years of our history have changed this country from independence to government dependence.

There are generally two things wrong in the American home — the clock and the father.

Don't you long for the "good old days" when Uncle Sam lived within his income and without most of yours?

The American family and the United States government are in agreement about one thing — neither of them can live within their income.

Income-tax forms should be more realistic by allowing the taxpayer to list Uncle Sam as a dependent.

Americans will pay a big price for an invention that will help them save time they don't know what to do with.

The people of the United States don't need more judges, but more sound judgment.

Everybody says the country has too many laws, and yet every man thinks he knows of a law that ought to be passed.

George Washington was first in war, first in peace, and first to have his birthday juggled to make a long weekend.

Mistakes aren't so bad. Columbus found America by mistake!

The principal export of the United States is money.

We need more watchdogs at the United States Treasury and fewer bloodhounds at the Internal Revenue Service.

The United States needs more tractors and fewer detractors.

It's beginning to look like America has too many parttime parents.

Which has made the biggest liars out of Americans — golf or the income tax?

The following is the revised edition of an American prayer: "Forgive us our debts, O Lord, as we forgive our international debtors."

If only men took the nation's problems as seriously as they do its sports!

The main difference between Russia and the United States is that in Russia the state owns everything and in the United States the finance companies do.

In Russia the people have only what the government gives them; in America the people have only what the government does not take away from them in taxes.

The thing raised most abundantly in the United States is taxes.

The president has the next to the hardest job in the United States. The taxpayer has the hardest.

The United States is in worse condition than we might think. Every time we dial a prayer we get a busy signal.

Anybody who thinks the United States isn't still the land of promise just hasn't been listening to political speeches lately.

The United States is running out of things our grandfathers never imagined anybody would need.

We should be extremely happy living in a country where we put chains on tires and not on people.

The United States is still the land of opportunity. Where else could you earn enough money to pay the interest on what you owe?

In 1776 our country was unsettled — it still is!

It often seems like the United States is building up its enemies and flattening its taxpayers.

We live in a wonderful country where lawns are well-kept — and laws aren't!

The United States would be better off if we had less conversation and more conservation.

What's wrong with our country isn't the people trying to get something for nothing — it's those who are succeeding.

The United States is a country of quiet majorities and vociferous minorities.

Relax, the United States will never run out of things to run out of.

U. S. now stands for Unlimited Spending.

What a great country this is! Anybody can have a second house, a second car, a second TV. All it takes is a second job, a second mortgage, and a second wind.

About all the United States is getting to see of the dove of peace is the bill.

A great man has said that the United States is having a rendezvous with destiny, but at times it seems more like it is having a blind date with fate.

The United States is a land with a President for a head, a Supreme Court for a backbone, and Congress for lungs.

The United States is determined that there shall be no more wars and is equally determined to be ready for the next one.

Americans

Americans have two chickens in every pot, two cars in every garage, and two headaches for every aspirin.

Not many Americans have been around the world but their money sure has.

Americans are now experiencing "shell-out shock."

If Americans bought only what they could afford it would destroy our economy.

Many Americans no longer celebrate the arrival of the New Year — they celebrate the survival of the old year.

Who but Americans can afford chairs that vibrate and cars that don't?

Most Americans are members of the debt set.

Millions of Americans aren't working, but thank heaven they've got jobs.

Americans are endowed with certain inalienable rights, but if we don't stick up for them somebody will come along and un-endow them.

Many Americans are trying to conserve energy as never before — they're now burning their morning toast only on one side.

Americans have the highest yearning power of any people on earth.

Millions of Americans are nervous wrecks. They're afraid the President will devalue trading stamps at any moment.

The average American would drive his car to the bathroom if the door was wide enough.

Americans have come to learn that it's easier to vote for something they want than to work for it.

Too many Americans go in for weightlifting with the wrong equipment — a knife and fork.

The average American takes an average of 19,689 steps daily — mostly in the wrong direction.

Every American has the right to make a fool of himself if he wants to, but too many folks are abusing the privilege.

Americans have more time-saving devices and less time than any other people in the world.

An American always makes sure his car is working whether he is or not.

One out of every two Americans is under twenty-five, and all women are under thirty.

If it weren't for picketing many Americans wouldn't walk at all.

Americans are getting bigger and broader, a fact which has filtered through to everybody except the people who mark off the seats in football stadiums.

The reason Americans don't own more elephants is that they have never been offered one for a dollar down and a dollar a week.

Many Americans are so nervous and restless they don't feel at home at home.

Most Americans have definite goals in life and attain them gradually — with the help of a finance company.

It's not difficult to recognize an American at a bullfight — he's the one who cheers for the bull.

A good American looks up to nobody, looks down on nobody, but looks straight into the eyes of everybody.

Those who complain that Americans are going too fast haven't been caught in a traffic jam lately.

The typical American knows when and where the Pilgrims landed but has no idea why.

Americans sink millions of dollars in unsound financial schemes, one of which is trying to keep up with the neighbors.

The American people are divided into two great classes: those who think they are as good as anybody, and those who think they are better.

Americans once shouted, "Give me liberty." Now they leave off the last word.

A patriotic American likes to discuss the Constitution of the United States despite the fact he has never taken the time to read it.

Americans have more food to eat than any other people on earth, and more diets to keep them from eating it.

The first thing the typical American will ask when he gets to heaven is the amount of the down-payment on a harp.

Americans are getting stronger. Twenty years ago it took two people to carry fifteen dollars worth of groceries. Today, a child can do it.

Fewer Americans are drunk with wealth nowadays. It's just the price of everything that causes them to stagger.

The vanishing American is one who pays cash for everything he buys.

Most Americans are vitally interested in space problems — especially parking and closet.

The average American doesn't really believe he is having a good time unless he is doing something he can't afford.

There are two kinds of Americans: one hopes the government will do something *for* them, the other hopes the government won't do something *to* them.

A well-informed American knows the lineup of baseball teams and about half the words of the "Star-Spangled Banner."

A patriotic American never orders anything from a menu that he can't spell.

Americans everywhere are now in a daze from INTAXICATION.

One day an American worries about going to the poorhouse, and the next day he buys a new automobile.

Americans believe in life, liberty, and the purchase of happiness.

Isn't it remarkable how our pioneering ancestors built up a great nation without asking Congress for help?

The kind of ancestors we have is not as important as the kind of descendants our ancestors have.

Some folks are as proud of their ancestors as if they were responsible for them.

There are few Americans who have never seen an automobile, but plenty who have not seen one soon enough.

American farmers don't need protection from competition to survive. They need protection from their own government.

Thousands of Americans are trying to find peace in a pill.

It is the secret ambition of every loyal American to discover the stream in which a president should never be changed in the middle of.

Only Americans have mastered the art of being prosperous and broke at the same time.

You can always tell when an American is prosperous. He fills his home with old furniture and new whiskey.

You can tell Americans trust in God by the way they drive.

Maybe one reason the Russians are so confident is they've watched our TV programs and figure all Americans have tired blood, indigestion, bad breath, and a nagging backache.

An American can consider himself a success when it costs him more to support the government than to support a wife and children.

A certain Senator recently informed us that the average American is not "tax conscious," and this is doubtless true. If he shows signs of coming to, he is immediately struck down with another tax.

People in other countries are not really rude; they are just trying to imitate some of our American tourists.

The American people should worry less about the population explosion and more about the tax explosion.

Ancestors

You can't choose your ancestors, but that's fair enough. They probably wouldn't have chosen you.

The man who has nothing to boast about but his ancestors is like a potato — the only good belonging to him is underground.

Our ancestors had to haul the washwater from the well, but they didn't have to sit up nights figuring out how to meet the payments on the bucket.

The man who boasts only of his roots is conceding that he belongs to a family that's better dead than alive.

The measure of a man's character is not what he gets from his ancestors, but what he leaves his descendants.

It's so sad that our ancestors did not live long enough to realize how smart we are.

A miser might be pretty tough to live with, but he often makes a nice ancestor.

Everybody thinks thrift is a wonderful virtue, especially in our ancestors.

Anger

"Anger" is just one letter short of *danger*.

He is a fool who cannot get angry, but he is a wise man who will not.

Never strike a child! You might miss and hurt yourself.

Hot words never resulted in cool judgment.

He who has a sharp tongue soon cuts his own throat.

We never weather the storm by storming the weather.

You can't put things across by getting cross.

When a man is wrong and won't admit it, he always becomes angry.

Speak when you are angry and you will make the best speech you will ever regret.

To take the wind out of an angry man's sails — stay calm.

The size of a man is measured by the size of the thing that makes him angry.

An angry man is seldom reasonable; a reasonable man is seldom angry.

Anger is a state that starts with madness and ends with regret.

The best way to get rid of a hothead is to give him the cold shoulder.

You shouldn't get angry at someone who knows more than you do. After all, it's not his fault.

Anger is like the fire extinguisher in a building — it is to be used only in case of emergency.

When angry count ten before speaking. When very angry count one hundred and then don't speak.

For every minute you're angry, you lose sixty seconds of happiness.

Men with clenched fists cannot shake hands.

No one can be reasonable and angry at the same time.

Striking while the iron is hot may be all right, but don't strike while the head is hot.

You are not a dynamic person simply because you blow your top.

Have you noticed that a fire department never fights fire with fire?

The world needs more warm hearts and fewer hot heads.

People who fly into a rage always make a bad landing.

Anyone who angers you conquers you.

To be angry with a weak man is proof that you are not very strong yourself.

When you see a married couple who's coming down the street, the one two or three steps ahead is the one who's mad.

The man who cannot be angry at evil usually lacks enthusiasm for good.

Be strong enough to control your anger instead of letting it control you.

No matter whether you are on the road or in an argument, when you begin to see red, STOP!

The emptier the pot, the quicker the boil — watch your temper!

Anger is a wind that blows out the lamp of the mind.

Every time you give someone a piece of your mind you make your head a little emptier.

The fellow who gets on a high horse is riding for a fall.

One of the sorriest spectacles imaginable is the anger of two people who have gotten into an argument over something that neither of them knows anything about.

Anger makes your mouth work faster than your mind.

There are two things that a man should never be angry at — what he can help, and what he cannot.

The man who loses his head is usually the last one to miss it.

It's easy to get up in the air. Coming down is what hurts.

We have found that it's much easier to restrain our wrath when the other fellow is bigger than we are.

When a person strikes in anger, he usually misses the mark.

Form the habit of closing your mouth firmly when angry.

The greatest remedy for anger is delay.

As a general rule, the angriest person in a controversy is the one who is wrong.

The difference between a prejudice and a conviction is that you can explain a conviction without getting angry.

Forgiveness saves the expense of anger, the high cost of hatred, and the waste of energy.

It is impossible to express love with a clenched fist.

The measure of a man is the size of the thing it takes to get his goat.

Patience strengthens the spirit, sweetens the temper, stifles anger, subdues pride, and bridles the tongue.

Blowing your stack adds to air pollution.

Animals

A Shetland pony is nothing but a compact horse.

Animals are such agreeable friends; they ask no questions, they make no criticisms.

An elephant never forgets. After all, what does it have to remember?

Many people don't like horses because they're uncomfortable in the middle and dangerous at both ends.

An ape is an animal with the effrontery to resemble man.

A gorilla in a Dallas zoo watches a TV set near his cage. He appears to be almost human — except that he seems to enjoy the commercials.

A racehorse is an animal that can take several thousand people for a ride at the same time.

One nice thing about a horse is that its body won't rust after just one winter on salted roads.

Many a bee has been drowned in his own honey.

The bee that makes the honey doesn't hang around the hive.

Bees can't make honey and sting at the same time.

It's real nice for children to have pets until the pets start having children.

People love goldfish because they like to see something with a mouth open that's not complaining.

The reason the cow jumped over the moon was because there was a short circuit in the milking machine.

If you have occasion to criticize a mule, do it to his face.

For the holidays, why not give the gift that keeps on giving? — a female cat.

Man is the only animal that laughs, but when you look at some people, it's hard to understand how the animals keep from laughing.

Veterinarians now prescribe birth-control pills for dogs — it's part of an anti-litter campaign.

A mule is an animal that has no pride in ancestry and no hope of posterity.

A farmer once said his mule was awfully backward about going forward — and this is also true of a lot of people today.

A mule makes no headway while he's kicking; neither does a man.

The donkey and the elephant play important roles in American politics. The bull plays a major role too.

A scientist recently crossed a carrier pigeon with a woodpecker. The bird not only carries messages, but he knocks on the door.

Antiques

Antique is a magic word that makes something worthless suddenly priceless.

The best antique is an old friend.

Antiques are things that one generation buys, the next generation gets rid of, and the following generation buys again.

The difference between antiques and junk depends on who's selling what to whom.

Sign on an antique shop in Stockton, California: "Come in and buy what your grandmother threw away."

An antique is something people forget to throw away until it becomes valuable.

Some people who buy modern furniture have antiques by the time they finish paying for it.

An antique is a fugitive from the junk yard with a price on its head.

Sign in an antique shop in Baltimore: "Our prices are firm. The management is not emotionally equipped to haggle."

Generally speaking, an antique is anything that has outlasted its warranty period.

Things would be a lot nicer if antique people were valued as highly as antique furniture.

Anybody could get rich if he could guess the exact moment at which a piece of junk becomes an antique.

Appearance

Life not only begins at forty — it begins to show.

Appearances can be deceiving — a dollar bill looks the same as it did twenty-five years ago.

A long face and a broad mind are rarely found under the same hat.

Nothing improves a man's appearance as much as the photograph the newspapers use with his obituary.

A father is usually more pleased to have his child look like him than act like him.

Nothing changes a small boy's appearance as much as soap.

Happier faces are seen on bottles of iodine than on some Christians.

A few Christians give the impression they have been baptized in vinegar.

The world will not be convinced of your faith by the sourness of your face.

A real friend will tell you when you have spinach stuck in your teeth.

Any girl can be glamorous. All she has to do is stand still and look stupid.

Some girls are so homely they could sue their parents for damages.

The Lord gives us our faces, but we must provide the expression.

The surest sign that a man is not great is when he strives to *look* great.

When happiness gets into your system, it is bound to break out on your face.

A beautiful heart more than offsets the handicap of a homely face.

It is a mistake to trust a man with an honest face. After all, that may be the only honest part of him.

Don't judge a man by the clothes he wears. God made one; the tailor, the other.

Some people will never live to be as old as they look.

A plastic surgeon increases your face value.

Some preachers are so sad of voice and countenance that they should apply for membership in the embalmer's union.

As a general rule, a green salesman is a better producer than a blue one.

If plenty of sleep is an aid to good looks, it seems that a considerable number of people are suffering from insomnia.

Many folks contend that sleeping out of doors makes one beautiful. That explains the charming appearance of the town drunk.

There's a face-lift you can perform yourself that is guaranteed to improve your appearance. It is called a smile.

People seldom notice old clothes if you wear a big smile.

The shorter the time to April 15, the longer the face of the taxpayer.

Few women believe what their mirrors and bathroom scales tell them.

The real secret of looking young is being young.

Applause

There's a new alarm clock on the market for actors. It doesn't ring — it applauds.

Applause at the beginning of a speech is a manifestation of faith. If it comes in the middle of the speech it's a sign of hope. If it comes at the end it's always charity.

It is more important to deserve the applause of people than to obtain it.

Appreciation

You must speak up to be heard, but sometimes you have to shut up to be appreciated.

Appreciate what you have before you haven't.

The best way to appreciate your job is to imagine yourself without one.

Don't forget that appreciation is always appreciated.

Appreciation is like an insurance policy. It has to be renewed occasionally.

If you want to really appreciate what an enormous job it is to clean up the environment, start cleaning out your garage.

The world's most unsatisfied hunger is the hunger for appreciation.

Appreciation is what some people lack when you do them a favor.

It is better to appreciate something you have than to have something you can't appreciate.

Some wives appreciate their husbands the most while they are away at work.

Appreciation makes people feel more important than almost anything you can give them.

A slap on the back often pushes out the chest.

A single rose for the living is better than a costly wreath at the grave.

Happiness will never come to those who fail to appreciate what they already have.

Carve your name on hearts — not on marble.

School teachers are not fully appreciated by parents until it rains all day Saturday.

Arguments

When you see a married couple who's coming down the street, the one two or three steps ahead is the one who's mad.

No matter whether you are on the road or in an argument, when you begin to see red, STOP!

One of the sorriest spectacles imaginable is the anger of two people who have gotten into an argument over something that neither of them knows anything about.

A lot of good arguments are spoiled by some fool who knows what he's talking about.

The only people who really listen to an argument are the neighbors.

Nothing makes an argument so one-sided as telling about it.

It will do no good to argue if you're in the wrong and if you're right — you don't need to.

The best way to win an argument with a woman is to hit her over the head with a new mink coat.

Many an argument is sound — and only sound!

The more arguments you win, the fewer friends you'll have.

A word to the wise usually starts an argument.

Before you have an argument with your boss, you'd better take a good look at both sides — his side and the outside.

The weaker the argument, the stronger the words.

Married couples who claim they've never had an argument in forty years either have poor memories or a very dull life to recall.

When you're arguing with your wife, make absolutely sure you're right — and then let the matter drop.

The best way to get the best of an argument is to listen to it at a safe distance.

Sometimes when you're arguing with a fool, he's doing the same thing.

An argument produces plenty of heat, but not much light.

Never argue with a woman. You might win — and then you'll really be in trouble.

It is impossible to defeat an ignorant man in an argument.

You get out of an argument exactly what you put into it — a lot of hot air.

In an argument the best weapon to hold is your tongue.

Discussion is an exchange of knowledge; argument is an exchange of ignorance.

A husband and wife in Montana make it a point not to argue over anything not worth arguing about. Of course, this leads to some dandy fights over whether or not a subject is worthwhile.

The argument you just won with your wife isn't over yet.

There are a lot of hot arguments over "cold cash."

An argument is where two people are trying to get in the last word first.

Some people are so argumentative they won't even eat food that agrees with them.

People who know the least always argue the most.

An argument is a collision in which two trains of thought are derailed.

One thing a man learns from an argument with a woman is how to be a good loser.

If you must argue, the best way to win is to start by being right.

An argument is a question with two sides — and no end.

Don't argue at the dinner table. The one who is not hungry always wins the argument.

In most cases all an argument proves is that two people are present.

When an argument flares up, the wise man quenches it with silence.

It is a rare thing to win an argument and the other fellow's respect at the same time.

A woman has the last word in any argument. Anything a man says after that is the beginning of a new argument.

It is fair to hear both sides of an argument, it is heavenly to hear the end of it.

Never argue with your doctor; he has inside information.

Arguing with your wife is as useless as trying to blow out a lightbulb.

A sure way to stop a red-hot argument is to lay a few cold facts on it.

The only thing worse than being on the wrong side of an argument is being in the middle.

Many a family argument has been saved by the doorbell or telephone.

After winning an argument with his wife, the wisest thing a man can do is apologize.

An argument is like a country road; you never know where it'll lead.

The hottest arguments over Canasta start after the guests depart.

Nothing will add heat to an argument like rubbing car fenders together.

Never start an argument with a woman when she's tired — or when she's rested!

It is never worthwhile to argue about the religion you haven't got.

There are a lot more marital arguments over a wink than a mink.

The easiest way to start an argument these days is to get two economists together.

When a wise man argues with a woman, he says nothing!

Nothing is so apt to start an argument with your wife as winning one.

Before arguing with your boss, make absolutely sure you're right — then let the matter drop.

Now there's a book on the market for people who disagree — a CONTRADICTIONARY.

A diplomat doesn't think it's necessary to understand anything in order to argue about it.

An ounce of facts is worth a ton of arguments.

A fanatic is one who can't change his opinions and won't change the subject.

To be a gentleman is a worthy trait, but it is a great handicap in an argument.

Nursing a grudge is like arguing with a policeman — the more you do it, the worse things get.

A married couple in Montana is so concerned with their health that whenever they have an argument, she jogs to her mother's.

A certain Hollywood couple is so incompatible they can't even agree on what to argue about.

More homes are destroyed by fusses than by funerals or fires.

There's one thing to be said for ignorance — it causes a lot of interesting arguments.

It is impossible to win an argument with an ignorant man.

We once settled our problems over coffee and cigarettes — now, they're our problems.

When a man uses profanity to support an argument, it indicates that either the man or the argument is weak — probably both.

What a great world this would be if people would spend as much energy practicing their religion as they spend quarreling about it.

Arguing about religion is much easier than practicing it.

It must be wonderful to be a wife. Just imagine knowing that every time there's an argument you are going to win.

Atheists
see also Unbelief

What do atheists do with their money? Surely they wouldn't carry around anything that says, "In God We Trust."

The atheist can't find God for the same reason that a thief can't find a policeman.

A good question for an atheist is to serve him a delicious meal and then ask him if he believes there is a cook.

An atheist is the fellow who shakes his fist and defies the God he claims doesn't exist.

An atheist hopes the Lord will do nothing to disturb his disbelief.

If there are any good traits about the atheist, he got them from Christianity.

The trouble with being an atheist is you have nobody to talk to when you're alone.

It may be hard to believe in God, but it's much harder not to believe in Him.

The worst possible moment for an atheist is when he feels grateful and has no one to thank.

There's a service, similar to Dial-A-Prayer, called Dial-A-Doubt. It's for atheists who aren't sure.

Attention

If you would like to get your wife's attention — just look comfortable!

The only thing some people pay is attention.

It is extremely easy for us to give our major attention to minor matters.

A good listener is one who can give you his full attention without hearing a word you say.

The easiest way to get a kid's attention is to stand in front of the TV set.

Pay attention to what a man is, not what he has been.

It's hard, if not impossible, to get a child to pay attention to you, especially when you're telling him something for his own good.

The quickest way to get a lot of individual attention is to make a big mistake.

Troubles and weeds thrive on lack of attention.

When a child pays attention to his parents, they're probably whispering.

Everybody likes friendly attention and cooperation. We always get it when we give it.

There would be fewer divorces if men gave as much loving attention to their wives as they do to their cars, boats, and dogs.

To get maximum attention, it's hard to beat a big mistake.

The quickest way for a mother to get her children's attention is to sit down and look comfortable.

While science has made giant strides in communication in recent years, there's still a lot to be said for paying attention.

It's no fun to suffer in silence unless you first make enough noise to attract attention — and sympathizers!

Authority

Nothing intoxicates some people like a sip of authority.

Authority is like a bank account. The more you draw on it, the less you have.

Some men who speak with authority at work know enough to bow to a higher authority at home.

There is just as much authority in the family today as there ever was — only now the children exercise it.

Give authority to some people and they grow; give it to others and they swell.

Nothing pleases a little man more than an opportunity to crack a big whip.

If there's anything small, shallow, or ugly about a person, giving him a little authority will bring it out.

The time to teach obedience to authority is in the playpen instead of the State pen.

Autobiographies

An autobiography is a book that reveals nothing bad about its writer except his memory.

Autobiography is an excellent medium for revealing *some* of the truth about yourself.

Anyone who's written an autobiography learns you can make two kinds of enemies with such a book — the people you mention and those you don't.

An autobiography, like charity, covers a multitude of sins.

Automation

Automation has opened up a whole new field of unemployment.

We often wonder if automation will ever replace the taxpayer!

It's true that automation creates new jobs. It takes more people to correct the mistakes.

Another advantage of automation is that the machines don't take time out for coffee breaks.

Automation is man's effort to make work so easy that women can do it.

Teachers in the lower grades needn't worry about automation until someone invents a machine that can blow noses and remove snowsuits and boots.

We are now told that automation is a process that gets all the work done while you just stand there. When we were younger, this process was called MOTHER.

Automobiles

It is simply remarkable how the apostle Paul covered so much territory and accomplished so much without a car.

One way to reduce motor accidents is to build cars so they can't go any faster than the average person thinks.

According to sales reports, automobile manufacturers had a bang-up year. According to accident reports, so did their customers.

Some men achieve distinction by the kind of car they drive — others by the kind of wife that is driving them.

No two people in a car can agree on which window should be open — and how much.

An American always makes sure his car is working whether he is or not.

One day an American worries about going to the poorhouse, and the next day he buys a new automobile.

One nice thing about a horse is that its body won't rust after just one winter on salted roads.

There may be fewer cars on the road nowadays, but the number of nuts driving them hasn't diminished.

If you think your automobile is expensive to operate, try operating a shopping cart in a supermarket.

It seems that our modern cars won't start until the seat belt is fastened — and the pocketbook is emptied.

The nicest looking car is the one pulling out of a parking space you want.

What the average man wants to get out of his new car is the kids.

Every year the cars get lower and wider, while the payments get longer and higher.

The first thing you'll notice in the glove compartment of your new car is a little booklet telling you how to lie about your gas mileage.

Driving an automobile would be a much greater pleasure if each motorist would use his head as much as he uses his horn.

One advantage of the compact car is that when any of the kids start acting up they can be reached by hand.

Automobiles continue to be driven at two speeds — lawful and awful.

Many people are having trouble with their new cars. The engine won't start and the payments won't stop.

Automobiles are like men — the less substantial they are, the more knocking they do.

There are too many middle-of-the-roaders in America, and they all drive cars.

A man in Alabama complains that his new car has been recalled by the dealer — there was a defect in his bank account.

The automobile has had a great influence on public morals; it has completely stopped horse stealing.

Perhaps the most necessary automobile accessory is a wallet.

Modern automobiles have every convenience — except a push button to lower the payments.

Bumper sticker on a 1950 Ford: "When passing, watch out for flying parts."

An elderly gentleman in Nevada calls his car Abe. It's a Lincoln.

After pricing new cars it begins to look like the economy model is the one you're now driving.

There was a time when $200 was the down-payment on a car; now it's the sales tax.

By the time a man can afford to buy one of those little sports cars, he's too fat to get into it.

There are a lot of nuts rattling around inside automobiles that the manufacturers didn't put there.

Nothing lengthens the life of your car like marrying-off the last of your children.

The easiest way to lose control of a car is to forget to make the payments.

Don't get discouraged and sell your car. Any day now you may find a place to park it.

There are two finishes for automobiles: lacquer and liquor.

The reason the automobile is so popular today is that you can drive one without owning it.

If you think a seat belt is uncomfortable, you've never tried a stretcher!

The difference between learning to drive a car and learning to play golf is that when you learn to play golf you don't hit anything.

The automobile has certainly discouraged walking, particularly among pedestrians.

Bumper sticker on an old car: "Don't pass — push!"

Most of our modern cars have so many warning lights and buzzers around the dashboard that just driving it makes you feel half-nagged to death.

What we want most in a new car is us.

It's not the used cars that are a menace on the highways — it's the mis-used cars.

Many an old car suffers from "rattle fatigue."

One of the major car manufacturers has an unusual problem on its hands. It recently re-called its faulty cars — and got back 5,000 more than it built.

The most popular model next year may be a compact car — with payments to match.

There was a time when you could rent a car for a week for what it now costs to park it for a day.

Some automobile manufacturers have a sneaky way of lowering the list price. For instance, on one model the steering wheel is an optional extra.

Statistics show that in 1940 each car on the road had an average of 2.2 persons; in 1950 it was 1.4. At this rate, by 1985 every third car on the road will be empty.

Scientists are working on the ultimate economy car. It will just sit in the driveway and impress the neighbors.

Soon after purchasing a used car a man finds out how hard it is to drive a bargain.

A cheap old car can be quite annoying. But so can a new expensive one.

The used car business is on the boom. Old cars that no longer run are rented to young couples who just want to park.

One thing we've learned about compact cars is that it takes twice as many of them to make a traffic jam.

Nothing depreciates a car faster than having a neighbor buy a new one.

Automobiles did away with horses and now they're working on people.

An automotive invention that is sorely needed is brakes that will automatically get tight when the driver does.

The auto industry accounts for one out of every twenty jobs in the United States — and this does not include morticians.

A limousine is a car with a glass partition to shut out stupid remarks from the backseat.

The springs of the late-model cars are of such high quality that you can hardly feel the bump when you run over a pedestrian.

There are few Americans who have never seen an automobile, but plenty who have not seen one soon enough.

Bumper sticker on the back of a car in Guthrie, Oklahoma: "Watch out for the driver in the car following me."

It is generally agreed that the first thing a new car runs into is money.

Automobiles are gradually doing away with absent-minded people.

One percent of the automobiles on the highways are rented — the others are mortgaged.

In these days of high speed and crowded highways, it doesn't take much of a car to last a lifetime.

Anybody who thinks the automobile has made people lazy never had to pay for one.

Present-day cars are so quiet that the only noise you hear is from the finance company.

Isn't it wonderful that our new cars are almost completely automatic? This leaves your mind free to worry about how you're going to make the monthly payments.

The first thing that strikes a visitor in New York City is a big car.

Today's cars keep a person strapped without safety belts.

Engineers are trying to build a car that will stop smoking. We would all like to own a car that would stop drinking.

It is estimated that by 1985 there will be more than 190 million automobiles in the United States. If you want to cross the street, you'd better do it now.

There are too many people in too many cars in too much of a hurry going too many directions to get nowhere for nothing.

Some automobiles have fluid drives; others just have a drip at the wheel.

Everybody should learn to drive an automobile. This is especially true of those who sit behind the steering wheel.

A good way to make your present car run better is to have a salesman quote you the price of a new one.

Automobiles wouldn't be so dangerous if the horsepower of the engine was proportioned to the horse-sense of the driver.

Nowadays every man wants life, liberty, and an automobile in which to pursue happiness.

You have to take your hat off to some of these new compact cars — or get it knocked off as you enter.

There are still a few people who can remember when it cost more to operate a car than to park it.

Any day now we expect to see power steering for backseat drivers.

Our grandparents never dreamed that the steering wheel would become America's only family circle.

It's not only the cost and the upkeep of a car that worries you, but also the possible turnover.

Is there any music as sweet as that of a car starting on a cold morning?

Car sickness is that feeling you get every month when the payment is due.

Some of our new cars are so classy the motor no longer purrs — it sneers!

New cars these days have a longer guarantee than the people who drive them.

Power brakes may stop a car on a dime, but it usually costs more than a hundred dollars to get the rear end fixed.

Nothing reduces the value of a car like trading it in.

An automobile has been described as a four-wheeled vehicle that runs up hills and down pedestrians.

It was more fun driving a car in the old days when the crank was in front of the engine.

Even the best running cars have some jerks in them.

The trouble with bucket seats in automobiles is that not everyone has the same size bucket.

In adding safety devices to automobiles, why not re-design the steering wheel into the shape of a harp?

The most dangerous thing about an automobile is one nut — the one behind the steering wheel.

Sign in a car on an out-of-the-way street: "Attention car thieves — this car is already stolen."

An automobile can help you see the world, but it's up to you to decide which world!

Always look at the brighter side of things — whenever a car is stolen, it creates another parking place.

A new car isn't a barometer of how much money a fellow has, but it's a pretty good indication of how much he owes.

An automobile dealer in Nevada offers a big extra — he supplies two friendly witnesses for your first accident.

Some auto mechanics can estimate the cost of repairs very closely. They can usually get within a dollar or two of what you have in your pocket.

You get a pretty good idea of eternity when you start paying for an $8,000 car on the installment plan.

Thank heaven! More people get autos than autos get people.

Having a big car doesn't always mean you have money; it may mean you once *had* money.

The biggest need in auto safety is the recall of a few million defective drivers.

Owning a compact car can be very economical. If you go out with another couple, you have to use their car.

If you think it's tough making the payments on your car, try not making them.

Sign in an automobile showroom in Little Rock, Arkansas: "Let's all fight poverty together. Buy a new car.

The new cars give you more room by removing the bulge in your wallet.

The most effective auto-safety measure is accidentally locking the keys inside the car.

One of the best automobile insurance policies is a Sunday afternoon nap.

Whoever called them "pleasure cars" never drove them in traffic.

Drive-in banks were established so that automobiles could see their real owners occasionally.

Soon after purchasing a used car a man finds out how hard it is to drive a bargain.

Don't drive as if you owned the road — drive as if you owned the car.

Caution is one automobile accessory you can't buy.

If Congress really wants to help the auto industry sell more cars, it should start building more parking lots.

In the old days the young fellow who went courting turned down the gas. Now he steps on it.

Have you noticed how delicately balanced the economy is? The minute auto prices go down, gasoline prices go up.

Walking is good exercise if you can dodge those who aren't.

The family that stays together probably has only one car.

The worst fault of a motorist is his belief that he has none.

The most dangerous wheel of chance is the steering wheel.

If all gambling were illegal, we would all have to stop driving cars and getting married.

The time was when the perfect gift for a sixteen-year-old girl was a compact. It still is — if it has four wheels.

At the last count, gossip was running down more people than automobiles.

The value of horse sense is shown by the fact that the horse was afraid of the automobile at the time the pedestrian laughed at it.

The wheel was man's greatest invention until he got behind it.

The juvenile delinquent is a mixed-up kid, a victim of mixed drinks — mostly alcohol and gasoline.

The only way you can get the same gas mileage in your car as your friends say they get in theirs is to lie about it.

Life is one dodge after another — cars, taxes, and responsibilities.

What we need in this country is a car that eats oats.

Automobile dealers say that motorists are demanding lighter cars. So are the pedestrians.

Detroit has finally come up with a 100 percent effective anti-pollution device. It's an ignition key that doesn't fit.

There should be just half as much horse sense behind the wheel as there is horsepower under the hood.

All forward motion isn't necessarily progress. Did your brakes ever go out as you were driving down a hill?

A rumor is afloat that we have a new trade agreement with Russia. We will send them 10,000 automobiles from Detroit, and they will send us 20,000 parking spaces from Siberia.

We have more cars in the United States, but Russia has more vacant parking places.

Nowadays when you tell a teen-ager he must shift for himself, he thinks you're going to buy him a new sports car.

The best way to keep teen-agers home is to make their surroundings pleasant — and let the air out of the tires.

A few teen-agers think they know all about driving a car once they learn where the horn is located.

The worst car trouble is when the engine won't start and the payments won't stop.

How far a young man goes these days depends on how much gas was left in the car.

B

Baby Sitters
Bachelors
Baldness
Banks
Banquets
Barbers
Bargains
Behavior
Bible

Bigamy
Bigotry
Birthdays
Blushing
Boasting
Books
Bores
Borrowing

Bosses
Boys
Brains
Budgets
Burdens
Bureaucracy
Business
Businessmen

Baby Sitters

A baby sitter is not experienced until she knows which kid to sit with and which kid to sit on.

There's an art to baby sitting. It isn't easy to watch TV, read a book, and eat a sandwich while the kids are crying.

A baby sitter is a teen-ager you hire to let your children do whatever they are big enough to do.

Baby sitting is a big business because it meets a crying need.

It's extremely difficult for a baby sitter to wake up five or ten minutes before the parents return home.

A baby sitter feeds the baby at ten, twelve, and two — and herself at nine, eleven, and one.

A baby sitter is a teen-ager who behaves like an adult, while the adults are out behaving like teen-agers.

Little Willie is at the awkward age — too young to leave him home alone, and too old to trust with baby sitters.

One of life's mysteries is why a girl who has done baby-sitting ever gets married.

A grandmother is a baby sitter who watches the kids instead of the television.

Bachelors

It may be that bachelors make more mistakes than married men — but they don't make the big one.

A bachelor usually wants one single thing in life — himself!

A bachelor is a guy who leans toward women, but not far enough to lose his balance.

An old bachelor in Kentucky finally fell in love. He got a cortisone shot so he could propose on bended knees.

Bachelors have no idea what married bliss is, and that's also true of a lot of husbands.

To the bachelor, horror films are pictures of a wedding.

A wealthy bachelor is a guy who saved money to get married, and then changed his mind.

For a man to remain a bachelor calls for a cool head — or cold feet!

Bachelors, like detergents, work fast and leave no rings.

A bachelor wishes he had as much fun as his married friends imagine he has.

A bachelor in Denver advertised for a wife in a newspaper: "Bachelor with waterbed desires to meet a nice, hard-working girl with short toenails."

Married men can't understand why every bachelor isn't a millionaire.

A bachelor is a rolling stone that gathers no boss.

Most bachelors have no ties except those that need pressing.

All bachelors expect to get married just as soon as they can find a girl who loves them as much as they love themselves.

A bachelor looks before he leaps, then stays where he is.

It isn't the "good old days" a bachelor fears he'll miss if he marries — it's the good old nights.

A bachelor never gets over the idea that he is a thing of beauty and a boy forever.

The bachelor's favorite dish is any dish that's already washed.

A bachelor may have no buttons on his shirt, but a married man often has no shirt.

All a bachelor has to do to discover his hidden faults is to get married.

A bachelor gets tangled up with a lot of women in order to avoid getting tied up with one.

You can always tell a man who's head of the house. He's a bachelor.

A bachelor is a man who has cheated some worthy woman out of her alimony.

Many a bachelor longs for a wife who will take care of him — and so does many a husband.

A bachelor is a man who makes his own bed and lies in it — at least a couple of times a week.

Nowadays it's easy for a bachelor to remain single. Every time he turns his TV set on he hears that most women have stringy hair, rough red hands, bad breath, and are overweight.

A Florida bachelor sent his picture to a Lonely Hearts Club. They replied, "We're not that lonely."

Any bachelor knows that June rhymes with groom and doom.

A bachelor is a man who is completely dedicated to life, liberty, and the happiness of pursuit.

The happiest day of a bachelor's life is the one when he almost got married but didn't.

Bachelors avoid a woman who has a ring in her voice.

Any man who speaks without fear of contradiction is probably a bachelor.

Many bachelors claim they never got married because they couldn't afford the luxury of a divorce.

A man who refuses to fight used to be called a coward. Today they call him a bachelor.

There are two kinds of bachelors: those too fast to be caught, and those too slow to be worth catching.

Most bachelors have quit chasing girls — they can't find any that'll run.

Did you hear about the bachelor who said he could have married any girl he pleased, but he never could find one he pleased?

Lots of men are bachelors by choice — a choice some girls didn't want to make.

A bachelor is a man who takes advantage of the fact that marriage isn't compulsory.

Flattery is what makes husbands out of bachelors.

A girl admires the tone of a bachelor's voice when there's a ring in it.

In Hollywood it's difficult for a bachelor to remain a bachelor — and even more difficult for a husband to remain a husband.

When a husband dreams he's a bachelor, it's a sign he's going to be disappointed when he wakes up.

Kissing is a practice that shortens life — single life!

The thought of marriage frightens a lot of bachelors — and a few husbands too!

Kissing is a practice that shortens life — single life!

Warning to all single men: There's a new perfume on the market with a secret ingredient — it makes a man think he can support a wife.

A wife is a great comfort to a husband during the distressing times a bachelor never has.

Baldness

Nothing better has ever been developed for baldness than a hat.

There's one nice thing about baldness — it's neat.

Man's oldest fall-out problem is baldness.

Sadder than falling leaves is falling hair.

To the baldheaded man, dandruff is a thrill.

There's a new remedy on the market for baldness. It's made of alum and persimmon juice. It doesn't grow hair but it shrinks your head to fit what hair you have left.

Nature seems determined to make us work. The less hair we have, the more face we have to wash.

Baldheaded people should remember that when God made heads He covered up the ones He didn't like.

The advantage of being bald is this: When you expect callers, all you have to do is straighten your tie.

Our great problem is not production, but distribution. This strikes a baldheaded man with peculiar force every time he shaves.

The baldheaded man may be ridiculed, but he's the first in the group to know when it starts to rain.

Better a bald head than none at all.

A bald head is something nobody wants to have, and nobody wants to lose.

Baldheaded men never think of themselves as bald; they think everybody else is hairy.

Barbers seem to take great delight in calling attention to the bald spot that you're trying to forget.

A gentleman complains that when long hair became stylish his started to fall out.

A hair in the head is worth two in the brush.

Hair seems important only when we no longer have any.

A man in Nevada says that when he was a boy his hair was light; then it turned dark, then it turned grey, then it turned loose.

People worry about their gray hair, but it's actually great to have gray hair. Ask any man who's bald.

People are always telling a woman how pretty her hair looks — but the only time they comment about a man's hair is when he no longer has any.

No baldheaded man was ever converted by a sermon during the fly season.

Men usually worry more about losing their hair than their heads.

Banks

Some banks guarantee maximum interest rates for several years, which is more than a marriage license can do.

There's a bank in California that has a "western window" for those who are quick on the draw.

Bank interest on a loan is so high that if you can afford to pay it you don't need the loan.

Drive-in banks were established so that automobiles could see their real owners occasionally.

A bank is a place where you can keep the government's money until the IRS asks for it.

Many banks have a new kind of Christmas club in operation. The new club helps you save money to pay for last year's gifts.

A bank is a financial institution where you can borrow money if you can present sufficient evidence to show that you don't need it.

Said a banker's son, "My pop went on a diet; there was too much collateral in his blood."

Many people seem to think a home is only good to borrow money on.

Modern prosperity means two cars in the garage, a boat in the driveway, and a note due at the bank.

Being prosperous means your credit is good enough to borrow money at the bank.

Banquets

At most banquets you'll find more after-dinner speakers than after-dinner listeners.

Too often a banquet is a plate of cold chicken and peas surrounded by warm appeals for funds.

The banquet's honored guest was introduced as follows: "We're very pleased to have as our guest speaker a man who has to catch a plane in twenty minutes."

A banquet is an affair where you eat a lot of food you don't want before talking about something you don't understand to a crowd of people who don't want to hear what you have to say.

No man is as smart as he sounds at his alumni banquet.

Barbers

A barber's remarks are sometimes more keen and cutting than his razor.

Barbers seem to take great delight in calling attention to the bald spot that you're trying to forget.

Most barbers have a scraping acquaintance with a great many people.

Sign in a Baltimore barber shop: "Six Barbers — Panel Discussions."

The only difference between a "hair stylist" and a regular barber is the price.

One guy who always goes to the top is a barber.

Then there's the barber whose specialty is "roadmap shaves"; when he's done, your face is full of short cuts.

Nothing makes a barber suffer in silence as much as not talking.

Bargains

A bargain is anything that costs no more today than it did last week.

Nowadays everything is a bargain — because by the time you get it home the price has gone up.

A bargain is when two people are sure they got the better of each other.

It's easy to tell when you've got a bargain — it doesn't fit.

Soon after purchasing a used car a man finds out how hard it is to drive a bargain.

A bargain sale is where women fight for merchandise that's reduced in price because nobody wanted it in the first place.

Anything you buy at a low price that you don't need is not a bargain.

A bargain is something you can't use at a price you can't resist.

One of the best bargains you can get these days is parking on what's left of the other fellow's dime.

A bargain is anything that is only moderately overpriced.

A bargain is something that looks better than it is and sells for less than it was.

A bargain is defined as a "ludicrous transaction in which each party thinks he has cheated the other."

There would be fewer divorces if women hunted for husbands with as much thought as they hunt for bargains.

The best exercise today is hunting for bargains.

Good government is a bargain at any price.

Heaven is a bargain, however great the cost.

One of the problems of modern life is for a husband to teach his wife that even bargains cost money.

Don't buy it for a song — unless you're sure you know what the pitch is.

One of the most difficult tasks in the world is to convince women that even a bargain costs money.

Behavior
see also Human Nature

Think what others ought to be like, then start being like that yourself.

To know what is right and not do it is as bad as doing wrong.

Statistics show there are three ages when men misbehave: young, old, and middle.

The surest way to gain respect is to earn it by conduct.

It's nice to be important, but it's more important to be nice.

A lot of good behavior is due to poor health.

Folks would enjoy us more if we gave as much thought to our own behavior as we do to our neighbor's.

No matter what you do, someone always knew you would.

When you make a mountain out of a molehill, don't expect anyone to climb up to see the view.

Let's all sympathize with the poor girl who spent four years learning how to behave in polite society and the rest of her life trying to locate it.

Most of us don't put our best foot forward until we get the other one in hot water.

No man is as smart as he sounds at his alumni banquet.

No one can stay young very long, but some manage to act like children all their lives.

What a scarcity of news there would be if everybody obeyed the Ten Commandments!

Actually there's only a slight difference between keeping your chin up and sticking your neck out, but it's worth knowing.

When in Rome do as the Romans do, that is, if the Romans do as they ought to do.

The kind of behavior that once brought shame and disgrace now brings a book, movie, or a television contract.

To really know a man, observe his behavior with a woman, a flat tire, and a child.

Most of us want other people's children to behave the way ours should.

Behavior is a mirror in which everyone reflects his own image.

When adults behave like children we call them juvenile; when children behave like adults we call them delinquents.

There are no detour signs along the straight and narrow path.

Anybody whose behavior is normal these days is probably considered to be slightly eccentric.

Behavior is what a man does, not what he thinks, feels, or believes.

How did people ever get along before they had all those government bureaus to tell them what to do?

It sometimes looks foolish for folks to be spending so much time loving their enemies when they should be treating their friends a little better.

A father is usually more pleased to have his child look like him than act like him.

None of us is responsible for all the things that happen to us, but we are responsible for the way we act when they do happen.

We count our blessings on our fingers and our miseries on an adding machine.

Men and nations do behave wisely, once all other alternatives have been exhausted.

We try to see some good in everybody we meet, but occasionally there are some folks who make us realize our eyesight isn't as good as it once was.

The behavior of some children suggests that their parents embarked on the sea of matrimony without a paddle.

Don't be a carbon copy of something. Make your own impressions.

Always hold your head up, but be careful to keep your nose at a friendly level.

You can't hold another fellow down in the ditch unless you stay down there with him.

Some people never say anything bad about the dead, or anything good about the living.

Wouldn't it be wonderful if everybody behaved as he thinks the other fellow ought to behave?

No man has a right to do as he pleases, except when he pleases to do right.

When people speak evil of you, live so that no one will believe them.

It's easy to save face. Just keep the lower half of it tightly closed.

Blowing out the other fellow's candle won't make yours shine any brighter.

By the time most folks learn to behave themselves they're too old to do anything else.

Good behavior gets a lot of credit that really belongs to a lack of opportunity.

You are young only once. If you act foolish after that you'll have to find some other excuse.

There's nothing consistent about human behavior except its tendency to drift toward evil.

Judging from the way some people behave these days, they must think that hell is air-conditioned!

We should never assume that people are going to behave as we expect them to.

Many pious people would rather study the Bible than practice what it teaches.

The business to stay out of is the other fellow's.

Some people continue to change jobs, mates, and friends — but never think of changing themselves.

A true test of a man's character is not what he does in the light, but what he does in the dark.

It isn't what you have, but what you are, that makes life worthwhile.

Children disgrace us in public by behaving just like we do at home.

The better we understand Christianity, the less satisfied we are with our practice of it.

If people have to ask you if you're a Christian — you're probably not.

Every Christian occupies some kind of a pulpit and preaches some kind of a sermon every day.

Conventions are something a lot of people leave behind when they attend one.

A person's faith is not judged by what he says about it, but by what he does about it.

Faith with works is a force. Faith without works is a farce.

No one will ever know of your honesty unless you give out some samples.

A sense of humor can help you overlook the unattractive, tolerate the unpleasant, cope with the unexpected, and smile through the unbearable.

There are two kinds of husbands: one brings his wife a gift when he returns from a convention, and the other behaved himself.

Better a little kindness while living than an extravagant floral display at the grave.

Learn to speak kind words — nobody resents them.

Statistics show that men who kiss their wives goodby in the morning live five years longer than those who don't. Some of you men had better pucker-up before you tucker-out.

As a general rule, the freedom of any people can be judged by the volume of their laughter.

If the world laughs at you, laugh right back — it's as funny as you are.

When you laugh, be sure to laugh at what people do and not at what people are.

No law, however stringent, can make the idle industrious, the shiftless provident, or the drunkard sober.

Lawyers would have a hard time making a living if people behaved themselves and kept their promises.

When you hear bells ringing, feel butterflies fluttering, and act as though you have bees in your bonnet — that's real love!

Combine common sense and the Golden Rule and you will have very little bad luck.

Just why do men lie about each other when the plain truth would be bad enough?

Man spends his life reasoning with the past, complaining about the present, and trembling for the future.

Man is the only member of the animal kingdom that apologizes — or needs to.

It is easier to hide mistakes than to prevent their consequences.

A man must be big enough to admit his mistakes, smart enough to profit from them, and strong enough to correct them.

A man who has made a mistake and doesn't correct it is committing another mistake.

Our mistake is loving things and using people, when we should use things and love people.

Do all you can and make no fuss about it.

Money not only changes hands — it changes people.

The value of a dollar will never drop as low as some people will stoop to get it.

It's not surprising that dollar bills wear out so quickly. Americans keep passing the buck.

A typical mother, seeing there are only four pieces of pie for five people, promptly announces she never did care for pie.

It's a pity more people can't travel the straight and narrow path without becoming strait-laced and narrow-minded.

Nature gave men two ends — one to sit on and one to think with. Man's success or failure is dependent on the one he uses most.

To keep young, stay around young people. To get old, try to keep up with them.

People may grow old gracefully, but seldom gratefully.

A fellow can't keep people from having a bad opinion of him, but he can keep them from being right about it.

Patience is the ability to remain silent and hungry while everybody else in the restaurant gets served.

Be the first to praise and the first to deserve praise.

Prayer does not need proof, it needs practice.

Bending our knees in prayer keeps us from breaking under the load of cares.

Wonderful things happen to us when we live expectantly, believe confidently, and pray affirmatively.

A preacher who will not try to practice what he preaches is not fit to listen to.

He who practices what he preaches may have to put in some overtime.

Those who don't practice what they preach don't have anything worthwhile to preach about.

Instead of uprooting his prejudices, the average person whitewashes them and presents them as principles.

Temper gets people into trouble, but pride keeps them there.

We all might as well face our problems. We can't run fast or far enough to get away from them all.

There's a growing suspicion that what the world needs now is a religion that will cover the other six days of the week.

A man has no more religion than he acts out in his life.

We are more comfortable with Christ in print than in practice.

True religion is the life we live, not the creeds we profess.

People don't really pay much attention to what we say about our religion, because they'd rather watch what we do about it.

Your religion doesn't amount to very much unless it causes you to come out of the grandstand onto the playing field.

If some folks lost their reputation, they should consider themselves very lucky.

What chance can a man have to control his destiny when he can't control himself?

You never have to take a dose of your own medicine if you know when to keep your mouth shut.

An open mind and a closed mouth make a happy combination.

Spending half of the time keeping quiet and the other half saying nothing is one way to keep out of trouble.

Might as well keep your mouth shut. If you talk about yourself you're a bore, and if you talk about others you're a gossip.

A man's conscience, and not his mattress, has most to do with his sleep.

If you can't crown yourself with laurels, you can wreathe your face in smiles.

To succeed — keep your head up and your overhead down.

A successful man continues to look for work after he has found a job.

Some men succeed by what they know, some by what they do, and a few by what they are.

One secret of success is to be able to put your best foot forward without stepping on anybody's toes.

It takes a big man to sympathize — a little man can criticize, and usually does.

Formula for tact: Be brief, politely; be aggressive, smilingly; be emphatic, pleasantly; be positive, diplomatically; be right, graciously.

Teen-agers haven't changed very much. They still grow up, leave home, and get married. The big difference is that today they don't always do it in that order.

Trouble causes some people to go to pieces; others to come to their senses.

The best way to surprise your wife is frequently.

Will power cannot be furnished by anyone but you.

What a nice world this world would be if we loved others as we love ourselves.

Perpetual worry will get you to one place ahead of time — the cemetery.

We are only young once. This is all society can stand.

Being young comes only once in life. The trick is to make it last as long as you can.

About the only way to stay young is to live honestly, eat sensibly, sleep well, work hard, worship regularly, and lie about your age.

Bible

A small town newspaper in Texas advertised, "Read your Bible to know what people ought to do. Read this paper to know what they actually do."

The Bible is most helpful when it is open.

A Bible that's falling apart often belongs to one who isn't.

Thousands of people don't like the Bible because it cramps their lifestyle.

Carrying a Bible will never take the place of reading it.

The most desirable time to read the Bible is as often as possible.

Keep your Bible open and you will not find the door to heaven shut.

A Bible in the hand is worth two in the bookcase.

If you couldn't get another Bible, what would yours be worth?

Dust on your Bible is not evidence that it is a dry book.

Many Christians expect the world to respect a book they neglect.

How can you have faith in the Bible unless you know what's in it.

A book which will lift men up to God must have come down from God.

Satan can quote Scripture for his purpose.

The Bible contains the vitamins for a healthy soul.

Bible verses will save you from spiritual reverses.

It's a terrible responsibility to own a Bible.

We should study the Bible as a privilege, not as a duty.

Don't criticize the Bible; let the Bible criticize you.

The Bible has nothing to fear — except neglect.

Read your Bible. A chapter a day keeps Satan away.

The Bible is the constitution of Christian civilization.

A Bible known is worth a dozen merely owned.

The Bible is not only the world's best seller, it is man's best purchase.

A Bible stored in the mind is worth a dozen stored in the bottom of a trunk.

The Bible promises no loaves to the loafer.

One evidence of the value of the Bible is the character of those who oppose it.

Satan is not afraid of a Bible with dust on it.

Those who *don't* read the Bible have no advantage over those who *can't* read it.

Study the Bible to be wise, believe it to be safe, practice it to be holy.

Men do not reject the Bible because it contradicts itself, but because it contradicts them.

No one is saved by buying a Bible he does not use, nor is one saved by reading a Bible he does not obey.

Go to your Bible regularly, open it prayerfully, read it expectantly, live it joyfully.

An aged grandfather explained why he reads the Bible several hours every day, "You might say I am cramming for my final examination."

One of the best evidences of the inspiration and infallibility of the Bible is that it has survived the fanaticism and ignorance of its friends.

Bumper stick on a car in Tyler, Texas: "Read the Bible — it'll scare hell out of you."

There are a number of splendid translations of the Bible. However, the most effective is its translation into the lives of people.

A person who merely samples the Word of God never acquires much of a taste for it.

The family Bible can be passed from generation to generation because it gets so little wear.

The Bible is a book of prayers. Out of 667 recorded prayers, there are 454 recorded answers.

Other books were given to us for information, but the Bible was given to us for transformation.

The value of the Bible doesn't consist in merely knowing it, but in obeying it.

If you will carry the Bible while you are young, it will carry you when you are old.

The study of the Bible is a postgraduate course in the richest library of human experience.

You can't understand all you read in the Bible, but you can obey what you do understand.

The Bible finds us where we are, and, with our permission, will take us where we ought to go.

Our forefathers built this country with three tools: an ax, a plow, and a book. That book was the Bible.

Many pious people would rather study the Bible than practice what it teaches.

If all the neglected Bibles in this country were dusted off at the same time, we would suffer the worst dust storm in years.

The Gideons should send a Bible to those hotel authorities who determine the room rates.

A thumbprint on the Bible is more important than a footprint on the moon.

The way some people use the "Sword of the Spirit," one would think it was made for splitting hairs.

If the Bible is mistaken in telling us from whence we came, how can we trust it to tell us where we are going?

It is impossible to mentally and socially enslave a Bible-reading people.

There's a vast difference between books that men make and the BOOK that makes men.

Noah was the first businessman mentioned in the Bible. He floated a company at a time when the rest of the world was under liquidation.

In the Book of Revelation we read of a book which no man could open. Some believe this was the pocketbook.

Our Lord does not open the windows of heaven to the person who keeps his Bible closed.

The knowledge, understanding, and appropriation of God's Word are the means by which a Christian grows.

A real highbrow is a person who can quote Shakespeare without attributing it to the Bible.

The Bible has vitamins for a healthy soul.

If some Christians knew as little about their jobs as they do the Bible, they would have to be guided to their work benches every morning.

A critically-ill lawyer was found frantically leafing through the Bible in his hospital room. When asked the reason, he replied, "Looking for loopholes."

The Bible admonishes us to love our neighbors, and also to love our enemies — probably because they are generally the same people.

An immoral man is dangerous whether he is armed with a rifle or a Bible.

The sword of the Spirit never becomes dull from use.

Be careful how you live. You may be the only Bible some people will ever read.

No matter how many new translations of the Bible are made, the people still sin the same way.

The three greatest sins of today are indifference to, neglect of, and disrespect for the Word of God.

The only way to succeed in life is to work hard, stay clean, walk with your back to the wall, and keep your Bible handy.

The student of truth keeps an open Bible, an open dictionary, and an open mind.

Bigamy

The penalty for bigamy is two mothers-in-law.

A bigamist is a chap who has had one too many.

A southern maiden married five GI's. She told the judge that Cupid must have shot her with a shrapnel.

Bigamy is having one wife too many — monogamy is often the same.

Nothing makes a man faster on his feet than politics, unless it's bigamy.

Bigamy is the only crime on the books where two rites make a wrong.

Most men would like to have a wife who's beautiful, understanding, economical, and a good cook. Unfortunately, the law allows a man only one wife!

Bigotry

Bigotry is being certain of something you know nothing about.

The bigot agrees there are two sides to every question — his side and the wrong one.

A bigot is a person who slams his mind in your face.

The mind of the bigot is like the pupil of the eye; the more light you shine into it, the more it will contract.

People who brag about having an open mind should close it occasionally and think.

A first-class mistake is to treat anyone as a second-class person.

Birthdays

Our beloved country recently celebrated its two-hundredth birthday, and all we've learned in that time is how to go fast, work less, waste more, and die quicker.

The least likely way for a middle-aged woman to celebrate her birthday is annually.

George Washington was first in war, first in peace, and first to have his birthday juggled to make a long weekend.

The design on a woman's birthday cake is often very beautiful, but the arithmetic is terrible.

Birthdays are nice to have, but too many of them will kill a person.

When a man has a birthday he may take a day off. When a woman has a birthday she may take as much as five years off.

Sign in a florist's window: "Smoking, or forgetting your wife's birthday, can be hazardous to your health."

At the birthday party of a prominent spinster, many of the guests were overcome by the heat of the candles.

A woman bakes a child's birthday cake big enough to hold all the candles — and her own small enough not to.

The best way to remember your wife's birthday is to forget it once!

A diplomatic husband said to his wife, "How do you expect me to remember your birthday when you never look any older?"

Her birthday cake had so many candles on it she was fined for air pollution.

Blushing

A baby sitter is a teen-ager who behaves like an adult, while the adults are out behaving like teen-agers.

A blush is one thing that can't be counterfeited.

When a modern girl blushes she's probably been caught doing something proper.

Judging from some of the specimens they select, can you blame brides for blushing?

Man is the only animal that blushes, and the only one that needs to.

An old-fashioned girl blushes when she is embarrassed, but a modern girl is embarrassed when she blushes.

A blush is the color of virtue.

The modern girl has all her blushing done for her by her parents, brothers, and sweethearts.

Boasting

One form of advertising that's a liability instead of an asset is a person blowing his own horn.

The man who has nothing to boast about but his ancestors is like a potato — the only good belonging to him is underground.

Those who have a right to boast don't need to.

A boaster and a liar are first cousins.

Folks who boast of being self-made usually have a few parts missing.

The trouble with blowing one's horn is that it seldom leaves any wind for climbing.

When we hear a man boasting about how much liquor he can hold, we get a mental picture of an animated garbage can.

A lot of people who boast they never go back on their word don't mind going around it a little.

The man who never boasts is always bragging about it.

Before you start tooting your own horn, be sure there's plenty of juice in your battery.

The husband who boasts that he never made a mistake has a wife who did.

There are very few who boast of having been born in a log cabin who still live in them.

The fellow who boasts of running things at his home most likely means the lawn mower, washing machine, vacuum cleaner, and errands.

He who boasts of being self-made relieves the Lord of a lot of responsibility.

The hen that laid the biggest egg usually does the least cackling about it.

Most men brag about their hunting experiences, though they're chiefly confined to shooting pool, craps, and bull.

Some people would rather blow their own horn than listen to the Marine Band.

The fellow who boasts of his open mind may only have a vacant one.

The person who boasts of having no religious prejudice quite often has no religion.

A businessman boasts that he and his wife started out with absolutely nothing, "And we've got most of it left."

The man who boasts only of his roots is conceding that he belongs to a family that's better dead than alive.

A Hollywood star boasts he's been happily married for twenty years. Of course, it took him five marriages to do it.

It's difficult to figure out who does more bragging — those who have lost weight or those who have quit smoking.

For every person who brags about being bright, there are a dozen ready to polish him off.

People who brag about having an open mind should close it occasionally and think.

The fellow who brags about how smart he is wouldn't if he was.

When a man brags that he wears the pants at home, the chances are his wife tells him which pants to put on.

Anybody who brags about what he's going to do tomorrow probably did the same thing yesterday.

The fellow who blows his horn the loudest is usually in the biggest fog.

People who brag about taking a middle-of-the-road position tend to forget they're setting themselves up for being hit from both directions.

It takes most men about two years to completely quit smoking cigarettes and twice as long to quit bragging about it.

The only time you should blow your horn is when you're in the band.

Duty is a task we look forward to with distaste, perform with reluctance, and brag about afterwards.

He who toots his own horn has everybody dodging him.

Don't brag and blow; it isn't the whistle that pulls the train.

Some proud folks are always letting off esteem.

The bouquet you hand yourself usually looks like weeds to the other fellow.

An egotist is like a ship in a fog — always blowing his horn.

Boasting and sleeping are the forerunners of failure.

Flattery will get you nowhere. This is especially true when you give it to yourself.

A fool tells you what he will do; a boaster, what he has done. The wise man does it and says nothing.

The Lord loves a cheerful giver — until he brags about it.

The trouble with people who have broken a habit is that they usually have the pieces mounted and framed.

You can't judge an automobile by the sound of its horn — nor a man!

A modest person hardly ever blows his "knows" in public.

There are a few people among us who are like boats — they toot the loudest when in a fog.

People should not forget the mama whale's advice to the baby whale, "Remember, it's only when you spout that you get harpooned."

Politics is the only profession in which a man can make a living solely by bragging.

The less power a man has, the more he brags of what he'd do if he had it.

The man who sings his own praises may have the right tune but the wrong words.

Did you ever suspect that folks who repent loud and long are really just bragging?

When selling yourself don't misrepresent the goods.

Self-praise can be put in the same class as anything else you get for nothing.

Praising yourself to the sky is not going to get you there.

When a man sings his own praise, he usually pitches the tune too high.

Self-praise is the only way some folks get any.

Few people need voice lessons to sing their own praise.

The man who sings his own praise invariably sings an unaccompanied solo.

Success doesn't always go to the head; sometimes it goes to the mouth.

A person interrupts and endangers his climb up the ladder of success when he stops to pat himself on the back.

The worst use that can be made of success is to boast of it.

Books

The Bible is not only the world's best seller, it is man's best purchase.

The book *How to Beat Inflation* has just gone from $1.75 to $2.95.

Nowadays it seems that more books are read in laundromats than in libraries.

There are a lot of books telling you how to manage when you retire. What most people want is one that'll tell them how to manage in the meantime.

How-to-get-rich books are now filed under FICTION.

The one book that always has a sad ending is a checkbook.

Sign in a South Dakota bookstore, "Read a good novel before Hollywood ruins it."

The trouble with speed reading is that by the time you realize a book is boring, you've finished reading it.

Some of our new books are so down-to-earth they should be plowed under.

In a library the books that aren't dirty are the ones that are dusty.

A poor appetite for good books eventually leads to intellectual malnutrition.

So many books are now being written on how to speak that there ought to be a market for one on how to shut up.

We've truly become a nation of book lovers — provided they're filled with trading stamps.

Some books you can't put down, and others you dare not put down when there are children in the house.

A reference book is one in which we can quickly find what it doesn't contain.

If you enjoy reading a spicy book, read a Mexican cookbook.

The only book that really tells you where you can go on your vacation is your checkbook.

There might be more good books if there were more good people to read them.

A classic is a book which people praise highly but never read.

Some books are not to be lightly thrown aside; they should be thrown with great force.

A country hick sent the following request to a public library: "Please send me the name of a good book on personal hygiene. I'm afraid I have it."

A rare volume is a borrowed book that comes back.

We should be as careful of the books we read as we are of the company we keep.

A good test of the worth of a book is the number of times you can read it with profit.

There is one good thing you can say for a book. It does not interrupt at the most interesting part for a word from the sponsor.

A book is a success when people who haven't read it pretend they have.

It is a good book when it is opened with expectation, and closed with delight and profit.

Now there's a book on the market for people who disagree — a CONTRADICTIONARY.

For many books the backs and covers are by far the best parts.

Confession is not only good for the soul; in Washington it can be turned into a bestseller.

Some folks commit a crime and go to jail; others commit a crime, write a book, and get rich.

Generally, women don't like the dictionary, because it has the first and the last word.

There's no sense in reading a dictionary; if you've read one, you've read them all.

All that some people lose when they buy a book on dieting is the price of the book.

An economist in Los Angeles recently completed writing a book titled *The Short Story of Money.* The book contains only seven words, "Here it is and there it goes."

When an egotist doesn't understand something in a book, he decides it *must* be a misprint.

Many a man thinks he has become famous when he merely happened to meet an editor who was hard-up for material.

To the average girl the most helpful books are mother's cookbook and father's checkbook.

In today's novels the boy always gets the girl — at least once in every chapter.

Today's novels contain a lot of details that were once told exclusively to the family doctor.

A lot of modern novels have one common failing — their covers are too far apart.

The one book that really tells you where you can go on your vacation is your pocketbook.

Bores

A bore only stops talking to see if you're still listening.

There are two kinds of bores — those who talk too much and those who listen too little.

A bore is as hard to get rid of as a summer cold.

Someone described a bore: "He reminds me of a toothache I once had."

A bore keeps you from feeling lonely and makes you wish you were.

One nice thing about bores is that they don't talk about other people.

A bore always lights up the room when he leaves.

Have you noticed that a bore doesn't stop talking when you've stopped listening?

A bore never runs out of talk — only out of listeners.

It isn't so much *what* we say as the number of times we say it that makes us a bore.

A bore is someone who boasts about his accomplishments when he should be boasting about yours!

It's easy to keep from being a bore. Just praise the person to whom you're talking.

A bore is like a TV commercial — often loud and dull.

Have you noticed that a bore always takes his time taking your time?

A bore is a guy with a cocktail glass in one hand, and your lapel in the other.

A bore is someone who holds a conversation and won't let go.

There is only one thing worse than a bore and that's a bore with bad breath.

A bigshot may also be a big bore.

One of the troubles with small talk is that it usually comes in large doses.

Some folks are so highly educated they can bore you on any subject.

Usually the man who howls loudest about free speech has nothing worth saying.

Too many people confuse free speech with loose talk.

Talking about others and being a gossip is probably better than talking about yourself and being a bore.

One of the best ways for some people to make others happy is to shut up and go home.

A man without a single idea is less of a bore than a man with only one idea.

Some people never let ideas interrupt the easy flow of their conversation.

When an idler sees a job completed, he's sure he could have done it better.

A person who never makes a mistake is pretty boring.

Some people can stay longer in an hour than others can in a week.

Many public speakers can talk for hours without any notes — or knowledge!

A speaker who doesn't strike oil in twenty-five minutes should stop boring.

Might as well keep your mouth shut. If you talk about yourself you're a bore, and if you talk about others you're a gossip.

Borrowing

An acquaintance is a person whom we know well enough to borrow from, but not well enough to lend to.

Bank interest on a loan is so high that if you can afford to pay it you don't need the loan.

A bank is a financial institution where you can borrow money if you can present sufficient evidence to show that you don't need it.

A rare volume is a borrowed book that comes back.

If you have to borrow, always borrow from a pessimist. He doesn't expect to be paid anyway.

Anybody who thinks all forms of larceny are illegal doesn't understand borrowing.

When a man borrows money from a bank he pays interest, but when he borrows from a friend he often loses interest.

The trouble with a chronic borrower is that he always keeps everything but his word.

It is a fraud to borrow when you know that you will be unable to repay.

A borrower is a person who exchanges hot air for cold cash.

The slogan of the borrowing nations today is, "See America First."

If it's as easy to borrow money from a bank as the advertisements claim, why should anybody want to rob it?

Lots of people think a house is only good to borrow money on.

A boy becomes a man when he stops asking his father for an allowance and requests a loan.

Some people feel that a cigarette is not harmful if they borrow it from somebody else.

The cancer scare has increased the use of borrowed cigarettes.

If you listen to the loan company commercials, you'll almost believe you can borrow yourself out of debt.

It's easier to love your enemies if you remember that they never try to borrow from you.

Warm friends often freeze up at the mention of cash.

Friends last longer the less they are used.

You can usually tell how close your closest friend is if you ask him for a loan.

A friend in need is a drain on the pocketbook.

A lifelong friend is someone you haven't borrowed money from yet.

The quickest way to wipe out a friendship is to sponge on it.

Many people seem to think a home is only good to borrow money on.

It takes a heap o' livin' to make a house a home, but before that, it takes a lot o' borrowin'.

We should always strive to live within our incomes, even if we have to borrow money to do so.

If life is ever found on the planet Mars, they're certain to ask us for a loan.

It's strange how much better our memory becomes as soon as a friend borrows money from us.

Everytime you lend money to a friend you damage his memory.

The reason it is called "cold cash" is because of the way the temperature drops when you try to borrow some.

If you want to know the value of money, try and borrow it.

Before borrowing money from a friend, decide which you need more.

It's easy to borrow money from the government. All you have to do is pretend you're a foreign power.

A good neighbor is one who doesn't expect you to return the things you borrow.

A cooperative neighbor is one who advises you on what to buy, so he can borrow it later.

Borrowing neighbors will take anything but a hint.

A neighbor likes to borrow your equipment and loan you his troubles.

When the new neighbors move in, it's only friendly to keep a close check on what they have that's worth borrowing.

The man who borrows trouble is always in debt.

A good neighbor is one who, when he wants to borrow your corkscrew, asks you to bring it over.

Sympathy is what you give to a man when you don't want to lend him money.

The reward for saving your money is being able to pay your taxes without borrowing.

Nothing makes time pass faster than vacations and short-term loans.

Time may be money, but it's much easier to persuade a man to give you his time than to lend you his money.

Bosses

Ability is what will get you to the top if the boss has no daughter.

Before you have an argument with your boss, you'd better take a good look at both sides — his side and the outside.

Before arguing with your boss, make absolutely sure you're right — then let the matter drop.

The only time it's safe to tell the boss where to get off is when he falls asleep on the bus.

Watch the man who says he's the boss at home. He may lie about other things too.

The hardest job in the world is telling the boss the computer proved him wrong.

A certain boss when asked how many people work for him replied, "About half of them."

Pity the boss. He has to come in early to see who comes in late.

In any office you can tell who the boss is: he's the one watching the clock during the coffee break.

Nothing makes a man the boss of his house like living alone.

An overbearing boss seldom fires you — he just makes you wish he had.

Some bosses are so mean that if they pay you a compliment they expect to get a receipt.

The wife isn't always boss in the American home. Sometimes it's her mother.

If your boss doesn't pay you what you deserve, be thankful!

Some bosses take great pains — and give them to others.

Be loyal to your boss because the next one might be worse.

The worst boss anyone can have is a bad habit.

A certain boss said to his secretary, "Congratulations! This is the earliest you've been late in a long time."

Computers will never replace man entirely until they learn to laugh at the boss's jokes.

A man's best boss is a well-trained conscience.

Being diplomatic is telling your boss he has an open mind instead of telling him he has a hole in the head.

Nothing is quite as embarrassing as watching your boss do something you assured him couldn't be done.

The fellow who is fired with enthusiasm for his work is seldom fired by his boss.

Enthusiasm for hard work is most sincerely expressed by the person who is paying for it.

The fellow who can beat his boss at golf is usually prudent enough not to.

The man is still boss in the American home — as long as he allows his wife to make all the decisions.

A husband often thinks he bosses the house — but actually he only houses the boss.

A husband wanted to show his wife who was boss so he bought her a mirror.

Imagination is what makes the average man think he can run the business better than his boss.

Nothing improves a joke more than telling it to your employees.

The fellow who knows more than his boss should be careful to conceal it.

You may know more than your employer, but his knowledge pays off.

The man who laughs at his boss's jokes doesn't necessarily have a sense of humor, but he surely has a sense of direction.

It is generally understood that leisure time is what you have when the boss is on vacation.

The best time to start thinking about retirement is before your boss does.

He who laughs last at the boss's jokes probably isn't very far from retirement.

Ulcers are contagious. You can get them from your boss.

Vacations are easy to plan — the boss tells you when, and the wife tells you where.

The reason a great many men don't bring their boss home for dinner is because she is already there.

If you do all the work and somebody else gets the credit — he's probably your boss.

A few people are enthusiastic about work, but most of the time they're the bosses.

About the only folks who work like a horse these days have a boss riding them.

One way to boost production in this country would be to put the labor bosses to work.

Hard work and devotion to duty will surely get you a promotion — unless, of course, the boss has a relative who wants the job.

Boys

The ambition of every small boy is to wash his mother's ears.

Many have said that boys will be boys, but they don't have to be the James boys.

Nothing changes a small boy's appearance as much as soap.

A boy loves a dog because it's the only thing around the house that doesn't find fault with him.

Many a boy is the kind of kid his mother tells him not to play with.

A small boy is a pain in the neck when he's around and a pain in the heart when he's not.

It's easy to believe that any American boy can become president when you observe some of them who have.

One way to keep young boys from getting on the wrong track is to use better switching facilities.

The thing a little boy outgrows fastest is his allowance.

What a small boy saves for a rainy day is apt to be mischief.

A boy is like a canoe — he behaves better if paddled from the rear.

If anything is as dirty as a small boy, it's probably his bath towel.

Nothing makes a boy smarter than being a grandson.

More boys would follow in their father's footsteps if they weren't afraid of being caught.

Many boys are flunking geometry. They just don't know the angles.

A boy becomes a man when he stops asking his father for an allowance and requests a loan.

Give a boy a rope and he'll tie a stray dog to it.

Any parent will tell you there are two kinds of boys — noisy and not yet.

A small boy's lament: "While there's life, there's soap."

The boy who takes a bath willingly is probably bathing his dog.

Waiting to be whipped is the most uninteresting period in any boy's life.

Boys are often a problem. Some are so slow you want to scream; others are so fast you have to.

A boy is the only thing God can use to make a man.

Anybody who thinks there is no such thing as a bad boy either doesn't understand boys or doesn't know exactly what bad is.

When a small boy puts something down in black and white it's apt to be a towel.

Boys will be boys, particularly when they're away from their wives.

On his examination paper a boy wrote, "A natural death is where you die by yourself without a doctor's help."

A boy handed his report card to his parents and said, "Look this over and see if I can sue for defamation of character."

Small boys are washable, but a lot of them shrink from it.

The time to start worrying about a boy is when he leaves the house without slamming the door.

A boy has two jobs. One is just being a boy. The other is growing up to be a man.

Having your boy follow in your footsteps can be very disconcerting, especially when you *think* you've covered your tracks — but aren't absolutely certain.

Do you know what happens to little boys who continually interrupt? They grow up and make a fortune doing TV commercials.

While there may be no such thing as a bad boy, there are some who could be with a little encouragement.

A boy becomes a man when he decides it's more fun to steal a kiss than second base.

To keep a small boy out of the cookie jar, lock it and hide the key under a cake of soap.

For every boy with a spark of genius, there are a dozen others with ignition trouble.

About the only time a boy manages to stay off the lawn is when you want him to mow it.

It used to be when a boy couldn't learn at his mother's knee he found himself over his father's.

When a boy begins to "feel his oats," he should strongly resist the urge to sow a few wild ones.

When a small boy doesn't mind soap, he's probably blowing bubbles.

The footsteps a boy follows are apt to be those his father thought he'd covered up.

A boy is a magical creature. You can lock him out of your workshop, but you can't lock him out of your heart.

A small boy said to his best friend, "It may be unconstitutional, but I always pray before an exam."

Of course there's no such thing as a bad boy. But an awful lot of them haven't given up trying.

College is the only vacation a boy gets between his mother and his wife.

There is no such thing as a problem boy. He's just a boy with a problem.

Every boy, in his heart, would rather steal second base than an automobile.

A boy's mind is a wonderful thing. It starts working the minute he gets up, and never stops until he gets to school.

A small boy prayed, "Lord, if you can't make me a better boy, don't worry about it. I'm having a good time as it is."

Little boys who don't always tell the truth will probably grow up and become weather forecasters.

Some boys seem to have dentists confused with barbers — they see both twice a year.

To a young boy there is no such period as "between meals."

Brains

Age stiffens the joints and thickens some brains.

There's no tax on brains; the take would be too small.

Be sure your brain is engaged before putting your mouth in gear.

It's unfortunate that rusty brains do not squeak.

Always remember that a man is not rewarded for having brains, but for using them.

Brains are what a man looks for in a wife, after not using any in selecting one.

The human brain is the apparatus with which we think we think.

Will our brains start shrinking now that machines do our thinking?

Nowadays most brains are suffering from chronic unemployment.

Most folks would benefit themselves and others if they would synchronize their tongues with their brains.

The human brain is like a freight car — guaranteed to have a certain capacity but often running empty.

If there is a substitute for brains it has to be silence.

Use your brain. It's the little things that count.

The marble business must be booming — many people seem to have lost theirs.

Brains and beauty are nature's gifts; character is your own achievement.

Keeping clean *between* the ears may be more important than keeping clean *behind* the ears.

A cheap but top-rate computer is the one between your ears.

Nature abhors a vacuum. When a head lacks brains, nature fills it with conceit.

If a person has no education he is forced to use his brains.

As the chest swells, the brain and the heart shrink.

Fishing stimulates the brain — also the imagination!

There are relatively few cases of mental indigestion. The brain is seldom overworked like the stomach.

There are more idle brains than idle hands.

Your brain becomes a mind when it's fortified with knowledge.

Some people have open minds; others just don't have anything between their ears.

Some people have more money than brains — but not for long.

Nature often makes up for a nugget-size brain with a bucket-size mouth.

God gave eloquence to some, brains to others.

Sometimes a handful of patience is worth more than a bucket full of brains.

Profanity is an evidence of the lack of a sufficient vocabulary — and brains.

There is no real substitute for brains, but silence does pretty well.

The mouths of many people seem to have the habit of going on active duty while their brains are on furlough.

Big mouths do not advertise big brains.

The human tongue is only a few inches from the brain, but when you listen to some people talk, they seem miles apart.

When you're up to your ears in trouble, try using the part that isn't submerged.

Budgets

There's nothing tighter than next year's budget and this year's bikini.

It's a cinch to balance your budget, if you can earn as much as you yearn.

A budget enables you to spend money without enjoying it.

Balancing the budget is when money in the bank and the days of the month come out together.

The trouble with a budget is that it won't budge.

Nowadays if the family budget balances you can be sure of one thing — you've made a mistake in your figures.

A budget is an orderly way of discovering that you can't live on what you're earning.

Balance your budget — rotate your creditors!

Most people look on budgeting as a nervous breakdown on paper.

A family budget is a device to make you worry about money before you spend it.

A married couple usually works out a budget together and then breaks it separately.

Budgeting doesn't take the whipped cream out of life. It simply means that you can have only the whipped cream you can afford.

If it weren't for keeping a budget, a lot of people wouldn't know how much they owe.

The tax collectors take up so much of your earnings to balance the budget that you just can't budget the balance.

A budget helps you pay as you go if you don't go anywhere.

Many people say a budget is a form of fiction that seldom turns out right in the end.

A budget is an attempt to live below your yearnings.

No wife objects to being put on a budget as long as she isn't expected to stay within it.

A budget is like a girdle — not enough room for everything.

Nothing helps to stabilize the family budget like an economy drive by the closest neighbors.

A budget is what you stay within if you go without.

Budgeting is the most orderly way of going into debt.

Living on a budget is the same as living beyond your means except that you have a record of it.

A budget is an aim that rarely shows good marksmanship.

The family budget tells us what we can't afford, but it doesn't keep us from buying it.

A budget is like a conscience — it doesn't keep you from spending, but it makes you feel guilty about it.

A budget is like a girdle — you take care of the bulge in one place and it pops up in another.

A budget is a plan by which you worry about expenditures before you make them — instead of afterwards.

A balanced budget is when the month and the money run out together.

Keeping a budget is an orderly way of getting through part of the month.

About all you can do is dream of a white Christmas, for it seems like it always leaves most of us in the red.

It seems that everytime Congress sets out to trim the budget, the knife slips and trims the taxpayers instead.

With food, rent, and gas prices so high, when you balance the budget there's nothing left to budget the balance.

We could get along better with fewer economists and more economizers.

You can enjoy a glorious vacation and stay within your budget — but not both in the same summer.

The old-fashioned wife is one who can stay on a budget and a diet.

Burdens

Life's heaviest burden is to have nothing to carry.

When God allows a burden to be put upon you, He will put His arms underneath you to help you carry it.

You will find that if you share your brother's burden, both of you will walk a little straighter.

It's not the load that breaks you down, it's the way you carry it.

The heaviest burdens in life are the things that might happen but don't.

A burden must be carried before we can put it down.

Let us pray, not for lighter burdens, but for stronger backs.

There will always be enough for today without taking on yesterday and tomorrow's burdens.

The burdens that appear easiest to carry are those borne by others.

Bearing one another's burdens is very different from bearing down on them.

It's better to complain occasionally and carry your own burdens than cheerfully push them off on someone else.

Few burdens are heavy when everybody lifts.

Some people carry their religion like a burden on their backs, when they should carry it like a song in their hearts.

Religion at its best is a lift and not a load.

Secrets are a burden. That's the reason we are so anxious to have somebody help us carry them.

Bureaucracy

How did people ever get along before they had all those government bureaus to tell them what to do?

In a bureaucracy, they shoot the bull, pass the buck, and make seven copies of everything.

The proper way to greet a visiting bureaucrat is to roll out the red tape.

A sure sign of bureaucracy is when the first person who answers the phone can't help you.

Bureaucracy is based on a willingness to either pass the buck or spend it.

Bureaucrats live on the fat of the land, while the rest of us stay skinny laboring to pay their salaries.

Business needs more orders from customers and fewer from the government.

Organized crime can very easily be stopped. All we have to do is form a government agency to run it — then stand back and watch it choke itself to death on red tape.

What's needed in government is more horse sense and less nonsense.

One solution to the energy problem is to bale up all the government red tape and use it for fuel.

A promise cannot be made more binding by using a lot of red tape.

Scientists have found a petrified man sitting with his feet elevated. He was probably a primitive bureaucrat.

A scientist recently revealed that it took millions of years to carve out the Grand Canyon — a government job, no doubt.

Washington is not going to get rid of any bureaucrats and bureaus — there has to be some place to put the shirts they are taking off our backs.

Business

A man's accomplishment in business depends partly on whether he keeps his mind or his feet on the desk.

Doing business without advertising is like winking at a girl in the dark. You know what you're doing, but she doesn't.

Never give advice — sell it!

A "gentleman's agreement" is a deal which neither party cares to put in writing.

Baby sitting is a big business because it meets a crying need.

If you want to go far in business, you'll have to stay close to it.

Business is "sound," the experts say, but at times the sound is a little mournful.

Business know-how is when a fellow knows his business and what's none of his business.

A store window sign in Jackson, Mississippi: "Staying-in-business sale now in progress."

The marble business must be booming — many people seem to have lost theirs.

A business is too big when it takes a week for gossip to go from one end of the office to the other.

In the business world transactions speak louder than words.

Sign on the door of a business office in Omaha: "You might as well come in — everything else has gone wrong today."

The reason business conditions are so unsettled is because so many accounts are.

In modern business it isn't the crook that we fear, but the honest man who doesn't know what he's doing.

If you would like to know how to operate a big business, ask the man who hasn't any.

Competition may be the life of trade, but it's often the death of profit.

A scissor sharpener is the only person whose business is good when things are dull.

Business is something which, if you don't have any, you go out of.

It isn't the number of people employed in a business that makes it successful. It's the number working.

Business is like a wheelbarrow — it stands still unless somebody pushes it.

It isn't the business you get that counts, it's the business you hold.

Not too long ago business got so bad that some men went bankrupt, and some went back to their wives.

The business to stay out of is the other fellow's.

A man who is immersed in business all week should come up for a breath of fresh air on Sunday — at church.

A good business manager hires optimists as salesmen and pessimists to run the credit department.

Business needs more orders from customers and fewer from the government.

Modern business has made buying easy, but paying is as hard as it ever was.

Business is like a bicycle — when it isn't moving forward at a good speed it wobbles.

A person or persons may decide to go into business, but the public decides whether or not a business stays in business.

The secret of business is to count your blessings while others are adding up their troubles.

Business will continue to go where invited and will remain where appreciated.

The reason some folks can't mind their own business is because they have very little mind and no business.

A shady business never produces a sunny life.

Business is the only thing which can be dead and still have a chance to survive.

During the depression business was so quiet you could even hear the passing of the dividends.

People would be delighted to attend to their own business if the government would give it back to them.

The best way for any business to keep on the upgrade is to stay on the level.

Anyone who thinks the customer isn't important should try doing without him for a period of ninety days.

Business is made good by yearning, learning, and earning.

The best way to go into business is with high hopes and low overhead.

A successful executive in business is the one who can delegate all the responsibility, shift all the blame, and appropriate all the credit.

Business is a lot like tennis — those who don't serve well wind up losing.

He who has the habit of smiling at the cash register instead of the customer won't be smiling long.

One trouble with credit business is that there is too much stall in installments.

Business forecasters are uncertain about the future and hazy about the present.

Business is like an automobile. It won't run itself, except downhill.

It isn't exactly true to say that business came back. Certain people went after it.

Business is the art of extracting money from another man's pocket without resorting to violence.

Most people find that running a business is no trouble at all — as long as it's the other fellow's.

The trouble with the business world is that there are too many one-ulcer men holding down two-ulcer jobs.

Business is tough these days. If a man does something wrong he gets fined; if he does something right he gets taxed.

In the hectic confusion of modern society it would be nice to experience a few dull moments occasionally.

Crime seems to be the only big business to escape government meddling.

A dentist is a man who runs a filling station. He is also a collector of old magazines.

The economy is not as bad as we are led to believe. Many merchants report this year's going-out-of-business sales are much better than last year's.

An efficiency expert is smart enough to tell you how to run your own business, and too smart to start one of his own.

An efficiency expert is a man hired by an executive who is too tenderhearted to fire his own employees.

The average efficiency expert is a person who has no business of his own to wreck.

Sign on a company bulletin board in Grand Rapids: "To err is human, to forgive is not company policy."

When they say a man is a "born executive," they mean his father owns the business.

A good executive is judged by the company he keeps — solvent.

In the language of flowers, the yellow rose means friendship, the red rose means love, and the orchid means business.

A business genius is a man who knows the difference between being let in on a deal and *taken* in on one.

Golf is a game that gives you something to do while you're nailing down a business deal.

An honest merchant is one who puts up a "going out of business" sign — and then goes out of business.

Honesty is one business policy that will never have to be changed to keep up with the times.

A disgruntled housewife suspects her butcher of using phony scales, "Just recently I didn't buy anything and it weighed three pounds."

Humor is the lubricating oil of business. It prevents friction and wins good will.

A husband seldom tells his wife about his business troubles until she wants to buy something expensive.

Imagination is what makes the average man think he can run the business better than his boss.

Nothing gives a man more leisure time than always being on time for appointments.

Nightclub business is so slow these days that even the waiters are insulting each other.

No business opportunity is ever lost. If you fumble it your competitor will find it.

What we need is less government in business and more business in government.

Patriotism is the willingness to make any sacrifice as long as it won't hurt business.

The trouble with mixing business and pleasure is that pleasure usually comes out on top.

The man who lives only for himself runs a very small business.

Businessmen

Executive ability is a talent for deciding something quickly and getting someone else to do it.

Executive ability is the art of getting credit for all the hard work that somebody else does.

In good times businessmen want to advertise; in bad times they have to.

When two men in business always agree about everything, one of them is unnecessary.

A businessman boasts that he and his wife started out with absolutely nothing, "And we've got most of it left."

A successful executive in business is the one who can delegate all the responsibility, shift all the blame, and appropriate all the credit.

Many businessmen refuse to cash personal checks because sometimes the checks come back but the customers don't.

An efficient businessman who found a machine that would do half his work bought two.

A businessman in Seattle says he has a rotten sense of timing. "Just as the recession began, I started manufacturing money belts."

Every businessman ought to sit back, close his eyes, and meditate for a while every day — and try not to snore.

Noah was the first businessman mentioned in the Bible. He floated a company at a time when the rest of the world was under liquidation.

An Oklahoma businessman reports that if his business gets any worse he won't have to lie on his next income-tax return.

The American businessman has a problem: if he comes up with something new the Russians invent it six months later and the Japanese make it cheaper.

Sign on a businessman's desk: "My decision is maybe — and that's final."

Many a businessman wanted his son to share in the business but the government beat him to it.

A certain businessman complained about his partner, "He's a real phony — I wouldn't believe him if he said he was lying."

There's a certain businessman in Houston who had to stop attending baseball games. He just couldn't stand hearing the umpire call a strike.

A businessman who came up the hard way observes that about all you can do on a shoestring these days is trip.

A Chicago businessman grumbled, "Things are so bad I can hardly wait for them to improve so I can afford a nervous breakdown."

The businessman is coming to realize that education is to business what fertilizer is to farming.

A modern executive is a man who wears out his clothes at the seat of his pants first.

Many men are able to solve big problems at the office, but are unable to settle little ones at home.

Prosperity is something that businessmen create for politicians to take the credit for.

Retirement has cured many a businessman's ulcers — and given his wife one!

Among the chief worries of today's business executives is the large number of unemployed still on the payrolls.

C

Capital Punishment
Careful Driving
Caution
Censors
Change
Character
Charity
Cheerfulness
Children
Child Training
Chivalry
Choice
Christianity
Christians
Christmas
Church
Church Attendance
Church Members
Cigarettes
Civilization

Class Reunions
Cleanliness
Clothing
Coffee Breaks
College Professors
Colleges
College Students
Committees
Common Sense
Communism
Communists
Complaining
Compliments
Compromise
Computers
Conceit
Conclusions
Conferences
Confession
Confidence

Confusion
Congress
Congressmen
Conscience
Contentment
Conventions
Conversation
Conviction
Cooperation
Cost of living
Courage
Courtesy
Courtship
Crime
Criminals
Criticism
Critics
Curiosity
Cynics

Capital Punishment

The death penalty may not eliminate crime but it stops repeaters.

Capital punishment is when Washington comes up with a new tax.

According to the best evidence available, the death penalty is definitely a deterrent to crime. Not one of the 162 killers executed in Kentucky has killed anyone since.

Capital punishment is when the government taxes you to get capital so that it can go into business in competition with you, and then taxes the profit on your business in order to pay its losses.

One sensible reason for abolishing the electric chair is the energy it would save.

It might lessen crime if an occasional jury would suspend the criminal instead of the sentence.

In the old days judges would suspend the bad men instead of the sentence.

Juvenile delinquency starts in the highchair and could end in the electric chair.

Careful Driving

Drive toward others as you would have others drive toward you.

To drive carefully — just drive like everybody else is crazy.

Your wife will drive more carefully if you tell her that in accident reports they always give the driver's age.

Glasses can make driving a lot safer. Providing, of course, they're worn instead of emptied.

By driving carefully you can help preserve two of our most valuable resources — gasoline and you.

A careful driver is a guy in a car that isn't insured yet.

Sign on a florist truck, "Drive carefully. The next load may be yours."

If we'd drive right, there would be more people left.

Often a man considers himself a careful driver if he slows down as he passes through a red light.

Drive carefully! Motorists can be recalled by their maker.

A good safety slogan: "Drive scared."

A gentleman driver always tips his headlights.

Driving is a lot like baseball — it's the number of times you get home safely that counts.

Drive carefully! The life you save could be someone who owes you money.

Better be patient on the road than a patient in the hospital.

The careful driver stops at a railroad crossing for a minute; the careless one, forever.

A good driver is the one who obeys all the traffic rules and is quick enough to dodge those who don't.

You should drive your car as if your family was in the other car.

A good driver keeps his eyes on two things when he comes to a traffic light — red lights and green drivers.

Always drive so that your license will expire before you do.

When driving near schools, open your eyes and save the pupils.

Nothing improves your driving like a police car following you.

Shrink your speed and stretch your life.

Safe driving will keep your car out of the junkyard and your body out of the graveyard.

Highway sign in Florida: "Drive carefully! You never know when life will be worth living again."

Baseball honors its no-hit pitchers. Why shouldn't we offer some recognition to our no-hit motorists?

A tip to young male drivers: Forget the girl and hug the road.

If you drive carefully, all you need is a strong rear bumper.

Drive with care. Life has no spare.

A light foot on the gas beats two under the grass.

The best safety device ever invented for automobiles is a careful driver.

Drive carefully if you'd rather be than was.

Forty years ago people were amazed when someone drove thirty miles-per-hour. They still are.

A Tennessee husband gave his wife the following instructions when teaching her how to drive his car: "Go on green, stop on red, slow down when I turn white."

Brains and brakes prevent pains and aches.

The best way to stay alive on the highway is to limit the speed — not speed the limit.

A careful driver is known by the fenders he keeps.

All the safety devices on a car can be replaced by one careful driver.

What many automobiles need is not four-wheel brakes but foresighted drivers.

Drive carefully! If motorists would give more ground, there'd be fewer in it.

Don't drive as if you owned the road — drive as if you owned the car.

If you drive carefully you avoid the "mourning after."

Driver! Please give the pedestrian a break instead of a fracture.

If you want the rest of the world to go by, just drive within the legal speed limit.

A good driver is one who, after seeing a wreck, drives carefully for several blocks.

Drive sensibly. The chance-taker is the accident-maker.

Please drive carefully — the IRS needs you.

Defensive driving is looking both ways before crossing a one-way street.

Sign on a laundry truck: "Drive carefully. Blood stains are the hardest to get out."

Safety note for motorists: "Watch out for children — especially if they're driving cars."

Caution is one automobile accessory you can't buy.

A railroad crossing is a place where it's better to be dead-sure than sure-dead.

The best way to stay alive on the highway is to limit the speed — not speed the limit.

There should be just half as much horse sense behind the wheel as there is horsepower under the hood.

Advice to motorists: If you want to stay in the pink, watch the red and the green.

It's better to be last in the traffic jam than first in the funeral procession.

The best rule in driving through five o'clock traffic is to try and avoid being a part of the six o'clock news.

Caution

Watch your step. Everybody else does.

Don't try to cross any bridges until you're sure one is there.

Bumper sticker on a car in Atlanta: "Caution — keep back! I drive like your wife."

A man never knows how careful he can be until he buys a new car or wears white shoes.

It's all right to be cautious — but even a turtle never gets anywhere until he sticks his head out.

Caution is one automobile accessory you can't buy.

It is well for a girl with a future to avoid the man with a past.

Caution is what we call cowardice in others.

A railroad crossing is a place where it's better to be dead-sure than sure-dead.

A cautious man is one who hasn't let a woman pin anything on him since he was a baby.

Be careful as you slide down the banister of life, lest you get a splinter in your career.

Be cautious in choosing friends, and be even more cautious in changing them.

Caution is a good risk to take.

A person can save himself from many hard falls by refraining from jumping to conclusions.

Always take plenty of time to make a snap decision.

When we're afraid we say we're cautious. When others are afraid we say they're cowardly.

You've reached middle age when all you exercise is caution.

Be careful where you inquire for directions along the road of success.

Censors

A censor is a guy who finds three meanings in a joke that has only two.

It is the business of a censor to acquaint us with vices we didn't know we had.

A censor has the peculiar faculty of banning just what we want to hear, see, and read.

Someone has described a censor as a man who knows more than he thinks other people ought to know.

Change

Some people continue to change jobs, mates, and friends — but never think of changing themselves.

Some things never change — like the taste of postage-stamp glue.

Constant change is here to stay.

Many people hate any change that doesn't jingle in their pockets.

The world changes so fast that you couldn't stay wrong all the time if you tried.

All some people need to make them happy is a change — and most of the time that's all a baby needs.

New ideas hurt some minds the same as new shoes hurt some feet.

One way to have a clean mind is to change it now and then.

About the only opinions that do not eventually change are the ones we have about ourselves.

Most people are willing to change, not because they see the light, but because they feel the heat.

What we want is progress, if we can have it without change.

The price of progress is change, and it is taking just about all we have.

Everybody is in favor of progress. It's the change they don't like.

There have been many changes for the better in recent years, and some people have been against all of them.

There's a small town in Nevada where so little ever changes that the local radio station is still running last year's weather forecasts.

Change is what a person wants on a vacation — and a lot of currency too.

We can only change the world by changing men.

Character

Be big enough to admit and admire the abilities of people who are better than you are.

What lies behind us and what lies before us are tiny matters compared to what lies within us.

Where we go and what we do advertises what we are.

The kind of ancestors we have is not as important as the kind of descendants our ancestors have.

The size of a man is measured by the size of the thing that makes him angry.

A long face and a broad mind are rarely found under the same hat.

Pay attention to what a man is, not what he has been.

One evidence of the value of the Bible is the character of those who oppose it.

A big shot is frequently an individual of small caliber and immense bore.

It's not the load that breaks you down, it's the way you carry it.

Have character — don't be one!

Character is easier kept than recovered.

Reputation is precious, but character is priceless.

Many people have character who have nothing else.

The collapse of character often begins on compromise corner.

A well-rounded character is square in all his dealings.

You can easily judge the character of a man by how he treats those who can do nothing for him.

A true test of a man's character is not what he does in the light, but what he does in the dark.

Only you can damage your character.

Character is made by many acts; it may be lost by a single act.

There is no royal road to character — but there is a road.

Character is not made in a crisis — it is only exhibited.

Think right, act right; it is what you think and do that makes you what you are.

To change one's character, you must begin at the control center — the heart.

It is not by a man's purse, but by his character, that he is rich or poor.

You can buy ready-made clothes, but you can't buy ready-made character.

Reputation is what you need to get a job; character is what you need to keep it.

A good past is the best thing a man can use for a future reference.

Character, like embroidery, is made stitch by stitch.

One of the surest marks of good character is a man's ability to accept personal criticism without feeling malice toward the one who gives it.

Every man has three characters: that which he exhibits, that which he has, and that which he thinks he has.

Brains and beauty are nature's gifts; character is your own achievement.

A person is never what he ought to be until he is doing what he ought to be doing.

Character is like glass — even a little crack shows.

A person's character is put to a severe test when he suddenly acquires or quickly loses a considerable amount of money.

A pat on the back will develop character if given young enough, often enough, low enough — and hard enough.

The measure of a man's character is not what he gets from his ancestors, but what he leaves his descendants.

Character grows in the soil of experience, with the fertilization of example, the moisture of desire, and the sunshine of satisfaction.

Much may be known of a man's character by what excites his laughter.

A man's character and his garden both reflect the amount of weeding that was done during the growing season.

Character cannot be purchased, bargained for, inherited, rented, or imported from afar. It must be home-grown.

Your character is what you have left when you've lost everything you can lose.

Character does not reach its best until it is controlled, harnessed, and disciplined.

Take care of your character and your reputation will take care of itself.

Men of genius are admired; men of wealth are envied; men of power are feared; but only men of character are trusted.

It's what you do when you have nothing to do that reveals what you are.

You can tell a man's character by what he turns up when offered a job — his nose or his sleeves.

The measure of a man's character is what he would do if he knew he would never be found out.

There are two very difficult things in this world. One is to make a good name for one's self, and the other is to keep it.

Character is the one thing we make in this world and take with us into the next.

How a man plays the game shows something of his character. How he loses shows all of it.

The address of character is often carved on the corner of Adversity Avenue and Determination Drive.

A man may be better than his creed, his company, or his conduct. But no man is better than his character.

There's no limit to the height a man can attain by remaining on the level.

A man's character, like rich topsoil, can erode so gradually he doesn't notice it until it's almost gone.

You can no more blame your circumstances for your character than you can blame the mirror for the way you look.

The two great tests of character are wealth and poverty.

You can't see the flaw in a bridge until it falls down, or the flaw in a man's character until he meets with temptation.

Ability will enable a man to get to the top, but it takes character to keep him there.

Nearly all men can stand adversity, but if you want to test a man's character, give him power.

People determine your character by observing what you stand for, fall for, and lie for.

A person's character is like a fence. All the whitewash in the world won't strengthen it.

Show how strong you are by not noticing how weak the other fellow is.

It isn't what you have, but what you are, that makes life worthwhile.

Youth and beauty fade; character endures forever.

A flaw in one's character will show up under pressure.

If a man's character is to be abused, there's nobody like a relative to get the job done.

Few things are more dangerous to a person's character than having nothing to do and plenty of time in which to do it.

Character, like sweet herbs, should give off its finest fragrance when pressed.

A golden character needs no gilding.

Character is never erected on a neglected conscience.

One of the main troubles with modern civilization is that we so often mistake respectability for character.

College is a place that's presumed to mold character, and some of the characters turn out to be very moldy.

Contentment is something that depends a little on position and a lot on disposition.

It is important that people know what you stand for; it is equally important that they know what you won't stand for.

The true test of moral courage is the ability to ignore an insult.

Courage is the quality it takes to look at yourself with candor, your adversaries with kindness, and your setbacks with serenity.

Greatness is not found in possessions, power, position, or prestige. It is discovered in goodness, humility, service, and character.

Happiness does not come from what you have, but from what you are.

It's not *where* you are but *what* you are that determines your happiness.

No one can make you feel inferior without your consent.

What you laugh at tells, plainer than words, what you are.

You cannot control the length of your life, but you can control its breadth, depth, and height.

It isn't how high you go in life that counts, but *how* you got there.

A man shows what he is by doing what he can with what he has.

The true measure of a man is the height of his ideals, the breadth of his sympathy, the depth of his convictions, and the length of his patience.

You can usually determine the caliber of a man by ascertaining the amount of opposition it takes to discourage him.

The measure of a man is the size of the thing it takes to get his goat.

Another great need of this country is guns of smaller caliber and men of larger.

The test of any man's character is how he takes praise.

It is strange that in our prayers we seldom ask for a change in character, but always a change in circumstances.

No man is better than his principles.

If a man's character is to be smeared, there's nobody like a relative to do the job.

Many a man's reputation would not recognize his character if they met in the dark.

Your reputation can be damaged by the opinions of others. Only you yourself can damage your character.

No amount of riches can atone for poverty of character.

Something of a person's character may be discovered by observing how he smiles.

Any man who is honest, fair, tolerant, charitable of others, and well-behaved is a success no matter what his station in life might be.

Some men succeed by what they know, some by what they do, and a few by what they are.

A sense of values is the most important single element in human personality.

The real measure of a man's wealth is how much he would be worth if he lost all his money.

Charity

Giving good advice does not qualify as charity.

Giving advice to the poor is not the best form of charity.

An autobiography, like charity, covers a multitude of sins.

Charity begins at home, and generally dies from lack of outdoor exercise.

Many a man's idea of charity is to give advice to others that he can't use himself.

Maybe we were better off when charity was a virtue instead of a deduction.

Charity is twice blessed — it blesses the one who gives and the one who receives.

It is better to give than to lend, and it costs about the same.

Charity often consists of a generous impulse to give away something for which we have no further use.

Unless a man is a recipient of charity, he should be a contributor to it.

Charity should begin at home, but most people don't stay at home long enough to begin it.

Real charity doesn't care if it's deductible or not.

Charity is injurious unless it helps the recipient become independent of it.

In the old days charity was a virtue instead of an industry.

Charity is the sterilized milk of human kindness.

Giving advice to the poor is about as close to charity as some people get.

True charity is helping those you have every reason to believe would not help you.

Christian charity knows no iron curtain.

Feel for others — in your pocketbook!

Charity begins at home and usually winds up in some foreign country.

Sincere charity is the desire to be useful to others without any thought of recompense.

Faith, hope, and charity — if we had more of the first two we'd need less of the last.

For a community leader, life is one big bowl of charities.

Cheerfulness

Cheerfulness greases the axles of the world.

Some people are able to spread cheer wherever they don't go.

Cheerfulness is contagious, but don't wait to catch it from others. Be a carrier!

Lots of people get credit for being cheerful when they are just proud of their teeth.

Your day goes the way the corners of your mouth turn.

The man who gets along in the world is the one who can look cheerful and happy when he isn't.

Keep your face to the sunshine and you will never see the shadows.

Remember the steam kettle! Though up to its neck in hot water, it continues to sing.

Few cases of eyestrain have been developed by looking on the bright side of things.

Cheerfulness is contagious, but it seems like some folks have been vaccinated against the infection.

Some people grow up and spread cheer; others just grow up and spread.

Children

There are three ways to get something done: do it yourself, hire someone to do it, or forbid your kids to do it.

Adolescence is when children start bringing up their parents.

Life's golden age is when the children are too old to need baby sitters and too young to borrow the family car.

An alarm clock is a device for awakening people who don't have small children.

Never strike a child! You might miss and hurt yourself.

The easiest way to get a kid's attention is to stand in front of the TV set.

It's hard, if not impossible, to get a child to pay attention to you, especially when you're telling him something for his own good.

When a child pays attention to his parents, they're probably whispering.

There is just as much authority in the family today as there ever was — only now the children exercise it.

Teachers in the lower grades needn't worry about automation until someone invents a machine that can blow noses and remove snowsuits and boots.

What the average man wants to get out of his new car is the kids.

One advantage of the compact car is that when any of the kids start acting up they can be reached by hand.

Nothing lengthens the life of your car like marrying-off the last of your children.

A baby sitter is not experienced until she knows which kid to sit with and which kid to sit on.

A baby sitter is a teen-ager you hire to let your children do whatever they are big enough to do.

Most of us want other people's children to behave the way ours should.

Some books you can't put down, and others you dare not put down when there are children in the house.

A small boy is a pain in the neck when he's around and a pain in the heart when he's not.

Safety note for motorists: "Watch out for children — especially if they're driving cars."

Too often an abandoned child is one who is still living with his parents.

Children love to break things — especially rules.

Watch the kid who's cutting classes at school — he may be in training to be a congressman later in life.

Children are unpredictable. You never know how high up the wall they're going to drive you.

Some kids are like ketchup bottles. You have to slap their bottoms a few times to get them moving.

All children don't disobey their parents. Some are never told what to do.

The child who always complains he's getting the short end of the stick should be given more of it.

Today's kids call it "finding themselves." In the "good old days" it was called loafing.

Reasoning with children is what gives you something to do while discovering that you can't.

When children are seen and not heard it's apt to be through binoculars.

A child's ear is a delicate instrument that can't hear a parent's shout from the next room, but picks up the faintest tingle of the ice cream man's bell.

Children always brighten up a home. They never turn out the lights.

Children who are reared in homes of poverty have only two mealtime choices — take it or leave it.

The school kids in some towns are getting so tough that teachers are playing hooky.

Children are like wet cement. Whatever falls on them makes an impression.

An unusual child is one who asks his parents questions they can answer.

The only thing that children wear out faster than shoes are parents and teachers.

A kid who learns the value of a dollar these days is certain to grow up cynical.

Small children start to school these days with a big advantage. They already know two letters of the alphabet — TV.

One thing most children save for a rainy day is lots of energy.

Children of today play a game called Zip Code. It's like Post Office but faster.

A child, like your stomach, doesn't need all you can afford to give it.

Some children grow like weeds and are about as well cared for.

The reason some parents want their children to play the piano instead of the violin is that it's harder to lose a piano.

Children may be deductible, but they're still taxing.

Modern kids are so TV-oriented they think there are two kinds of rainbows. One in color and the other in black and white.

The trouble with having outspoken children is that you're frequently left holding the bag they let the cat out of.

The first thing a child learns when he gets a drum is that he's never going to get another one.

Children disgrace us in public by behaving just like we do at home.

It now costs more to amuse a child than it once did to educate his father.

Children brought up in Sunday school are seldom brought up in court.

There are many "bright children" who should be applauded with one hand.

Children may tear up a house, but they never break up a home.

Few children are guilty of thoughtless mischief. They plan it.

The best time to put the children to bed is when you can.

Babies are angels whose wings grow shorter as their legs grow longer.

Children are very much like airplanes; you hear only of the ones that crash.

Most kids can't understand why a country that makes atomic bombs would ban firecrackers.

Nothing seems to make children more affectionate than sticky hands.

Not all children sass their parents. Some don't pay that much attention.

Children will be children — even after they are fifty years old.

When parents can't or won't control their children in the home, it's extremely difficult for the government to control them on the streets.

If some children are as bright as their parents think they are, they should be looked at through sunglasses.

No two children are alike — particularly if one is yours and the other one isn't.

Some children are running everything around the house except errands.

Children are a comfort to us in our old age, and they help us to reach it a lot sooner.

One important way for us to help our children grow up is for us to grow up first.

There are only two things children will share willingly — communicable diseases and their mother's age.

If you are disgusted and upset with your children, just imagine how God must feel about His!

Infant prodigies are young people with highly imaginative parents.

In the old days a father didn't have to take his kid to a psychiatrist to find out that he was a little stinker.

There are no illegitimate children — only illegitimate parents.

The trouble with children is that when they're not bringing a lump to your throat they're a pain in the neck.

There are still a few people who can remember when a child misbehaved to get attention — and got it!

Children are a great deal more apt to follow your lead than the way you point.

The best time to put kids to bed is very late — when they're too tired to fight back.

It's real nice for children to have pets until the pets start having children.

Children are unpredictable. You never know when they're going to catch you in a lie.

Childhood is that wonderful period when all you need to do to lose weight is take a bath.

The children of today think they have it rough in school if they have to walk more than a block to park their cars.

Someday science may be able to explain why a child can't walk around a mud puddle.

Spoiled kids soon become little stinkers.

There's no child so bad that he can't be used as an income-tax deduction.

More twins are being born these days than ever before. Maybe kids lack the courage to come into the world alone.

A baby may not be able to lift very much, but it can hold a marriage together.

If brushing up on manners doesn't help some children, the brush should be moved down a bit.

One reason so many children are seen on the streets at night is because they're afraid to stay home alone.

Children need strength to lean on, a shoulder to cry on, and an example to learn from.

You can get any child to run an errand for you — if you ask him at bedtime.

Maybe children could keep on the straight and narrow path if they could get information from someone who's been over the route.

Children are natural mimics; they act like their parents in spite of every effort to teach them good manners.

Some of today's children don't smart in the right place.

Nothing grieves a child more than to study the wrong lesson and learn something he wasn't supposed to.

The trouble with a child is that he can't grow up to be anything but an adult.

If you don't want your children to hear what you're saying, pretend you're talking to them.

If children didn't ask questions, they would never know what little adults know.

Children are about the only things in a modern home that have to be washed by hand.

Rearing children is the biggest "heir-conditioning" job ever undertaken.

You can tell your kids are growing up when they stop asking where they came from and start refusing to say where they're going.

When a child listens to his mother, he's probably on the telephone extension.

Modern parents think children should be seen, not heard; children think parents should be neither seen nor heard.

Many children have grown up to be fairly levelheaded because their parents couldn't find the guidance book they were looking for.

What most children learn by doing is how to drive their parents almost crazy.

It's extremely difficult for a child to live right if he has never seen it done.

Children these days seem to grow up bigger and faster, yet remain children longer than ever before.

It's always charming to see little children lined up waiting to talk to the department store Santa Claus — some with parents, some with lists, and some with chicken pox.

Nowadays children are called bright when they make remarks that used to call for a good spanking.

The chief trouble with children is they are human.

It's great to have your children home from school. It takes your mind off your other troubles.

The best thing to spend on children is your time.

Telling children that school days are the happiest days of their lives doesn't give them much to look forward to.

Any child who gets raised strictly by the book is probably a first edition.

The latest class of underprivileged children are those whose parents own two cars — but no speedboat.

Almost every child would learn to write sooner if allowed to do homework on wet cement.

There's nothing thirstier than a child who has just gone to bed.

More children are spoiled because the parents won't spank Grandma.

A "brat" is a child who acts like your own but belongs to your neighbor.

Most children seldom misquote you; they repeat what you shouldn't have said word for word.

We can't understand why today's children are complaining so much. They're not old enough to remember what prices used to be.

Among the best home furnishings are children.

Infant care is another thing that has to be learned from the bottom up.

Many children would take after their parents if they knew where they went.

When children get on the wrong track it's time to use the switch.

Little Willie is at the awkward age — too young to leave him home alone, and too old to trust with baby sitters.

Children always know when company is in the living room — they can hear their mother laughing at their father's jokes.

It's very difficult to teach children the alphabet these days. They think V comes right after T.

Children are so tough in big cities they no longer use bunnies for Easter — they use porcupines.

Parents are embarrassed when their children tell lies, but sometimes it's even worse when they tell the truth.

A child's definition of a torture chamber is a living room or den without a TV set.

If the church neglects the children, it is certain the children will neglect the church.

Cleanliness may be next to godliness, but in childhood it's next to impossible.

A modern son is one who finishes college and his dad at the same time.

Sending your child to college is like sending your clothes to the laundry. You get what you put in, but sometimes you can hardly recognize it.

With the world in such a confused state, no wonder babies cry when they come into it.

Most kids think a balanced diet is a hamburger in each hand.

Every father should remember that one day his son will follow his example instead of his advice.

A great many children face the hard problem of learning good table manners without seeing any.

We learn from experience. A man never wakes up his second baby just to see it smile.

In some families it would be best if the children were properly spaced — about one hundred yards apart.

The advantage of a large family is that at least one of the children may not turn out like the others.

As the gardener is responsible for the products of his garden, so the family is responsible for the character and conduct of its children.

Families with babies and families without babies are sorry for each other.

Every part of the family constitutes a part of the family tree. Father is the rough bark and fiber, the rugged part which supports and protects it. Mother is the heart, which must be sound and true or the tree will die. The daughter may be likened to the leaves and flowers that adorn it. The son is almost always the sap.

A lucky farmer is one who has raised a bumper crop of good boys.

There's a new babyfood on the market. It's half orange juice and half garlic. It not only makes the baby healthier, but also easier to find in the dark.

Jelly is a food usually found on bread, children, and piano keys.

No family should have less than three children. If there is one genius among them, there should be two to support him.

Playing golf is like raising children — you keep thinking you'll do better next time.

All some people need to make them happy is a change — and most of the time that's all a baby needs.

The best possible infant care is to keep one end full and the other end dry.

Nothing creates a firmer belief in heredity than having a good-looking child.

Home is a man's refuge, a place of quiet and rest, says a certain writer. That's true except for the telephone, the children, the vacuum cleaner, and the salesman at the door.

The honeymoon is definitely over when all the babytalk around the house is done only by the baby.

If you plan to teach your children the value of a dollar, you'll have to do it awfully fast.

A much-needed invention for the American scene is an automatic childwasher.

We need tougher child abuse laws — parents have taken enough abuse from their children.

A real family man is one who looks at his new child as an addition rather than a deduction.

Children often hold a marriage together by keeping their parents so busy they don't have time to quarrel.

A "miracle drug" is any medicine you can get the kids to take without screaming.

Another reason men don't live as long as women is that they suffer so much waiting around in hospitals for their wives to have babies.

A mother in Colorado is so ashamed of her unruly kids that she attends the PTA under an assumed name.

There are still a few old-fashioned mothers who would like to tuck their children in bed, but they can't stay awake that late.

When it comes to music lessons, most kids make it a practice not to practice.

Who said kids aren't obedient? They'll obey any TV commercial about buying a new toy.

You are quite old if you can remember when children were strong enough to walk to school.

When all the kids have grown up, married, and moved away, many parents experience a strange new emotion; it's called ecstacy.

All a parent has to do to make a child thirsty is to fall asleep.

Parents would not have to worry so much about how a kid turns out if they worried more about when he turns in.

You have to give American parents credit — they know how to obey their children.

People who say they sleep like a baby haven't got one.

There's only one perfect child in the world and every mother has it.

A good way for your daughter to be popular is for you to be rich.

A major problem facing housewives is that ovens are self-cleaning but kids aren't.

Psychiatry has certainly changed things. The kid who used to be just a chatterbox is now a "compulsive talker."

It's incredible when we think how little our parents knew about child psychology and how wonderful we turned out to be!

Child psychology is what children manage their parents with.

Where do kids get all those questions parents can't answer?

Little Junior brought home what is now remembered as his Watergate report card. First, he denied there was one; then he couldn't find it. When he finally located it, three grades had been erased.

The hardest people to convince that they're ready to retire are children at bedtime.

If your youngster asks how Santa Claus gets into your house, tell him he comes in through a hole in daddy's wallet.

It's invariably the little devil in your neighborhood who starts the fight with your little angel.

Sleep is something that science cannot abolish — but babies can.

Efficient school teachers may cost more, but poor school teachers cost the most.

A teacher's constant task is to take a roomful of live wires and see to it that they're grounded.

Nothing improves a television program as much as getting the children to bed.

Children who watch television every night will go down in history — not to mention arithmetic, geography, and science.

You don't know what trouble is until your kids reach the age of consent, dissent, and resent — all at the same time.

The guy whose troubles are all behind him is probably a school bus driver.

The child who knows the value of a dollar these days must be terribly discouraged.

The trouble with teaching a child the value of a dollar is you have to do it almost every week.

Every child comes into the world endowed with liberty, opportunity, and a share of the war debt.

The two agencies now being used to redistribute wealth are taxation and offspring.

Things are pretty well evened up in this world. Other people's troubles are not as bad as ours, but their children are a lot worse.

Child Training

Some adolescents become bad eggs because they have been set on too long — or not long enough.

Never strike a child! You might miss and hurt yourself.

It's hard, if not impossible, to get a child to pay attention to you, especially when you're telling him something for his own good.

One advantage of the compact car is that when any of the kids start acting up they can be reached by hand.

The behavior of some children suggests that their parents embarked on the sea of matrimony without a paddle.

A boy loves a dog because it's the only thing around the house that doesn't find fault with him.

One way to keep young boys from getting on the wrong track is to use better switching facilities.

A boy is like a canoe — he behaves better if paddled from the rear.

It used to be when a boy couldn't learn at his mother's knee he found himself over his father's.

A pat on the back will develop character if given young enough, often enough, low enough — and hard enough.

Some kids are like ketchup bottles. You have to slap their bottoms a few times to get them moving.

All children don't disobey their parents. Some are never told what to do.

The child who always complains he's getting the short end of the stick should be given more of it.

Some children grow like weeds and are about as well cared for.

Children brought up in Sunday school are seldom brought up in court.

There are many "bright children" who should be applauded with one hand.

One important way for us to help our children grow up is for us to grow up first.

There are still a few people who can remember when a child misbehaved to get attention — and got it!

Spoiled kids soon become little stinkers.

If brushing up on manners doesn't help some children, the brush should be moved down a bit.

Some of today's children don't smart in the right place.

Rearing children is the biggest "heir-conditioning" job ever undertaken.

Many children have grown up to be fairly levelheaded because their parents couldn't find the guidance book they were looking for.

Nowadays children are called bright when they make remarks that used to call for a good spanking.

Any child who gets raised strictly by the book is probably a first edition.

When children get on the wrong track it's time to use the switch.

Child training is chiefly a matter of knowing which end of the child to pat — and when.

Training a child to follow the straight and narrow way is easy for parents — all they have to do is lead the way.

In bringing up children it's best not to let them know it.

Sometimes the best way to straighten out a child is by bending him over.

Never slap a child in the face. Remember, there's a *place* for everything.

It is extremely difficult to train a boy in the way his father does not go.

If a child annoys you, quiet him by brushing his hair — if this doesn't work, use the other side of the brush on the other end of the child.

It's better to teach children the roots of labor than to hand them the fruits of yours.

Theories on how to rear children usually end with the birth of the second child.

Every child has a right to be both well-fed and well-led.

To train children at home, it's necessary for both the children and the parents to spend some time there.

Someone has defined spanking as "stern" punishment.

The surest way to make it hard for your children is to make it soft for them.

You train a child until age ten; after that you only influence him.

Train your child in the way you now know you should have gone yourself.

The best way to bring up children is never to let them down.

Teaching children to count is not as important as teaching them *what* counts.

Another thing a modern child learns at his mother's knee is to watch out for cigarette ashes.

A switch in time saves crime.

Psychiatrists tell us that discipline doesn't break a child's spirit half as often as the lack of it breaks a parent's heart.

Discipline is what you inflict on one end of a child to impress the other.

A modern home is a place where a switch controls everything but the children.

A typical home is where the TV set is better adjusted than the kids.

One reason for juvenile delinquency is that many parents are raising their children by remote control.

One of the problems of juvenile delinquency is children running away from home. It is entirely possible they may be looking for their parents.

Most juvenile delinquents are youngsters who have been given a free hand, but not in the proper place.

In the days when a woodshed stood behind the American home, a great deal of what passes as juvenile delinquency was settled out of court.

When a youth begins to sow wild oats it's time for father to start the threshing machine.

Juvenile delinquency is the result of parents trying to train their children without starting at the bottom.

Juvenile delinquency was unheard of many years ago because the problem was thrashed-out in the woodshed.

Did the conversion of so many woodsheds into garages have anything to do with the alarming increase in juvenile delinquency.?

The man who remembers what he learned at his mother's knee was probably bent over at the time.

A mother should be like a quilt — keep the children warm but don't smother them.

The time to teach obedience to authority is in the playpen instead of the State pen.

Too many parents tie up their dogs and allow their children to run loose.

The ability to say no is perhaps the greatest gift a parent has.

Some parents begin with giving in and end with giving up.

Some parents bring their children up, others let them down.

Judging by what we read in the papers, the reason some parents "spare the rod" is because Junior is carrying one.

By the time some parents get around to putting a foot down, the child already has his on the accelerator.

Applied child psychology was more effective when the applicator was a small razor strap.

We've given our youngsters too much too soon, and now it's too late.

The best way to stop kids from seeing dirty movies is to label them "Educational."

Chivalry

Chivalry is a man's inclination to defend a woman against every man but himself.

The age of chivalry is certainly not dead. If a college girl drops one of her books, almost any boy in her class will be delighted to kick it back to her.

Chivalry is what a husband displays toward somebody else's wife.

In the "good old days" men stood up for women — but there were no buses then.

Chivalry is when a man picks up a girl's handkerchief, even if she's not pretty.

Chivalry is opening the door and standing aside so some female can rush in and get the job you're after.

Choice

Sign on a businessman's desk: "My decision is maybe — and that's final."

Few people make a deliberate choice between good and evil; the choice is between what we want to do and what we ought to do.

Choice, not chance, determines destiny.

When you need to make a choice and don't make it, that in itself is a choice.

The choice is simple — you can either stand up and be counted, or lie down and be counted out.

It is much wiser to choose what you say than to say what you choose.

There comes a time when a nation, as well as an individual, must choose between tightening the belt or losing the pants.

A conference is a meeting to decide when and where the next meeting will be held.

A conference is nothing more than an organized way of postponing a decision.

Generally speaking, a conference is a gathering of people who singly can do nothing, but together can decide that nothing can be done.

When a man decides to marry, it may be the last decision he'll ever be allowed to make.

No one can grow by allowing others to make his decisions.

Nothing great was ever done without an act of decision.

Always take plenty of time to make a snap decision.

It's pretty hard for the Lord to guide a man if he hasn't made up his mind which way he wants to go.

A man can't go anywhere while he's straddling a fence.

If you're going to pull decisions out of a hat, be sure you're wearing the right hat.

Almost everybody knows the difference between right and wrong, but some hate to make decisions.

Current events are so grim that we can't decide whether to watch the six o'clock news and not be able to eat, or the ten o'clock news and not be able to sleep.

Many a woman's final decision is not the last one she makes.

Be cautious in choosing friends, and be even more cautious in changing them.

A good executive is one who can make decisions quickly — and sometimes correctly.

An executive is a fellow who can take as long as he wants to make a snap decision.

If fate throws a knife at you, there are two ways of catching it — by the blade or by the handle.

If fate hands you a lemon, try to make lemonade.

Wise people sometimes change their minds — fools, never.

Nature gives man corn, but man must grind it; God gives man a will, but man must make the right choices.

Intuition is that gift which enables a woman to arrive instantly at an infallible, irrevocable decision without the aid of reason, judgment, or discussion.

In most marriages the husband is the provider and the wife is the decider.

Nine out of ten people who change their minds are wrong the second time too.

Patience may be simply the inability to make decisions.

Christianity

If there are any good traits about the atheist, he got them from Christianity.

The Bible is the constitution of Christian civilization.

Christian charity knows no iron curtain.

If your Christianity won't work where you are, it won't work anywhere.

One of the best things about Christianity is that it must function or fizzle.

If you want to convince others of the value of Christianity — live it!

A genuine Christian is the best evidence of the genuineness of Christianity.

An empty tomb proves Christianity; an empty church denies it.

Christianity is a way of walking as well as a way of talking.

The true expression of Christianity is not a sigh, but a song.

If you want to defend Christianity, practice it.

Christianity is a roll-up-your-sleeves religion.

A Chicago gangster was recently converted to Christianity. He confessed that he had sown enough wild oats to make a grain deal with Russia.

Christianity is not a life insurance policy from which one benefits only by dying.

Those who say they believe in Christianity and those who practice it are not always the same people.

Christianity requires the participants to come down out of the grandstand and onto the playing field.

The better we understand Christianity, the less satisfied we are with our practice of it.

Christianity has been studied and practiced for ages, but it has been studied far more than it has been practiced.

The spirit of Christianity is not to impose some kind of a creed, but to share a life.

Christianity, like a watch, needs to be wound regularly if it is to be kept running.

Satan is perfectly willing to have a person confess Christianity as long as he does not practice it.

Christianity helps us face the music, even when we don't like the tune.

Some people can talk Christianity by the yard but they can't, or won't, walk it by the inch.

Foreign missionaries will be more successful when they can *show* Christianity to the heathen and not merely tell them about it.

Too much of the Christian faith has become trimming on the dress of life instead of a part of the fabric.

The hope is that some day the Christian ideal will be put into practice.

Christ was one child who knew more than His parents — yet He obeyed them.

People always get into trouble when they think they can handle their lives without God.

The sermon will be better if you listen to it as a Christian rather than a critic.

When tempers grow hot, Christianity grows cold.

Christians

Many Christians expect the world to respect a book they neglect.

No one can become a Christian on his own terms.

A Christian must get on his knees before he can get on his feet.

Christians are the light of the world, but the switch must be turned on.

To feel sorry for the needy is not the mark of a Christian — to help them is.

The Christian who is pulling the oars doesn't have time to rock the boat.

Christians may not see eye to eye, but they can walk arm in arm.

We are not to consider ourselves Christians simply because we think we are.

A Christian shows what he is by what he does with what he has.

The true Christian is a person who is right-side-up in a world that is upside-down.

If people have to ask you if you're a Christian — you're probably not.

Every Christian occupies some kind of a pulpit and preaches some kind of a sermon every day.

A Christian must carry something heavier on his shoulder than a chip.

There are a lot of Christians who haven't stored up enough treasures to make a down-payment on a harp.

A Christian is one who makes it easier for other people to believe in God.

What most Christians need is fewer platitudes and better attitudes.

A lukewarm Christian makes a good bench-warmer but a poor heart-warmer.

It does not take much of a man to be a Christian, but it takes all there is.

Happier faces are seen on bottles of iodine than on some Christians.

What the world needs is not more Christianity but more Christians who practice Christianity.

The Christian's walk and talk must go together.

A Christian has not lost the power to sin, but the desire to sin.

Satan is never too busy to rock the cradle of a sleeping Christian.

If you were arrested for being a Christian, would there be enough evidence to convict you?

A real Christian is as horrified by his own sins as he is by his neighbor's.

There are some Christians who can't be called "pilgrims" because they never make any progress.

An idle Christian is the raw material of which backsliders are made.

Christians are like pianos — grand, square, upright, and no good unless in tune.

The Christian should learn two things about his tongue — how to hold it and how to use it.

It's a little difficult to reconcile the creed of some Christians with their greed.

Two marks of a Christian: giving and forgiving.

It's good to be a Christian and know it, but it's better to be a Christian and show it.

Too many Christian soldiers fraternize with the enemy.

A few Christians give the impression they have been baptized in vinegar.

No Christian is strong enough to carry a cross and a prejudice at the same time.

Beware of a Christian with an open mouth and a closed pocketbook.

A genuine Christian is like a good watch: he has an open face, busy hands, is made of pure gold, is well-regulated, and is full of good works.

A Christian is a mind through which Christ thinks, a heart through which Christ loves, a voice through which Christ speaks, a hand through which Christ helps.

When Christians feel safe and comfortable, the church is in its greatest danger.

Some Christians who should be wielding the sword of the Spirit are still tugging at the nursery bottle.

The cross is easier to the Christian who takes it up than to the one who drags it along.

A Christian is like ripening corn: the riper he grows, the lower he bows his head.

Every Christian should have two planks in his platform: one is for what he will stand for; the other is for what he will not stand for.

A Christian is a living sermon, whether or not he preaches a word.

No one is a Christian just because he goes to church, any more than one is a calf because he drinks milk.

A Christian should live so that instead of being a part of the world's problems he will be a part of the answer.

Some Christians have will power; others have *won't* power.

A Christian is not necessarily a man who is better than someone else, but one who is better than he would be if he were not a Christian.

Some Christians wish to be counted *in,* but not to be counted *on.*

The Christian life is like an airplane — when you stop you drop!

Many churches are plagued with a lot of "retired" Christians.

No garment is more becoming to a Christian than the cloak of humility.

Communism will be defeated in America and in all countries where Christians are more interested in being mobilized than in being tranquilized.

God is not only a present help in time of trouble, but also a great help in keeping us out of trouble.

The knowledge, understanding, and appropriation of God's Word are the means by which a Christian grows.

To feel sorry for the needy is not the mark of a Christian — to help them is.

A wise man said that humility is Christian clothing. It never goes out of style.

If some Christians knew as little about their jobs as they do the Bible, they would have to be guided to their work benches every morning.

The weekend religion of some Christians is weak at both ends, and unreliable between the two ends.

The Lord prepares a table for His children, but too many of them are on a diet.

Nowadays we have sermonettes by preacherettes for Christianettes.

Some people seem willing to do anything to become a Christian except to give up their sins.

Christmas

Many banks have a new kind of Christmas club in operation. The new club helps you save money to pay for last year's gifts.

Nothing destroys the Christmas spirit faster than looking for a place to park.

Christmas is a race to see which gives out first — your money or your feet.

The Christmas season is only as meaningful as we make it.

Christmas carolers sing about peace on earth, but they don't tell us where.

Can you remember when Christmas was so simple that one Santa Claus could work an entire town?

What most of us want for Christmas is the day after.

Anyone who thinks Christmas doesn't last all year doesn't have a charge account.

About all you can do is dream of a white Christmas, for it seems like it always leaves most of us in the red.

The average couple splits the Christmas chores. She signs the cards and he signs the checks.

Christmas shopping should include buying toys for the children that their father would enjoy playing with.

Last year a big store in Milwaukee started its Christmas sale so early that Santa Claus wore Bermuda shorts.

Christmas is a time when everybody wants his past forgotten and his present remembered.

Always mail your Christmas gift early. It will give the receiver time to reciprocate.

Christmas is the time of the year when Santa Claus comes down the chimney and your savings go down the drain.

When we throw out the Christmas tree we should be especially careful not to throw out the Christmas spirit with it.

Christmas holidays mean: anticipation, preparation, recreation, prostration, and recuperation.

A Christmas shopper's complaint is one of long-standing.

Christmas is when we celebrate the birth of the Prince of Peace by giving our kids rockets, machine guns, atom-bomb kits, and tanks.

Perhaps the best Yuletide decoration is being wreathed in smiles.

79

An unbreakable Christmas toy is one that's guaranteed to last through the New Year.

This year Americans are planning the biggest Christmas they ever charged.

The battle of Christmas shopping is a time when the casualty list grows in the War on Poverty.

When you pay twenty-five dollars for a Christmas tree, you've been trimmed more than the tree has.

Many a parent sighs for the "good old days" when a stocking could hold what a child wanted for Christmas.

The Christmas season reminds us that a demonstration of religion is often better than a definition of it.

Christmas shoppers are people with the "brotherly shove."

Smart kids will be hanging up stretch stockings next Christmas.

Christmas is the time of year when both trees and husbands get trimmed. Sometimes both get lit up too.

You might as well do your Christmas hinting early.

Christmas is a time for sportsmanship because we don't always get everything we want.

We feel close to everybody at Christmas — especially on a bus.

What many a store clerk gets for Christmas is an ulcer.

The Christmas spirit that goes out with the dried-up Christmas tree is just as worthless.

There have always been some Christmas stockings that provided Santa with a few problems, but one wonders about his reaction to panty hose!

The exchange of Christmas gifts ought to be reciprocal rather than retaliatory.

Keeping Christmas is good, but sharing it with others is much better.

The best Christmas gift of all is the presence of a happy family all wrapped up with one another.

Christmas is a time when a lot of others besides Santa find themselves in the red.

It's a soul-stirring experience to hear Yule carolers standing in a Los Angeles smog singing, "It Came upon a Midnight Clear."

The *way* you spend Christmas is far more important than *how much.*

One thing about Christmas shopping — it toughens you up for the January sales.

Let's all have an old-fashioned Christmas this year, but not the kind that comes in bottles.

At Christmas most parents spend more money on their children than they did on the honeymoon that started it all.

A father's biggest difficulty at Christmas time is convincing the children that he is Santa Claus and his wife that he is not.

A family in San Francisco is reliving its Christmas holidays — the man of the house is showing colored slides of his cancelled checks.

On Christmas Eve Santa carries the bag. After Christmas dad is holding it.

"Good Will Toward Men" is the spice in the Christmas season.

Christmas is a time for exchanging a lot of things you can't afford for a lot of things you don't want.

One of the nice things about Christmas is that you can make people forget the past with a present.

God shocked the world with a babe, not a bomb.

Church

A man who is immersed in business all week should come up for a breath of fresh air on Sunday — at church.

Children brought up in Sunday school are seldom brought up in court.

When Christians feel safe and comfortable, the church is in its greatest danger.

The man who says he's just as good as half the folks in the church seldom specifies which half.

Many churches are plagued with a lot of "retired" Christians.

Church is where you go to find out what your neighbors should do to lead better lives.

Many church services today are marked by lameness, tameness, and sameness.

It's disconcerting to fall asleep in church and have a fly buzz into one's open mouth.

Every church has all the success it prays for and pays for.

A fortune awaits the person who will design a church building without any front pews.

The church offers you something you simply can't get elsewhere.

Not many people are attracted to churches which are as cold as ice or by preachers who are as dry as dust.

Sign on a church bulletin board in Benton, Wisconsin: "For God so loved the world that He didn't send a committee."

The less religion a church has, the more ice cream and cake it takes to keep it going.

All churches grow old, but some never grow up.

A church that is not reaching out is passing out.

The church needs workers, not a wrecking crew.

It is easy to lose interest in the church if you have never made an investment in it.

One place where people seem to think they can get as much as ever for a quarter is in the church.

What the church needs is more men who talk less and work more.

The business of the church is to get rid of evil, not to supervise it.

A cold church is like cold butter — never spreads very well.

Sign on a church lawn in Des Moines, Iowa: "Keep off the grass. This means thou."

Separation of church and state could hardly be more complete. The church teaches that money isn't everything, and the government keeps telling us it is.

The church cannot afford the luxury of loafing.

If the church neglects the children, it is certain the children will neglect the church.

Some churches seem to be sound in doctrine, but they are also sound asleep.

Did you know that the church is a workshop and not a dormitory?

A nodding congregation may or may not mean assent to what the preacher is saying.

When the church ceases to be in touch with another world, it is no longer in touch with this world.

The great task of the church is not only to get sinners into heaven, but to get saints out of bed.

Sign in front of a Chicago church: "The competition is terrible, but we're still open for business."

Too many churches have become distribution points for religious aspirin.

All church buildings should be air-conditioned; it is unhealthy to sleep in a stuffy room.

What the church needs today is more calloused hands and fewer calloused hearts.

The carriers and the carried are in every church.

You need the church, the church needs you, the world needs both.

If the church were perfect, you could not belong.

Sign outside a Dallas church: "Last chance to pray before entering the freeway."

Don't stay away from the church because you have the idea that there are too many hypocrites in it. There's always room for one more.

If you make the church important, it is quite likely to return the favor.

The collection is a church function in which many people take only a passing interest.

We are sometimes so interested in creating the machinery of the church that we let the fire go out in the boiler.

When the churches discover they can't successfully compete with the theater, perhaps they will try religion again.

Don't knock your church — it may have improved since the last time you were there.

The church is a building and loan association to help you build a mansion in heaven.

Many churches are now serving coffee after the sermon. Presumably this is to get the people thoroughly awake before they start to drive home.

Sign on a church bulletin board in Denver: "If you have troubles, come in and tell us about them. If you have none, come in and tell us how you do it."

Many folks think that what the church has is for somebody else.

The church will improve when its members improve.

Church is a place where you can meet old friends you never saw before.

The church does not necessarily consist of the good, but of those who want to be better and do better.

Notice in a church bulletin: "The Lord loveth a cheerful giver. He also accepteth from a grouch."

The church is paralyzed with timidity and gradually dying of dignity.

If the church is ever to get on its feet, it must get on its knees.

The church of today is an institution supported largely by the husbands of its members.

It seems that our modern churches are full of willing people; some are willing to work, and others are willing to let them.

Announcement on the bulletin board of a church in Ohio: "This is a segregated church — for sinners only. All welcome."

How often have you met a critic of the church who tried to make it better?

When someone says he diets religiously, he probably means he doesn't eat anything while in church.

Your faith gets a real test when you find yourself in church with nothing less than a twenty dollar bill in your wallet.

The way some people give, you would think the church is coin-operated.

One reason we have so many pennies in the church collection basket is because we have no smaller coins.

Many people give a tenth to the Lord — a tenth of what they ought to give.

From the amount that some people give to the Lord, they must be positive that it's the little things that count.

Support the church with your money. You can't take it with you, but you can send it on ahead.

Some people will bring a hymnbook or a prayerbook — but not a pocketbook to church.

If it rained dollar bills, some people would try to get one changed before going to church.

A really good golfer is one who goes to church on Sunday first.

Golf is a wonderful game — for one thing it keeps men from falling asleep in church on Sunday mornings.

The surest steps toward happiness are the church steps.

Every human being should have three homes: a domestic home, a church home, and an eternal home.

It's funny how a dollar can look so big when you take it to church and so small when you take it to the supermarket.

Anybody who thinks there's a shortage of coins hasn't been to church lately.

The woman who starts putting on her shoes when the preacher says, "And now in conclusion," is a real optimist.

Perfect poise is not looking self-conscious in the front pew.

If you gave the same amount of time to your work as you do your church, how long would you hold your job?

Many people spend the first six days of each week sowing wild oats — then go to church on Sunday and pray for a crop failure.

The world at its worst needs the church at its best.

A place of worship should be of such character that it will be easy for men to find God and difficult for them to forget Him.

Church Attendance

Blessed is the man who can hear his alarm clock on Sunday as well as on Monday.

An empty tomb proves Christianity; an empty church denies it.

No one is a Christian just because he goes to church, any more than one is a calf because he drinks milk.

No one is too bad to go to church; neither is anyone good enough to stay away.

Everybody has to be somewhere, so how about being at church next Sunday?

Sign on a church lawn in Atlanta: "Come to church next Sunday. If you have no sins, bring someone who has."

It seems that some people refuse to come to the front of the church unless escorted by pallbearers.

One reason it's often difficult to coax men to go to church is that men aren't interested in what other men are wearing.

Many come to church to bring their new clothes rather than themselves.

The great task of the church is not only to get sinners into heaven, but to get saints out of bed.

The church service is not a convention to which a family should merely send a delegate.

If you would like to hear all about the troubles in the church, ask someone who hasn't been there for several months.

The most expensive piece of furniture in the church is the empty pew.

Sign outside a Louisiana church: "Heaven knows when you were here last."

Sign outside a church in Dallas: "Join our sit-in demonstration every Sunday."

Many people go to church; fewer go to worship.

A man may attend church services regularly, but this does not necessarily mean he attends religiously.

Every person ought to go to church occasionally to get away from himself.

Some people go to church to see who didn't.

Church attendance is determined more by desire than by distance.

The automobile does not take people away from the church against their will.

Judging by church attendance, heaven won't be crowded with men.

Perhaps you had never thought of going to church as a beauty treatment, but it is a wonderful way to get your faith lifted.

Some are late for church service because they have to change a tire; others, because they have to change a dollar.

Many people who demand a front seat in a night club try to even things up by taking a back seat in church.

Depressions, funerals, weddings, and covered-dish suppers keep most people attending church regularly.

Your willful absence from church is a vote to close its doors.

Too many men who talk of finding God in nature rather than in church go hunting for Him with rod or gun.

Some folk's churchgoing is like ice cream — it disappears when the weather gets hot.

If absence makes the heart grow fonder, some church members are deeply in love with the church.

On December 22, 1977, the following sign appeared in a Los Angeles church: "Come in and pray today. Beat the Christmas rush."

If a church member expects to answer when the roll is called up yonder, he had better be present when the roll is called down here.

No person can fully and completely discharge his debt to Almighty God, but surely he can make regular payments on it.

There are some whose faith is not strong enough to bring them to church services, but they expect it to take them to heaven.

Religious freedom is the right of each individual to attend the church of his choice, or go fishing.

More time in God's house will bring better times in our house.

A religion that won't take you to church services on Sunday certainly won't take you to heaven when you die.

Blessed is the man whose watch keeps church time as well as business time.

Church Members

Church membership is not necessarily an elevator to heaven.

Church membership is now at an all-time high; but so is political and social corruption.

Many churches today gain more members by generation than by regeneration.

Some church members are so introverted they can't even lead a silent prayer.

There are four classes of church members: the tired, the retired, the tiresome, and the tireless.

The undertaker is the only person who ought to take names off the church roll.

Church members are stockholders in the church, not merely spectators.

Judging by the way some church members live, they need fire insurance.

A sickly saint is likely to be a healthy hypocrite.

When a church member rests, he rusts.

"Not good if detached" is true of church members as well as railroad tickets.

It is far better to be a weak church member than a strong sinner.

Too many church members have "teflon minds" — nothing seems to stick.

Did you hear about the church member who attends church occasionally to discount his blessings?

There are still a few church members who are like the farmer's pond — dried up in the summer and frozen in the winter.

There are two kinds of people in your church: those who agree with you and the bigots.

A lot of church members know the twenty-third psalm much better than they know the Shepherd.

The inactive church member is of no more use than a corpse — and takes up more room.

Some church members are like wheelbarrows — they go only when they are pushed.

Many church members could appropriately begin all church services by singing, "Nothing in my hand I bring."

It seems that some church members have been starched and ironed, but not all have been washed.

Many churches have three kinds of members: pickers, kickers, and stickers.

Have you noticed that some church members are like balloons — full of wind and ready to blow up at any time!

Why is it that so many church members who say "Our Father" on Sunday go around the rest of the week acting like orphans?

A great many church members are in the salvation train, but too many of them are traveling in the sleeper.

There are a few church members who may be described as the farmer described his mule: "Awfully backward about going forward."

Some church members are like footballs — you never know which way they'll bounce.

Church members who need defrosting should hear a few "red-hot" sermons.

Some church members are like a tire with a slow leak — it takes a lot of pumping to keep them inflated.

Many church members have enough religion to make them decent but not enough to make them dynamic.

Beware of the church member with an open mouth and a closed pocketbook.

Cigarettes

It takes most men about two years to completely quit smoking cigarettes and twice as long to quit bragging about it.

When everything else fails as a cure for smoking cigarettes, try carrying wet matches.

The best way to stop smoking cigarettes is to marry a woman who objects to it.

It doesn't take very long to save enough cigarette coupons to get a radio to listen to while you're propped up in bed with emphysema.

Most people who give up cigarettes substitute something for them — such as irritability.

There's a new cigarette package containing ear plugs for those who don't want to hear reasons why they should quit smoking.

Some people feel that a cigarette is not harmful if they borrow it from somebody else.

Just about as many people will quit smoking cigarettes this week as last week — and a lot of them will be the same people.

Sign in an Iowa munitions factory: "If you insist on smoking in this building, be prepared to leave this world through a hole in the ceiling."

Many fat people have cut down to five cigarettes a day — one after each meal.

People who quit smoking cigarettes have the same problem as newcomers to nudist camps — they don't know what to do with their hands.

Remember, when you stop smoking cigarettes you're creating a hardship for others — the people who mooch cigarettes from you.

A man promised his wife five hundred dollars if she'd stop smoking cigarettes — and she did. Now he's offering her one thousand dollars if she'll stop talking about it.

If you don't think smoking cigarettes makes a woman's voice harsh, try dropping cigarette ashes on her rug.

The tobacco industry would really be doing something if it could come up with a cigarette that eliminated tar, nicotine, and taxes.

Cigarettes are killers that travel in packs.

A new cigarette offers coupons good for a cemetery lot.

Worrying about smoking cigarettes can be beneficial — it takes your mind off lung cancer.

Medical reports don't make people quit smoking cigarettes, but they cut down on the enjoyment.

Now there's a group called Smokers Anonymous. When you feel a strong urge to smoke, you dial a number and hear a lot of coughing.

A person pays twice for his cigarettes. Once when he gets them and, second, when they get him.

One thing can be said for smoking three packs of cigarettes every day. It gives your hands something to do — like shake.

The mortality rate of cigarette smokers and non-smokers is 100 percent. The only difference is the timing.

As kids we started smoking cigarettes because we thought it was smart. Why don't we stop smoking for the same reason?

The cancer scare has increased the use of borrowed cigarettes.

Another thing a modern child learns at his mother's knee is to watch out for cigarette ashes.

The best way to give up cigarettes is to smoke cigars.

Walking a mile for a cigarette may be healthier than smoking one.

At last one of the tobacco companies has found a way to make its cigarettes less irritating; it filters the commercials.

Anti-cigarette commercial: "Truth or cancer-quences."

The trouble with people who have broken a habit is that they usually have the pieces mounted and framed.

A health nut in Idaho has specified in his will that he wishes to be buried in a "no smoking" section of the cemetery.

Sign in a Boston hospital: "We don't sell cigarettes — we love you too much."

A modern mother is one who can hold a safety pin and a cigarette in her mouth at the same time.

A major scientific advancement would be the development of cigarette ashes that would match the color of the rug.

Self-control is giving up smoking cigarettes; extreme self-control is not telling anybody about it.

A tobacco chewer in North Carolina has agreed that if smokers won't blow smoke in his face he won't spit on them.

One of the nice things about smoking a pipe is that you can't light the wrong end.

Why is it that someone who has the will power to give up smoking doesn't have the will power to stop bragging about it?

Civilization

The main hope of civilization is that people may get together some day and try it.

Civilization is a state of affairs where nothing can be done without first being financed.

Another measure of civilization's progress is the way the cost of relaxing goes up.

One of the main troubles with modern civilization is that we so often mistake respectability for character.

A sociologist says civilization will last fifty thousand more years, but he didn't say when it would begin.

There have been twenty-five civilizations before ours, and all have been destroyed — not from without but from within.

Perhaps the supreme product of civilization is people who can endure it.

If we are to preserve civilization, we must remain civilized.

Civilization has brought us guided rockets and misguided rackets.

Some historians say the Egyptians contributed more to civilization than any other people. They invented soap.

If we saved civilization in two world wars, we wonder where it is hiding now!

The greatest lesson we learn from past civilizations is ingratitude.

There is some argument over the origin of civilization — but this is unimportant compared with the question of when it will resume operation.

In another hundred years civilization will have reached all peoples except those who have no resources worth stealing.

Civilization has now reached the point where miracle drugs and get-well cards have a hard time keeping up with each other.

The coating of civilization is so thin it often comes off with a little alcohol.

Civilization is a state of society in which the only people who speak about the future with any degree of confidence are the fortunetellers.

In our civilization man came first, then the machine — then the ambulance.

The path of civilization is paved with tax receipts.

Sometimes we get the feeling that Scotch tape and staples are all that's holding civilization together.

The march of civilization is slow because so many are out of step.

The world seldom notices who the teachers are; but civilization depends on what they do and what they say.

The biggest farce of man's history has been the argument that wars are fought to save civilization.

The greatest paradox of them all is to speak of "civilized warfare."

Class Reunions

True happiness is going to a high school class reunion and learning that the boy who was voted most likely to succeed — didn't.

Description of a thirty-year class reunion: "Same old faces, many new teeth."

A class reunion is where everybody gets together to see who is falling apart.

The most irritating person at a class reunion is the guy who has both hair and money.

A satisfying class reunion is one where you discover all your former classmates have bigger problems than yours.

Class reunions are going to be very confusing fifteen years from now when everybody has a haircut.

A class reunion is a gathering where you come to the conclusion that most of the people your age seem to be a lot older than you are.

After attending his class reunion a Texas gentleman reported, "My classmates have all gotten so fat and bald they didn't even recognize me."

A class reunion is when nothing helps you recognize your old classmates as much as their nametags.

Cleanliness

If you want to really appreciate what an enormous job it is to clean up the environment, start cleaning out your garage.

There's one nice thing about baldness — it's neat.

Nature seems determined to make us work. The less hair we have, the more face we have to wash.

A country hick sent the following request to a public library: "Please send me the name of a good book on personal hygiene. I'm afraid I have it."

Nothing changes a small boy's appearance as much as soap.

Nothing seems to make children more affectionate than sticky hands.

Children are about the only things in a modern home that have to be washed by hand.

Some historians say the Egyptians contributed more to civilization than any other people. They invented soap.

Keeping clean *between* the ears may be more important than keeping clean *behind* the ears.

Cleanliness may be next to godliness, but in childhood it's next to impossible.

The most difficult thing imaginable is to keep clean of debt, dirt, and the devil all at the same time.

Cleanliness once lived next to godliness, but both tenants vacated some time ago.

Cleanliness may be next to godliness, but it is not a substitute.

Clothing

Many actresses won't wear a dress that's not original, but they'll take a secondhand husband.

You're getting along in years when the only urge you feel in the spring is to climb out of your long underwear.

Nothing better has ever been developed for baldness than a hat.

It's easy to tell when you've got a bargain — it doesn't fit.

There's nothing tighter than next year's budget and this year's bikini.

Many come to church to bring their new clothes rather than themselves.

Bathing suits are really something — if you call nothing something.

Clothes do not make the man. Particularly an apron.

The nicest things in men's clothing are women.

Nothing seems to last as long as a pair of shoes that doesn't fit.

When a man has torn socks and buttons missing from his shirt, he should do one of two things — either get married or get a divorce.

A dear old lady in Montana says she's worn the same dress so many years it's been in style five times.

Many women suffer discomfort because they often buy shoes to fit the occasion instead of the feet.

Sign in a dress shop in New Orleans: "Wedding gowns for all occasions."

Pants are like molasses. They are thinner in hot weather and thicker in cold weather.

Where do clothing stores get those tricky mirrors that make old suits look so shabby?

A music magazine recently took a poll to name the best-dressed rock star — and nobody won.

One woman to another at a party: "That's lovely material in the dress you're wearing. I wonder if the style will ever come back!"

A bikini is the difference between not very much and nothing at all.

It's extremely difficult to design a gown for a girl who rides the backseat of a motorcycle.

When you see a man wearing a baggy suit, either he has a great diet or a terrible tailor.

About the only thing we can't figure out about those new strapless evening gowns is what keeps them up.

A woman's hat tells you something about her, including whether her husband was along when she bought it.

The only clothing permitted in a nudist camp is a coat — of tan.

A hat is something the average man covers his head with, the beggar passes around, and the politician talks through.

Why do they sell knee socks and Bermuda shorts only to men with knobby knees?

Many husbands prefer clinging gowns for their wives — the kind that cling for at least three years.

A lady shopper in a shoe store expressed a desire to buy an expensive pair of shoes — to go with a cheap husband!

About the only thing concealed in a modern bikini is the manufacturers label.

Clothes, particularly walking shorts, don't make the man.

Sometimes a woman gets a mink coat the hard way — by being nice to her husband.

Nothing lasts as long as a necktie you don't like.

Modern girls wear as many clothes as grandma, but not all at once.

A vest gives a man more pockets to look through for whatever it is that's in his other suit.

No garment is more becoming to a Christian than the cloak of humility.

The reason nobody wears old clothes anymore is because the kind being sold wear out before they get old.

Trousers are more important to a man than his wife is because there are lots of places he can go without his wife.

Sign in a sportswear store: "Buy your girlfriend a bikini — it's the least you can do for her."

Women buy their husbands loafer shoes and leisure slacks — and then call them lazy when they play the part they're dressed for.

Wearing shorts reveals nothing about a man so much as his indifference to public opinion.

The clothes that make a woman break a man.

Sign in a women's clothing shop in Laramie, Wyoming: "We have everything for tall women — except tall men."

One thing we know for sure — there is no way they can make those bikinis any smaller.

New shoes hurt the most when you have to buy them for the whole family.

There is one good thing about pants that are too tight — they teach you not to drop anything on the floor.

Clothes may make the man, but we've seen some where the job still wasn't finished.

If a woman looks good in slacks, she would probably look better in something else.

In summer mosquitoes put more clothes on people than modesty.

It's a pretty safe bet that the husbands of the ten best-dressed women won't show up on the list of the ten best-dressed men.

A man hates to see a woman in cheap clothes, unless, of course, it's his wife.

The old-fashioned mother who saved her wedding togs for her daughter now has a daughter who tries to make them outlast three husbands.

A woman's slacks are what usually makes us wonder why they aren't called something else.

What the well-dressed woman is wearing this year is less.

The reason so many wives have new fur coats is that husbands give in before their wives give up.

If Mother Nature could have foreseen Bermuda shorts, she surely would have done a better job on the male knee.

Many a husband doesn't know a thing about women's clothes, except what they cost.

Fabulous wealth and fame await the man who designs a woman's shoe that's bigger on the inside than it is on the outside.

A Tennessee woman recently complained, "My fur coat is so old it's paid for."

Men no longer hide behind women's skirts; neither do women.

A girdle is a garment to hold a woman in when she goes out.

The wife who dresses to please her husband wears last year's clothes.

It isn't the clothes that make a man stare; it's the women in them.

Some women say they have nothing to wear — others demonstrate it.

Some dresses aren't so bad for the shape they're on.

Most husbands wouldn't object to their wives wearing their skirts a little shorter if they would wear them a little longer.

Preachers who formerly gave lectures on women's clothes have been compelled to turn to other subjects. There just wasn't enough material.

Thirty years ago "halfway to the knees" meant from the ground up, not from the shoulders down.

In some foreign countries girls dress like their mothers, but in America it's the other way around.

Most husbands would like for their wives to wear their dresses longer — about three years longer.

The new bikinis make women look better — and men look longer.

When some women show up in stretch pants, they sure do.

Evening gowns are getting longer, and so are the shoulder straps.

You can't judge some women by their clothes these days — there isn't enough evidence.

If women are so fond of clothes, why don't they wear more of them?

Just about the time you convince your youngsters that they can't put more in a container than it will hold, along comes a woman in stretch pants.

Fashion designers for women's clothing aren't running out of ideas — they're running out of material.

Some dresses are described as stunning because of the effects they have on husbands.

A woman with a new mink coat can't wait to show it to the man she likes most and the woman she likes least.

Even low shoes are very high these days.

Nowadays when a girl says her new evening gown is nothing, she means it.

Nothing makes a woman's clothes go out of style faster than her husband's raise in salary.

By the time a husband is in shape to buy his wife beautiful clothes, she isn't.

An evening dress is more gone than gown.

Ten years from now we'll laugh at the clothes women wear today, but can we hold it that long?

A girl who priced some of the new bikinis reports the tags are bigger than the togs.

In a women's shoe store the most comfortable pair in the house is usually worn by the salesman.

Anybody who says you never get more out of it than you put into it isn't talking about a bikini.

A survey shows that college students prefer ties with dots, suits with stripes, and letters with checks.

Attention wives: If your husband complains about the tie you gave him last Christmas — give him a sock!

A Nevada husband complains that there are two reasons why his wife won't wear last year's dresses — she doesn't want to, and she can't.

The electric computer saves a man a lot of guesswork — but so does a bikini.

A style expert can make a woman feel modest when she doesn't look it.

Fashion experts tell us that women dress to express themselves — but on that basis, some have very little to say.

The nicest thing that can be said about some of today's fashions is that they can't possibly last.

Some women have what it takes to wear the latest fashions — rich husbands.

If women's fashions continue at the present rate, the next creation is likely to be a gownless strap.

With the return of the vest to men's fashions, ties are going to be much freer of gravy stains.

Overheard in a dress shop: "But madam, looking ridiculous is the fashion this year."

When husbands talk about the height of fashion, they probably mean the price.

Some girls show a lot of style, and some styles show a lot of girl.

Many a girl has made it to the top because her dress didn't.

Some of our present-day girls wear less on the streets than their grandmothers wore in bed.

The old-fashioned girl is one who stayed at home when she had nothing to wear.

Girls wear bikinis for the same reason stores have glass showcases.

After the honeymoon the girl usually stops wondering what she should wear and starts wondering how long it will last.

A wise man said that humility is Christian clothing. It never goes out of style.

Don't judge a man by the clothes he wears. God made one; the tailor, the other.

We shouldn't judge a modern girl by her clothes; there really isn't enough evidence.

Any man who laughs at women's clothes has never paid the bill for them.

It may be true that life begins at forty, but everything else starts to wear out, fall out, or spread out.

One advantage of being a man is that you don't run the risk of catching a cold in evening clothes.

Women wear rings to show they're married, while men wear last year's clothes for the same reason.

The nice thing about money is that it never clashes with anything you're wearing.

You have poise when you buy a new pair of shoes without seeming conscious of the hole in your sock.

Isn't it strange how some people insist on having expensive clothes, yet are perfectly satisfied with a shoddy religion?

You're never fully dressed in the morning until you put on a smile.

People seldom notice old clothes if you wear a big smile.

The only thing you can wear that's never out of style is a smile.

The best way to forget all about your troubles is to wear a pair of tight shoes.

Those who put on the most style sometimes put off the most creditors.

It seems that some women would rather be out of money than out of style.

When a woman's toe sticks out of her shoes, she's considered fashionable. When a man's toe sticks out of his shoes, he's a bum.

If you're not in style, the chances are you're out of debt.

Many a woman shows a lot of style, but many a style shows a lot of woman.

A woman's dress usually stays in style until the next time she goes shopping.

There are some things that never go out of style. A feminine woman is one of them.

A woman isn't usually impressed by a new style of clothes unless it's uncomfortable or unreasonable.

If you want to succeed, wear out two pairs of shoes to every suit.

A distressed father said to his teen-age daughter, "Young lady, either that dress is too short or you're not in it far enough."

There are very few certainties in this world, but one of them is that no woman is wearing shoes that are too large for her.

It's obvious that on some women stretch pants have no other choice.

Youth is like fashion. Both fade quickly.

Coffee Breaks

Another advantage of automation is that the machines don't take time out for coffee breaks.

In any office you can tell who the boss is: he's the one watching the clock during the coffee break.

The only break some people get these days is a coffee break.

If some folks aren't careful, they'll stretch their coffee break to the unemployment office.

If coffee breaks get much longer, employees will be late for quitting time.

A conference is just a high-falutin' name for the executives' coffee break.

An employee in Chicago stretched his coffee break all the way to the unemployment office.

Gossip is always brewing at coffee break.

Science has never come up with a better office communication system than the coffee break.

Work is the annoyance people have to endure between coffee breaks.

College Professors

A college professor in Michigan says he has found five different kinds of dumbness. It seems incredible that an educated man like that should have met so few people.

College professors are not made overnight. They reach the height of their profession by degrees.

College professors are the persons who get paid with what's left over after the athletic director and football coaches are paid.

The perfect college professor's wife is the one who, each morning, lays out her husband's slacks, sweater, and picket sign.

Those who go to college and never get out are called professors.

In America a street sweeper can become a college professor — if he's willing to make the financial sacrifice.

The average college professor leads a simple sober life because he never has enough money to make a fool of himself.

Some wit has said that a college professor is little more than a textbook wired for sound.

A college professor isn't really smarter than other people. He just has his ignorance better organized.

We'll be in trouble as long as we pay the best professors less than the worst football coach.

Oh, how this world needs a computer that can figure out all the things in life that don't add up!

Colleges

If the cost of a college education continues to snowball, a person can make a profit by remaining ignorant.

One nice thing about a college education is that it enables us to worry more intelligently about things all over the world.

It's possible that a college education doesn't always pay off, but that doesn't release dad from his financial obligation.

Some people have to carry their diplomas with them to prove they have a college education.

It seems that all a college education does is help folks become confused on a higher plane.

A college education costs thousands of dollars, and sometimes all it yields is a quarterback.

Said a girl graduate, "Four years of college! And *whom* has it got me?"

A college education is very educational. It teaches the parents of the student how to do without a lot of things.

It has been said that a college education is nothing but a four-year plan of confusing young minds methodically.

One of the fine things about a college education is that it shows a person how little other people know.

Nowadays you have to pass a tougher exam to get into college than old-timers did to get out.

A college doesn't give you knowledge, it just shows you where it is.

Don't worry about crowded colleges. Hopefully, they'll empty by degrees.

The college campus of today is one of the biggest supporters of wild life.

Attending college has become so expensive that even football players are writing home for money.

Colleges are attempting to raise huge sums of money to stop the professors from envying the janitors.

Colleges don't make fools, but they occasionally develop a few.

The head of a Mississippi college says he is trying to develop an educational institution the football team can be proud of.

College is the only vacation a boy gets between his mother and his wife.

Many colleges have two serious problems: too many dropouts and too few kickouts.

We're still waiting for a college to come up with a march protesting student ignorance.

Soon the colleges will be forced to offer degrees in the ancient art of loafing.

A college is truly a fountain of knowledge, and a great many go there to drink.

The college of hard knocks is about the only one that doesn't let the student drop out if the course gets tough.

College never hurts a young man — unless, of course, he meets his future wife there.

Most college campuses are getting to be so crowded that if a student wants to be alone, he has to go to class.

Colleges try to find out what their graduates do after graduation. Employers are trying too.

One thing that keeps a lot of people from going to college is high school.

In today's colleges the freshmen are smarter than the seniors; everything the seniors have learned is already outmoded.

A country boy was afraid to go to college because he was told he would be compelled to matriculate.

College is a place that's presumed to mold character, and some of the characters turn out to be very moldy.

What this country needs are colleges that teach everything the students think they already know.

It seems a bit odd for a college to give a man with a wife and three kids a Bachelor's Degree.

Going to college won't guarantee you a job, but it'll give you four years to worry about getting one.

College debts are obligations that with diligence, economy, and stern self-denial, father will be able to pay.

Sending children to college educates parents. It teaches them how to do without a lot of things.

Parents of college students get poorer by degrees.

In college football the real triple threat is one who can run, kick, and pass all his exams!

The young man who is able to work his way through college is a pretty good bet to be able to work his way through life.

College Students

The age of chivalry is certainly not dead. If a college girl drops one of her books, almost any boy in her class will be delighted to kick it back to her.

A college boy in Ohio reported to his parents that he was about to flunk out — because he found out he had a klinker in his thinker.

Advice to college students: Be kind to your parents. After sending you through college, you're all they have left.

A modern son is one who finishes college and his dad at the same time.

Commencement is when the college students who learned all the answers discover that there are a new set of questions.

A college student who hadn't heard from home in several weeks wrote to his father, "Please send me a check so I'll know you're well and happy.

In the old days students went to college to get an education from the professors, but now it seems like some students think they ought to educate the professors.

A college girl may be poor in history, but great on dates.

Many college students can write home for money in four or five languages.

Nothing irks the college boy more than shaking out the envelope from home and finding nothing but news and love.

It takes a college student twenty minutes longer to say what he thinks than to tell what he knows.

Sending your child to college is like sending your clothes to the laundry. You get what you put in, but sometimes you can hardly recognize it.

A survey shows that college students prefer ties with dots, suits with stripes, and letters with checks.

Some college girls pursue learning and some others learn pursuing.

There was a time when college students thought they were living dangerously when they cut classes.

Coeds are college students who sign up for the romance languages.

A real surprise is when the college boy comes home and discovers people sleep at night rather than in the daytime.

A father is often a man who is working his son's way through college.

Committees

Sign on a church bulletin board in Benton, Wisconsin: "For God so loved the world that He didn't send a committee."

As a rule, the best things are done by a committee of one.

A committee usually keeps minutes and wastes hours.

Perpetual motion can be found in any committee meeting.

A committee is composed of five persons — one does the work, three give him moral support, and the fifth gives the story to the newspapers.

If Moses had been a committee, the Israelites would still be in Egypt.

The chairman of a committee is like the official at a bullfight whose job it is to open and close the gate so the bull can come in or go out.

There are more than 200,000 useless words in the English language, and at some committee meetings you hear all of them.

A committee usually consists of three persons, each of whom thinks the others talk a lot of nonsense.

A committee is a group of the unfit, appointed by the unwilling, to do the unnecessary.

Another nice thing about being quiet and dumb is that you won't be picked to head a committee.

A committee of three gets things done if two don't show up.

Committee work is like a soft chair — easy to get into but hard to get out of.

Committees have become so important that a subcommittee has to be appointed to do the work.

It's hard to say exactly what a Congressional Committee does — but if your wife did it, you'd call it nagging.

Our Congress is continually appointing "fact-finding" committees when what they really need are some "fact-facing" committees.

If a bomb wiped out the entire population except two politicians, they'd form a committee.

Politicians wonder how the Lord can run the world without appointing committees.

It is generally agreed that progress is what most inactive committees report.

The best way to slow progress is to form a committee to do something about it.

One reason why the Ten Commandments are so short and to the point is the fact they did not come out of a committee.

Of all the one hundred thousand useless words in the English language, you hear almost all of them at some committee meetings.

Our greatest need is an investigating committee to investigate investigating committees.

Common Sense

Automobiles wouldn't be so dangerous if the horsepower of the engine was proportioned to the horse-sense of the driver.

The biggest shortage of all is the shortage of common sense.

Common sense is the knack of seeing things as they are, and doing things as they ought to be done.

It seems that common sense isn't as common as it used to be.

An unusual amount of common sense is sometimes called wisdom.

Most people have good common sense, but they use it only in an emergency.

It is a thousand times better to have common sense without an education than to have an education without common sense.

Common sense is something you want the other fellow to show by accepting your ideas and conclusions.

Emotion makes the world go round, but common sense keeps it from going too fast.

Common sense could prevent a great many divorces; but, on the other hand, it could also prevent a great many marriages.

Common sense is the sixth sense, given to us by the Creator to keep the other five from making fools of themselves — and us.

It's unfortunate that common sense isn't more common.

There is more need today for common sense than at any time since man stopped having a lot of it.

Common sense is genius dressed in its working clothes.

A little common sense would prevent most divorces — and marriages too.

It is extremely embarrassing to come to your senses and find out you haven't any.

Horse sense is what keeps horses from betting on what people will do.

Horse sense means stable thinking.

There is just as much horse sense as ever, but the horses have it.

Horse sense deserts when you begin to feel your oats.

There should be just half as much horse sense behind the wheel as there is horsepower under the hood.

Horse sense is just the ability to say "neigh."

A rabbit's foot is a poor substitute for horse sense.

The value of horse sense is shown by the fact that the horse was afraid of the automobile at the time the pedestrian laughed at it.

Horse sense is what keeps a woman from being a nag.

A wise man once said that intuition is something that women have in place of common sense.

Love quickens all the senses — except common sense.

Combine common sense and the Golden Rule and you will have very little bad luck.

Philosophy is nothing but common sense in a dress suit.

A suggested prayer: "Oh God, give the world a lot more common sense, beginning with me."

Psychiatry is just common sense clothed in a language no one can understand.

Modern man has the genius to make rain, but often lacks enough common sense to come in out of it.

Science is nothing but trained and organized common sense.

Society is always taken by surprise by any new example of common sense.

The kind of wealth most of us need isn't dollars as much as sense.

It is generally agreed that some people are wise and some otherwise.

Wisdom is nothing more than common sense refined by learning and experience.

The door to wisdom swings on hinges of common sense and uncommon thoughts.

One of the advantages of being young is that you don't let common sense get in the way of doing things everybody else knows are impossible.

Communism

America is a country where Groucho Marx has more followers than Karl Marx.

Communism is freedom — Russian style!

In America it's "Believe it or not," but in communist countries it's "Believe it or else."

Communism is socialism with a gun to make you take it.

All that communism in Russia lacks for success is something for the people to eat, something to wear, and something constructive for the people to do.

Communism is the product of the apathy of many and the audacity of the few.

The difference between communism and democracy is — plenty!

Communism will be defeated in America and in all countries where Christians are more interested in being mobilized than in being tranquilized.

If communism were as successful as they claim, they'd put up a plate glass window instead of an iron curtain.

Russia reports that life under the communistic system is longer than under capitalism. On the other hand it may just *seem* longer.

The Russians have one big advantage over us. They don't have to spend half their time and money fighting communism.

Communists

A Communist is a person who has given up all hope of becoming a capitalist.

Communists seem to be laboring under the impression that everybody wants to die poor.

The Communists want to have their cake and eat ours too.

One reason why the Russian Communists are increasingly adopting free-market practices in their economy is that they'd rather be fed than "red."

The strongest objection Communists have against capital is that they don't have any.

A Communist is a Socialist in a hurry.

The average Communist is a fellow who is willing to divide his thirst and hunger with your beer and sandwich.

Communists may not know how to make "Reds" out of us, but they sure know how to put us in the red.

A Communist in the United States is a person who says everything is perfect in Russia but stays in this country because he likes to rough it.

If the Communists had as much to eat as they have to swallow they'd be a lot better off.

How often do you hear of a protest march in a Communist country?

A Communist is one who borrows your pot to cook your goose in.

Communist countries are where the people name a street for you one day and chase you down it the next.

Complaining

see also Criticism, Grumbling

About the only thing people in every walk of life will agree about is that they are underpaid and overcharged.

An alarm clock is a device that makes men rise and whine.

A boy loves a dog because it's the only thing around the house that doesn't find fault with him.

It's better to complain occasionally and carry your own burdens than cheerfully push them off on someone else.

A Christmas shopper's complaint is one of long-standing.

A man complains about the food when he eats at home and about the price when he eats out.

Attention wives: If your husband complains about the tie you gave him last Christmas — give him a sock!

A gentleman complains that when long hair became stylish his started to fall out.

The people who talk most about the "good old days" are the first to complain when their TV set goes on the blink.

When someone complains about prices today, one thing is certain — he's buying, not selling.

A Nevada husband complains that there are two reasons why his wife won't wear last year's dresses — she doesn't want to, and she can't.

The woman who complains about the man she married should realize that she could have caught a bigger fish if she had used better bait.

Many people complain about the fuel mileage they get on their riding lawn mower — only a yard to the gallon.

Complaining is the thing to try when all else fails.

Don't complain because you have to get up early every morning. The time may come when you can't get up — period!

The poor complain about the money they can't get, and the rich complain about the money they can't keep.

Some complain that the stepping stones to success bruise their feet.

Don't complain. Every time the lamb bleats he loses a mouthful of hay.

A factory worker in Akron complained, "If there's one more deduction from my take-home pay, I won't have any home to take my pay to."

Don't complain if your brother-in-law comes to visit you from Christmas to New Year's — he might stay with you from New Year's to Christmas.

Those who complain about the way the ball bounces are often the ones who dropped it.

Some people complain because God puts thorns on roses, while others praise God for putting roses among the thorns.

A lot of people go through life standing at the complaint counter.

Some of those old codgers who keep complaining that things are not what they used to be always forget to include themselves.

Don't pray for rain if you're going to complain about the mud.

Some people who had no shoes have been known to complain until they met someone who had no feet.

It is usually not so much the greatness of our troubles as the littleness of our spirit which causes us to complain.

A Missouri man complains that he was married fifteen years ago by a Justice of the Peace, and since that time he has had neither justice nor peace.

People make enemies by complaining too much to their friends.

Don't complain. The wheel that squeaks the loudest often gets replaced.

A man in Colorado complains that the only thing lit up on his block after 11 P.M. is his neighbor.

The pain in your neck you complain about may be the result of looking back too much.

People love goldfish because they like to see something with a mouth open that's not complaining.

An Arizona man complained, "My wife always has the last word — and all the words before it."

A Kansas wife complained that her husband is extremely forgetful. "He keeps forgetting things — like being married."

A customer in a cafeteria complained that everything there was terrible, including the self-service.

Computers will never replace human beings entirely. Someone has to complain about the errors.

Any fool can criticize, condemn, and complain — and most fools do.

A critic is one who finds fault without a search warrant.

Ours is a democracy where the rich and the poor are alike — both complain about taxes.

One of the easiest things to find is fault.

The person who is always finding fault seldom finds anything else.

If faultfinding were electrified, some people would be a powerhouse.

Before finding fault with another person, stop and count ten — of your own.

Faultfinding is as dangerous as it is easy.

The way some people find fault you'd think there was a reward.

An expert faultfinder has no reason to be proud of his accomplishment.

Faultfinding without suggestions for improvement is a waste of time.

Two things are bad for the heart — running upstairs and running down people.

Faultfinding is one talent that ought to be buried, and the grave forgotten.

Don't find fault with what you don't understand.

When it comes to spotting the faults of others, everybody seems to have 20-20 vision.

We do not get rid of our faults by calling attention to the faults of others.

It's a pity that some folks never learn that uncovering the other fellow's faults will never cover up their own.

Some people find fault as if it were a buried treasure.

If you have occasion to criticize a mule, do it to his face.

Happiness comes when we stop wailing about the troubles we have, and offer thanks for all the troubles we don't have.

There are two kinds of people in every hospital; those who are desperately ill, and those who complain about the food.

You can send your marriage to an early grave with a series of little digs.

A mule makes no headway while he's kicking; neither does a man.

Compliments

Don't forget that appreciation is always appreciated.

A diplomatic husband said to his wife, "How do you expect me to remember your birthday when you never look any older?"

It's easy to keep from being a bore. Just praise the person to whom you're talking.

The best way to compliment your wife is frequently.

A compliment a day keeps divorce far, far away.

Some pay a compliment as if they expected a receipt.

It's ironic but the toughest thing to take gracefully is a compliment.

Be sincere with your compliments. Most people can tell the difference between sugar and saccharine.

A compliment is the soft soap that wipes out a dirty look.

Compliments are like perfume: to be inhaled, not swallowed.

A hammer sometimes misses its mark — a bouquet, never.

It is all right to be always looking for compliments — to give to somebody else.

A compliment is something you say to another which both of you know isn't true.

No person is so poor that he cannot give a compliment.

There's a difference between paying compliments and paying *for* them.

Nobody has ever been bored by someone paying them a compliment.

Some people exceed the limit when fishing for compliments.

When you consider the shape it's in, it's no longer a compliment to be told someone thinks the world of you.

Man works like a zipper — better after a little "soft soap."

Compromise

The collapse of character often begins on compromise corner.

A compromise is the art of dividing a cake in such a way that everybody believes he got the biggest piece.

Why should some people be willing to compromise when they're the ones who are always right?

A compromise is a deal in which two people get what neither of them wanted.

Compromise is always wrong when it means sacrificing a principle.

Many things are worse than defeat, and compromise with evil is one of them.

Peace won by the compromise of principles is a short-lived achievement.

Computers

The hardest job in the world is telling the boss the computer proved him wrong.

Will our brains start shrinking now that machines do our thinking?

The computer is a great invention. There are as many mistakes as ever, but now they're nobody's fault.

The electric computer saves a man a lot of guesswork — but so does a bikini.

There is now a female computer on the market. You don't ask it anything, but it tells you anyway.

There's nothing wrong with a computer that a little competency on the part of the operator couldn't cure.

Computers will never replace human beings entirely. Someone has to complain about the errors.

Some computers are almost human. When they make a mistake they put the blame on another computer.

With computers doing our thinking, all we need now is a worrying machine.

A cheap but top-rate computer is the one between your ears.

Computers will never replace man entirely until they learn to laugh at the boss's jokes.

To err is human. But to really louse it up, it takes a computer.

Some big executives have computers to do all their thinking for them. Some just have wives.

A girl said to her boyfriend, "Remember, I'm a computer date, and I don't want to be bent, folded, or spindled."

Modern science is simply wonderful. It would take fifty people twenty years to make the same mistake a computer can make in only two seconds.

Have you heard about those computer arranged weddings? The couple promises not to fold, spindle, or mutilate?

Conceit
see also Egotists

Many people doubt their ability, but few have any misgivings about their importance.

A certain Hollywood actor would really become a big star if the public liked him as much as he does.

You can pick out actors by the glazed look that comes to their eyes when the conversation wanders away from themselves.

A Hollywood actor denies he is egotistical. He says he just deeply admires people with great talent.

Some actors think they are elevating the stage when they're merely depressing the audience.

A young actress in a southern state insists she's not conceited, "although you understand I have every right to be."

We all like the person who comes right out and admires us.

Admiration is our polite recognition of another person's resemblance to ourselves.

The self-made man always seems to admire his maker.

Adversity is the only diet that will reduce a fat head.

A man is usually as young as he feels but seldom as important.

The American people are divided into two great classes: those who think they are as good as anybody, and those who think they are better.

The fellow who gets on a high horse is riding for a fall.

Give authority to some people and they grow; give it to others and they swell.

A bachelor usually wants one single thing in life — himself!

All bachelors expect to get married just as soon as they can find a girl who loves them as much as they love themselves.

A bachelor never gets over the idea that he is a thing of beauty and a boy forever.

A big shot is frequently an individual of small caliber and immense bore.

There isn't anything as effective for subduing a big shot as confronting him with somebody he used to go to school with.

The fellow who blows his horn the loudest is usually in the biggest fog.

There is something pathetic about a man who turns on his charm when he has none.

Some church members are like a tire with a slow leak — it takes a lot of pumping to keep them inflated.

Why should some people be willing to compromise when they're the ones who are always right?

A sure cure for conceit is a visit to the cemetery, where eggheads and boneheads get equal billing.

One good thing about conceited people — they don't go around talking about other people.

When the other fellow talks that way it's conceit. When we do it's merely self-appraisal.

An eye specialist in Chicago is a trifle conceited. Instead of an eye chart, he makes you read his diploma.

Conceit is generally thought of as God's gift to little people.

You can always get someone to love you — even if you have to do it yourself.

A conceited person never gets anywhere because he thinks he is already there.

The person who sings his own praises is likely to be a soloist.

A bigshot may also be a big bore.

Nature abhors a vacuum. When a head lacks brains, nature fills it with conceit.

Just because you are puffed up with conceit doesn't mean you are a swell guy.

The strength that comes from confidence can be quickly lost in conceit.

The head never begins to swell until the mind stops growing.

The person who is all wrapped up in himself is overdressed.

One thing that's hard to keep under your hat is a big head.

Have you ever noticed that the most conceited person is one whose opinions differ from your own?

A conceited person knows a good thing when he sees himself in the mirror.

Heads that are filled with knowledge and wisdom have little space left for conceit.

Talk to a man about himself, and he will listen for hours.

The line between self-confidence and conceit is very narrow.

Conceit is the only disease known to man that makes everybody sick except the person who has it.

The world's most conceited man was the fellow who celebrated his birthday by sending his mother a telegram of congratulations.

Conceit may puff a man up, but it never props him up.

A certain young fellow in Texas was so conceited he joined the Navy so the world could see him.

The only time you should blow your horn is when you're in the band.

To be unusually pleased with yourself is the surest way of offending everybody else.

Take the conceit out of a man and he will be like an umbrella with the ribs gone.

Conceit is nature's compensation for inferiority.

Occasionally you meet a fellow who thinks he is all seven wonders of the world.

Conceit is what makes a little squirt think he's a fountain of knowledge.

The best remedy for conceit is to sit down and make a list of all the things you don't know.

If you will hide your conceit as much as possible, people will give you credit for knowing more than you do.

Conceit is a form of "I" strain that doctors can't cure.

Psychiatrists tell us that conceit is a disease. It's a mighty strange ailment; the victim usually feels all right, but it makes his associates sick.

If you think you are important, just remember that a lot of famous men of a century ago have weeds growing over their graves today.

Conceit in a man is a sure sign that he still hopes to become successful someday.

Many people spend a lot of time just letting off esteem.

Belief in yourself is a fine thing, but see to it that you are not too easily convinced.

Many a man labors under the delusion that standing on one's dignity will enable him to see over the heads of the crowd.

Many divorces are caused by the marriage of two people who are in love with themselves.

Education will broaden a narrow mind, but there is no known cure for a big head.

Some people are in sore need of surgery; they need about half of their ego removed.

Many a little squirt thinks he's a fountain of wisdom.

Pat others on the back, not yourself.

An expert knows all the answers — if you ask the right questions.

It's difficult, if not impossible, to have faith in God if a man has too much faith in himself.

The man who believes in nothing but himself lives in a very small world.

When a person starts to rest on his laurels, he discovers they are poison ivy.

A gentleman in South Carolina said, "Most people won't admit their faults. I'd admit mine if I had any."

The man who thinks he has no faults has at least one.

The greatest fault is to be conscious of none.

Flattery is hearing from others the things you have already thought about yourself.

Flattery will get you nowhere. This is especially true when you give it to yourself.

Most of us like a person who comes right out and says what he thinks — especially when he thinks like we do.

A prominent gentleman in Dayton, Ohio, denies that he is conceited, but says he's absolutely convinced that if he had never been born people would want to know why.

Some men achieve greatness, others are born great, and a few have greatness thrust upon them. The rest of us just think we're great.

People whose main concern is their own happiness seldom find it.

No big ideas over come from swelled heads.

The head never begins to swell until the mind stops growing.

It's unfortunate that swelled heads aren't painful.

There's more hope for a confessed sinner than a conceited saint.

Ideas are like children. No matter how much you like other people's, you can't help thinking your own are best.

A slap on the back often pushes out the chest.

When an idler sees a job completed, he's sure he could have done it better.

Looking in the mirror isn't exactly the best way to convince yourself that things are improving.

There is nothing so irritating as somebody with less intelligence and more sense than we have.

The person who knows everything has a lot to learn.

The fellow who is too deeply in love with himself ought to get a divorce.

He who falls in love with himself will have no rivals.

It probably would be all right if we'd love our neighbors as we love ourselves — but could they stand that much affection?

You can always get someone to love you — even if you have to do it yourself.

Some men grow; others just swell.

A certain man in Texas has such a big mouth he can sing a duet by himself.

You don't have to be much of a musician to toot your own horn.

Nature never intended for us to pat ourselves on the back. If she had, our hinges would be different.

The man who has a good opinion of himself is usually a poor judge.

It's not difficult to pick out the best people. They'll help you do it.

If biologists are right in their assertion that there is not a perfect man on earth today, a lot of personal opinions will have to be altered.

Some people grow under responsibility, while others only swell.

One of the most difficult secrets for a man to keep is his opinion of himself.

A person interrupts and endangers his climb up the ladder of success when he stops to pat himself on the back.

A person who thinks too much of himself isn't thinking enough.

Conclusions

A person can save himself from many hard falls by refraining from jumping to conclusions.

The fellow who is always jumping to conclusions isn't always sure of a happy landing.

Jumping to conclusions is about the only exercise some people get.

The chief hazard of jumping to conclusions is the high percentage of misses.

Jumping to conclusions is a dangerous form of mental acrobatics.

Digging for facts is better mental exercise than jumping to conclusions.

Why don't we jump at opportunities as quickly as we jump to conclusions?

Conferences

A conference is a meeting to decide when and where the next meeting will be held.

When all is said and nothing done, it's time for the conference to adjourn.

A conference room is a place where everybody talks, nobody listens, and everybody disagrees afterward.

A conference is nothing more than an organized way of postponing a decision.

A conference is a meeting at which people talk about things they should be doing.

Generally speaking, a conference is a gathering of people who singly can do nothing, but together can decide that nothing can be done.

A conference is a big business term for swapping stories in somebody's office.

A conference is just a high-falutin' name for the executives' coffee break.

Definition of a conference: "The confusion of one man multiplied by the number present."

When a conference of diplomats announce they have "agreed in principle," it means nothing has been done.

Confession

Confess your sins to the Lord, and you will be forgiven; confess them to men, and you will be laughed at.

Confessing your sins is no substitute for forsaking them.

An honest confession is not always good for the soul, but, in most cases, it's cheaper than hiring a high-powered lawyer.

An open confession is good for the soul, but bad for the reputation.

Confession is not only good for the soul; in Washington it can be turned into a bestseller.

To err is understandable; to admit it is unlikely.

There's more hope for a confessed sinner than a conceited saint.

Few things in life are more difficult for some of us than admitting a mistake.

An innovative priest in San Francisco has a fast confession line for those with three sins or less.

Confess your sins, not your neighbor's.

Unless sin is confessed it will fester.

Confidence

You must first be a believer if you would be an achiever.

The strength that comes from confidence can be quickly lost in conceit.

The line between self-confidence and conceit is very narrow.

Misplaced confidence is seldom found again.

Always trust a fat man. He'll never stoop to anything low.

Confidence is the feeling you have before you fully understand the situation.

Belief in yourself is a fine thing, but see to it that you are not too easily convinced.

There are two reasons why we don't trust people: one, because we don't know them; and the other, because we do.

We had complete confidence in reaching the moon. Now if we could only feel the same way about getting to the other side of the street.

Confidence is that quiet, absolutely assured feeling you have just before you fall flat on your face.

Faith gives us the courage to face the present with confidence, and the future with expectancy.

Belief in God will help you most if you also believe in yourself.

A good leader inspires men to have confidence in him; a great leader inspires them to have confidence in themselves.

Confusion

It seems that all a college education does is help folks become confused on a higher plane.

It has been said that a college education is nothing but a four-year plan of confusing young minds methodically.

Definition of a conference: "The confusion of one man multiplied by the number present."

A wise man is never confused by what he can't understand, but a fool is sure to be.

In the hectic confusion of modern society it would be nice to experience a few dull moments occasionally.

Why did they have to admit to the Union the State of Confusion?

The only thing that isn't hard to get these days is confusion.

No one is more confusing than the fellow who gives good advice while setting a bad example.

"All the world is a stage," and everybody is in a wild scramble trying to get on it.

When lost it is better to stand still than to run in the wrong direction. This applies to governments as well as individuals.

Some folks think they are busy when they are only confused.

With the world in such a confused state, no wonder babies cry when they come into it.

Even if this is the dawn of a bright new world, most of us are still in the dark.

If this world becomes any more confused than it is now, don't be surprised to see monkeys tossing peanuts to people.

It's a confused world. We're running out of electricity — and nobody even knows what it is.

Nothing confuses a man more than to drive behind a woman who does everything right.

A man never gets so confused in his thinking that he can't see the other fellow's duty.

It is a mistake to trust a man with an honest face. After all, that may be the only honest part of him.

An expert can take something you already know and make it sound confusing.

An expert is always able to create confusion out of simplicity.

After all, life is really simple; we ourselves create the circumstances that complicate it.

Many people look ahead, some look back, but most look confused.

World problems are so confusing that even computers are asking questions.

In our generation the popular religion is CONFUSIONISM.

Statisticians collect facts, then draw their own confusions.

Congress

Isn't it remarkable how our pioneering ancestors built up a great nation without asking Congress for help?

If Congress can pay farmers not to raise crops, why can't we pay Congress not to raise taxes?

Besides adjourning, what other good thing has Congress done this year?

Members of Congress meet more often than they get together.

Congress fighting inflation is like the Mafia fighting crime.

The trouble with Congress today is that the members don't want to get involved.

It appears that Congress has found it's a lot easier to trim the taxpayers than expenses.

Now that Congress has made it possible for Americans to buy gold, somebody should suggest they make it possible for us to buy groceries.

If Congress really wants to help the auto industry sell more cars, it should start building more parking lots.

Congress does some strange things — it puts a high tax on liquor, and raises the other taxes that drive people to drink.

Wouldn't it be nice if Congress would divert some of that foreign aid to the Postal Service!

Congress has figured out the right system. When the members encounter a problem they can't solve, they subsidize it.

What this country needs is more men in Congress with throat trouble.

Congress would accomplish more with fewer "blocs" and more tackle.

The trouble with Congress is that it can't remain calm and cool when collected.

Congress is like a country fair. Nothing gets as much attention as the bull.

Seniority, as practiced by Congress, is one of those things you're for if you have it and against if you don't.

There wouldn't be very much objection to increasing the size of Congress if there were any chance of improving its quality.

It's hard to say exactly what a Congressional Committee does — but if your wife did it, you'd call it nagging.

Congress is proof that women don't do all the talking.

Our Congress is continually appointing "fact-finding" committees when what they really need are some "fact-facing" committees.

Congress must not improve our lot in life any further. We simply can't afford it.

There are two periods when Congress does no business: one is before the holidays; and the other, after.

The biggest job Congress has is how to get money from the taxpayers without disturbing the voters.

Congress will not know what a real filibuster is until women members are in the majority.

The attitude of Congress toward hidden taxes is not to do away with them, but to hide them better.

The latest report is that the manufacturers of aspirin want to sponsor televised sessions of Congress on one of the major networks.

Congress is a legislative body whose members make the laws and whose chaplain prays for the country.

Sitting in Congress is the privilege of the few; sitting on Congress, the prerogative of the many.

Congress seems to favor a stable government, judging from the amount of stalling it does.

It seems that everytime Congress sets out to trim the budget, the knife slips and trims the taxpayers instead.

Congress is confronted with the unsolved problem of how to get the people to pay taxes they can't afford for services they don't need.

It's getting harder and harder to railroad legislation through Congress now that it has installed the "bloc system."

Some members of Congress would best promote the country's peace by holding their own.

Congress is unpredictable. You never know what urgent problem they're not going to do anything about.

One wonders what the crime statistics would be if they included all the holdups in Congress.

Modern political theory seems to hold that the best way to keep the economy in the pink is to run the government in the red.

Would you enjoy reading one of America's foremost humor publications? If so, subscribe to the *Congressional Record.*

Just when you think you've found a hedge against inflation, Congress decided to trim.

The man who says there are no new jokes probably hasn't read the latest batch of bills before Congress.

Natural law is a fundamental force that Congress constantly tries to amend.

Economists tell us that we may have to devalue the dollar. What do they think Congress has been doing for the past twenty-five or thirty years?

Occasionally an innocent man is sent to the legislature.

The chaplains who pray for the United States Senate and the House of Representatives might speak a word now and then on behalf of the taxpayers.

A congressional speech is one printed by the government without profit and read the same way.

When Congress tries to decide between two new taxes, it's like a woman deciding between two dresses — she usually decides to take both.

If Congress would repeal the nuisance tax, we wouldn't have any taxes to pay.

The United States is a land with a President for a head, a Supreme Court for a backbone, and Congress for lungs.

One thing about death — it doesn't get worse every time Congress meets.

As we pay our taxes, most of us are not worried about Congress letting us down — but we often wonder if it will ever let us up.

In the near future Congress is expected to raise the legal limit on the taxpayer's patience.

We often wonder what the Ten Commandments would look like today if Moses had been compelled to submit them to a hostile legislature!

You can lead a man to Congress but you can't make him think.

Congressmen

According to recent reports, America produces 92 percent of the world's natural gas — not counting the speeches of our senators and congressmen.

Watch the kid who's cutting classes at school — he may be in training to be a congressman later in life.

The little boy who was sent to the store and could never remember what he went for finally grew up to be a congressman.

Nowadays the truly forgotten man is a congressman who isn't investigating somebody.

A veteran congressman told a freshman colleague, "In Washington, if you're not confused, you haven't heard all the facts.

It might be more worthwhile if we stopped wringing our hands and started ringing our congressman.

A congressman gets a lot of money for a man who gets up to speak, says nothing, nobody listens, and then everybody disagrees.

The average congressman's idea of government waste is a dollar spent in another congressman's district.

What's wrong with this country is that you can't sue a congressman for breach of promise.

You can lead a horse to water, but you can't make him drink. You can send a man to Congress, but you can't make him think.

How much a congressman's political fence needs mending depends on how much he has straddled it.

Now that they've gotten the lead out of gasoline, we ought to give them the names and addresses of a few of our congressmen.

A congressman made the following brilliant statement: "Lynching deprives a man of his constitutional rights. It also interferes with his plans for the future.

New congressmen go home frequently to find out what their constituents think about what they have done. The older and wiser ones remain safely in Washington.

A congressman is always in favor of economy, but not when it involves his own district.

The average man has quit dreaming of having enough money to last him the rest of his life. He'd settle for enough to last him the rest of the month.

No drunken sailor ever spent money as fast as a sober congressman.

Our legislators would practice more economy if they weren't so out of practice.

The United States Constitution is a great document with one defect. It does not require intelligence tests for congressional candidates.

Too many Model-T congressmen are drawing Cadillac salaries.

Nowadays many taxpayers are writing letters of protest to their congressmen — and some are so hot they're steaming themselves open.

Conscience

To know what is right and not do it is as bad as doing wrong.

A budget is like a conscience — it doesn't keep you from spending, but it makes you feel guilty about it.

Character is never erected on a neglected conscience.

Conscience keeps more people awake than coffee.

With some people a clear conscience is nothing more than a poor memory.

Conscience is like a baby. It has to go to sleep before you can.

If it weren't for your conscience, you'd probably do everything you want to do right away.

Conscience is what hurts when everything else feels good.

To remove the conscience from some people would be only a minor operation.

No one works his conscience so hard that it needs a vacation.

Happy is the man who renounces everything that places a strain on his conscience.

The line is often too busy when conscience wishes to speak.

A man's conscience tells him what he shouldn't do — but it does not keep him from doing it.

Conscience, like a pencil, needs to be sharpened occasionally.

When a man won't listen to his conscience, it's usually because he doesn't want advice from a stranger.

Conscience helps, but the fear of getting caught doesn't do any harm either.

Some folks who say they have a clear conscience may have a good "forgetter."

Thousands of people become hard of hearing when conscience speaks.

When you have a fight with your conscience and get licked, you win.

The best tranquilizer is a good conscience.

A gash in the conscience may disfigure the soul.

Many people would listen to the voice of conscience if they knew what channel it was on.

Conscience is that small inner voice that tells you the IRS might check your return.

It's a good idea to keep on good terms with everybody, but especially with your wife, your banker, your stomach, and your conscience.

The testimony of a good conscience is worth more than a dozen character witnesses.

Quite often when a man thinks his mind is getting broader, it is only his conscience stretching.

Your conscience doesn't really keep you from doing anything; it merely keeps you from enjoying it.

Conscience is that still, small voice that makes you feel even smaller.

The greatest tormentor of the human soul is a guilty conscience.

A fellow's conscience works best while he's being watched.

One should be more concerned about what his conscience whispers than about what other people shout.

A conscience is a safe guide only when God is the guide of the conscience.

Conscience is that sixth sense that comes to our aid when we are doing something wrong and tells us we are about to get caught.

Most people follow their conscience as a man follows a wheelbarrow — pushing it along before him the way he wants to go.

Conscience does not get its guidance from a Gallup poll.

Most things that broaden the mind also narrow the conscience.

Conscience is not the voice of God; it is the gift of God.

Conscience is the voice that tells you not to do something after you've done it.

As long as your conscience is your friend, never mind about your enemies.

Nobody's conscience ever kept him awake at night for having exaggerated the good qualities of his friends.

There's no substitute for conscience — unless it's knowing you're being watched.

Nothing goes to sleep as easy as one's conscience.

Conscience is the only mirror that doesn't flatter.

Many people have trained their conscience to roll over and play dead.

Conscience is something inside that bothers you when nothing outside does.

A man's best boss is a well-trained conscience.

The world would be better off if people paid as much attention to their conscience as they do to their neighbors' opinions.

One of the most painful wounds in the world is a stab of conscience.

In the courtroom of our conscience, we call only witnesses for the defense.

Conscience is that still, small voice that yells so loud the morning after.

Many people claim that the best substitute for a conscience is cold feet.

Conscience is that still, small voice that tells you what other people should do.

It is your conscience that warns you to be careful about what it can't stop you from doing.

Fear is the tax that conscience pays guilt.

Those who remember the past with a clear conscience need have no fear of the future.

The world is composed of the takers and the givers. The takers may eat better, but the givers sleep better.

The head usher to happines is a well-kept conscience.

Happiness is a healty mental attitude, a grateful spirit, a clear conscience, and a heart full of love.

Ignorance is an opiate that lulls a conscience to sleep.

What the world needs is an amplifier for the still, small voice.

Preachers don't talk in their sleep; they talk in other people's sleep.

Most reformers insist that their conscience be your guide.

With some people it's rheumatism more than conscience that keeps them on the right path.

If a sermon pricks the conscience, it must have good points.

God may forgive your sin, but your nervous system won't.

A man's conscience, and not his mattress, has most to do with his sleep.

Too many teen-agers don't pay any more attention to their conscience than they do their parents.

Contentment

Contentment is often the result of being too lazy to stir up a fuss.

If you can't be content with what you have received, be thankful for what you have escaped.

Many of us won't be content with our lot in life until it's a lot more.

Contentment is something that depends a little on position and a lot on disposition.

When you can think of yesterday without regret and tomorrow without fear, you are near real contentment.

Contentment is when your earning power equals your yearning power.

It is right to be content with what you have, never with what you are.

The greatest wealth is contentment with a little.

Some folks aren't content with the milk of human kindness — they want the cream.

Contentment has been praised more and practiced less than any other condition of life.

If you would be content, do what you ought, not what you please.

The best way for a person to have a contented state of mind is for him to count his blessings, not his cash.

It's difficult to be content if you don't have enough, and it's impossible if you have too much.

When we cannot find contentment in ourselves, it is useless to seek it elsewhere.

Contentment is a matter of hoping for the best and making the best of what we get.

A contented neighborhood is one in which each man thinks he is doing just a little better than the man next door.

Contentment in life consists not in great wealth, but in simple wants.

In order to become perfectly content, it is necessary to have a poor memory and no imagination.

A dish towel will certainly wipe a contented look off a married man's face.

The secret of contentment is knowing how to enjoy what you have, and to be able to lose all interest in things beyond your reach.

A contented person is one who has all the things his neighbor has.

If everyone were perfectly contented there would be no progress.

To be content, just think how happy you would be if you lost everything you have right now, and then got it back again!

Patience, forbearance, and understanding are companions to contentment.

The happiest people are those who are too busy to notice whether they are happy or not.

Some people find happiness by making the most of what they don't have.

Happiness is in the heart, not in the circumstances.

How to be happy: Keep your heart free from hate, your mind from worry, live simply, expect little, give much, sing often, pray always, forget self, think of others and their feelings, fill your heart with love, scatter sunshine. These are tried links in the golden chain of contentment.

There's nothing like a dish towel for wiping that contented look off a husband's face.

The greatest lesson we learn from past civilizations is ingratitude.

All the world lives in two tents: content and discontent.

Conventions

Attending a convention in your home city is like kissing your own wife.

A convention is where people pass a lot of resolutions, but few bars.

Conventions are something a lot of people leave behind when they attend one.

At a convention the "delegate-at-large" is the man who has come without his wife.

When a man takes his wife to a convention, he has twice the expense — and half as much fun.

Conversation

You can pick out actors by the glazed look that comes to their eyes when the conversation wanders away from themselves.

The trouble with being an atheist is you have nobody to talk to when you're alone.

A barber's remarks are sometimes more keen and cutting than his razor.

Some people never say anything bad about the dead, or anything good about the living.

People love goldfish because they like to see something with a mouth open that's not complaining.

Fascinating conversation is the art of telling people a little less than they want to know.

One of the troubles with small talk is that it usually comes in large doses.

Nine-tenths of the people couldn't start a conversation if the weather didn't change occasionally.

An intelligent conversationalist is one who nods his head in agreement while you're talking.

If you have to think twice before you speak, you'll never get into the conversation.

The man who said the art of conversation is dead never stood outside a telephone booth waiting for a woman to finish talking.

A thin conversation is usually made by a person with a thick head.

The average dinner conversation is a series of cold cuts — her spiced tongue and his baloney.

It's all right to hold a conversation, but you should let go of it now and then.

If you are not a charming conversationalist, you may still be a big hit as a charmed listener.

About the only gas rationing most of us would favor concerns useless conversations.

A conversation should be like a good meal. You should leave it just before you've had enough.

The secret of polite conversation is never to open your mouth unless you have something to say.

Anybody who thinks conversation is a lost art in America doesn't play bridge.

The real art of conversation is not only saying the right thing in the right place, but to leave unsaid the wrong thing at the tempting moment.

Nothing lowers the level of conversation more than raising the voice.

Women have one main topic of conversation — how thin they used to be, or how thin they're gonna be.

The real spirit of conversation consists in building on another man's observation, not overturning it.

Conversation is when three women are talking; gossip is when one of them leaves.

A form of communication in which men never stop to think and women never think to stop is otherwise known as conversation.

The woman who constantly interrupts a man's conversation is either already married or never will be.

If you want all the conversation you can handle, put a bandage on your forehead.

Conversation between Adam and Eve must have been difficult at times because they had nobody to talk about.

Some people never let ideas interrupt the easy flow of their conversation.

Conversation is an exercise of the mind, but gossiping is merely an exercise of the tongue.

Saying it with flowers doesn't mean throwing bouquets at yourself.

If you wish to get along with people, pretend not to know whatever they tell you.

There's one thing to be said about ignorance — it gives rise to almost 90 percent of the world's conversations.

Our country needs more soil conservation and not so much soiled conversation.

Profanity is the mark of a conversational cripple.

A breath of scandal makes conversation breezy for some people.

If you think television has killed conversation, you've never heard people trying to decide which program to watch.

People who talk about things they can't afford sometimes forget that the list should include pride, envy, and malice.

Conviction

A conviction is that commendable quality in ourselves that we call bullheadedness in others.

Conviction is a belief that you hold or that holds you.

People generally have too many opinions and not enough convictions.

If there is anything stronger than your convictions, it's the heat of your prejudices.

If you don't stand for something, you will likely fall for anything.

The difference between a prejudice and a conviction is that you can explain a conviction without getting angry.

It is important that people know what you stand for; it is equally important that they know what you won't stand for.

At the age of fifty, one settles down into certain well-defined convictions — most of which are wrong.

Many convictions are family hand-me-downs.

What some people call a conviction may be just a prejudice.

Be bold in what you stand for, but careful in what you fall for.

The true measure of a man is the height of his ideals, the breadth of his sympathy, the depth of his convictions, and the length of his patience.

An open mind is sometimes too porous to hold a conviction.

If you want to convince others of the value of Christianity — live it!

Salesmanship is transferring a conviction from a seller to the buyer.

Cooperation

You will find that if you share your brother's burden, both of you will walk a little straighter.

Few burdens are heavy when everybody lifts.

Everybody likes friendly attention and cooperation. We always get it when we give it.

It's difficult for men of different nations to work shoulder to shoulder when they carry a chip on one shoulder and a gun on the other.

No one can whistle a symphony. It takes an orchestra to play it.

Even freckles would make a nice coat of tan if they would get together.

Cooperation is doing what I tell you to do, and doing it quickly.

If you don't think cooperation is necessary, watch what happens to a wagon if one wheel comes off.

A minority of the people usually carry a majority of the load.

You'll find that the big potatoes are on top of the heap because there are a lot of little potatoes holding them up.

We cannot all play the same instrument, but we can all be in the same key.

Cost of living
see also Inflation

It seems the only thing that hasn't increased in cost is free advice.

About the only thing people in every walk of life will agree about is that they are underpaid and overcharged.

Airplane fares have been increased considerably. Even the cost of going up is going up.

The average man's modest ambition is to make his weekly paycheck last a week.

What is hurting America today is the high cost of low living.

Americans are now experiencing "shell-out shock."

Fewer Americans are drunk with wealth nowadays. It's just the price of everything that causes them to stagger.

If you think your automobile is expensive to operate, try operating a shopping cart in a supermarket.

It seems that our modern cars won't start until the seat belt is fastened — and the pocketbook is emptied.

Every year the cars get lower and wider, while the payments get longer and higher.

A man in Alabama complains that his new car has been recalled by the dealer — there was a defect in his bank account.

After pricing new cars it begins to look like the economy model is the one you're now driving.

There was a time when $200 was the down-payment on a car; now it's the sales tax.

Some automobile manufacturers have a sneaky way of lowering the list price. For instance, on one model the steering wheel is an optional extra.

A cheap old car can be quite annoying. But so can a new expensive one.

Anybody who thinks the automobile has made people lazy never had to pay for one.

Today's cars keep a person strapped without safety belts.

A good way to make your present car run better is to have a salesman quote you the price of a new one.

There are still a few people who can remember when it cost more to operate a car than to park it.

Power brakes may stop a car on a dime, but it usually costs more than a hundred dollars to get the rear end fixed.

Nothing reduces the value of a car like trading it in.

Some auto mechanics can estimate the cost of repairs very closely. They can usually get within a dollar or two of what you have in your pocket.

Having a big car doesn't always mean you have money; it may mean you once *had* money.

The new cars give you more room by removing the bulge in your wallet.

Bank interest on a loan is so high that if you can afford to pay it you don't need the loan.

A businessman who came up the hard way observes that about all you can do on a shoe-string these days is trip.

It now costs more to amuse a child than it once did to educate his father.

We can't understand why today's children are complaining so much. They're not old enough to remember what prices used to be.

Christmas is the time of the year when Santa Claus comes down the chimney and your savings go down the drain.

Christmas is a time when a lot of others besides Santa find themselves in the red.

One place where people seem to think they can get as much as ever for a quarter is in the church.

Another measure of civilization's progress is the way the cost of relaxing goes up.

If the cost of a college education continues to snowball, a person can make a profit by remaining ignorant.

A man complains about the food when he eats at home and about the price when he eats out.

When someone complains about prices today, one thing is certain — he's buying, not selling.

Now that Congress has made it possible for Americans to buy gold, somebody should suggest they make it possible for us to buy groceries.

Congress must not improve our lot in life any further. We simply can't afford it.

It's now costing Americans twice as much to live beyond their means as it did twenty years ago.

The way things are now you're lucky if you can make one end meet.

Nothing seems to make the cost of living as reasonable as pricing funerals.

If two can live as cheaply as one — why don't they?

You look at today's prices and the only thing you can get more of for a dollar is mad.

Have you seen anybody lately who wants to stop living on account of the cost?

With food, rent, and gas prices so high, when you balance the budget there's nothing left to budget the balance.

It's hard to understand how an Alabama cemetery raised its burial charges — and blamed it on the cost of living.

We are told that two can live as cheaply as one — and at today's prices they'd better.

The cost of operating a car is high, but it's not at all bad in comparison with the low mileage-per-dollar when you push a grocery cart.

Foreign aggressors don't realize that even if they invaded the United States they couldn't afford to live here.

If life is worth what it's costing now, people were getting a bargain in grandpa's day.

About the only thing you can build now at the same old price is a mansion in the sky.

With telephone rates due to go up again, we begin to wonder if what we have to say is still worth saying.

The only way to beat the high cost of living is to stop living.

They call it a "dream house" because it usually costs twice as much as you dreamed it would.

Beware of the high cost of low living.

It's easy to make money these days — it's only hard to make a living.

If two can live as cheaply as one, it's because they have to.

Whatever the cost of living is, it's worth it.

Today one can buy ten cents worth of almost anything for thirty cents.

It is really no longer the high cost of living. The problem today is one of existence.

The biggest obstacle to the return of the five cent cup of coffee is the cost of the water.

It's not difficult to meet expenses these days. In fact, you can meet them everywhere.

After all, the high cost of living seems unimportant when we consider all of life's fringe benefits.

As soon as the average person pays one fiddler, another one begins to tune up.

The cost of living remains fairly constant — all we have.

110

It's almost as difficult to live within an income today as it was to live without one in the early 1930s.

Prices seem to think there is plenty of room at the top.

The cost of living is usually what one makes plus 10 percent.

Air is still free, but it costs more and more to breathe it.

If the law of supply and demand is responsible for existing prices, it ought to be repealed.

Two can live as cheaply as one if one doesn't eat.

Descending prices, like falling stars, always seem to fall in some other place.

The cost of living is the only thing that defies the law of gravitation; it keeps going up without ever coming down.

Economists tell us that Jones is having a hard time keeping up with himself.

Have you ever noticed that the things you never wanted are considerably cheaper?

At today's prices the shopper is left holding the bag — and there's very little left in it.

There's no better diet than eating only what you can afford.

There's a new diet that will reduce weight like nothing else. It's called the high price of food.

One thing about those thirty-day diets — by the time you go back to eating you're shocked at the price of food.

Everybody is suffering from a new ailment called COSTROPHOBIA. It's the fear of rising prices.

It's becoming more difficult each passing day to find a disease we can afford.

Human diseases are the same as they were a thousand years ago, but doctors have selected more expensive names for them.

You have a very common disease, if you're sick of high doctor fees.

The only part of our economy that seems to be looking up is living costs.

Speaking of higher education, here's hoping it doesn't go much higher.

Many people are beginning to learn that the cost of experience has gone up like everything else.

Nowadays the family that buys together cries together.

A gardener raises a few things, a farmer raises many things, and the middleman raises everything.

The boys would stay down on the farm if prices wouldn't.

When husbands talk about the height of fashion, they probably mean the price.

If food prices go any higher, toothpicks may become a status symbol.

At today's pork prices, being called a pig is more of a compliment than an insult.

Just buying all those expensive diet foods can be very flattening.

In some meat markets today a good steak costs you twenty-five cents a bite.

Most of us can't afford to eat out any more, but sometimes we park near a restaurant and inhale.

If today's food prices haven't driven you to dieting, nothing will.

Look at the price of bread and you'll realize that never before has so much "dough" bought so little dough.

Sign in a bakery window in Houston: "Cakes — 66 cents. Upside down cakes — 99 cents."

The last time beef was this high was when the cow jumped over the moon.

A hamburger by any other name is more expensive.

At today's prices, spilled milk is worth crying over.

Vegetables grow in the ground, but they are not dirt cheap.

Many people have given up meat for Lent. Others have given it up for rent.

To market, to market/ my groceries to buy/ home again, home again/ to sit down and cry.

If a hen knew the current price of eggs, she wouldn't cackle — she'd crow!

The only thing wrong with $5 steaks these days is they cost $9.50.

These days there are two kinds of people cutting down on food — those who can't afford the calories, and those who can't afford the prices.

Judging by the high price of eggs, somebody must have told the hens how much a bricklayer gets for laying bricks.

In meat markets the meat may be tender, but the price is tough.

Nothing makes food less fattening than being too expensive.

At today's food prices, the man who goes bankrupt can blame it on what he ate.

What we need in this country is an inexpensive substitute for food.

It's not the coffee that keeps folks awake these days, but the price of it.

It's beginning to look like porkchop prices have gone "hog wild."

The way food prices are going up, more people are being put on diets by their accountants than by their doctors.

When you stop to consider what you pay for steak, it's easy to understand why cows are sacred in India.

At today's prices everybody's putting his money where his mouth is.

Doctors who tell us never to eat when we're unhappy should revise restaurant prices.

Grocer checking a ten dollar grocery order: "Is this take-out, or will you eat it here?"

Inflated food prices are hard to swallow.

If food prices keep going up, TV dinners will soon cost more than TV sets.

The happiest man in the world is a vegetarian looking at the prices in a meat market.

No matter how you order it, nowadays you get your steak served expensively.

Food prices are so high that it's no longer possible to bite off more than you can chew.

Visit the frozen-food department in any supermarket and you'll find everything is frozen except the prices.

If all men are born free, why doesn't somebody tell the hospitals and doctors about it?

At current prices, a friend in need is practically anybody.

Nothing is dirt cheap anymore except gossip.

Two heads are not better than one, considering the present price of haircuts.

Nothing in recent years seems to have improved the health of the American people as much as the staggering cost of being sick.

With auto and gasoline prices going up and up, we ought to find a better word than *freeway*.

Seems like every time history repeats itself the price doubles.

In the old days history was made for a tenth of what it costs today.

Nothing makes you feel that your home is your castle more than getting an estimate to have it repaired.

After building a new home these days, a man is likely to be "house-broke."

The average income of Americans is at a high point. In fact, it's almost as high as their expenses.

If we can't win the war against inflation — how about a cease-fire?

At today's nightclub prices it's harder than ever for a comedian to make people laugh.

If the law of supply and demand is responsible for existing prices, it ought to be amended.

The best things in life are free, of course, but isn't it a pity that most of the next best things are so expensive?

The way the cost of living and taxes are today, you might as well marry for love.

The average man has quit dreaming of having enough money to last him the rest of his life. He'd settle for enough to last him the rest of the month.

Maybe what we liked most about the old movies was the admission price.

Nothing is as dead as yesterday's news — except yesterday's prices.

An old-timer is someone who once believed that whatever went up must come down.

Nowadays an optimist is any supermarket customer who holds out his hand for the change.

What this country needs is a good five-cent anything.

Our greatest need at the present time is a cheap substitute for food.

There was a time when parents taught their children the value of a dollar. Today they try to keep the bad news from the kids as long as possible.

Some people find their cholesterol problem nearly solved by the high cost of meat, eggs, and butter.

The problem the average housewife faces is that she has too much month left over at the end of the money.

The question we all must face sooner or later is how to fit a long vacation into a short bankroll.

Prices in some restaurants are now so high that you'd be wiser to watch your steak than your hat and topcoat.

Have you noticed how today's restaurant prices seem to make home cooking taste a lot better?

Remember that when you eat out in a swanky restaurant the food may be plain, but the prices will be fancy.

Next Christmas Santa Claus won't be the only one in the red.

Those who say sleep is nature's greatest gift to man have not priced very many motels lately.

The only time where ends meet nowadays is on a football field.

The cart in the supermarket is rapidly becoming the most expensively operated vehicle in the world.

The only walk more expensive than a walk down a church aisle is a walk down a supermarket aisle.

It's true that the market is hitting new highs, that is, the supermarket.

The reason why the supermarket calls it an "express line" is that your money goes so fast.

Supermarkets are like churches. People walk down the aisles saying, "Lord, help us."

Supermarkets are very convenient. They permit a shopper to go broke in one store.

Always get in the shortest line at the supermarket. That way you stand a chance to get to the cashier before the prices go up.

When you hear about somebody who took a financial beating in the market, they might be talking about the supermarket.

When two women used to get together, they talked about another woman; now they talk about supermarket prices.

Have you noticed that most supermarket shopping carts are just the right size — big enough to kill one paycheck?

A supermarket used to be a place where people came out with a bundle. Now it's where they go in with a bundle — of money!

The newest and most popular game these days is called "Supermarket Roulette," which consists of trying to get all the groceries in your basket before the prices go up.

Maybe the reason supermarkets now sell underwear, magazines, and cosmetics is that many people can't afford to buy groceries.

Sign at a checkout counter in a Chicago supermarket: "English and Spanish are spoken here. Tears understood."

Today millions of Americans are suffering from respiratory problems. It comes from standing at supermarket check-out counters holding their breath.

Sometimes the most imaginative thing about TV is the repairman's bill.

At today's prices people don't take vacations — vacations take people.

Most folks need higher wages to pay the higher prices caused by higher wages.

Courage

Actually there's only a slight difference between keeping your chin up and sticking your neck out, but it's worth knowing.

It's all right to be cautious — but even a turtle never gets anywhere until he sticks his head out.

More twins are being born these days than ever before. Maybe kids lack the courage to come into the world alone.

The true test of moral courage is the ability to ignore an insult.

Courage is being the only one who knows you're afraid.

The courage to speak must be matched by the wisdom to listen.

Be bold in what you stand for, but careful in what you fall for.

Courage is something you always have until you need it.

Unfortunately, courage is all too often composed of equal parts of bourbon and water.

Too many people consider themselves daring when they are only delirious.

Remember, you are your own doctor when it comes to curing cold feet.

Courage is not the absence of fear, but the conquest of it.

Many a man who is proud of his right to say what he pleases wishes he had the courage to do so.

Courage makes both friends and foes.

The Supreme Court of the United States gives a husband the right to open his wife's letters — but it doesn't give him the courage.

Courage is the quality it takes to look at yourself with candor, your adversaries with kindness, and your setbacks with serenity.

Courage is what it takes for a woman to show friends the old Family Bible containing the date of her birth.

Don't be afraid to go out on a limb. That's where the fruit is.

Keep your fears to yourself, but share your courage with others.

A man who says what he thinks is courageous — but friendless.

Freedom is the sure possession of only those who have the courage to defend it.

Keep your chin up and your knees down.

When your knees are knocking, it might help to kneel on them.

Prayer gives strength to the weak, faith to the fainthearted, and courage to the fearful.

It takes more courage to repent than to keep on sinning.

The test of courage comes when you are in the minority; the test of tolerance comes when you are in the majority.

A military inductee, when asked if he had any physical defects, replied, "No guts."

Courtesy

He who has the habit of smiling at the cash register instead of the customer won't be smiling long.

Some people are so naturally courteous they even say thank you when the automatic door at the supermarket opens for them.

They tell us that courtesy is contagious. So why not start an epidemic?

Be nice and courteous to people on your way up because you'll meet many of them on your way down.

There is no law against being courteous, even when you aren't a candidate for office.

Practice courtesy. You never know when it might become popular again.

A little of the oil of courtesy will save a lot of friction.

Courtesy costs nothing, yet it buys things that are priceless.

A man gave a woman his seat on the bus; she fainted. When she revived, she thanked him; then he fainted.

Courtesy is the quality that keeps a woman smiling when a departing guest stands at the open door and lets the flies in.

It is getting harder and harder to find a courteous person who isn't trying to sell you something.

Why are husbands and wives more courteous to strangers than to each other?

Life is not so short that there isn't time for courtesy.

Be courteous to everybody. You never know who might show up on the jury.

One civil right we can all practice is courtesy to the other fellow.

The measure of a truly great man is the courtesy with which he treats lesser men.

A little courtesy goes a long way, which is just as well since it's in such short supply.

Gratitude is the most exquisite form of courtesy.

The measure of a truly great man is the courtesy with which he treats lesser men.

To be humble to superiors is duty; to equals, courtesy; to inferiors, nobility.

If you wish to get along with people, pretend not to know whatever they tell you.

Courtship

More and more lovely courtships sail into the sea of matrimony, and finally sink into the rocky storms of divorce.

Courtship is that period during which the female decides whether or not she can do any better.

In the old days the young fellow who went courting turned down the gas. Now he steps on it.

Courtship, unlike proper punctuation, is a period before a sentence.

Courtship is that part of a girl's life which comes between the lipstick and the broomstick.

Divorce records show that many married couples spend too much time in court and not enough time courting.

Platonic friendship is the name given the period between the first look and the first kiss.

The fellow who once enjoyed chasing girls now has a son who can't find any who will run.

An old-fashioned girl is one who will not hold hands on the first date — unless it's absolutely necessary.

If men acted after marriage as they do during courtship there would be fewer divorces — and more bankruptcies.

A newspaper reporter says it's dangerous for a young man to propose to a girl while he's driving a car. It's dangerous anywhere, son!

Running for president is like asking a girl to marry you — you may say a lot of things you later wish you hadn't.

Time changes things. Nowadays the couple has the honeymoon first, and if it's a success, they have the engagement, and if that works out all right, they *may* have a wedding.

Today young people start going steady with the opposite sex as soon as they learn there is one.

Young man, don't continue to tell your best girl friend that you are unworthy of her. Let it be a surprise!

Crime

A shady business never produces a sunny life.

Business is tough these days. If a man does something wrong he gets fined; if he does something right he gets taxed.

Many businessmen refuse to cash personal checks because sometimes the checks come back but the customers don't.

The death penalty may not eliminate crime but it stops repeaters.

According to the best evidence available, the death penalty is definitely a deterrent to crime. Not one of the 162 killers executed in Kentucky has killed anyone since.

Congress fighting inflation is like the Mafia fighting crime.

Some folks commit a crime and go to jail; others commit a crime, write a book, and get rich.

The crime situation is so bad in some American cities you could walk five blocks and never leave the scene of the crime.

Crime seems to be the only big business to escape government meddling.

One wonders what the crime statistics would be if they included all the holdups in Congress.

Crime may cost billions of dollars each year, but you've got to admit we're getting plenty for our money.

The rising crime rate would be slowed down considerably if we'd put as many cops on the streets as there are on television.

Organized crime can very easily be stopped. All we have to do is form a government agency to run it — then stand back and watch it choke itself to death on red tape.

Crime doesn't pay but it sure costs.

If we can't win the war against crime, how about a cease-fire?

Crime's story would be shorter if the sentences were longer.

Crime begins in the mind. A man has to think wrong before he acts wrong.

The average crime expert seems to know everything about crime except how to reduce it.

It might lessen crime if an occasional jury would suspend the criminal instead of the sentence.

We'll never stop crime until we get over the idea that we can hire or elect people to stop it.

The best way to put down crime is to stop putting up with it.

Some people seem to think that crime is not crime until discovery makes it so.

The reason crime doesn't pay is that when it does it's called something more respectable.

Let's nationalize crime so it won't pay!

Everybody seems to speak with conviction on the subject of crime, except the courts.

Anybody who thinks crime doesn't pay probably doesn't realize what a good living politicians make.

We don't seem to be able to check crime, so why not legalize it and then tax it out of business?

A crooked path is the shortest way to the penitentiary.

Following a good example is not always the wisest course — look what happens to a counterfeiter!

Faith in mankind will be a reality when they stop hauling money in armored cars.

Gossip is one form of crime for which the law provides no punishment.

It is reported that many resort hotels have towels so thick and fluffy that you can hardly close your suitcase.

Inflation is when a counterfeiter buys ink, paper, a printing press, and runs off a few thousand dollars — and loses money on the deal.

Judges certainly are getting tougher on criminals. They're giving them much longer suspended sentences.

If juvenile delinquency gets any worse, parents will have to post a five thousand dollar bail bond everytime a child is born.

A juvenile delinquent usually prefers vice to advice.

The delinquents of today are the same as the delinquents of fifty years ago — only they have better weapons.

Why keep on enacting laws when we already have more than we can break?

It's beginning to look like America has too many part time parents.

A doctor in Chicago turned kidnapper but was not very successful. Nobody could read the ransom notes.

The work of the preacher and the policeman is similar. The policeman usually gets the preacher's dropouts.

Once we thought the world was flat, then round. Now we know a lot of it is crooked.

Criminals

In America we'll try anything once — except criminals.

America has turned out some great men, but there are others not so great that ought to be turned out.

The automobile has had a great influence on public morals; it has completely stopped horse stealing.

Sign in a car on an out-of-the-way street: "Attention car thieves — this car is already stolen."

Some folks commit a crime and go to jail; others commit a crime, write a book, and get rich.

Anyone old enough to commit a man's crime is old enough to take a man's punishment.

Why do men take up crime when there are so many legal ways to be dishonest?

In this country we're willing to try anything once, except the criminals.

Criminals seem to know their rights better than their wrongs.

The dumbest criminal on earth is the one who would hold up a group of tourists on their way home from Las Vegas.

If a man defrauds you one time, he's a rascal; if he does it twice, you're a fool.

A grafter seldom improves the family tree.

A criminal doesn't care who makes the laws of this country so long as they are not enforced.

Judges and criminals are the only people who take the law into their own hands.

Some wit said that society invites the crime, and criminals accept the invitation.

Criticism
see also Complaining, Grumbling

Animals are such agreeable friends; they ask no questions, they make no criticisms.

Automobiles are like men — the less substantial they are, the more knocking they do.

Blowing out the other fellow's candle won't make yours shine any brighter.

Don't criticize the Bible; let the Bible criticize you.

One of the surest marks of good character is a man's ability to accept personal criticism without feeling malice toward the one who gives it.

If you can get anything for a song these days, it's probably criticism.

Most people don't object to criticism if it's favorable.

Criticism from a friend is better than flattery from an enemy.

Some of the older generation's criticism of the younger generation is heavily tinged with envy.

No one appreciates the value of constructive criticism more thoroughly than the one who's giving it.

Criticism is a blunt instrument, and on hard heads it makes little impression.

Nobody likes to criticize the medical profession, *but* — it has failed to conquer the common cold and babies continue to be born at the most outlandish hours.

Criticism is like dynamite. It has its place, but should be handled only by experts.

Don't criticize too quickly — even a clock that's out of order is right twice a day!

If you're not mature enough to take criticism, you're too immature for praise.

Adverse criticism from a wise man is more to be desired than the enthusiastic approval of a fool.

Criticism should always leave a person with the feeling he has been helped.

The person who is never criticized is not breathing.

It doesn't take brains to criticize; any old vulture can find a carcass.

Everybody should have a hobby of some kind, even if it's only criticizing the government.

Criticism is the disapproval of people, not for having faults, but for having faults different from your own.

Attention men: Before you criticize another, look closely at your sister's brother!

Criticizing another's garden doesn't keep the weeds out of your own.

The best place to criticize is in front of your own mirror.

Constructive criticism is when I criticize you. Destructive criticism is when you criticize me.

You might possibly avoid criticism by saying nothing, doing nothing, and being nothing.

Never fear criticism when you're right; never ignore criticism when you're wrong.

Before criticizing your wife's faults, you must remember it may have been those very defects which prevented her from getting a better husband than the one she married.

Criticizing an egg is a lot easier than laying one.

No need to criticize yourself; others will be glad to do that for you.

You can always tell a failure by the way he criticizes success.

Throwing mud at another man only soils your own hands.

The generation that criticizes the younger generation is always the one that raised it.

Those who can — do. Those who can't — criticize.

The difference between coaching and criticism is your attitude.

Small minds are the first to criticize large ideas.

The trouble with most of us is that we'd rather be ruined by praise than saved by criticism.

Any fool can criticize, condemn, and complain — and most fools do.

The mud-thrower never has clean hands.

Don't criticize the other fellow's plan unless you have a better one to offer.

When the other fellow finds a flaw in almost everything, he's cranky; when you do, you're discriminating.

Many people have the mistaken idea that they can make themselves great by showing how small someone else is.

Don't criticize anyone for wishing for what he doesn't have. What else could he wish for?

A person usually criticizes the individual whom he secretly envies.

Criticism is one thing most of us think is more blessed to give than to receive.

Don't mind criticism. If it's untrue, disregard it; if it's unfair, keep from irritation; if it's ignorant, smile; if it's justified, learn from it.

If your head sticks up above the crowd, expect more criticism than bouquets.

It's a pity that some folks never learn that uncovering the other fellow's faults will not cover up their own.

If you have occasion to criticize a mule, do it to his face.

Nobody has a right to criticize the government unless he voted in the last election.

One of the hardest things to take is one of the easiest things to give — criticism.

You can't stop people from criticizing you — but you can make them appear silly for doing it.

If you are afraid of criticism, you'll die doing nothing.

It is better to be criticized than to be ignored.

Criticism wouldn't be so hard to take if it weren't so often right.

You don't have time to criticize when you harmonize, sympathize, and evangelize.

Sometimes criticism is nothing but a mild form of envy.

Don't mind the fellow who belittles you; he's only trying to cut you down to his size.

Envy is blind and knows nothing except to depreciate the excellence of others.

Instead of letting their light shine, some people spend their time trying to put out the lights of others.

One of the easiest things to find is fault.

The person who is always finding fault seldom finds anything else.

Before finding fault with another person, stop and count ten — of your own.

Faultfinding without suggestions for improvement is a waste of time.

The worst fault of some people is telling others about theirs.

Any person can criticize, complain, and find fault — and most of them do.

Fear of criticism is the kiss of death in the courtship of achievement.

Nobody can make a fool out of another person if he isn't the right kind of material for the job.

A valuable friend is one who'll tell you what you should be told even if it momentarily offends you.

It's smart to pick your friends — but not to pieces.

The best way to lose a friend is to tell him something for his own good.

Knock your friends often enough and soon you'll find no one at home.

You can't cultivate a friend by digging up dirt around him.

Reprove a friend in secret, but praise him before others.

Running down your friends is the quickest way to run them off.

One form of generosity that can lead to trouble consists in giving others a piece of your mind.

Sometimes a reprimand is only a grouch in disguise.

It is easier to point the finger than to offer a helping hand.

How good a red-hot idea is depends on how much heat it loses when somebody throws cold water on it.

Time invested in improving ourselves cuts down on time wasted in disapproving of others.

What a blessing it would be if someone would invent anti-knock gas for people.

Hard knocks won't hurt you — unless you're doing all the knocking.

It isn't necessary to blow out the other person's light to let your own shine.

Opportunity never knocks at the door of a knocker.

Some people, even after they come in, keep on knocking.

You can't hold a man down indefinitely without staying down with him.

Often our mistakes serve a useful purpose. Our friends find great satisfaction in pointing them out to us.

It is usually best to be generous with praise, but cautious with criticism.

You'll never move up if you're continually running somebody down.

You can't carve your way to success with cutting remarks.

A successful man is one who can lay a firm foundation with the bricks that others throw at him.

It takes a big man to sympathize — a little man can criticize, and usually does.

Teen-agers are young people who get too much of everything, including criticism.

The critical tongue gets its wrapping orders from an untrained eye, an unthoughtful mind, and an ungrateful heart.

Critics

How often have you met a critic of the church who tried to make it better?

When nature made great men she made critics out of the chips that were left over.

If it were not for the doers, the critics would soon be out of business.

A literary critic is a person who finds meaning in literature that the author didn't know was there.

There's only one way to handle the ignorant or malicious critic. Ignore him.

A critic is one who finds fault without a search warrant.

The critic who begins with himself will be too busy to take on outside contracts.

A critic is one who would have you write it, sing it, play it, or paint it as he would — if he could.

The friend who is constantly trying to correct your faults is not a friend — he's a critic.

Curiosity

Half the world doesn't know how the other half lives but is trying to find out.

Enough curiosity may enable you to learn, but too much of it can get you into trouble.

Curiosity often gets mice into a trap — just like it does men and women.

The things most people want to know about are usually none of their business.

Bright eyes indicate curiosity, and black eyes indicate too much curiosity.

Few people suffer as do people in a small town when a stranger drops in and won't tell his business.

Curiosity is nothing more than freewheeling intelligence.

Nothing so excites a man's curiosity as a woman's complete silence.

Cynics

A cynic is a person who knows everything and believes nothing.

Most cynics look both ways before crossing a one-way street.

A cynic believes other people are as bad as he is.

In Hollywood there's a group called Divorce Anonymous. If a male member feels the urge to get a divorce, they send over an accountant to talk him out of it.

An onion is the only thing that will make a cynic shed tears.

A pessimist expects nothing on a silver platter except tarnish.

D

Dancing
Days
Death
Debts
Deeds
Defeat
Democracy
Dentists
Diets
Difficulties

Dignity
Diplomacy
Diplomats
Disagreement
Disappointments
Disarmament
Discipline
Discretion
Diseases

Divorce
Divorce Courts
Dogs
Doubt
Dreams
Drivers
Drunkards
Drunken Driving
Duty

Dancing

With some of today's dance steps you don't know if the guy on the floor is a good dancer or a bad drunk.

The rhumba is a foxtrot with the backfield in motion.

Dancing is the art of getting your feet out of the way faster than your partner can step on them.

He who dances must pay the fiddler — also the waiter, the florist, the hat check girl, the doorman, and the parking attendant.

The difference between wrestling and dancing is that some holds are barred in wrestling.

Those who perform the modern dance exercise everything except discretion.

A jitterbug is not an insect. It's a human being acting like one.

Judging from present-day dancing, familiarity doesn't breed as much contempt as it ought to.

The belly dance was originated by someone trying to take off a union suit in an upper berth.

The dance called the twist created an interesting phenomenon. For the first time in history clothes were worn out from the inside.

A Los Angeles girl described her dancing partner as follows, "He does a terrific tango — no matter what the band is playing."

The latest new dance craze is called, "The Politician." It's two steps forward, one step backward, and then a sidestep.

Belly dancing is the only profession where the beginner starts in the middle.

Days

When you come to the end of a perfect day, it probably isn't over yet.

Make each day count, but don't count each day.

The safest way to start the day is to go back to bed.

There ought to be a better way of starting the day than having to get up.

The best thing about the "good old days" is that they are forever gone.

The longest days are those you start with a grouch.

Don't put off until tomorrow what you can do today; by tomorrow there may be a law against it.

How beautiful a day can be when kindness touches it.

The most utterly lost of all days is the one in which you have not once laughed.

About all some people can say at the end of the day is that it's done.

It's old age when each day makes you feel two days older.

Death

There are two places the jet planes have brought closer together — this world and the next.

Nothing improves a man's appearance as much as the photograph the newspapers use with his obituary.

On his examination paper a boy wrote, "A natural death is where you die by yourself without a doctor's help."

Drive carefully! Motorists can be recalled by their maker.

A new cigarette offers coupons good for a cemetery lot.

A sure cure for conceit is a visit to the cemetery, where eggheads and boneheads get equal billing.

Nothing seems to make the cost of living as reasonable as pricing funerals.

It's hard to understand how an Alabama cemetery raised its burial charges — and blamed it on the cost of living.

The person who is never criticized is not breathing.

The nearer the time comes for our departure from this life, the greater our regret for wasting so much of it.

Death is not a period but a comma in the story of life.

People who are afraid of death are usually afraid of life.

Make this your motto: Don't die until you are dead.

Some people have been dead for several years, but they just prefer not to have it known.

So live that when death comes the mourners will outnumber the cheering section.

No one is dead as long as he is remembered by someone.

When we die we leave behind us all that we have and take with us all that we are.

Natural death is now defined as being killed by an automobile.

A hunter in West Virginia climbed a fence while carrying a cocked rifle. He's survived by his wife, five kids, and one rabbit.

Everyone should fear death until he has something that will live on after his death.

Depending on how a man lives, he may die old at forty or young at eighty.

There are worse things than death for some people — take life, for instance.

A person can survive almost everything except death.

If you drink before you drive, you are 'putting the quart before the hearse.'

Fame is chiefly a matter of dying at the right time.

A single rose for the living is better than a costly wreath at the grave.

A grouch never goes where he's told until he dies.

In a world where death is, we should have no time to hate.

Be as kind as you can today; tomorrow you may not be here.

You can't live without lawyers, and certainly you can't die without them.

The one thing certain about life is that we must leave it.

A man in Louisiana explained why he refuses to buy life insurance, "When I die I want it to be a sad day for everybody."

The only thing worse than growing old is to be denied the privilege.

Having problems may not be so bad after all. There's a special place for folks who have none — it's called a cemetery.

The easiest way to commit suicide is to take gas or step on it.

In preaching a funeral sermon, a preacher made the following remarks, "We have here before us only the shell — the nut is gone."

We are told the wages of sin is death — shouldn't you quit before payday?

Another difference between death and taxes is that death is frequently painless.

Death and taxes are inevitable, but death is not a repeater.

One thing about death — it doesn't get worse every time Congress meets.

A taxpayer resents the fact that death and taxes don't come in that order!

Nothing is certain in this world except death, taxes, and teen-agers.

Perpetual worry will get you to one place ahead of time — the cemetery.

Debts

Alimony is another war debt a lot of husbands would like to see cancelled.

America may be the land of the free, but not the debt-free.

America unquestionably has the highest standard of living in the world. Too bad we can't afford it.

The man who borrows trouble is always in debt.

America is rapidly proving to be a place with two cars in every garage — and none of them paid for.

Most Americans are members of the debt set.

A new car isn't a barometer of how much money a fellow has, but it's a pretty good indication of how much he owes.

If it weren't for keeping a budget, a lot of people wouldn't know how much they owe.

Budgeting is the most orderly way of going into debt.

The reason business conditions are so unsettled is because so many accounts are.

Drive carefully! The life you save could be someone who owes you money.

The most difficult thing imaginable is to keep clean of debt, dirt, and the devil all at the same time.

One thing America isn't running out of is debts.

Every year around April 15 Americans have a rendezvous with debt.

It's comforting to know that when we get up every morning we are no deeper in debt than we were when we went to bed.

If you don't go into debt these days you're probably doing something illegal.

Nowadays it seems to take half as long to get into debt and twice as long to get out.

The trouble with public debt is that private individuals have to pay for it.

Things bought on convenient terms always fall due at inconvenient times.

Debt is what you get into if you spend as much as you tell your friends you earn.

We owe a great deal to our forefathers, and that's another debt we'll probably never re-pay.

Running into debt is no trouble. Running into creditors is.

The best possible thing to do with a debt is pay it.

If you think you won't be missed, move away leaving a few unpaid bills.

Many people have learned to their sorrow that it's a great deal easier to run into debt than it is to outrun bill collectors.

In these modern times a man is considered out of debt when he owes no more but the doctor and dad.

The government debt is so huge the next generation will have to help pay it off — which explains why a baby yells when it's born.

They ought to make it as hard to get into debt as it is to get out of it.

Next to debt, the hardest thing to get out of is a warm bed on a cold morning.

If you listen to the loan company commercials, you'll almost believe you can borrow yourself out of debt.

All that many people will have when the rainy days come are a lot of debts they made when the sun was shining.

Some people use one half of their ingenuity to get into debt and the other half to avoid paying it.

Debt is like quicksand, and just about as hard to get out of.

No person can fully and completely discharge his debt to Almighty God, but surely he can make regular payments on it.

What you don't owe won't hurt you.

Everybody agrees the huge national debt should be reduced and hopes some future generation will do it.

College debts are obligations that with diligence, economy, and stern self-denial, father will be able to pay.

Every person born in the United States is endowed with life, liberty, and a substantial share of the national debt.

Many who are quick to run into debt find it takes a long time to crawl out.

Debts are about the only thing we can acquire without money.

It might seem hard to believe, but there was once a time when being over your head in debt was a catastrophe rather than an ordinary condition in life.

Molehills of debt build mountains of worry.

We had better go easy on piling up the national debt. With the life span steadily increasing, we may have to pay it ourselves.

Dentists claim the best collector of old bills is a new toothache.

Some friends stick together until 'debt do them part.'

Never forget a friend — especially if he owes you anything.

Future generations will be born free, equal, and in debt.

Debts of gratitude are the most difficult to collect.

Real happiness is getting a reminder about a bill you've already paid so you can sit down and write the store a nasty letter.

A husband seldom worries about the national debt. What bothers him is the way his wife keeps trying to localize it.

Yesterday's luxuries are today's debts.

Creditors have a better memory than debtors.

Isn't it funny how some people can remember a joke, but can't seem to remember an unpaid bill?

Once upon a time it was hard to save money. Now it's difficult just to stay broke without going into debt.

The younger generation will learn the value of a dollar when it begins paying off our debts.

About all you can do with money nowadays is owe it.

Money may not make a person happy, but it keeps his creditors in a better frame of mind.

Modern political theory seems to hold that the best way to keep the economy in the pink is to run the government in the red.

The following is the revised edition of an American prayer: "Forgive us our debts, O Lord, as we forgive our international debtors."

As a general rule, prosperity is what keeps us in debt.

The Reds won't have to bury us if we keep going deeper in the hole.

A good salesman can talk you to debt.

If you're not in style, the chances are you're out of debt.

Most people find they can scale the ladder of success quicker when they're debt-propelled.

Let's be thankful we don't have to pay taxes on our debts.

Blessed are the teen-agers, for they shall inherit the national debt.

Television sets are three dimensional. They give you height, width, and *debt*.

There's always something to be thankful for. If you can't pay your bills, you can be thankful you're not one of your creditors.

The man who borrows trouble is always in debt.

The United States is still the land of opportunity. Where else could you earn enough money to pay the interest on what you owe?

For a vacation some will go to the mountains, while others go to the seashore, but most of us will go in the hole.

Every child comes into the world endowed with liberty, opportunity, and a share of the war debt.

We've had wars to end all wars — why not have one to end all debts?

The only thing you can get without work is debt.

And there was the poor old man who worried so much about his debts that the hair began to fall out of his wig.

Deeds

Kind words can never die, but without kind deeds they can sound mighty sick.

Those who say they believe in Christianity and those who practice it are not always the same people.

You always remember a kind deed — particularly if it was yours.

Evil deeds, like fire, can be hidden for a short time — but the smoke can't.

Small deeds done are better than great deeds planned.

Some men are known by their deeds; others, by their mortgages.

Good deeds speak for themselves. The tongue only interprets their eloquence.

Few people ever get dizzy from doing too many good turns.

Superior to a kind thought is a kind word; better than both is a kind deed.

There are a lot of people who never forget a kind deed — if they did it!

A good deed gets about as much attention these days as a homely face.

He who does a kind deed should be silent; he who has received one should shout it from the housetop.

The smallest good deed is better than the grandest intention.

Some of the world's greatest deeds have been accomplished by two types of men — those who were smart enough to know it could be done, and those too dumb to know it couldn't.

It is vain to use words when deeds are expected.

Defeat

Many things are worse than defeat, and compromise with evil is one of them.

Defeat never comes to any man until he admits it.

You are never defeated unless you defeat yourself.

He took his defeat like a man; he blamed it on his wife.

The highway of fear is the shortest route to defeat.

Democracy

The difference between communism and democracy is — plenty!

Democracy is a wonderful system. It permits you to vote for a politician, and then sit on the jury that tries him.

A democracy is a form of government that believes at least part of what you earn belongs to you.

While living in a democracy, you can say what you think without thinking.

Democracy is a word all politicians use, and very few seem to understand.

Too many people see democracy as a chance to push other people around for their own personal benefit.

A democracy is a place where you can say what you please but don't have to listen unless you want to.

Democracy cannot be safe anywhere until it is safe everywhere.

A democracy is government that is run by all the people and run down by some of them.

Democracy would not need so many to defend it if it had more on whom it could depend.

One of the great blessings about living in a democracy is that we have complete control over how we pay our taxes — cash, check, or money order.

A democracy is a country in which everybody has an equal right to feel superior to the other fellow.

Ours is a democracy where the rich and the poor are alike — both complain about taxes.

Democracy, like love, can survive almost any attack — except neglect and indifference.

The most important principle of democracy is that even a wrong guy has rights.

One of the disadvantages of a democracy is that the minority has the say and the majority has to pay.

A democracy is a system where a fellow who didn't vote can spend the rest of the year kicking about the candidate the other fellows elected.

Dentists

As a man gets older he suspects that nature is plotting against him for the benefit of doctors and dentists.

Dentists are often driven to extraction.

When dentists start advertising they'll probably promise painless commercials.

Many people are so afraid of dentists they need an anesthetic just to sit in the waiting room.

Dentists claim the best collector of old bills is a new toothache.

Every time we go to a dentist we get *bored* to tears.

Dentistry means drilling, filling, and billing.

The dentist is one guy who's always ready to get back to the old grind.

Dentists have more faith in people than anybody. It's a miracle that more of them don't get their fingers bitten off.

A dentist expects you to answer his questions after he fills your mouth with everything but the kitchen sink!

Many young men would like to become dentists but they don't seem to have enough pull.

Wouldn't you say a romance between a dentist and a manicurist is a tooth-and-nail affair?

A dentist always looks down at the mouth.

Members of the dental profession are the only men on earth who can tell a woman to open or close her mouth and get away with it.

A dentist is a man who runs a filling station. He is also a collector of old magazines.

Almost any dentist has more pull than a politician.

The dentist's favorite marching song is "The Yanks Are Coming."

When a dentist makes an extraction, you hope he pulls the tooth, the whole tooth, and nothing but the tooth.

Nature may have known what she was doing, but sometimes it looks like she deliberately constructed mankind for the benefit of doctors and dentists.

You've got a problem when your dentist tells you that you need a bridge, and you can't pay his toll.

Diets

Advice to men over fifty: Keep an open mind and a closed refrigerator.

Too many Americans go in for weightlifting with the wrong equipment — a knife and fork.

Americans have more food to eat than any other people on earth, and more diets to keep them from eating it.

Childhood is that wonderful period when all you need to do to lose weight is take a bath.

When you see a man wearing a baggy suit, either he has a great diet or a terrible tailor.

You can't reduce by talking about it. You must keep your mouth shut.

Diets are so strict nowadays that the only thing dieters are allowed to have is hunger pains.

One of the best reasons for going on a diet is the money you'll save on food.

There's no better diet than eating only what you can afford.

The odds against a diet succeeding are three to one — knife, fork, and spoon.

With all the diets we hear and read about, it appears there are more problem eaters than problem drinkers.

There's a new diet that includes tranquilizers. You don't lose much weight — but you really don't care.

One thing you can be sure of — there will always be more people going on a diet tomorrow than those on a diet today.

People who diet go to great lengths to avoid great widths.

Dieting is the time when the days seem longer and the meals seem shorter.

When you go on a diet the first thing you're apt to lose is your sense of humor.

A diet helps people gain weight slower.

There's one thing to be said for a diet — it certainly improves the appetite.

A husband in New Mexico explained why his wife went on a diet: "She went from a size ten to a size tent.

Nowadays almost everybody is on a diet — due to high prices or high cholesterol.

It's strange how people always announce they're going on a diet after a big meal.

Most kids think a balanced diet is a hamburger in each hand.

Many with the strength to diet lack the strength to keep it quiet.

It's time to go on a diet when you notice you're puffing going *down* stairs.

The one thing rougher than being on a diet is listening to someone else who is.

Dieting is merely a matter of keeping your mouth shut at the right time — such as breakfast, lunch, and dinner.

Everybody is so diet-conscious these days that if someone says you're not half the man you used to be, it's considered a compliment.

Many people are on the new "see-food" diet — you see food, but you don't eat it.

Any dieter will tell you that the one thing worse than a menu offering nothing you like is a menu offering everything you like.

A nutritionist in India has the perfect new diet food. You open a can, and there's nothing in it.

A diet is something you went off yesterday — or expect to start tomorrow.

Anybody who has ever gone on a diet knows which meal is the hardest one to skip — the next one.

A Kansas dieter says, "I watch everything I eat, and wish I could eat everything I watch."

A diet is what you keep putting off while you keep putting on.

Those on a diet are the only people who gain from losing.

The first few days of a thousand-calorie diet are like a bunion — it doesn't show, but you can't forget it.

Diet tip: To indulge is to bulge.

When someone says he diets religiously, he probably means he doesn't eat anything while in church.

There's a new diet that will reduce weight like nothing else. It's called the high price of food.

When you go on a diet the first thing you lose is your temper.

No people feel more close and more friendly than those who are on the same diet.

Your diet should be a very simple matter — if the food tastes good, spit it out.

A diet is something that will take the starch out of you.

Some women diet to keep their girlish figure; others, to keep their boyish husbands.

Being on a diet requires great *won't* power.

The trouble with dieting is that your diet calls for less food while your appetite calls for more.

Probably nothing in the world arouses more false hopes than the first six hours of a diet.

The best way to lose weight is to eat all you want of everything you don't like.

People who can't stay on a diet do the next best thing — they stay off the scales.

According to science, the second day of a diet is easiest. By that time you are off it.

Mother and daughter have a tougher time keeping their figures straight than a public accountant.

Most of us don't know what poor losers we are until we try dieting.

One thing about those thirty-day diets — by the time you go back to eating you're shocked at the price of food.

The ideal diet is expressed in four words: "No more, thank you."

All that some people lose when they buy a book on dieting is the price of the book.

Destiny shapes our ends, but calorie intake is what shapes our middle.

The worst part of a diet isn't watching your food — it's watching everybody else's.

A dieter recently quit his onion diet. He lost fifteen pounds and thirty-five friends in sixteen days.

Said a banker's son, "My pop went on a diet; there was too much collateral in his blood."

You have to have patience on a diet — especially if it's your wife who's on it.

Successful dieting requires that you do the opposite of baseball players — stay away from the plate!

When some people go on a diet they don't lose anything except a lot of time.

A diet is the only thing that shows a gain by showing a loss.

A diet is like a ball game. You're the umpire behind the "home plate."

The best exercise is to exercise discretion at the dining table.

Just buying all those expensive diet foods can be very flattening.

If today's food prices haven't driven you to dieting, nothing will.

These days there are two kinds of people cutting down on food — those who can't afford the calories, and those who can't afford the prices.

Nothing makes food less fattening than being too expensive.

The way food prices are going up, more people are being put on diets by their accountants than by their doctors.

Scientists tell us we are what we eat. Nuts must be more common in diets than we thought.

We have more food in the United States per person than any other country — and more diets to keep us from eating it.

To feel "fit as a fiddle" you must tone down your middle.

Nothing gives you more false hope than the first day of a diet.

A man hopes that his lean years are behind him; a woman, that hers are ahead.

An Illinois man complained about inflation, "Last year it was my doctor who put me on a diet. This year it was my accountant."

A great invention for dieters would be a refrigerator that weighs you every time you open the door.

Overweight people don't like to hear four-letter words — such as diet.

An overweight woman was told by her doctor, "Under my new diet you can eat anything you like. Now, here's a list of what you're going to like."

It's funny how people on a diet are never reduced to silence.

Wouldn't it be nice if two weeks on vacation seemed to last as long as two weeks on a diet?

The old-fashioned wife is one who can stay on a budget and a diet.

It isn't a woman's will that makes her diet — it's her ego.

The modern woman seems to go through three stages — her first crush, her first divorce, and her first diet.

People who are forced to eat their own words should find it a good diet to reduce their big mouths.

Difficulties

Troubles and weeds thrive on lack of attention.

Many people are having trouble with their new cars. The engine won't start and the payments won't stop.

Most of us don't put our best foot forward until we get the other one in hot water.

We count our blessings on our fingers and our miseries on an adding machine.

The secret of business is to count your blessings while others are adding up their troubles.

The American businessman has a problem: if he comes up with something new the Russians invent it six months later and the Japanese make it cheaper.

Remember the steam kettle! Though up to its neck in hot water, it continues to sing.

It's great to have your children home from school. It takes your mind off your other troubles.

A father's biggest difficulty at Christmas time is convincing the children that he is Santa Claus and his wife that he is not.

Sign on a church bulletin board in Denver: "If you have troubles, come in and tell us about them. If you have none, come in and tell us how you do it."

It is usually not so much the greatness of our troubles as the littleness of our spirit which causes us to complain.

Have you ever noticed how extremely difficult it is for a person to keep his mind open and his mouth shut at the same time?

In youth we run into difficulties. In old age difficulties run into us.

Tackle any difficulty at first sight, for the longer you gaze at it the bigger it grows.

The most difficult thing to open is a closed mind.

One of the most difficult mountains for people to climb is the one they make out of a molehill.

The difficulties of life are intended to make us better — not bitter.

There are two ways of meeting difficulties: alter the difficulties, or alter yourself to meet them.

Some people would have us believe that there's no difficulty in the world that cannot be overcome. How about trying to squeeze toothpaste back into the tube?

The best way out of difficulty is through it.

Education enables a person to get into more intelligent trouble.

Efficiency experts can cope with everybody's troubles, but not with their own.

When you feel yourself turning green with envy, you're ripe for trouble.

The school of experience never changes; it always issues its diplomas on the roughest grade of sandpaper.

All men need a faith that will not shrink when washed in the waters of affliction and adversity.

How would a person ever know whether his faith was weak or strong unless it has been tried and tested?

There are some flowers that will not yield their perfume till they are bruised.

Having no food to eat will take your mind off other troubles.

Don't make your friends a dumping ground for your troubles.

It's a pity that happiness isn't as easy to find as trouble.

The secret of happiness is to count your blessings while others are adding up their troubles.

One thing is certain. If you can laugh at your troubles, you will always have something to laugh at.

Those who can laugh at trouble must be having a hilarious time nowadays.

A lie is a coward's way of getting out of trouble.

Despite all the pain and trouble, life is still better than any alternative.

The triumphal song of life would lose its melody without its minor keys.

The ladder of life is full of splinters, but you never realize it until you begin to slide down.

Liquor is nothing but trouble in liquid form.

Have you noticed that an optimist is always able to see the bright side of other people's troubles?

Patience is the greatest of all shock absorbers. About the only thing you can get in a hurry is trouble.

It's easy to have a balanced personality. Just forget your troubles as easily as you do your blessings.

A person's most fervent prayers are not said when he is on his knees, but when he is flat on his back.

He who does not pray when the sun shines will not know how to pray when the clouds come.

Prayer can *keep* us out of trouble a lot easier than it can *get* us out of trouble.

The man who smiles in the face of trouble is either brave or covered by insurance.

Few people travel the road to success without a puncture or two.

Three cases where supply exceeds demand are: taxes, trouble, and advice.

The worst car trouble is when the engine won't start and the payments won't stop.

One thing you are never asked to return is borrowed trouble.

Going out to meet trouble is one of life's shortest walks.

There aren't many troubles in the world more alarming than an empty stomach.

Trouble defies the law of gravity. It's easier to pick up than to drop.

Invite trouble and it will usually come.

If nobody knows the trouble you've had, you don't live in a small town.

There are few troubles that can't be relieved by an understanding friend, a good night's sleep, or a steak dinner.

You can save yourself a lot of trouble by not borrowing any.

Men's troubles are largely due to three things: women, money — and both.

Another thing about trouble — you don't have to get rid of the old ones to make room for the new ones.

It's much easier to borrow trouble than to give it away.

Most of modern man's troubles come from the fact that he has too much time on his hands and not enough on his knees.

Nothing costs more than buying trouble.

It's a lot easier to fall into trouble than it is to work out of it.

The person who is always looking for trouble may someday discover that he's it.

There's a lot of trouble in this country nowadays, and it seems everybody is trying to fix the blame instead of the trouble.

Anytime you try to borrow trouble, you soon learn that your credit is in good standing.

Many people these days are jumping into trouble mouth first.

You don't know what trouble is until your kids reach the age of consent, dissent, and resent — all at the same time.

Don't bother people by telling them about your troubles. Half of them don't care, and the other half figure you probably had it coming to you.

Don't advertise your troubles — people are already oversupplied.

Be happy when your troubles are at their worst — it means that anything that happens will be an improvement.

Tackle your troubles one day at a time; there will always be enough to last the rest of your life.

Examine your troubles and you'll probably find your name stamped on them as the manufacturer.

There's no such thing as a little trouble — especially if you're the one that's in it.

To really know a man, observe his behavior with a woman, a flat tire, and a child.

"Double trouble" is a mother-in-law with a twin sister.

A lot of trouble is caused by combining a narrow mind with a wide mouth.

Borrowing trouble is as easy as pie, but the carrying charge runs pretty high.

Never meet trouble halfway. It will gladly make the entire trip.

Almost everything comes ready-mixed these days — including trouble.

The guy whose troubles are all behind him is probably a school bus driver.

Say what you will about trouble; it always gives you something to talk about.

If we could only forget our troubles as easily as we do our blessings!

Troubles are like babies — the more you nurse them, the larger they grow.

Trouble is usually produced by those who produce nothing else.

Never bear more than one kind of trouble at a time. Some people bear three: all they have now, all they have had, and all they expect to have.

About the only thing you're sure to get by asking for it is trouble.

Much trouble is caused by our yearnings getting ahead of our earnings.

Why does trouble always come at the wrong time?

This world would be different if people were required to have a license to hunt for trouble.

Half our troubles come in wanting our way; the other half comes in getting it.

The fellow who is always telling us about his troubles is of some use — he keeps us from thinking about our own.

You can't keep trouble from coming, but you needn't give it a chair to sit in.

Before you begin to tell your troubles to another person, ask yourself if you would like to listen to his.

We'll be in trouble as long as we pay the best professors less than the worst football coach.

Don't borrow trouble. Be patient and you'll soon have some of your own.

When you brood over your troubles you are certain to hatch despair.

People would have very little trouble if it weren't for other people.

A good way to forget your troubles is to help others out of theirs.

Most of us listen to the troubles of other people just for the chance to get back at them with our own.

If your troubles are deep-seated and long-standing, try kneeling.

One trouble with trouble is that it usually starts out like fun.

The only thing you can get in a hurry is trouble.

When the commencement orator tells the graduating class that the world is their oyster, he should also explain the difficulty of cracking the shell.

Troubles teach you two things: how many friends you have, and how many people are waiting to catch you bent over.

The way some people go out of their way to look for trouble, you'd think trading stamps came with it.

The best way to forget all about your troubles is to wear a pair of tight shoes.

The easiest way to get into trouble is to be in the right place at the wrong time.

Don't bore your friends with your troubles. Tell them to your enemies, who will be delighted to hear about them.

If you would like to know who is responsible for most of your troubles, take a look in the mirror.

To avoid trouble and insure safety, breathe through your nose. It keeps your mouth shut.

One thing is certain — if you laugh at your troubles you will always have something to laugh at.

Most of our troubles are caused by too much done in the head and not enough in the back.

In a small town people will sympathize with you in trouble, and if you don't have any they will hunt some up for you.

When you look for trouble, you don't need a search warrant.

Trouble is like muddy water: be patient, don't stir it, and it will soon clear up.

Maybe the Lord allows some people to get into trouble because that is the only time they ever think of Him.

The only people who enjoy hearing your troubles are lawyers, and they're paid for it.

The person who persists in courting trouble will soon find himself married to it.

If you think you have trouble supporting a wife, just try not supporting her!

Everybody shuns trouble unless it comes to him disguised as money.

If half of your wishes came true, your troubles would probably double.

If you could kick the person who is most responsible for your troubles, you wouldn't be able to sit down for a week.

Looking for trouble is wasted energy. All a guy has to do is to sit down and wait.

Responsibility for a considerable portion of the world's troubles rests upon two people of the past. One of them invented credit; the other, taxes.

Did you ever feel yourself turning green with envy? If so, you were ripe for trouble.

May your troubles in the coming New Year be as short-lived as your resolutions.

Those who court trouble will never come out with a hung jury.

Why does it always seem that our blessings can be counted on our fingers, while we need a computer to count our troubles.

God is not only a present help in time of trouble, but also a great help in keeping us out of trouble.

When you're up to your ears in trouble, try using the part that isn't submerged.

Trouble causes some people to go to pieces; others to come to their senses.

There are a lot of people who get into trouble trying to keep up with the Joneses — especially the Dow Joneses.

It's not the people who tell all they know who start trouble — it's the people who tell more than they know.

When you help the fellow who's in trouble, he'll never forget you when he's in trouble again.

A cool head may sometimes keep a man out of trouble, but more often it's cold feet.

People always get into trouble when they think they can handle their lives without God.

One of your troubles is that it took six days to create the world and we're trying to run it on a five-day basis.

Imaginary troubles become real by telling them too often.

Of all the troubles great or small, the greatest are those that don't happen at all.

The man who borrows trouble is always in debt.

A lot of trouble arises from workers who don't think, and from thinkers who don't work.

Most of our troubles arise from loafing when we should be working, and talking when we should be listening.

What a different world this would be if people would only magnify their blessings the way they do their troubles.

Things are pretty well evened up in this world. Other people's troubles are not as bad as ours, but their children are a lot worse.

Worry is interest paid on trouble before it falls due.

Dignity

The church is paralyzed with timidity and gradually dying of dignity.

Anybody who stands on his dignity isn't going anywhere.

Dignity is often a mask we wear to hide our ignorance.

Many a man labors under the delusion that standing on one's dignity will enable him to see over the heads of the crowd.

A man may get a reputation for dignity when he's merely suffering from a stiff neck.

Dignity is one thing that cannot be preserved in alcohol.

It has been said that dignity is the ability to hold back from the tongue that which never should have been on the mind in the first place.

The fellow who stands on his dignity will find he has poor footing.

Diplomacy

Diplomacy is simply letting the other fellow have his way.

Being diplomatic is telling your boss he has an open mind instead of telling him he has a hole in the head.

Diplomacy is the art of taking sides without anyone knowing it.

Secret diplomacy is never secret and seldom diplomatic.

Diplomacy is the art of making others believe that you believe what you don't believe.

Diplomacy is simply saying nothing nicely.

Diplomacy is to do and say the nastiest things in the nicest way.

Diplomacy is convincing a man he's a liar without actually saying so.

Diplomacy couldn't prevent the last war, but it usually does a good job of preventing the peace.

Diplomacy is the art of saying things in such a way that nobody knows exactly what you mean.

A smile is the magic language of diplomacy that even a baby understands.

Diplomats

A diplomatic husband said to his wife, "How do you expect me to remember your birthday when you never look any older?"

When a diplomat lays his cards on the table, he usually has another deck up his sleeve.

A diplomat is the person who says, "I will take the matter under advisement," instead of saying no.

Diplomats are frequently decorated in European countries. We'd like to crown some of ours here in this country.

A diplomat doesn't think it's necessary to understand anything in order to argue about it.

When two diplomats shake hands we aren't sure whether it's friendship or time for the fight to start.

A diplomat is usually a wealthy person assigned to meddle in other people's business.

It's difficult for a diplomat to smoke the pipe of peace while he has his foot in his mouth.

If you can pat a guy on the head when you feel like bashing it in, you're a diplomat.

A diplomat can juggle a hot potato long enough for it to become a cold issue.

When a conference of diplomats announce they have "agreed in principle," it means nothing has been done.

A diplomat is a man who can make his wife believe she would look fat in a fur coat.

There is something wrong in international relations when a diplomat is called courageous if he speaks the truth.

A diplomat remembers a lady's birthday but forgets her age.

If a diplomat says yes, he means perhaps; when he says perhaps, he means no; and when he says no, he is no diplomat.

A diplomat can keep his shirt on while getting something off his chest.

An experienced diplomat is one who can pronounce the names of all the countries in the world that are mad at us.

A diplomat is a parent with two boys on different Little League teams.

It is only on matters of great principle that a diplomat lies with a clear conscience.

A diplomat is usually an old worn-out politician who, when he's being run out of town, can make it look like he's leading a parade.

A diplomat is one who can put his cards on the table without showing his hand.

A foolish man tells a woman to stop talking so much, but a tactful man tells her that her mouth is extremely beautiful when her lips are closed.

Disagreements

The safest way to disagree with your wife is very quietly.

It's better to disagree than agree and *all* be wrong.

One of the things we need to realize is that people can disagree with us without being crazy, rude, crude, or crooked.

The only way to settle a disagreement is on the basis of what's right, not who's right.

The most foolhardy way to disagree with your wife is out loud.

Everybody claims they're being logical, especially when they're in complete disagreement.

It's annoying when folks disagree with you — especially when they're right.

Disappointments

Some of the most disappointed people in the world are those who get what is coming to them.

Just about the time we think we can make both ends meet, somebody moves the ends.

When we get what we want, we are always disappointed to find out it was not what we wanted.

Disappointments should be cremated, not embalmed.

Nothing worthwhile is achieved without patience, labor, and disappointment.

Few people travel the road to success without a puncture or two.

Disarmament

Many Americans are in favor of disarmament — especially if it starts with those noisy "Westerns" on TV.

The first step in disarmament is to get nations to remove the chips from their shoulders.

Nations could safely lose their arms if statesmen wouldn't lose their heads.

Each nation seems to favor disarmament for all other nations.

If the disarmament conference wants quick results, it ought to meet in a muddy trench.

If disarmament doesn't make us love one another, it will at least make it safer to hate one another.

The next disarmament conference might be a great success if the delegates were representative taxpayers.

Friendship is the only cement that will hold the world together.

Discipline

Never strike a child! You might miss and hurt yourself.

One way to keep young boys from getting on the wrong track is to use better switching facilities.

A boy is like a canoe — he behaves better if paddled from the rear.

A pat on the back will develop character if given young enough, often enough, low enough — and hard enough.

Character does not reach its best until it is controlled, harnessed, and disciplined.

The child who always complains he's getting the short end of the stick should be given more of it.

There are many "bright children" who should be applauded with one hand.

There are still a few people who can remember when a child misbehaved to get attention — and got it!

Spoiled kids soon become little stinkers.

If brushing up on manners doesn't help some children, the brush should be moved down a bit.

Some of today's children don't smart in the right place.

Nowadays children are called bright when they make remarks that used to call for a good spanking.

When children get on the wrong track it's time to use the switch.

Child training is chiefly a matter of knowing which end of the child to pat — and when.

Sometimes the best way to straighten out a child is by bending him over.

If a child annoys you, quiet him by brushing his hair — if this doesn't work, use the other side of the brush on the other end of the child.

Dieting is merely a matter of keeping your mouth shut at the right time — such as breakfast, lunch, and dinner.

Being on a diet requires great *won't* power.

Successful dieting requires that you do the opposite of baseball players — stay away from the plate!

If you can pat a guy on the head when you feel like bashing it in, you're a diplomat.

Discipline yourself so others won't have to.

When a man praises discipline, nine times out of ten this means he is prepared to administer it rather than submit to it.

Discipline is something that can be learned during the first year of school or the first year of married life.

Psychiatrists tell us that discipline doesn't break a child's spirit half as often as the lack of it breaks a parent's heart.

Discipline is what you inflict on one end of a child to impress the other.

Nothing is harder on a grandparent than having to watch a grandchild being disciplined.

All that the overwhelming majority of people are doing about juvenile delinquency is reading about it.

Most juvenile delinquents are youngsters who have been given a free hand, but not in the proper place.

In the days when a woodshed stood behind the American home, a great deal of what passes as juvenile delinquency was settled out of court.

Juvenile delinquency is the result of parents trying to train their children without starting at the bottom.

Juvenile delinquency was unheard of many years ago because the problem was thrashed-out in the woodshed.

Did the conversion of so many woodsheds into garages have anything to do with the alarming increase in juvenile delinquency.?

The man who remembers what he learned at his mother's knee was probably bent over at the time.

A really good parent is a provider, a counselor, an adviser, and when necessary, a disciplinarian.

Applied child psychology was more effective when the applicator was a small razor strap.

One sure way to test your will power is to see a friend with a black eye and not ask any questions.

Human beings have will power while a mule has won't power.

Why is it that someone who has the will power to give up smoking doesn't have the will power to stop bragging about it?

Will power cannot be furnished by anyone but you.

Most of the time our will power suffers from generator trouble.

What kids need today is plenty of LSD — Love, Security, and Discipline.

Discretion

Those who perform the modern dance exercise everything except discretion.

Discretion is something that comes to a person after he's too old for it to do him any good.

The age of discretion is when you make a fool of yourself in a more dignified way.

Discretion is putting two and two together and keeping your mouth shut.

Discretion is simply leaving a few things unsaid.

Definition of discretion: "Closing your eyes to a situation before someone else closes them for you."

Discretion is the art of forgiving your enemies — especially those you can't whip.

Discretion is like a man's beard — it doesn't show up until he grows up.

The best exercise is to exercise discretion at the dining table.

And there was the girl who was so lazy she wouldn't even exercise discretion.

Diseases
see also Sickness

There are only two things children will share willingly — communicable diseases and their mother's age.

Conceit is the only disease known to man that makes everybody sick except the person who has it.

Psychiatrists tell us that conceit is a disease. It's a mighty strange ailment; the victim usually feels all right, but it makes his associates sick.

Germs attack the weakest part of your body — which is the reason for head colds.

Sometimes we get the feeling that swine flu was thought up by somebody who couldn't spell pneumonia.

Virus is a Latin word used by doctors, meaning, "Your guess is as good as mine."

Fatal diseases kill more people than any other kind.

Everybody is suffering from a new ailment called COSTROPHOBIA. It's the fear of rising prices.

It's becoming more difficult each passing day to find a disease we can afford.

The inevitable has happened. An artificial kidney has come down with kidney stones.

Human diseases are the same as they were a thousand years ago, but doctors have selected more expensive names for them.

The most wonderful thing for the common cold is a common handkerchief.

We called it "swine flu" because it made us so sick we just laid around and grunted.

It seems that almost everybody you meet has a cure for the common cold — except your doctor.

The best way to avoid the flu is to visit a night club. No flu bug can live in that environment.

The occupational disease of politicians is SPENDICITIS.

A bad cold wouldn't be so annoying if it weren't for the advice of your friends.

You have a very common disease if you're sick of high doctor fees.

A summer cold isn't much different from a winter cold, except that we talk about it more.

Arthritis is nothing more than twinges in the hinges.

Among the most popular remedies that won't cure a cold is advice.

Why is the virus that causes the common cold so hard to find, when it's so easy to catch?

The best way to get rid of a cold is to contract pneumonia, which the doctor can do something about.

People with bad colds don't go to the doctor — they go to the theater.

If gambling is a disease, as some contend, can you deduct your losses as a medical expense?

Why not cultivate health instead of treating disease?

If we had our way, we would make health "catching" instead of disease.

An indecisive hypochondriac is one who just can't make up his mind which disease he wants to have next.

Kissing is the most pleasant way of spreading germs yet devised.

Now that we have Medicare we can enjoy diseases that once we couldn't afford.

Said a weight watcher, "I'm fat because I have a hand-to-mouth disease."

Human diseases are the same as they were five thousand years ago, but doctors have selected more expensive names for them.

A cynic in New Jersey asks, "If science is so smart, why doesn't it discover an ailment that can be cured only by smoking and drinking?"

Some ulcers are caused by inflammation of the wishbone.

Divorce

An actress in Hollywood described her ex-husband, "He's six feet tall in his socks and $2,000 short in his alimony payments."

Did you hear about the movie actress who was so sentimental she got divorced in the same dress her mother was wearing when she got her divorce?"

An actress in New York City has broken up so many homes that she's listed in the Yellow Pages under "Demolition Experts."

America is a country where permanent waves are increasing and permanent wives are decreasing.

A bachelor is a man who has cheated some worthy woman out of her alimony.

Many bachelors claim they never got married because they couldn't afford the luxury of a divorce.

Common sense could prevent a great many divorces; but, on the other hand, it could also prevent a great many marriages.

A compliment a day keeps divorce far, far away.

More and more lovely courtships sail into the sea of matrimony and finally sink into the rocky storms of divorce.

The only thing a divorce proves is whose mother was right in the first place.

A divorce is what couples agree on when they can't agree on anything else.

The best and surest way to save a marriage from divorce is not to show up for the wedding.

There would be fewer divorces if women hunted for husbands with as much thought as they hunt for bargains.

It's true that some people get divorced for trivial reasons. But, then, some of them got married for trivial reasons.

The first step toward divorce is getting engaged.

Did you hear about the father of three sets of twins who sued his wife for a divorce on the grounds that she was overbearing?

The most terrible thing about a divorce is that somewhere, maybe miles apart, two mothers are nodding their heads and saying, "See? I told you so."

Judging by the divorce rate, a lot of people who said, "I do" — didn't!

A man and his wife were divorced because of illness — they got sick of each other.

A little common sense would prevent most divorces — and marriages too.

All a girl needs for a divorce these days is a husband.

A divorce is what happens when what you thought was a marriage turns out to be a conglomerate.

Most divorce cases are only antitrust suits.

A "Hollywood divorce" means that the wife is asking for custody of the money.

With as many divorces as we have nowadays, it seems that more parents are running away from home than children.

The divorce rate would be lower if, instead of marrying for better or worse, people would marry for good.

Divorce is when you'd rather switch than fight.

You have only to mumble a few words in church to get married and a few in your sleep to get divorced.

The high divorce rate indicates that the modern woman hasn't made up her mind whether to have a man for a hubby or a hobby.

Divorce is the hash made from domestic scraps.

There would be fewer divorces if the husband tried as hard to keep his wife as he did to get her.

Those who are so perturbed over the present divorce rate evidently do not understand the law of supply and demand. There are more lawyers in this country than there are preachers.

The story is going around about a couple whose divorce was so amicable that he proposed to her again.

There would be fewer divorces if men gave as much loving attention to their wives as they do to their cars, boats, and dogs.

A Georgia woman got a divorce because of religious differences. She worshiped money, and he didn't have a dime.

Judging by the number of divorces, too many couples were mispronounced husband and wife.

Love is the quest, marriage the conquest, divorce the inquest.

A woman no longer says she's getting a divorce — now she says she's being recycled.

Divorce is a custom so common nowadays that smart people are staying single in order to be different.

The way divorces keep climbing someday the marriage ceremony will change from "I do" to "Perhaps."

Many divorces are caused by the marriage of two people who are in love with themselves.

The divorce problem exists because there are too many married couples and too few husbands and wives.

Two Hollywood children were talking. One of them said quite boastfully, "I've got two brothers and one little sister, how many do you have?" The other child answered, "I don't have any brothers and sisters, but I have three daddies by my first mother, and four mothers by my last daddy."

Desertion is the poor man's method of divorce.

A divorce is like a fire escape — you only use it when things get too hot.

A wealthy father didn't know what to give his daughter as a wedding present, so he promised to pay for her divorce.

Americans have always been willing to pay any price for freedom. If you don't believe it, look at the divorce statistics!

A girl becomes a woman when she stops living on her allowance and starts living on her alimony.

Nowadays some girls seem more particular about choosing their divorce lawyers than choosing their husbands.

Some girls get married for financial security; others get divorced for the same reason.

A modern miracle would be a golden wedding anniversary in Hollywood.

In Hollywood the bride tossing the bouquet is just as likely to be the next one to get married as the girl who catches it.

A couple in Hollywood got divorced; then they got married again. The divorce didn't work out to the complete satisfaction of both parties.

The secret of a successful Hollywood marriage is for the couple to have something in common — such as the same divorce lawyer.

There's many a girl who got married because she didn't like to spend her evenings alone — and then got a divorce for the same reason.

Love at first sight usually ends with divorce at first slight.

Too many people are finding it easier to get married than to stay married.

A couple recently had their marriage annulled, and sued the officiating minister for malpractice.

A man in Montana has been married so many times his last marriage license was made out TO WHOM IT MAY CONCERN.

Marriage often results when a man meets a woman who understands him. So does divorce.

When it comes to broken marriages most husbands will split the blame — half his wife's fault, and half her mother's.

Some men get married because they're tired of going to the laundromat, eating in restaurants, and wearing socks with holes in them. Other men get divorces for the same reasons.

In the old days a woman married a man for his money, but now she divorces him for it.

A man in New Hampshire complained about slow mail delivery, "Today, I received an invitation to the wedding of a couple who are already divorced."

Distressed wife to her attorney: "My husband always said everything he has is mine, and now I want it."

It takes only a few words mumbled in church and you're married. It takes only a few words mumbled in your sleep and you're divorced.

Divorce Courts

If it weren't for the divorce courts separating people, the police would have to.

Divorce records show that many married couples spend too much time in court and not enough time courting.

Black and blue are very effective colors when worn in the divorce courts.

In much divorce-court testimony the couples seem to think they were married by an injustice of the peace.

The divorce courts are filled with people who thought they had been bitten by the love bug, and then found out they had only been bitten.

A divorce court is where the "little woman" who was once considered *incomparable* suddenly becomes *incompatible.*

Dogs

It's hard to believe, but some people claim their dogs are almost human — and they mean it as a compliment!

Isn't it wonderful how dogs can win friends and influence people without ever reading a book.

A dog is the only thing on earth that loves you more than he loves himself.

If dogs could talk, perhaps we'd find it just as hard to get along with them as we do with people.

A dog is smarter than some people. It wags its tail and not its tongue.

The noblest of all animals is the dog, and the noblest of all dogs is the hotdog. It feeds the hand that bites it.

If dogs can think, how can we account for their love for man?

Another reason why a dog is man's best friend is because he's not always calling for explanations.

How did dogs learn to bark their loudest during a television news bulletin?

Doubt

When in doubt, tell the truth.

Never put a question mark where God has put a period.

Some folks demand the benefit of the doubt when there isn't any.

When in doubt, don't.

Doubt makes the mountain which faith can move.

Many people believe their doubts and doubt their beliefs.

If you doubt the propriety of doing a thing, you'd better give yourself the benefit of the doubt and not do it.

Think of doubt as an invitation to think.

Feed your faith and your doubts will starve to death.

No one can live in doubt when he has prayed in faith.

Twin fools: one doubts nothing, the other doubts everything.

Hope is putting faith to work when doubting would be easier.

Dreams
see also Goals, Ideals

Castles in the air are all right until you try to move into them.

Too many of us forget to put foundations under our air castles.

It's more fun building castles in the air than on the ground.

Castles in the air are great until you step out the door.

They call it a "dream house" because it usually costs twice as much as you dreamed it would.

The American dream is owning a British sports car, smoking a Havana cigar, and drinking Russian vodka on the French Riviera.

Some people dream in technicolor — others add sound effects.

Don't be unhappy if your dreams never come true — just be thankful your nightmares don't.

Some men believe in dreams until they marry one.

It doesn't do any harm to dream, providing you get up and hustle when the alarm goes off.

We cannot dream ourselves into what we could be.

We may have a lot of excitement in our dreams, but nobody ever wakes up in the morning breathless.

If you want your dreams to come true, don't oversleep.

No dream comes true until you wake up and go to work.

The world would be happier if its leaders had more dreams and fewer nightmares.

A house is made of walls and beams; a home is built with love and dreams.

Man is like a tack; he can go only as far as his head will let him.

Between tomorrow's dream and yesterday's regret is today's opportunity.

Those who think they are dreamers are usually just sleepers.

People who are always walking on clouds leave too many things up in the air.

There is more pleasure in building castles in the air than on the ground.

Day dreams at the steering wheel lead to nightmares in the hospital.

Oversleeping is a mighty poor way to make your dreams come true.

Success is the ability to hitch your wagon to a star while keeping your feet on the ground.

Men who dream of hitching their wagon to a star would be better off to hitch up their pants and go to work.

Drivers
see also Women Drivers

Driving an automobile would be a much greater pleasure if each motorist would use his head as much as he uses his horn.

Some automobiles have fluid drives; others just have a drip at the wheel.

Any day now we expect to see power steering for backseat drivers.

Bumper sticker on a car in Atlanta: "Caution — keep back! I drive like your wife."

Nothing confuses a man more than to drive behind a woman who does everything right.

The worst fault of a motorist is his belief that he has none.

The horse would have a good laugh if he could see motorists adjusting their shoulder harnesses.

All the world loves a lover except when he is driving his automobile in crowded traffic — with his arm around his girlfriend.

A safety belt is a device some motorists wear religiously for about twenty minutes after they pass an accident.

American motorists take the best possible care of their cars — and they keep pedestrians in good running condition too.

Nowadays when a motorist goes looking for a parking place, it's a good idea to have someone go along to share the driving.

Too many motorists figure they have an engine to move their own car and a horn to move everybody else's.

The only reason some motorists slow down for pedestrians is because they're afraid they'll damage their cars.

Quite often a motorist will knock a pedestrian down because his windshield is obscured by safety stickers.

An expert has predicted that in twenty years every motorist will be flying. And by that time every pedestrian will be playing a harp.

Motorists are people in such a hurry to get into the next county that they often end up in the next world.

A motorist recently admitted running over the same man twice. The time evidently has come when there aren't enough pedestrians to go around.

Give a motorist an inch and he'll take off one of your fenders.

It's strange that a motorist never remembers he was once a pedestrian.

America needs a car that can't go any faster than a driver can think.

One traffic hazard that drivers seem determined to eliminate is the pedestrian.

A polite driver is one who honks his horn before he forces you off the road.

Maybe the reason we have traffic problems is because the traffic has become as dense as the drivers.

The way motorists drive, it pays to look both ways when your cross a one-way street.

Too many youngsters who have passed their driving test think they can pass anything.

Drunkards

Advice to hunters: Don't get loaded when your gun is.

With some of today's dance steps you don't know if the guy on the floor is a good dancer or a bad drunk.

The higher you get in the evening, the lower you feel in the morning.

A drunkard can live neither with alcohol nor without it.

There's nothing more stubborn than a drunkard trying to convince you he isn't.

Pity the poor drunkard who started out to get mellow, then he got ripe, and ended up rotten.

A drunkard can't make both ends meet because he's too busy making one end drink.

Some men become fishermen because they're not allowed to drink at home.

A fool and a drunkard are two of the most mistaken human beings on earth. One thinks he is wise, and the other thinks he is sober.

Some folks drink liquor as if they want to be mentioned in "BOOZE WHO."

A Montana man who seldom takes more than one drink explained, "One drink is just right, two are too many, and three are not enough."

You've had too much drink when you feel exhilarated, but can't spell or pronounce it.

Warning: Boozers are losers.

Heavy drinkers have what is known as saloon arthritis — every night they get stiff in a different joint.

A boozer insisted that his liquor bill was deductible as a medical expense. "My friends and I drink to each other's health."

Without his big bank account the "problem drinker" would be called a drunken bum.

If the price of liquor continues to go up, a certain drunk complains that it would be enough to drive him *not* to drink.

The reason some people drink booze is that they don't know what else to do with it.

Many people have so much alcohol in their system that they ought to be charged a liquor tax for crossing state lines.

The man who downs bottles of liquor will find that the liquor returns the favor.

Booze makes a man colorful; it gives him a red nose, a white liver, a yellow streak, and a blue outlook.

It's when a man gets tight as a drum that he makes the most noise.

Booze-befuddled brains mean brawls, bumps, and bruises.

Our next Thanksgiving menu will probably consist of roast turkey, yams, and pickled relatives.

Drinking is something that makes one lose inhibitions and give exhibitions.

When a man drinks too much liquor he can approach you from several directions at once.

It is useless for alcoholics to worry about the future for there will soon be no future for them to worry about.

Many folks contend that sleeping out of doors makes one beautiful. That explains the charming appearance of the town drunk.

Drunken Driving

Fewer accidents are caused by traffic jams than by pickled drivers.

An automotive invention that is sorely needed is brakes that will automatically get tight when the driver does.

Cars and bars mean stars and scars.

If you must drive while drinking, drive a nail. Then the only thing you'll hit is your finger.

When a drunken driver runs into a telephone pole, he blames the pole.

It's better to sit tight than to attempt to drive tight.

If you drink like a fish, swim — don't drive.

If you drink before you drive, you are 'putting the quart before the hearse.'

One reason why the courts don't handle more drunken driver cases is that the undertaker gets them first.

Loose brakes and tight drivers cause most of the accidents.

Another dangerous habit of drunken drivers is taking a curve at high speed when there isn't a curve.

The hand that lifts the cup that cheers, should not be used to shift the gears.

Watch out for Sunday drivers who started out Saturday night.

A loose nut at the wheel isn't as dangerous as a tight one.

Traffic warning sign: "Heads you win — cocktails you lose."

There is only one way to drink and drive — hazardously!

The driver who has "one for the road" will have state troopers as a chaser.

Drivers are safer when highways are dry, and highways are safer when drivers are dry.

The hand that lifts the cup that "cheers" should not be used to shift the gears.

One gallon of gas plus one pint of liquor often adds up to a first-class funeral.

There are two finishes for automobiles: lacquer and liquor.

Duty

The value of the Bible doesn't consist in merely knowing it, but in obeying it.

Many people see their duty in plenty of time to dodge it.

Some who do their duty as they see it must have a blind spot.

When duty calls some people are never at home.

Generally speaking, duty is what we expect of others.

You can do anything you ought to do.

The fellow who believes he is exerting himself beyond the call of duty is apt to be a poor judge of distance.

God never imposes a duty without giving time and strength to perform it.

A man never gets so confused in his thinking that he can't see the other fellow's duty.

Many people spend more time trying to dodge duty than would be required to discharge it.

The best way to get rid of your duties is to discharge them.

Duty is a task we look forward to with distaste, perform with reluctance, and brag about afterwards.

Some folks who do their duty as they see it need to consult an eye specialist.

An excuse is a statement given to cover up for a duty not well done or not done at all.

Happiness will never come your way as long as your back is turned on duty.

To be humble to superiors is duty; to equals, courtesy; to inferiors, nobility.

Duty makes us do things well, but love makes us do them beautifully.

It is our duty to obey God's commands, not to direct His counsels.

A reformer sees his duty and overdoes it.

Hard work and devotion to duty will surely get you a promotion — unless, of course, the boss has a relative who wants the job.

The trouble with the world is that so many people who stand up for their rights fall down miserably on their duties.

E

Economists
Economy
Education
Efficiency Experts
Egotists
Elections
Embarrassment
Employees
Encouragement

Enemies
Energy
Enjoyment
Enthusiasm
Envy
Equality
Error
Evil
Evolution

Exaggeration
Example
Excuses
Executives
Exercise
Experience
Experts
Extravagance

Economists

The easiest way to start an argument these days is to get two economists together.

Economists predict the year ahead will reward hard workers. What a frightening outlook for many!

An economist is a man who figures out tomorrow why the things he predicted yesterday didn't happen today.

We could get along better with fewer economists and more economizers.

An economist usually has a plan to do something with somebody else's money.

Economists now say we move in cycles instead of running in circles. It may sound better, but it means the same thing.

An economist can tell you what to do with your money after you've done something else with it.

The average economist thinks he knows more about money than the people who have it.

An economist in Los Angeles recently completed writing a book titled *The Short Story of Money.* The book contains only seven words, "Here it is and there it goes."

Economists say we must devalue the dollar. What do they think Congress has been doing the past twenty years?

An economist talks about something he doesn't understand and tries to make you think it's your fault.

An economist is uncertain about the future and hazy about the present.

Economists tell us that we may have to devalue the dollar. What do they think Congress has been doing for the past twenty-five or thirty years?

Economy

Millions of Americans are nervous wrecks. They're afraid the President will devalue trading stamps at any moment.

Scientists are working on the ultimate economy car. It will just sit in the driveway and impress the neighbors.

Owning a compact car can be very economical. If you go out with another couple, you have to use their car.

There comes a time when a nation, as well as an individual, must choose between tightening the belt or losing the pants.

A congressman is always in favor of economy, but not when it involves his own district.

Perhaps what's wrong with our economy is that there isn't any.

The only part of our economy that seems to be looking up is living costs.

Our economy has reached the point where a counterfeiter can't even make a profit.

The changing economy has made bill collectors of just about everybody.

Experts say our economy is bottoming out. Some of us already know that by the patches on the seats of our pants.

The more government in the economy, the less economy in the government.

Many people don't start economizing until they run out of money.

Have you noticed how delicately balanced the economy is? The minute auto prices go down, gasoline prices go up.

Economizing to some people is not working hard enough to need a deodorant.

The economy is not as bad as we are led to believe. Many merchants report this year's going-out-of-business sales are much better than last year's.

Economy size means large in soap and small in automobiles.

The economy is moving so slow these days that the Postal Service is getting jealous.

Our present economy is terrible. We're making more and more dollars and less and less money.

The way the American economy is going, we'll soon have a system of checks and bounces.

How can political candidates discuss the economy when there isn't any?

Most people might practice economy if they had something left to practice with.

The trouble with today's managed economy is the mismanagement.

A balanced economy is one in which there are as many people working as there are striking.

Economy is defined as a reduction in some other fellow's salary.

If you want economy, never let an economic question get into politics.

The only thing wrong with our economy is that nobody wants to economize.

Planned economy is fast becoming calculated extravagance.

The secret of economy is to live as cheaply the day after payday as you did the day before.

The economy is as confusing as a cross-eyed Ping-Pong player. The stock market keeps going down and the supermarket keeps going up.

We never knew what real extravagance was until we had this so-called planned economy.

Economizing is easier when you're broke.

Don't cheat the Lord and call it economy.

We never knew what real extravagance was until we had this so-called planned economy.

It is difficult to predict the future of an economy in which it takes more brains to figure out the tax on our income than it does to earn it.

Political economy are two words that should be divorced on the grounds of incompatibility.

Our legislators would practice more economy if they weren't so out of practice.

Modern political theory seems to hold that the best way to keep the economy in the pink is to run the government in the red.

It is poor economy to cut down on schools and use the money later on jails and reformatories.

Some practice economy only with the truth.

Education
see also Learning

Let's all sympathize with the poor girl who spent four years learning how to behave in polite society and the rest of her life trying to locate it.

An aged grandfather explained why he reads the Bible several hours every day, "You might say I am cramming for my final examination."

Many boys are flunking geometry. They just don't know the angles.

Small children start to school these days with a big advantage. They already know two letters of the alphabet — TV.

Nothing grieves a child more than to study the wrong lesson and learn something he wasn't supposed to.

It's very difficult to teach children the alphabet these days. They think V comes right after T.

Teaching children to count is not as important as teaching them *what* counts.

A college education never hurt anybody who was willing to learn after he got it.

In the old days students went to college to get an education from the professors, but now it seems like some students think they ought to educate the professors.

It is a thousand times better to have common sense without an education than to have an education without common sense.

Education is a funny thing. At eighteen we knew all the answers — forty years later even the questions confuse us.

Among the few things more expensive than an education these days is the lack of it.

A person should have enough education so he doesn't have to look up to anyone. He should also have enough to be wise enough not to look down on anyone.

Some folks are so highly educated they can bore you on any subject.

A good education is important. It enables you to pick out the most important things to worry about.

Education is what folks have left after they've forgotten most of what they learned in school.

If you get a good education, you can become prosperous — if you marry a rich widow.

Education is a wonderful thing but it doesn't go far enough. It merely teaches a man *how* to speak, not *when* or *how long.* And neither does it teach him exactly when to shut up.

Everybody should get at least a high school education — even if they already know everything.

Don't call it education unless it has taught you life's true values.

A person isn't educated unless he has learned how little he already knows.

If you think getting an education is expensive, try not getting one.

Abraham Lincoln had great difficulty getting an education — but what can you expect from a guy who didn't play football or basketball?

Since the advent of sex education, the old fellow who drives the local school bus can't tell whether the kids are talking dirty or discussing their lesson assignment!

Adult education got its start in a household with teen-age children.

Education enables a person to get into more intelligent trouble.

The least expensive education is to profit from the mistakes of others — and ourselves.

Education is what you get from reading the small print in a contract. Experience is what you get from not reading it.

All true education is a delayed-action bomb, assembled in the classrooms for explosion at a later date.

One way to get an education in a hurry is to drive a school bus.

You can buy education, but wisdom is a gift from God.

An educated person is one who knows a great deal and says little about it.

Education pays less when you are an educator.

Those who don't read have no advantage over those who can't.

Many a brilliant young man has his BA and MA, but he's still living with his PA.

Many people don't know what an education could do for them because they've never tried it.

An educated person is one who knows how to be ignorant intelligently.

The chief benefit of education is to discover how little we know.

Education should include knowledge of what to do with it.

An educated man will sit up all night and worry over things a fool never dreamed of.

Education can't make us all leaders — but it can teach us which leader to follow.

Shortchange your education now and you may be short of change the rest of your life.

Education is not received. It is *achieved.*

An educated man is one who has finally discovered that there are some questions to which nobody has the answer.

Education will broaden a narrow mind, but there is no known cure for a big head.

It is not the I.Q. but the I WILL that is important in education.

A person with a reservoir of knowledge is not well-educated unless he knows when to turn the spigot on and off.

No man is fully educated until he learns to read himself.

It's what we learn after we know it all that really counts.

May education never become as expensive as ignorance.

The true object of education should be to train one to think clearly and act rightly.

The businessman is coming to realize that education is to business what fertilizer is to farming.

The money saved this year on education will be spent later on jails and reformatories.

Speaking of higher education, here's hoping it doesn't go much higher.

It's a pity so many people get college training without getting an education.

Education is not a head full of facts, but knowing *how* and *where* to find facts.

It's not what is poured into a student that counts, but what is planted.

You can always spot an educated man. His views are the same as yours.

An educational system isn't worth a great deal if it teaches young people how to make a living but doesn't teach them how to make a life.

As an educational institution, nothing beats the stock market.

Education is an ornament in prosperity and a refuge in adversity.

The trick is to get education out of politics — and get it into politicians.

Education is going forward from cocksure ignorance to thoughtful uncertainty.

Many people were blue and down in the dumps before they became educated. Now they are depressed and despondent.

Education helps you earn more. But not many school teachers can prove it.

Sometimes an adult education begins with a teen-age marriage.

If a person has no education he is forced to use his brains.

Education means developing the mind, not stuffing the memory.

Not all educated people are intelligent.

By nature all men are much alike, but by education they become different.

Education has produced a vast population able to read but unable to distinguish what is worth reading.

True education enrolls men at the cradle and graduates them at the grave.

Education makes people easy to lead but difficult to drive; easy to govern but impossible to enslave.

An intellectual is so smart he doesn't understand the obvious.

Education is knowing what you want, knowing where to get it, and knowing what to do with it after you get it.

We'll be in trouble as long as we pay the best professors less than the worst football coach.

At the rate we're going, the day may come when everybody has a college degree and nobody has an education.

Education is one commodity of which we can never have a surplus.

The mark of an educated man is the ability to make a reasoned guess on the basis of insufficient information.

Education is something you get when your father sends you to college, but it isn't complete until you send your own son.

The roots of education are sometimes bitter, but the fruits are sweet.

Perhaps sex education does have a place in our schools. If that won't get the kids to read, nothing will.

The truly educated man is that rare individual who can separate reality from illusion.

We've had adult education for several thousand years. It's called marriage.

Experience has been described as "Compulsory Education."

A highbrow is one who is educated beyond his intelligence.

A hypochondriac is now attending a medical college in Kansas City. He is studying to be a patient.

The only thing more expensive than education is ignorance.

The only known cure for ignorance is education.

A little learning may be a dangerous thing — but it's still safer than total ignorance.

The difference between education and intelligence is that intelligence will make you a living.

Nothing makes a *little* knowledge as dangerous as examination time.

Some students drink at the fountain of knowledge. Others just gargle.

Only hungry minds can become educated.

The mind is like the stomach. It's not how much you put into it that counts, but how much it digests.

If people learn from their mistakes, many are getting a fantastic education.

A hundred mistakes are a liberal education — if you learn something from each one.

The best way to stop kids from seeing dirty movies is to label them "Educational."

When the commencement orator tells the graduating class that the world is their oyster, he should also explain the difficulty of cracking the shell.

Many men are able to solve big problems at the office, but are unable to settle little ones at home.

School and education should not be confused; it is only school that can be made easy.

It's said that society will achieve the kind of education it deserves. Heaven help us if this is true!

It's not so much what is poured into the student, but what is planted, that really counts.

As an educational device, TV rates above everything else. No nation in history has ever known as much as we do about detergents and deodorants.

Efficiency Experts

An efficiency expert is smart enough to tell you how to run your own business, and too smart to start one of his own.

The efficiency expert is a man whose work, if it were done by a woman, would be called nagging.

A layman can't understand why efficiency experts don't go into business for themselves and monopolize the world.

The real efficiency expert is the woman who finds what she wants in her handbag at the first swoop.

An efficiency expert is a man hired by an executive who is too tenderhearted to fire his own employees.

Efficiency experts can cope with everybody's troubles, but not with their own.

The average efficiency expert is a person who has no business of his own to wreck.

An efficiency expert's idea of lowering costs is to cut the other fellow's salary.

The world's work must be done by some of us. We can't all be politicians and efficiency experts.

Egotists
see also Conceit

The beauty of America is that the average man always thinks he's above average.

A bachelor usually wants one single thing in life — himself!

Egotism is that quality which causes a person to think he's in the groove when he's actually in a rut.

One way to deflate your ego is to read the want ads in the newspapers and discover all the jobs you're not equipped to handle.

Egotism is what makes other people *think* they're as intelligent as we know we are.

Some people are in sore need of surgery; they need about half of their ego removed.

The emptiest man in all the world is the man who is full of himself.

A stiff neck usually supports an empty head.

Egotism is obesity of the head.

One of the hardest secrets for a man to keep is his opinion of himself.

The bigger a man's head gets, the easier it is to fill his shoes.

A man likes his wife to be just clever enough to comprehend his cleverness and just stupid enough to admire it.

The more praise a man is willing to take, the less he deserves it.

He who toots his own horn has everybody dodging him.

The strange thing is that man is satisfied with so little in himself but demands so much in others.

The cemeteries are full of people who thought the world couldn't get along without them.

You're never going to get anywhere if you think you're already there.

The only thing that can keep on growing without nourishment is an ego.

Some of us veer to the left and some of us swing to the right, but most of us are self-centered.

Egotism is an internally-generated anesthetic which enables a conceited person to live painlessly with himself.

Any smart woman will tell you that the best way to a man's heart is through his ego.

151

The kind of success that turns a man's head always leaves him facing the wrong direction.

Staring up to admire your halo usually creates a pain in the neck.

The minute a man begins to feel his importance, his friends begin to doubt it.

It's so sad that our ancestors did not live long enough to realize how smart we are.

Egotism is the world's most poorly-kept secret.

There never was a person with an inflated ego who wasn't full of hot air.

The bigger the head, the smaller the heart.

A man who is self-centered is off-centered.

We have observed that many self-made men made their heads oversize.

When a man gets too big for his "britches," his hat doesn't fit either.

Don't brag and blow; it isn't the whistle that pulls the train.

When a man tries himself, the verdict is usually in his favor.

Some proud folks are always letting off esteem.

The more you speak of yourself, the more you are likely to lie.

Egotism is the ability to see those things in yourself that others cannot see.

Those who are sold on themselves still have to find a buyer's market.

The man who thinks he has no faults has at least one.

Some folks get carried away by the sound of their own voices — but not far enough.

Egotism is a disease that often kills men before they know they have it.

As the chest swells, the brain and the heart shrink.

Egotism is partly enthusiasm — but mostly ignorance.

The bouquet you hand yourself usually looks like weeds to the other fellow.

Egotism is the glue with which you get stuck on yourself.

Many a little squirt thinks he's a fountain of wisdom.

Some folks are like the rooster who thought the sun rose every morning just to hear him crow.

Egotism is the anesthetic that dulls the pain of stupidity.

It doesn't pay to get "stuck up." The peacock of today is the feather duster of tomorrow.

Neither an egg nor an ego is any good until you break it.

There are only two kinds of egotists — those who admit it and the rest of us.

An egotist is a man who talks so much about himself that he gives us no time to talk about ourselves.

Some folks are so proud of themselves they can strut sitting down.

An egotist is like a ship in a fog — always blowing his horn.

To hear some snobs talk, you'd think they begat their own ancestors.

An egotistical person persists in telling you things about himself that you had planned on telling him about yourself.

Some people are so egotistical that every time they look in the mirror they take a bow.

An egotist is a person who thinks as much of himself as you think of yourself.

Any egotist will tell you there is no satisfactory substitute for himself.

There's something to be said for the egotist, and he's usually saying it.

No matter what effect the egotist has on others, he always fascinates himself.

The biggest egotist of all is the one who thinks that if he hadn't been born people would wonder why.

An egotist is a guy who keeps holding himself over by popular demand.

An egotist is a person who is his own best friend.

When two egotists meet it's a case of an "I" for an "I."

When an egotist doesn't understand something in a book, he decides it *must* be a misprint.

Pride hides a man's faults to himself and magnifies them to everyone else.

It seems that when a fellow claims to know all the answers some fool comes along and asks the wrong questions.

An egotist is a person who plays too big a part in his own life.

The eyes of an egotist look in instead of out.

An egotist is not necessarily a man who thinks too much of himself; he is a man who thinks too little of other people.

Not even an egotist is all bad. At least he doesn't go around talking about other folks.

An egotist is a man who thinks he's smarter than you are — though you know very well he isn't.

You can always spot an egotist, but seldom soon enough.

An egotist is an inferior person with a superiority complex.

A prominent gentleman in Dayton, Ohio, denies that he is conceited, but says he's absolutely convinced that if he had never been born people would want to know why.

The man doesn't live who has not, at some time, thought he had the elements of greatness in him.

Some men achieve greatness, others are born great, and a few have greatness thrust upon them. The rest of use just think we're great.

Mental cases hardest to cure are those who are crazy about themselves.

Too many people are humble — and know it.

No big ideas ever came from swelled heads.

The fellow who thinks he is full of knowledge is especially annoying to those of us who are.

The more you talk about yourself, the more apt you are to lie.

If your life is an open book, don't bore your friends by reading out of it.

The fellow who is too deeply in love with himself ought to get a divorce.

He who falls in love with himself will have no rivals.

You can usually recognize a self-made man. He has arms long enough to pat himself on the back.

A self-made man is usually a horrible example of unskilled labor.

You don't have to be much of a musician to toot your own horn.

We are sorely in need of a special encyclopedia with blank pages for the fellow who knows everything.

The only time some people don't interrupt is when you're praising them.

It's not difficult to pick out the best people. They'll help you do it.

People who are carried away by their own importance seldom have far to walk back.

If biologists are right in their assertion that there is not a perfect man on earth today, a lot of personal opinions will have to be altered.

Remember, whenever you're praised to the sky, it's best to keep your feet on the ground.

A song that never gets an encore is when you sing your own praises.

Reputation is a large bubble which bursts when you try to blow it up yourself.

When selling yourself don't misrepresent the goods.

The biggest obstacle many of us stumble over are our own faults.

The trouble with most people is that every time they think, they think only of themselves.

It isn't a woman's will that makes her diet — it's her ego.

Elections

A democracy is a system where a fellow who didn't vote can spend the rest of the year kicking about the candidate the other fellows elected.

The cheapest way to have your family tree traced is to run for public office.

People are not against political jokes — they just wonder how they get elected.

Everybody makes mistakes. That's why we keep having political elections.

If we could use the money political candidates spend on their campaigns, we could cure a lot of the ills they complain about.

We are sorely in need of a voting machine with a space for "Remarks."

It's useless to try to hold some people to anything they say while they're madly in love, drunk, or running for office.

You can't fool all the people all the time, but politicans figure that once every four years is good enough.

Everytime a politician expresses a growing concern for something the price goes up.

The election isn't very far away when a candidate can recognize you across the street.

Wasn't it too bad about the politician in Ohio who ran for reelection unopposed — and lost?

An election year is when a lot of politicians get free speech mixed up with cheap talk.

We are all ready to vote a straight ticket next election — as soon as we can find out which party is straight.

It's about time that voters start electing candidates for what they won't stand for.

Don't vote a straight ticket unless it's filled with straight men.

We should hold elections every year because there never seem to be tax increases in an election year.

An election year is a period when all the Democrats and all the Republicans devote their time saving the country from each other.

During an election year the political races get rough, and many candidates develop straddle sores.

The guy who never votes is the first to tell you what's wrong with the government.

The whole purpose of any political campaign is to stay calm, cool, and elected.

In this country only half of the voters vote and generally it's the wrong half.

An election is a system which allows us to decide which politicians we prefer to mess things up for us.

The most dangerous vote in America is the vote that is not used.

Ballot boxes in America are more often starved than stuffed.

Be thankful American elections are by ballots — not bullets. We count the returns — not the remains.

It's nice to have four years between elections. It takes people that long to regain their faith.

During political elections all political parties campaign for better education. When we take a close look at some of the men elected, we have to admit it's needed.

It is reported that someone recently broke into the Kremlin and stole next year's election.

Russia is just about the only country in the world where nobody sits up all night to see how the elections come out.

Russia is a gambler's paradise; you'd never lose an election bet.

Embarrassment

The most embarrassing moment in your life was probably when you spit out of a car window when it wasn't open.

It's always embarrassing for a man to run unexpectedly into a girl he was once engaged to.

The height of embarrassment is when two eyes meet at the same keyhole.

Real embarrassment is when you tell a girl her stockings are wrinkled when she's not wearing any.

Nothing is quite as embarrassing as watching your boss do something you assured him couldn't be done.

It is extremely embarrassing to come to your senses and find out you haven't any.

Parents are always embarrassed when their children tell lies, but sometimes it's even worse when they tell the truth.

Poise is often being too stupid to know you should be embarrassed.

If thoughts could be read, faces might be redder.

Employees

Millions of Americans aren't working, but thank heaven they've got jobs.

A certain boss when asked how many people work for him replied, "About half of them."

It isn't the number of people employed in a business that makes it successful. It's the number working.

If coffee breaks get much longer, employees will be late for quitting time.

Colleges try to find out what their graduates do after graduation. Employers are trying too.

White House employees are no longer permitted to use the polite expression "Pardon me."

The best employees work for their employers as though they were self-employed.

When a distillery employee works overtime, does he get time and a *fifth?*

If things don't change for the better, the day is not far off when employees will demand the deductions instead of the pay.

An employee in Chicago stretched his coffee break all the way to the unemployment office.

There is something all employees should know. There is a big difference between finishing a job and wrecking it.

Most employees would get more work done if they didn't have to spend so much time filling out work schedules.

The executive most hated by those around him is the one who is always annoying office workers by asking them to do something.

Nothing improves a joke more than telling it to your employees.

You may know more than your employer, but his knowledge pays off.

Executives of large industrial firms are looking for men between twenty-five and thirty with forty years of experience.

Some workers are trying to make both weekends meet.

It's predicted that in twenty years people will work two days a week and relax five. Some employers think that's happening now.

Encouragement

A slap on the back often pushes out the chest.

A slap on the back doesn't always mean encouragement — mosquitoes get it too!

Encouragement is like premium gasoline. It helps to take the knock out of living.

Pat others on the back, not yourself.

The best thing to do behind a person's back is pat it.

A pat on the back, though only a few vertebrae removed from a kick in the pants, is miles ahead in results.

Don't forget that a pat on the back can cause a chin to go up and shoulders to go back.

Patting a fellow on the back is the best way to get a chip off his shoulder.

A friend will strengthen you with his prayers, bless you with his love, and encourage you with his hope.

Keep your ideals high enough to inspire you, and low enough to encourage you.

Enemies

Anyone who's written an autobiography learns you can make two kinds of enemies with such a book — the people you mention and those you don't.

It sometimes looks foolish for folks to be spending so much time loving their enemies when they should be treating their friends a little better.

People make enemies by complaining too much to their friends.

As long as your conscience is your friend, never mind about your enemies.

Discretion is the art of forgiving your enemies — especially those you can't whip.

It's easier to love your enemies if you remember that they never try to borrow from you.

155

Love your enemies — it will drive them nuts!

If you simply must make enemies, pick lazy ones.

Blessed are our enemies, for they tell us the truth when our friends flatter us.

Always speak well of your enemies; remember you made them.

No enemy is more dangerous than a friend who isn't quite sure whether he's for you or against you.

Love your enemies, but if you really want to make them mad, ignore them completely.

When you bury the hatchet, don't bury it in your enemy's back.

It is possible to learn from an enemy things we can't learn from a friend.

Some people make enemies instead of friends because it's less trouble.

The enemy you make today may be the only one who can help you twenty-five years from now.

Nobody can have too many friends, but one enemy may constitute a surplus.

If you want an enemy, just try to convince a fool he's wrong.

There is only one reason why your enemy can't become your friend — YOU!

We make more enemies by what we say than friends by what we do.

You can meet friends everywhere, but you can't meet enemies anywhere — you have to make them.

Love your enemies and they will wonder what kind of a deal you are trying to pull.

It's a lot easier for a fellow to love his enemies than to make them love him.

Mankind's worst enemy is fear — of work!

Forgive your enemies — if you can't get back at them any other way!

Always forgive your enemies; nothing annoys them quite so much.

Folks who are friends usually have the same virtues, the same enemies, or the same faults.

The difference between our friends and our enemies is this: Our friends love us in spite of our faults, and our enemies hate us in spite of our virtues.

No one should judge another person by what that person's enemies say about him.

You can judge a man by his enemies as well as by his friends.

Kindness is the ability to treat your enemy decently.

Always speak kindly to your enemy and maybe he'll come close enough for you to box his ears!

The Bible admonishes us to love our neighbors, and also to love our enemies — probably because they are generally the same people.

Love your enemies. It'll sure make them feel foolish.

Beware of the man who continues to tell you he's on your side. So is appendicitis.

Man is that foolish creature who tries to get even with his enemies and ahead of his friends.

The best medicine in the world is to love your work and your enemies.

A man's reputation is a blend of what his friends, enemies, and acquaintances say behind his back.

A still tongue makes no enemies.

Energy

America's number one energy crisis is Monday morning.

Many Americans are trying to conserve energy as never before — they're now burning their morning toast only on one side.

Engineers are trying to build a car that will stop smoking. We would all like to own a car that would stop drinking.

One sensible reason for abolishing the electric chair is the energy it would save.

One thing most children save for a rainy day is lots of energy.

Many people complain about the fuel mileage they get on their riding lawn mower — only a yard to the gallon.

It's a confused world. We're running out of electricity — and nobody even knows what it is.

About the only gas rationing most of us would favor concerns useless conversations.

Those who are most successful in making excuses have no energy left for anything else.

Forgiveness saves the expense of anger, the high cost of hatred, and the waste of energy.

Sign on a California freeway: "All in favor of conserving gasoline please raise your right foot."

The only way you can get the same gas mileage in your car as your friends say they get in theirs is to lie about it.

A concert pianist in Chicago claims he's doing his part to conserve energy. He's now playing the piano with only one hand.

One solution to the energy problem is to bale up all the government red tape and use it for fuel.

Some restaurants are now saving energy — drink two or three of their cocktails and the lights go out.

Windmills in Washington could ease the energy crisis. Washington has an abundance of wind and hot air.

Enjoyment

Your conscience doesn't really keep you from doing anything; it merely keeps you from enjoying it.

Enjoy today and don't waste it grieving over a bad yesterday — tomorrow may be even worse.

Why not learn to enjoy the little things — there are so many of them?

Don't expect to enjoy life if you keep your milk of human kindness all bottled up.

If you don't enjoy what you have, how could you be happier with more?

Not what we have, but what we enjoy, constitutes our abundance.

Enjoy yourself. These are the "good old days" you're going to miss in the years ahead.

The good things of life were made to enjoy. Enjoying a thing means sharing it with others.

There are a lot of folks in the world who spend so much time watching their health that they haven't time to enjoy it.

It's a grand person indeed who can laugh at himself with others and enjoy it as much as they do.

Enthusiasm

The cross is easier to the Christian who takes it up than to the one who drags it along.

A cold church is like cold butter — never spreads very well.

Enthusiasm is contagious — and so is the lack of it.

We have never learned to support the things we support with the enthusiasm with which we oppose the things we oppose.

A wise man once said that enthusiasm is nothing but faith with a tin can tied to its tail.

Enthusiasm is a good engine, but it needs intelligence for a driver.

There's always a good crop of food for thought. What we need is enough enthusiasm to harvest it.

He who has no fire in himself cannot warm others.

If it were as easy to arouse enthusiasm as it is suspicion, just think what could be accomplished!

We won't go far without enthusiasm, but neither will we go far if that's all we have.

Enthusiasm is apt to breed more action than accuracy.

The fellow who is fired with enthusiasm for his work is seldom fired by his boss.

Enthusiasm is the propelling force necessary for climbing the ladder of success.

An enthusiast is a fellow who feels perfectly sure of the things he is mistaken about.

The gap between enthusiasm and indifference is filled with failures.

A wave of enthusiasm is seldom a permanent wave.

Years wrinkle the skin, but lack of enthusiasm wrinkles the soul.

An enthusiast is one who believes about four times as much as he can prove, and can prove about eight times as much as anyone will ever believe.

Enthusiasm for hard work is most sincerely expressed by the person who is paying for it.

The road to failure is greased with the slime of indifference.

Genius is nothing more than inflamed enthusiasm.

Some folks get into the sea of matrimony on a wave of enthusiasm.

Envy

Americans sink millions of dollars in unsound financial schemes, one of which is trying to keep up with the neighbors.

Nothing depreciates a car faster than having a neighbor buy a new one.

Some of the older generation's criticism of the younger generation is heavily tinged with envy.

A person usually criticizes the individual whom he secretly envies.

Sometimes criticism is nothing but a mild form of envy.

The only person worth envying is the person who doesn't envy.

When you feel yourself turning green with envy, you're ripe for trouble.

Love looks through a telescope; envy, through a microscope.

Don't mind the fellow who belittles you; he's only trying to cut you down to his size.

Envy is blind and knows nothing except to depreciate the excellence of others.

We underrate that which we do not possess.

Envy provides the mud that failure throws at success.

Don't envy anybody. Every person has something no other person has. Develop that one thing and make it outstanding.

The only person worth envying is the one who has found a cause bigger than himself.

After a man makes his mark in the world, a lot of people will come around with an eraser.

Instead of letting their light shine, some people spend their time trying to put out the lights of others.

Being overcome with envy is like running into the ocean; the deeper you go in, the harder it is to get out.

Envy is usually the mother of gossip.

Most of us would be better off financially if it weren't for the extravagance of our neighbors.

There are many roads to hate, but envy is one of the shortest of them all.

A good idea is one that hits the other fellow with a bolt of envy.

Jealousy is to the soul what sickness is to the body.

Love is the glue that cements friendship; jealousy keeps it from sticking.

The sunlight of love will kill all the germs of jealousy and hate.

The thing that keeps some men broke is not the wolf at the door but the silver fox in the window.

The smart politician keeps envy out of his voice when he accuses his opponents of fooling the public.

Most of us aren't prepared to accept success — especially somebody else's.

Did you ever feel yourself turning green with envy? If so, you were ripe for trouble.

Some ulcers are caused by inflammation of the wishbone.

People who talk about things they can't afford sometimes forget that the list should include pride, envy, and malice.

A San Francisco woman says she's allergic to furs. Every time she sees a friend wearing a new mink coat she gets sick.

One blessing in being poor, honest, and hardworking is that nobody envies you.

Equality

A good American looks up to nobody, looks down on nobody, but looks straight into the eyes of everybody.

A sure cure for conceit is a visit to the cemetery, where eggheads and boneheads get equal billing.

A democracy is a country in which everybody has an equal right to feel superior to the other fellow.

Ours is a democracy where the rich and the poor are alike — both complain about taxes.

Creating all men free and equal isn't enough. Some means must be devised to keep them free and equal.

Freedom is indivisible. It is for all or none.

Future generations will be born free, equal, and in debt.

The reason they say the income tax is the fairest tax of all is that it gives every individual an even chance at poverty.

There's justice for all, but it doesn't seem to be equally distributed.

All men are born equal. The tough job is to outgrow it.

In an atomic war all men will be cremated equal.

Error

All childish errors are not made by children.

To err is human; to blame it on others is even more human.

Sign on a company bulletin board in Grand Rapids: "To err is human, to forgive is not company policy."

Sometimes we learn more from a man's errors than from his virtues.

To err is understandable; to admit it is unlikely.

It is one thing to show a man he is in error, and quite another thing to put him in possession of the truth.

An error doesn't become a mistake until you refuse to correct it.

To err is human; to forget, routine.

It's true that to err is human — but it can be overdone.

The longer a man is in error, the surer he is he's right.

To err is human; to cover it up is even more human.

Things could be worse. Suppose your errors were counted and published every day like those of a baseball player!

To err is human. But to really louse it up, it takes a computer.

It may be true that to err is human, but to remain in error is stupid.

Defending your faults and errors only proves that you have no intention of quitting them.

Stupid mistakes are made by others — we only make "unavoidable errors."

The man who never makes an error never plays ball.

Few people seek to discover truth; most of us seek to confirm our errors and perpetuate our prejudices.

Evil

One of the secret ambitions of many people is to be able to enjoy some of the evils which go with having too much money.

The man who cannot be angry at evil usually lacks enthusiasm for good.

There's nothing consistent about human behavior except its tendency to drift toward evil.

Few people make a deliberate choice between good and evil; the choice is between what we want to do and what we ought to do.

The business of the church is to get rid of evil, not to supervise it.

Many things are worse than defeat, and compromise with evil is one of them.

Evil deeds, like fire, can be hidden for a short time — but the smoke can't.

The chief evil of many people consists not so much in doing evil, but in permitting it.

Between two evils, choose neither; between two goods, choose both.

Supervising evil does not make it good.

Evil can never be disguised.

A necessary evil is one we like so well we do not care about abolishing it.

The man who cannot be angry at evil usually lacks enthusiasm for good.

Evil flourishes in the world because the good people allow their differences to divide them instead of allowing the things on which they agree to unite them.

The evils of men are divided into two classes: openly bad and secretly bad.

It seems that the roots of all evil are planted very deeply.

The best way to escape evil is to pursue good.

Shakespeare said that the evil men do lives after them. On TV this is called.a rerun.

Facts are troublesome things to the evildoer.

A man who is unable to choose between two evils often hunts up a third.

The love of money, and the lack of it, is the root of all kinds of evil.

The saxophone was invented a century ago, thus proving that "the evil which men do lives after them."

Evolution

Darwin's theory of evolution suggests that first came the baboon and then man. Politics is proving that it can go either way.

Life started from a cell, and, if justice is done, a lot of it is going to end there.

One objection to evolution is that it is too slow for this age.

Evolution is the descent of man from monkey, which some people forgot to make.

It's difficult to contend that man hasn't descended from some sort of an animal as long as one half of the world goosesteps and the other half pussyfoots.

The question is not whether man descended from the monkey, but when is he going to stop descending?

If evolution works, nature will eventually produce a pedestrian who can jump three ways at once.

Exaggeration

When you make a mountain out of a molehill, don't expect anyone to climb up to see the view.

One of the most difficult mountains for people to climb is the one they make out of a molehill.

There are people so addicted to exaggeration that they can't tell the truth without lying.

Exaggeration is a blood relative to falsehood, and almost as bad.

Never exaggerate your faults — leave that for your friends.

Some folks never exaggerate. They just think big.

Some people get all their mental exercise by climbing up and down molehills.

It's a well-known fact that the older a man gets, the faster he could run as a boy.

Our own faults are not minimized by magnifying the faults of others.

Rare is the person who can weigh the faults of others without putting his thumb on the scales.

The faults of others are like headlights on a passing car. They seem more glaring than our own.

No fisherman who tells the truth about his catches can make his story very interesting.

How far a fisherman stretches the truth depends on the length of his arms.

Nothing makes a fish bigger than almost being caught.

Nothing grows faster than a fish from the time he bites until he gets away.

Anyone who finds it easy to improve his golf game probably does it with a pencil.

Some of the world's best golf scores are made with a lead pencil.

Gossip is like a balloon — it grows bigger with every puff.

Gossip is when someone gets wind of something and treats it like a cyclone.

It isn't difficult to make a mountain out of a molehill — just add a little dirt.

Some people are always indebted to their imagination for facts.

If a Texan had an inferiority complex, rest assured it would be the biggest one you can get.

African natives fish lying down, but in this country fishermen lie standing up with their arms outstretched.

Man is inclined to exaggerate almost everything — except his own mistakes.

Most politicians spend half their time making promises and the other half making excuses.

There must be a shortage of truth the way so many folks are stretching it these days.

Some people stretch the truth; others mutilate it.

When you stretch the truth, watch out for the snap back.

Example

It's difficult to inspire others to accomplish what you haven't been willing to try.

When a man gets too old to set a bad example, he usually starts giving good advice.

More boys would follow in their father's footsteps if they weren't afraid of being caught.

The footsteps a boy follows are apt to be those his father thought he'd covered up.

Character grows in the soil of experience, with the fertilization of example, the moisture of desire, and the sunshine of satisfaction.

Children are a great deal more apt to follow your lead than the way you point.

Children need strength to lean on, a shoulder to cry on, and an example to learn from.

Maybe children could keep on the straight and narrow path if they could get information from someone who's been over the route.

Children are natural mimics; they act like their parents in spite of every effort to teach them good manners.

It's extremely difficult for a child to live right if he has never seen it done.

Many children would take after their parents if they knew where they went.

Training a child to follow the straight and narrow way is easy for parents — all they have to do is lead the way.

Every child has a right to be both well-fed and well-led.

You train a child until age ten; after that you only influence him.

If your Christianity won't work where you are, it won't work anywhere.

If you want to convince others of the value of Christianity — live it!

A genuine Christian is the best evidence of the genuineness of Christianity.

Christianity is a way of walking as well as a way of talking.

If you want to defend Christianity, practice it.

Those who say they believe in Christianity and those who practice it are not always the same people.

Christianity requires the participants to come down out of the grandstand and onto the playing field.

Satan is perfectly willing to have a person confess Christianity as long as he does not practice it.

Some people can talk Christianity by the yard but they can't, or won't, walk it by the inch.

Christians are the light of the world, but the switch must be turned on.

A Christian shows what he is by what he does with what he has.

What the world needs is not more Christianity but more Christians who practice Christianity.

No one is more confusing than the fellow who gives good advice while setting a bad example.

The self-made man is usually a pathetic example of unskilled labor.

Example is a language all men can read.

A good example is the best sermon you can preach.

Every father should remember that one day his son will follow his example instead of his advice.

None of us is entirely useless. Even the worst of us can serve as horrible examples.

The worst danger that confronts the younger generation is the example set by the older generation.

A good example has twice the value of good advice.

A great many children face the hard problem of learning good table manners without seeing any.

The greatest gift we can bestow on others is a good example.

What can't be done by advice can often be done by example.

Always remember there are certain people who set their watches by your clock.

Following a good example is not always the wisest course — look what happens to a counterfeiter!

People seldom improve when they have no model but themselves.

Foreign missionaries will be more successful when they can *show* Christianity to the heathen and not merely tell them about it.

We are less convinced by what we hear than by what we see.

What the world wants is not advice but examples. Any fool can talk.

Example is not the main thing in influencing others. It is the only thing.

No one is more confusing than the fellow who gives good advice while setting a bad example.

A pint of example is worth a gallon of advice.

People take your example far more seriously than they take your advice.

We do more good by being good than in any other way.

People are guided to heaven more by footprints than by guideposts.

No one will ever know of your honesty unless you give out some samples.

People seldom improve when they have no model to copy but themselves.

It is impossible for you to influence others to live on a higher level than that on which you live yourself.

Just one act of yours may turn the tide of another person's life.

Juvenile delinquency would disappear if kids followed their parent's advice instead of their examples.

Delinquents are children who have reached the age when they want to do what papa and mama are doing.

There would be less juvenile delinquency if parents led the way instead of pointing to it.

The reason parents don't lead their children in the right direction is because the parents aren't going that way themselves.

Love is more easily demonstrated than defined.

Nothing worries a parent more than the uneasy feeling that his children are relying more on his example than his advice.

It never occurs to some politicians that Lincoln is worth imitating as well as quoting.

The greatest power for good is the power of example.

The prayers a man lives on his feet are just as important as those he says on his knees.

Prayer does not need proof, it needs practice.

Practical prayer is harder on the soles of your shoes than on the knees of your trousers.

The world looks at preachers out of the pulpit to know that they mean in it.

He who practices what he preaches may have to put in some overtime.

People are won to your religious beliefs less by description than by demonstration.

A man has no more religion than he acts out in his life.

True religion is the life we live, not the creeds we profess.

What a great world this would be if people would spend as much energy practicing their religion as they spend quarreling about it.

The hardest job that people have is to move their religion from their throats to their muscles.

People don't really pay much attention to what we say about our religion, because they'd rather watch what we do about it.

It's time for us to stop putting more saints in stained glass and start putting more in shoe leather.

It's extremely difficult to sell anyone a product you've never used — or a religion you've never lived.

To really know a man, observe his behavior with a woman, a flat tire, and a child.

We talk a great deal of religion in this country, but we need to stop long enough to let our feet catch up with our mouths.

It is easier to preach ten sermons than it is to live one.

All sermons should have handles on them so people could pick them up and carry them home.

You can preach a better sermon with your life than with your lips.

As a general rule, teachers teach more by what they are than by what they say.

The worst danger facing the younger generation is the example of the older generation.

Excuses

If you have an excuse, don't use it.

Most failures are expert at making excuses.

Excuses fool no one but the person who makes them.

There are always excuses available if you are weak enough to use them.

A real man is one who finds excuses for others, but never for himself.

You can catch some men without money, without tobacco, but never without an excuse.

There aren't really enough crutches in the world for all the lame excuses.

Never give an excuse that you would not be willing to accept.

An excuse is usually a thin skin of falsehood stretched tightly over a bald-faced lie.

It is soon going to be too hot to do the job it was too cold to do last winter.

An excuse is a statement given to cover up for a duty not well done, or not done at all.

When you don't want to do anything, one excuse is as good as another.

The man who really wants to do something finds a way; the other man finds an excuse.

If you need some kind of an excuse, see your preacher; he has heard more than anybody else.

The most unprofitable item ever manufactured is an excuse.

Those who are most successful in making excuses have no energy left for anything else.

Time wasted thinking up excuses would be better spent avoiding the need for them.

The most prolific inventors are those who invent excuses for their failures.

For every sin Satan is ready to provide an excuse.

A flimsy excuse is one that your wife can see through.

Great riches await the man who will manufacture crutches for lame excuses.

Some executives call passing the buck delegating authority.

People are great manufacturers. Some make good, others make trouble, and some just make excuses.

Executives

When they say a man is a "born executive," they mean his father owns the business.

A good executive is one who can make decisions quickly — and sometimes correctly.

Plaque on the desk of an executive: "Once I thought I was wrong — but I was mistaken."

Some executives call passing the buck delegating authority.

A certain ineffective executive was recently fired. No one filled his vacancy. He didn't leave one.

An executive is a fellow who can take as long as he wants to make a snap decision.

One of the greatest failings of our present-day executive is his inability to do what he's supposed to do.

A survey shows that slender executives make more money than fat ones. The chunky son of the president is apt to be an exception.

Sign on a junior executive's desk: "It's not whether you win or lose — it's how you place the blame.

An executive refused an employee's request for a raise, adding, "I know you can't get married on what I pay you —and some day you'll thank me."

An executive reports that his secretary is making two hundred a week. Not dollars — mistakes!

Some big executives have computers to do all their thinking for them. Some just have wives.

The executive most hated by those around him is the one who is always annoying office workers by asking them to do something.

A business executive in Denver gave his employees long vacations to find out which ones he could do without.

Executives of large industrial firms are looking for men between twenty-five and thirty with forty years of experience.

Sign on an executive's desk: "Don't tell me what I mean. Let me figure it out myself."

If you want a job done fast, give it to a busy executive. He'll have his secretary do it.

A good executive is judged by the company he keeps — solvent.

Slogan of a new executive: "If you haven't developed ulcers, you're not carrying your share of the load."

An honest executive is one who shares the credit with the man who did all the work.

An executive is one who hires others to do the work he's supposed to do.

A modern executive is a man who wears out his clothes at the seat of his pants first.

Sign on a Chicago executive's desk: "It's too late to agree with me. I've already changed my mind."

The best executive is the one who has sense enough to pick good people to do what he wants done, and self-restraint enough to keep from meddling with them while they do it.

An executive is a man who talks to the visitors while others are doing the work.

The chief executive of a large business firm in Milwaukee told his underlings at an office meeting, "The day of the yes-man is over. Does everybody agree?"

With some executives the real test of a good idea is whether they thought of it first.

Exercise

If it weren't for picketing many Americans wouldn't walk at all.

Walking a mile for a cigarette may be healthier than smoking one.

Jumping to conclusions is about the only exercise some people get.

Those who perform the modern dance exercise everything except discretion.

It's time to go on a diet when you notice you're puffing going *down* stairs.

Walking is good exercise if you can dodge those who aren't.

Digging for facts is better mental exercise than jumping to conclusions.

If exercise is so good for us, why do so many athletes retire at thirty-five?

The exercise that wears most people out is *running* out of cash.

There's nothing like a little exercise to change a man's life — especially if it's a walk down a church aisle.

The best exercise today is hunting for bargains.

If it weren't for giving directions, some people wouldn't get any exercise at all.

The stock market gives you a lot of exercise — you run scared, lift your hopes, and push your luck.

About the only exercise some young fellows get is running out of money and after women.

Some people get all their mental exercise by climbing up and down molehills.

The best thing to get out of exercise is rest.

Thanks to jogging more people are collapsing in perfect health than ever before.

A woman in Montana recently complained that the only exercise her husband gets is changing the dial on their TV set.

Too many people confine their exercise to jumping to conclusions, running up bills, stretching the truth, bending over backward, lying down on the job, sidestepping responsibility, and pushing their luck.

If some people didn't lift their eyebrows they never would get any exercise.

The only exercise some people get in the morning is brushing their teeth and sharpening their tongues.

Many a man who is too tired to help around the house plays golf for exercise.

Violent exercise after sixty is apt to be harmful — especially if you do it with a knife and fork.

Exercise doesn't make you nearly as hungry as thinking does — especially thinking about food.

The only exercise some people get is pulling ice trays out of the refrigerator.

About the only part of the body that is over-exercised is the lower jaw.

The trouble with some wives is that their idea of exercise is making bank withdrawals.

The best exercise is to exercise discretion at the dining table.

Many men hire someone to mow their lawns so they can play golf for exercise.

The trouble with being physically fit is that you're apt to wear yourself out trying to stay that way.

The physical condition of a man can best be judged from what he takes two of at a time — stairs or pills.

If you must exercise, why not exercise kindness?

You've reached middle age when all you exercise is caution.

A sleepwalker is the only person who gets his rest and his exercise at the same time.

Experience

The best advice you'll get is from someone who made the same mistake himself.

Sixty-five is the age when one acquires sufficient experience to lose his job.

The study of the Bible is a postgraduate course in the richest library of human experience.

Character grows in the soil of experience, with the fertilization of example, the moisture of desire, and the sunshine of satisfaction.

Train your child in the way you now know you should have gone yourself.

The least expensive education is to profit from the mistakes of others — and ourselves.

Education is what you get from reading the small print in a contract. Experience is what you get from not reading it.

Executives of large industrial firms are looking for men between twenty-five and thirty with forty years of experience.

If experience is the best teacher, many of us are mighty poor pupils.

Experience has been described as "Compulsory Education."

Trying to give people the benefit of your experience is one way of getting a lot more.

Experience is about the cheapest thing a fellow can get if he's smart enough to get it secondhand.

One thing about the school of experience is that it will repeat the lesson if you flunk the first time.

Experience is what helps you make an old mistake in a new way.

The wealth of experience is one possession that has not yet been taxed.

About all some of us get from experience is experience.

Experience is what you have left after you've pulled the boner.

Past experience should be a guidepost — not a hitching post.

Don't expect to buy experience at a discount house — it can't be done.

A wise man learns by the experience of others. An ordinary man learns by his own experience. A fool learns by nobody's experience.

Every time you think you've graduated from the school of experience, somebody thinks up a new course.

Experience is the best teacher, and considering what it costs, it should be.

It requires experience to know how to use it.

It was bitter experience that put the "prod" into the prodigal son.

There is no way to get experience except through experience.

Experience makes a person better or bitter.

Experience is not only an expensive teacher, but by the time you get through her school, life is over.

One thorn of experience is worth a whole wilderness of warning.

Experience is sometimes a very costly commodity that rarely has little resale value.

Some people speak from experience; others, from experience don't speak.

Experience increases our wisdom but doesn't seem to reduce our follies.

Some people profit by their experiences; others never recover from them.

Experience may be a thorough teacher, but no man lives long enough to graduate.

If a man could sell his experiences for what they cost him, he would never need Social Security.

Experience is often what you get when you were expecting something else.

The school of experience would be more pleasant if there were a vacation once in a while.

Experience is what you've got when you're too old to get a job.

The school of experience never changes; it always issues its diplomas on the roughest grade of sandpaper.

If experience is the best teacher, how is it that some husbands still think they're the boss of the family?

We learn from experience. A man never wakes up his second baby just to see it smile.

Experience may not be worth what it costs, but we can't seem to get it for any less.

Many people are beginning to learn that the cost of experience has gone up like everything else.

Experience is a form of knowledge acquired in only two ways — by doing and by being done.

One reason experience is such a good teacher is that she doesn't allow any dropouts.

Experience is what prevents you from making the same mistake again in exactly the same way.

There is no free tuition in the school of experience.

By the time you learn all the lessons of life, you're too old and weak to walk to the head of the class.

Experience is what makes your mistakes so familiar.

Very few people listen to the voice of experience — they heed only the kick in the pants.

Experience surely teaches that there's a small but important difference between keeping your chin up and sticking your neck out.

About the time one makes good marks in the school of experience he is old enough to retire.

Experience is a great teacher, but the fees are high.

Unused experience is a dead loss.

Experience is one thing you can't get on the easy payment plan.

The proof that experience teaches us nothing is that the end of one love affair does not prevent us from beginning another.

Experience is what teaches you that you need a lot more.

Another reason why experience is the best teacher — she is always on the job.

Experience is what tells you to watch your step, and it is also what you get if you don't.

When you pay for experience, be sure to keep the receipt.

Experience may be the best teacher, but she's not the prettiest.

A failure is a man who has blundered and is not able to cash in on the experience.

Old fools are the biggest fools. This is quite natural because they've had more experience.

One-fifth of the population of the United States is in the schools, and the other four-fifths are in the school of experience.

The most difficult school is the school of hard knocks. One never graduates.

A person becomes wise by observing what happens when he isn't.

Our wisdom usually comes from our experience, and our experience comes largely from our foolishness.

The man who has to eat his own words never asks for another serving.

Experts

A style expert can make a woman feel modest when she doesn't look it.

An expert can take something you already know and make it sound confusing.

An expert knows all the answers — if you ask the right questions.

The public would have greater respect for the judgments of experts if the experts would agree.

Often an expert is the fellow you employ to do what you'd rather not.

Be careful about calling yourself an expert. An *ex* is a has-been, and a *spurt* is a drip under pressure.

The trouble with being an expert is that you can't turn to anybody else for advice.

An expert is someone who doesn't know any more than you do but is better organized.

Fashion experts tell us that women dress to express themselves — but on that basis, some have very little to say.

An expert is always able to create confusion out of simplicity.

What this country needs today is fewer experts on what this country needs.

An expert is a man who doesn't know all the answers, but is sure that if he's given enough money he can find them.

The function of an expert is not to be right more than other people, but to be wrong for more sophisticated reasons.

An expert is a man from another city; the farther away the city, the greater the expert.

Have you noticed that an expert will gladly give you his advice fee-ly?

If you want to know how to handle a big fortune, ask the man who hasn't any.

If the world blew itself up, the last audible voice would be that of an expert saying it couldn't be done.

Extravagance

The remarkable thing about most of us is our ability to live beyond our means.

The average man's ambition is to be able to afford what he's spending.

America may be the land of the free, but not the debt-free.

America unquestionably has the highest standard of living in the world. Too bad we can't afford it.

America is rapidly proving to be a place with two cars in every garage — and none of them paid for.

America is the land of the spree and the home of the crave.

If Americans bought only what they could afford it would destroy our economy.

The average American doesn't really believe he is having a good time unless he is doing something he can't afford.

Living on a budget is the same as living beyond your means except that you have a record of it.

The American dream is owning a British sports car, smoking a Havana cigar, and drinking Russian vodka on the French Riviera.

Planned economy is fast becoming calculated extravagance.

167

Americans sink millions of dollars in unsound financial schemes, one of which is trying to keep up with the neighbors.

Extravagance is anything you buy that you can't put on a credit card.

The extravagant girl usually makes a poor mother and a bankrupt father.

One reason why a great many American families don't own an elephant is that they have never been offered one for a dollar down and a dollar a week.

Buying what you don't need often ends up in needing what you can't buy.

Most of us would be better off financially if it weren't for the extravagance of our neighbors.

We never knew what real extravagance was until we had this so-called planned economy.

The thing that keeps some men broke is not the wolf at the door but the silver fox in the window.

Extravagance is buying whatever is of no earthly value to your wife.

Most husbands know what an extravaganza is. They married one.

Thanks to inflation it's costing more than ever to live beyond our means.

Too many of us spend our time the way politicians spend our money.

Increased earnings nearly always lead to increased yearnings.

It is especially hard to work for money you've already spent for something you didn't need.

F

Facts
Failure
Faith
Fame
Families
Family Trees
Fanatics
Farmers
Fast Living

Fate
Faults
Fear
Fishermen
Fishing
Flattery
Flirting
Flowers
Food

Fools
Forgiveness
Frankness
Freedom
Free Speech
Friends
Friendship
Future

Facts

A sure way to stop a red-hot argument is to lay a few cold facts on it.

Our Congress is continually appointing "fact-finding" committees when what they really need are some "fact-facing" committees.

A veteran congressman told a freshman colleague, "In Washington, if you're not confused, you haven't heard all the facts.

Education is not a head full of facts, but knowing *how* and *where* to find facts.

Digging for facts is better mental exercise than jumping to conclusions.

The hardest thing about facts is to face them.

There is nothing as effective as a bunch of facts to spoil a good rumor.

It's a well-known fact that the older a man gets, the faster he could run as a boy.

Facts do not cease to exist just because they are ignored.

When people agree as to what the facts are, they often disagree as to what the facts mean.

People should keep their mouths shut and their pens dry until they know the facts.

Getting the facts is only half the job; the other half is to use them intelligently.

Facts mean nothing unless they are rightly understood, rightly related, and rightly interpreted.

Every man has a right to his opinion, but no man has a right to be wrong about the facts.

Facts are troublesome things to the evildoer.

An ounce of facts is worth a ton of arguments.

A thousand possibilities do not make one fact.

Fact is fact and feeling is feeling; never does the second change the first.

There's one thing for which you should be thankful — only you and God have all the facts about yourself.

It's easier to get facts than to face them.

It's easier to believe a lie that one has heard a thousand times than to believe a fact that no one has heard before.

Facts are worthless to a man if he has to keep running to somebody else for advice on how to use them.

Facts that are not frankly faced have a habit of stabbing us in the back.

Facts, when combined with ideas, constitute the greatest force in the world.

Facts do not change; feelings do.

A gossip is one who can give you all the details without knowing any of the facts.

History is nothing more than the art of reconciling fact with fiction.

Some people are always indebted to their imagination for facts.

Overheard: "I wouldn't exactly call him a liar. Let's just say he lives on the wrong side of the facts."

It is easier to believe a lie that one has heard a thousand times than a fact no one ever heard before.

It's a lot easier to form an opinion when you have only a few of the facts.

An opinion is usually a prejudice with a few unrelated facts.

An opinion is often a minimum of facts combined with prejudice and emotion.

Our present generation is so smart it can form an opinion without consulting any of the facts.

To be a successful orator one must be able to cover indefinite facts with infinite words.

Give a politician some facts and he'll draw his own confusions.

To be extremely popular, one must be more tactful than truthful.

Prejudice is a great timesaver. It enables you to form opinions without bothering to get the facts.

Prejudice is an unwillingness to be confused with facts.

Let's keep our mouths shut and our pens dry until we know the facts.

Facts are stubborn, but statistics are more pliable.

Statisticians collect facts, then draw their own confusions.

Failure

The only thing in life achieved without effort is failure.

You can always tell a failure by the way he criticizes success.

The gap between enthusiasm and indifference is filled with failures.

Envy provides the mud that failure throws at success.

Most failures are expert at making excuses.

The most prolific inventors are those who invent excuses for their failures.

One of the greatest failings of our present-day executive is his inability to do what he's supposed to do.

The train of failure usually runs on the track of laziness.

Many of life's failures are men who did not realize how close they were to success when they gave up.

Failure is a better teacher than success, but she seldom finds an apple on her desk.

A failure is a man who has blundered and is not able to cash in on the experience.

Failure always overtakes those who have the power to do without the will to act.

There are a great many more trapdoors to failure than there are shortcuts to success.

Life's greatest failure is failing to be true to the best you know.

Failures are divided into those who thought and never did, and those who did and never thought.

Formula for failure: Try to please everybody.

Sometimes a noble failure serves the world as faithfully as a distinguished success.

People don't accidentally stumble into failure. They think their way into it.

There are a lot of ways to become a failure, but never taking a chance is the most successful.

No man ever fails until he fails on the inside.

Failure is not necessarily missing the target, but aiming too low.

Stopping at third base adds no more to the score than striking out.

If you have tried your hand at something and failed, the next best thing is to try your head.

Four word story of failure: Hired, tired, mired, fired.

Falling down doesn't make you a failure, but staying down does.

A man is a failure who goes through life earning nothing but money.

Failure is not the worst thing in the world. The very worst is not to try.

No one is a failure who can truly say, "I have done my best."

Many people are not failures. They just started at the bottom and liked it there.

The difference between failure and success is doing a thing almost right and doing it exactly right.

Many a man has failed because he has a wishbone where his backbone ought to have been.

The road to failure is greased with the slime of indifference.

There are only two kinds of failures: the man who will do nothing he is told, and the man who will do nothing else.

A failure in life is one who lives and fails to learn.

Fear of failure is the father of failure.

Failure always catches up with those who sit down and wait for success.

Boasting and sleeping are the forerunners of failure.

The last time you failed, did you stop trying because you failed — or did you fail because you stopped trying?

Failure is more frequently from want of energy than want of capital.

The fact that a man can do as he pleases often accounts for his lack of success.

There is something to be gained from just about everything, even our failures.

Failure is the path of least persistence.

Most of us don't fear failure as much as we dread getting blamed for it.

It's difficult, if not impossible, to have faith in God if a man has too much faith in himself.

Love does not keep a ledger of the sins and failures of others.

The man who tried his hand at something and failed might try using his head for a change.

Nature gave men two ends — one to sit on and one to think with. Man's success or failure is dependent on the one he uses most.

Success isn't necessarily permanent — but neither is failure.

If the truth were known, most successes are built on a multitude of failures.

Men sometimes credit themselves for their successes, and God for their failures.

The man who fails while trying to do good has more honor than he who succeeds by accident.

Success makes failures out of too many people.

The reason some men don't go very far in life is that they sidestep opportunity and shake hands with temptation.

Wisdom is learned more from failure than from success.

Right is a bigger word than either success or failure.

Faith

Christianity helps us face the music, even when we don't like the tune.

No one can become a Christian on his own terms.

The Christian life is like an airplane — when you stop you drop!

We are sometimes so interested in creating the machinery of the church that we let the fire go out in the boiler.

Perhaps you had never thought of going to church as a beauty treatment, but it is a wonderful way to get your faith lifted.

Dentists have more faith in people than anybody. It's a miracle that more of them don't get their fingers bitten off.

Feed your faith and doubt will starve to death.

Doubt makes the mountain which faith can move.

A wise man once said that enthusiasm is nothing but faith with a tin can tied to its tail.

No one has more faith than the person who plays a slot machine.

It is when men stop having faith in one another that they stop having faith in their government.

The world will not be convinced of your faith by the sourness of your face.

Before a person sets out to test his faith by trying to move a mountain, he should begin with a molehill and work up.

Too much of the Christian faith has become trimming on the dress of life instead of a part of the fabric.

A person's faith is not judged by what he says about it, but by what he does about it.

When you cease to use your faith, you lose it.

Faith is to the soul what a mainspring is to a watch.

The greatest act of faith takes place when a man finally decides that he is not God.

Genuine faith is assuring, insuring, and enduring.

All men need a faith that will not shrink when washed in the waters of affliction and adversity.

The greatness of our fears shows us the littleness of our faith.

Feed your faith and your doubts will starve to death.

Faith keeps the man who keeps his faith.

How would a person ever know whether his faith was weak or strong unless it has been tried and tested?

Faith without works is like an automobile without gas.

It is sickly faith that is shaken because some frail human being goes wrong.

Faith gives us the courage to face the present with confidence, and the future with expectancy.

There is no better demonstration of faith than a man planting seed in a field.

Faith builds a bridge from this world to the next.

There are a thousand ways of pleasing God, but not one without faith.

Faith does not demand miracles, but it often accomplishes them.

If your faith cannot move mountains, it ought to at least climb them.

What is faith but to believe what you do not see?

There are some whose faith is not strong enough to bring them to church services, but they expect it to take them to heaven.

Believe that life is worth living and your belief will help create the fact.

Faith is the daring of the soul to go farther than it can see.

Your faith gets a real test when you find yourself in church with nothing less than a twenty dollar bill in your wallet.

When a man wants to believe something, it doesn't take much to convince him.

In all relationships of life, faith is worthless unless it leads to action.

Faith is better company than imagination for the wife whose husband fails to come home on time.

The man who believes in nothing but himself lives in a very small world.

Every tomorrow has two handles. We can take hold of it by the handle of anxiety, or by the handle of faith.

Faith is the wind that blows the sail of our ship of hope toward the desired destination.

When you become wrinkled with care and worry, it's time to have your *faith* lifted.

Faith either moves mountains or tunnels through.

Both faith and fear sail into the harbor of your mind, but only faith should be allowed to anchor.

Faith is the hinge that holds the believer to a personal relationship with God.

Faith is something like electricity. You can't see it, but you can see the light.

Living without faith is like driving in a fog.

Faith is the effort to believe what your common sense tells you isn't true.

Faith with works is a force. Faith without works is a farce.

When you pin your faith on some folks you ought to use a safety pin.

Faith gives man a harbor where he can drop anchor and feel safe.

Not as many people have lost faith in America as you might think. An awful lot of them still sign up for a thirty-year mortgage.

Faith in mankind will be a reality when they stop hauling money in armored cars.

No one can live in doubt when he has prayed in faith.

Faith helps us walk fearlessly, run confidently, and live victoriously.

Our faith deals with what God says — not what learned men say.

Faith is the magic formula that supplies starch to the spine.

Thinking will get us to the foot of the mountain; faith will get us to the top.

Faith, hope, and charity — if we had more of the first two we'd need less of the last.

Belief in God will help you most if you also believe in yourself.

The greatness of our fear shows us the littleness of our faith.

Fear falls before the fortress of faith.

The future holds something in store for the individual who keeps faith in it.

When we do what we can, God will do what we can't.

It should be a great comfort to know that God still has His hands on the steering wheel of the universe.

God doesn't call us to be successful. He calls us to be faithful.

God makes a promise — faith believes it, hope anticipates it, patience quietly awaits it.

Some people ask the Lord to guide them; then they grab the steering wheel.

Hope is putting faith to work when doubting would be easier.

Prayer gives strength to the weak, faith to the fainthearted, and courage to the fearful.

Faith may move mountains, but only hard work can put a tunnel through.

Fame

If you think you are important, just remember that a lot of famous men of a century ago have weeds growing over their graves today.

An expert is a man from another city; the farther away the city, the greater the expert.

Behind every famous man there's a woman — telling him he's not so hot.

When a person starts to rest on his laurels, he discovers they are poison ivy.

Fame is chiefly a matter of dying at the right time.

One can always tell a truly great man by the fact that at least ten thousand persons went to school with him in the small town where he grew up.

No one ever traveled the road to fame on a free pass.

Many a man thinks he has become famous when he merely happened to meet an editor who was hard-up for material.

Some men's names appear in the paper only three times: when they're too young to read, when they're too dazed to read, and when they're too dead to read.

The fame of great men ought always to be estimated by the means used to acquire it.

Money, achievement, fame, and success are important, but they are bought too dearly when acquired at the cost of health.

While some people rise to the pinnacle of fame, others reach the height of folly.

Families

Many a family argument has been saved by the doorbell or telephone.

There is just as much authority in the family today as there ever was — only now the children exercise it.

What the average man wants to get out of his new car is the kids.

You should drive your car as if your family was in the other car.

Charity should begin at home, but most people don't stay at home long enough to begin it.

Children may tear up a house, but they never break up a home.

The best Christmas gift of all is the presence of a happy family all wrapped up with one another.

In some families it would be best if the children were properly spaced — about one hundred yards apart.

If you go to the beach just remember that the family that bakes together aches together.

The family that stays together probably has only one car.

A family consists of a husband who gets an idea, the kids who say it can't be done, and the wife who does it.

Nowadays the family that buys together cries together.

The trouble with some American families is that they have Cadillac tastes and compact incomes.

It really doesn't matter who wears the pants in the family, just so there's money in the pockets.

The greatest institution in the world is the human family.

A religious family has been described as one where the father says grace before every meal, and the mother says "Amen" when the football game is over.

It's hard to raise a family — especially in the morning.

The advantage of a large family is that at least one of the children may not turn out like the others.

As the gardener is responsible for the products of his garden, so the family is responsible for the character and conduct of its children.

The family altar would alter many a family.

Modern families don't seem to worry about the wolf at the door anymore. They just feed him on installments.

A happy family is like a baseball team — with Mom pitching, Dad catching, the kids fielding, and everyone taking a turn at bat.

Families that pray together stay together, and families that work together — eat.

The head of the American family should speak in a loud, firm voice — and she does!

Nowadays families seem to be either multiplying or dividing.

Families with babies and families without babies are sorry for each other.

A lot of American families are so poor they have only one automobile and one boat.

Growing families have a way of outgrowing everything — especially their incomes.

Can you remember when the family meals were thought out carefully instead of thawed out?

If you're wondering what happened to the old-fashioned girl, you'll probably find her at home with her husband and children.

Nowadays there are more model homes than model families.

It's a happy home where the only scraps are those brushed off the dining table.

The American family and the United States government are in agreement about one thing — neither of them can live within their income.

In today's world of inflation a big spender is any man who supports a wife and kids.

Happy laughter and family voices in the home will keep more kids off the streets at night than the strictest curfew.

There's no sure cure for laziness in a man, but a wife and children often help.

A real family man is one who looks at his new child as an addition rather than a deduction.

The most wonderful thing ever made by man is a living for his family.

One of life's major mistakes is being the last member in the family to get the flu — after all the sympathy has run out.

It takes a raft of money to keep the family afloat these days.

Some people never change their opinions because they've been in the family for generations.

Keeping peace in the family requires patience, love, understanding, and at least two television sets.

Domestic peace is the luxury you enjoy between the children's bedtime and your own.

There aren't many old-fashioned family doctors around these days largely because there aren't many old-fashioned families.

The remarkable thing about family pride is that so many people can be so proud of so little.

It seems that Satan first makes friends with the parents to make it easier to get their boys and girls.

Family Trees

You can't make a place for yourself under the sun if you keep sitting in the shade of the family tree.

When some people talk about their family tree, they trim off a branch here and there.

People who depend on their family tree for status should shake it first.

The fellow who's always leaning on his family tree never seems to get out of the woods.

A man in Montana recently paid a research outfit one thousand dollars to have his family tree traced — and in a few days, another five hundred dollars to forget what it found.

Some family trees suffered from lack of trimming.

The best thing to do with the average family tree is to spray it.

A grafter seldom improves the family tree.

If we climb high enough in our family tree we are likely to find something hanging there that is not an apple.

A good family tree is a useful object to climb into society with.

What this country needs is more family trees that will produce more lumber and fewer nuts.

Even the best family tree has its sap.

Some families can trace their ancestry back three hundred years, but can't tell you where their children were last night.

One thing most family trees have in common is a shady branch.

It takes about five or six years for a tree to produce nuts, but this doesn't apply to a family tree.

Most family trees have had at least one crop failure.

A family tree is something you pay a little to have looked up, and then pay more to have hushed up.

The cheapest way to have your family tree traced is to run for public office.

The appearance of the sap is a sign of continued vigor in all trees except the family tree.

Family trees seem to produce a variety of nuts.

Every part of the family constitutes a part of the family tree. Father is the rough bark and fiber, the rugged part which supports and protects it. Mother is the heart, which must be sound and true or the tree will die. The daughter may be likened to the leaves and flowers that adorn it. The son is almost always the sap.

Fanatics

Motivation without knowledge produces fanaticism.

Fanaticism is redoubling your efforts when you have forgotten your aim.

Fanaticism is the false fire of an overheated mind.

Have you ever noticed that a fanatic sticks to his guns whether they're loaded or not?

A fanatic is one who can't change his opinions and won't change the subject.

A fanatic usually has such a huge chip on his shoulder that it causes him to lose his balance.

A fanatic is a man who does what he thinks the Lord would do if He knew all the facts in the case.

Zeal without knowledge is fanaticism.

Farmers

What this country needs is more people raising beans and fewer people spilling them.

If Congress can pay farmers not to raise crops, why can't we pay Congress not to raise taxes?

There is no better demonstration of faith than a man planting seed in a field.

There is no need for a farmer to retire and move to the city. If he will stay where he is the city will soon come and annex him.

A wise farmer puts as much thought to sowing as he does to reaping.

About the only farm movement which will benefit the farmers are those that start about daybreak and end at sunset.

A lucky farmer is one who has raised a bumper crop of good boys.

The farmer doesn't go to work. He wakes up every morning surrounded by it.

One thing farmers aren't raising enough of is farmhands.

As soon as a farmer's crop starts coming up in the field, it starts going down in the market.

A gardener raises a few things, a farmer raises many things, and the middleman raises everything.

Today's farmer must not only remember what he didn't grow but also in what field he didn't grow it.

Another reason why men don't go back to the farm is that it cost them all they had to get away.

No farmer ever plowed a field by turning it over in his mind.

Even if a farmer intends to loaf, he gets up in time to get an early start.

A gentleman farmer is a man with more hay in the bank than in the barn.

People who believe what goes down must come up are sometimes called farmers.

The American farmer prefers getting bent from hard work rather than getting crooked from trying to avoid it.

The boys would stay down on the farm if prices wouldn't.

A gentleman farmer raises nothing but his hat.

American farmers don't need protection from competition to survive. They need protection from their own government.

A farmer makes his money in the country and blows it when he comes to town.

Farmers are so closely inspected by the federal government that the country teen-agers hesitate to sow any wild oats.

Any girl who wants to be sure she will never be unemployed should marry a farmer.

Like farmers we need to learn that we can't sow and reap the same day.

Our politicians have thought of just about everything to help the farmer but to leave him alone so he can operate his own business.

The farm bloc in Congress does more blocking than farming.

Fast Living

If you burn the candle at both ends you are not as bright as you think.

The higher you get in the evening, the lower you feel in the morning.

Lots of people don't have to look at the world through rose-colored glasses — their eyes are already bloodshot.

Doctors tell us that Americans are living too fast. Traffic statistics show they are dying the same way.

A slow day always follows a fast night.

Most people seem to have plenty of speed, but they don't seem to know what direction they're going.

You can't rise with the lark if you have been on one the night before.

Bad news travels fast. In many instances, it concerns people who did the same.

If you've mortgaged the future to buy folly, don't complain when the foreclosure comes.

Life doesn't begin at forty for those who went eighty when they were twenty.

Life is like an overnight bag — if you try to cram too much into it, something has got to give.

Many people who are pleasure-bent tonight will end up pleasure-broke tomorrow morning.

Fate

Man blames most accidents on fate — but feels a more personal responsibility when he makes a hole-in-one on the golf course.

Never before has the fate of so many been at the whim of so few.

If fate throws a knife at you, there are two ways of catching it — by the blade or by the handle.

A man should never resign himself to fate because the resignation might be accepted.

Beware of fate — it loves to take advantage of anyone who believes in it.

If fate hands you a lemon, try to make lemonade.

Faults

All a bachelor has to do to discover his hidden faults is to get married.

A man who has faults he doesn't know about probably doesn't listen to his wife.

Almost all our faults are more pardonable than the methods we use to hide them.

We confess small faults to convey the impression that we have no big ones.

A gentleman in South Carolina said, "Most people won't admit their faults. I'd admit mine if I had any."

The worst fault of some people is telling others about theirs.

When looking for faults use a mirror, not a telescope.

The worst fault of a motorist is his belief that he has none.

We can do more for other people by correcting our own faults than by trying to correct theirs.

Women's faults are many. Men have only two: everything they say and everything they do.

To be swift to discuss the faults and follies of others does not necessarily imply that we are superior.

Most of our faults can be hidden, except over-eating.

Never exaggerate your faults — leave that for your friends.

The man who thinks he has no faults has at least one.

You can shut your eyes to your own faults, but the neighbors always refuse to cooperate.

The size of the other man's faults depends on how much they annoy you.

Defending your faults and errors only proves that you have no intention of quitting them.

Be patient with the faults of others; they may have to be patient with yours.

Each one of us finds in others the very faults others find in us.

Justifying a fault doubles it.

We usually tell the faults of others because it takes less time than telling our own.

After counting another person's faults, multiply by two and you will have a fair estimate of your own.

Some of us who have few faults make the most of what we've got.

If you must publish someone's faults, publish your own.

A fault which humbles a man is of more use to him than a virtue which puffs him up.

The greatest fault is to be conscious of none.

Nature couldn't make us perfect, so she did the next best thing: she made us blind to our faults.

Every man should keep a cemetery in which to bury the faults of his friends.

We can't put our faults behind us until we face them.

If the faults we see in other people were not so much like our own, we would not recognize them so easily.

The biggest obstacle many of us stumble over are our own faults.

If you want people to notice your faults, start giving advice.

The sincere man suspects that he, too, is sometimes guilty of the faults he sees in others.

Rare is the person who can weigh the faults of others without putting his thumb on the scales.

Any person can criticize, complain, and find fault — and most of them do.

Close your eyes to the faults of others and watch the doors of friendship swing wide.

The faults of others are like headlights on a passing car. They seem more glaring than our own.

Most of us can live peacefully with our own faults, but the faults of others get on our nerves.

Few people have good enough sight to see their own faults.

Deal with the faults of others as gently as you do with your own.

Our faults irritate us most when we see them in others.

Folks who are friends usually have the same virtues, the same enemies, or the same faults.

A fault which humbles a man is of more use to him than a good action which puffs him up.

Isn't it true that we judge ourselves by our best intentions and others by their worst faults?

People will overlook the faults of anyone who is kind.

Marriage is the world's most expensive way of discovering your faults.

Nature didn't make us perfect, so she did the next best thing. She made us blind to our faults.

Human nature seems to endow every man with the ability to size up everybody but himself.

We all agree that the nicest people in the world are those who minimize our faults and magnify our virtues.

Pride hides a man's faults to himself and magnifies them to everyone else.

A lot of people who boast they never go back on their word don't mind going around it a little.

You can be 100 percent certain of being a success if you decide to go into faultfinding.

It seems that many teen-agers still have faults we older people have outgrown.

Fear

One of the Ringling Brothers trapeze artists refuses to travel by plane — even if they put a net under it.

A man who refuses to fight used to be called a coward. Today they call him a bachelor.

When you can think of yesterday without regret and tomorrow without fear, you are near real contentment.

Courage is being the only one who knows you're afraid.

Remember, you are your own doctor when it comes to curing cold feet.

Courage is not the absence of fear, but the conquest of it.

Many people are so afraid of dentists they need an anesthetic just to sit in the waiting room.

Fear of failure is the father of failure.

The greatness of our fears shows us the littleness of our faith.

Both faith and fear sail into the harbor of your mind, but only faith should be allowed to anchor.

Don't be afraid to go out on a limb. That's where the fruit is.

Fear of criticism is the kiss of death in the courtship of achievement.

The one thing worse than a quitter is the man who is afraid to start.

If you're not afraid to face the music, you may someday lead the band.

Those who fear the future are likely to fumble the present.

The greatness of our fear shows us the littleness of our faith.

Fear is the darkroom where negatives are developed.

Fear falls before the fortress of faith.

The function of fear is to warn us of danger, not to make us afraid to face it.

Keep your fears to yourself, but share your courage with others.

Fear is the only thing that multiplies faster than rabbits.

The highway of fear is the shortest route to defeat.

Who is more foolish — the child who is afraid of the dark, or a man who is afraid of the light?

We fear man so much because we fear God so little.

Fear of what is called consequences keeps most of us sober, true, and *dull.*

The kind of man who doesn't know the meaning of fear is usually the kind who doesn't know the meaning of many other words either.

Fear makes fools of two kinds of men: the one who is afraid of nothing, and the other who is afraid of everything.

If you fear people will know it, don't do it.

He who is afraid of doing too much always does too little.

Fear is the tax that conscience pays guilt.

When we're afraid we say we're cautious. When others are afraid we say they're cowardly.

Fear tends to produce the thing that it's afraid of.

Many people are so filled with fear that they go through life running from something that isn't after them.

The man who is afraid of his past may have reason to be afraid of his future.

Mankind's worst enemy is fear — of work!

Folks shouldn't be fearful of tomorrow because when it comes it'll be today.

The only thing we have to fear is not doing something about the fear we have.

While fear slows down our thinking process, it greatly improves our footwork.

Fear of the future is a waste of the present.

We used to fear God; now we fear our fellow-man.

Fear not tomorrow. God is already there.

Don't let the future scare you — it's just as shaky as you are.

Don't let the future frighten you — you only face it a little at a time.

The greatest mistake you can make in this life is to be constantly fearful you will make one.

When you can think of yesterday without regret, and of tomorrow without fear, you are well on the road to success.

A cool head may sometimes keep a man out of trouble, but more often it's cold feet.

Fishermen

There are two kinds of fishermen: those who fish for sport, and those who catch something.

A Florida fisherman was arrested for fishing without a license. He denied the charge stating that he was only trying to drown the worms.

George Washington was not a fisherman — he never told a lie!

No fisherman who tells the truth about his catches can make his story very interesting.

How far a fisherman stretches the truth depends on the length of his arms.

Some fishermen don't catch anything until they get home.

It is generally agreed that no honest men are successful fishermen.

Some men become fishermen because they're not allowed to drink at home.

The typical fisherman is long on optimism and short on memory.

An honest fisherman, if there is such a thing, is a very uninteresting person.

Note from a fisherman's wife: "Wouldn't it be great if all men showed as much patience with their wives as they do with fish?"

To be a successful fisherman you should get there yesterday when the fish were biting.

A golfer has one advantage over the fisherman; he doesn't have to show anything to prove his success.

The ability to lie differs among people. For instance, a short-armed fisherman isn't as big a liar as a long-armed one.

African natives fish lying down, but in this country fishermen lie standing up with their arms outstretched.

An optimist is a fisherman who takes along a camera.

This would be a wonderful world if men showed as much patience in all things as they do in waiting for a fish to bite.

Too many men who talk of finding God in nature rather than in church go hunting for Him with rod or gun.

Fishing

There is probably no better way to loaf, without attracting a lot of criticism and unfavorable attention, than to go fishing.

Nothing makes a fish bigger than almost being caught.

Fishing stimulates the brain — also the imagination!

Any man who pits his intelligence against a fish and loses has it coming.

Fishing is the art of doing almost nothing.

It's a crime to catch fish in some lakes and a miracle in others.

Fishing is a sport that makes men and truth strangers.

Nothing grows faster than a fish from the time he bites until he gets away.

Fishing is just a jerk at one end of the line waiting for a jerk at the other end.

It's always good fishing just before you get there and just after you leave.

Fishing is a laborious way of taking it easy.

Since three-fourths of the earth's surface is water and one-fourth land, it's perfectly clear the good Lord intended that man spend three times as much time fishing as he does plowing.

Fishing is like romance; the next best thing to experiencing it is talking about it.

Religious freedom is the right of each individual to attend the church of his choice, or go fishing.

If you would like to stimulate your imagination, why not try fishing?

A liar is the type of person who gets the most enjoyment out of fishing.

Nothing improves a man's luck like fish that are in a biting mood.

Every man has three secret wishes — to outsmart racehorses, women, and fish.

Many a problem will solve itself if we forget it and go fishing.

A model wife is one who, when she spades the garden, picks up the fish worms for her husband.

Flattery

Conscience is the only mirror that doesn't flatter.

Criticism from a friend is better than flattery from an enemy.

Blessed are our enemies, for they tell us the truth when our friends flatter us.

Flattery is like chewing gum — enjoy it briefly, but don't swallow it.

However much a man may scoff at flattery, deep down in his heart he is pleased with the thought that some of it might be true.

Flattery is what makes husbands out of bachelors.

If you can't think of any other way to flatter a man, tell him he's the kind of man who can't be flattered.

Flattery is now called an "artificial sweetener."

The flattery that gets you nowhere is the kind you listen to.

Many people soft-soap their friends until they can't see anything for the suds.

Flattery looks like friendship — just like a wolf looks like a dog!

If flattery is the food of fools, why are we so starved for it?

Flattery makes you think you are better than you are, and no living person can be that!

Nothing makes it harder to detect flattery than being flattered.

Most women despise flattery, especially when it's directed toward other women.

Flattery is hearing from others the things you have already thought about yourself.

If you would like to flatter somebody, just look serious and ask them what they think of the general situation.

Flattery will get you nowhere. This is especially true when you give it to yourself.

Flattery is a commodity that makes everybody sick except those who swallow it.

Flattery is like perfume; you're supposed to smell it, not swallow it.

Flattery is the art of stretching the truth without letting anybody see through it.

A breath of kindness is more moving than a gale of flattery.

Modesty is the triumph of mind over flatter.

More people are flattered into virtue than bullied out of vice.

Insincere praise is worse than no praise at all.

The man who requests truth instead of flattery should be careful or he might get it.

Flirting

There are a lot more marital arguments over a wink than a mink.

Flowers

A rose by any other name would mean that you're ignorant about flowers.

When a man brings his wife flowers for no reason — he'd better have one.

Sign in a florist's window: "Send flowers to the one you love. While you're at it, don't forget your wife."

A single rose for the living is better than a costly wreath at the grave.

All the flowers of all the tomorrows are in the seeds of today.

Flowers are the most beautiful things that God ever made that He didn't give a soul.

Our national flower is the concrete cloverleaf.

In the language of flowers, the yellow rose means friendship, the red rose means love, and the orchid means business.

A chrysanthemum by any other name would be easier to spell.

There are some flowers that will not yield their perfume till they are bruised.

When a man brings flowers to his wife, she figures it's because of something he did or something he forgot to do.

Sign in a Florida flower shop: "Bring flowers home to your wife. She must be mad at you for something."

Saying it with flowers doesn't mean throwing bouquets at yourself.

Food

The worst thing about accidents in the kitchen is that you usually have to eat them.

Most of us are too fond of people who agree with us and food that doesn't.

Americans have more food to eat than any other people on earth, and more diets to keep them from eating it.

Americans are getting stronger. Twenty years ago it took two people to carry fifteen dollars worth of groceries. Today, a child can do it.

Don't argue at the dinner table. The one who is not hungry always wins the argument.

A baby sitter feeds the baby at ten, twelve, and two — and herself at nine, eleven, and one.

Children who are reared in homes of poverty have only two mealtime choices — take it or leave it.

A child, like your stomach, doesn't need all you can afford to give it.

A man complains about the food when he eats at home and about the price when he eats out.

Most kids think a balanced diet is a hamburger in each hand.

There's a new diet that will reduce weight like nothing else. It's called the high price of food.

The noblest of all animals is the dog, and the noblest of all dogs is the hotdog. It feeds the hand that bites it.

Violent exercise after sixty is apt to be harmful — especially if you do it with a knife and fork.

Exercise doesn't make you nearly as hungry as thinking does — especially thinking about food.

The best exercise is to exercise discretion at the dining table.

Nothing lasts as long as a box of cereal you don't like.

The trouble with square meals is that they make you round.

Some steaks are so tough it becomes necessary to tenderize the gravy.

The best thing to put into a homemade pie is your teeth.

When it comes to food for thought, some folks are on a hunger strike most of the time.

At today's pork prices, being called a pig is more of a compliment than an insult.

Carrots are definitely good for the eyes. Have you ever seen a rabbit with glasses?

More and more food is coming canned or prepackaged — including food for thought.

Most of us can't afford to eat out any more, but sometimes we park near a restaurant and inhale.

Pie isn't fattening — not the way some restaurants slice it.

There is now a margarine on the market for people over forty. It's called the "Middleage Spread."

Among life's mysteries is how a two pound box of candy can make a woman gain five pounds.

There's a new babyfood on the market. It's half orange juice and half garlic. It not only makes the baby healthier, but also easier to find in the dark.

Our next Thanksgiving menu will probably consist of roast turkey, yams, and pickled relatives.

Having no food to eat will take your mind off other troubles.

We'd better go easy on "stick to the ribs" food, because that's not where it usually sticks.

Most of us don't like fancy food covered with various sauces. We don't like to eat anything we can't see.

The people in England have hundreds of different kinds of food — much of which tastes the same.

The trouble with health foods is that you have to be healthy and strong to screw the lid off the jars.

Turnip greens are better than nothing. Ask the people who have tried both.

The best way to eat garlic is sparingly.

A chef is a man with a big enough vocabulary to give the soup a different name every day.

There's a new margarine on the market named RUMOR — because it spreads so easily and quickly.

Eating plenty of onions and garlic will help you live longer, claim dietary authorities — but you will die very lonely.

There was a time when people ordered steaks rare. Now they order steaks rarely.

Scientists tell us we are what we eat. Nuts must be more common in diets than we thought.

The best way to serve spinach is to someone else.

Spaghetti is the stuff you wind around your fork and then drop in your lap.

Wealthy people don't get enough roughage in their food, and poor people don't get enough food in their roughage.

What to eat in hot weather is a problem to some people, but what to eat in all kinds of weather is a problem to others.

Some housewives serve only those foods that are low in calories and high in trading stamps.

An onion is a vegetable that builds you up physically and tears you down socially.

An old gentleman in the hospital refused to eat a bowl of quivering jello. Pressed for an explanation by the nurse, he replied, "I'm not going to eat anything that's more nervous than I am."

Health rule: Eat like a king for breakfast, a prince for lunch, and a pauper for dinner.

The Agriculture Department says the average American eats 1,148 pounds of food a year. Of course, a lot of it goes to *waist*.

Can you remember when the family meals were thought out carefully instead of thawed out?

Soup should be seen and not heard.

Jelly is a food usually found on bread, children, and piano keys.

Many people seem to be allergic to food for thought.

Many restaurants are now listing hash on the menu as "Today's Conglomerate."

Sign in a Chicago delicatessen: "If you can't smell it, we don't have it."

We have more food in the United States per person than any other country — and more diets to keep us from eating it.

Recipe for salad from The Hippie Cookbook: "Cut up lettuce, cucumbers, green peppers, and tomatoes. Add a little marijuana and let the salad toss itself."

A wedding cake is the only cake that can give you indigestion for the rest of your life.

Have you ever thought what Swiss cheese might smell like if it were not ventilated?

A fool and his money are soon parted. The rest of us wait until we reach the supermarket.

After a good meal one can forgive anybody, even one's relatives.

A girl can win a man with the smell of perfume, but she can't keep him without the smell of good food.

Happiness is like a potato salad — when shared with others, it's a picnic.

Hash is an enthusiastic food — the cook puts all she has into it.

Home is really the only place where you can enjoy corn-on-the-cob and soup!

It's hard to keep a man's love with cold food.

Table manners must have been invented by people who were never hungry.

This year about the only thing not enriched, fortified, or reinforced is money.

The old-fashioned mother who used to have prunes every morning now has a granddaughter who has dates every night.

Some folks go *starch* raving mad when they see food.

A Christian is like ripening corn: the riper he grows, the lower he bows his head.

Our greatest need at the present time is a cheap substitute for food.

Sign in a South Carolina restaurant: "Don't make fun of our coffee. You may be old and weak yourself someday."

Some wives do wonderful things with left-overs — they throw them out.

Fools

Advice is that which the wise don't need and fools won't take.

The trouble with America today is that all the stupid people are cocksure of everything and all the intelligent people are full of doubt.

Every American has the right to make a fool of himself if he wants to, but too many folks are abusing the privilege.

He is a fool who cannot get angry, but he is a wise man who will not.

A lot of good arguments are spoiled by some fool who knows what he's talking about.

Sometimes when you're arguing with a fool, he's doing the same thing.

It is impossible to defeat an ignorant man in an argument.

People who know the least always argue the most.

Colleges don't make fools, but they occasionally develop a few.

A wise man is never confused by what he can't understand, but a fool is sure to be.

Adverse criticism from a wise man is more to be desired than the enthusiastic approval of a fool.

Any fool can criticize, condemn, and complain — and most fools do.

If a man defrauds you one time, he's a rascal; if he does it twice, you're a fool.

The age of discretion is when you make a fool of yourself in a more dignified way.

An educated man will sit up all night and worry over things a fool never dreamed of.

If you want an enemy, just try to convince a fool he's wrong.

What the world wants is not advice but examples. Any fool can talk.

A wise man learns by the experience of others. An ordinary man learns by his own experience. A fool learns by nobody's experience.

Who is more foolish — the child who is afraid of the dark, or a man who is afraid of the light?

The kind of man who doesn't know the meaning of fear is usually the kind who doesn't know the meaning of many other words either.

Fear makes fools of two kinds of men: the one who is afraid of nothing, and the other who is afraid of everything.

If flattery is the food of fools, why are we so starved for it?

A fool and his money are soon parted. The rest of us wait until we reach the supermarket.

A selfish fool is a man who says it's nobody's business what he does.

It's impossible for a man to make a fool of himself without knowing it — not if he's married.

As you grow older you can make a fool of yourself in a more dignified way.

You've never heard of a woman making a fool out of a man without a lot of cooperation.

It's bad to act like a fool, but it's worse when you're not acting.

Preachers and lawyers are paid for zeal, but fools dish it out for nothing.

It is reported that 75 percent of the people are fools, and the rest of us are in great danger of contamination.

A fool tells you what he will do; a boaster, what he has done. The wise man does it and says nothing.

Under the Constitution of the United States every man has the right to make a fool of himself as he sees fit.

Sometimes when we argue with a fool, he is doing the same thing.

A fool is a person whose brand of folly differs from your own.

Wise men think without talking; fools reverse the order.

There was a time when a fool and his money were soon parted. Now it happens to everybody.

Some people can't wait until April to make fools of themselves.

There are so many different ways of being a fool that no man can hope to dodge all of them.

Many folks display a lot of unexpected talent when it comes to acting the fool.

Twin fools: one doubts nothing, the other doubts everything.

Women make fools of some men. Other men are the do-it-yourself type.

Fools sometimes make money, but money also sometimes makes fools.

It's a man's inalienable right to make a fool of himself, but he shouldn't abuse the privilege.

Wise people sometimes change their minds — fools, never.

Old fools are the biggest fools. This is quite natural because they've had more experience.

Fools rush in where angels wouldn't even send a calling card.

Nobody can make a fool out of another person if he isn't the right kind of material for the job.

The greatest lesson in life is to realize that even fools are right sometimes.

A wise man can sometimes learn from a fool — as soon as it can be detemined which is which.

More painful than acting the fool is the sudden realization that you weren't acting.

A fool and a drunkard are two of the most mistaken human beings on earth. One thinks he is wise, and the other thinks he is sober.

There are two kinds of fools: those who can't change their opinions, and those who won't.

If anybody calls you a fool, don't insist on his proving it. He might do it.

There is no fool like an old fool. Ask any young fool.

No law has ever been passed that will keep a man from acting the fool.

A fool and his money are soon parted. The rest of us wait until income-tax time.

Nature never makes any blunders; when she makes a fool, she means it.

Let's be thankful for the fools that have lived and are now living in the world. Had it not been for them, the rest of us might not have succeeded.

A wise man reflects before he speaks; a fool speaks and then reflects on what he has uttered.

If there is a greater fool than one who is always changing his mind, it is one who never changes it.

For every woman who makes a fool out of a man, there's another woman who makes a man out of a fool.

A fool empties his head just about every time he opens his mouth.

The biggest fool of all is the person who refuses to profit by his mistakes.

There is only one way to acquire wisdom. But when it comes to making a fool of yourself, you have your choice of thousands of different ways.

There may be no fool like an old fool, but some members of our younger generation seem to be doing a pretty good job.

When one wishes to be regarded as learned he has to prove himself repeatedly, while the fool can establish his character in a single performance.

A fool may have a knowing look — until he opens his mouth.

We know that a fool and his money are soon parted, but how did they ever get together?

A fellow who is always declaring he's no fool usually has his suspicions.

We have an abundance of freedom in this country, even the freedom to make fools of ourselves.

Why is it that when a fellow's cup of happiness is full, some fool will come along and nudge his elbow?

Heredity is something a father believes in until his son begins to act the fool.

You are certain to get the worst of the bargain when you exchange ideas with a fool.

Nobody ever made a law that could prevent a man from making a fool of himself.

It's not the ups and downs of life that bother the average man — it's the jerks!

Everybody is liable to make mistakes, but fools practice them.

The main difference between a wise man and a fool is that a fool's mistakes never teach him anything.

A fool and his money are soon parted — especially with the government to expedite matters.

It's funny how we never get too old to learn some new ways to be foolish.

A foolish opinion shared by thousands is still a foolish opinion.

Only the foolish and the dead never change their opinions.

While some people rise to the pinnacle of fame, others reach the height of folly.

Some of our politicians who act foolish aren't acting.

Take one natural-born fool and one high-powered automobile. Soak fool in liquor, place in car, and turn loose. After due time, remove fool from wreckage, place in a satin-lined box, and garnish with flowers.

A man is a selfish fool who says it's nobody's business what he does.

The man who treats himself when he is sick has a fool for a physician — but at least he doesn't have to wait for an appointment.

There isn't anything more becoming for a fool than a closed mouth.

It's better to be silent like a fool than to talk like one.

If at first you don't succeed, try, try again. Then quit. There's no point in making a fool of yourself.

A foolish man tells a woman to stop talking so much, but a tactful man tells her that her mouth is extremely beautiful when her lips are closed.

Wise men always know more than they tell, but fools tell more than they know.

A wise man is not as certain of anything as a fool is of everything.

A wise man is never confused by what he doesn't understand, but a fool is sure to be.

The young people of today are no worse than we were; they just have more and different ways of making fools of themselves.

Zeal is fit only for wise men, but is found mostly in fools.

Forgiveness

Men with clenched fists cannot shake hands.

Two marks of a Christian: giving and forgiving.

Christmas is a time when everybody wants his past forgotten and his present remembered.

When you bury the hatchet, don't bury it in your enemy's back.

Sign on a company bulletin board in Grand Rapids: "To err is human, to forgive is not company policy."

Have you noticed that it's much easier to forgive an enemy after you get even with him?

The trouble with people forgiving and forgetting is that they keep reminding us they're doing it.

Forgive your enemies — if you can't get back at them any other way!

Forgiveness is a funny thing. It warms the heart and cools the sting.

After a good meal one can forgive anybody, even one's relatives.

We should forgive and then forget what we have forgiven.

We are like beasts when we kill. We are like men when we judge. We are like God when we forgive.

Forgiveness is the perfume that the trampled flower casts upon the heel that crushed it.

It is far better to forgive and forget than to hate and remember.

Forgiveness saves the expense of anger, the high cost of hatred, and the waste of energy.

Always forgive your enemies; nothing annoys them quite so much.

It isn't necessary to put a marker at the grave when we forgive and bury the hatchet.

It has been rightly said that forgiveness is the quality of heart that forgets the injury and forgives the offender.

Forgiveness is the key that unlocks the door of resentment and the handcuffs of hate. It is a power that breaks the chains of bitterness and the shackles of selfishness.

Our Lord is in the cleansing business, not the whitewashing business.

The kindest people are those who forgive and forget.

When a friend makes a mistake, don't rub it in. Rub it out.

Frankness

Frankness doesn't require being brutally so.

It's too bad those who speak straight from the shoulder can't speak from a little higher up.

Most of us like a person who comes right out and says what he thinks — especially when he thinks like we do.

Another thing that isn't worth what it costs is telling a man what you think of him.

Getting down to brass tacks is a good way to produce a puncture.

A man who says what he thinks is courageous — but friendless.

People who say what they think would not be so bad if they thought.

Freedom

It is impossible to mentally and socially enslave a Bible-reading people.

Under the Constitution of the United States every man has the right to make a fool of himself as he sees fit.

Freedom also includes the right to mismanage your own affairs.

Americans have always been willing to pay any price for freedom. If you don't believe it, look at the divorce statistics!

Freedom, like soap, can lose its strength if watered down.

We may rest assured that freedom is worth whatever it costs.

Freedom is a package deal — with it comes responsibilities and consequences.

Men fight for freedom and then start making laws to get rid of it.

Too many people are clamoring for freedom to do what ought not to be done.

The freedom of slaves is measured by the length of their chains.

Whether or not this is a free country depends on what you want to do.

Freedom is not the right to do as you please, but the liberty to do as you ought.

If all men are born free, why doesn't somebody tell the hospitals and doctors about it?

Freedom is like the air we breathe; we don't miss it until we're deprived of it.

Freedom ends when it begins to deprive another of his freedom.

This country is as free today as it ever was — unless you happen to be a taxpayer.

Freedom is not worth having if it does not include the freedom to make mistakes.

When freedom grows flabby, the tyrants become grabby.

The freedom of the press these days is the freedom to be sure that all the propaganda is on one side.

We have an abundance of freedom in this country, even the freedom to make fools of ourselves.

Creating all men free and equal isn't enough. Some means must be devised to keep them free and equal.

Freedom is not only the right to use your judgment, but the obligation to live with the consequences.

Freedom is the right all people have to be as happy as they can.

Freedom is indivisible. It is for all or none.

As a rule, the freedom of any people can be judged by the volume of their laughter.

Religious freedom is the right of each individual to attend the church of his choice, or go fishing.

Freedom is the sure possession of only those who have the courage to defend it.

Freedom is a jealous mistress. To possess her, we must reject her ancient competitor, slavery. She will not accept a divided allegiance.

If freedom is important when we don't have it, why shouldn't it be just as important when we do have it?

Freedom departs when we are no longer worthy of possessing it.

Our freedoms are lost unless they are continually fought for.

One of the best freedoms is the freedom from bad habits.

No freedom is so outrageously and so often abused as the freedom of speech.

Future generations will be born free, equal, and in debt.

As a general rule, the freedom of any people can be judged by the volume of their laughter.

The tree of liberty is one shrub that won't stand very much grafting.

No man should govern another man without the other's consent.

Newspapers are owned by individuals and corporations, but freedom of the press belongs to the people.

We should be extremely happy living in a country where we put chains on tires and not on people.

Free Speech

You can say what you please in America — but nobody listens.

Many a man who is proud of his right to say what he pleases wishes he had the courage to do so.

While living in a democracy, you can say what you think without thinking.

A democracy is a place where you can say what you please but don't have to listen unless you want to.

If you think free speech costs you nothing, try listening to some of it.

Usually the man who howls loudest about free speech has nothing worth saying.

No freedom is so outrageously and so often abused as the freedom of speech.

It's fortunate that we have freedom of speech, but it's unfortunate that the supply usually exceeds the demand.

In this country you are still privileged to free speech, but that's as far as the Constitution goes. It doesn't guarantee listeners.

Freedom not to listen is just as precious as freedom of speech.

Too many people confuse free speech with loose talk.

Why shouldn't speech be free? Very little of it is worth anything.

The only place in America where you don't have free speech is in a telephone booth.

Freedom of speech is useless unless you have something to say.

Freedom of speech is the right to argue about issues you don't understand.

Some wit has said that freedom of speech means that even a donkey has a right to bray!

The fact that you know what to say does not guarantee your right or obligation to say it.

An election year is when a lot of politicians get free speech mixed up with cheap talk.

A long-winded speaker should realize that, while the Constitution guarantees free speech, it doesn't guarantee listeners.

189

Freedom of speech is still guaranteed in Russia. You can say anything you want — at least once.

We're thankful we have free speech here in America — and equally thankful that there's no law requiring us to listen to it.

No nation is so poor that it cannot afford free speech.

The greatest danger to free speech is that many people who have it are too free with it.

Some women regard free speech, not as a right, but as a continuous obligation.

Anybody who thinks there's free speech everywhere in this country has never been on a psychiatrist's couch.

Sometimes free speech is greatly overpriced.

We ought to be thankful that we are living in a country where folks can say what they think without thinking.

Friends

When you're down and out something always turns up — and it's usually the noses of your friends.

Animals are such agreeable friends; they ask no questions, they make no criticisms.

The best antique is an old friend.

The more arguments you win, the fewer friends you'll have.

It sometimes looks foolish for folks to be spending so much time loving their enemies when they should be treating their friends a little better.

Be cautious in choosing friends, and be even more cautious in changing them.

People make enemies by complaining too much to their friends.

As long as your conscience is your friend, never mind about your enemies.

Nobody's conscience ever kept him awake at night for having exaggerated the good qualities of his friends.

The minute a man begins to feel his importance, his friends begin to doubt it.

An egotist is a person who is his own best friend.

Blessed are our enemies, for they tell us the truth when our friends flatter us.

No enemy is more dangerous than a friend who isn't quite sure whether he's for you or against you.

It is possible to learn from an enemy things we can't learn from a friend.

Some people make enemies instead of friends because it's less trouble.

Nobody can have too many friends, but one enemy may constitute a surplus.

There is only one reason why your enemy can't become your friend — YOU!

We make more enemies by what we say than friends by what we do.

Never exaggerate your faults — leave that for your friends.

Some people are very generous. They are constantly giving away their friends.

Every man should keep a cemetery in which to bury the faults of his friends.

Many people soft-soap their friends until they can't see anything for the suds.

Warm friends often freeze up at the mention of cash.

A friend will see you through after others see you are through.

A friend that isn't in need is a friend indeed.

Why not make friends before you need them?

A valuable friend is one who'll tell you what you should be told even if it momentarily offends you.

You never really know how many friends you have until you buy a house with a swimming pool and a tennis court.

Friends are like a priceless treasure; he who has none is a social pauper.

Friends last longer the less they are used.

The best recipe for making friends is to be one yourself.

Everybody should have at least two friends — one to talk *to* and one to talk *about*.

A real friend warms you by his presence, trusts you with his secrets, and remembers you in his prayers.

God gives us our relatives, but thank heaven we can choose our friends.

A good friend is one who can tell you all his problems — but doesn't.

Folks who are friends usually have the same virtues, the same enemies, or the same faults.

A true friend thinks of you when all others are thinking of themselves.

You can usually tell how close your closest friend is if you ask him for a loan.

A friend will joyfully sing with you when you are on the mountain top, and silently walk beside you through the valley.

It's smart to pick your friends — but not to pieces.

A good friend is like a tube of toothpaste — comes through in a tight squeeze.

At current prices, a friend in need is practically anybody.

The friend we admire most is the one who asks us important questions that we are able to answer.

Don't make your friends a dumping ground for your troubles.

A friend is one who is there to care.

Constant use will wear out anything — especially friends.

A real friend is one who sticks by you, even when you become successful.

You can win more friends with your ears than with your mouth.

The best way to lose a friend is to tell him something for his own good.

Knock your friends often enough and soon you'll find no one at home.

A real friend never gets in your way — unless you happen to be on the way down.

Friends are like radios — some have volume and some have tone.

With money you can buy all the friends you want, but they are never worth the price.

We hope our friends can find a way to unwind without falling apart.

Some friends stick together until 'debt do them part.'

Having money and friends is easy. Having friends and no money is an accomplishment.

A man's hair and teeth are just about his best friends, but even the best of friends fall out.

The friends you make in prosperity are those you lose in adversity.

A friend is like a dollar — hard to get and easy to throw away.

A friend will strengthen you with his prayers, bless you with his love, and encourage you with his hope.

Promises may get friends, but it is performance that keeps them.

A true friend is one who sticks by you even when he gets to know you real well.

False friends are those who roll out the carpet for you one day — and pull it out from under you the next.

When the average man becomes thoroughly acquainted with himself, he ceases to wonder why he has so few friends.

Never forget a friend — especially if he owes you anything.

Sometimes friends are just two people who are mad at the same person.

A friend in need is a drain on the pocketbook.

A friend is one who walks in when the rest of the world walks out.

A man never gets so rich that he can afford to lose a friend.

Time separates the best of friends, and so does money — and marriage!

Friends are what you think you have oodles of until you happen to be badly in need of just one.

You can't cultivate a friend by digging up dirt around him.

A friend you can buy can be bought from you.

There are three faithful friends: an old wife, an old dog, and ready cash.

A friend takes an interest in you — but not a controlling one.

It seems that a friend in need is about the only kind a person has these days.

Real friends are those who, when you've made a fool of yourself, don't feel that you've done a permanent job.

A man can have no better epitaph than that which is inscribed in the hearts of his friends.

Reprove a friend in secret, but praise him before others.

Friends are those who speak to you after others don't.

A true friend says nasty things to your face, instead of saying them behind your back.

The difference between friends and fiends is often just a typographical error.

A real friend will tell you when you have spinach stuck in your teeth.

If you were another person, would you like to be a friend of yours?

A friend is a person who knocks before he enters, not after he has taken his departure.

The difference between our friends and our enemies is this: Our friends love us in spite of our faults, and our enemies hate us in spite of our virtues.

Our friends judge us by what we are capable of doing; our enemies, by what we have done.

Sensible folks would rather have friends than money — especially friends with money.

A real friend will tell you your faults and follies in times of prosperity, and assist you with his hand and heart in times of adversity.

A good place to keep your friends is out of politics.

It is not how many friends you've won in life that counts, but how many you have left.

You can have no two better friends than the twin brothers, PULL and PUSH.

The greatest objection to many of our friends is their friends.

Prosperity makes friends; adversity tries them.

The ornaments of a house are the friends that frequent it.

You'd be surprised how you can win friends and influence people if you have some idea of what you're talking about.

The friend who is constantly trying to correct your faults is not a friend — he's a critic.

Untried friends are like uncracked eggs — you can't be sure what they're like on the inside.

You will never have a friend if you must have one without a fault.

If you really want your friends to remember you, give them something cheap.

Friends are made by many acts — they can be lost by one.

The friends we treasure most are the few who "guess" it's time to go — and do!

Be slow in choosing friends, slower in changing them.

It's better to keep a friend from falling than to help him up after he falls.

A trusted friend thinks you're a good egg — even though you might be slightly cracked.

Friends that you can buy are a dime a dozen, and will shortchange you if given a chance.

A friend is someone to have in time of need; when you're prosperous he needs you.

Your neighbor friend will continue to talk to you over the back fence even though he knows he's missing his favorite TV program.

If a fellow can't say nice things about his friends he ought to get some new friends.

Running down your friends is the quickest way to run them off.

A loyal friend is someone who sticks up for you even when you're not there.

The friend who is really worth having is the one who will listen to your deepest hurts, and feel that they are his too.

A true friend is like a good book — the inside is better than the cover.

Everybody can use friends — and almost everybody does!

The best thing one friend can do for another is to refrain from giving advice.

You can't keep your friends if you give them away.

It's nice to have close friends, but it's nicer to have generous ones.

Treat your friends like a bank account — refrain from drawing too heavily on either.

Don't bore your friends with your troubles. Tell them to your enemies, who will be delighted to hear about them.

Some friends are like your shadow — you see them only when the sun shines.

A lifelong friend is someone you haven't borrowed money from yet.

The open hand holds more friends than the closed fist.

Some people are very generous. They are constantly giving away their friends.

If all men knew what each said about the other, there wouldn't be five friends in the whole world.

The trouble with being a grouch is that you have to make new friends every few months.

It is best to test new ideas on old friends.

Judge not your friend until you stand in his place.

You can judge a man by his enemies as well as by his friends.

A task worth doing and friends worth having make life worthwhile.

If anything lucky happens to you, don't forget to tell your friends in order to annoy them.

Beware of the man who continues to tell you he's on your side. So is appendicitis.

When the average man has become thoroughly acquainted with himself, he ceases to wonder why he has so few friends.

Man is that foolish creature who tries to get even with his enemies and ahead of his friends.

Often our mistakes serve a useful purpose. Our friends find great satisfaction in pointing them out to us.

When a friend makes a mistake, don't rub it in. Rub it out.

When a man is broke he can count his friends on his thumb.

Friendless indeed is the man who has friends only because he has money.

Before borrowing money from a friend, decide which you need more.

Money separates more friends than it unites.

It may be easy to become the most popular citizen in town — if you can only find a town small enough.

Your popularity will depend on *how* you treat your friends — and how often!

There is one thing about poverty — it sticks to a fellow even after most of his friends leave him.

Until he becomes prosperous, a man doesn't realize how many old friends he has.

A man's reputation is a blend of what his friends, enemies, and acquaintances say behind his back.

It is folly to believe that the bosom of a friend can hold a secret your own could not contain.

Selfish individuals have a very easy time of it — if they can get along without friends.

People who can hold their tongues rarely have any trouble holding their friends.

When a man has climbed high on the ladder of success, quite often some of his friends begin to shake the ladder.

Success is the only thing some people cannot forgive in a friend.

It is extremely difficult for a man who loses his temper to hold his friends.

Hot tempers will mean cool friends.

Long tongues will mean short friends.

Troubles teach you two things: how many friends you have, and how many people are waiting to catch you bent over.

Some people may still have their first dollar, but the man who is really wealthy is the fellow who still has his first friend.

Friendship

The world needs more warm hearts and fewer hot heads.

Bees can't make honey and sting at the same time.

Always hold your head up, but be careful to keep your nose at a friendly level.

When a man borrows money from a bank he pays interest, but when he borrows from a friend he often loses interest.

No people feel more close and more friendly than those who are on the same diet.

Close your eyes to the faults of others and watch the doors of friendship swing wide.

Flattery looks like friendship — just like a wolf looks like a dog!

In the language of flowers, the yellow rose means friendship, the red rose means love, and the orchid means business.

Friendships will last if they are put first.

The best way to be sure of a man's friendship is not to put it to the test.

Friendship is like money — easier made than kept.

Ties of friendship begin to slip the moment you begin to pull on them.

No matter how useless a man is, his friendship is worth more than his hatred.

Broken friendships may be patched up, but the patch is likely to show.

Friendship is a living thing that lasts only as long as it is nourished with kindness, sympathy, and understanding.

The quickest way to wipe out a friendship is to sponge on it.

Wise is the man who fortifies his life with friendships.

The world is round so that friendship may encircle it.

Platonic friendship is the name given the period between the first look and the first kiss.

Friendship that is bought will not stay bought; sooner or later there will be a higher bidder.

You can only extend the hand of friendship; you cannot force the other fellow to grasp it.

We are on the wrong track when we think of friendship as something to get — rather than something to give.

Genuine friendship is like sound health; its value is seldom known until it is lost.

Friendships cemented together with sin do not hold.

Another good way to preserve friendship — don't work it to death.

Friendship is usually a plant of slow growth.

The bank of friendship cannot exist for long without deposits.

The best rule for friendship: Keep your heart a little softer than your head.

Friendship is the only cement that will hold the world together.

Gossip is a torpedo that has sunk many friendships.

One man's idea of humor is another man's idea of a broken friendship.

The man who has strong opinions and always says what he thinks is courageous — and friendless.

Future

It's better to look where you're going than to see where you've been.

It is useless for alcoholics to worry about the future for there will soon be no future for them to worry about.

Telling children that school days are the happiest days of their lives doesn't give them much to look forward to.

Civilization is a state of society in which the only people who speak about the future with any degree of confidence are the fortunetellers.

A congressman made the following brilliant statement: Lynching deprives a man of his constitutional rights. It also interferes with his plans for the future.

The enemy you make today may be the only one who can help you twenty-five years from now.

Faith gives us the courage to face the present with confidence and the future with expectancy.

Those who fear the future are likely to fumble the present.

The man who is afraid of his past may have reason to be afraid of his future.

Folks shouldn't be fearful of tomorrow because when it comes it'll be today.

Fear of the future is a waste of the present.

If we don't care for the future, the future won't care for us.

Don't let the future scare you — it's just as shaky as you are.

Judging from the way things look, it's a good thing the future doesn't come all at once.

No matter how much a person dreads the future, he usually wants to be around to see it.

It's disheartening to think that sometime in the future we may look back on these as the "good old days."

A lot of people who are worrying about the future ought to be preparing for it.

Most of us spend a lot of time dreaming of the future, never realizing that a little of it arrives each day.

It's better to construct the future than to varnish the past.

Fortune-tellers deserve a lot of credit. Who else would have the nerve to look into the future?

The future is the time when folks will be wishing they'd done all the things they ain't doin' now!

In the "good old days" we were told to think about the future; but if a fellow stops to think these days, the future is already here.

Hats off to the past, coats off to the future.

Never be afraid to trust an unknown future to a known God.

The trouble with the future is that it keeps getting closer and closer.

We make our future by the best use of the present.

Future generations will be born free, equal, and in debt.

Whatever your past has been, you have a spotless future.

When all is lost, the future still remains.

Some folks looking forward to a bright future may find the heat terrific!

Some carve out a future, while others just whittle away the time.

Never before has the future so rapidly become the past.

Those who remember the past with a clear conscience need have no fear of the future.

It's a good idea to take an interest in the future — that's where you will spend the rest of your life.

The future holds something in store for the individual who keeps faith in it.

It's such a tragedy that so many really nice people have such a bright future behind them.

The trouble with the future is that it usually arrives before we're ready for it.

You can't have rosy thoughts about the future when your mind is full of the blues about the past.

Some folks are so far behind, the future is gone before they get there.

The future will be different if we make the present different.

Stop fretting about the future — there'll probably be as much of it as you can stand when you get there.

There is no future in the past.

The time to get primed for the future is when you're still in your prime.

If you've mortgaged the future to buy folly, don't complain when the foreclosure comes.

You can't have a better tomorrow if you are thinking about yesterday all day today.

The future frightens only those who prefer living in the past.

Perhaps the best thing about the future is that it comes only one day at a time.

Don't take tomorrow to bed with you.

Don't let the future frighten you — you only face it a little at a time.

There is no future in any job. The future is in the man who holds the job.

We may not know *what* the future holds, but we know *who* holds the future.

Why worry about the future? Between the bomb and pollution, there may not be any.

It is a mistake to look too far ahead. Only one link in the chain of destiny can be handled at a time.

Let's not think of the future. It comes too soon!

Many fortune-tellers are quitting the business. They claim the future isn't what it used to be.

It is doubtful that you will ever carve out much of a future trying to cut too many corners.

Have you noticed that your future just keeps right on getting shorter?

Most of us are still planning for the future after it is in the past.

More people worry about the future than prepare for it.

The only way to judge the future is by the past, but if some people are judged that way, they won't have any future.

A lot of people are worrying about the future of the world, as though it had one.

The best thing to save for the future is your soul.

The only way to judge the future is by the past, but if some people are judged that way, they won't have any future.

A kindness done today is the surest way to a brighter tomorrow.

A lie may take care of the present, but it has no future.

Man spends his life reasoning with the past, complaining about the present, and trembling for the future.

The trouble with growing old is that there's not much future in it.

People who look back know where they've been but not where they're going.

A pessimist burns his bridges before he gets to them.

A pessimist can hardly wait for the future so he can look back with regret.

One way to cover up a bad past is to build a big future over it.

Why worry about the future? The present is more than most of us can handle.

One good rule for living is not to worry about the future until we have learned to manage the present.

Don't worry too much about what lies ahead. Go as far as you can see, and when you get there, you can see farther.

G

Gambling

Generosity

Genius

Gentlemen

Gifts

Girls

Giving

Goals

God

Golden Rule

Golf

Goodness

Gossip

Government

Government Spending

Grandparents

Gratitude

Greatness

Grouches

Growth

Grudges

Grumbling

Gambling

see also Las Vegas

A racehorse is an animal that can take several thousand people for a ride at the same time.

No one has more faith than the person who plays a slot machine.

Gambling is pretty much like liquor; you can make it illegal but you can't make it unpopular.

Some people will gamble on anything. Now they're saving money with the hope that it'll be worth something someday.

Never gamble in heavy traffic. The cars may be stacked against you.

The best throw of the dice is to throw them away.

Gambling is just plain stealing by mutual consent.

People who can afford to gamble don't need money, and those who need money can't afford to gamble.

Las Vegas has all kinds of gambling devices, such as dice, roulette, slot machines — and wedding chapels.

Never bet on a sure thing unless you can afford to lose.

If gambling is a disease, as some contend, can you deduct your losses as a medical expense?

It is hard to decide whether gambling is a means of getting something for nothing or nothing for something.

The first time a man bets he bets to win. The rest of the time he's trying to get even.

Gambling is the child of avarice, the brother of iniquity, and the father of mischief.

A Texas man reports he had terrible luck in Las Vegas. He lost everything he had but his cold.

Gambling is like diving into an empty swimming pool. The chances that you'll hit bottom are about the same.

No horse can go as fast as the money you bet on him.

Gamblers are like toilets — broke one day and flush the next.

He who hopes to win what belongs to another deserves to lose.

The safest bet is the one you didn't make.

Many people are violently opposed to gambling for the simple reason that they can never win anything at it.

No wife can endure a gambling husband — unless he's a steady winner.

The best way to get out of a poker game with a small fortune is to start with a large one.

Playing with dice is a *shaky* business.

The young people of the United States squander over ten billion dollars a year on games of chance. This does not include weddings, starting a business, passing cars on a hill, or buying a television set.

There is no thrill in gambling unless you are betting more than you can afford to lose.

You do not really make money in the stock market. You merely take it from somebody who guessed wrong.

The most dangerous wheel of chance is the steering wheel.

Gambling is frequently a means of getting nothing for your money.

All forms of gambling are frowned upon by preachers — except marriage.

There are two times in a man's life when he shouldn't gamble: when he can't afford it and when he can.

A slot machine is a steel trap for catching dumb animals.

Horse sense is what keeps horses from betting on what people will do.

The worst evil of gambling is that the odds are always with the house.

If it weren't for betting on horses, some people wouldn't contribute to anything.

If all gambling were illegal, we would all have to stop driving cars and getting married.

Sometimes a person goes to Las Vegas out of curiosity and comes home out of funds.

A visitor to Las Vegas received the "cook's tour" — he was baked in the sun, stewed at the bar, and burned at the crap tables.

Some people are luckier with cards than with horses — because they can't shuffle the horses.

Every man has three secret wishes — to outsmart racehorses, women, and fish.

An Arizona wit says people shouldn't get married on Sunday because it's not right to gamble on a Holy Day.

Most newspapers condemn gambling on the editorial page and print racing tips on the sports page.

Russia is a gambler's paradise; you'd never lose an election bet.

In case of an air raid, go to the nearest slot machine. It hasn't been hit in years.

A Texan, just back home from a Nevada vacation, says he underwent a bit of "Las Vegas Surgery". He had his bankroll painlessly removed.

All vices are of personal origin. Playing cards do not make the gambler, nor a bottle of liquor the drunkard.

Generosity

Feel for others — in your pocketbook!

When a man is generous, the last one to find it out is usually his wife.

A lot of folks think they are generous because they give free advice.

The open hand holds more friends than the closed fist.

Some people feel they deserve a medal for generosity if they give somebody the time of day.

Generosity will always leave a more pleasant memory than stinginess.

The true test of generosity is to give the hat-check girl a quarter without wondering if a dime would have been enough.

One form of generosity that can lead to trouble consists in giving others a piece of your mind.

Some people are very generous. They are constantly giving away their friends.

He who gives only when he is asked has waited too long.

The hardest thing to give is *in.*

Giving until it hurts is not a true measure of generosity. Some are easier hurt than others.

A typical mother, seeing there are only four pieces of pie for five people, promptly announces she never did care for pie.

Wisdom enables one to be thrifty without being stingy, and generous without being wasteful.

Genius

For every boy with a spark of genius, there are a dozen others with ignition trouble.

Men of genius are admired; men of wealth are envied; men of power are feared; but only men of character are trusted.

Common sense is genius dressed in its working clothes.

Most of us are spared the torment of genius.

A genius is a guy who solves a problem you didn't know you had and in a manner you can't understand.

Some of these young fellows whose mothers think they have a spark of genius seem to be having ignition trouble.

Genius is nothing more than inflamed enthusiasm.

A business genius is a man who knows the difference between being let in on a deal and *taken* in on one.

Genius may have its limits, but not so with stupidity.

No family should have less than three children. If there is one genius among them, there should be two to support him.

Genius is the tag we put on a bright person — which allows him to act like a nut.

A genius is any man who can adjust the thermostat to please his wife.

It is solemnly hoped that someday a genius will come along and invent something that will make golf unnecessary.

A genius shoots at something no one else sees — and hits it!

Genius is 1 percent inspiration and 99 percent perspiration.

A genius remains a crackpot until he hits the jackpot.

Often GENIUS is just another way of spelling perseverance.

So few people think. When we find one who really does, we call him a genius.

A genius is someone who thinks exactly as you do.

Gentlemen

A gentleman is a man who makes it a cinch for a woman to remain a lady.

The final test of a gentleman is his respect for those who can be of no possible service to him.

One of the marks of a gentleman is his refusal to make an issue out of every difference of opinion.

A prominent gentleman in Dayton, Ohio, denies that he is conceited, but says he's absolutely convinced that if he had never been born people would want to know why.

The first duty of a gentleman is to put back into the world the equivalent of what he has taken out of it.

If a man cannot be a gentleman where he is, he cannot be a gentleman anywhere.

There is only one way to be a gentleman — there are hundreds of ways not to be.

To be born a gentleman is an accident — to die one is an accomplishment.

To be a gentleman is a worthy trait, but it is a great handicap in an argument.

A gentleman in Georgia says he's at the age where he's too old for castor oil and too young for Geritol.

The real gentleman is the fellow who is courteous and affable even when he isn't trying to sell you something.

It takes at least three generations to create a genuine gentleman, but only one to make a bum.

Gentlemen prefer blondes — especially gentlemen who are married to brunettes.

A popular gentleman is one who can tell you all about his problems — but doesn't.

Gifts

Christmas is a time when everybody wants his past forgotten and his present remembered.

The greatest gift we can bestow on others is a good example.

A small gift will do if your heart is big enough.

For the holidays, why not give the gift that keeps on giving? — a female cat.

The gift people appreciate most is something you made yourself – such as money.

A "rare gift" is any kind a woman gets from her husband after ten years of marriage.

You'll never convince a newlywed bride that someday she might prefer a dishwasher to a mink coat.

The parents gave their daughter a new car as a birthday present. On the windshield was a card signed, "With all our love. Mama and Pauper."

Birthday gifts generally fall into two categories: those you don't like, and those you didn't get.

A practical gift is one you can afford.

Among the most expensive gifts on earth is the gift of gab.

Nothing adds to a guest's popularity like a punctual arrival — with an armful of gifts.

If we bestow a gift or a favor and expect a return for it, it's not a gift but a trade.

We buy gifts we think are swell, hoping our friends will do as well.

The time was when the perfect gift for a sixteen-year-old girl was a compact. It still is — if it has four wheels.

Nothing makes the average wife so suspicious of her husband as an unexpected gift.

The perfect gift for a man who has everything would be a girl who knows what to do with it.

A lasting gift to a child is the gift of a parent's listening ear — and heart.

It's true that gifts to charity are deductible on your income tax; the trouble is they are also deductible from your income.

The best gift for a man who has everything is a burglar alarm.

Did you hear about the wife who lamented, "My husband once showered me with gifts, but lately there's been a long dry spell."

A wise husband buys his wife fine china so she won't trust him to wash the dishes.

A good husband meets a marital crisis with a firm hand — full of candy and flowers.

Many a husband has learned that an ironclad alibi isn't as effective as a diamond-studded one.

Money is an ideal gift — everything else is too expensive!

Girls
see also Women

When a modern girl blushes she's probably been caught doing something proper.

An old-fashioned girl blushes when she is embarrassed, but a modern girl is embarrassed when she blushes.

A child of the feminine gender may be the picture of her father and have the soundtrack of her mother.

It's extremely difficult to design a gown for a girl who rides the backseat of a motorcycle.

Modern girls wear as many clothes as grandma, but not all at once.

In some foreign countries girls dress like their mothers, but in America it's the other way around.

Said a girl graduate, "Four years of college! And *whom* has it got me?"

A college girl may be poor in history, but great on dates.

Some college girls pursue learning and some others learn pursuing.

Cosmetics is used by teen-age girls to make them look older sooner, and by their mothers to make them look younger longer.

Courtship is that part of a girl's life which comes between the lipstick and the broomstick.

Real embarrassment is when you tell a girl her stockings are wrinkled when she's not wearing any.

The extravagant girl usually makes a poor mother and a bankrupt father.

Some girls can't take a joke, but others prefer one to no husband at all.

It's amazing how many things a girl can do without until she gets married.

Give a girl enough rope and she'll ring the wedding bell.

A girl can win a man with the smell of perfume, but she can't keep him without the smell of good food.

A girl becomes a woman when she stops living on her allowance and starts living on her alimony.

There never was an athletic girl who thought she was strong enough to do indoor work.

Any normal girl would rather be looked over than overlooked.

A modern girl isn't afraid of anything except a stack of dirty dishes.

Some girls think it is better to be well-formed than well-informed.

Almost any girl who has a nice steady job has no trouble getting married.

When a girl starts calling a man by his first name, she may have her eye on his last name.

One way a girl can stop a man from making love to her is to marry him.

A smart girl knows all the hazards of parking.

And there was the girl who was so lazy she wouldn't even exercise discretion.

A girl needs to keep on her toes to avoid heels.

The easier a girl is to pick up, the harder she is to drop.

To the average girl the most helpful books are mother's cookbook and father's checkbook.

Many a girl is looking for a man with a strong will — made out to her!

A career girl is one who is more interested in plots and plans than in pots and pans.

Any girl can be glamorous. All she has to do is stand still and look stupid.

When a girl marries she gives up the attention of several men for the inattention of one.

Most girls seem to marry men like their fathers. Maybe that's the reason so many mothers cry at weddings.

When you see the men some girls marry, you realize how they must hate working for a living.

A girl who is looking for a husband has to know how to play tennis, golf, the piano, and dumb.

Girls are creatures who can make up their faces more easily than their minds.

A girl is judged by the company she keeps — at a distance.

If you're wondering what happened to the old-fashioned girl, you'll probably find her at home with her husband and children.

Some girls are so homely they could sue their parents for damages.

When a girl casts her bread upon the waters, she expects it to come back to her in the shape of a wedding cake.

The girl who thinks no man is good enough for her may be right, but she is more often left.

Some of our modern girls turn a man's head with charm — and his stomach with their cooking.

Some girls feel that they might as well make a fool out of a man as to let some other girl do it.

One of life's mysteries is why a girl who has done baby-sitting ever gets married.

Some girls show a lot of style, and some styles show a lot of girl.

The old-fashioned girl who darned her husband's socks now has a daughter who socks her darned husband.

The man who wants a girl who is good, clever, and beautiful doesn't want one; he wants three.

Did you hear about the girl who was so slow she didn't even get to be a juvenile delinquent until she was twenty-three?

Any girl who wants to be sure she will never be unemployed should marry a farmer.

The fellow who once enjoyed chasing girls now has a son who can't find any who will run.

One girl to another: "I love your hair. Is it home-grown?"

A girl can catch a man with face powder, but it takes baking powder to keep him.

When a girl is single, she's pensive. After she gets married, she's ex-pensive.

Can you remember when a girl's charms were hidden?

The old-fashioned girl who used to go to the city and stop at the YMCA now has a daughter who goes to the city and stops at nothing.

Many girls are trying to break their boyfriends of a bad habit — eating alone.

Girls have an unfair advantage over men. If they can't get what they want by being smart, they get it by being dumb.

The girl who remembers her first kiss now has a daughter who can't even remember her first husband.

Why are girls so eager to get married and swap an eight-hour day for a fourteen-hour day?

Some girls will scream at a mouse and then climb in a car with a wolf.

A girl who is free for the evening can be one of the most expensive things in the world.

Most modern girls detest four-letter words such as wash, iron, cook, and dust.

Many a girl has made it to the top because her dress didn't.

Then there was the good little girl who had been saying no so long that she almost loused up her wedding ceremony.

The modern girl has all her blushing done for her by her parents, brothers, and sweethearts.

Some of our present-day girls wear less on the streets than their grandmothers wore in bed.

A girl admires the tone of a bachelor's voice when there's a ring in it.

You can tell when a girl is nice — you have to whistle at her at least twice.

Nowadays some girls seem more particular about choosing their divorce lawyers than choosing their husbands.

Girls who fall in love with a fellow at first sight sometimes wish they had taken a second look.

A girl said to her boyfriend, "Remember, I'm a computer date, and I don't want to be bent, folded, or spindled."

There are two kinds of girls: those who can get any man they like, and those who like any man they can get.

Some of our modern girls are so hard the only thing that will make an impression on them is a diamond.

The old-fashioned girl is one who stayed at home when she had nothing to wear.

Some girls get married for financial security; others get divorced for the same reason.

The modern girl's hair may look like a mop, but that doesn't seem to worry her — she doesn't know what a mop looks like.

For some girls the idea of housework is to sweep the floor with a glance.

Any girl who knows how to cook can certainly find a man who knows how to eat.

Many of our modern girls have plenty of polish — on their fingernails.

A girl certainly has a wide choice of vacations. She can go to the mountains and see the scenery, or go to the beach and be the scenery.

One of life's unsolved mysteries is what young girls giggle about.

A girl can have both a career and a successful marriage if she knows how to put both of them first.

Attention girls: Always save a boyfriend for a rainy day — and another one in case it doesn't rain.

The girl in Mississippi explained the breakup with her boyfriend, "Once he was all the world to me — but I've learned a lot of geography since."

A girl's face may be her fortune, but some of her other features draw the most interest.

A lot of girls who say they'll wait for a man who's tall and handsome finally settle for one who's short and willing.

Any girl can tell you that the only thing harder than a diamond is getting one.

The average girl would rather have beauty than brains because the average man can see better than he can think.

An old-fashioned girl is one who will not hold hands on the first date — unless it's absolutely necessary.

The girl who tends to her knitting isn't apt to have the wool pulled over her eyes.

A girl knows she's been on the right road when it turns into a bridal path.

"Girls" is what women over forty-five call each other.

Girls wear bikinis for the same reason stores have glass showcases.

Many a girl who elopes wishes later she had just let her imagination run away with her.

In these days of inflation, it's virtually an insult to tell a girl she looks like a million dollars.

There are three things most men love but never understand: females, girls, and women.

A girl may love you from the bottom of her heart, but there's always room for some other fellow at the top.

Many mothers had their daughters vaccinated in places they wrongly thought would never show.

An old-timer is one who can remember when a girl with hidden charms hid them.

For the modern girl, opportunity doesn't knock. It parks in front of her home and honks the horn.

One advantage of today's high postal rates is that when you write a girl a love letter, she knows you mean it.

Every year many American girls resolve that they're going to give up rich foods and poor boyfriends.

Football is popular with girls. They like to see men making passes.

The way taxes are now, you seldom hear any more about a girl getting married for money.

Giving

Too many people are cheerful givers only when they get a chance to hand out free advice.

Advice is the one thing which is "more blessed to give than to receive."

Charity begins at home, and generally dies from lack of outdoor exercise.

Charity is twice blessed — it blesses the one who gives and the one who receives.

It is better to give than to lend, and it costs about the same.

Two marks of a Christian: giving and forgiving.

The exchange of Christmas gifts ought to be reciprocal rather than retaliatory.

One of the nice things about Christmas is that you can make people forget the past with a present.

Notice in a church bulletin: "The Lord loveth a cheerful giver. He also accepteth from a grouch."

Criticism is one thing most of us think is more blessed to give than to receive.

We are on the wrong track when we think of friendship as something to get — rather than something to give.

The bank of friendship cannot exist for long without deposits.

If it weren't for betting on horses, some people wouldn't contribute to anything.

Blessed are those who can give without remembering, and receive without forgetting.

Always remember that it is better to give than to receive. Besides, you don't have to write thank-you notes.

The best thing you can give someone is a chance.

About all some people are giving these days is advice.

Nothing makes people more sensitive to pain than giving until it hurts.

Give with no strings attached, and you will receive in the same manner.

The way some people give, you would think the church is coin-operated.

One reason we have so many pennies in the church collection basket is because we have no smaller coins.

The devil also loves a cheerful giver — providing he is the receiver.

Where there is no interest, there is no investment.

Many people give a tenth to the Lord — a tenth of what they ought to give.

There are many nerves in the human body, but the most sensitive is the one that goes from the brain to the pocketbook.

We need to get God off the charity list and put Him on the payroll.

You receive in proportion and in kind as you have given.

When it comes to giving, some people stop at nothing.

The hardest thing to give is *in*.

From the amount that some people give to the Lord, they must be positive that it's the little things that count.

He who gives only when he is asked has waited too long.

Feel for others — in your pocketbook.

The world is composed of the takers and the givers. The takers may eat better, but the givers sleep better.

Don't give till it hurts — give till it feels good.

The Lord loves a cheerful giver — until he brags about it.

A collection at a church service is one in which many take a passing interest.

Support the church with your money. You can't take it with you, but you can send it on ahead.

Some people will bring a hymnbook or a prayerbook — but not a pocketbook to church.

A lot of people are willing to give God the credit, but not too many are willing to give him the cash.

Give not from the top of your purse, but from the bottom of your heart.

It may be more blessed to give than to receive, but it sure costs more.

When it comes to giving until it hurts, most of us have a very low threshold of pain.

Some give their mite; some give with all their might; and some who might don't give.

If it rained dollar bills, some people would try to get one changed before going to church.

"It is more blessed to give than to receive" is often quoted but seldom practiced.

More people would give to charity anonymously if it were well-publicized.

He who keeps close to God will not be "close" with God.

Give your best to the world, and the best will be given back to you.

We make a living by what we get, but we make a life by what we give.

Some folks give according to their means, and some give according to their meanness.

It is better to give than to lend, and the cost is about the same.

Giving until it hurts is not a true measure of generosity. Some are easier hurt than others.

We should give freely and generously — and in accordance with what we reported on our income tax.

Giving help to the enemy used to be called treason. Now it is called "foreign aid."

What you give lives!

Nothing makes you want to talk about it as much as giving to charity anonymously.

God looks not to the quantity of the gift but to the quality of the giver.

You can give without loving, but you can't love without giving.

In the Book of Revelation we read of a book which no man could open. Some believe this was the pocketbook.

The manner of giving is worth more than the gift.

Giving is the thermometer of our love.

There is a sense in which no gift is ours till we have thanked the giver.

The surest way to have happiness and peace of mind is to give them to somebody else.

Every man who expects to receive happiness is obligated to give happiness. You have no right to consume it without producing it.

We make a living by what we get, but we make a life by what we give.

The world is composed of givers and takers. The takers may eat better, but the givers sleep better.

Goals
see also Ideals

Some fellows dream of worthy accomplishments, while others stay awake and do them.

Having a great aim in life is important. So is knowing when to pull the trigger.

It's better to aim at a good thing and miss it than to aim at a bad thing and hit it.

There's no sense aiming for a goal with no arrow in your bow.

Following the path of least resistance is what makes rivers and men crooked.

Many people aim to do right but are just poor shots.

We never see the target a man aims at in life; we see only the target he hits.

A person going nowhere can be sure of reaching his destination.

Having the right aim in life doesn't mean a thing if you're loaded with blanks.

It is useless to have an aim in life unless one has ammunition to back it up.

There is no point in carrying the ball until you learn where the goal is.

The greatest danger for most of us is not that our aim is too high and we miss it, but that our aim is too low and we reach it.

You seldom hit anything unless you aim at it.

Anyone can be a sure shot if he shoots first and draws the circle afterwards.

Our aim should be service, not success.

Many people have a good aim in life, but for some reason they never pull the trigger.

Our aim in life improves as we grow older, but it seems that we soon run out of ammunition.

Too many of us shoot blanks when aiming at our goals.

A man with a burning ambition is seldom fired.

Few people make a deliberate choice between good and evil; the choice is between what we want to do and what we ought to do.

Most Americans have definite goals in life and attain them gradually — with the help of a finance company.

A budget is an aim that rarely shows good marksmanship.

Enthusiasm is apt to breed more action than accuracy.

Failure is not necessarily missing the target, but aiming too low.

A genius shoots at something no one else sees — and hits it!

Do not be simply good — be good for something.

A hypocrite never intends to be what he pretends to be.

The goal of the defense in a court trial is to get at least one stubborn man on the jury.

If you don't know where you're going, you may miss it when you get there.

The elevator operator has his ups and downs, but he's one of the few who knows where he's going.

The lazy man aims at nothing and generally hits it.

Before following a leader it is wise to see if he is headed in the right direction.

There are plenty of leaders, but *where* are they leading us?

Your life can't go according to plan if you have no plan.

It has been said that life is a game — but how can we play it if we don't know where the goal posts are?

Most people would rather look backward than forward because it's easier to remember where you've been than to figure out where you're going.

Men, like tacks, are useful if they have good heads and are pointed in the right direction.

The best ammunition to fight poverty is a load of ambition fired with effort toward a definite goal.

It is not enough to make progress; we must make it in the right direction.

Progress has little to do with speed, but much to do with direction.

Keep your head and your heart going in the right direction and you'll not have to worry about your feet.

Success is the ability to hitch your wagon to a star while keeping your feet on the ground.

Success comes from having the proper aim as well as the right ammunition.

God

We increase our ability, stability, and responsibility when we increase our sense of accountability to God.

Man's maximum achievement often falls short of God's minimum demands.

We cannot do everything we want to do, but we should do everything God wants us to do.

God gives us the ingredients for our daily bread, but He expects us to do the baking.

Don't sit back and take what comes. Go after what you want.

What do atheists do with their money? Surely they wouldn't carry around anything that says, "In God We Trust."

The atheist can't find God for the same reason that a thief can't find a policeman.

A boy is the only thing God can use to make a man.

When God allows a burden to be put upon you, He will put His arms underneath you to help you carry it.

If you are disgusted and upset with your children, just imagine how God must feel about His!

No one can become a Christian on his own terms.

A Christian is one who makes it easier for other people to believe in God.

The church offers you something you simply can't get elsewhere.

Sign on a church bulletin board in Benton, Wisconsin: "For God so loved the world that He didn't send a committee."

Too many men who talk of finding God in nature rather than in church go hunting for Him with rod or gun.

Why is it that so many church members who say "Our Father" on Sunday go around the rest of the week acting like orphans?

Common sense is the sixth sense, given to us by the Creator to keep the other five from making fools of themselves — and us.

Some people complain because God puts thorns on roses, while others praise God for putting roses among the thorns.

Conceit is generally thought of as God's gift to little people.

Confess your sins to the Lord, and you will be forgiven; confess them to men, and you will be laughed at.

A conscience is a safe guide only when God is the guide of the conscience.

Conscience is not the voice of God; it is the gift of God.

No person can fully and completely discharge his debt to Almighty God, but surely he can make regular payments on it.

It's pretty hard for the Lord to guide a man if he hasn't made up his mind which way he wants to go.

God never imposes a duty without giving time and strength to perform it.

Don't cheat the Lord and call it economy.

You can buy education, but wisdom is a gift from God.

There's one thing for which you should be thankful — only you and God have all the facts about yourself.

It's difficult, if not impossible, to have faith in God if a man has too much faith in himself.

The greatest act of faith takes place when a man finally decides that he is not God.

There are a thousand ways of pleasing God, but not one without faith.

Faith is the hinge that holds the believer to a personal relationship with God.

Our faith deals with what God says — not what learned men say.

A fanatic is a man who does what he thinks the Lord would do if He knew all the facts in the case.

We fear man so much because we fear God so little.

We used to fear God; now we fear our fellow-man.

Fear not tomorrow. God is already there.

Since three-fourths of the earth's surface is water and one-fourth land, it's perfectly clear the good Lord intended that man spend three times as much time fishing as he does plowing.

Flowers are the most beautiful things that God ever made that He didn't give a soul.

We are like beasts when we kill. We are like men when we judge. We are like God when we forgive.

Never be afraid to trust an unknown future to a known God.

We may not know *what* the future holds, but we know *who* holds the future.

We need to get God off the charity list and put Him on the payroll.

If you are disgusted, frustrated, and upset about your children, just imagine how God feels about some of His!

At times we may not know where God is, but we can be confident that He knows where we are.

God doesn't expect us to solve all the world's problems — He only expects us not to create them.

There is no need to nervously pace the deck of the ship of life when the Great Pilot is at the wheel.

God created the world in six days — which probably never could have happened if there had been labor unions.

If God now seems far away, who made the first move?

God shocked the world with a babe, not a bomb.

God cares for people through people.

Sooner or later we must learn that God makes no deals.

God still speaks to those who take the time to listen.

Nature gives man corn, but man must grind it; God gives man a will, but man must make the right choices.

Sometimes a nation abolishes God, but, fortunately, God is more tolerant.

God was at His best when He made man. He made four holes in the head for information to go in, and only one for it to go out.

The Lord calls for us to stand, though not always to understand.

When we do what we can, God will do what we can't.

It should be a great comfort to know that God still has His hands on the steering wheel of the universe.

The birth of a baby is God's vote of confidence in the future of man.

If God is kept outside, something must be wrong inside.

The Lord gives us our faces, but we must provide the expression.

God is more interested in inner grace than in outer space.

God's main problem with the laborers in His vineyard is absenteeism.

Our Lord does not open the windows of heaven to the person who keeps his Bible closed.

When God measures a man, He puts the tape around his heart instead of his head.

God never gives you anything bigger to do than you have resources to handle.

If God is small enough for us to understand, He isn't big enough for us to worship.

God writes with a pen that never blots, speaks with a tongue that never slips, and acts with a hand that never fails.

The Lord prepares a table for His children, but too many of them are on a diet.

God honors no drafts where there are no deposits.

Our Lord is in the cleansing business, not the whitewashing business.

God never intended that we do as we please, but as *He pleases.*

God is never more than a prayer away.

Many people want an affidavit from God proving that He really exists.

When you get to the end of your rope, be thankful — God is there!

God often visits us, but most of the time we are not at home.

The promises of God are certain, but they don't all mature in ninety days.

Whatever God wants us to do, He will help us do it.

God often tries us with a little to see what we would do with a lot.

Many people want God's blessings, but they don't want Him.

God has called us to play the game, not to keep the scores.

Our Lord can't go to war with an army of tin soldiers.

Some think God is like medicine; you don't need Him when you're feeling well.

God promises a safe landing but not a calm voyage.

It is not the wolfishness of the wolves that bothers God so much as the sheepishness of the sheep.

God doesn't call us to be successful. He calls us to be faithful.

Never put a question mark where God has put a period.

God makes a promise — faith believes it, hope anticipates it, patience quietly awaits it.

Some people ask the Lord to guide them; then they grab the steering wheel.

God will never allow anything to come to you that you and He can't handle.

It may be hard to believe in God, but it's much harder not to believe in Him.

God is not a cosmic bellboy for whom we can press a button whenever we need something.

Our Lord is needed on the avenue as much as in the alley.

God has two dwelling places; one in heaven, and the other in a meek and thankful heart.

When we let God *guide* He will *provide.*

The only way to be good is to obey God, love your fellowman, and hate the devil.

Lots of people who once looked to God to save them now expect the government to do it.

God helps those who help themselves, and the government helps those who don't.

Gratitude to God should be as regular as our heartbeat.

Two people can't hate each other if they both love God.

Medical doctors measure physical health by how the tongue looks. The Great Physician measures spiritual health by how the tongue acts.

God is not only a present help in time of trouble, but also a great help in keeping us out of trouble.

The most essential element in any home is God.

No man can truly stand erect until he has first bent the knee to Almighty God.

The person who looks up to God rarely looks down on people.

The man who bows humbly before God is sure to walk uprightly before men.

The best way to stand up before the world is to kneel down before God.

The darkest ignorance is man's ignorance of God.

The greatest thing a man can do for his heavenly Father is to be kind to His children.

The highest knowledge is the knowledge of God.

God's laws last longer than those who break them.

Those who go against the grain of God's law shouldn't complain when they get splinters.

Liberty is not a gift of God but a hard-won achievement with the help of God.

Why not let God have your life? He can do more with it than you can.

The love of God cannot be merited or earned, but it can be spurned.

Love is the fairest flower that blooms in God's garden.

In nature we hear the speech of God.

A patient cannot accept the physician and, at the same time, reject his remedy.

God makes opportunities, but He expects us to hunt for them.

God gave eloquence to some, brains to others.

There will be no peace as long as God remains unseated at the conference table.

What the nations of the world need is a peace conference with the "Prince of Peace."

Politicians wonder how the Lord can run the world without appointing committees.

A lot of little prayers as we go along through life would save a lot of long ones in case of emergencies.

A lot of kneeling keeps you in good standing with God.

Prayer must mean something to us if it is to mean anything to God.

When leading a public prayer, speak loudly enough to be heard of men and sincerely enough to be heard of God.

God never tires of hearing us in prayer.

We must live with people to know their problems and live with God to solve them.

Your promise to God should be as binding as those you make at the bank.

God's promises are like life preservers. They keep the soul from sinking in the sea of trouble.

Practicing psychiatry without faith in God is like meeting a hungry man and giving him a toothpick.

God wants spiritual fruit, not religious nuts.

God holds us responsible, not for what we have, but for what we could have; not for what we are, but for what we might be.

Man is responsible to God for becoming what God has made possible for him to become.

The only way to be good is to obey God, love your fellowman, and hate the devil.

No man can be at peace with God without getting into an argument with the devil.

Russia has abolished God, but so far God has been more tolerant of Russia.

Some people are willing to serve God, but only as His consultant.

God may forgive your sin, but your nervous system won't.

God gave to man five senses: touch, taste, smell, sight, and hearing. The successful man has two more — horse and common.

Men sometimes credit themselves for their successes, and God for their failures.

When the Lord gave us the Ten Commandments, He didn't mention amendments.

Maybe the Lord allows some people to get into trouble because that is the only time they ever think of Him.

God is not only a present help in time of trouble, but also a great help in keeping us out of trouble.

People always get into trouble when they think they can handle their lives without God.

The Lord didn't burden us with work. He blessed us with it.

What the world needs is an amplifier for the still, small voice.

Golden Rule

One of the troubles with the world today is that we have allowed the Golden Rule to tarnish.

Practicing the Golden Rule is not a sacrifice; it's an investment.

The Golden Rule is what we want everybody else to practice.

Do unto others as though you were the others.

We commit the Golden Rule to memory and forget to commit it to life.

The trouble with the Golden Rule is that before men are ready to live by it they have lead in their legs and silver in their hair.

People who live by the Golden Rule today never have to apologize for their actions tomorrow.

The Golden Rule may be old but it hasn't been used enough to show any signs of wear.

More golden wedding anniversaries would be celebrated if more couples practiced the Golden Rule.

The Golden Rule is of little value unless you realize that you must make the first move.

The Golden Rule of friendship is to listen to others as you would have them listen to you.

Lie about others as you would like them to lie about you.

Combine common sense and the Golden Rule and you will have very little bad luck.

Tolerance is really nothing but putting the Golden Rule into practice.

Golf

Man blames most accidents on fate — but feels a more personal responsibility when he makes a hole-in-one on the golf course.

Many a man who is too tired to help around the house plays golf for exercise.

Anyone who finds it easy to improve his golf game probably does it with a pencil.

Nothing handicaps you so much in golf as honesty.

Golf is a lot like taxes — you drive hard to get to the green and then wind up in the hole.

The only way some golfers can drive down the fairway is in a cart.

Few golfers play golf — most of them work at it.

Golf is a sport in which a small white ball is chased by men who are too old to chase anything else.

A Sunday golfer is a person who is more interested in a hole-in-one than the Holy One.

Some of the world's best golf scores are made with a lead pencil.

All golfers should refrain from picking up lost balls until they have stopped rolling.

Many men consider it a good day at golf if they don't fall out of the cart.

A fat man is no good at golf because if he tees the ball where he can hit it, he can't see it; and if he tees the ball where he can see it, he can't hit it.

The most difficult part of golf is learning not to talk about it.

A great many men have switched from golf to bowling — because they don't lose nearly as many balls.

One of the quickest ways to meet new people is to pick up the wrong ball on the golf course.

Many men hire someone to mow their lawns so they can play golf for exercise.

Golf is the game that turned the cows out of the pasture and let the bull in.

The difference between learning to drive a car and learning to play golf is that when you learn to play golf you don't hit anything.

Golf was invented so that even the man who isn't in politics would have something to lie about.

There are many golfers who play a fair game — if you watch them.

Golf consists of a lot of walking — broken up by disappointments and bad arithmetic.

About the time a man gets his temper under control, he goes out and plays golf again.

A woman in Nevada explains why she doesn't play golf: "I have more important things to lie about."

Many a man who formerly played golf to keep him in the pink has now given it up to keep out of the red.

If swearin' and cussin' and cheatin' are crimes, then golf should be outlawed.

Golf is like a love affair — if you don't take it seriously, it's fun; if you do take it seriously, it's apt to break your heart.

A golfer has one advantage over the fisherman; he doesn't have to show anything to prove his success.

If there is any larceny in a man, golf will bring it out.

A golfer is a guy who can walk several miles toting a hundred pounds or more of equipment, but who has little Junior bring him the ashtray.

If you watch a game, it's fun. If you play it, it's recreation. If you work at it, it's golf.

The best thing about golf is that it isn't compulsory.

In Africa certain of the native tribes practice the strange custom of beating the ground with clubs and uttering wild bloodcurdling yells. Anthropologists call this a form of primitive expression. In America we call it golf.

A really good golfer is one who goes to church on Sunday first.

A New Yorker recently explained why he gave up golf: "I have enough crises in my life without volunteering for eighteen of them on my day off."

Golf is a wonderful game — for one thing it keeps men from falling asleep in church on Sunday mornings.

No wonder golf is so popular. It's one of the few games where the participant keeps his own score.

Golf is a good game. It gives a fellow a chance to be a pedestrian without the danger of being run over.

Old golfers never die. They just tee off and putt away.

Golf is a game that gives you something to do while you're nailing down a business deal.

The fellow who can beat his boss at golf is usually prudent enough not to.

Playing golf is like raising children — you keep thinking you'll do better next time.

By the time a man can afford to lose a golf ball, he's too old to hit one that far.

One good thing about golf — a man doesn't get into any holes he can't get out of.

A golf ball leaves the club at 125 miles per hour, or just a little faster than some golfers leave the office.

The income tax has made more liars out of the American people than golf.

Which has made the biggest liars out of Americans — golf or the income tax?

Locating a doctor these days is a matter of course — the golf course.

A male retiree says he's been playing golf occasionally — but only on days ending with y.

Goodness

The man who cannot be angry at evil usually lacks enthusiasm for good.

Few people make a deliberate choice between good and evil; the choice is between what we want to do and what we ought to do.

Between two evils, choose neither; between two goods, choose both.

The best way to escape evil is to pursue good.

We do more good by being good than in any other way.

There is no limit to the amount of good a man can do if he doesn't care who gets the credit.

Do not be simply good — be good for something.

There must be a lot of good in some folks — because so little of it has ever come out.

Goodness consists not so much in the outward things we do, but in the inward things we are.

The only way to be good is to obey God, love your fellowman, and hate the devil.

There is some good in everyone, though in some it takes a little longer to find.

There isn't a man alive who is as good as he knows he ought to be.

People seldom get dizzy spells from doing good turns.

Greatness is not found in possessions, power, position, or prestige. It is discovered in goodness, humility, service, and character.

There is not true greatness where simplicity, goodness, and truth are absent.

A hypocrite at least appreciates goodness enough to imitate it.

Public opinion is the greatest force for good — when it happens to be on that side.

There must be a lot of good in some people because very little of it ever comes out.

Gossip
see also Slander

A casual acquaintance is a person you know well enough to talk *about* but not *to.*

Nothing makes an argument so one-sided as telling about it.

Some people never say anything bad about the dead, or anything good about the living.

One nice thing about bores is that they don't talk about other people.

A business is too big when it takes a week for gossip to go from one end of the office to the other.

The reason some folks can't mind their own business is because they have very little mind and no business.

One good thing about conceited people — they don't go around talking about other people.

A conference is a big business term for swapping stories in somebody's office.

Conversation is when three women are talking; gossip is when one of them leaves.

Conversation between Adam and Eve must have been difficult at times because they had nobody to talk about.

Conversation is an exercise of the mind, but gossiping is merely an exercise of the tongue.

Not even an egotist is all bad. At least he doesn't go around talking about other folks.

The best thing to do behind a person's back is pat it.

Envy is usually the mother of gossip.

Everybody should have at least two friends — one to talk *to* and one to talk *about.*

The quickest way to stop gossip is for everybody to shut up.

Gossip is always brewing at coffee break.

Some people seldom repeat gossip — the way they heard it.

Most people don't approve of gossip. Enjoying it is enough.

Many people are gossips; however, some of us are merely being informative.

Gossip is the art of saying nothing in a way that leaves practically nothing unsaid.

The most useless thing in the world is gossip that isn't worth repeating.

Gossip is nothing more than mouth-to-mouth recitation.

Those who gossip are often caught in their own "mouth-trap."

Gossip is like an old joke — there's always somebody around who hasn't heard it.

The only time some people dislike gossip is when you gossip about them.

An Oklahoma husband says the only thing his wife ever got secondhand was gossip.

One gossip to another: "I won't bore you with details. In fact, I've already told you more than I heard myself."

It is always difficult to sling mud with clean hands.

Much gossip that is aired should also be fumigated.

A gossiper is a newscaster without a sponsor.

A gossip is a person who tells you everything you suspected.

In most beauty parlors the gossip alone would curl your hair.

Gossip always seems to travel fastest over grapevines that are slightly sour.

Gossip is sometimes referred to as halitosis of the mind.

You can't believe everything you hear — but you can repeat it.

Gossip is like a balloon — it grows bigger with every puff.

If we all said to people's faces what we say behind their backs, society would be impossible.

Gossip is one form of crime for which the law provides no punishment.

The hard of hearing are not so unfortunate as it might seem. About all they miss is a lot of gossip and smalltalk.

If folks didn't carry gossip, it wouldn't go so far.

Nothing is more annoying than to have someone fail to tell you a piece of gossip you said you didn't want to hear.

One half of the world knows how the other half lives because of backyard fences, front porches, bridge parties, and sewing circles.

At the last count, gossip was running down more people than automobiles.

A gossip always creates the smoke in which other people assume there's a fire.

Confirmed gossipers never gossip about their inferiors; they have none.

Talking about others and being a gossip is probably better than talking about yourself and being a bore.

Without the tale-hearers there would be no tale-bearers.

Gossip is like mud thrown on a clean wall. It may not stick but it always leaves a dirty mark.

There's a fortune awaiting any man who can find something to do with gossip besides repeating it.

The expert gossiper knows just how much to leave out of a conversation.

Gossip is almost anything that goes in one ear and out over the back fence.

It is a good idea to believe only half of what you hear, but be sure the half you believe isn't the wrong half.

Gossip is when someone gets wind of something and treats it like a cyclone.

Even when gossip isn't worth repeating, what else can you do with it?

There isn't much to see in a small town, but what you hear makes up for it.

The little bird that is always giving away secrets must be a stool pigeon.

Gossip research is conducted in a BLABORATORY.

A person can't help the size of his ears, or the length of his nose or tongue, but he can keep them out of other people's business.

Spreading gossip is impossible if we refuse to listen — or to believe it.

If all men knew what each said about the other, there wouldn't be five friends in the whole world.

It isn't difficult to make a mountain out of a molehill — just add a little dirt.

The difference between gossip and news is whether you hear it or tell it.

Gossip is what might be called "ear pollution."

A gossip is one who can give you all the details without knowing any of the facts.

Conversation is an exercise of the mind; gossiping is merely an exercise of the tongue.

Idle gossip sure does keep some folks busy.

Nothing is dirt cheap anymore except gossip.

A gossip is a person who puts two and two together whether they were or not.

It takes a secondhand person to deliver firsthand gossip.

Gossip is a "negative" that is developed and then enlarged.

When we stop to think that it requires dirt to grow things, we understand why gossip thrives.

A gossip is a person with a strong sense of rumor.

Gossip is like grapefruit — it has to be juicy to be good.

Plant a little gossip and you will reap a harvest of regret.

Much of history is just gossip that has grown old gracefully.

Most great men come from small towns. We don't know whether it's because of ambition or gossip.

Some people seem to think a fertile mind requires a lot of dirt.

Public opinion is private gossip which has reached epidemic proportions.

Some people seem to get an awful lot of pleasure being shocked by other people's sins.

Just think how speechless some politicians would be if they didn't say nasty things about each other!

A churchman in Florida reports that his minister recently preached on the subject of gossip, followed by the hymn, "I Love to Tell the Story."

All women don't repeat rumors. Some originate them.

A scandal is a breeze whipped by two or more windbags.

A scandal-monger is one who pours social sewage into people's ears.

Usually the half of a scandal that has not been told is the better half.

Might as well keep your mouth shut. If you talk about yourself you're a bore, and if you talk about others you're a gossip.

Confess your sins, not your neighbor's.

Slander, like coffee, is usually handed to you without grounds.

The slanderer differs from the assassin only in that he murders the reputation instead of the body.

A tongue four inches long can kill a man six feet tall.

Everybody likes to hear the truth — especially about somebody else.

Government

In America today there is a surplus of food, a surplus of manufactured goods, and a surplus of people who think they know how to run the government.

Not many Americans have been around the world but their money sure has.

There are two kinds of Americans: one hopes the government will do something *for* them, the other hopes the government won't do something *to* them.

Men and nations do behave wisely, once all other alternatives have been exhausted.

The slogan of the borrowing nations today is, "See America First."

In a bureaucracy, they shoot the bull, pass the buck, and make seven copies of everything.

People would be delighted to attend to their own business if the government would give it back to them.

Many a businessman wanted his son to share in the business but the government beat him to it.

Capital punishment is when the government taxes you to get capital so that it can go into business in competition with you, and then taxes the profit on your business in order to pay its losses.

Charity begins at home and usually winds up in some foreign country.

With all the laws and government regulations, a fellow is downright stupid to steal when there are so many legal ways to cheat.

Most kids can't understand why a country that makes atomic bombs would ban firecrackers.

When parents can't or won't control their children in the home, it's extremely difficult for the government to control them on the streets.

Separation of church and state could hardly be more complete. The church teaches that money isn't everything, and the government keeps telling us it is.

When lost it is better to stand still than to run in the wrong direction. This applies to governments as well as individuals.

The average congressman's idea of government waste is a dollar spent in another congressman's district.

Crime seems to be the only big business to escape government meddling.

Everybody should have a hobby of some kind, even if it's only criticizing the government.

A democracy is government that is run by all the people and run down by some of them.

Diplomacy couldn't prevent the last war, but it usually does a good job of preventing the peace.

The more government in the economy, the less economy in the government.

The money saved this year on education will be spent later on jails and reformatories.

It is when men stop having faith in one another that they stop having faith in their government.

There is no need for a farmer to retire and move to the city. If he will stay where he is the city will soon come and annex him.

American farmers don't need protection from competition to survive. They need protection from their own government.

Farmers are so closely inspected by the federal government that the country teen-agers hesitate to sow any wild oats.

Never before has the fate of so many been at the whim of so few.

Giving help to the enemy used to be called treason. Now it is called "foreign aid."

Lots of people who once looked to God to save them now expect the government to do it.

It's getting harder and harder to support the government in the style to which it is accustomed.

There is one fixed rule in government — the less it's worth, the more it costs.

Many young college graduates who planned a career in government have changed their minds and are going into something legitimate.

There seems to be a consensus these days that the government is doing more *to* the average citizen than it does *for* him.

It's a mistake to believe that government can give things to some people without first taking it away from others.

The government will soon conduct a survey as to why people get bored on the job. Just thinking about this survey makes one drowsy.

Few things get kicked as much as the seat of government.

The government advocates putting our pictures on our Social Security cards. Wouldn't that constitute cruel and unusual punishment?

Some folks feel the government owes them a living. The rest of us would gladly settle for a small tax refund.

Government machinery has been described as a marvelous laborsaving device which enables ten men to do the work of one.

There's little danger of our government being overthrown. There's too much of it.

One great thing about our form of government is that everybody gets something out of it, even if it's only free income-tax forms.

Good government is a bargain at any price.

The only government that will ever benefit mankind permanently is self-government.

Every nation has the kind of government it deserves.

Government is an institution through which sound travels faster than light.

The government should supply a slide rule, prayerbook, and a Ouija Board with each income-tax form.

President Herbert Hoover was the first President to give his salary back to the government. Now the government would like everybody to do it.

There are four branches of government today: the executive, the legislative, the judicial, and the investigative.

Everybody works for the government, either on the payroll or the taxroll.

Good government is dependent on the office-holders and fewer freeloaders.

The government is concerned about the population explosion, and the population is concerned about the government explosion.

Heavy taxes and government expenses are still cheaper than the cost of chaos and anarchy.

God helps those who help themselves, and the government helps those who don't.

One of the things we have to be thankful for is that we don't get as much government as we pay for.

In the old days it was two chickens in every pot; now it's two government employees for every taxpayer.

How can a government know what the people want when the people don't know?

More people now depend on the government than once supported it.

Government is another thing that needs much more pruning and much less grafting.

If people are the right kind of people, almost any kind of government can be made to work.

The truth about government of the people, by the people, and for the people is that we are being billed in triplicate. This is not what "Honest Abe" had in mind.

Any government big enough to give you everything you want is big enough to take everything you've got.

The people who look to government to bring them security and prosperity ought to remember what happened to the American Indians.

What's needed in government is more horse sense and less nonsense.

The hardest job an independent man has today is trying to keep the government from taking care of him.

The government appears to want to regulate everybody and everything — except government.

There is nothing quite as permanent as a "temporary" government program.

Most businessmen want their sons to inherit their business, but the government beats them to it.

The cost of government won't go down until the voters rise up.

The real trouble with government is that we have too few ideals and too many deals.

It's the fathead, not the overhead, that makes government costly.

The government can take our business away from us faster than our competitors can.

Whatever the faults of our government, we are primarily to blame because it is our government.

Our government has operated in red ink so long that the federal ledger looks like a slaughterhouse.

Government is a lot like your digestive system — if it works right, you hardly know you have it.

The trouble with government is that it has too many heads and too few brains.

The only federally-controlled enterprise that ever made money is the mint.

A government is a large-scale operation with too many small-scale minds.

Two good reasons for a change in government: first, too much overhead; second, too much underhand.

A government official is a man who has risen from obscurity to something worse.

The trouble with government is that it thinks everybody owes it a living.

Government regulations are a lot like catsup — you either get none or a lot more than you want.

According to a number of old-timers, the only thing wrong with government today is the same thing that's always been wrong with it.

Big government isn't the answer — it's the problem.

In many ways the past two hundred years of our history have changed this country from independence to government dependence.

Honesty is also the best foreign policy.

Ignorance of law is no excuse — neither is the ignorance of the lawmakers.

The American family and the United States government are in agreement about one thing — neither of them can live within their income.

When making out your income-tax report, be sure you don't overlook your most expensive dependent — the government.

Income-tax forms are nothing more than the government's quiz program.

We wouldn't mind paying income tax if we could know which country it's going to.

Said an old lady to the IRS clerk, "I do hope you will give my money to a nice country."

A serious impediment to a successful marriage these days is the difficulty of supporting both the government and a wife on one small income.

Recently a Medicare patient underwent surgery. When he awoke he found this placard on his incision, "This is a federal project showing your tax dollars at work."

A fool and his money are soon parted — especially with the government to expedite matters.

It's easy to borrow money from the government. All you have to do is pretend you're a foreign power.

Some people's finances are in such a mess they must be getting advice from the government.

The principal export of the United States is money.

George Washington set a poor precedent when he threw that dollar across the Potomac. Since then our government has felt impelled to throw billions of them across the oceans.

An old-timer is one who can remember when going to the eternal rest didn't mean landing a job with the government.

What we need is less government in business and more business in government.

Modern political theory seems to hold that the best way to keep the economy in the pink is to run the government in the red.

Apparently the government has abandoned the idea of abolishing poverty. Investigation has shown it was the only thing within reach of everybody.

Everything is much simpler today. Instead of solving problems, we just subsidize them.

How easy it would be for governments to reform if there were nothing to grab.

A scientist recently revealed that it took millions of years to carve out the Grand Canyon — a government job, no doubt.

Sign on a desk in the Pentagon. "The secrecy of my job does not permit me to know what I am doing."

Our government could raise unlimited revenue simply by taxing sin.

Being a success today means the government takes away in taxes what you used to dream of earning.

When a man becomes a success, his wife takes most of the credit and the government takes most of the cash.

Patrick Henry ought to come back and see what taxation *with* representation is like.

Is there any human activity that isn't taxed, licensed, regulated, or restricted?

Stay on your job and pay your taxes promptly. Thousands of workers in the government bureaus are counting on you.

A California taxpayer recently moaned, "I owe the government so much money it doesn't know whether to throw me out or recognize me as a foreign power."

The only people who don't have to pass the Civil Service exams to work for the government are taxpayers.

After the government takes enough to balance the budget, the taxpayer has the job of budgeting the balance.

If Washington D. C. is the seat of government, then the taxpayer is the pants pocket.

Most American taxpayers gladly support their own government by paying their taxes promptly, but they resent having to support the government of several other countries.

Pity the poor taxpayer who has the whole government on his payroll.

A saver is a farsighted person who lays money away for the government's rainy day.

The United States is a land with a President for a head, a Supreme Court for a backbone, and Congress for lungs.

One reason many of us can't afford a European vacation is because our dollars made the trip without us.

The mess in Washington shouldn't be blamed on one man. It took real teamwork.

Everybody has to work for the government — but only the bureaucrats get paid for it.

Nowadays when you miss a day's work the government loses as much as you do.

If the creation of the world had been a federal project it probably would have taken six years instead of six days.

It's a weird world. The strong take away from the weak, the clever take away from the strong, and the government takes away from everybody.

Government Spending

The government that gives too much costs too much.

Only big government could advocate spending our way to prosperity while being broke.

In government the next step after planned economy is planned extravagance.

There is one fixed rule in government — the less it's worth, the more it costs.

The government is a strong believer in ESP — Extra Spending Power.

Why can't the government cut down on its spending? It forced the rest of us to cut down on ours.

Government bulletins are available on almost every subject except on curbing government expenses.

Can you remember way back when the government got along without something if it cost too much?

Wouldn't it be wonderful if the government was half as fussy about how it spends money as it is about how we spend ours?

Everything seems to be under government control except the national debt and the budget.

Our government has operated in red ink so long that the federal ledger looks like a slaughterhouse.

Ours is no longer a government of checks and balances, but a government of checks and deficits.

Our government was founded on a system of checks and balances; nowadays the checks are so big there aren't any balances.

Just because the Declaration of Independence says everyone is entitled to the pursuit of happiness, it doesn't mean the government should finance the chase.

Grandparents

A man begins to show his age at about the same time he begins to show pictures of his grandchildren.

Nothing makes a boy smarter than being a grandson.

More children are spoiled because the parents won't spank Grandma.

Just about the time a woman thinks her work is done, she becomes a grandmother.

Grandparents are people who come to your house, spoil the children, and then go home.

No cowboy was ever faster on the draw than a grandparent pulling a baby picture out of a wallet.

Another thing "so simple a child can operate" is a grandparent.

Nothing is harder on a grandparent than having to watch a grandchild being disciplined.

Some of our modern grandmothers are so young and spry they help the Boy Scouts across the street.

A grandmother is a baby sitter who watches the kids instead of the television.

Grandchildren don't make a man feel old — it's knowing that he's married to a grandmother.

Grandpa and grandma were too busy scratching for a living to need books on how to stop worrying.

Gratitude
see also Thankfulness

The greatest lesson we learn from past civilizations is ingratitude.

If you can't be content with what you have received, be thankful for what you have escaped.

A man gave a woman his seat on the bus; she fainted. When she revived, she thanked him; then he fainted.

There's one thing for which you should be thankful — only you and God have all the facts about yourself.

Our favorite attitude should be gratitude.

He who is not grateful for the good things he has would not be happy with what he wishes he had.

Debts of gratitude are the most difficult to collect.

Gratitude to God should be as regular as our heartbeat.

He who forgets the language of gratitude can never be on speaking terms with happiness.

There is a sense in which no gift is ours till we have thanked the giver.

Gratitude is the rarest of all virtues, and yet we invariably expect it.

Express gratitude generously and sincerely; receive gratitude humbly and graciously; expect gratitude rarely, if ever.

He who receives a good turn should never forget it; he who does one should never remember it.

The worst possible moment for an atheist is when he feels grateful and has no one to thank.

Be grateful for what you have, not regretful for what you haven't.

If you can't be grateful for what you receive, be grateful for what you escape.

Gratitude is not only the greatest of virtues, but the parent of all the others.

Be grateful for the doors of opportunity — and for friends who oil the hinges.

If you have nothing to be thankful for, make up your mind that there is something wrong with you.

Gratitude is the most exquisite form of courtesy.

Happiness comes when we stop wailing about the troubles we have, and offer thanks for all the troubles we don't have.

Heaven is a state of thankfulness for having received what we did not deserve, and for not receiving what we did deserve.

Greatness

It takes a great man to give sound advice tactfully, but a greater man to accept it graciously.

The measure of a truly great man is the courtesy with which he treats lesser men.

Many people have the mistaken idea that they can make themselves great by showing how small someone else is.

Nothing great was ever done without an act of decision.

One can always tell a truly great man by the fact that at least ten thousand persons went to school with him in the small town where he grew up.

Abraham Lincoln was great, not because he once lived in a cabin, but because he got out of it.

The surest sign that a man is not great is when he strives to *look* great.

Greatness lies not in being strong, but in the right use of strength.

We cannot all be great, but we can attach ourselves to a great cause.

Greatness is not found in possessions, power, position, or prestige. It is discovered in goodness, humility, service, and character.

The man doesn't live who has not, at some time, thought he had the elements of greatness in him.

There are not great men except those who have rendered service to mankind.

A great man is one who can have power and not abuse it.

He who would be great must be fervent in his prayers, fearless in his principles, firm in his purposes, and faithful in his promises.

There is not true greatness where simplicity, goodness, and truth are absent.

Great men see where small men sigh.

The measure of a man's greatness is not the number of servants he has, but the number of people he serves.

Some men achieve greatness, others are born great, and a few have greatness thrust upon them. The rest of us just think we're great.

Greatness is largely by comparison. A ship looks huge at the dock, but tiny when at sea.

If you would attain greatness, think no little thoughts.

The measure of a truly great man is the courtesy with which he treats lesser men.

Humility makes a man feel smaller as he becomes greater.

No man is too big to be kind, but many men are too little.

Knowledge humbles great men, astonishes the common man, and puffs up the little man.

A good leader inspires men to have confidence in him; a great leader inspires them to have confidence in themselves.

Most great men come from small towns. We don't know whether it's because of ambition or gossip.

This country has turned out some great men in the past, and there are some others who are not so great that ought to be turned out as well.

Great men, like the tallest mountain, retain their majesty and stability during the most severe storm.

Great minds have purposes; others have wishes.

A man must be big enough to admit his mistakes, smart enough to profit from them, and strong enough to correct them.

The greater the man's talent, the more becoming his modesty.

Every great person first learned how to obey, whom to obey, and when to obey.

Great principles do not need men and women as much as men and women need great principles.

Grouches

Notice in a church bulletin: "The Lord loveth a cheerful giver. He also accepteth from a grouch."

The longest days are those you start with a grouch.

A grouch is always unhappy and dissatisfied, especially when he gets what he deserves.

An old grouch in Alabama had a telephone installed — just so he could hang up on people.

A grouch thinks the world is against him — and it is.

We all know that sourness spoils milk — and it has the same effect on human beings.

The trouble with being a grouch is that you have to make new friends every few months.

A grouch never goes where he's told until he dies.

Sometimes a reprimand is only a grouch in disguise.

A grouch spreads cheer wherever he doesn't go.

The longest days are those you start with a grouch.

A grouch distrusts people who flatter him and dislikes those who don't.

When you feel dog-tired at night, it may be because you growled and grumbled all day.

If you would like to spoil the day for a grouch, give him a smile.

Growth

If you're going to climb, you've got to grab the branches, not the blossoms.

Give authority to some people and they grow; give it to others and they swell.

A man's character and his garden both reflect the amount of weeding that was done during the growing season.

There's no limit to the height a man can attain by remaining on the level.

Children these days seem to grow up bigger and faster, yet remain children longer than ever before.

There are some Christians who can't be called "pilgrims" because they never make any progress.

Some Christians who should be wielding the sword of the Spirit are still tugging at the nursery bottle.

No one can grow by allowing others to make his decisions.

Anybody who stands on his dignity isn't going anywhere.

Don't envy anybody. Every person has something no other person has. Develop that one thing and make it outstanding.

Past experience should be a guidepost — not a hitching post.

Friendship is usually a plant of slow growth.

If only our minds instead of our waistlines would grow with the passing of the year.

Some people grow up and spread cheer. Others just grow up and spread.

To grow tall spiritually, a man must first learn to kneel.

Many cities have grown so fast that their outskirts no longer cover their extremities.

The knowledge, understanding, and appropriation of God's Word are the means by which a Christian grows.

Some people grow up and still remain both juvenile and delinquent.

There is a vast difference between growth and inflation.

Spiritual growth soars when we have prayed up, made up, and paid up.

Many people grow small by trying to be big.

The head never begins to swell until the mind stops growing.

Why is it we never experience growing pains in the head?

At no time is a little knowledge more dangerous than when you are using it to start a rumor.

Knowledge has to be improved, challenged, and increased constantly or it vanishes.

All men are born equal. The tough job is to outgrow it.

Some men grow; others just swell.

Grudges

Men with clenched fists cannot shake hands.

The first step in disarmament is to get nations to remove the chips from their shoulders.

Patting a fellow on the back is the best way to get a chip off his shoulder.

A fanatic usually has such a huge chip on his shoulder that it causes him to lose his balance.

Nursing a grudge is like arguing with a policeman — the more you do it, the worse things get.

The heaviest thing a person can carry is a grudge.

If you would quit nursing that grudge of yours, it might die.

It doesn't take a doctor to tell you it's better to remove a grudge than to nurse it.

One of the fastest ways to get round-shouldered is to carry a grudge.

No matter how long you nurse a grudge it won't get better.

Many men get more fun out of grinding the ax than in burying the hatchet.

When you take responsibility on your shoulders there is not much room left for chips.

It's extremely difficult for men of different nations to work together when they carry a rifle on one shoulder and a chip on the other.

Grumbling
see also Complaining, Criticism

When opportunity knocks a grumbler complains about the noise.

Some grumble because they don't get what's coming to them; others, because they do.

It requires no musical talent to be always harping on something.

When you get the daily bread you've been praying for, don't grumble because it's not cake.

When you feel dog-tired at night, it may be because you growled and grumbled all day.

There is no place like home — where we are treated the best and grumble the most.

H

Habits

Hair

Happiness

Hatred

Heads

Health

Heart

Heaven

Hell

Helpfulness

Heredity

Hick Towns

Highbrows

Highways

History

Hollywood

Home

Honesty

Honeymoon

Hope

Hospital Costs

Hospitals

Hotels

Housewives

Human Nature

Humility

Humor

Hunting

Husbands

Hypochondriacs

Hypocrites

Habits

It is possible that a man could live twice as long if he didn't spend the first half of his life acquiring habits that shorten the other half.

The worst boss anyone can have is a bad habit.

Many girls are trying to break their boyfriends of a bad habit — eating alone.

The easiest and best way to break a habit is to drop it.

A habit is something a fellow hardly notices until it's too strong to break.

There's only one good thing that can be said for bad habits. If it weren't for them we couldn't make New Year's resolutions.

When a habit begins to cost money, it is called a hobby.

Bad habits, like chiggers and cockleburrs, are easy to acquire but difficult to shake off.

The only way to avoid bad habits is to make it a point to avoid them.

Good habits are usually formed; bad habits we fall into.

Many people look forward to the new year for a new start on old habits.

One can conquer a bad habit easier today than tomorrow.

We first make our habits, and then our habits make us.

Habits are either the best of servants or the worst of masters.

Nothing needs reforming as much as other people's habits.

A man spends the first half of his life learning habits that shorten the other half.

Form good habits; they're as hard to break as bad ones.

Habits are either bobbers or sinkers, corks or lead. They hold you up or pull you down.

A bad habit is first a caller, then a guest, and, finally a master.

Changing our habits, like climbing a long flight of stairs, is something easier to do when we're young.

It's easier to form good habits than reform bad ones.

A habit cannot be tossed out the window; it has to be coaxed down the stairs one step at a time.

The trouble with people who have broken a habit is that they usually have the pieces mounted and framed.

Habits are like a soft bed — easy to get into but hard to get out of.

If there's anything harder than breaking a bad habit, it's trying not to tell how you did it.

Habit is a cable. We weave a thread of it every day until it is extremely difficult to break.

Few of us are proud of our bad habits, but without them there wouldn't be anything for the doctor to tell us to give up when we aren't feeling well.

What is it about human nature that makes it easier to break a commandment than a habit?

Marriage is a case of two people agreeing to change each other's habits.

Middle age is when you've given up all your bad habits and still don't feel good.

It's not so bad making mistakes so long as you don't make a habit of it.

The New Year gives people a fresh start on their old habits.

To avoid old age keep taking on new thoughts and throwing off old habits.

A toast: MAY ALL YOUR PLEASURES BECOME HABITS.

There is nothing so easy to acquire and so difficult to drop as prejudice.

Serious trouble comes when the New Year's resolutions collide with the old year's habits.

Some who have a habit of thinking out loud make others appreciate how golden silence really is.

Hair

A rock and roll singer had a bad accident recently. His partner slammed the car door on his hair.

Class reunions are going to be very confusing fifteen years from now when everybody has a haircut.

A gentleman complains that when long hair became stylish his started to fall out.

A man's hair and teeth are just about his best friends, but even the best of friends fall out.

One girl to another: "I love your hair. Is it home-grown?"

A hair in the head is worth two in the brush.

Sadder than falling leaves is falling hair.

Hair seems important only when we no longer have any.

A guaranteed hair-restorer is now on the market. The manufacturer gives a comb with every bottle.

Not since Indians collected scalps have so many people walked around with hair that's not their own.

Gray hair usually comes along about twenty years after you thought it would make you look distinguished.

Why worry if your hair falls out? Suppose it ached and you had to have it pulled like teeth.

A man in Nevada says that when he was a boy his hair was light; then it turned dark, then it turned grey, then it turned loose.

You're not going to get anywhere telling your teen-age son his hair looks like a mop. He probably doesn't know what a mop is.

People worry about their gray hair, but it's actually great to have gray hair. Ask any man who's bald.

The best thing for gray hair is a sensible head.

Did you hear about the teen-age boy who let his hair down — and smothered?

People are always telling a woman how pretty her hair looks — but the only time they comment about a man's hair is when he no longer has any.

Two heads are not better than one, considering the present price of haircuts.

It may be true that life begins at forty, but everything else starts to wear out, fall out, or spread out.

When a middle-aged man says he's worried about fallout, he probably means hair, not atoms.

You can recognize the golden years by all the silver in your hair.

Nowadays a parent can remember his son's first haircut — but not his last.

Some boys seem to have dentists confused with barbers — they see both twice a year.

Just a glance at this generation makes us realize we're living in hair-raising times.

Did you hear about the young fellow who spent two years trying to find himself? He got a haircut and there he was!

Happiness

Americans believe in life, liberty, and the purchase of happiness.

For every minute you're angry, you lose sixty seconds of happiness.

Nowadays every man wants life, liberty, and an automobile in which to pursue happiness.

A shady business never produces a sunny life.

The man who gets along in the world is the one who can look cheerful and happy when he isn't.

True happiness is going to a high school class reunion and learning that the boy who was voted most likely to succeed — didn't.

Happy is the man who renounces everything that places a strain on his conscience.

If you don't enjoy what you have, how could you be happier with more?

The happiest man in the world is a vegetarian looking at the prices in a meat market.

Freedom is the right all people have to be as happy as they can.

He who forgets the language of gratitude can never be on speaking terms with happiness.

People are always telling a woman how pretty her hair looks — but the only time they comment about a man's hair is when he no longer has any.

All some people need to make them happy is a change — and most of the time that's all a baby needs.

People whose main concern is their own happiness seldom find it.

To be happy, do not add to your possessions but subtract from your desires.

In life we eventually learn that there is a speed limit in the pursuit of happiness.

Happiness is the result of being too busy to be miserable.

The surest path to happiness is in losing yourself in a cause greater than yourself.

Happiness is a healthy mental attitude, a grateful spirit, a clear conscience, and a heart full of love.

It seems that some people can't be happy unless they're unhappy.

The roots of happiness grow deepest in the soil of service.

Happiness is a place somewhere between too much and too little.

It's difficult for any of us to go through life without either increasing or diminishing somebody's happiness.

He who continually searches for happiness will never find it. Happiness is made, not found.

A small house will hold as much happiness as a big one.

Two things contribute to happiness: what we can do without and what we can do with.

Real happiness is getting a reminder about a bill you've already paid so you can sit down and write the store a nasty letter.

Happiness is home-brewed.

A man has happiness in the palm of his hands if he can fill his days with real work and his nights with real rest.

The search for happiness is one of the chief sources of unhappiness.

Happiness consists of living each day as if it were the first day of your honeymoon and the last day of your vacation.

Genuine happiness is when a wife sees a double chin on her husband's old girl friend.

It's a pity that happiness isn't as easy to find as trouble.

Pursuing happiness would be a lot easier if everybody slowed down a little.

Happiness is like the common cold — it's catching!

True happiness may be sought, thought, or caught — but never bought.

It isn't your position that makes you happy or unhappy. It's your *disposition.*

Happiness is discovering that the slip of paper under your windshield is just an advertisement.

The heart is happiest when it beats for others.

Everybody you know can make you happy, some by arriving and some by leaving.

The happiest people are those who are too busy to notice whether they are happy or not.

If you cannot find happiness along the way, you will not find it at the end of the road.

Real happiness is cheap enough, yet how dearly we pay for its counterfeit.

A lot of happiness is overlooked because it doesn't cost anything.

No one can define happiness. You have to be unhappy to understand it.

Happiness is not something you have in your hands; it is something you carry in your heart.

The world would be happier if its leaders had more dreams and fewer nightmares.

Some pursue happiness — others create it.

Even if money could buy happiness, just think what a luxury tax there'd be!

High-octane happiness is a blend of gratitude, service, friendship, and contentment.

Happiness is like a potato salad — when shared with others, it's a picnic.

Do something every day to make other people happy, even if it's only to let them alone.

You can't sprinkle the perfume of happiness on others without getting a few drops on yourself.

Some people find happiness by making the most of what they don't have.

Keep your happiness in circulation.

It's pretty hard to tell what brings happiness; poverty and wealth have both failed.

The plain fact is that human beings are happy only when they are striving for something worthwhile.

Happiness is in the heart, not in the circumstances.

The secret of happiness is to count your blessings while others are adding up their troubles.

Happiness does not come from what you have, but from what you are.

If happiness could be bought, few of us could pay the price.

The place to be happy is here, the time to be happy is now, the way to be happy is to make others so.

Basis for happiness: something to do, something to love, something to look forward to.

Happiness is getting something you wanted but didn't expect.

Just because the Declaration of Independence says everyone is entitled to the pursuit of happiness, it doesn't mean the government should finance the chase.

Happiness is not perfected until it is shared with others.

True happiness comes not from having much to live on, but from having much to live for.

You can live happily ever after if you're not after too much.

The surest steps toward happiness are the church steps.

You will be happier if you will give people a bit of your heart rather than a piece of your mind.

People are generally about as happy as they've made up their minds to be.

Happiness is learning that your daughter's boyfriend has had his electric guitar repossessed by the finance company.

If happiness could be bought, most of us would be unhappy because of the price.

Happiness is no easy matter; it's hard to find it within ourselves and impossible to find elsewhere.

The surest way to have happiness and peace of mind is to give them to somebody else.

To find happiness you must be willing to ignore what life owes you and think about what you owe life.

Happiness is within us, but it does not get there by itself.

Wealth does not insure happiness, but neither does poverty.

Every man who expects to receive happiness is obligated to give happiness. You have no right to consume it without producing it.

The secret of happiness is to learn to accept the impossible, to do without the indispensable, and to bear the intolerable.

Happiness will never come your way as long as your back is turned on duty.

It's not *where* you are but *what* you are that determines your happiness.

Happiness is a by-product of achievement.

They tell us that money doesn't bring happiness, but it would be nice to find that out for yourself.

Happiness can never be found, because it was never lost.

It's true you can't buy happiness — at least not at today's prices.

Happiness will never come to those who fail to appreciate what they already have.

One of the best ways for some people to make others happy is to shut up and go home.

The really happy man is one who can enjoy the scenery on a detour.

Happiness is often punctured by a sharp tongue.

It's difficult to tell who gives some couples the most happiness, the preacher who married them or the judge who divorced them.

Why is it that when a fellow's cup of happiness is full, some fool will come along and nudge his elbow?

Happiness is where you find it, and very seldom where you seek it.

Happiness comes when we stop wailing about the troubles we have, and offer thanks for all the troubles we don't have.

How to be happy: Keep your heart free from hate, your mind from worry, live simply, expect little, give much, sing often, pray always, forget self, think of others and their feelings, fill your heart with love, scatter sunshine. These are tried links in the golden chain of contentment.

Happiness is the conviction that we are loved in spite of ourselves.

Happiness adds and multiplies as we divide it with others.

All we are guaranteed is the pursuit of happiness. You have to catch up with it yourself.

When happiness gets into your system, it is bound to break out on your face.

The heart is happiest that beats for others.

If ignorance was bliss, we'd all be a whole lot happier.

To love others makes us happy; to love ourselves makes us lonely.

A wise man never enjoys himself so much, or a fool so little, as when he is alone.

One does not find happiness in marriage, but takes happiness into marriage.

So live that your memories will be a part of your happiness.

Money never did buy happiness, and credit cards aren't doing much better.

Money can't buy happiness, but it helps you to be unhappy in comfort.

Money won't buy real friends, but it does help you if you want to lease a few nice acquaintances.

Money won't buy happiness, but it will keep you from being more than moderately sullen and depressed.

Money brings happiness to those who find happiness earning it.

Money may be used as a universal passport to everywhere except heaven and as a universal provider for everything except happiness.

Money alone will not bring happiness, but it will attract interesting companions.

A restaurant owner in a southern state grumbled about poor business, "If I could drop dead right now I'd be the happiest man alive."

The secret of success and happiness lies not in doing what you like, but in liking what you do.

Any person who looks happy when he isn't is well on the road to success.

The best way for a person to have happy thoughts is to count his blessings and not his cash.

Wealth may not bring happiness, but it seems to bring a pleasant kind of misery.

Some wives are so concerned about their husband's happiness that they hire private detectives to find out the cause of it.

Hatred

It is far better to forgive and forget than to hate and remember.

Forgiveness saves the expense of anger, the high cost of hatred, and the waste of energy.

Forgiveness is the key that unlocks the door of resentment and the handcuffs of hate. It is a power that breaks the chains of bitterness and the shackles of selfishness.

No matter how useless a man is, his friendship is worth more than his hatred.

The head usher to happiness is a well-kept conscience.

The big question is: Where can we put our hatred while we say our prayers?

Hatred is a boomerang which is sure to hit you harder than the one at whom you throw it.

Two people can't hate each other if they both love God.

Hate is a luxury no one can afford.

Hate is the most inefficient use a person can make of his mind.

If you want to be miserable, hate somebody.

Doctors tell us that hating people can cause cancer, heart attacks, headaches, skin rashes, and asthma. It doesn't make the people we hate feel too good either.

Hatred is cancer of the intellect.

Hatred does a great deal more damage to the vessel in which it is stored than the object on which it is poured.

There are many roads to hate, but envy is one of the shortest of them all.

Hatred is like a rifle with a plugged barrel. The backfire can be much more dangerous than the shot.

It's extremely difficult to endure hatred without resentment and a desire to reciprocate.

In a world where death is, we should have no time to hate.

Hate pollutes the mind.

The sunlight of love will kill all the germs of jealousy and hate.

Some people are so intelligent they can speak on any subject — others don't seem to need a subject.

Heads

Baldheaded people should remember that when God made heads He covered up the ones He didn't like.

A bald head is something nobody wants to have, and nobody wants to lose.

Germs attack the weakest part of your body — which is the reason for head colds.

A stiff neck usually supports an empty head.

Egotism is obesity of the head.

The bigger a man's head gets, the easier it is to fill his shoes.

We have observed that many self-made men made their heads oversize.

Some of our modern girls turn a man's head with charm — and his stomach with their cooking.

Some people have flat feet — and heads to match.

Empty heads are always the hardest to fill.

Soft heads do more harm than soft muscles.

It's hard to get ahead if you don't have one.

No big ideas over come from swelled heads.

Two heads are better than one — except when both are behind the same steering wheel.

There is an unusually large assortment of heads on the current scene: egg, meat, fat, sore, and swell, among others.

The head never begins to swell until the mind stops growing.

Everybody agrees that it's bad enough to have a skeleton in the closet, but worse to have a bonehead in the family.

Why is it we never experience growing pains in the head?

It isn't easy for an idea to squeeze itself into a head that is filled with prejudice.

The only thing some people keep in their heads overnight is a cold.

Folks who hide their heads in the sand won't leave any footprints.

Two heads are not better than one, considering the present price of haircuts.

It's unfortunate that swelled heads aren't painful.

There is only one quality worse than hardness of the heart, and that is softness of the head.

The man who is always losing his head probably has a screw loose.

A "hangover" is something that occupies the head you neglected to use last night.

The man who tried his hand at something and failed might try using his head for a change.

Many men manage to keep their heads above water because wood floats.

Have you noticed that many people have flat feet — and heads to match?

Heads, hearts, and hands could settle the world's problems better than arms.

The lighter the motorist's head, the heavier his foot.

Much of the sickness people experience in this life is located immediately north of the neck.

The person who loses his head probably doesn't miss it.

A cool head may sometimes keep a man out of trouble, but more often it's cold feet.

The greatest area of unemployment in the United States is just above the shoulders.

Health

A lot of good behavior is due to poor health.

Don't complain because you have to get up early every morning. The time may come when you can't get up — period!

If health is wealth, how come it's tax-free?

Any man who can get out of bed in the morning is in pretty good shape. Ask any man who can't.

Anybody with normal blood pressure these days just isn't paying attention.

To feel "fit as a fiddle" you must tone down your middle.

A health nut in Idaho has specified in his will that he wishes to be buried in a "no smoking" section of the cemetery.

Why not cultivate health instead of treating disease?

If you want to be the picture of health, you'd better have a happy frame of mind.

A lot of people lose their health trying to become wealthy, and then lose their wealth trying to get back their health.

A married couple in Montana is so concerned with their health that whenever they have an argument, she jogs to her mother's.

Many people suffer poor health, not because of what they eat, but from what is eating them.

By the way they talk about it, you'd think some people enjoy bad health.

The physical condition of a man can best be judged from what he takes two of at a time — stairs or pills.

Specialization has reached such a state today that patients have to learn to diagnose themselves before they know which specialist to call.

There are only two classes of people — those who have ulcers, and those who give them.

Money, achievement, fame, and success are important, but they are bought too dearly when acquired at the cost of health.

The only way to keep your good health is to eat what you don't want, drink what you don't like, and do what you'd rather not do.

The way some people treat their bodies you'd think they were opposed to good health.

If you drink too often to other people's health, you'll ruin your own.

The best health insurance is moderation.

It is generally believed that Medicare will soon bring nervous breakdowns within the reach of everybody.

The secret of good health is to leave the table hungry, the bed sleepy, and the tavern thirsty.

The first health hazard in smoking a pipe is high blood pressure caused by trying to keep the thing lit.

A great deal of poor health in this country may be attributed to heavy meals and light work.

The trouble with our health is not that we are all run down, but that we are all wound up.

The human body, with proper care, will last a lifetime.

Mental health has become such an issue today that many people go crazy in pursuit of it.

Nothing in recent years seems to have improved the health of the American people as much as the staggering cost of being sick.

The relative values of health and wealth depend on which you have left.

You need to start worrying about health if you can't sleep when it's time to get up.

Our health always seems much more valuable after we lose it.

Health is the thing that makes you feel that *now* is the best time of the year.

By the time most people discover that good health is everything, they've lost it.

Those who ignore health in the pursuit of wealth usually wind up losing both.

There are a lot of folks in the world who spend so much time watching their health that they haven't time to enjoy it.

The best possible infant care is to keep one end full and the other end dry.

If we had our way, we would make health "catching" instead of disease.

Medical doctors measure physical health by how the tongue looks. The Great Physician measures spiritual health by how the tongue acts.

Good health just doesn't take care of itself, and it is most often lost by assuming that it will.

A beautiful heart more than offsets the handicap of a homely face.

Anybody who thinks money is everything has never been sick.

The secret of good health is to eat onions. The trouble is to keep it a secret.

Stretching may be an aid to health, but it doesn't seem to help the truth.

The relative value of health and wealth depends on which you have left.

A good wife and good health are a man's best wealth.

Heart

Don't forget that people will judge you by your actions, not your intentions. You may have a heart of gold — but so does a hard-boiled egg.

Hardening of the heart ages people more quickly than hardening of the arteries.

It is not by the gray of the hair that one knows the age of the heart.

To change one's character, you must begin at the control center — the heart.

What the church needs today is more calloused hands and fewer calloused hearts.

The bigger the head, the smaller the heart.

As the chest swells, the brain and the heart shrink.

Two things are bad for the heart — running upstairs and running down people.

Forgiveness is a funny thing. It warms the heart and cools the sting.

It has been rightly said that forgiveness is the quality of heart that forgets the injury and forgives the offender.

A man can have no better epitaph than that which is inscribed in the hearts of his friends.

The best rule for friendship: Keep your heart a little softer than your head.

A small gift will do if your heart is big enough.

A lasting gift to a child is the gift of a parent's listening ear — and heart.

Give not from the top of your purse, but from the bottom of your heart.

When God measures a man, He puts the tape around his heart instead of his head.

God has two dwelling places; one in heaven, and the other in a meek and thankful heart.

Happiness is a healthy mental attitude, a grateful spirit, a clear conscience, and a heart full of love.

The heart is happiest when it beats for others.

Happiness is not something you have in your hands; it is something you carry in your heart.

Happiness is in the heart, not in the circumstances.

You will be happier if you will give people a bit of your heart rather than a piece of your mind.

There is only one quality worse than hardness of the heart, and that is softness of the head.

A heart enlarged by sympathy has never yet killed anyone.

Some people have a heart as big as all outdoors — and just as polluted!

The door to the human heart can be opened only from the inside.

People take heart when you give them yours.

Keep your head and your heart going in the right direction and you'll not have to worry about your feet.

There is no better exercise for the heart than reaching down and lifting people up.

Hope springs eternal in the human heart, but with some the spring is getting very weak.

If it were not for hope, the heart would break.

In judging others it's always wise to see with the heart as well as with the eyes.

Kindness is the insignia of a loving heart.

A kiss is a contraction of the mouth due to an enlargement of the heart.

Our trouble today is that we have our heads filled with knowledge, but our hearts are empty.

No constitution, no court, no law can save liberty when it dies in the hearts and minds of men and women.

The most lonely place in the world is the human heart when love is absent.

We do not need more money in our pockets as much as we need more grace in our hearts.

A man cannot touch his neighbor's heart with anything less than his own.

Peace is not made in documents, but in the hearts of men.

It's not the body's posture, but the heart's attitude, that counts when we pray.

It is difficult for a preacher to break a hard heart and mend a broken one at the same time.

Heads, hearts, and hands could settle the world's problems better than arms.

The gospel of Jesus Christ breaks hard hearts and heals broken hearts.

There is no passion of the human heart that promises so much and pays so little as that of revenge.

The greatest reward for serving others is the satisfaction found in your own heart.

A smile is the lighting system of the face and the heating system of the heart.

If there is a smile in your heart, your face will show it.

The smile that lights the face will also warm the heart.

What is in the well of your heart will show up in the bucket of your speech.

If success made the heart swell like it does the head, this world would be a far better world.

Sympathy is two hearts tugging at the same load.

Sympathy is the result of thinking with your heart.

Sympathy is the golden key that unlocks the hearts of others.

There are many tears in the heart that never reach the eye.

Tears are the safety valves of the heart when too much pressure is put upon them.

It isn't what you have in your pocket that makes you thankful, but what you have in your heart.

Tolerance is seeing things with your heart instead of your eyes.

Truth is something which must be known with the mind, accepted with the heart, and enacted in life.

Heaven

The first thing the typical American will ask when he gets to heaven is the amount of the down-payment on a harp.

Keep your Bible open and you will not find the door to heaven shut.

When the church ceases to be in touch with another world, it is no longer in touch with this world.

Judging by church attendance, heaven won't be crowded with men.

Faith builds a bridge from this world to the next.

There are some whose faith is not strong enough to bring them to church services, but they expect it to take them to heaven.

Our Lord does not open the windows of heaven to the person who keeps his Bible closed.

God promises a safe landing but not a calm voyage.

God has two dwelling places; one in heaven, and the other in a meek and thankful heart.

Heaven on earth would be something like this: 1977 wages, 1932 prices, 1928 dividends, and 1910 taxes.

People are guided to heaven more by footprints than by guideposts.

A senior citizen in Alabama says if he makes it to heaven he hopes he won't have to stand in line and fill out a bunch of forms.

Going to heaven is like riding a bicycle — you must either go on or get off.

233

Many a person's idea of heaven would be nothing to do and an eternity to do it in.

Heaven is a place many Americans wouldn't want to go if they couldn't send back picture postcards.

If you wish to dwell in the house of many mansions, you must make your reservation in advance.

Some people talk about heaven being so far away. It is within speaking distance of those who belong there.

You can't get into heaven by naturalization papers.

He who seldom thinks of heaven is not likely to get there.

When you get to heaven you will be surprised to see many people there you did not expect to see. Many may be just as surprised to see you there.

It is easier to write a guidebook to heaven than it is to get there.

There is no reaching heaven except by traveling the road that leads there.

Many people hope to be elected to heaven who are not even running for the office.

The road to heaven is never overcrowded.

Some people want to go to heaven for the same reason they want to go to California — they have relatives there.

The distance from earth to heaven is not so much a matter of altitude as it is attitude.

Almost everybody is in favor of going to heaven, but many people are hoping they'll live long enough to see easing of the entrance requirements.

The man who expects to go to heaven must take the time to study the route that will get him there.

You can't cash checks on heaven's bank without first making a deposit.

There will be no crown-wearers in heaven who were not cross-bearers here on earth.

Heaven is a bargain, however great the cost.

Heaven is a state of thankfulness for having received what we did not deserve, and for not receiving what we did deserve.

Every human being should have three homes: a domestic home, a church home, and an eternal home.

It may be well to stand tall in this life, but heaven is entered only on the knees.

The best some of us can expect on the Day of Judgment is a suspended sentence.

If heaven is a place to rest, many people are going to be all practiced up for it.

Marriages are made in heaven, but they are lived on earth.

Marriages are made in heaven — so are thunder and lightning.

Money may be used as a universal passport to everywhere except heaven and as a universal provider for everything except happiness.

The main object of religion is not to get a man into heaven, but to get heaven into him.

Hell

Judging from the way some people behave these days, they must think that hell is air-conditioned!

Judging by the way some church members live, they need fire insurance.

Hell will be populated by two classes of people: those who will do anything, and those who will not do anything.

Judging from the general behavior we see in this world, hell must be experiencing a population explosion.

Hell is heaven's junkyard.

About the time people ceased to believe in hell, along came the Great Depression.

Since the old-time evangelist has almost disappeared from the scene, hell doesn't seem half as hot as it used to.

Hell is getting out of date by today's thinking, but it is not out of business.

You will not go to hell because you made a bad start, but because you made a bad finish.

The man who tries to prove there is no hell usually has a personal reason for doing so.

There is a way to stay out of hell, but no way to get out.

If there is no hell, many preachers are obtaining money under false pretense.

Religion is a cloak used by some people in this world who will be warm enough without one in the next.

Helpfulness

Too many people are anxious to give you advice when what you really need is help.

Offering good advice may be noble and grand, but it's not the same as a helping hand.

True charity is helping those you have every reason to believe would not help you.

To feel sorry for the needy is not the mark of a Christian — to help them is.

A Christian is a mind through which Christ thinks, a heart through which Christ loves, a voice through which Christ speaks, a hand through which Christ helps.

A church that is not reaching out is passing out.

Criticism should always leave a person with the feeling he has been helped.

Many a man who is too tired to help around the house plays golf for exercise.

It's better to keep a friend from falling than to help him up after he falls.

A Christian should live so that instead of being a part of the world's problems he will be a part of the answer.

To feel sorry for the needy is not the mark of a Christian — to help them is.

It is easier to point the finger than to offer a helping hand.

The best place to find a helping hand is at the end of your arm.

It's nice to know that when you help someone up a hill you are a little nearer the top yourself.

Everybody is ready to lend a helping hand to the fellow who has trouble opening his pocketbook.

The open hand holds more friends than the closed fist.

About the only farm movement which will benefit the farmers are those that start about daybreak and end at sunset.

The enemy you make today may be the only one who can help you twenty-five years from now.

God helps those who help themselves, and the government helps those who don't.

A good way to forget your troubles is to help others out of theirs.

When you help the fellow who's in trouble, he'll never forget you when he's in trouble again.

Heredity

There seems to be a cure for everything but heredity.

Having teen-agers is often what undermines a parent's belief in heredity.

When a person has nothing else to blame, he falls back on his heredity.

Nothing creates a firmer belief in heredity than having a good-looking child.

The law of heredity is that all undesirable traits come from the other parent.

Heredity is what makes a father wonder more than ever about his wife's parents.

Parents of brilliant children are great believers in heredity.

Heredity is what makes the father and mother of teen-agers wonder a little about each other.

The frightening thing about heredity and environment is that parents provide both.

It is impossible to make wisdom hereditary.

Hick Towns

A hick town is where you can park as long as you want to, but don't want to.

There isn't very much to do in a hick town — but there are plenty of people to talk about it when you do.

235

A hick town in Oklahoma is so small they had to do away with the citizen of the year award. Everybody in town had already won it twice.

In a hick town a man is known by his first name and last scandal.

A hick town is a place where the only thing that goes out after 10 P.M. is the lights.

There's a hick town in North Carolina so tough there are no "innocent bystanders."

A hick town in a western state has no crime in the streets. In fact, it doesn't have any streets.

Recently a hick town in Idaho decided to go big time and install a traffic light, but the authorities didn't know whether to make it red or green.

A hick town in Virginia had such a depression last year the poorhouse went bankrupt.

There's a hick town in Alabama so quiet and easygoing that the roosters are still drowsy at noon.

In a small town people will sympathize with you in trouble, and if you don't have any they will hunt some up for you.

There's a small town in Nevada so dull and unexciting that the favorite pastime is yawning.

A newspaper reporter recently made mention of a hick town in Arkansas so slow that Sunday School is held on Monday.

In a hick town they give you credit for resisting temptation — and a lot more credit for finding any.

A hick town is usually a place that is divided by a railroad, a main street, two churches, and a lot of opinions.

A hick town is where they have to widen the street so they can put a white line down the middle.

Highbrows

A highbrow is the person who can tell whether the symphony orchestra is playing or merely tuning up.

Highbrows use expletives — lowbrows use cusswords.

A real highbrow is a person who can quote Shakespeare without attributing it to the Bible.

Highways, Freeways

Sign outside a Dallas church: "Last chance to pray before entering the freeway."

Our national flower is the concrete cloverleaf.

There were millions of people on the highways last weekend — most of them asking for directions.

With auto and gasoline prices going up and up, we ought to find a better word then *freeway*.

Drivers are safer when highways are dry, and highways are safer when drivers are dry.

Most highway signs are understandable to the people who already know which way to go.

The best way to stay alive on the highway is to limit the speed — not speed the limit.

Our highway engineers are performing miracles these days, but they are still building highways that don't curve when the driver does.

Highway sign near San Antonio: "Thirty days hath September, April, June, and November — and anyone exceeding the speed limit."

A highway is a road that can make bad manners fatal.

On some freeways you can drive miles and not leave the scene of the accident.

Highway billboards must go — we need the room for roadsigns, garbage dumps, and junkyards.

An expressway is a highway with three lanes — a right lane, a left lane, and the one you're in when you see the exit.

The old narrow trails where two cars could barely pass without colliding are happily being replaced by splendid wide highways on which six or eight cars can collide at the same time.

Sign on a California freeway: "All in favor of conserving gasoline please raise your right foot."

By the time you see what's coming at you on the freeway it already has.

Our highways are fine for getting to a place in a hurry, if you can get off them when you get there.

There are two kinds of highways in this country: under construction and under repair.

If they really want to beautify our highways, they might start by removing those toll booths.

Sign at highway construction site: "Men working — we hope."

Vacation time is when the highway department closes all the roads and opens up all the detours.

History

The typical American knows when and where the Pilgrims landed but has no idea why.

Isn't it remarkable how our pioneering ancestors built up a great nation without asking Congress for help?

Seems like every time history repeats itself the price doubles.

We are told that history always repeats itself. But, then, so does television.

Why is it that nobody listens when history repeats itself?

History repeats it self — and that's one of the things wrong with history.

History books which contain no falsehoods are extremely dull.

Perhaps no one has changed the course of history as much as the historian.

History is simply a record of man's intelligence — or lack of it.

Isn't it discouraging to contemplate that tomorrow's history will consist of today's current events?

There are three stages in American history: the passing of the buffalo, the passing of the Indian, and the passing of the buck.

Learning history is easy; learning its lessons is almost impossible.

History shows that war is better at abolishing nations than nations are at abolishing war.

History does repeat itself, but not as often as old movies.

Much of history is just gossip that has grown old gracefully.

History is to a nation what memory is to the individual.

One good place to study ancient history is in a doctor's waiting room.

After you hear two witnesses to an automobile accident testify in court, you're not so sure about history.

History is now costing us more than the stuff is worth.

A lot of history isn't fit to repeat itself.

With history piling up so fast, almost every day is the anniversary of something awful.

The reason history repeats itself is that most people weren't listening the first time.

Sometimes the only difference between history and hysteria is the spelling.

The advantage of studying history is that it keeps you from feeling too important.

History is nothing more than the art of reconciling fact with fiction.

The short history of some men is that they live so tense they soon become past tense.

In many ways the past two hundred years of our history have changed this country from independence to government dependence.

We sincerely hope that history will repeat itself at longer intervals.

In the old days history was made for a tenth of what it costs today.

Leaders go down in history — some farther down than others.

History records only one indispensable man — Adam.

Our forefathers should have fought for representation without taxation!

The biggest farce of man's history has been the argument that wars are fought to save civilization.

History reveals that wars create more problems than they solve.

Hollywood

A "Hollywood divorce" means that the wife is asking for custody of the money.

Two Hollywood children were talking. One of them said quite boastfully, "I've got two brothers and one little sister, how many do you have?" The other child answered, "I don't have any brothers and sisters, but I have three daddies by my first mother, and four mothers by my last daddy."

Hollywood is just one great big family. Everybody is related by marriage — or soon will be.

Times are tough in Hollywood these days. People are marrying people they've never met before.

Hollywood is where the movies have happy endings and marriages don't.

Sign on a Hollywood car: "Just remarried."

Even in Hollywood people are having financial trouble. Executives who once pinched girls are now pinching pennies.

A Hollywood celebrity recently hired two press agents to tell the world how modest he is.

Hollywood is where a boy grows up and marries the girl next door — and the girl next door to her.

In Hollywood a happy marriage is one in which the husband loves his wife more than somebody else's.

The best acting job done in Hollywood is done by the man congratulating his ex-wife's husband on the choice he made.

Some Hollywood people compare marriage to eating salted peantus — it's hard to stop at one.

In Hollywood there's a group called Divorce Anonymous. If a male member feels the urge to get a divorce, they send over an accountant to talk him out of it.

A certain Hollywood couple is so incompatible they can't even agree on what to argue about.

Many girls in Hollywood didn't exchange gifts last Christmas — they exchanged husbands.

In Hollywood they figure a marriage has a chance of succeeding if the couple leaves the church together.

A certain Hollywood actor carries a note in his wallet, "I am a celebrity. In case of an accident — call a reporter."

In Hollywood it's difficult for a bachelor to remain a bachelor — and even more difficult for a husband to remain a husband.

Hollywood is a strange place. Many couples live together and don't get married — and many get married and don't live together.

The kid who used to get spanked for writing obscenities in restrooms is now cleaning up as a writer in Hollywood.

Success in Hollywood consists in having your name in the gossip columns and out of the phonebook.

A modern miracle would be a golden wedding anniversary in Hollywood.

In Hollywood the bride tossing the bouquet is just as likely to be the next one to get married as the girl who catches it.

A couple in Hollywood got divorced; then they got married again. The divorce didn't work out to the complete satisfaction of both parties.

Hollywood is now the town of ex-wives, ex-husbands, and x-ratings.

The secret of a successful Hollywood marriage is for the couple to have something in common — such as the same divorce lawyer.

In Hollywood husbands are as hard to keep as secrets.

Nothing makes for undying love in Hollywood like the prompt arrival of alimony checks.

There's a new jewelry store in Hollywood where business has suddenly leaped ahead of all competition. It rents engagement rings.

In Hollywood people get married for better or for worse, or as an excuse to throw a party.

A producer in Hollywood plans a film entitled "Marriage, Hollywood Style." It will be short.

Nostalgia has really caught on in show business. Some Hollywood actors are remarrying their ex-wives.

A Hollywood wedding is one where they take each other for better or worse — but not for long.

Home

The number of accidents in the home are rising; people aren't spending enough time there to know their way around.

A man in Mississippi was told that most accidents happen within twenty miles of home — so he moved to another town fifty miles away.

Many Americans are so nervous and restless they don't feel at home at home.

Some men who speak with authority at work know enough to bow to a higher authority at home.

Nothing makes a man the boss of his house like living alone.

Charity should begin at home, but most people don't stay at home long enough to begin it.

Children may tear up a house, but they never break up a home.

Among the best home furnishings are children.

To train children at home, it's necessary for both the children and the parents to spend some time there.

A small house will hold as much happiness as a big one.

Can you remember when day-care centers were called home?

Home is where you scratch anything that itches.

Almost every American home has all kinds of laborsaving devices, but very few have moneysaving devices.

Home is where a fellow should hang his hat, not his head.

Nothing makes you feel that your home is your castle more than getting an estimate to have it repaired.

Nowadays there are more model homes than model families.

Home is a place where teen-agers go to refuel.

Many people seem to think a home is only good to borrow money on.

The average American home is so modernized that the only thing left to wash by hand is the kids.

A modern home is one that gives you half the space for twice the money.

One nice thing about going home is that you don't have to make a reservation.

The average man has probably thought twice about running away from home — once as a child and once as a husband.

A man's home is his castle. At least that's how it seems when he pays taxes on it.

Sign on the front door of a Georgia home: "We shoot every third salesman, and the second one just left."

After building a new home these days, a man is likely to be "house-broke."

A typical American home is where the parakeet is taught to talk and the kids are told to shut up.

"Home Sweet Home" is where you can put up your feet and let down your hair.

The most essential element in any home is God.

In most homes it's a fifty-fifty proposition. The husband tells the wife what to do, and the wife tells the husband where to go.

The warmth of a home is not necessarily determined by its heating system.

Home is a place where you can take off your new shoes and put on your old manners.

It's a happy home where the only scraps are those brushed off the dining table.

The factory that produces the most important product is the home.

Homes are now being built with every known convenience except low payments.

The trouble with owning a home is that no matter where you sit, you're looking at something you should be doing.

A large number of people live in all-electric homes; everything in them is *charged.*

The easiest way to feel at home is to stay there.

Money can build a house, but it takes love to make it a home.

Many homes seem to be on three shifts — father is on the night shift, mother is on the day shift, and the children shift for themselves.

It takes a heap o' livin' to make a house a home, but before that, it takes a lot o' borrowin'.

A happy home is one in which each spouse entertains the possibility that the other may be right, though neither believes it.

It would be better if the overstuffed things in the home were confined to furniture.

Happy homes are built with blocks of patience.

In the gramatically-correct home the wife says, "You shall," and the husband says, "I will."

There is no place like home if you haven't got the money to go out.

A house is made of walls and beams; a home is built with love and dreams.

Home is where folks go when they get tired of being nice to people.

It takes a lot of living to make a house a home — without a mortgage.

Some of today's happiest reunions occur when the children find their parents at home.

Our greatest need today is for more home-builders and fewer home-wreckers.

A real home is more than just a roof over your head — it's a foundation under your feet.

Home is a place where a man is free to say and do anything he pleases, because no one will pay the slightest attention to him.

It seems that many people these days are building new homes on the outskirts of their incomes.

Every human being should have three homes: a domestic home, a church home, and an eternal home.

In some unfortunate homes, husbands and wives aren't talking. In others, it's just the husband who isn't talking.

Home is a man's refuge, a place of quiet and rest, says a certain writer. That's true except for the telephone, the children, the vacuum cleaner, and the salesman at the door.

Things would be a lot better if more folks at home felt at home.

A modern home is a place where a switch controls everything but the children.

By the time a family pays for a home in the suburbs, it isn't.

Home is a place where women work in the absence of men, and men rest in the presence of women.

There are generally two things wrong in the American home — the clock and the father.

More homes are destroyed by fusses than by funerals or fires.

The modern home is a place where nothing can be accomplished if the electricity goes off.

A typical home is where the TV set is better adjusted than the kids.

The worst trouble about living in a mobile home is that there's no place to put anything except where it belongs.

The man is still boss in the American home — as long as he allows his wife to make all the decisions.

Modern homes are wonderful. They're equipped with gadgets that do everything except make the monthly payments.

There are so many laborsaving devices in the home today that a man has to devote much of his time to repairing them.

The new homes being built have the latest innovations — from wall-to-wall carpeting to back-to-wall payments.

A split-level home is half yours and half the bank's.

Home is a place where you don't have to stifle a yawn and try to cover it up with a smile.

Juvenile delinquency is like charity — it often begins at home.

Like charity, obesity begins at home.

Forbidding prayers in school won't hurt our country half as much as forgetting prayers at home.

Honesty

Our country was in better condition when there were more whittlers and fewer chiselers.

The best way for any business to keep on the upgrade is to stay on the level.

A well-rounded character is square in all his dealings.

There's no limit to the height a man can attain by remaining on the level.

Always trust a fat man. He'll never stoop to anything low.

An honest executive is one who shares the credit with the man who did all the work.

It is generally agreed that no honest men are successful fishermen.

An honest fisherman, if there is such a thing, is a very uninteresting person.

We should give freely and generously — and in accordance with what we reported on our income tax.

Nothing handicaps you so much in golf as honesty.

The most important person to be honest with is yourself.

It takes a mighty honest man to tell the difference between when he's tired and when he's just plain lazy.

Honesty pays, but it doesn't seem to pay enough to suit some people.

There are no degrees of honesty.

An honest merchant is one who puts up a "going out of business" sign — and then goes out of business.

We always hear about "old-fashioned honesty" — but dishonesty has a long genealogy too.

Honesty is also the best foreign policy.

It pays more than it costs to be honest.

Honesty gives a person strength but not always popularity.

Some folks who are "as honest as the day is long" sure have to be watched after the sun goes down.

There is no acceptable substitute for honesty; there is no valid excuse for dishonesty.

A policy of absolute honesty can make a man's character and ruin his golf game.

Nobody ever got hurt on the corners of a square deal.

Most men would be willing to earn their money honestly if it didn't take so long.

Common honesty should be more common.

When you sell yourself, be sure that you don't misrepresent the goods.

To be honest with the world, one must give it at least the equivalent of what he receives from it.

The world will be a better place to live when the "found" ads in the newspapers begin to outnumber the "lost" ads.

No one will ever know of your honesty unless you give out some samples.

We cannot have an honest horserace until we develop an honest human race.

If you are honest only because you think it's the best policy, your honesty has already been corrupted.

There's no place a man values honesty more than in a competitor.

All men are honest — until they are faced with a situation tempting enough to make them dishonest.

There is a right way to settle our problems, most of which are caused by trying to avoid that way.

A commentary on the times in which we live is that the noun *honesty* is usually preceded by *old fashioned*.

It is not enough to be "as honest as the day is long." You should behave yourself at night too.

An honest man alters his ideas to fit the truth, and a dishonest man alters the truth to fit his ideas.

Honesty is one business policy that will never have to be changed to keep up with the times.

The practice of honesty is more convincing than the profession of holiness.

It is a mistake to trust a man with an honest face. After all, that may be the only honest part of him.

Honesty is a question of right and wrong, not a matter of policy.

If honesty could be bottled, boxed, or canned, how many would you buy?

So live your life that your autograph will be wanted instead of your fingerprints.

The person who is straightforward and honest doesn't have to worry about a faulty memory.

The honesty of many politicians has never been questioned. In fact, it's never been mentioned.

Honeymoon

The honeymoon is over when the bride begins to suspect that she was never anything to him but a tax deduction.

After the honeymoon the girl usually stops wondering what she should wear and starts wondering how long it will last.

The honeymoon is over when he finds out he married a big spender and she finds out she didn't.

A honeymoon is the short period between the bridal toast and the burnt toast.

The honeymoon is over when you realize that everything she says or cooks disagrees with you.

The honeymoon is a period of doting between dating and debating.

It's easy to spot honeymooners in Las Vegas. The man kisses his wife even when he's losing.

The honeymoon is over when a wife stops making a fuss *over* her husband and begins to make a fuss *with* him.

The honeymoon is definitely over when all the babytalk around the house is done only by the baby.

A woman in Arizona married so late in life that Medicare paid for her honeymoon.

There is nothing so unromantic as a seasick bride.

Hope

Probably nothing in the world arouses more false hopes than the first six hours of a diet.

Faith, hope, and charity — if we had more of the first two we'd need less of the last.

God makes a promise — faith believes it, hope anticipates it, patience quietly awaits it.

Nothing gives you more false hope than the first day of a diet.

There are those who cast their bread upon the waters, hoping it will be returned to them toasted and buttered.

Hope springs eternal in the human heart, but with some the spring is getting very weak.

There's more hope for a confessed sinner than a conceited saint.

Hope sees the invisible, feels the intangible, and achieves the impossible.

Lost hope is the undertaker's best friend.

A lot of people no longer hope for the best. They just hope to avoid the worst.

You can't live on hope alone, nor can you live without it.

A man hopes that his lean years are behind him; a woman, that hers are ahead.

We may as well hope for the best, be prepared for the worst, and take what comes with a grin.

Hope is the anchor of the soul, the stimulus to action, and the incentive to achievement.

If it were not for hope, the heart would break.

Hope is putting faith to work when doubting would be easier.

Hope is faith holding out its hand in the dark.

The hope is that some day the Christian ideal will be put into practice.

Ideals may be beyond our reach but never beyond our fondest hopes.

There is hope for any man who can look in a mirror and laugh at what he sees.

Hope for the best, and be ready for the worst.

The best bridge between despair and hope is a good night's sleep.

Hospital Costs

A fellow recently released from the hospital says he learned what a disturbed patient is — one who has just received his bill!

A hospital should have a recovery room adjoining the cashier's office.

Most surgical operations in the hospital are minor. The bills are always major.

No patient should leave the hospital until he's strong enough to face the cashier.

Any patient can tell you that a hospital bed is the closest thing to a parked taxi with the meter running.

Most hospitals are now so expensive that when you're brought in they interview you to see which ailment you can afford to have.

Wouldn't it be wonderful to open a few discount hospitals?

Hospitals can put both you and your bankroll on the critical list.

These days they carry you into a hospital "fee first."

Hospital costs are high, but where else can you get breakfast in bed?

If you have to go to the hospital, it may help you to remember there is no such thing as a dangerous operation for less than eleven hundred dollars.

Why doesn't science come up with a painkiller for medical and hospital bills?

The people of this nation are sick of the high cost of being sick.

If you plan to finance your forthcoming heart attack, it's absolutely necessary that you work ten hours a day, seven days a week.

Hospitals

An old gentleman in the hospital refused to eat a bowl of quivering jello. Pressed for an explanation by the nurse, he replied, "I'm not going to eat anything that's more nervous than I am."

If all men are born free, why doesn't somebody tell the hospitals and doctors about it?

Time has proven that it pays to be honest even though you may be a long time collecting.

A fellow recently released from the hospital says he learned what a disturbed patient is — one who has just received his bill!

You're ready to leave the hospital when the food begins to taste good.

Some hospitals are so crowded that the only way you can get in is by accident.

A hospital emergency room is a place where you can receive medical attention just as fast as you can prove your ability to pay for it.

A hypochondriac is now attending a medical college studying to be a patient.

A hospital is where they wake a patient at the crack of dawn so that he can lie there wondering why they did it!

A hospital is a place where people who are run-down wind up.

There are two kinds of people in every hospital; those who are desperately ill, and those who complain about the food.

A hospital room is a place where friends of the patient congregate to tell him what their symptoms are.

Some hospitals are so highly specialized they have one man who doesn't do anything but take out stitches.

If folks had more patience the hospitals wouldn't have so many patients.

Hotels

The Gideons should send a Bible to those hotel authorities who determine the room rates.

It is reported that many resort hotels have towels so thick and fluffy that you can hardly close your suitcase.

The price of some luxury hotels is so high that it takes three or four credit cards to pay your bills.

Resort hotels in Florida are usually surrounded by tropical plants — mostly outstretched palms.

A hotel is a place where you're paying seventy-five dollars a day — and they call you a "guest."

Business has been so dull at one major hotel that the management is stealing the towels back from the guests.

Some of our swanky hotels are so expensive you can go broke just sleeping.

When people go to a resort hotel for a change and a rest, the bellboys get the change and the hotel gets the rest.

A hotel is an establishment where a guest gives up good dollars for poor quarters.

A housewife in Utah says her silverware isn't sterling — it's Early Holiday Inn.

One of Moscow's finest hotels proudly boasts that there is a television set in every room — only it watches you!

Those who say sleep is nature's greatest gift to man have not priced very many motels lately.

Housewives

Nothing annoys a housewife more than to have friends drop in unexpectedly and find the house looking like it usually does.

A housewife in Utah says her silverware isn't sterling — it's Early Holiday Inn.

Many modern housewives press buttons instead of clothes.

A harried housewife in Nebraska sighed, "I have so many problems that if something terrible happened to me it would be at least two weeks before I could get around to worrying about it."

Most housewives are very careful about money. They're afraid their husbands might lose it, so they spend it as soon as possible.

A disgruntled housewife suspects her butcher of using phony scales, "Just recently I didn't buy anything and it weighed three pounds."

Did you hear about the wife who lamented, "My husband once showered me with gifts, but lately there's been a long dry-spell."

A major problem facing housewives is that ovens are self-cleaning but kids aren't.

The problem the average housewife faces is that she has too much month left over at the end of the money.

Housework is something you do that nobody notices unless you don't do it.

Human Nature

Many people doubt their ability, but few have any misgivings about their importance.

We all like the person who comes right out and admires us.

Admiration is our polite recognition of another person's resemblance to ourselves.

We learn some things from prosperity, but we learn many more from adversity.

It's a pleasure to give advice, humiliating to need it, normal to ignore it.

Some people never take advice from anybody; others take advice from everybody.

We naturally admire the wisdom and good judgment of those who come to us for advice.

Youth looks ahead, old age looks back, and middle age looks tired.

How come only the most sensible people agree with us?

The greatest danger for most of us is not that our aim is too high and we miss it, but that our aim is too low and we reach it.

The beauty of America is that the average man always thinks he's above average.

An angry man is seldom reasonable; a reasonable man is seldom angry.

An ape is an animal with the effrontery to resemble man.

No matter what you do, someone always knew you would.

Men and nations do behave wisely, once all other alternatives have been exhausted.

We should never assume that people are going to behave as we expect them to.

Man is the only animal that blushes, and the only one that needs to.

A bore is someone who boasts about his accomplishments when he should be boasting about yours!

A good driver is one who, after seeing a wreck, drives carefully for several blocks.

Caution is what we call cowardice in others.

Some people continue to change jobs, mates, and friends — but never think of changing themselves.

Character cannot be purchased, bargained for, inherited, rented, or imported from afar. It must be home-grown.

A man may be better than his creed, his company, or his conduct. But no man is better than his character.

There are two kinds of people in your church: those who agree with you and the bigots.

Common sense is something you want the other fellow to show by accepting your ideas and conclusions.

Cooperation is doing what I tell you to do, and doing it quickly.

When the other fellow finds a flaw in almost everything, he's cranky; when you do, you're discriminating.

If dogs can think, how can we account for their love for man?

You can always spot an educated man. His views are the same as yours.

By nature all men are much alike, but by education they become different.

An egotist is a man who talks so much about himself that he gives us no time to talk about ourselves.

An egotistical person persists in telling you things about himself that you had planned on telling him about yourself.

Don't forget that a pat on the back can cause a chin to go up and shoulders to go back.

To err is human; to cover it up is even more human.

Man, being unable to choose between two evils, often hunts up a third.

The question is not whether man descended from the monkey, but when is he going to stop descending?

Too many people confine their exercise to jumping to conclusions, running up bills, stretching the truth, bending over backward, lying down on the job, sidestepping responsibility, and pushing their luck.

Experience makes a person better or bitter.

Some people profit by their experiences; others never recover from them.

It is when men stop having faith in one another that they stop having faith in their government.

Faith in mankind will be a reality when they stop hauling money in armored cars.

We confess small faults to convey the impression that we have no big ones.

We can do more for other people by correcting our own faults than by trying to correct theirs.

If the faults we see in other people were not so much like our own, we would not recognize them so easily.

There are two kinds of fishermen: those who fish for sport, and those who catch something.

Have you noticed that it's much easier to forgive an enemy after you get even with him?

The trouble with people forgiving and forgetting is that they keep reminding us they're doing it.

We are like beasts when we kill. We are like men when we judge. We are like God when we forgive.

God was at His best when He made man. He made four holes in the head for information to go in, and only one for it to go out.

The birth of a baby is God's vote of confidence in the future of man.

Many people are gossips; however, some of us are merely being informative.

There are no great men except those who have rendered service to mankind.

Some pursue happiness — others create it.

The plain fact is that human beings are happy only when they are striving for something worthwhile.

By the time most people discover that good health is everything, they've lost it.

Why is it that nobody listens when history repeats itself?

What is it about human nature that makes it easier to break a commandment than a habit?

Human nature is what makes kids like to write on wet cement.

It's easy to understand human nature when we bear in mind that almost everybody thinks he's an exception to most rules.

Human nature is harder to change than a thousand dollar bill.

Our five senses are incomplete without the sixth — a sense of humor.

The normal reaction to a new idea is to think of reasons why it can't be done.

You can't judge an automobile by the sound of its horn — nor a man!

Some people use language to express thought, some to conceal thought, and others instead of thought.

If you can laugh at it you can live with it.

Man is the only animal that laughs, but when you look at some people, it's hard to understand how the animals keep from laughing.

No law, however stringent, can make the idle industrious, the shiftless provident, or the drunkard sober.

Laws are man's guidelines, but, unfortunately, too many try to read between them.

A good deal of what passes for even temper is nothing but laziness.

Followers do not usually go any farther than their leaders.

A liar is hard not to believe when he says nice things about you.

We lie loudest when we lie to ourselves.

It's easier to love humanity as a whole than to love one's neighbor.

Of all human passions love is the strongest, for it attacks simultaneously the head, the heart, and the senses.

The weakness of man is the thing to be feared, not his strength.

Modern man meets a crisis face-to-face — after taking a pill.

Man is a book telling the world about its author.

It may be true that every man has his price, but too many people seem to be holding bargain sales.

Many a man saves everything but his soul.

Man starts life young and broke and winds up old and bent.

The average man thinks he isn't.

No matter how much he's got, a man never gets over wanting something for nothing.

Man has learned to fly like a bird and swim like a fish — now all he needs to do is learn to live like a man.

A man who is unable to choose between two evils often hunts up a third.

Man is that foolish creature who tries to get even with his enemies and ahead of his friends.

The trouble with man is twofold. He cannot, or will not, learn truths which are too complicated, and he forgets truths which are too simple.

Perched on the loftiest throne in the world, man is still sitting on his behind.

Most people make the mistake of looking too far ahead for things close by.

The man who invented the eraser had the human race pretty well sized up.

You can't change human nature, but perhaps you can improve it.

Man has conquered almost every dangerous thing in nature except human nature.

It's easier to understand human nature by bearing in mind that almost everybody thinks he's an exception to most rules.

Every man has a right to his opinion — if it parallels ours!

It's easy to spot a person with a lot of personality — he always reminds you so much of yourself.

Politeness is to human nature what warmth is to wax.

It is strange that in our prayers we seldom ask for a change in character, but always a change in circumstances.

We should exchange problems. Everybody seems to know how to solve the other fellow's.

Most of us are broad-minded enough to admit there are two sides to every question — our own side, and the side that no intelligent, informed, sane, and self-respecting person could possibly hold.

When folks clamor for a new religion, what they really want is a religion that isn't too religious.

246

It is much easier to repent of sins that we have already committed than to repent of those we intend to commit.

The eminent scientist who once said we all behave like human beings obviously never drove a car.

The nice thing about wearing a smile is that one size fits everybody.

It is almost impossible to smile on the outside without feeling better on the inside.

Success is a matter of luck. Ask any failure.

God gave to man five senses: touch, taste, smell, sight, and hearing. The successful man has two more — horse and common.

Everybody wants to talk, few want to think, and nobody wants to listen.

Most people can resist everything but temptation.

Think small and you'll remain small.

Five percent of the people really think, ten percent think they think, and the remainder would rather die than think. It's the five percent who change things.

There are few troubles that can't be relieved by an understanding friend, a good night's sleep, or a steak dinner.

Don't bother people by telling them about your troubles. Half of them don't care, and the other half figure you probably had it coming to you.

The person who persists in courting trouble will soon find himself married to it.

A sense of values is the most important single element in human personality.

Those at war with others are seldom at peace with themselves.

One of the most difficult tasks in the world is to convince women that even a bargain costs money.

Fortunately, in our work there is always a choice. We can do it willingly or unwillingly.

The only thing wrong with the world is the people.

Nothing makes us wonder if this is really a man's world as much as watching him trying to run it.

The typical American youth is always ready to give those who are older than himself the full benefit of his inexperience.

Humility

It is when we forget ourselves that we do things that are most likely to be remembered.

The fellow who does things that count doesn't usually stop to count them.

We usually admire the other fellow more after we have tried to do his job.

The hen that laid the biggest egg usually does the least cackling about it.

No garment is more becoming to a Christian than the cloak of humility.

One of the hardest secrets for a man to keep is his opinion of himself.

Greatness is not found in possessions, power, position, or prestige. It is discovered in goodness, humility, service, and character.

To grow tall spiritually, a man must first learn to kneel.

Humility is the ability to look properly shy when you tell people how wonderful you are.

To be humble to superiors is duty; to equals, courtesy; to inferiors, nobility.

Humility is like underwear. We should have it — but not let it show.

No man can truly stand erect until he has first bent the knee to Almighty God.

Those traveling the highway of humility won't be bothered by any heavy traffic.

Humility is elusive. It is such a fragile plant that the slightest reference to it causes it to wilt and die.

Sincere humility attracts. Lack of humility subtracts. Artificial humility detracts.

The person with true humility never has to be shown his place; he is always in it.

When you know you've got humility, you've lost it.

Stay humble or stumble.

A wise man said that humility is Christian clothing. It never goes out of style.

Humility is one of the qualities often left out of the "self-made" man.

Humility is a wonderful trait, but it doesn't help you get waited on at a crowded store.

The person who looks up to God rarely looks down on people.

A fault which humbles a man is of more use to him than a good action which puffs him up.

The best way to be right or wrong is humbly.

Humility makes a man feel smaller as he becomes greater.

Too many people are humble — and know it.

Humility and self-denial are always admired but seldom practiced.

The man who bows humbly before God is sure to walk uprightly before men.

Humility is the ability to look embarrassed while bragging.

No matter how humble you think you are, it always comes as a shock to find out some people don't like you.

The best way to stand up before the world is to kneel down before God.

The best sense of humor belongs to the person who can laugh at himself.

Power is dangerous unless you have humility.

Humor

America is a country where Groucho Marx has more followers than Karl Marx.

When you go on a diet the first thing you're apt to lose is your sense of humor.

Some folk's sense of humor doesn't make sense.

The best sense of humor belongs to the person who can laugh at himself.

Humor is like a needle and thread — deftly used it can patch up just about everything.

Would you enjoy reading one of America's foremost humor publications? If so, subscribe to the *Congressional Record.*

Writing TV humor isn't as hard as listening to it.

Our five senses are incomplete without the sixth — a sense of humor.

One man's idea of humor is another man's idea of a broken friendship.

A man with a sense of humor doesn't make jokes out of life; he merely recognizes the ones that are there.

Humor is the hole that lets the sawdust out of a stuffed shirt.

A genuine sense of humor is the pole that adds balance to our steps as we walk the tightrope of life.

Real humor enables you to laugh when someone takes your best joke and improves on it.

A sense of humor reduces people and problems to their proper proportions.

God gave women a sense of humor — so they could understand the jokes they married.

A sense of humor is what makes you laugh at something which would make you mad if it happened to you.

Every survival kit should include a sense of humor.

Humor is the lubricating oil of business. It prevents friction and wins good will.

A sense of humor is a test of sanity.

Humor is truth in an intoxicated condition.

A sense of humor can help you overlook the unattractive, tolerate the unpleasant, cope with the unexpected, and smile through the unbearable.

Genuine humor is always kindly and gracious. It points out the weakness of humanity, but shows no contempt and leaves no sting.

Imagination was given to man to compensate for what he is not, and a sense of humor to console him for what he is.

It's strange how a man with no sense of humor can come up with such funny answers on his income-tax returns!

Nature must have a sense of humor to let spring fever and house cleaning come at the same time.

Get-well cards have become so humorous that if you don't get sick you're missing a lot of fun.

Writing TV humor isn't as hard as listening to it.

Hunting

Accidents happen every hunting season because both hunter and gun are loaded.

Advice to hunters: Don't get loaded when your gun is.

Most men brag about their hunting experiences, though they're chiefly confined to shooting pool, craps, and bull.

A hunter in West Virginia climbed a fence while carrying a cocked rifle. He's survived by his wife, five kids, and one rabbit.

Husbands
see also Marriage, Wives

Some men achieve distinction by the kind of car they drive — others by the kind of wife that is driving them.

The best time to do the dishes is right after your wife tells you to.

A man whose actions leave his wife speechless has really done something!

Advice to the bridegroom: No matter how she treats you, always try to look a little hurt.

A California woman says her husband is at the dangerous age when all females look alike to him — desirable!

Many a husband has learned that an ironclad alibi isn't as effective as a diamond-studded one.

Some wives appreciate their husbands the most while they are away at work.

Married couples who claim they've never had an argument in forty years either have poor memories or a very dull life to recall.

When you're arguing with your wife, make absolutely sure you're right — and then let the matter drop.

The argument you just won with your wife isn't over yet.

Sign in a florist's window: "Smoking, or forgetting your wife's birthday, can be hazardous to your health."

A diplomatic husband said to his wife, "How do you expect me to remember your birthday when you never look any older?"

The fellow who boasts of running things at his home most likely means the lawn mower, washing machine, vacuum cleaner, and errands.

Watch the man who says he's the boss at home. He may lie about other things too.

Boys will be boys, particularly when they're away from their wives.

When a man brags that he wears the pants at home, the chances are his wife tells him which pants to put on.

Chivalry is what a husband displays toward somebody else's wife.

The average couple splits the Christmas chores. She signs the cards and he signs the checks.

A lady shopper in a shoe store expressed a desire to buy an expensive pair of shoes — to go with a cheap husband!

Sometimes a woman gets a mink coat the hard way — by being nice to her husband.

Women buy their husbands loafer shoes and leisure slacks — and then call them lazy when they play the part they're dressed for.

It's a pretty safe bet that the husbands of the ten best-dressed women won't show up on the list of the ten best-dressed men.

A man hates to see a woman in cheap clothes, unless, of course, it's his wife.

The reason so many wives have new fur coats is that husbands give in before their wives give up.

Many a husband doesn't know a thing about women's clothes, except what they cost.

The wife who dresses to please her husband wears last year's clothes.

Most husbands would like for their wives to wear their dresses longer — about three years longer.

Attention wives: If your husband complains about the tie you gave him last Christmas — give him a sock!

A Kansas wife complained that her husband is extremely forgetful. "He keeps forgetting things — like being married."

The Supreme Court of the United States gives a husband the right to open his wife's letters — but it doesn't give him the courage.

He took his defeat like a man; he blamed it on his wife.

The high divorce rate indicates that the modern woman hasn't made up her mind whether to have a man for a hubby or a hobby.

There would be fewer divorces if the husband tried as hard to keep his wife as he did to get her.

When a husband's ego needs a little boosting, he asks his wife to describe the fellow she turned down to marry him.

Many a man who is too tired to help around the house plays golf for exercise.

If experience is the best teacher, how is it that some husbands still think they're the boss of the family?

Faith is better company than imagination for the wife whose husband fails to come home on time.

A man who has faults he doesn't know about probably doesn't listen to his wife.

Flattery is what makes husbands out of bachelors.

Sign in a florist's window: "Send flowers to the one you love. While you're at it, don't forget your wife."

No wife can endure a gambling husband — unless he's a steady winner.

Gentlemen prefer blondes — especially gentlemen who are married to brunettes.

A "rare gift" is any kind a woman gets from her husband after ten years of marriage.

Nothing makes the average wife so suspicious of her husband as an unexpected gift.

Some girls can't take a joke, but others prefer one to no husband at all.

Most girls seem to marry men like their fathers. Maybe that's the reason so many mothers cry at weddings.

Nowadays some girls seem more particular about choosing their divorce lawyers than choosing their husbands.

In Hollywood it's difficult for a bachelor to remain a bachelor — and even more difficult for a husband to remain a husband.

In some unfortunate homes, husbands and wives aren't talking. In others, it's just the husband who isn't talking.

The man is still boss in the American home — as long as he allows his wife to make all the decisions.

A husband controls his wife just like a barometer controls the weather.

Some husbands are living proof that a woman can take a joke.

When a husband has the last word, he's probably talking to himself.

A husband who still calls his wife the "little woman" very likely hasn't looked lately.

A devoted husband is one who assures his wife every morning that she's right.

Most husbands are interested in politics. In fact, many of them are already the minority leader in the house.

A Wyoming husband reports that his wife thinks swimming is good for his health. She's always telling him to go jump in the river.

Many a husband comes home from work and hopes the kitchen stove is as warm as the TV set.

When a husband says he can't do something due to circumstances beyond his control, he means his wife won't let him.

A henpecked husband washes the dishes — even when they use paper plates.

It can be dangerous for a husband to come home late at night — especially if he promised his wife he'd be home early.

Most husbands never even think of other women. They're too decent, too refined, too old.

When a husband sees the kind of men most women marry, he is sure his wife did pretty well.

A husband who doesn't know what's wrong with him hasn't been listening.

The reason many husbands never speak out of turn is because they never have one.

An Alabama husband recently remarked, "I'm concerned about my wife; she no longer nags me with the same dedication she used to."

Husbands are like sour pickles; the older they get, the sourer they get.

A young Georgia husband is mad at the minister who performed his marriage ceremony. The minister asked his bride, "Do you take this man for better, or probably worse?"

It takes a smart husband to have the last word — and not use it.

Views expressed by husbands are not necessarily those of the management.

A husband seldom worries about the national debt. What bothers him is the way his wife keeps trying to localize it.

The ideal husband is the one who understands every word his wife isn't saying.

When a husband has the last word it's probably in his will.

Marriage counselors say husbands should wear a ring or other indication to show they're wed. How about a worried look?

It's a wise husband who puts his foot down only to shift positions.

A husband seldom tells his wife about his business troubles until she wants to buy something expensive.

Husbands are like wood fires. When unattended they go out.

Many husbands go broke on the money their wives save at sales.

A wise husband not only allows his wife to get in the last word, he's relieved when she finally gets it in.

If more husbands had self-starters, fewer wives would have to be cranks.

A husband often thinks he bosses the house — but actually he only houses the boss.

A henpecked husband in Illinois won't even eat anything that disagrees with his wife.

A husband is just a guy who smiled back once too often.

Some husbands irritate their wives by staying out too much; and others, by staying in too much.

A husband wishes he had as much fun when he's out as his wife thinks he does.

One of a husband's hardest problems is getting back some of his take-home pay after he takes it home.

A good husband is one who will wash up when asked and shut up when told.

As any husband knows, one way to make a long story short is to stop listening.

The man who boasts that he never made a mistake has a wife who did.

Technically, the husband is the head of the house, but the technicality is often overruled.

A happily married man is one who helps his wife into her fur coat — which she bought before they were married.

There are two kinds of husbands: one brings his wife a gift when he returns from a convention, and the other behaved himself.

A wise husband buys his wife fine china so she won't trust him to wash the dishes.

A devoted husband is one who stands by his wife in troubles she wouldn't have had if she hadn't married him.

The only time some husbands put their foot down is when spading the garden.

A good husband meets a marital crisis with a firm hand — full of candy and flowers.

The world is a stage all right, with husbands always playing the supporting role.

A husband is like an egg — if kept in hot water continually, he becomes hard-boiled.

Any husband who expects to pull the wool over his wife's eyes had better be sure he's using a good yarn.

An ideal husband is one who treats his wife with the same consideration as his pretty secretary.

Husbands are awkward things to deal with. Even keeping them in hot water will not make them tender.

Most husbands remember where and when they got married. What stumps them is why.

When a husband dreams he's a bachelor, it's a sign he's going to be disappointed when he wakes up.

In selecting a husband, a woman should shut both eyes, grab hard, and trust the Lord.

About the only voice some husbands have around the house is the invoice.

There's nothing like a dish towel for wiping that contented look off a husband's face.

Getting a husband is like buying a house. You don't see it the way it is, but the way you think it's going to be when you get it remodeled.

Most husbands know what an extravaganza is. They married one.

A Kentucky wife described her husband, "He doesn't smoke, curse, drink, or go out with women — including me."

A husband is a wolf who paid too much for his whistle.

A California husband complained that his wife is leading a double life — hers and his.

Advice on holding a husband: Treat him as you would any other pet — three meals a day, plenty of affection, and a loose leash.

Many a henpecked husband feels like his birthstone is the grindstone.

There are two reasons why husbands leave home — wives who can cook and won't, and wives who can't cook and do.

A husband should tell his wife everything he thinks she'll find out.

Give some husbands enough rope and they'll skip.

The average husband considers the ideal household appliance something his wife can repair.

The new husband soon learns that his bride may be too cute for words — but not for arguments.

Many a husband has learned that an ironclad alibi isn't as effective as a diamond-studded one.

A husband is never as good as his wife thought he was before marriage, and never as bad as she thinks him to be after marriage.

Whether or not a husband considers his wife a necessity or a luxury depends on whether she's cooking his dinner or asking for a new dress.

Give a man enough rope and he'll claim he was tied up at the office.

The husband who sits under a tree while his wife mows the lawn could be called a "shady character."

A husband wanted to show his wife who was boss so he bought her a mirror.

What puzzles a husband is how he can put his foot down and end up with it in his mouth.

Imagination is something that sits up with a wife when her husband comes home late.

The man who says his wife can't take a joke forgets that she took him.

If you think the average American woman can't take a joke, take a look at the average American husband.

Don't trust your wife's judgment — look at whom she married!

Treat a dog with kindness, pet him often, feed him well, and he'll never leave you. The same system usually works with husbands.

When a woman laughs at her husband's jokes, either they're good jokes or she's a good wife.

Husbands lay down the law, but wives usually repeal it.

A widow in Oklahoma remarked that her husband was a total loss — he died without life insurance.

A man may be drinking because his wife walked out on him — or because she walked in on him.

A husband knows his wife loves him when she returns a dress he can't afford.

A timid man said to his wife, "We're not going out tonight and that's semi-final."

There would be a lot more happy marriages if husbands tried to understand their wives and wives tried to understand football.

Married men can't understand why every bachelor isn't a millionaire.

The husband who brags that he never made a mistake has a wife who did.

All men make mistakes — husbands just find out about them sooner.

When his wife nags the civilized man goes to a club instead of reaching for one.

The reason some husbands are overweight is that the only time they get to open their mouths is when they're eating.

There are two kinds of people — the "haves" and the "have nots." Or to put it more simply — wives and husbands.

Two Texas political candidates were having a heated debate. One shouted, "What about the powerful interests that control you?" The other screamed back, "You leave my wife out of this."

One of the problems of modern life is for a husband to teach his wife that even bargains cost money.

Some husbands quarrel with their wives, and others have learned to say, "Yes, dear."

A certain radio station phoned one thousand men, asking to whom they were listening. Ninety-seven percent said they were listening to their wives.

A super salesman is a husband who can convince his wife that she's too young for a mink coat.

Silence is a wife's best weapon. It upsets her husband.

If TV doesn't start getting better, husbands may go back to listening to their wives.

Nothing makes a wife more skeptical than when her husband tells the exact truth.

A good wife is one who believes her husband, who does all the work, should get at least half the credit.

A wife can often surprise her husband on their wedding anniversary by merely mentioning it.

A woman in Maryland recently gave birth to her tenth child and has run out of names — to call her husband.

By the time a woman is wise enough to select a husband, she has been married for years.

Some women have very little regard for husbands, especially if they already have one.

How long a woman works after her marriage is often determined by the number of payments still due on her husband's car.

The world's a stage all right, with husbands playing the supporting role.

The average husband worries about what his wife spends and what the government spends. The difference is he's not afraid to criticize the government.

A yawn is nature's provision for making it possible for husbands to open their mouths.

A young man spends at least twelve years in school learning the English language, then becomes a husband and never gets a chance to use it.

Hypochondriacs

Never ask a hypochondriac how he feels unless you want to hear an "organ recital."

A real hypochondriac is one who wants to be buried next to a doctor.

An Ohio hypochondriac recently exclaimed to a friend, "I had the most wonderful dizzy spell yesterday."

An indecisive hypochondriac is one who just can't make up his mind which disease he wants to have next.

A hypochondriac is now attending a medical college in Kansas City. He is studying to be a patient.

There's a hypochondriac in Wyoming who has an annual checkup every week.

Inscription on the tombstone of a hypochondriac: "Now will you believe I was sick?"

A hypochondriac reports that her doctor cured her illness with one sentence, "Your insurance doesn't cover it."

A true hypochondriac is the guy who can tell you exactly how many measles he had.

A recent wedding between two hypochondriacs was very touching. They exchanged vows and symptoms.

A Louisiana hypochondriac reports that the best thing he got for his birthday was a gift certificate to the Mayo Clinic.

A man might be considered just a little bit mean when he sends get-well cards to a hypochondriac.

Hypocrites

Actors are the only honest hypocrites.

As soon as you observe that everybody agrees with you, you can be sure they don't mean it.

Don't stay away from the church because you have the idea that there are too many hypocrites in it. There's always room for one more.

A sickly saint is likely to be a healthy hypocrite.

A hypocrite is a person who preaches by the yard, but practices by the inch.

A hypocrite prays on his knees on Sunday — and on his neighbors the rest of the week.

If you cause a man to think he is right when he is wrong, you are a hypocrite.

A hypocrite at least appreciates goodness enough to imitate it.

A man who smiles when he hands his paycheck over to his wife might be classified as a hypocrite!

A hypocrite never intends to be what he pretends to be.

A hypocrite is someone who writes a book in praise of atheism, and then prays it'll sell.

It must be a problem for two-faced people to put their best face forward.

Even the hypocrite admires righteousness. That is why he imitates it.

I

Ideals

Ideas

Idleness

Ignorance

Imagination

Improvement

Income

Indigestion

Inferiority Complex

Inflation

Influence

Installment Plans

Intelligence

Intentions

Internal Revenue
Service

Intuition

Inventions

Ideals
see also Goals

Much has been said about what America stands for. Let's not forget some things that America won't stand for.

Nobody has a right to criticize the government unless he voted in the last election.

The real trouble with government is that we have too few ideals and too many deals.

The ideal of some men is to marry a rich girl who is too proud to have her husband work.

The hope is that some day the Christian ideal will be put into practice.

Keep your ideals high enough to inspire you, and low enough to encourage you.

Ideals may be beyond our reach but never beyond our fondest hopes.

Most of us have high ideals and will stand by them as long as it pays.

If you are satisfied with yourself, you had better change your ideals.

Our ideals are too often like an antique chair — nice to talk about and show off, but too fragile to use.

The ideal summer resort is where the fish bite and the mosquitoes don't.

Ideals are like tuning forks; you must sound them frequently to keep your life up to pitch.

The true measure of a man is the height of his ideals, the breadth of his sympathy, the depth of his convictions, and the length of his patience.

It's a sad fact that many politicians are more concerned with deals than with ideals.

If you are satisfied with yourself, you had better change your ideals.

Ideas
see also Thoughts

You can judge your age by the amount of pain you feel when you come in contact with a new idea.

What America really needs most are those things which money can't buy.

Some people never let ideas interrupt the easy flow of their conversation.

Facts, when combined with ideas, constitute the greatest force in the world.

Only hungry minds can become educated.

It's easier to get people to exchange ideas than to change them.

Another war worth waging is one against the poverty of ideas.

The man with a new idea is often considered a crank until the idea succeeds.

Ideas are like children. No matter how much you like other people's, you can't help thinking your own are best.

Too many people run out of ideas long before they run out of words.

The real crown jewels are ideas.

Unexpressed ideas are of no more value than kernels in a nut before it has been cracked.

Nothing dies quicker than a new idea in a closed mind.

Some people entertain ideas; others put them to work.

New ideas hurt some minds the same as new shoes hurt some feet.

It is possible that you could stop an army of a million men, but you can't stop a good idea when it comes along.

A "sensational new idea" is sometimes just an old idea with its sleeves rolled up.

An idea isn't responsible for the people who believe in it.

Good ideas need landing gear as well as wings.

It is better to have no ideas at all than to have false ones.

A good idea poorly expressed often sounds like a poor one.

A man without a single idea is less of a bore than a man with only one idea.

Some people never let ideas interrupt the easy flow of their conversation.

The mind stretched by a new idea never returns to its original dimensions.

Ideas are funny things. They don't work unless you do.

The normal reaction to a new idea is to think of reasons why it can't be done.

257

Many a good idea has been smothered to death by words.

The best way to put an idea across is to wrap it up in a person.

A new idea is delicate. It can be killed by a sneer or a yawn; it can be terribly distorted by a quip; or it can be crushed by a frown.

Have you ever noticed that the smaller the idea, the bigger the words used to express it?

If you can't think up a new idea, try finding a way to make better use of an old one.

You can kill men and cripple nations, but you cannot kill a good idea.

There are more warmed-over ideas than hot ones.

The real test of a good idea is whether or not it's your own.

You are certain to get the worst of the bargain when you exchange ideas with a fool.

The reason ideas die quickly in some heads is because they can't stand solitary confinement.

How good a red-hot idea is depends on how much heat it loses when somebody throws cold water on it.

The soundness of your ideas is more important than the sound of your words.

No big ideas ever came from swelled heads.

A good idea is one that hits the other fellow with a bolt of envy.

It is best to test new ideas on old friends.

There is nothing in the world more powerful than an idea. No weapon can destroy it; no power can conquer it, except the power of another idea.

Every time one man expresses an idea, he finds ten men who thought of it before — but they only thought.

Old ideas, like old medicine, can be dangerous to have around after they've done their job.

An idea is more than information; it is information with legs, and — it is headed somewhere.

An idea is the only lever which really moves the world.

It isn't easy for an idea to squeeze itself into a head filled with prejudice.

Many great ideas have been lost because the people who had them couldn't stand being laughed at.

Ideas are not truly alive if they remain locked in a single mind.

Nothing is more valuable than a workable idea.

Profanity is a means of escape for the person who runs out of ideas.

The difficulty with amplifiers is that they amplify the speaker's voice but not his ideas.

Too many speakers have diarrhea of words and constipation of ideas.

The unhappiest man is the one whose expenditure of speech is too great for his income of ideas.

Another form of wastefulness is the expenditure of words beyond the income of ideas.

Idleness

Do something. Either lead, follow, or get out of the way!

It pays to keep your feet on the ground, but keep them moving.

It doesn't do any good to sit up and take notice if you keep on sitting.

No thoroughly occupied man has ever been known to be miserable.

A person going nowhere can be sure of reaching his destination.

The bee that makes the honey doesn't hang around the hive.

The Bible promises no loaves to the loafer.

It's what you do when you have nothing to do that reveals what you are.

Few things are more dangerous to a person's character than having nothing to do and plenty of time in which to do it.

An idle Christian is the raw material of which backsliders are made.

The church cannot afford the luxury of loafing.

When you don't want to do anything, one excuse is as good as another.

The road to failure is greased with the slime of indifference.

Fishing is the art of doing almost nothing.

Fishing is a laborious way of taking it easy.

Some carve out a future, while others just whittle away the time.

Many a person's idea of heaven would be nothing to do and an eternity to do it in.

There are more idle brains than idle hands.

The chief reward for idleness is poverty.

Stand still and watch the world go by — and it will!

Don't wait for your ship to come in if you haven't sent one out.

The hardest job of all is trying to look busy when you're not.

Doing nothing is the most tiresome job in the world because you can't stop and rest.

A loafer is always glad when Monday comes. He has another whole week to loaf.

Most of the people who sit around and wait for the harvest haven't planted anything.

When an idler sees a job completed, he's sure he could have done it better.

The man who has nothing to do always gives it his personal attention.

Idleness travels so slowly that poverty soon overtakes it.

Idleness is the nest in which mischief lays its eggs.

The Bible promises no loaves to the loafer.

Easy Street is still mighty hard to find.

A man is truly poor, not when he *has* nothing, but when he *does* nothing.

It's too bad that the only men who can solve the world's problems are too busy sitting on the front porch whittling.

To get collective bargaining, men sometimes engage in collective loafing.

The idle person is not much better than a dead one and takes up a lot more room.

It's easy to take a day off but extremely difficult to put it back.

No one ever stumbled onto anything worthwhile sitting down.

Even if you are on the right track, you may get run over if you sit there long enough.

A loafer is one who continues to live even though he complains that he can't live on the wages he turns down.

You can't make a hit with the bat on your shoulder.

It does a man no good to sit up and take notice — if he keeps on sitting.

Sign on a minister's desk: "If you have nothing to do, please don't do it here."

Loafing is the only way to beat the income tax.

A little knowledge that acts is worth infinitely more than much knowledge that is idle.

Entirely too many people fashion their lives after French bread — one long loaf!

The fellow who fiddles around seldom gets to lead the orchestra.

Never has a man who lived a life of ease left a name worth remembering.

All some people do is grow old.

A lot of people do nothing in particular but they do it well.

Some people stand on the promises; others just sit on the premises.

Did you ever know of an idle rumor that remained idle?

A lot of trouble arises from workers who don't think, and from thinkers who don't work.

Most of our troubles arise from loafing when we should be working, and talking when we should be listening.

Worry kills more people than work. Some people play it safe by doing neither.

Among the chief worries of today's business executives is the large number of unemployed still on the payrolls.

Ignorance

No one gives advice with more enthusiasm than an ignorant person.

It is impossible to defeat an ignorant man in an argument.

Discussion is an exchange of knowledge; argument is an exchange of ignorance.

A Tennessee husband gave his wife the following instructions when teaching her how to drive his car: "Go on green, stop on red, slow down when I turn white."

Dignity is often a mask we wear to hide our ignorance.

Among the few things more expensive than an education these days is the lack of it.

An educated person is one who knows how to be ignorant intelligently.

May education never become as expensive as ignorance.

Education is going forward from cocksure ignorance to thoughtful uncertainty.

It may be true that to err is human, but to remain in error is stupid.

A rose by any other name would mean that you're ignorant about flowers.

All of us know a few people who hold the Doctor of Ignorance degree.

Very few people have learned to use ignorance intelligently.

Many of the most firmly held beliefs are based solidly on ignorance.

If you don't know, simply say so.

There's one thing to be said about ignorance — it gives rise to almost 90 percent of the world's conversations.

Ignorance is no excuse. Almost invariably it's the real thing.

Don't forget the fact that ignorance of the law is what keeps our higher courts functioning.

More people get into trouble by covering up their ignorance than by admitting it.

It's all right to be ignorant, but it's stupid to make a career out of it.

Ignorance is not the real problem. It's not knowing we're ignorant that causes the difficulty.

If ignorance was bliss, we'd all be a whole lot happier.

The recipe for perpetual ignorance is to be satisfied with your opinions and content with your knowledge.

Unless you are willing to admit your ignorance, you will never be able to acquire knowledge.

Ignorance needs no introduction; it always makes itself known.

It seems that some people were born ignorant — and later had a relapse.

Poverty is no disgrace, but ignorance is.

It's not necessary for some people to put out the light to be in the dark.

The only thing more expensive than education is ignorance.

A person can accumulate a lot of ignorance in the course of a lifetime.

There is nothing more terrifying than ignorance in action.

What you don't know won't hurt you, but it may cause you to look pretty silly.

The darkest ignorance is man's ignorance of God.

It is better to be silent and thought ignorant than to speak and remove all doubt.

Being ignorant is not so shameful as being unwilling to learn.

It is a very common thing for ignorance to denounce what it does not understand.

The fellow who knows nothing soon repeats it.

A man doesn't always get paid for what he knows, but he seldom escapes paying for what he doesn't know.

It's harder to conceal ignorance than to acquire knowledge.

Speak softly and only those closest to you will ever know how little you know.

There are a lot of things we don't know, but there are also a lot of things we do know that we never use.

The less you know about your own future and the other fellow's past, the better off you are.

Ignorance is an opiate that lulls a conscience to sleep.

The average man has more money than sense; the trouble is that he doesn't know it.

Ignorance of law is no excuse — neither is the ignorance of the lawmakers.

The more ignorant a person is about a subject under discussion, the more convinced he is that he's right.

Knowledge may have its limits — but not so with ignorance.

Too many fellows pop up with "I think I know" when they haven't the ability to think or to know.

It's remarkable how large a part ignorance plays in making a man satisfied with himself.

Ignorance is when you don't know anything, and somebody finds it out.

If ignorance is no excuse, there doesn't seem to be much use for it.

There's one thing to be said for ignorance — it causes a lot of interesting arguments.

The only known cure for ignorance is education.

Folks who don't know anything should keep it to themselves.

Many a man is not suspected of being ignorant till he starts to talk.

People who know the very least seem to know it the loudest.

Ignorance must not be bliss or lots of people would be jumping for joy all the time.

A person must have a certain amount of intelligent ignorance to get anywhere.

If some Christians knew as little about their jobs as they do the Bible, they would have to be guided to their work benches every morning.

Nothing pleases an ignorant man as much as a chance to hand out information.

Lots of people play dumb. Unfortunately, many aren't playing.

Never have so many understood so little about so much.

One of the hardest things in the world to face is our own ignorance.

One advantage of being ignorant is that you never feel alone.

A little learning may be a dangerous thing — but it's still safer than total ignorance.

Ignorance of the law is no excuse, but it's better than no alibi at all.

Some days you run into so many stupid people you're amazed there's enough ignorance to go around.

It is impossible to win an argument with an ignorant man.

The most effective way to conceal ignorance is to listen and shake your head when asked for an opinion.

You can't help but admire the fellow who is stupid but knows it.

It's beginning to look like many people are fighting fiercely to preserve their ignorance.

The quickest way for a man to reveal his ignorance is to try to tell someone how much he knows.

The more we study, the more we discover our ignorance.

There is no limit to either intelligence or ignorance.

A jury is a group of twelve men and women of average ignorance.

One part of knowledge consists in being ignorant of things that are not worth knowing.

The best part of our knowledge is that which teaches us where knowledge leaves off and ignorance begins.

The first step to knowledge is to know that you are ignorant.

It's better to know nothing than to know what isn't so.

Ignorance of the law is no excuse, except for judges.

A truly great leader is one who never allows his followers to discover that he is as ignorant as they are.

It's a lot easier to form an opinion when you have only a few of the facts.

If you wish to get along with people, pretend not to know whatever they tell you.

A philosopher thinks in order to believe. He formulates his prejudices and systematizes his ignorance.

Prejudice is essentially an outgrowth of ignorance.

Silence is the best and surest way to hide ignorance.

Keeping one's mouth shut keeps a lot of ignorance from leaking out.

Sin is mothered by ignorance.

Wisdom is knowing when and how to appear ignorant.

There is no zeal so intemperate and cruel as that which is backed by ignorance.

Imagination

Infant prodigies are young people with highly imaginative parents.

In order to become perfectly content, it is necessary to have a poor memory and no imagination.

Fishing stimulates the brain — also the imagination!

If you would like to stimulate your imagination, why not try fishing?

Imagination was given to man to compensate for what he is not, and a sense of humor to console him for what he is.

Anybody who thinks Americans lack imagination has never worked for the IRS.

Imagination is what makes you think you're having a wonderful time when you are only spending money.

Unlike an aircraft, your imagination can take flight day or night and in any kind of weather.

Many a girl who elopes wishes later she had just let her imagination run away with her.

Some people are always indebted to their imagination for facts.

Imagination is something that sits up with a wife when her husband comes home late.

A man's life is dyed the color of his imagination.

Imagination is what makes the average man think he can run the business better than his boss.

The imagination is the powerhouse that supplies the mysterious force which we call "inspiration."

Stretch your imagination too far and it will snap back at you.

No stretch of the imagination is as complete as the one used in filling out income-tax forms.

You can't depend on your evaluation of a person when your imagination is out of focus.

A liar is one who forgets to keep a partition between his imagination and the true facts.

Man is like a tack; he can go only as far as his head will let him.

About the only thing that modern movies leave to the imagination is the plot.

When temptation knocks, imagination usually answers.

Improvement

People seldom improve when they have no model but themselves.

Time invested in improving ourselves cuts down on time wasted in disapproving of others.

There is a mad scramble to improve just about everything in the world except people.

One way to make the world better is by improving yourself.

People seldom improve when they have no model to copy but themselves.

Improvement is what you see a need for in other people, but can't see the same need in yourself.

Looking in the mirror isn't exactly the best way to convince yourself that things are improving.

Nobody ever does his best; that's why we all have a good chance to do better.

The world might be improved with less television and more vision.

Each person has the chance to improve himself, but some just don't believe in taking chances.

There are times when you just aren't feeling like yourself, which can be quite an improvement.

The largest room in the world is the room for improvement.

By improving yourself the world is made better.

The human race seems to be improving everything except people.

Silence is one of the most beautiful, impressive, and inspiring things known to man. Don't break it unless you can improve on it.

Income

Growing families have a way of outgrowing everything — especially their incomes.

It's true that gifts to charity are deductible on your income tax; the trouble is they are also deductible from your income.

If you live within your income you'll live without worry — and without a lot of other things.

The way most people manage to live within their income is partially.

Just about the time your income reaches the point where food prices don't matter — calories do.

The trouble with fixed incomes is that they are not very well-fixed.

A guaranteed income is nothing new in this country. We've had alimony for years.

Living within your income is likely to cause people to wonder if there is anything else peculiar about you.

Most people could live within their incomes if they were as economical all year round as they are right after their vacations.

The outcome of the income depends on the outgo for the upkeep.

Nothing makes it harder to live within your income than being paid what you're really worth.

Don't you long for the "good old days" when Uncle Sam lived within his income and without most of yours?

People not only can't live within their income, they can't even live within their credit cards.

The two most important things about your income are: make it first and then make it last.

Nothing makes a man so modest about his income as a tax form to fill out.

Sometimes it's hard to decide which is worse — living within an income or without one.

The American family and the United States government are in agreement about one thing — neither of them can live within their income.

When it comes to income these days, about all you can keep is quiet.

The easiest way to live within your income is to have a big one.

We should always strive to live within our incomes, even if we have to borrow money to do so.

The average income of Americans is at a high point. In fact, it's almost as high as their expenses.

Anyone on a fixed income is in a bad fix these days.

Pity the guy in the middle-income bracket — earning too much to avoid paying taxes, and not enough to afford paying taxes.

A dyed-in-the-wool patriot is one who says he's sorry he has only one income to give to his country.

The world is full of people making a good living but poor lives.

Indigestion

Our new faster-than-sound jet planes are wonderful. You can eat dinner in London and get indigestion in New York City.

There are relatively few cases of mental indigestion. The brain is seldom overworked like the stomach.

A lot of indigestion is caused by people having to eat their own words.

Indigestion is like charity. It, too, begins at home.

A lot of "food for thought" being dished out these days is giving our country a bad case of mental indigestion.

Indigestion is the failure to adjust a square meal to a round stomach.

In some restaurants you'll notice three shakers on every table — salt, pepper, and Alka-Seltzer.

Inferiority Complex

An inferiority complex would be a mighty fine thing if only the right people had it.

No one can make you feel inferior without your consent.

The typical inferiority complex in Washington results from not having a telephone worth tapping.

Some men think they have an inferiority complex, when, in fact, they are just inferior.

If a Texan had an inferiority complex, rest assured it would be the biggest one you can get.

Psychiatrists don't fare too well in Texas — no inferiority complexes!

Inflation
see also Cost of living

Airplane fares have been increased considerably. Even the cost of going up is going up.

Americans are getting stronger. Twenty years ago it took two people to carry fifteen dollars worth of groceries. Today, a child can do it.

Appearances can be deceiving — a dollar bill looks the same as it did twenty-five years ago.

Every year the cars get lower and wider, while the payments get longer and higher.

There was a time when you could rent a car for a week for what it now costs to park it for a day.

A bargain is anything that costs no more today than it did last week.

Nowadays everything is a bargain — because by the time you get it home the price has gone up.

The book *How to Beat Inflation* has just gone from $1.75 to $2.95.

Congress fighting inflation is like the Mafia fighting crime.

It's now costing Americans twice as much to live beyond their means as it did twenty years ago.

If life is worth what it's costing now, people were getting a bargain in grandpa's day.

Today one can buy ten cents worth of almost anything for thirty cents.

It's almost as difficult to live within an income today as it was to live without one in the early 1930s.

Our present economy is terrible. We're making more and more dollars and less and less money.

Inflated food prices are hard to swallow.

There is a vast difference between growth and inflation.

With today's inflation, it's a question of which is more costly — investing in the stock market or shopping in a supermarket.

Inflation has even created a new law of gravity — what goes *up* gets *us* down.

There is only one sure way to slow down inflation — turn it over to the Post Office.

You know inflation is getting worse when they sell apples on the street — by the bite.

No matter where you go these days, you'll find that inflation got there first.

Inflation is a period when you can go broke in a prosperous way.

The "good old days" were when inflation was something you did to a balloon.

Inflation is an economic situation which occurs when the prices you get look good, and the prices you pay look awful.

If we can't win the war against inflation — how about a cease-fire?

Inflation is when a counterfeiter buys ink, paper, a printing press, and runs off a few thousand dollars — and loses money on the deal.

In today's world of inflation a big spender is any man who supports a wife and kids.

Inflation is like getting stuck in a traffic jam. You're part of the problem, but you don't know what to do about it.

In these days of inflation, it's virtually an insult to tell a girl she looks like a million dollars.

Inflation is getting so bad that even guys who never pick up a check are complaining.

Inflation is when petty cash is the only kind there is.

Inflation is when the buck doesn't stop anywhere.

Trying to curb inflation by raising taxes is like giving a drunk another drink to sober him up.

Inflation is when sitting on your nest egg doesn't give you much to crow about.

Let's hope inflation flattens out before our wallets do.

Inflation seems to affect everything. The fellow who used to be as phony as a three dollar bill is now up to six dollars.

How much better off we all would be if quality were inflated instead of prices!

Inflation is when "never having it so good" never cost us so much.

An Illinois man complained about inflation, "Last year it was my doctor who put me on a diet. This year it was my accountant."

Inflation is what makes balloons bigger and candy bars smaller.

Inflation is the period when a fellow goes broke by just staying even.

If you plan to teach your children the value of a dollar, you'll have to do it awfully fast.

Inflation is when wallets are getting bigger and shopping bags are getting smaller.

Inflation is a state of affairs in which you never had it so good or parted with it so fast.

Production is one answer to inflation. That's why rabbit fur is cheaper than mink.

Inflation is just now striking home. Many of us are receiving our bank statements in an envelope edged in black.

Not everybody has been affected by inflation. We still have two-bit politicians.

Note on inflation: The best time to buy anything seems to be about a year ago.

There's one consolation in inflation — the money you haven't got isn't worth what it was once worth.

Inflation is when you do more for a dollar than a dollar does for you.

Thanks to inflation it's costing more than ever to live beyond our means.

There is one thing we can all say about inflation — it has completely eliminated the generation gap. We are all crying like babies.

Inflation is something like the flu — hard to trace and harder to stop.

One of the benefits of inflation is that kids can no longer get sick on a nickel's worth of candy.

Unless inflation is stopped soon, we'll have to do some more fixing on these fixed incomes.

About the only way Washington will ever be able to stop inflation is to stop inflating.

Something that cost five dollars to buy a few years ago now cost ten dollars to repair.

Let's stop inflation. It's hazardous to our wealth.

Just when you think you've found a hedge against inflation, Congress decided to trim.

There's one comforting thought about inflation — the money you pay back isn't worth nearly as much as the money you borrowed.

Inflation is making the green pastures of retirement look parched.

If George Washington never told a lie, what's his picture doing on a dollar bill that's worth about forty-three cents?

More marriages will be inevitable if postage continues to increase. It'll be cheaper to marry the girl than to write to her.

Even with inflation money still talks, but it carries on a quieter conversation.

The more money is inflated, the less it can be stretched.

Have you found a penny in the street lately? It was probably a dime when someone dropped it.

You can tell it's an old movie when the doctor tells the patient, "You're as sound as a dollar."

Fat people have the kind of inflation that even the government can't keep down.

No wonder politicians pass the buck — it's now worth only forty-three cents.

Politics is like inflation. The more we have of it, the more things cost.

Even the price of being poor today has gone up at least 20 percent.

Inflation has affected everything except the wages of sin.

Increasing taxes to stop inflation makes about as much sense as fanning a fire to cool its heat.

Despite inflation a penny for the thoughts of many people is still a fair price.

The salary we used to dream of is the one we can't live on today.

Washington is recalling all the one dollar bills. There's a defect in the value.

Influence

Every action of our lives touches some chord that will vibrate in eternity.

Example is not the main thing in influencing others. It is the only thing.

Please don't try to use your influence until you're sure you have it.

One sure way for you to gain adherents to your cause is to start winning.

It is impossible for you to influence others to live on a higher level than that on which you live yourself.

Influence is something you *think* you have until you try to use it.

Influence is like a savings account. The less you use it, the more you've got.

A man lives as long as there are those who bear the stamp of his influence.

Just one act of yours may turn the tide of another person's life.

It's sad when a person has a head like a door-knob — anybody can turn it.

Installment Plans

Nothing makes installment buying as easy as the advertising.

The reason Americans don't own more elephants is that they have never been offered one for a dollar down and a dollar a week.

Most Americans have definite goals in life and attain them gradually — with the help of a finance company.

The first thing the typical American will ask when he gets to heaven is the amount of the down-payment on a harp.

The vanishing American is one who pays cash for everything he buys.

Our ancestors had to haul the washwater from the well, but they didn't have to sit up nights figuring out how to meet the payments on the bucket.

Some people who buy modern furniture have antiques by the time they finish paying for it.

Every year the cars get lower and wider, while the payments get longer and higher.

Many people are having trouble with their new cars. The engine won't start and the payments won't stop.

Modern automobiles have every convenience — except a push button to lower the payments.

The easiest way to lose control of a car is to forget to make the payments.

The reason the automobile is so popular today is that you can drive one without owning it.

Some people nowadays buy a new car with one down payment and thirty-five *darn* payments.

The most popular model next year may be a compact car — with payments to match.

One percent of the automobiles on the highways are rented — the others are mortgaged.

Present-day cars are so quiet that the only noise you hear is from the finance company.

Isn't it wonderful that our new cars are almost completely automatic? This leaves your mind free to worry about how you're going to make the monthly payments.

266

Car sickness is that feeling you get every month when the payment is due.

You get a pretty good idea of eternity when you start paying for an $8,000 car on the installment plan.

If you think it's tough making the payments on your car, try not making them.

Drive-in banks were established so that automobiles could see their real owners occasionally.

Modern business has made buying easy, but paying is as hard as it ever was.

One trouble with credit business is that there is too much stall in installments.

Anyone who thinks Christmas doesn't last all year doesn't have a charge account.

Civilization is a state of affairs where nothing can be done without first being financed.

A Tennessee woman recently complained, "My fur coat is so old it's paid for."

The man who first called it the "easy payment plan" was mighty careless with his adjectives.

Things bought on convenient terms always fall due at inconvenient times.

One reason why a great many American families don't own an elephant is that they have never been offered one for a dollar down and a dollar a week.

Not as many people have lost faith in America as you might think. An awful lot of them still sign up for a thirty-year mortgage.

Modern families don't seem to worry about the wolf at the door anymore. They just feed him on installments.

Homes are now being built with every known convenience except low payments.

Modern homes are wonderful. They're equipped with gadgets that do everything except make the monthly payments.

The new homes being built have the latest innovations — from wall-to-wall carpeting to back-to-wall payments.

We're using sign language more and more. We sign for just about everything we buy.

The drinking man commits suicide on the installment plan.

A luxury becomes a necessity if we can make the down-payment on it.

Old-timers well remember when a family that couldn't afford to own a car didn't.

This is still the land of opportunity. Where else could you earn enough to pay the interest on what you owe?

Many people don't do anything on time, except buy.

We are living in an unprecedented era of prosperity. Never before have people acquired so many unpaid for things.

Prosperous times are when we pay installments on ten things instead of one.

Prosperity is that short period of time between the final installment and the next purchase.

The paramount question before the country today is, "How much is the down-payment?"

Don't drive as if you owned the road — drive as if you owned the car.

The main difference between Russia and the United States is that in Russia the state owns everything and in the United States the finance companies do.

Life's greatest satisfactions include getting the last laugh, having the last word, and paying the last installment.

Television is with us to stay — if we can keep up the payments.

Pay television has been with us for years. It's called the installment plan.

Some folks never do anything on time but buy.

Nothing makes time go faster than buying on it.

Time is what passes rapidly between the "easy monthly payments."

Wealthy people miss one of the greatest thrills of life — paying the last installment.

You can't pay cash for wisdom. It comes to you on the installment plan.

How long a woman works after her marriage is often determined by the number of payments still due on her husband's car.

Intelligence

An intelligent person not only knows how to take advice, but also how to reject it.

As kids we started smoking cigarettes because we thought it was smart. Why don't we stop smoking for the same reason?

Curiosity is nothing more than freewheeling intelligence.

It is not the I.Q. but the I WILL that is important in education.

Not all educated people are intelligent.

An intellectual is so smart he doesn't understand the obvious.

It is extremely embarrassing to come to your senses and find out you haven't any.

Enthusiasm is a good engine, but it needs intelligence for a driver.

Getting the facts is only half the job; the other half is to use them intelligently.

Facts mean nothing unless they are rightly understood, rightly related, and rightly interpreted.

Any man who pits his intelligence against a fish and loses has it coming.

History is simply a record of man's intelligence — or lack of it.

It is incredible how much intelligence is used in this world to prove a lot of nonsense.

There is nothing so irritating as somebody with less intelligence and more sense than we have.

It's not enough to be smart — one must know *when* to be smart.

Intelligence is very much like money — if you don't reveal how little you've got people will treat you as though you have a lot.

Human intelligence is thousands of years old, but it doesn't seem to act its age.

A lot of people are smarter than they look — and they ought to be!

Intelligence is like a river — the deeper it is, the less noise it makes.

The difference between education and intelligence is that intelligence will make you a living.

Don't always assume that the other person has equal intelligence. He might have more.

There is no limit to either intelligence or ignorance.

If library cards were used more and credit cards less, it would tend to raise the level of intelligence.

A man is seldom as smart as his mother thinks, or as dumb as his mother-in-law says he is.

An eminent scientist has announced that, in his opinion, intelligent life is possible on several of our planets — including the earth!

Some of us learned many years ago that the only substitute for intelligence is to keep your mouth shut.

Intentions

Don't forget that people will judge you by your actions, not your intentions. You may have a heart of gold — but so does a hard-boiled egg.

When you say that you agree to a thing in principle, you mean that you do not have the slightest intention of carrying it out.

A conference is a meeting at which people talk about things they should be doing.

Small deeds done are better than great deeds planned.

The smallest good deed is better than the grandest intention.

There are few people who are fast enough to keep up with their good intentions.

Good intentions die unless they are executed.

Make sure your intentions are not just pretensions.

Many good intentions die young, but not because they were executed.

Isn't it true that we judge ourselves by our best intentions and others by their worst faults?

The kindness we resolve to show tomorrow cures no headaches today.

When a man says he is going to do this or that tomorrow, ask him what he did yesterday.

No one can build a reputation on what he's going to do tomorrow.

What a fine world this would be if today we did as well as we expect to do tomorrow.

It's rather odd how temptation always seems to get action quicker than good intentions.

Internal Revenue Service
see also Taxes

As the IRS sees it, America is a land of untold wealth.

A bank is a place where you can keep the government's money until the IRS asks for it.

Please drive carefully — the IRS needs you.

Conscience is that small inner voice that tells you the IRS might check your return.

Anybody who thinks Americans lack imagination has never worked for the IRS.

Just thinking about income taxes often taxes the mind — which is something people once said the IRS couldn't do.

The new theme song of the IRS is titled, "I've Got My Eyes on You."

If you think you can keep everything to yourself, the IRS doesn't.

A certain IRS office has two signs over the door. The one going in says, "Watch your step." The one going out says, "Watch your language."

Why doesn't the IRS offer us our money back if we're not satisfied?

A San Francisco millionaire requested that he be cremated and his ashes sent to the IRS with a note, "Now you have it all."

The first "touch" of spring is the IRS.

If the IRS gave green stamps, thousands of Americans would look forward to paying their income tax.

You may not know when you're well off, but the IRS does.

Behind every successful man stands a woman and the IRS. One takes the credit, and the other takes the cash.

Said an old lady to the IRS clerk, "I do hope you will give my money to a nice country."

If a person wishes to die poor, the IRS is organized and qualified to help him.

The IRS recently celebrated its fiftieth anniversary as a federal agency. Tax officials noted that no one sent them best wishes for many happy *returns.*

Some people are always taking the joy out of life, and a good many of them are in the IRS.

With a billion dollar budget, it ought to be possible to set aside enough money to teach the IRS the basic English necessary to write a readable income-tax form.

Psychologists say that no one should try to keep too much to himself. The IRS is of the same opinion.

Can you remember way back when a revenue agent chased moonshiners instead of checking your income?

The IRS can put the screws on you quicker than an undertaker.

Does the IRS permit a double exemption for a split personality?

The Lord giveth, and the IRS taketh away.

The IRS received a batch of buttons in the mail with this notation, "You got the shirt last year."

The first person to say "You can't take it with you" was probably a representative of the IRS.

The IRS must love poor people — it makes so many of them.

When it comes to profiting from your mistakes, you can be sure that the IRS will.

We need more watchdogs at the United States Treasury and fewer bloodhounds at the Internal Revenue Service.

If our President wants to abolish poverty, he can do it by abolishing the IRS.

Those who are well-versed in psychology tell us no one should keep too much to himself. As long as the IRS is around, nobody is likely to do so.

At no time is it easier to keep your mouth shut than during an audit of your income-tax return.

A man owes it to himself to become successful. Once successful, he owes it to the IRS.

Intuition

If women's intuition is so good, how come they ask so many questions?

It is intuition that enables a woman to put two and two together and come up with any answer that suits her.

Intuition is the strange power a woman has that enables her to guess right — and wrong!

The only time a woman's intuition doesn't work is when trying to decide which way to turn at the street intersection.

Intuition is what tells a wife her husband has done something wrong before he even thinks of doing it.

That so-called female intuition is just the old habit of being suspicious.

Women's intuition is the result of thousands of years of not thinking.

Intuition is that gift which enables a woman to arrive instantly at an infallible, irrevocable decision without the aid of reason, judgment, or discussion.

A wise man once said that intuition is something that women have in place of common sense.

Intuition enables a woman to contradict her husband before he says anything.

Woman's intuition often gets the credit that belongs to eavesdropping.

A woman's intuition is merely a guess that made good.

Inventions

A fortune awaits the inventor of an alarm clock that can't go off.

An automotive invention that is sorely needed is brakes that will automatically get tight when the driver does.

Engineers are trying to build a car that will stop smoking. We would all like to own a car that would stop drinking.

Any day now we expect to see power steering for backseat drivers.

In adding safety devices to automobiles, why not re-design the steering wheel into the shape of a harp?

There's a new remedy on the market for baldness. It's made of alum and persimmon juice. It doesn't grow hair but it shrinks your head to fit what hair you have left.

The American businessman has a problem: if he comes up with something new the Russians invent it six months later and the Japanese make it cheaper.

The best safety device ever invented for automobiles is a careful driver.

A fortune awaits the person who will design a church building without any front pews.

A nutritionist in India has the perfect new diet food. You open a can, and there's nothing in it.

It is solemnly hoped that someday a genius will come along and invent something that will make golf unnecessary.

Another American invention is the permanent temporary tax.

The wheel was man's greatest invention until he got behind it.

A great invention for dieters would be a refrigerator that weighs you every time you open the door.

What a blessing it would be if someone would invent anti-knock gas for people.

The guy who invented the boomerang was probably the same one who invented the credit card.

There's a new invention on the market — a pencil with an eraser on both ends. It's for people who do nothing but make mistakes.

Americans will pay a big price for an invention that will help them save time they don't know what to do with.

Modern inventions are simply great. Once you had to dig the toast out of the toaster. Today the burnt toast pops up automatically.

Here's a new invention — a solar-powered clothes dryer. It's called a clothes line.

Of all the laborsaving devices invented for women, none has ever been as popular as a devoted man.

A much-needed invention for the American scene is an automatic childwasher.

One of the greatest laborsaving inventions of all time is tomorrow.

The man who invented the eraser had the human race pretty well sized up.

The new era of peace will begin when somebody invents a way to get all the axes on the grindstone at the same time.

The most humiliating thing about science is that it keeps filling our homes with gadgets smarter than we are.

A major scientific advancement would be the development of cigarette ashes that would match the color of the rug.

Inventions are coming so fast that the ladder of success may soon be replaced by an escalator.

Any company that manufactures a mechanical taxpayer will make a fortune in a hurry!

J

Jobs
Jokes
Judges

Judging
Judgment
Jury

Justice
Juvenile Delinquency

Jobs

A man with a burning ambition is seldom fired.

The best way to appreciate your job is to imagine yourself without one.

Before you have an argument with your boss, you'd better take a good look at both sides — his side and the outside.

Before arguing with your boss, make absolutely sure you're right — then let the matter drop.

You can tell a man's character by what he turns up when offered a job — his nose or his sleeves.

Going to college won't guarantee you a job, but it'll give you four years to worry about getting one.

Belly dancing is the only profession where the beginner starts in the middle.

No dream comes true until you wake up and go to work.

Economists predict the year ahead will reward hard workers. What a frightening outlook for many!

One way to deflate your ego is to read the want ads in the newspapers and discover all the jobs you're not equipped to handle.

Nothing is quite as embarrassing as watching your boss do something you assured him couldn't be done.

The fellow who is fired with enthusiasm for his work is seldom fired by his boss.

Four word story of failure: Hired, tired, mired, fired.

There is no future in any job. The future is in the man who holds the job.

The government will soon conduct a survey as to why people get bored on the job. Just thinking about this survey makes one drowsy.

It's always hard to find a job for the fellow who doesn't want one.

Some workers are trying to make both weekends meet.

There may be luck in getting a job, but there's no luck involved in keeping it.

The nearest to perfection that most people ever come is when filling out a job application.

Stick to your job until one of you is through.

The best time to start thinking about retirement is before your boss does.

The most dangerous position in which to sleep is with your feet on your office desk.

According to the latest statistics, there are five million Americans who aren't working. And there are even more if you count those with jobs.

Be thankful if your job is a little harder than you like. A razor can't be sharpened on a piece of velvet.

Ulcers are contagious. You can get them from your boss.

A lot of folks are flocking to Washington to ask what they can do for their country — and what the salary will be!

Don't worry about the job you don't like. Someone else will soon have it.

It seems a lot of young people want an occupation that doesn't keep them occupied.

Jokes

Computers will never replace man entirely until they learn to laugh at the boss's jokes.

Some girls can't take a joke, but others prefer one to no husband at all.

A man with a sense of humor doesn't make jokes out of life; he merely recognizes the ones that are there.

Real humor enables you to laugh when someone takes your best joke and improves on it.

Some husbands are living proof that a woman can take a joke.

The man who says his wife can't take a joke forgets that she took him.

If you can't remember a joke — don't dismember it.

A good wife laughs at her husband's jokes, not because they are clever, but because she is.

275

Anybody who thinks a joke about a plumber is funny hasn't had a faucet replaced lately.

People are not against political jokes — they just wonder how they get elected.

Old jokes never die. They just smell that way.

The most discouraging thing about repeating a good story is that it reminds some idiot of a "better" one.

The man who says there are no new jokes probably hasn't read the latest batch of bills before Congress.

Nothing helps you laugh at an old joke as much as telling it.

In the old days a comedian took a dirty joke and cleaned it up for radio. Today he hears a clean joke and dirties it up for television.

If you think the average American woman can't take a joke, take a look at the average American husband.

Other people's jokes, like other people's kids, are more difficult to enjoy than our own.

Nothing improves a joke more than telling it to your employees.

You can judge a man not only by the company he keeps, but by the jokes he tells.

If you don't think people have good memories, try repeating a joke you told them about a month ago.

Isn't it funny how some people can remember a joke, but can't seem to remember an unpaid bill?

He who laughs last at the boss's jokes probably isn't very far from retirement.

Judges

It's difficult to tell who gives some couples the most happiness, the preacher who married them or the judge who divorced them.

For every judge operating in an official capacity, there are a hundred who are self-appointed.

In the old days judges would suspend the bad men instead of the sentence.

A judge is a man of great trials and many convictions.

Four things are required of a judge: to hear courteously, to answer wisely, to consider soberly, and to decide impartially.

A judge is an official who should lay down the law, not lay down *on* the law.

Judges certainly are getting tougher on criminals. They're giving them much longer suspended sentences.

Ignorance of the law is no excuse, except for judges.

Judges and criminals are the only people who take the law into their own hands.

If you can't get a lawyer who knows the law, get one who knows the judge.

A good lawyer knows the law; a clever one takes the judge to lunch.

The people of the United States do not need more judges but more judgment.

Judging

Be sure to judge yourself before you judge others.

No one should judge another person by what that person's enemies say about him.

Judge each day, not by the harvest, but by the seeds you plant.

The only way to judge the future is by the past, but if some people are judged that way, they won't have any future.

Never judge a man by his relatives; he did not choose them.

You can judge a man not only by the company he keeps, but by the jokes he tells.

Isn't it true that we judge ourselves by our best intentions and others by their worst faults?

You can't depend on your evaluation of a person when your imagination is out of focus.

Never judge a summer resort by its post cards.

It's easier to judge people by what they fall for than by what they stand for.

Don't judge a man by the clothes he wears. God made one; the tailor, the other.

Judge not your friend until you stand in his place.

In judging others it's always wise to see with the heart as well as with the eyes.

It's a mistake to try to judge a man's horsepower by the size of his exhaust.

Too many people are unable to judge what a man is because of what he has.

We shouldn't judge a modern girl by her clothes; there really isn't enough evidence.

People are also judged by the company they keep away from.

It's easy to misconstrue the actions and words of those we dislike.

You can judge a man by his enemies as well as by his friends.

Never judge a man's actions until you know his motives.

Don't judge a man by what he says; try and find out *why* he said it.

The best way to judge a man is not by what other men say about him, but by what he says about other men.

You will make a mistake if you judge a man by his opinion of himself.

Don't judge your wife too harshly for her weaknesses. If she didn't have them, chances are she wouldn't have married you.

You can't judge an automobile by the sound of its horn — nor a man!

We usually see things, not as they are, but as we are.

You can't always judge a dinner by the price.

We are sure to judge wrong if we do not feel right.

Judgment

The only way to judge the future is by the past, but if some people are judged that way, they won't have any future.

Men of good judgment seldom rely wholly on their own.

The people of the United States don't need more judges, but more sound judgment.

If you must go against your better judgment, do it when *she's* not around!

A man's judgment is no better than his information.

Snap judgments would be all right if they didn't come unsnapped so often.

Don't condemn the judgment of another because it differs from your own. You both may be wrong.

Don't trust your wife's judgment — look at whom she married!

It's pretty hard to make a fellow see that his bad judgment wasn't just bad luck.

The best some of us can expect on the Day of Judgment is a suspended sentence.

Rare is the man who is governed by sound judgment.

Your neighbor will seem like a better man when you judge him as you judge yourself.

The man who has a good opinion of himself is usually a poor judge.

The judgment of a man on a subject on which he is prejudiced isn't really worth much.

Before passing judgment on a sermon, be sure to try it out in practice.

The world we live in is old-fashioned. It still judges a man by what he does.

Jury

A jury is a body of twelve men and women selected to decide which of the contestants had the better lawyer.

The goal of the defense in a court trial is to get at least one stubborn man on the jury.

If you believe that a woman hasn't a mind of her own, you've never served on a jury.

A jury is a group of twelve men and women of average ignorance.

Puzzled as to the cause of death in a murder trial, a jury finally gave its findings in these words, "An act of God under very suspicious circumstances."

A jury recently reported back to the judge, "We don't want to get involved."

One great flaw in the jury system — it's a little frightening to know your fate is in the hands of twelve people who weren't smart enough to get excused.

Be kind to everybody. You never know who might show up on the jury at your trial.

Justice

Crime's story would be shorter if the sentences were longer.

Justice is blind, so they say, but seldom is it too blind to distinguish between the defendant who has a roll of bills and the one who is dead broke.

Everybody is for justice, thinking it will bring them rewards and give the neighbors what they have coming to them.

Justice is what we get when the decision is in our favor.

There's justice for all, but it doesn't seem to be equally distributed.

If a cause is just it will eventually triumph in spite of all the propaganda issued against it.

Justice is something that is too good for some people and not good enough for others.

Injustice is relatively easy to bear. What stings is justice!

It is just as well that justice is blind; she might not like some of the things done in her name if she could see them.

Life started from a cell, and, if justice is done, a lot of it is going to end there.

There doesn't seem to be any justice. If you fill out an income-tax return correctly, you go to the poorhouse. If you don't, you go to jail.

Juvenile Delinquency

Some adolescents become bad eggs because they have been set on too long — or not long enough.

When adults behave like children we call them juvenile; when children behave like adults we call them delinquents.

Juvenile delinquency is like charity — it often begins at home.

One reason for juvenile delinquency is that many parents are raising their children by remote control.

All that the overwhelming majority of people are doing about juvenile delinquency is reading about it.

There is no such thing as a problem boy. He's just a boy with a problem.

Juvenile delinquency starts in the highchair and could end in the electric chair.

An enemy could not afford to take the risk of invading our country. Our juvenile delinquents are too well-armed.

One of the problems of juvenile delinquency is children running away from home. It is entirely possible they may be looking for their parents.

Happy laughter and family voices in the home will keep more kids off the streets at night than the strictest curfew.

The favorite cereal of juvenile delinquents is "Wild Oats."

Juvenile delinquency would disappear if kids followed their parent's advice instead of their examples.

Very few old people are qualified to discuss juvenile delinquency. They've been away from it too long.

Some people grow up and still remain juvenile.

Most juvenile delinquents are youngsters who have been given a free hand, but not in the proper place.

Delinquents are children who have reached the age when they want to do what papa and mama are doing.

Every boy, in his heart, would rather steal second base than an automobile.

In the days when a woodshed stood behind the American home, a great deal of what passes as juvenile delinquency was settled out of court.

Another trouble with juvenile delinquency is that it's harder to say than "just plain cussedness."

Juvenile delinquency is a modern term for what we did when we were kids.

When a youth begins to sow wild oats it's time for father to start the threshing machine.

When a child always gets what he wants, you can be sure he is well on his way toward delinquency.

Juvenile delinquency is now defined as a situation where the youngsters stop asking their parents where they came from and start telling them where to go.

One way to curb juvenile delinquency is to take the parents off the streets at night.

Do you remember the "good old days" when a juvenile delinquent was a boy who played the saxophone too loud?

If juvenile delinquency gets any worse, parents will have to post a five thousand dollar bail bond everytime a child is born.

A juvenile delinquent usually prefers vice to advice.

Juvenile delinquency is the result of parents trying to train their children without starting at the bottom.

There would be less juvenile delinquency if parents led the way instead of pointing to it.

Juvenile delinquency was unheard of many years ago because the problem was thrashed-out in the woodshed.

A juvenile delinquent is a minor who is a major problem.

The trouble with the average juvenile delinquent is not always apparent — sometimes it's two parents!

A juvenile delinquent sows his wild oats and his parents pray for a crop failure.

Juvenile delinquency is no mystery. Mama is so busy keeping up with the Joneses and Papa is so busy keeping up with Mama that neither of them has any time left for keeping up with John and Mary.

The delinquents of today are the same as the delinquents of fifty years ago — only they have better weapons.

A juvenile delinquent is a teen-ager who wants what he wants when he wants it and won't wait to get it.

When parents cannot control their children in the home, it is extremely difficult for the government to control them in the streets.

The juvenile delinquent is a mixed-up kid, a victim of mixed drinks — mostly alcohol and gasoline.

Can you remember way back when a juvenile delinquent was a kid with an overdue library book?

Did the conversion of so many woodsheds into garages have anything to do with the alarming increase in juvenile delinquency?

K

Kindness   Kisses   Knowledge

Kindness

Kind actions begin with kind thoughts.

Kind words can never die, but without kind deeds they can sound mighty sick.

Charity is the sterilized milk of human kindness.

Some folks aren't content with the milk of human kindness — they want the cream.

In this country we're willing to try anything once, except the criminals.

Don't expect to enjoy life if you keep your milk of human kindness all bottled up.

Friendship is a living thing that lasts only as long as it is nourished with kindness, sympathy, and understanding.

Be kind to unkind people — they need it the most.

Kindness is the ability to treat your enemy decently.

One of the most difficult things to give away is kindness; it usually comes back to you.

If you were arrested for being kind, would enough evidence be found to convict you?

Kindness is the world's greatest unused capital.

The person who sows seeds of kindness enjoys a perpetual harvest.

Kindness has influenced more people than eloquence.

Kindness is the ability to love people more than they really deserve.

A breath of kindness is more moving than a gale of flattery.

Be as kind as you can today; tomorrow you may not be here.

The only way we can erase unkindness is with kindness. Don't lose the eraser.

Remember the kindness of others; forget your own.

The kindness planned for tomorrow doesn't count today.

People will overlook the faults of anyone who is kind.

Kindness makes a fellow feel good whether it's being done to him or by him.

The greatest thing a man can do for his heavenly Father is to be kind to His children.

If you must exercise, why not exercise kindness?

The kindest people are those who forgive and forget.

Kindness is a warm breeze in a frigid climate, a radiant heat that melts the icebergs of fear, distrust, and unhappiness.

Treat a dog with kindness, pet him often, feed him well, and he'll never leave you. The same system usually works with husbands.

Kindness is the insignia of a loving heart.

A kindness done today is the surest way to a brighter tomorrow.

Let all your words be kind, and you will always hear kind echoes.

No man is too big to be kind, but many men are too little.

The milk of human kindness never curdles.

Remember, there has never been an overproduction of kind words.

Kindness is the oil that takes the friction out of life.

Money will buy a fine dog, but only kindness will make him wag his tail.

Kindness is the golden chain by which society is bound together.

One way to get along better in the world is to be just a little kinder than necessary.

Kindness is never wasted. If it has no effect on the recipient, at least it benefits the bestower.

Better a little kindness while living than an extravagant floral display at the grave.

This is a dangerous age in which we live, but we don't stand in much danger of being killed by kindness.

The cow knows she has to be milked, but she will give her milk more freely when treated with kindness.

You cannot do a kindness too soon, because you never know how soon it will be too late.

There's nothing so kingly as kindness, and nothing so royal as truth.

Kindness is a language which the deaf can hear and the blind can see.

Learn to speak kind words — nobody resents them.

Never part without loving words. They might be your last.

It's too bad that so many folks who pass out the milk of human kindness always skim it first.

Be kind. Every person you meet is fighting a difficult battle.

Kindness pays most when you don't do it for pay.

Be kind to people until you make your first million. After that, people will be kind to you.

What this country needs is more of the milk of human kindness in the cream of society.

Kindness is like snow; it makes everything it covers beautiful.

The kindness you spread today will be gathered up and returned to you tomorrow.

A kindness put off until tomorrow may become only a bitter regret.

Kindness often goes a long way when it ought to stay at home.

Milk can be kept in cold storage indefinitely. That's the way a lot of the milk of human kindness is kept.

Be kind to everybody. You never know who might show up on the jury at your trial.

Happy is the person who has a good supply of the milk of human kindness and knows how to keep it from souring.

The milk of human kindness beats cold cream for wrinkles.

Always speak kindly to your enemy and maybe he'll come close enough for you to box his ears!

How beautiful a day can be when kindness touches it.

The kindness we resolve to show tomorrow cures no headaches today.

A good memory test is to recall all the kind things you have said about your neighbor.

Kind words are short to speak, but their echoes are endless.

Kind words do not wear out the tongue — so speak them.

A kind word picks up a man when trouble weighs him down.

There has never been an overproduction of kind words.

Kisses

A boy becomes a man when he decides it's more fun to steal a kiss than second base.

Kissing a girl is like opening a jar of olives — hard to get the first one, but the rest come easy.

A kiss is a contraction of the mouth due to an enlargement of the heart.

The word *kiss* is a word invented by poets to rhyme with *bliss*.

Sign at the New Orleans airport: "Start kissing goodby early, so the plane can leave on time."

A kiss is what a husband struggled for before marriage and what his wife struggles for after marriage.

The difference between a man kissing his sister and a pretty girl is about fifty-five seconds.

Stealing a kiss may be petty larceny, but sometimes it's grand.

Kissing is the most pleasant way of spreading germs yet devised.

A prominent physician says that in fifty years kissing will be unheard of — but in fifty years, who cares?

It's impossible to kiss a girl unexpectedly — only sooner than she thought you would.

All the legislation in the world will not abolish kissing.

Statistics show that men who kiss their wives goodby in the morning live five years longer than those who don't. Some of you men had better pucker-up before you tucker-out.

It's nice to kiss the kids goodnight — if you don't mind waiting up for them.

Kissing is a practice that shortens life — single life!

A psychologist says kissing is where two people get so close together they can't see anything wrong with each other.

Knowledge

Knowing without doing is like plowing without sowing.

A lot of good arguments are spoiled by some fool who knows what he's talking about.

Discussion is an exchange of knowledge; argument is an exchange of ignorance.

A college doesn't give you knowledge, it just shows you where it is.

Heads that are filled with knowledge and wisdom have little space left for conceit.

Conceit is what makes a little squirt think he's a fountain of knowledge.

The best remedy for conceit is to sit down and make a list of all the things you don't know.

If you will hide your conceit as much as possible, people will give you credit for knowing more than you do.

Even if this is the dawn of a bright new world, most of us are still in the dark.

Everybody should get at least a high school education — even if they already know everything.

A person isn't educated unless he has learned how little he already knows.

The chief benefit of education is to discover how little we know.

Education should include knowledge of what to do with it.

A person with a reservoir of knowledge is not well-educated unless he knows when to turn the spigot on and off.

Education is not a head full of facts, but knowing *how* and *where* to find facts.

Education is knowing what you want, knowing where to get it, and knowing what to do with it after you get it.

Experience is a form of knowledge acquired in only two ways — by doing and by being done.

Don't find fault with what you don't understand.

The recipe for perpetual ignorance is to be satisfied with your opinions and content with your knowledge.

Unless you are willing to admit your ignorance, you will never be able to acquire knowledge.

What you don't know won't hurt you, but it may cause you to look pretty silly.

It's harder to conceal ignorance than to acquire knowledge.

Knowledge may have its limits — but not so with ignorance.

You can't help but admire the fellow who is stupid but knows it.

If you don't know where you're going, you may miss it when you get there.

The fellow who thinks he is full of knowledge is especially annoying to those of us who are.

You have to know the ropes in order to pull the strings.

Knowledge becomes wisdom only after it has been put to practical use.

At no time is a little knowledge more dangerous than when you are using it to start a rumor.

Knowledge, like lumber, is best when well-seasoned.

The fellow who knows more than his boss should be careful to conceal it.

By the time you know what it's all about, it's about over.

The wise carry their knowledge as they do their watches — not for display but for their own use.

Knowledge has to be improved, challenged, and increased constantly or it vanishes.

No one is ever too old to learn, but many people keep putting it off anyway.

Knowledge comes by taking things apart, but wisdom comes by putting things together.

Your brain becomes a mind when it's fortified with knowledge.

Knowing your limitations is the first step toward overcoming them.

A little knowledge is not as dangerous as the man who has it.

The highest knowledge is the knowledge of God.

A smart person doesn't tell everything he knows, but he knows everthing he tells.

Firsthand knowledge does not become secondhand when used.

Most of us have knowledge about everything except the things that matter most.

If a little knowledge is dangerous, a lot of dangerous people are wandering about.

One part of knowledge consists in being ignorant of things that are not worth knowing.

It is not necessary to know everything, but you had better know almost all the important things.

A little knowledge that acts is worth infinitely more than much knowledge that is idle.

As long as a little knowledge is a dangerous thing, not many of us can really feel safe.

Knowledge is power only when it is turned on.

What you don't know doesn't hurt you — until you find out someone is getting paid for knowing what you don't.

The best part of our knowledge is that which teaches us where knowledge leaves off and ignorance begins.

Knowledge advances by steps, not by leaps.

It is impossible for anyone to learn what he thinks he already knows.

Knowledge not put into practice is useless.

The more a man knows, the more modest he is inclined to be.

Knowing what's none of your business is just as important as knowing what is.

When people don't want knowledge, no man can give it to them.

The larger the island of knowledge, the longer the shoreline of wonder.

Nothing makes a *little* knowledge as dangerous as examination time.

When a man's knowledge is not in order, the more of it he has, the greater will be his confusion.

Those who really thirst for knowledge always get it.

Knowledge is like a snapshot. It can be enlarged, but if it gets out of focus, everything becomes a blur.

If you want to know how to handle a big fortune, ask the man who hasn't any.

The fact that you know what to say does not guarantee your right or obligation to say it.

A good listener is not only popular, but after a while he knows something.

Knowledge without wisdom is as dangerous as an automobile with neither steering wheel nor brakes.

A little knowledge properly applied is more important than a tremendous number of facts accumulated and not utilized.

Some students drink at the fountain of knowledge. Others just gargle.

What you don't know you can learn.

You may not know all the answers, but you probably won't be asked all the questions either.

It's not so much what we know as how we use what we know.

Our trouble today is that we have our heads filled with knowledge, but our hearts are empty.

Never get mad at anyone for knowing more than you do. It's not his fault!

Knowledge is knowing a fact. Wisdom is knowing what to do with that fact.

The first step to knowledge is to know that you are ignorant.

You may know more than your employer, but his knowledge pays off.

Knowledge humbles great men, astonishes the common man, and puffs up the little man.

The more you know, the more you know you ought to know.

Knowledge is information acquired by some people for the sake of knowing it and by other people for the sake of telling it.

The man who knows *how* will always find a place in life, but the man who knows *why* will likely be his boss.

What counts in knowledge is what you learn after you reach the point where you know it all.

Although psychologists tell us that man is afraid of the unknown — it is what we *know* that really scares us.

The only commodity on earth that does not deteriorate with use is knowledge.

Knowledge is like dynamite — dangerous unless handled wisely.

The elevator operator has his ups and downs, but he's one of the few who knows where he's going.

Sign on a high school bulletin board in Dallas: "Free every Monday through Friday — knowledge. Bring your own containers."

It is entirely possible to know more than you understand.

The world does not pay for what a person knows; it pays for what he does with what he knows.

Never carry your shotgun, or your knowledge, at half cock.

It's better to know nothing than to know what isn't so.

The person who knows everything has a lot to learn.

If just knowing the difference between right and wrong were enough, every jail in the country would be empty.

Money is like knowledge — the more you have, the less you need to brag.

A soapbox orator is a speaker who enjoys the advantage of being unhampered by any knowledge of the subject.

A man who knows his imperfections is just about as perfect as anyone can be.

Many public speakers can talk for hours without any notes — or knowledge!

Blessed is the man who does not speak until he knows what he is talking about.

Some men succeed by what they know, some by what they do, and a few by what they are.

Most of our suspicion of others is aroused by a knowledge of ourselves.

Wisdom is the right use of knowledge.

Knowledge is knowing a fact. Wisdom is knowing what to do with that fact.

Knowledge comes by taking things apart, but wisdom comes by putting things together.

Wisdom is knowledge in action.

Knowledge can be memorized. Wisdom must think things through.

Zeal without knowledge is like heat without light.

Zeal without knowledge is fanaticism.

Zeal without knowledge is the sister of folly.

L

Language

Las Vegas

Laughter

Laws

Lawyers

Laziness

Leaders

Learning

Leisure

Liars

Liberty

Lies

Life

Life Insurance

Liquor

Listening

Living

Loneliness

Love

Luck

Luxuries

Lying

Language

We're using sign language more and more. We sign for just about everything we buy.

People who spout filthy language in public are trespassing on our eardrums, and we don't like it.

Politicians should watch their language — they use so much of it.

Never poke fun at someone who misuses and abuses the English language. He may be in training to write tomorrow's hit songs.

A man's language is an index of his mind.

Language, like linen, looks best when it's clean.

Our language in America is called the "Mother Tongue" because father so seldom gets to use it.

Slang is just language stripped down to get more speed with less horsepower.

A synonym is a word you use in place of one you can't spell.

Some people use language to express thought, some to conceal thought, and others instead of thought.

Thousands of Americans can speak at least two languages — English and profanity.

Language is the dress of thought; every time you talk your mind is on parade.

The English language has far more lives than a cat. People have been murdering it for years, but it's far from being dead.

Many people get unlimited mileage out of a limited vocabulary.

We often show command of language when we say nothing.

Rhetoric is language in white tie, top hat, and tails.

Language is the apparel in which our thoughts parade before the public. Let's never clothe them in vulgar or shoddy attire.

There are no curse words in the Indian language. They don't need any because they don't pay taxes.

A noted jurist says our laws should be rewritten in simple language so that everybody could understand their meaning. If this were done, a great number of lawyers would have to go to work for a living.

Las Vegas
see also Gambling

The dumbest criminal on earth is the one who would hold up a group of tourists on their way home from Las Vegas.

Las Vegas has all kinds of gambling devices, such as dice, roulette, slot machines — and wedding chapels.

A Texas man reports he had terrible luck in Las Vegas. He lost everything he had but his cold.

Visitors to Las Vegas are divided into two groups — the *haves* and the *hads.*

Las Vegas is where you go the first time for fun — and the second time for revenge.

A gentleman in Nashville described his last Las Vegas vacation, "Out by jet. Back in debt."

The city of Las Vegas is now so crowded that strangers are sharing slot machines.

Sometimes a person goes to Las Vegas out of curiosity and comes home out of funds.

Almost everybody gets married while they're in Las Vegas. They figure as long as they're on a losing streak they might as well go all the way.

A visitor to Las Vegas received the "cook's tour" — he was baked in the sun, stewed at the bar, and burned at the crap tables.

Las Vegas is a place where people go broke trying to get rich.

In case of an air raid, go to the nearest slot machine. It hasn't been hit in years.

Why not spend your vacation in Las Vegas? You can't beat the sunshine, the climate, or the slot machines.

A Texan, just back home from a Nevada vacation, says he underwent a bit of "Las Vegas Surgery". He had his bankroll painlessly removed.

Laughter

Another thing learned in adversity is that a tire isn't the only thing you can patch.

Much may be known of a man's character by what excites his laughter.

As a rule, the freedom of any people can be judged by the volume of their laughter.

Happy laughter and family voices in the home will keep more kids off the streets at night than the strictest curfew.

A man isn't really poor if he can still laugh.

Laugh and the world laughs with you; cry and the other guy has an even better sob story.

As a general rule, the freedom of any people can be judged by the volume of their laughter.

If you can laugh at it you can live with it.

One thing is certain. If you can laugh at your troubles, you will always have something to laugh at.

Fortune smiles upon the man who can laugh at himself.

There are few things to laugh at these days, but the time to really worry is when this includes yourself.

A good laugh is the best medicine, whether you are sick or not.

Sometimes we get the feeling we laugh by the inch and cry by the yard.

He who laughs last didn't get the joke.

The horse would have a good laugh if he could see motorists adjusting their shoulder harnesses.

When you laugh at something that happens to somebody else, that's a sense of humor. If it happens to you, that's an outrage.

Laughter is like changing a baby's diaper — it doesn't permanently solve any problems, but it makes things more acceptable for a while.

Blessed is the man who can laugh at himself, for he will never cease to be amused.

Those who can laugh at trouble must be having a hilarious time nowadays.

The sourpuss informs us that laughter causes wrinkles.

When a woman laughs at her husband's jokes, either they're good jokes or she's a good wife.

He who laughs last is usually the dumbest.

At today's nightclub prices it's harder than ever for a comedian to make people laugh.

Laughter is a tranquilizer with no side effects.

It's a grand person indeed who can laugh at himself with others and enjoy it as much as they do.

The man who laughs at his boss's jokes doesn't necessarily have a sense of humor, but he surely has a sense of direction.

Laughter costs too much when it is purchased by sacrificing decency.

There is hope for any man who can look in a mirror and laugh at what he sees.

He who laughs last probably has an insecure upper plate.

Laughter is the shock absorber that eases the blows of life.

When a person can no longer laugh at himself, it is time for others to laugh at him.

If the world laughs at you, laugh right back — it's as funny as you are.

A laugh is worth a hundred groans in any market.

If you're too busy to laugh, you're entirely too busy.

Laugh with people — not at them.

Man is the only animal that laughs, but when you look at some people, it's hard to understand how the animals keep from laughing.

Many of us get a hearty laugh out of the old family album and then look in the mirror without so much as a grin.

Laughter is the sweetest music that ever greeted the human ear.

One good hearty laugh together could be the greatest insurance of lasting peace that men of all nations could contrive.

Don't laugh at the fallen; there may be slippery places in your path.

Laughter is but a frown turned upside down.

Any man who laughs at women's clothes has never paid the bill for them.

What you laugh at tells, plainer than words, what you are.

Laughter is to life what salt is to an egg.

We don't stop laughing because we grow old; we grow old because we stop laughing.

He who laughs last wanted to tell the same story.

It is better to be laughed at for not being married than to be unable to laugh because you are.

Laughter is the cheapest luxury that man has. It stirs up the blood, expands the chest, electrifies the nerves, clears away the cobwebs from the brain, and gives the whole system a cleansing rehabilitation.

The most utterly lost of all days is the one in which you have not once laughed.

Try to make the world laugh; it already has enough to cry about.

When you laugh, be sure to laugh at what people do and not at what people are.

Laughter is the remedy for many little ills. It can cure more quickly than the doctor's tiny pills.

Frequently he who laughs last didn't get the point at all but is just being polite.

Take time to laugh — it is the music of the soul.

A marriage seldom goes on the rocks when a couple finds something in common to laugh about. For instance, there's the old wedding pictures!

All of us like to see people smile and hear them laugh, but not when we're chasing our best hat down the street on a windy day.

Laugh and the world will laugh with you; think and you will almost die of loneliness.

Happy laughter and family voices in the home will keep more kids off the streets at night than the strictest curfew.

Your ulcers can't grow while you're laughing.

Laws

In America we'll try anything once — except criminals.

Maybe this country would not be in such a mess today if the Indians had adopted more stringent immigration laws.

With all the laws and government regulations, a fellow is downright stupid to steal when there are so many legal ways to cheat.

Congress is a legislative body whose members make the laws and whose chaplain prays for the country.

If the law of supply and demand is responsible for existing prices, it ought to be repealed.

No law has ever been passed that will keep a man from acting the fool.

Men fight for freedom and then start making laws to get rid of it.

Don't forget the fact that ignorance of the law is what keeps our higher courts functioning.

Ignorance of the law is no excuse, but it's better than no alibi at all.

A judge is an official who should lay down the law, not lay down *on* the law.

All the legislation in the world will not abolish kissing.

Of all the laws we have to contend with, the most troublesome are usually the in-laws.

Many objections to law arise from the impossibility of making them apply only to the other fellow.

The world needs a new law that would prevent any country from waging war unless it pays for it in advance.

Why keep on enacting laws when we already have more than we can break?

The arm of the law needs a little more muscle.

Too many laws are passed and then bypassed.

Ignorance of the law is no excuse, except for judges.

We need tougher child abuse laws — parents have taken enough abuse from their children.

It's beginning to look like we need a law so we can sue successful candidates for breach of promise.

Husbands lay down the law, but wives usually repeal it.

Mass production tends to cheapen almost everything, including laws.

Laws, like clothes, should be made to fit the people they are meant to serve.

There is too much talk about enforcing the laws and not enough said about obeying them.

Not all the teeth put into our laws these days are wisdom teeth.

Strict enforcement of the law against polluting the air should result in fewer, shorter, and better political speeches.

The law will protect everybody who can afford to hire a good lawyer.

Some recent laws would indicate the lawmakers not only passed the bar but also stopped there.

Everybody says the country has too many laws, and yet every man thinks he knows of a law that ought to be passed.

Where law ends, tyranny begins.

A bright young law student in a western university reports that an oral contract is not worth the paper it's written on.

God's laws last longer than those who break them.

The law of gravitation is the only law that everybody observes.

The law of supply and demand determines the price of everything; you supply what the profiteers demand.

Judges and criminals are the only people who take the law into their own hands.

English law prohibits a man from marrying his mother-in-law. This is the epitome of useless legislation.

No law, however stringent, can make the idle industrious, the shiftless provident, or the drunkard sober.

A man does not stumble over the moral law until he tries to cross it.

Many people believe in law and order as long as they can lay down the law and give the orders.

The best tax law is the one that gets the most feathers with the least squawking.

Natural law is a fundamental force that Congress constantly tries to amend.

The portion of a law found unconstitutional is usually the part with teeth in it.

This country might not be in such a mess if the Indians had adopted stricter immigration laws.

All laws of nature become our servants if we respect the law of their existence.

The execution of the law is more important than the making of laws.

Those who go against the grain of God's law shouldn't complain when they get splinters.

There's one law we don't have to enforce — the law of gravitation.

Laws are man's guidelines, but, unfortunately, too many try to read between them.

Nobody ever made a law that could prevent a man from making a fool of himself.

Laws are no stronger than the devotion to them by the people who live under them.

If the law of supply and demand is responsible for existing prices, it ought to be amended.

A noted jurist says our laws should be rewritten in simple language so that everybody could understand their meaning. If this were done, a great number of lawyers would have to go to work for a living.

Necessity knows no law, and neither does the average lawyer.

Many wives of young lawyers are buying sewing machines. They want to help their husbands make loopholes.

There is no liberty worth anything which is not liberty under law.

Liberty is the right to go just as far as the law allows.

The law gives the pedestrian the right-of-way but makes no provision for flowers.

Don't put off until tomorrow what you can do today; by tomorrow there may be a law against it.

We live in a wonderful country where lawns are well-kept — and laws aren't!

Lawyers

Doctors and lawyers are always giving *fee* advice.

An honest confession is not always good for the soul, but, in most cases, it's cheaper than hiring a high-powered lawyer.

Those who are so perturbed over the present divorce rate evidently do not understand the law of supply and demand. There are more lawyers in this country than there are preachers.

Preachers and lawyers are paid for zeal, but fools dish it out for nothing.

A jury is a body of twelve men and women selected to decide which of the contestants had the better lawyer.

The law will protect everybody who can afford to hire a good lawyer.

A noted jurist says our laws should be rewritten in simple language so that everybody could understand their meaning. If this were done, a great number of lawyers would have to go to work for a living.

A lawyer can dictate sixty-two single-spaced pages and call it a "brief."

Necessity knows no law, and neither does the average lawyer.

A lawyer in Utah recently reported that he is instructing his son in the "alleged" facts of life.

Practice does not make a lawyer perfect, but enough of it will make him rich.

If people would leave the bulk of their fortunes to lawyers, a lot of time would be saved on inheritance suits.

Some lawyers are just the opposite of laundrymen; they lose your suit and then take you to the cleaners.

If you can't get a lawyer who knows the law, get one who knows the judge.

Old lawyers never die. They just lose their appeal.

You can't live without lawyers, and certainly you can't die without them.

Lawyers would have a hard time making a living if people behaved themselves and kept their promises.

A lawyer is always willing to spend your last dollar to prove he's right.

Many wives of young lawyers are buying sewing machines. They want to help their husbands make loopholes.

A lawyer is a glib-tongued fellow who defends your property from an enemy in order to save it for himself.

A good lawyer knows the law; a clever one takes the judge to lunch.

A lawyer is the only man who gets rich fighting other people's battles.

A critically-ill lawyer was found frantically leafing through the Bible in his hospital room. When asked the reason, he replied, "Looking for loopholes."

Lawyers are like bread — they're best when they're young and fresh.

The lawyer agrees with the doctor that the best things in life are fees.

It's difficult to tell who gets the most pleasure out of marriage, the preacher who ties the knot, or the lawyer who severs it.

Of course you can't take it with you, and with high taxes, lawyer's fees, and funeral expenses you can't leave it behind either.

Moses was a great law giver. The way he was satisfied to keep the Ten Commandments short and to the point shows clearly that he was not an ordinary lawyer.

A successful criminal lawyer in Montana reports that he has found several loopholes in the Ten Commandments.

The only people who enjoy hearing your troubles are lawyers, and they're paid for it.

Why is it that everytime a witness offers to tell all the truth, some lawyer objects?

Laziness

Executive ability is a talent for deciding something quickly and getting someone else to do it.

295

Executive ability is the art of getting credit for all the hard work that somebody else does.

You can't make a place for yourself under the sun if you keep sitting in the shade of the family tree.

A man's accomplishment in business depends partly on whether he keeps his mind or his feet on the desk.

The only thing some people can achieve on their own is dandruff.

It doesn't do any good to sit up and take notice if you keep on sitting.

No one ever climbed a hill just by looking at it.

If you don't climb the mountain, you can't see the view.

Following the path of least resistance is what makes rivers and men crooked.

A person going nowhere can be sure of reaching his destination.

Millions of Americans aren't working, but thank heaven they've got jobs.

The average American would drive his car to the bathroom if the door was wide enough.

Anybody who thinks the automobile has made people lazy never had to pay for one.

The bee that makes the honey doesn't hang around the hive.

The Bible promises no loaves to the loafer.

A certain boss when asked how many people work for him replied, "About half of them."

It's what you do when you have nothing to do that reveals what you are.

Today's kids call it "finding themselves." In the "good old days" it was called loafing.

Soon the colleges will be forced to offer degrees in the ancient art of loafing.

Now that they've gotten the lead out of gasoline, we ought to give them the names and addresses of a few of our congressmen.

Contentment is often the result of being too lazy to stir up a fuss.

If you simply must make enemies, pick lazy ones.

The train of failure usually runs on the track of laziness.

Many people are not failures. They just started at the bottom and liked it there.

Failure always catches up with those who sit down and wait for success.

Failure is more frequently from want of energy than want of capital.

There is probably no better way to loaf, without attracting a lot of criticism and unfavorable attention, than to go fishing.

Fishing is a laborious way of taking it easy.

It takes a mighty honest man to tell the difference between when he's tired and when he's just plain lazy.

Doing nothing is the most tiresome job in the world because you can't stop and rest.

Most of the people who sit around and wait for the harvest haven't planted anything.

It's too bad that the only men who can solve the world's problems are too busy sitting on the front porch whittling.

A loafer is one who continues to live even though he complains that he can't live on the wages he turns down.

A new name for laziness is voluntary inertia.

Some people who get credit for being patient are just too lazy to start anything.

A man is considered lazy when he has to work up the energy to lie down and take a nap.

The best thing about spring fever is that it makes laziness respectable.

Some folks are so lazy that if their ship came in, they'd expect someone else to unload it for them.

Most lazy people have about as much initiative as an echo.

Laziness is like money — the more a man has of it, the more he seems to want.

If money grew on trees some people are so lazy they wouldn't shake a limb to get it.

The only thing lazy men do fast is get tired.

Be sure to watch for thorns when the flowery beds of ease begin to wilt.

About all some people can say at the end of the day is that it's done.

Times are especially trying for those who aren't trying.

The only bright spots in some men's lives are on the seats of their pants.

Entirely too many people fashion their lives after French bread — one long loaf!

Laziness is an overwhelming love for physical calm.

While some are standing on the promises, others just sit on the premises.

The lazier a man is, the more he is going to do tomorrow.

There's no sure cure for laziness in a man, but a wife and children often help.

The man who is able to distinguish between tiredness and laziness in himself will go far.

It's always hard to find a job for the fellow who doesn't want one.

Many people think they are broad-minded just because they are too lazy to form an opinion.

Did you hear about the fellow who was so lazy his self-winding watch stopped?

If heaven is a place to rest, many people are going to be all practiced up for it.

The first prize for being the laziest man in the world went to the fellow who sat at home and whittled with an electric knife.

The fellow who fiddles around seldom gets to lead the orchestra.

It was recently revealed that there are many volunteers in the army of the unemployed.

The man who falls down on the job usually starts from a sitting position.

Some people do nothing in particular, but they do it very well.

Laziness is a quality that prevents people from getting tired.

Too many people itch for what they want, but won't scratch for it.

The height of laziness is a fellow who gets up at five every morning so he can have more time to loaf.

The best thing you can do for spring fever is absolutely nothing.

Shiftless people seldom get into high gear.

The reason most people won't stand up and be counted is not that they're afraid to stand up — they're just too lazy.

Some workers are trying to make both weekends meet.

The trouble with Easy Street is that it often ends on Rotten Row.

One sure way to fall down on the job is to lie down on it.

A good deal of what passes for even temper is nothing but laziness.

The lazy man aims at nothing and generally hits it.

Most of us are lazier in mind than in body.

One trouble with the world is that laziness is so seldom fatal.

A group of doctors is trying to develop a cure for laziness. Somebody is always trying to take the joy out of life!

It's unfortunate that the symptoms of fatigue and laziness are almost identical.

Many people are as lazy as they can afford to be, but not as lazy as they want to be.

If a man is too lazy to think for himself, he should get married!

Then there was the fellow who said the only reason he was lazy was because it kept him from getting so tired.

Laziness is a luxury that few people can afford.

There is no such thing as leisure to people who do nothing.

There's enough leisure time for everybody, but the wrong people seem to have it.

Leisure originally meant an opportunity to do something. It has come to mean an opportunity to do nothing.

Some people treat life like a slot machine — putting in as little as possible while hoping for the jackpot.

Good luck is a lazy man's estimate of a worker's success.

Some men remind us of blisters; they don't show up until the work is done.

Some people never make a mistake, nor do they ever make anything else.

All some people do is grow old.

A great deal of laziness of mind is called liberty of opinion.

Lack of pep is often mistaken for patience.

The trouble with many people is they stop faster than they start.

Many people never learn to relax. Others never learn anything else.

A lot of people would pull their weight if some weren't so busy dragging their feet.

It takes too long for some people to start to begin to commence to get ready.

There are still a few people who believe in gittin' up and gittin', while a great many prefer sittin' down and sittin'.

It's rather strange how so many people go into a summer slump that lasts all winter.

If you don't rest as much as your doctor tells you, he says you're uncooperative. If you rest more than he advises, he says you're lazy.

Most people who sit around waiting for their ship to come in often find it is a hardship.

Some people stand on the promises; others just sit on the premises.

Some people call the world dirty because they're too lazy to clean their windows, windshields, and glasses.

Leaders

Education can't make us all leaders — but it can teach us which leader to follow.

If you're not afraid to face the music, you may someday lead the band.

The world would be happier if its leaders had more dreams and fewer nightmares.

Leaders go down in history — some farther down than others.

Don't ever follow any leader until you know whom he is following.

It's extremely difficult to lead farther than you have gone yourself.

A truly great leader is one who never allows his followers to discover that he is as ignorant as they are.

The business of a leader is to turn weakness into strength, obstacles into stepping stones, and disaster into triumph.

A real leader faces the music even when he dislikes the tune.

The trouble with being a leader today is that you can't be sure if people are following or chasing you.

A good leader takes a little more than his share of the blame, a little less than his share of the credit.

We herd sheep, we drive cattle, we lead men.

A leader is anyone who has two characteristics: first, he is going somewhere; second, he is able to persuade other people to go with him.

Followers do not usually go any farther than their leaders.

It is easier to follow the leader than to lead the followers.

There are two kinds of leaders in the world today: those who are interested in the fleece, and those who are interested in the flock.

A good leader inspires men to have confidence in him; a great leader inspires them to have confidence in themselves.

Before following a leader it is wise to see if he is headed in the right direction.

We can't lead someone else to the light while we are standing in the dark.

The reason parents don't lead their children in the right direction is because the parents aren't going that way themselves.

For a community leader, life is one big bowl of charities.

We spend half our time crying for leaders, and the other half nailing them to the cross of prejudice.

Leaders are ordinary people with extraordinary determination.

There are plenty of leaders, but *where* are they leading us?

Good leaders are so scarce that many people are just following themselves.

To determine the value of a leader, you must look at who's doing the following.

The world would be happier if its leaders had more vision and fewer nightmares.

The young people of today are tomorrow's leaders, but we sometimes wonder whether they're going to be followed or chased.

Learning
see also Education

Adversity is never pleasant, but sometimes it's possible to learn lessons from it that can be learned in no other way.

It's better to teach children the roots of labor than to hand them the fruits of yours.

Christianity has been studied and practiced for ages, but it has been studied far more than it has been practiced.

A college education never hurt anybody who was willing to learn after he got it.

Don't mind criticism. If it's untrue, disregard it; if it's unfair, keep from irritation; if it's ignorant, smile; if it's justified, learn from it.

Enough curiosity may enable you to learn, but too much of it can get you into trouble.

It's what we learn after we know it all that really counts.

It is possible to learn from an enemy things we can't learn from a friend.

If experience is the best teacher, many of us are mighty poor pupils.

A failure in life is one who lives and fails to learn.

Learning history is easy; learning its lessons is almost impossible.

Being ignorant is not so shameful as being unwilling to learn.

What you don't know you can learn.

The mind is like the stomach. It's not how much you put into it that counts, but how much it digests.

If people learn from their mistakes, many are getting a fantastic education.

More people would learn from their mistakes if they weren't so busy denying they made them.

Learn from the mistakes made by others. You won't live long enough to make them all yourself.

The man who says he's too old to learn new things probably always was.

Leisure

The best thing to get out of exercise is rest.

There is no such thing as leisure to people who do nothing.

Leisure is a beautiful garment, but it will not do for constant wear.

Everybody knows that leisure can be a real friend if you know how to use it, and a formidable enemy if you abuse it.

Nothing gives a man more leisure time than always being on time for appointments.

There's enough leisure time for everybody, but the wrong people seem to have it.

The real problem with your leisure time is how to keep other people from using it.

Leisure originally meant an opportunity to do something. It has come to mean an opportunity to do nothing.

It is generally understood that leisure time is what you have when the boss is on vacation.

The real problem with leisure time is how to keep other people from using it.

The reason why so many men can't work any harder in the office is because they wear leisure suits.

Liars

A boaster and a liar are first cousins.

A lot of people who boast they never go back on their word don't mind going around it a little.

An Oklahoma businessman reports that if his business gets any worse he won't have to lie on his next income-tax return.

Diplomacy is convincing a man he's a liar without actually saying so.

The income tax has made more liars out of the American people than golf.

George Washington never told a lie, but then he never had to file a Form 1040.

As a general rule, a liar is not believed even when he speaks the truth.

A liar is one who forgets to keep a partition between his imagination and the true facts.

Overheard: "I wouldn't exactly call him a liar. Let's just say he lives on the wrong side of the facts."

A liar is hard not to believe when he says nice things about you.

If a man is a liar it is useless to tell him so. He knew it all the time.

It's a lot more difficult to be a consistent liar than to tell the truth.

A pathological liar is a person so addicted to falsehood that he can't tell the truth without lying.

The kid who used to be the town's cutest fibber is now a bald-faced old liar.

There are many people who are not actually liars, but they keep a respectful distance from the truth.

Which has made the biggest liars out of Americans — golf or the income tax?

Some people are such liars you find it difficult to believe even the opposite of what they say.

A liar is the type of person who gets the most enjoyment out of fishing.

One of the differences between a liar and a publicity agent is that the publicity agent gets paid.

No man has a good enough memory to be a successful liar.

It is impossible for a man to be a successful liar unless someone believes him.

The ability to sin differs between people. A short-armed fisherman is not as big a liar as a long-armed one.

Liberty

The tree of liberty is one shrub that won't stand very much grafting.

Liberty doesn't work as well in practice as it does in speeches.

There is no liberty worth anything which is not liberty under law.

Every human being has the liberty to do that which is good, just, and honest.

Liberty is the right to go just as far as the law allows.

What this country needs is not more liberty, but fewer people who take liberties with liberty.

Let's not fight for more liberty until we learn how to handle what we've got.

Personal liberty ends where public safety begins.

If ever a new Statue of Liberty is designed, it will quite likely be holding the bag instead of the torch.

No constitution, no court, no law can save liberty when it dies in the hearts and minds of men and women.

Liberty is not a gift of God but a hard-won achievement with the help of God.

Those who are rooting up the tree of liberty will certainly be crushed by its fall.

Liberty is dearly bought, continually paid for, and difficult to keep.

The cradle of liberty needs more vigilant baby sitters.

Every child comes into the world endowed with liberty, opportunity, and a share of the war debt.

If we are going to fight for the liberty to worship, we ought to make use of that liberty.

Lies

Actions speak louder than words — and speak fewer lies.

The first thing you'll notice in the glove compartment of your new car is a little booklet telling you how to lie about your gas mileage.

Children are unpredictable. You never know when they're going to catch you in a lie.

The more you speak of yourself, the more you are likely to lie.

Exaggeration is a blood relative to falsehood, and almost as bad.

An excuse is usually a thin skin of falsehood stretched tightly over a bald-faced lie.

It's easier to believe a lie that one has heard a thousand times than to believe a fact that no one has heard before.

George Washington was not a fisherman — he never told a lie!

History books which contain no falsehoods are extremely dull.

When you sell yourself, be sure that you don't misrepresent the goods.

An honest man alters his ideas to fit the truth, and a dishonest man alters the truth to fit his ideas.

Nothing shows dirt like a white lie.

A man in Oklahoma admitted he lied on his income-tax return — he listed himself as the head of the household!

Sometimes a fib starts out as a little white lie and winds up as a double feature in technicolor.

The truth may hurt but a lie is agony.

A lie is the deliberate withholding of any part of the truth from someone who has the right to know.

The person who says he enjoys a cold shower early in the morning will lie about other things too.

A white lie soon gets tanned from exposure.

If George Washington never told a lie, what's his picture doing on a dollar bill that's worth about forty-three cents?

The only way you can get the same gas mileage in your car as your friends say they get in theirs is to lie about it.

Women are to blame for men telling lies. They keep asking questions!

We lie loudest when we lie to ourselves.

Truth often hurts, but it's the lie that leaves the scars.

Lie about others as you would like them to lie about you.

A lie may take care of the present, but it has no future.

Lies, like chickens, always come home to roost.

The devil is the father of lies, but he forgot to patent the idea.

Never chase a lie. Let it alone and it will run itself to death.

It takes at least three times as long to tell a lie on any subject as it does to tell the truth.

Sin has many tools, but a lie is a handle that fits them all.

A lie always has a certain amount of weight with those who wish to believe it.

Many people don't actually lie; they merely present the truth in such a way that nobody recognizes it.

The fellow who says he has never told a lie has just told one.

If you lie to people to get their money, that's fraud. If you lie to them to get their votes, that's politics.

The ability to lie differs among people. For instance, a short-armed fisherman isn't as big a liar as a long-armed one.

If you tell a big enough lie and tell it often enough, many will believe it.

It's not the land that lies, it's the real-estate agent.

Nothing lends the weight of truth to a lie like saying it in a whisper.

George Washington never told a lie — but then he entered politics when the country was very young.

A lie will go twice around the world while the truth is getting its boots on.

White lies are likely to leave black marks on a man's reputation.

It is easy to tell one lie but difficult to tell only one.

With many people telling lies is not a shortcoming but is one of their major achievements.

The most dangerous lies are those that most resemble the truth.

There are two things that cannot lie: the smile of a baby, and the wag of a dog's tail.

The man who always agrees with you lies to others also.

It is easier to believe a lie that one has heard a thousand times than a fact no one ever heard before.

A lie has no legs; it has to be supported by other lies.

The little white lie can slowly change to a tattletale gray.

If a man tells a woman she's beautiful, she'll overlook most of his other lies.

A lie is a coward's way of getting out of trouble.

The most terrible lie is not that which is uttered, but that which is lived.

A truthful woman is one who does not lie about anything but her age, her weight, and her husband's salary.

The more you talk about yourself, the more apt you are to lie.

Lies don't live nearly so long as the truth does, but their birthrate is much higher.

The color and caliber of a lie does not change its real character.

Some people remember a lie for ten years but forget the truth in ten minutes.

There are some people who can't tell a lie, some who can't tell the truth, and a few others who can't tell the difference.

The person who tells you how perfect he thinks you are will lie to others too.

The trouble with pulling the wool over the voter's eyes is that they soon recognize the yarn.

Our country has made great progress. George Washington couldn't tell a lie. Now, just about everybody tells them.

When selling yourself don't misrepresent the goods.

Of course truth hurts. You would too if you got stretched so much.

Truth is often violated by falsehood, but can be equally outraged by silence.

Some people stretch the truth; others mutilate it.

Truth crushed to earth will rise again — but so will a lie.

Some people do not lie — they merely present the truth in such a way that nobody recognizes it.

It is seldom as hard to tell the truth as it is to hide a lie.

Truth needs no crutches. If it limps it's a lie.

It is difficult to believe that a man is telling the truth when you know that you would lie if you were in his place.

A half-truth and a whole lie are congenial companions.

When a fellow tells you, "I'm going to tell you the truth," you wonder what he has been telling you since the conversation began.

They now have a lie detector without wires; it's called a wife!

Life

There are four steps to accomplishment: Plan purposefully. Prepare prayerfully. Proceed positively. Pursue persistently.

Advice to some people: If you had your life to live over — don't do it!

Life not only begins at forty — it begins to show.

Did you ever have one of those days when the only thing that goes off as planned is your alarm clock?

Americans believe in life, liberty, and the purchase of happiness.

There are too many people in too many cars in too much of a hurry going too many directions to get nowhere for nothing.

Nowadays every man wants life, liberty, and an automobile in which to pursue happiness.

There are a lot of books telling you how to manage when you retire. What most people want is one that'll tell them how to manage in the meantime.

Life's heaviest burden is to have nothing to carry.

Drive with care. Life has no spare.

Be careful as you slide down the banister of life, lest you get a splinter in your career.

The college of hard knocks is about the only one that doesn't let the student drop out if the course gets tough.

Whatever the cost of living is, it's worth it.

After all, the high cost of living seems unimportant when we consider all of life's fringe benefits.

Life is not so short that there isn't time for courtesy.

Death is not a period but a comma in the story of life.

People who are afraid of death are usually afraid of life.

There are worse things than death for some people — take life, for instance.

Believe that life is worth living and your belief will help create the fact.

Many people are so filled with fear that they go through life running from something that isn't after them.

We make a living by what we get, but we make a life by what we give.

We commit the Golden Rule to memory and forget to commit it to life.

A man spends the first half of his life learning habits that shorten the other half.

To find happiness you must be willing to ignore what life owes you and think about what you owe life.

A man's life is dyed the color of his imagination.

Laughter is the shock absorber that eases the blows of life.

Life is one dodge after another — cars, taxes, and responsibilities.

By the time a fellow is fixed for life during these trying times, he has just about worried himself to death.

Your life can't go according to plan if you have no plan.

Life is like a camel — it won't back up.

If life is ever found on the planet Mars, they're certain to ask us for a loan.

The trouble with life is that there are so many last minute details and so few last minutes.

Life is what you make it until somebody makes it worse.

No one finds life worth living; he must make it worth living!

Life not only begins at forty — that's when it really begins to show.

The best things in life are free, of course, but isn't it a pity that most of the next best things are so expensive?

About the only kicks some folks get out of life are from behind.

You cannot control the length of your life, but you can control its breadth, depth, and height.

It has been said that life is a game — but how can we play it if we don't know where the goal posts are?

Life allows us to ask for what we want, but usually gives us what we deserve.

The prime of life comes at a point between sixteen and sixty-five, depending on the age of the man doing the talking.

On the average, people who hurry through life get through it quicker.

If life were a bed of roses, some people wouldn't be happy until they developed an allergy.

Life is like a bank. You can't take out what you haven't put in.

Despite all the pain and trouble, life is still better than any alternative.

The triumphal song of life would lose its melody without its minor keys.

Life nowadays is just one tranquilizer after another.

The best things in life are free — plus tax, of course.

As you slide down the banister of life, may the splinters never point your way.

Life has become a struggle to keep our weight down and our spirits up.

The trouble with life is that by the time you know how to play the game you're too old to make the team.

If life were a bowl of cherries, chances are two to one that the pickers would go on strike.

We keep trying to find new ways to improve the quality of life — while neglecting the ways we already know.

Many people think life would be so much more enjoyable if we didn't have to work our way through it.

Life is like a poker game — if you don't put anything in the pot, there won't be anything to take out.

We get out of life what we put into it — that's the trouble!

Finding a way to live a simple life is today's most complicated job.

The great purpose of life is to make something that will outlast us.

Living in the past has one thing in its favor — it's cheaper.

Life is 10 percent what you make it and 90 percent how you take it.

If your life is an open book, don't bore your friends by reading out of it.

It isn't how high you go in life that counts, but *how* you got there.

Life is but a brief lull between the stork and the epitaph.

The best way to live a long life is to get somebody to do the worrying for you.

Life started from a cell, and, if justice is done, a lot of it is going to end there.

You can live in this world but once, but if you live it right once is enough.

Some people seem to know how to live everybody's life but their own.

Life is an eternal struggle to keep money coming in and teeth, hair, and vital organs from coming out.

If you break the rules in the game of life, the rules will eventually break you.

So live your life that your autograph will be wanted instead of your fingerprints.

Why not let God have your life? He can do more with it than you can.

When all the affairs of life are said and done, there is more said than done.

Life is like a mirror — we get the best results when we smile.

How tragic to give one's life to something the world does not want or need.

Some people don't go through life — they're *shoved* through it.

About the time we learn to make the most of life, the greater part of it is gone.

A long life is a gift of God; a full and fruitful life is your own doing.

In the game of life, one of the most humiliating experiences is to foul out when the bases are loaded.

The ladder of life is full of splinters, but you never realize it until you begin to slide down.

Life is tragic for those who have plenty to live on and nothing to live for.

Take life as you find it, but don't leave it so.

Life doesn't begin at forty for those who went eighty when they were twenty.

In the "good old days" life was what we made it, but now it's a case of *if* we make it.

You'll have a better life if you make the most of the best and the least of the worst.

Some of us may feel that life is a terrible disappointment, yet we want to stay here and be disappointed as long as we can.

Some people treat life like a slot machine — putting in as little as possible while hoping for the jackpot.

The best things in life are free — including the worst advice.

They tell us that life begins at forty, but they don't say what kind of life.

Life is like a radio comedy; it doesn't always follow the script.

Trying to make life easy is often what makes it so hard.

Life may not be worth living, but what else can you do with it?

If life were as easy as we would like, we could sleep all the way through it.

Life is as uncertain as a grapefruit's squirt.

There are three ingredients in the good life: learning, yearning, and earning.

Life is what you make it, or what it makes you.

Life is a cup to be filled, not drained.

Life is more like a ball of twine than a bowl of cherries. It has a tendency to come unraveled.

Life is like an overnight bag — if you try to cram too much into it, something has got to give.

Life would make more sense if we could live it backwards.

The things in life that count most are the things that can't be counted.

We make a living by what we get, but we make a life by what we give.

Life is like a mirror. If we frown at it, it frowns back. If we smile, it returns the greeting.

To love and to labor is the sum of life; and, yet, how many think they are living when they neither love nor labor?

The one thing certain about life is that we must leave it.

A task worth doing and friends worth having make life worthwhile.

It's not the ups and downs of life that bother the average man — it's the jerks!

After all, life is really simple; we ourselves create the circumstances that complicate it.

A man's life, like his barn, needs a little repair once in a while to keep it from falling apart.

Life is full of golden opportunities for doing what we don't want to do.

If your life looks cloudy, maybe the windows of your soul need washing.

The tragedy of life is what dies inside a man while he lives.

It may be true that life begins at forty, but everything else starts to wear out, fall out, or spread out.

Life is a bundle of little things, and the string is always coming untied.

The poorest way to face life is to face it with a sneer.

Life will lick you if you don't fight back.

To many people living life to the fullest simply means overeating.

Most of us go through life not knowing what we want, but feeling sure we don't have it.

The most important things in life aren't things.

Life has more questions than answers.

As one travels down the highway of life it becomes evident that there are far more toll roads than freeways.

The tragedy of life is not that it ends so soon, but that we wait so long to begin it.

Life can be understood backward but it must be lived forward.

The true measure of life is not its duration but its donation.

Life may begin at forty, but so does rheumatism.

Too many people attempt to fight the battles of life with a bottle.

Many a man saves everything but his soul.

Man starts life young and broke and winds up old and bent.

For most of us life is what we make it, but for the pedestrian it's *if* he makes it.

The world is full of people making a good living but poor lives.

Most pessimists are seasick during the entire voyage of their lives.

Life is fragile — handle with prayer.

When life knocks you to your knees, you're in position to pray.

Live prayerfully — the life you save may be your own.

Some people pray for a bushel, but carry a cup.

When the road of life is steep and slippery, prayer in action gives us traction.

Life's most difficult problem is to keep clean of debt, dirt, and the devil all at the same time.

Medical science is adding years to our lives, but it's up to us to add life to our years.

There's one consolation about life and taxes — when you finish the former, you're through with the latter.

The person who kills time hasn't learned the value of life.

Truth is something which must be known with the mind, accepted with the heart, and enacted in life.

Life Insurance

Depressions, funerals, weddings, and covered-dish suppers keep most people attending church regularly.

Most women don't buy life insurance — they marry it.

Life insurance keeps you poor all your life so you can die rich.

A man in Louisiana explained why he refuses to buy life insurance, "When I die I want it to be a sad day for everybody."

The uninsured are in no more peril than the insured, but their families are.

Life insurance is the last thing on earth a man wants, but it's too late then.

The only dependable fortuneteller is the life insurance agent. He tells you exactly what is going to happen — and it does.

Life insurance is like a football game — our relatives sit around and wait for us to "kick off."

A widow in Oklahoma remarked that her husband was a total loss — he died without life insurance.

Honesty may be the best policy, but life insurance is more satisfactory to the widow.

The longer a man goes without life insurance, the more he needs it, the less chance he has of getting it, and the more it costs him.

Liquor
see also Alcoholics

Which do you suppose ages faster — whiskey or the man who drinks it?

An alcoholic claims a little too much liquor is just about right.

There are two finishes for automobiles: lacquer and liquor.

When we hear a man boasting about how much liquor he can hold, we get a mental picture of an animated garbage can.

Glasses can make driving a lot safer. Providing, of course, they're worn instead of emptied.

Let's all have an old-fashioned Christmas this year, but not the kind that comes in bottles.

The coating of civilization is so thin it often comes off with a little alcohol.

A college is truly a fountain of knowledge, and a great many go there to drink.

Congress does some strange things — it puts a high tax on liquor, and raises the other taxes that drive people to drink.

A convention is where people pass a lot of resolutions, but few bars.

Out west corn is measured by the foot; down south, by the gallon; and on TV, by the hour.

Unfortunately, courage is all too often composed of equal parts of bourbon and water.

With some of today's dance steps you don't know if the guy on the floor is a good dancer or a bad drunk.

Dignity is one thing that cannot be preserved in alcohol.

The higher you get in the evening, the lower you feel in the morning.

Cars and bars mean stars and scars.

A drunkard can live neither with alcohol nor without it.

Gambling is pretty much like liquor; you can make it illegal but you can't make it unpopular.

If you drink too often to other people's health, you'll ruin your own.

The juvenile delinquent is a mixed-up kid, a victim of mixed drinks — mostly alcohol and gasoline.

Liquor is a lubricant only if a man is going downhill.

The reason so many people drink booze is because they are trying to cure a cold or prevent one.

Whiskey improves with age, but those who drink it don't.

Those who drown themselves in liquor don't have far to sink.

Why do they call it "going on a bender" when what actually happens is that one gets absolutely stiff?

Some folks drink liquor as if they want to be mentioned in "BOOZE WHO."

A Montana man who seldom takes more than one drink explained, "One drink is just right, two are too many, and three are not enough."

You've had too much drink when you feel exhilarated, but can't spell or pronounce it.

The only thing that keeps the bootlegger in business is customers.

Warning: Boozers are losers.

People who say that many things drive them to drink should walk.

Most folks know their capacity for drinking — the trouble is they get drunk before they reach it.

A man may be drinking because his wife walked out on him — or because she walked in on him.

Heavy drinkers have what is known as saloon arthritis — every night they get stiff in a different joint.

Despite the high price of whiskey, a twenty-five cent drink is still available in the mountain regions of the south — according to a recent autopsy!

When liquor talks in a business deal, don't pin your faith on what it says.

A boozer insisted that his liquor bill was deductible as a medical expense. "My friends and I drink to each other's health."

Vodka is colorless, odorless, tasteless, and too much of it leaves you senseless.

Too many people attempt to fight the battles of life with a bottle.

Liquor is nothing but trouble in liquid form.

Without his big bank account the "problem drinker" would be called a drunken bum.

Whiskey has more lovers and fewer friends than anything on earth.

It's better to sit tight than to walk tight.

Nothing can hold liquor as well as a bottle — so why not leave it there?

Get the best of liquor or it will get the best of you.

If the price of liquor continues to go up, a certain drunk complains that it would be enough to drive him *not* to drink.

When you come right down to it, the problem isn't alcohol — it's the people who drink it.

A cocktail lounge is a half-lit room full of half-lit people.

The reason some people drink booze is that they don't know what else to do with it.

Drinking liquor is legal, but some people seem to think it's compulsory.

A great many folks have no respect for age unless it's bottled.

The only person who can handle a pint or a quart while driving is the milkman.

Booze increases business for the hospitals, ambulance drivers, doctors, nurses, undertakers, and gravediggers.

If you take the time to follow the history of the man who says he drinks "now and then," you will find that he drinks more *now* than he did *then*.

Whiskey is by far the most popular of all the many remedies that absolutely won't cure a cold.

Glasses have an amazing effect on the eyes, especially after they've been emptied of liquor several times.

Many people have so much alcohol in their system that they ought to be charged a liquor tax for crossing state lines.

A cocktail party starts out with people mixing drinks and ends up with drinks mixing people.

Many men give up drinking on account of the wife and bad kidneys.

Any safety campaign that does not throttle booze overlooks the main cause of accidents and crime.

The man who downs bottles of liquor will find that the liquor returns the favor.

Booze makes a man colorful; it gives him a red nose, a white liver, a yellow streak, and a blue outlook.

It's when a man gets tight as a drum that he makes the most noise.

Some battle their way to the top; others bottle their way to the bottom.

Liquor will not drown sorrows; it only irrigates them.

Some people have a veneer that comes off easily with a little liquor.

The main trouble with liquor is that it makes you see double and feel single.

A weak moment with the bottle can mean several weeks in the jug.

Booze is the only enemy that man has succeeded in loving.

Booze-befuddled brains mean brawls, bumps, and bruises.

The hand that lifts the cup that "cheers" should not be used to shift the gears.

A "hangover" is something that occupies the head you neglected to use last night.

Liquor will kill germs, but you can't get them to drink it.

Anything can be pickled in alcohol. Just take a look at the guy next door!

You take a drink of booze and it makes a new man out of you — then the new man wants a drink.

The reason some men can't make both ends meet is because they're too busy making one end drink.

Drinking is a subject that floors a lot of people.

The difference between spirit doctors and doctored spirits is that the latter really shows you the next world.

Poverty never drives a man to drink unless he wants to go, but drink will drive a man to poverty whether he wants to go or not.

If you drink enough moonshine, you won't see the sunshine.

Drinking to another man's health isn't going to improve your own.

Nothing can be more frequent than an occasional drink.

The drinking man commits suicide on the installment plan.

All liquids seek the lowest level; alcohol takes the drinker with it.

Four reasons for not drinking: the head is clearer, the health is better, the heart is lighter, and the purse is heavier.

It is sometimes difficult to tell whether a red nose is caused by sunshine or moonshine.

Drinking is something that makes one lose inhibitions and give exhibitions.

The liquor of today is the hangover of tomorrow.

"Wild Oats" and "Old Rye" grow in the same field.

Liquor kills everything that's alive and preserves everything that's dead.

Many a man keeps on drinking till he hasn't a coat on his back or his stomach.

Don't think that things couldn't be worse — take a few drinks and they will be.

One thing is certain: you can't pull yourself out of trouble with a corkscrew.

Sign in a liquor store: "Preserve wild life — throw a party."

When a man drinks too much liquor he can approach you from several directions at once.

Liquor makes a man tight, and his tongue loose.

One gallon of gas plus one pint of liquor often adds up to a first-class funeral.

Some people drink when they have occasion, and sometimes when they have no occasion.

A cocktail party is an excuse to drink for people who don't need any excuse.

Liquor may not be so bad after all; it makes men fight and shoot at each other — and miss!

Did you hear about the old-timer in Kentucky who drank more than a quart of whiskey a day for sixty years? When he passed away at the age of ninety-seven they tried to cremate him, but he blew up and wrecked the place!

If you drink like a fish, swim. Don't drive.

It takes only one drink to make a person drunk — and usually it's the fourth one.

There's one thing about whiskey — it always looks so sober in a glass.

A gentleman in Iowa reports that his uncle will donate his body to science. He's now preserving it in alcohol till they need it.

Most people have no taste for liquor at all. They just gulp it down.

Pity the poor drunk who started out to get mellow, then he got ripe, and ended up rotten.

A drinking man is the last to be hired and the first to be fired.

The trouble with people who "drink like fish" is they don't drink what the fish drink.

A man is drunk when he feels sophisticated but can't pronounce it.

What silly things human beings utter when drunk or in love!

The New Year is when some people drop in for a call and others call in for a drop.

To many football fans the pint after the touchdown is the most important part of the game.

Football stadiums are usually filled to capacity — and so are some of the fans.

All vices are of personal origin. Playing cards do not make the gambler, nor a bottle of liquor the drunkard.

Vision is definitely affected by glasses, especially after they've been filled and emptied several times.

Listening

You can say what you please in America — but nobody listens.

A good listener is one who can give you his full attention without hearing a word you say.

There are two kinds of bores — those who talk too much and those who listen too little.

If you don't want your children to hear what you're saying, pretend you're talking to them.

If you are not a charming conversationalist, you may still be a big hit as a charmed listener.

In this country you are still privileged to free speech, but that's as far as the Constitution goes. It doesn't guarantee listeners.

You can win more friends with your ears than with your mouth.

A lasting gift to a child is the gift of a parent's listening ear — and heart.

God still speaks to those who take the time to listen.

The Golden Rule of friendship is to listen to others as you would have them listen to you.

Spreading gossip is impossible if we refuse to listen — or to believe it.

Knowledge without wisdom is as dangerous as an automobile with neither steering wheel nor brakes.

Take a tip from nature — your ears aren't made to shut, but your mouth is!

In nature we hear the speech of God.

Always listen to the opinions of others. It may not do you much good but it will them.

Opportunities are often missed because we are broadcasting when we should be listening.

One way to be popular is to listen attentively to a lot of things you already know.

If you would have God hear you when you pray, you must hear Him when He speaks.

Perhaps you can improve your preacher's preaching by being a better listener.

We reform others unconsciously when we walk uprightly.

It takes great listening, as well as great preaching, to make a great sermon.

A poor listener seldom hears a good sermon.

About all that's worth listening to these days is silence.

Nobody ever listens themselves out of a job.

Living

No man is fully accomplished until he has acquired the ability to attend to his own business.

People aren't really living any longer — it just seems that way.

What is hurting America today is the high cost of low living.

The kind of behavior that once brought shame and disgrace now brings a book, movie, or a television contract.

There are no detour signs along the straight and narrow path.

When people speak evil of you, live so that no one will believe them.

Thousands of people don't like the Bible because it cramps their lifestyle.

The Bible contains the vitamins for a healthy soul.

Go to your Bible regularly, open it prayerfully, read it expectantly, live it joyfully.

Our beloved country recently celebrated its two-hundredth birthday, and all we've learned in that time is how to go fast, work less, waste more, and die quicker.

A budget is an orderly way of discovering that you can't live on what you're earning.

Maybe children could keep on the straight and narrow path if they could get information from someone who's been over the route.

It's better to teach children the roots of labor than to hand them the fruits of yours.

Teaching children to count is not as important as teaching them *what* counts.

If you want to convince others of the value of Christianity — live it!

The spirit of Christianity is not to impose some kind of a creed, but to share a life.

The true Christian is a person who is right-side-up in a world that is upside-down.

There are a lot of Christians who haven't stored up enough treasures to make a down-payment on a harp.

A Christian should live so that instead of being a part of the world's problems he will be a part of the answer.

The *way* you spend Christmas is far more important than *how much*.

Judging by the way some church members live, they need fire insurance.

In today's colleges the freshmen are smarter than the seniors; everything the seniors have learned is already outmoded.

Have you seen anybody lately who wants to stop living on account of the cost?

The only way to beat the high cost of living is to stop living.

Beware of the high cost of low living.

Make this your motto: Don't die until you are dead.

Some people have been dead for several years, but they just prefer not to have it known.

So live that when death comes the mourners will outnumber the cheering section.

Depending on how a man lives, he may die old at forty or young at eighty.

There are no detours along the straight and narrow path.

Encouragement is like premium gasoline. It helps to take the knock out of living.

Believe that life is worth living and your belief will help create the fact.

Living without faith is like driving in a fog.

Faith helps us walk fearlessly, run confidently, and live victoriously.

A genuine sense of humor is the pole that adds balance to our steps as we walk the tightrope of life.

If you can laugh at it you can live with it.

The most terrible lie is not that which is uttered, but that which is lived.

No one finds life worth living; he must make it worth living!

Finding a way to live a simple life is today's most complicated job.

You can live in this world but once, but if you live it right once is enough.

Life is tragic for those who have plenty to live on and nothing to live for.

An upright man can never be a downright failure.

Man has learned to fly like a bird and swim like a fish — now all he needs to do is learn to live like a man.

Man was created a little lower than the angels and has been getting lower ever since.

Man is much like an automobile — just so much mileage in him whether he runs it out in forty years or eighty.

There is entirely too much worrying about unhappy marriages. All marriages are happy. It's only living together afterward that causes the trouble.

So live that your memories will be a part of your happiness.

Wonderful things happen to us when we live expectantly, believe confidently, and pray affirmatively.

Reckless drivers drive like living is going out of style.

If your religion means much to you, live so it will mean much to others.

It's better to live richly than to die rich.

A fellow ought to live so that anyone speaking against him would be recognized as a liar.

No man ever got lost on a straight road.

Straight living cannot come out of crooked thinking.

A lot of people would do right if they thought it was wrong.

It is better to be beaten in the right than to succeed in the wrong.

One may go wrong in many directions but right in only one.

Let's live our lives in such a way that we can laugh when we're together and smile when we're alone.

If people generally cared as much for their souls as they do their looks, the preachers would soon be out of a job.

The only way to be good is to obey God, love your fellowman, and hate the devil.

Always stand for the right; then you win even if you lose.

The fellow who stays on the straight and narrow path won't have many folks trying to pass him.

Always do right; it will gratify some people and astonish others.

No man can be at peace with God without getting into an argument with the devil.

Be careful how you live. You may be the only Bible some people will ever read.

Right living is better than high living — and cheaper.

The straight and narrow road has not yet developed enough traffic to require a four-lane highway.

Be on the level and you are not likely to go downhill.

What a fine world this would be if today we did as well as we expect to do tomorrow.

He who walks circumspectly by day need not fear the rap on the door at midnight.

So live that when the preacher has ended his remarks over your grave, those present will not think they have attended the wrong funeral.

Remember your spiritual system, forget your nervous system, and you'll have a place in God's heavenly system.

Live your life so that you won't be afraid to have your phone tapped.

People who live right never get left.

There is more chance for a cripple on the right road than for an athlete on the wrong road.

If you will live right each day, you will be neither afraid of tomorrow nor ashamed of yesterday.

So live that people will want your autograph and not your fingerprints.

Keep your head and your heart going in the right direction and you'll not have to worry about your feet.

Many men would turn over a new leaf if they could tear out some of the old pages.

A straight line is the shortest in moral problems as well as in geometry.

Usually it is on the detours that we pick up the tacks.

So live that you wouldn't be ashamed to sell the family parrot to the town gossip.

What do we live for if not to make the world less difficult for each other?

Go straight. Every crooked turn delays your arrival at success.

The straight and narrow road could be broadened a little if more people would walk on it.

People will usually take the right road when you lead them to it — not when you merely point to it.

To succeed — keep your head up and your overhead down.

The shortest route to success is the straight road.

When you meet temptation — turn to the right!

Which needs to be raised more — our standard of living or our standard of thinking?

The straight and narrow path is the only one that has no traffic problems.

Loneliness

A Florida bachelor sent his picture to a Lonely Hearts Club. They replied, "We're not that lonely."

A bore keeps you from feeling lonely and makes you wish you were.

It is better to be criticized than to be ignored.

Many people are lonely because they build walls and not bridges.

The reason many successful men are so lonely is because they sacrificed too many friends on the way up.

There's many a girl who got married because she didn't like to spend her evenings alone — and then got a divorce for the same reason.

The most lonely place in the world is the human heart when love is absent.

To love others makes us happy; to love ourselves makes us lonely.

Punctuality assures loneliness.

Laugh and the world will laugh with you; think and you will almost die of loneliness.

The surest way to be lonesome is to always tell the truth.

Love

Age is like love. It cannot be hidden.

The world needs more warm hearts and fewer hot heads.

You can always get someone to love you — even if you have to do it yourself.

Democracy, like love, can survive almost any attack — except neglect and indifference.

There would be fewer divorces if men gave as much loving attention to their wives as they do to their cars, boats, and dogs.

Love is the quest, marriage the conquest, divorce the inquest.

A dog is the only thing on earth that loves you more than he loves himself.

If dogs can think, how can we account for their love for man?

The fellow who is deeply in love with himself should get a divorce.

Love looks through a telescope; envy, through a microscope.

In the language of flowers, the yellow rose means friendship, the red rose means love, and the orchid means business.

You can give without loving, but you can't love without giving.

Happiness is a healthy mental attitude, a grateful spirit, a clear conscience, and a heart full of love.

Happiness is the conviction that we are loved in spite of ourselves.

Money can build a house, but it takes love to make it a home.

A house is made of walls and beams; a home is built with love and dreams.

Love is the glue that cements friendship; jealousy keeps it from sticking.

Kindness is the ability to love people more than they really deserve.

Kindness is the insignia of a loving heart.

To love and to labor is the sum of life; and, yet, how many think they are living when they neither love nor labor?

The most lonely place in the world is the human heart when love is absent.

Love at first sight may be all right, but it might be wise to take a second look.

To some people love is only the last word in a telegram.

Love is a little word; people make it big.

We are often told that love is blind — it can also be deaf and dumb.

Love makes a man think almost as much of a woman as he thinks of himself.

If you had it all to do over, would you fall in love with yourself again?

Nothing beats love at first sight except love with insight.

A man doesn't know the value of a woman's love until he starts paying alimony.

Love is an unusual game. There are either two winners or none.

A husband knows his wife loves him when she returns a dress he can't afford.

To love the world is no big chore. It's that miserable guy next door who's the problem!

The way the cost of living and taxes are today, you might as well marry for love.

If love is blind, why are so many men attracted to a beautiful woman?

Love is the beautiful story, and marriage is the "talkie" version of it.

The biggest drawback to budding love these days is the *blooming* expense.

Love may make the world go 'round, but so will a big swallow of tobacco juice.

The fellow who is too deeply in love with himself ought to get a divorce.

Love conquers all things except poverty and toothaches.

Don't underestimate love at first sight. Many of us might not pass a second inspection.

"Puppy love" is just a prelude to a dog's life.

A woman knowns the value of love, but a man knows its cost.

The sunlight of love will kill all the germs of jealousy and hate.

Love is sharing a part of yourself with others.

First love is a little foolishness and a lot of curiosity.

The love of God cannot be merited or earned, but it can be spurned.

It is impossible to express love with a clenched fist.

Love is oceans of emotions surrounded by expanses of expenses.

The trouble with blind love is that it doesn't stay that way.

True love doesn't consist of holding hands — it consists of holding hearts.

The most important thing a father can do for his children is to love their mother.

It's easier to love humanity as a whole than to love one's neighbor.

Love covers a multitude of sins — temporarily.

Those who deserve love least need it most.

Illicit love isn't very much fun once it gets into court.

Love at first sight is often cured by a second look.

He who falls in love with himself will have no rivals.

The Bible admonishes us to love our neighbors, and also to love our enemies — probably because they are generally the same people.

Of all human passions love is the strongest, for it attacks simultaneously the head, the heart, and the senses.

What silly things human beings utter when drunk or in love!

Everything in the household runs smoothly when love oils the machinery.

Duty makes us do things well, but love makes us do them beautifully.

Love is like a vaccination — when it takes hold, you don't have to be told.

It probably would be all right if we'd love our neighbors as we love ourselves — but could they stand that much affection?

Love quickens all the senses — except common sense.

It would be a happy world if love were as easy to keep as it is to make.

Another good way for a young man to waste his breath is trying to be reasonable about love.

Love is more easily demonstrated than defined.

One of the tragedies of American life is that love is being defined by those who have experienced so little of it.

Love is the fairest flower that blooms in God's garden.

Love at first sight usually ends with divorce at first slight.

It's much wiser to love thy neighbor than his wife.

The course of true love never runs smoothly — and the detours aren't much better.

Love is something different from delirium, but it's hard to tell the difference.

To love others makes us happy; to love ourselves makes us lonely.

There are three things most men love but never understand: females, girls, and women.

True love doesn't have a happy ending; true love doesn't have an ending.

Love is the only game in which two can play and both lose.

He loved a girl so much he worshiped the very ground her father discovered oil on.

Booze is the only enemy that man has succeeded in loving.

Love has been defined as something that makes a fellow feel funny and act foolish.

Love is a disease you can't "catch" without being properly exposed.

The course of true love never runs — it stops and parks!

Love doesn't really make the world go round. It just makes people so dizzy it looks like it.

A girl may love you from the bottom of her heart, but there's always room for some other fellow at the top.

Love may be blind but it seems to find its way around.

A woman cherishes the memory of her first love affair with the same zeal with which a man forgets his.

Love is a condition of the mind at a time when the mind is out of condition.

Love is a fabric which never fades, no matter how often it is washed in the water of adversity and grief.

When you hear bells ringing, feel butterflies fluttering, and act as though you have bees in your bonnet — that's real love!

Love intoxicates a man; marriage often sobers him.

All the world loves a lover except when he is driving his automobile in crowded traffic — with his arm around his girlfriend.

It's hard to keep a man's love with cold food.

Love does not keep a ledger of the sins and failures of others.

Love is a ticklish sensation around the heart that can't be scratched!

The train of brotherly love rides on the track of concern and compassion.

Love your enemies. It'll sure make them feel foolish.

A woman feels a man's love should be like a toothbrush. It shouldn't be shared.

Mother love is dangerous when it becomes *smother* love.

Works, not words, are the proof of love.

Marriage is too often a process whereby love ripens into vengeance.

It's useless to try to hold some people to anything they say while they're madly in love, drunk, or running for office.

There are two sides to every quesion, except when it happens to be a love triangle.

Service is nothing but love in work clothes.

You know a woman is in love with her husband if she smiles at him the way she does at a traffic cop.

What a nice world this world would be if we loved others as we love ourselves.

This will be a better world when the power of love replaces the love of power.

What kids need today is plenty of LSD — Love, Security, and Discipline.

Luck

You can always tell luck from ability by its duration.

Spilling the salt might be bad luck, but spilling the beans is much more dangerous.

Choice, not chance, determines destiny.

A rabbit's foot is a poor substitute for horse sense.

It's pretty hard to make a fellow see that his bad judgment wasn't just bad luck.

Many people are having such bad luck these days that even their artificial fruit is beginning to rot.

Luck is a wonderful thing. The harder a person works, the more of it he seems to have.

Good luck is a lazy man's estimate of a worker's success.

Some people are luckier with cards than with horses — because they can't shuffle the horses.

Luck always seems to be against the man who depends on it.

Combine common sense and the Golden Rule and you will have very little bad luck.

Depend on the rabbit's foot if you will, but remember it didn't work for the rabbit!

There may be luck in getting a job, but there's no luck involved in keeping it.

Good luck often has the odor of perspiration about it.

Luck is good planning, carefully executed.

The only sure thing about luck is that it will change.

Luck is what happens when preparation meets opportunity.

If anything lucky happens to you, don't forget to tell your friends in order to annoy them.

Ten minutes of good luck will make you forget all the bad luck you ever had.

Good luck, like inheriting a million dollars, always happens to someone else.

It's hard to recognize good luck. It looks so much like something you've earned!

Nothing improves a man's luck like fish that are in a biting mood.

Good luck is often with the man who doesn't include it in his plans.

Luck is that mysterious something that enables others to succeed at something we have failed to accomplish.

If "all the world were a stage," our luck would most likely give us a seat on the last row in the third balcony.

There's no such thing as luck, but, just in case, it's good to have it on your side.

Industry is the mother of success — luck, a distant relative.

Luxuries

Advertising is what tells us which luxuries we can't do without.

Hate is a luxury no one can afford.

Laughter is the cheapest luxury that man has. It stirs up the blood, expands the chest, electrifies the nerves, clears away the cobwebs from the brain, and gives the whole system a cleansing rehabilitation.

Laziness is a luxury that few people can afford.

Luxuries are what other people buy — not us!

Real luxury is living in a house with so many closets that one of them is empty.

A luxury is something you don't really need, and yet you can't do without it.

There, little luxury, don't you cry — you'll be a necessity by and by.

Yesterday's luxuries are today's debts.

A luxury is something the average person manages to pay for by buying his necessities on credit.

The difference between a luxury and a necessity depends on whether your neighbor has it and you don't.

A luxury becomes a necessity if we can make the down-payment on it.

Nowadays we spend so much on luxuries we can't afford to buy the necessities.

A necessity is almost any luxury you see in the home of a neighbor.

Lying

The time-tested method of slowing down advancing age seems to be misrepresentation.

A certain businessman complained about his partner, "He's a real phony — I wouldn't believe him if he said he was lying."

People determine your character by observing what you stand for, fall for, and lie for.

It is only on matters of great principle that a diplomat lies with a clear conscience.

There are people so addicted to exaggeration that they can't tell the truth without lying.

Anyone who finds it easy to improve his golf game probably does it with a pencil.

Some of the world's best golf scores are made with a lead pencil.

There are many golfers who play a fair game — if you watch them.

A woman in Nevada explains why she doesn't play golf: "I have more important things to lie about."

Any husband who expects to pull the wool over his wife's eyes had better be sure he's using a good yarn.

Lying about people annoys them very much, but sometimes telling the truth annoys them a lot more.

The next worst thing to lying is getting caught at it.

It's extremely difficult to believe that a man is telling the truth when you know that you would lie if you were in his place.

Just why do men lie about each other when the plain truth would be bad enough?

A woman usually starts lying about her age when her face begins telling the truth about it.

An ambitious young man in Oklahoma is determined to enter politics. He says he's looking for something where he won't get punished for lying.

People who do a lot of kneeling don't do much lying.

There must be a shortage of truth the way so many folks are stretching it these days.

M

Man–Average
Man–Self-Made
Manners
Marriage
Meanness
Medical Costs
Medicare
Medicine

Meekness
Memory
Men
Men and Women
Middle Age
Mind
Mistakes

Modesty
Money
Mother
Mother-in-law
Movies
Music
Musicians

Man — Average

What the average man wants to get out of his new car is the kids.

When the average man becomes thoroughly acquainted with himself, he ceases to wonder why he has so few friends.

The average man doesn't usually increase his average.

The average man now lives thirty-one years longer than he did in 1850. He has to in order to get his taxes paid.

The average man doesn't want much and usually gets less than that.

The average man is able to detect a rattle in his car more quickly than one in his head.

The average man thinks he isn't.

The average man is forty-two around the chest, forty-four around the waist, ninety-six around the golf course, and a nuisance around the house.

When the average man has become thoroughly acquainted with himself, he ceases to wonder why he has so few friends.

The worst thing about the average man is that there are so many of them.

The average man has sixty-nine pounds of muscle, forty-one pounds of bone, three pounds of brain — which seems to explain a lot of things.

Self-made men should be more careful in selecting the material they use.

Man — Self-Made

The self-made man always seems to admire his maker.

Folks who boast of being self-made usually have a few parts missing.

He who boasts of being self-made relieves the Lord of a lot of responsibility.

We have observed that many self-made men made their heads oversize.

The self-made man is usually a pathetic example of unskilled labor.

Humility is one of the qualities often left out of the "self-made" man.

You can usually recognize a self-made man. He has arms long enough to pat himself on the back.

A self-made man is usually a horrible example of unskilled labor.

The trouble with the self-made man is that he often quits the job too soon.

Of course everybody likes and respects a self-made man. It's a great deal better to be made that way than not to be made at all.

Many self-made men are apt to blame somebody else.

Some self-made men show poor architectural skill.

The best thing some self-made men could do is deny it.

Manners

Children are natural mimics; they act like their parents in spite of every effort to teach them good manners.

No one can find as many detours as a woman approaching middle age!

A great many children face the hard problem of learning good table manners without seeing any.

Soup should be seen and not heard.

A highway is a road that can make bad manners fatal.

Home is a place where you can take off your new shoes and put on your old manners.

Table manners must have been invented by people who were never hungry.

Good manners is being able to put up with bad ones.

Bad manners are like bad teeth. Nobody knows you have them if you keep your mouth shut.

It may be bad manners, but it sure tastes good to sop your biscuit in the gravy.

Good manners is what enables a person to wait at the counter patiently and quietly for service — while the blabber mouth gets all the service.

Some people insist on having the best of everything — except manners.

319

A Mississippi mother said to her children, "Mind your manners, they may come back in style someday."

Punctuality is like having bad manners. You're sure of having lots of time to yourself.

Some people take everything on a vacation except their manners.

Marriage

Most accidents occur in the home. Many men use this as an excuse to stay out late.

A Hollywood actress is now teaching a course on educational TV — husbandry!

There's an unusual actress in Hollywood — she's signed more marriage certificates than autographs.

On TV talk shows the Hollywood actresses always seem to mention either their last picture or their next husband.

Many actresses won't wear a dress that's not original, but they'll take a secondhand husband.

A Chicago actress says she's been so busy planning her sixth marriage she hasn't time to cook for her fifth husband.

Advertising is a good deal like marriage. There may be a better way, but what is it?

Any man who has to ask for advice probably isn't married.

Advice to the bridegroom: No matter how she treats you, always try to look a little hurt.

Some people think the proper age for a man to start thinking of marriage is when he's old enough to realize he shouldn't.

Many a husband has learned that an ironclad alibi isn't as effective as a diamond-studded one.

When you see a married couple who's coming down the street, the one two or three steps ahead is the one who's mad.

Married couples who claim they've never had an argument in forty years either have poor memories or a very dull life to recall.

When you're arguing with your wife, make absolutely sure you're right — and then let the matter drop.

A husband and wife in Montana make it a point not to argue over anything not worth arguing about. Of course, this leads to some dandy fights over whether or not a subject is worthwhile.

The argument you just won with your wife isn't over yet.

Arguing with your wife is as useless as trying to blow out a lightbulb.

After winning an argument with his wife, the wisest thing a man can do is apologize.

The hottest arguments over Canasta start after the guests depart.

There are a lot more marital arguments over a wink than a mink.

Some men who speak with authority at work know enough to bow to a higher authority at home.

It may be that bachelors make more mistakes than married men — but they don't make the big one.

Bachelors have no idea what married bliss is, and that's also true of a lot of husbands.

To the bachelor, horror films are pictures of a wedding.

A bachelor is a rolling stone that gathers no boss.

A bachelor may have no buttons on his shirt, but a married man often has no shirt.

Many a bachelor longs for a wife who will take care of him — and so does many a husband.

Some banks guarantee maximum interest rates for several years, which is more than a marriage license can do.

Bigamy is having one wife too many — monogamy is often the same.

Judging from some of the specimens they select, can you blame brides for blushing?

The husband who boasts that he never made a mistake has a wife who did.

A Hollywood star boasts he's been happily married for twenty years. Of course, it took him five marriages to do it.

Brains are what a man looks for in a wife, after not using any in selecting one.

A married couple usually works out a budget together and then breaks it separately.

Not too long ago business got so bad that some men went bankrupt, and some went back to their wives.

A baby may not be able to lift very much, but it can hold a marriage together.

Children always know when company is in the living room — they can hear their mother laughing at their father's jokes.

The old-fashioned mother who saved her wedding togs for her daughter now has a daughter who tries to make them outlast three husbands.

Common sense could prevent a great many divorces; but, on the other hand, it could also prevent a great many marriages.

The woman who complains about the man she married should realize that she could have caught a bigger fish if she had used better bait.

A Missouri man complains that he was married fifteen years ago by a Justice of the Peace, and since that time he has had neither justice nor peace.

A dish towel will certainly wipe a contented look off a married man's face.

At a convention the "delegate-at-large" is the man who has come without his wife.

Why are husbands and wives more courteous to strangers than to each other?

More and more lovely courtships sail into the sea of matrimony, and finally sink into the rocky storms of divorce.

Courtship, unlike proper punctuation, is a period before a sentence.

Before criticizing your wife's faults, you must remember it may have been those very defects which prevented her from getting a better husband than the one she married.

When a man decides to marry, it may be the last decision he'll ever be allowed to make.

The best and surest way to save a marriage from divorce is not to show up for the wedding.

It's true that some people get divorced for trivial reasons. But, then, some of them got married for trivial reasons.

Judging by the divorce rate, a lot of people who said, "I do" — didn't!

A divorce is what happens when what you thought was a marriage turns out to be a conglomerate.

The divorce rate would be lower if, instead of marrying for better or worse, people would marry for good.

You have only to mumble a few words in church to get married and a few in your sleep to get divorced.

Love is the quest, marriage the conquest, divorce the inquest.

Many divorces are caused by the marriage of two people who are in love with themselves.

A wealthy father didn't know what to give his daughter as a wedding present, so he promised to pay for her divorce.

Some men believe in dreams until they marry one.

Sometimes an adult education begins with a teen-age marriage.

We've had adult education for several thousand years. It's called marriage.

An executive refused an employee's request for a raise, adding, "I know you can't get married on what I pay you — and someday you'll thank me."

There's nothing like a little exercise to change a man's life — especially if it's a walk down a church aisle.

Faith is better company than imagination for the wife whose husband fails to come home on time.

A wedding cake is the only cake that can give you indigestion for the rest of your life.

It's impossible for a man to make a fool of himself without knowing it — not if he's married.

Time separates the best of friends, and so does money — and marriage!

Las Vegas has all kinds of gambling devices, such as dice, roulette, slot machines — and wedding chapels.

All forms of gambling are frowned upon by preachers — except marriage.

If all gambling were illegal, we would all have to stop driving cars and getting married.

321

Gentlemen prefer blondes — especially gentlemen who are married to brunettes.

You'll never convince a newlywed bride that someday she might prefer a dishwasher to a mink coat.

It's amazing how many things a girl can do without until she gets married.

One way a girl can stop a man from making love to her is to marry him.

When a girl marries she gives up the attention of several men for the inattention of one.

Most girls seem to marry men like their fathers. Maybe that's the reason so many mothers cry at weddings.

If you're wondering what happened to the old-fashioned girl, you'll probably find her at home with her husband and children.

When a girl casts her bread upon the waters, she expects it to come back to her in the shape of a wedding cake.

Some of our modern girls turn a man's head with charm — and his stomach with their cooking.

The girl who remembers her first kiss now has a daughter who can't even remember her first husband.

Girls who fall in love with a fellow at first sight sometimes wish they had taken a second look.

Some girls get married for financial security; others get divorced for the same reason.

More golden wedding anniversaries would be celebrated if more couples practiced the Golden Rule.

Genuine happiness is when a wife sees a double chin on her husband's old girl friend.

Hollywood is just one great big family. Everybody is related by marriage — or soon will be.

In Hollywood a happy marriage is one in which the husband loves his wife more than somebody else's.

Some Hollywood people compare marriage to eating salted peanuts — it's hard to stop at one.

In Hollywood they figure a marriage has a chance of succeeding if the couple leaves the church together.

The average man has probably thought twice about running away from home — once as a child and once as a husband.

A happy home is one in which each spouse entertains the possibility that the other may be right, though neither believes it.

The honeymoon is over when the bride begins to suspect that she was never anything to him but a tax deduction.

After the honeymoon the girl usually stops wondering what she should wear and starts wondering how long it will last.

The honeymoon is a period of doting between dating and debating.

God gave women a sense of humor — so they could understand the jokes they married.

Husbands are like wood fires. When unattended they go out.

The ideal of some men is to marry a rich girl who is too proud to have her husband work.

Many a girl who elopes wishes later she had just let her imagination run away with her.

A kiss is what a husband struggled for before marriage and what his wife struggles for after marriage.

Almost everybody gets married while they're in Las Vegas. They figure as long as they're on a losing streak they might as well go all the way.

It is better to be laughed at for not being married than to be unable to laugh because you are.

If a man is too lazy to think for himself, he should get married!

A man in Oklahoma admitted he lied on his income-tax return — he listed himself as the head of the household!

There's many a girl who got married because she didn't like to spend her evenings alone — and then got a divorce for the same reason.

The way the cost of living and taxes are today, you might as well marry for love.

Love is the beautiful story, and marriage is the "talkie" version of it.

Love intoxicates a man; marriage often sobers him.

One nice thing about being a man is that you don't have to kiss somebody who hasn't shaved in three days.

A well-informed man is one whose wife has just told him what she thinks of him.

There would be a lot more happy marriages if husbands tried to understand their wives and wives tried to understand football.

Marriage is like arthritis. You have to learn to live with it.

What frightens most men about marriage is not another mouth to feed — but another one to listen to!

Most men think they're marrying a cook; most women think they're marrying a banker.

Some men who say they're not interested in marriage have wives sitting home alone to prove it.

Marriage is perhaps the most expensive way to get advice for nothing.

In most marriages the husband is the provider and the wife is the decider.

The person who marries for money usually earns every penny of it.

When you see how willingly some young men go to the marriage bureau, the idea of a volunteer army doesn't seem so far-fetched.

The most difficult years of marriage are those following the wedding.

When a man and woman marry they become one — and they spend the rest of their lives trying to find out which one.

The thought of marriage frightens a lot of bachelors — and a few husbands too!

More marriages will be inevitable if postage continues to increase. It'll be cheaper to marry the girl than to write to her.

Anybody who thinks marriage is a fifty-fifty proposition doesn't understand women or fractions.

Some wives believe the secret of a happy marriage is doing things together — like opening a joint checking account.

An Ohio woman reports that she has a "glow-worm" marriage. The glow has gone, but the worm remains.

Too many people are finding it easier to get married than to stay married.

You can send your marriage to an early grave with a series of little digs.

Marriage is the difference between painting the town and painting the back porch.

Sign in a marriage bureau window: "Out to lunch — think it over!"

Engaged couples should realize that marriage will never be as good as *she* believes or as bad as *he* suspects.

Marriage is the world's most expensive way of discovering your faults.

Many people who suddenly realize that they can't afford to get married already are.

A couple recently had their marriage annulled, and sued the officiating minister for malpractice.

Before marriage the three little words are, "I love you." After marriage they are, "Let's eat out."

Marriage is a nice sort of life for a husband to lead — if only his wife would let him do a little leading.

A beefstew marriage is when she's always beefing, and he's always stewed.

Getting married is like buying on credit. You see something, you like it, you make it your own, and you pay for it later.

Marriage is a case of two people agreeing to change each other's habits.

A man in Montana has been married so many times his last marriage license was made out TO WHOM IT MAY CONCERN.

Marriage is an alliance between two people — one who never remembers a birthday and the other who never forgets them.

It's easy for a married couple to acquire mutual interests. All *he* has to do is what *she* likes.

A marriage seldom goes on the rocks when a couple finds something in common to laugh about. For instance, there's the old wedding pictures!

Marriage entitles a woman to the protection of a stalwart man who'll hold the ladder while she paints the ceiling.

On his fiftieth wedding anniversary an Arkansas husband explained his happy marriage, "At home I rule the roost — and my wife rules the rooster."

Marriage is like horseradish — men praise it with tears in their eyes.

The trouble with marriage is not the institution. It's the personnel.

An Arizona wit says people shouldn't get married on Sunday because it's not right to gamble on a Holy Day.

Marriage often results when a man meets a woman who understands him. So does divorce.

When it comes to broken marriages most husbands will split the blame — half his wife's fault, and half her mother's.

A sure sign your marriage is slipping is when you start bidding against each other at auctions.

An Oklahoma woman refused to marry her boyfriend for religious reasons. He was broke, and she worshipped money.

Marriage is too often a process whereby love ripens into vengeance.

Some men get married because they're tired of going to the laundromat, eating in restaurants, and wearing socks with holes in them. Other men get divorces for the same reasons.

Marriages are made in heaven, but they are lived on earth.

A good many things are easier said than done — including the marriage ritual.

What marriage needs is more open minds and fewer open mouths.

A marriage may be a holy wedlock or an unholy deadlock.

To marry a woman for her beauty is like buying a house for its paint.

An engagement is an urge on the verge of a merge.

Fewer marriages would skid if more who said "I do" did.

If men acted after marriage as they do during courtship there would be fewer divorces — and more bankruptcies.

Girls expect money with marriage because they have difficulty finding anything else worthwhile in a man.

Marriage was formerly a contract, but it's now regarded as a ninety-day option.

Nothing makes a marriage rust like distrust.

A typical marriage is where the husband keeps his mouth shut and his checkbook open.

There's one point at which both husband and wife are in perfect agreement — he thinks nothing is too good for her, and so does she.

Marriage is too often a case where cupidity meets stupidity.

There is entirely too much worrying about unhappy marriages. All marriages are happy. It's only living together afterward that causes the trouble.

When a boy marries, his mother thinks he's throwing himself away, and his sisters think the girl is.

Marriage may be inspired by music, soft words, and perfume; but its security is manifest in work, consideration, respect, and well-fried bacon.

It takes at least two people to make a marriage — a single girl and an anxious mother.

Something every couple should save for their old age is marriage.

Marriages are made in heaven — so are thunder and lightning.

The best things to get out of marriage are children.

One does not find happiness in marriage, but takes happiness into marriage.

The "good old days" date back to the time when marriage produced more triangles on the clothesline than in the courtroom.

Making marriage work is like operating a farm. You have to start all over again each morning.

A mother may hope that her daughter will get a better husband than she did, but she knows her son will never get as good a wife as his father did.

Marriage is seldom successful unless both parties get better mates than they deserve.

A model marriage is one in which the wife is the treasure and the husband the treasury.

One reason why so many marriages are failures is that so many inexperienced people get into them.

It's difficult to tell who gets the most pleasure out of marriage, the preacher who ties the knot, or the lawyer who severs it.

Why shouldn't a woman take her husband's name? She takes everything else!

A serious impediment to a successful marriage these days is the difficulty of supporting both the government and a wife on one small income.

Women wear rings to show they're married, while men wear last year's clothes for the same reason.

A married man was once accused of being a deserter, but it turned out that he was only a refugee.

Success in marriage is more than finding the right person. It's also a matter of being the right person.

Marriage is like canned hash — you've got to take a chance.

If a man's wife is his "better half," and he marries twice, what happens to him mathematically?

The story of some marriages should be told in a scrapbook.

Many marriages crack up when the bill collector cracks down.

The unhappiness in some marriages is due to illness — they're sick of each other!

Getting married is one mistake every man should make.

Many married couples never go out. The husband sits in front of the TV set and smokes. The wife sits in front of the TV set and fumes.

Trial marriages may be dangerous. They could lead to the real thing.

Another reason for unhappy marriages is that men can't fool their wives like they could their mothers.

Marriage is like twirling a baton, turning handsprings, or eating with chopsticks. It looks easy till you try it.

The bonds of matrimony are worthless unless the interest is kept up.

Even the thought of embarking on the sea of matrimony makes some men seasick.

The sea of matrimony is where many a poor fish gets hooked with his own line.

Speaking of "doubtful states" — there's the state of matrimony!

Some people don't take much stock in the bonds of matrimony.

On the rough sea of matrimony, many a husband or wife has vanished overboard.

Some of those who embark on the sea of matrimony know little about navigation.

The sea of matrimony is so called because husbands have such a hard time keeping their heads above water.

Some folks get into the sea of matrimony on a wave of enthusiasm.

The bonds of matrimony are like any other bond — they take a while to mature.

The state of matrimony is one state that permits a woman to work eighteen hours a day.

The medical world has its problems. It's hard to give a man shock treatments once he's seen his wife in hair curlers.

Even the men who aren't meek get married and get that way.

Memory is what tells a man his wedding anniversary was yesterday.

A woman always remembers where and when she got married; a man sometimes forgets why!

There was a middle-aged man in Ohio who married an eighteen-year-old girl. He didn't know whether to take her on a honeymoon or send her to camp.

Money is something a man saves so he can get married — and then be broke the rest of his life.

On the matrimonial sea, the hand that rocks the cradle seldom rocks the boat.

A producer in Hollywood plans a film entitled "Marriage, Hollywood Style." It will be short.

Marriage brings music into a man's life — he learns to play second fiddle.

The kind of music people should have in their homes is domestic harmony.

A real optimist is the husband who goes to the marriage bureau to see if his license has expired.

Two Texas political candidates were having a heated debate. One shouted, "What about the powerful interests that control you?" The other screamed back, "You leave my wife out of this."

Romance goes out the window when she stops knitting and starts needling.

There's nothing like a marriage to break up a beautiful romance.

Romance often begins by a splashing waterfall and ends over a leaky sink.

Romance is like a game of chess — one false move and you're mated.

Scientists tell us that the most devastating thing in the world is the A-bomb; the second most devastating thing is coming home with lipstick on your collar.

Another thing marriage brings out in a lot of men is silence.

A marriage counselor says a man should make his wife a silent partner in all his business affairs. It would be a great trick if he could do it.

Notice on a new TV set: "Warning — extended watching of basketball and baseball games may be harmful to your marriage."

What a married couple should save for their old age is each other.

Time separates the best of friends, and so does money — and don't forget marriage!

The most impressive evidence of tolerance is a golden wedding anniversary.

If a woman can be a sweetheart, valet, audience, cook, and nurse, she is qualified for marriage.

A woman marries the first time for love, the second time for companionship, the third time for support, and the rest of the time from habit.

A woman in Ohio says she's wearing her wedding ring on the wrong finger because she married the wrong man.

The only state that permits a woman to work more than eight hours a day is the state of matrimony.

Meanness

Some bosses are so mean that if they pay you a compliment they expect to get a receipt.

The meanest man on earth is the fellow who gives a friend with loose dentures a package of bubble gum.

When you have broken ribs, a hiccup is a crisis, a cough is a calamity, a sneeze is a disaster, and a slap on the back is the meanest thing one human being can do to another.

A man might be considered just a little bit mean when he sends get-well cards to a hypochondriac.

Medical Costs

One problem with some of the new wonder drugs is the side effects — such as bankruptcy.

Medication is so expensive these days that doctors are giving prescriptions with a note, "Take one pill as often as you can afford it."

The cost of allergy treatments are nothing to sneeze at.

Modern medicine is fascinating. The same operation can add ten years to your life and take ten years off your savings account.

Pharmacists tell us the cost of prescription drugs are sky-high because the little wad of cotton in the bottles costs so much.

At today's prices for medication, any pill is a bitter pill to swallow.

Medical costs are so high that it seems the first thing germs attack is your wallet.

Nowadays it costs about twenty dollars for a throat specialist to paint our throats. Many of us can remember when we could get a whole barn painted for that amount.

The biggest drug problem today is that drug stores charge too much for them.

The way medical costs keep rising is enough to make a person sick — if he could afford it.

Medicine has advanced to the point where an ounce of prevention is worth about $18.50.

One of the new "miracle drugs" is inexpensive. That's the miracle!

Things have changed with doctors — they once checked our pulse, now they check our purse.

What's the point in consulting a doctor for a cold if it gives you heart trouble when you get the bill?

A physician in San Francisco is doing so well financially that he can occasionally tell a patient there's noting wrong with him.

Everything is more expensive these days. Doctors have even raised the price of their free samples.

You may not be able to read your doctor's handwriting on a prescription, but you'll notice that his bills are neatly typewritten.

The majority of American doctors don't believe in acupuncture. They'd rather stick us with their bill.

Most doctors specialize today — and the specialty of some is banking.

Some doctors believe in shock treatments — mailed out the first of every month.

Many physicians don't pass the buck — they keep it.

A doctor's office is a place where your symptoms are diagnosed after a thorough examination of your assets.

A doctor recently gave one of his male patients only six months to live. When the guy didn't pay his bill, the doctor gave him another six months.

If doctors really want to give patients a pain-killer, let them tear up the bill!

A fashionable doctor in Houston charges fifty dollars a visit — and even more if you're really sick.

Why doesn't science come up with a pain-killer for medical and hospital bills?

The people of this nation are sick of the high cost of being sick.

If you plan to finance your forthcoming heart attack, it's absolutely necessary that you work ten hours a day, seven days a week.

Medicare

You have to be in perfect health to go through the red tape of Medicare.

It is generally believed that Medicare will soon bring nervous breakdowns within the reach of everybody.

Recently a Medicare patient underwent surgery. When he awoke he found this placard on his incision, "This is a federal project showing your tax dollars at work."

Now that we have Medicare we can enjoy diseases that once we couldn't afford.

Say what you will about Medicare — it's giving ulcers to the doctors.

A woman in Arizona married so late in life that Medicare paid for her honeymoon.

The older a man gets, the less room he has in his medicine cabinet.

Medicine

America is a land of six-lane highways, one-way streets, and four-way cold tablets.

Americans have two chickens in every pot, two cars in every garage, and two headaches for every aspirin.

The latest report is that the manufacturers of aspirin want to sponsor televised sessions of Congress on one of the major networks.

There's a new diet that includes tranquilizers. You don't lose much weight — but you really don't care.

Among the most popular remedies that won't cure a cold is advice.

There's a new pill on the market so powerful that you can't take it unless you're in perfect health.

A good laugh is the best medicine, whether you are sick or not.

Laughter is a tranquilizer with no side effects.

Laughter is the remedy for many little ills. It can cure more quickly than the doctor's tiny pills.

Life nowadays is just one tranquilizer after another.

The reason so many people drink booze is because they are trying to cure a cold or prevent one.

Modern man meets a crisis face-to-face — after taking a pill.

Today's miracle drugs sound so exciting you feel like you're missing something if you're in good health.

Can you remember when drug abuse was merely another dose of castor oil?

Some people only feel good when their pep pills forge ahead of their tranquilizers.

Has the popularity of "the pill" made the stork one of the endangered species?

Researchers have developed a medication which, when taken under a doctor's orders, is guaranteed not to make your cold any worse.

Following the doctor's orders to take a purgative and stay in bed can't be done.

When you have to swallow your own medicine, the spoon seems very large.

There is entirely too much specialization in medicine. When your head cold moves down to your chest you have to change doctors.

The best medicine in the world is to love your work and your enemies.

Penicillin is called a "wonder drug" because any time your doctor wonders what you've got, that's what you get.

There's a new medicine on the market called ZIP. It doesn't cure anything, but at least it's easy to spell.

Medical costs are so high that it seems the first thing germs attack is your wallet.

The latest tranquilizer works so well that people don't care whether they pay their doctor or not.

There can be little doubt that the medical profession made tremendous progress in the last twenty-five years. What used to be merely an itch is now an allergy.

A "miracle drug" is any medicine you can get the kids to take without screaming.

Old-timers can remember when the wonder drugs of the day were quinine and castor oil.

The medical world has its problems. It's hard to give a man shock treatments once he's seen his wife in hair curlers.

Veterinarians now prescribe birth-control pills for dogs — it's part of an anti-litter campaign.

One of the large drug companies has been asked to compound a pill to inhibit spending — by senators.

They tell you that drugs turn you on. They don't tell you that later they turn on you.

A few of us can still remember when the drugs of youth were sulphur and molasses.

A lot of people who switched from cyclamates to saccharin got artificial diabetes.

A "miracle drug" is any drug that'll do about half what the TV commercial promises it'll do.

There's now a Geritol for postmen — when they've lost their zip.

Music has been called medicine, and some of it is hard to take.

Above all, we need tranquility without tranquilizers.

Some people feel we don't need prayer any more since we now have penicillin!

The world has so many problems that if Moses had come down from Mount Sinai today — the two tablets he carried would be aspirin.

Some people think religion, like aspirin, should be taken only to relieve pain.

The best medicine for rheumatism is being thankful it isn't gout.

Science has found a tranquilizer to combat car sickness. You take it just before the car payment is due.

All some people do for a cold is sneeze.

To find what your doctor recommends, watch television.

The Ten Commandments were given to men in tablet form, and by following their directions, we could save a lot of other tablets from being used.

Tolerance is getting a lot of credit that belongs to tranquilizers.

Meekness

Blessed are the meek for they shall inherit the earth — less 40 percent inheritance tax.

No one would object to the meek inheriting the earth if we could be sure they would stay meek after they got it.

Even the men who aren't meek get married and get that way.

Many wish the meek would hurry up and inherit the earth. The un-meek are making such a mess of it!

Some of us wonder how long the meek can keep the earth after they inherit it!

When the time comes for the meek to inherit the earth, taxes will most likely be so high that they won't want it.

If people aren't meek when they inherit the earth, they will be when they get the mortgage paid off.

The meek may inherit the earth just in time to see it sold for taxes.

When the time comes for the meek to inherit the earth, taxes will be so high they won't want it.

Memory

An elephant never forgets. After all, what does it have to remember?

An autobiography is a book that reveals nothing bad about its writer except his memory.

With some people a clear conscience is nothing more than a poor memory.

Some folks who say they have a clear conscience may have a good "forgetter."

In order to become perfectly content, it is necessary to have a poor memory and no imagination.

You always remember a kind deed — particularly if it was yours.

Your creed may be interesting but your deeds are much more convincing.

There are a lot of people who never forget a kind deed — if they did it!

Education means developing the mind, not stuffing the memory.

To err is human; to forget, routine.

The typical fisherman is long on optimism and short on memory.

We commit the Golden Rule to memory and forget to commit it to life.

History is to a nation what memory is to the individual.

If you can't remember a joke — don't dismember it.

No man has a good enough memory to be a successful liar.

The reason people can remember the "good old days" is that there were so few of them.

It's remarkable how long people with even a bad memory can recall the favors they did for you.

You know that your memory is failing when you watch TV reruns and they seem new to you.

Nothing improves the memory more than trying to forget.

Memory is what tells a man his wedding anniversary was yesterday.

It's strange how much better our memory becomes as soon as a friend borrows money from us.

Memory is the faculty that enables you to give someone most of your zip code.

Some women have a terrible memory — they remember everything!

Memory is a faculty that reminds you that you've probably forgotten something.

A stroll down memory lane would be pleasant if we could detour around a few "rough spots."

There's an advantage in having a poor memory. You have less to forget.

Creditors have a better memory than debtors.

Nothing is more responsible for the "good old days" than a poor memory.

You never know how much a man can't remember till he is called as a witness.

Memory is a wonderful treasure chest for those who know how to pack it.

If you don't think people have good memories, try repeating a joke you told them about a month ago.

A woman always remembers where and when she got married; a man sometimes forgets why!

The man who remembers what he learned at his mother's knee was probably bent over at the time.

Some wives have such good memories that they can even remember things that never happened.

You must arrange in advance for pleasant memories.

A senior citizen in Nebraska says his memory is so poor he can't even remember all the words to Happy Birthday!

It is the memory that enables a person to gather roses in January.

Everytime you lend money to a friend you damage his memory.

The person who is straightforward and honest doesn't have to worry about a faulty memory.

So live that your memories will be a part of your happiness.

About the only thing a woman is sure to remember is another woman's age.

A good memory test is to recall all the kind things you have said about your neighbor.

Among the things that enable a man to be self-satisfied is a poor memory.

Isn't it funny how some people can remember a joke, but can't seem to remember an unpaid bill?

Most people would rather look backward than forward because it's easier to remember where you've been than to figure out where you're going.

It's difficult to remember when people didn't buy things they couldn't pay for.

Some people remember a lie for ten years but forget the truth in ten minutes.

About the only way a middle-aged woman can hold her school girl figure is in fond memory.

Anybody who tells you he never made a mistake in his life is probably relying on a poor memory — his or yours.

Nostalgia is remembering the pleasures of sitting in front of a big fireplace — without remembering you had to cut the wood for it.

Three things indicate we are getting old. First, the loss of memory — and we can't remember the other two.

A politician has a good memory, but hopes other people haven't.

There is no point in worrying about forgetting things as your grow older because you'll soon forget what you forgot.

Men

Most accidents occur in the home. Many men use this as an excuse to stay out late.

Advice to men over fifty: Keep an open mind and a closed refrigerator.

By the time a man finds greener pastures, he's too old to climb the fence.

A man is usually as young as he feels but seldom as important.

Some people think the proper age for a man to start thinking of marriage is when he's old enough to realize he shouldn't.

A man who correctly guesses a woman's age may be smart, but he's not very bright.

Nothing ages a man faster than trying to prove he's still as young as ever.

Few women admit their age. Few men act theirs.

Every man has a secret ambition to outsmart horses, fish, and women.

Automobiles are like men — the less substantial they are, the more knocking they do.

A bachelor is a guy who leans toward women, but not far enough to lose his balance.

Statistics show there are three ages when men misbehave: young, old, and middle.

No man is as smart as he sounds at his alumni banquet.

To really know a man, observe his behavior with a woman, a flat tire, and a child.

Most men brag about their hunting experiences, though they're chiefly confined to shooting pool, craps, and bull.

A boy becomes a man when he decides it's more fun to steal a kiss than second base.

A tip to young male drivers: Forget the girl and hug the road.

Judging by church attendance, heaven won't be crowded with men.

When a man has torn socks and buttons missing from his shirt, he should do one of two things — either get married or get a divorce.

When a man becomes a success, his wife takes most of the credit and the government takes most of the cash.

Any smart woman will tell you that the best way to a man's heart is through his ego.

About the only exercise some young fellows get is running out of money and after women.

Women's faults are many. Men have only two: everything they say and everything they do.

You've never heard of a woman making a fool out of a man without a lot of cooperation.

Women make fools of some men. Other men are the do-it-yourself type.

The perfect gift for a man who has everything would be a girl who knows what to do with it.

Some men think they have an inferiority complex, when, in fact, they are just inferior.

If love is blind, why are so many men attracted to a beautiful woman?

There are three things most men love but never understand: females, girls, and women.

By the time a man understands women, he's no longer interested.

To see through a man it takes an x-ray or an ex-wife.

A well-informed man is one whose wife has just told him what she thinks of him.

The average man is able to detect a rattle in his car more quickly than one in his head.

History records only one indispensable man — Adam.

A man is about halfway between what he thinks he is and what his secretary knows he is.

The average man is forty-two around the chest, forty-four around the waist, ninety-six around the golf course, and a nuisance around the house.

When the average man has become thoroughly acquainted with himself, he ceases to wonder why he has so few friends.

One advantage of being a man is that you don't run the risk of catching a cold in evening clothes.

The man with PUSH will pass the man with PULL.

The sea of matrimony is where many a poor fish gets hooked with his own line.

Some men don't need to be out in the rain to be all wet.

Few men are ever satisfied when they get what they deserve.

Married men can't understand why every bachelor isn't a millionaire.

Listen men: Maybe you'll never be as big a hero as your son thinks you are but you'll never be as big a fool as your mother-in-law thinks you are either!

Many men are doing well on TV today. They have great faces for acid indigestion commercials.

Most men are either old and bent, or young and broke.

About the only time some men ever look up to a woman is from their seat in a bus.

Most men have a way with women, but it's seldom their own.

Men, like tacks, are useful if they have good heads and are pointed in the right direction.

Many men manage to keep their heads above water because wood floats.

Another reason men don't live as long as women is that they suffer so much waiting around in hospitals for their wives to have babies.

Men often congregate in the kitchen because it's one of the few places thay can get away from women.

Most great men come from small towns. We don't know whether it's because of ambition or gossip.

There are a lot more counterfeit men than money in this country.

Many men are slow but sure. Others are just slow.

Men are endowed by their creator with certain inalienable rights, all of which they must fight for.

Many men get more fun out of grinding the ax than in burying the hatchet.

This country has turned out some great men in the past, and there are some others who are not so great that ought to be turned out as well.

Men are born collectors. First, they collect bugs, toads, and marbles; then girls, kisses, and ties; then money, worries, and a family; then golf trophies, dirty jokes, and hair tonics; and, finally, pains, symptoms, and memories.

There are three kinds of men in the world: fits, misfits, and counterfeits.

There are a lot of men in this world who started at the bottom — and stayed there.

The one thing most men can do better than anybody else is to read their own handwriting.

Some men prefer learning the tricks of the trade rather than the trade itself.

Great men, like the tallest mountain, retain their majesty and stability during the most severe storm.

Some men remind us of blisters; they don't show up until the work is done.

Most men can't tell the difference between working up steam and generating fog.

All men are born equal. The tough job is to outgrow it.

Some men close their eyes when they ride the bus. They hate to see women standing.

Warning to all single men: There's a new perfume on the market with a secret ingredient — it makes a man think he can support a wife.

Some men grow; others just swell.

Some men keep up with the Joneses by wearing last year's suits and driving this year's car on next year's salary. This is real progress.

A lot of friction on the highway is caused by half the drivers trying to go fast enough to thrill their girl friends, and the other half trying to go slow enough to placate their wives.

A young man was arrested while necking with his girl friend on a freeway. He was charged with driving while "infatuated."

Men sometimes credit themselves for their successes, and God for their failures.

Teen-age boys who whistle at girls are just going through a stage which will probably last fifty years.

Most men wish they were as wise as they think their wives think they are.

Maybe one of the things wrong with the world is that there are not enough leaders of men and too many chasers of women.

Men usually worry more about losing their hair than their heads.

Men and Women

A California woman says her husband is at the dangerous age when all females look alike to him — desirable!

The ambition of some girls is to make a man a good husband.

The best way to win an argument with a woman is to hit her over the head with a new mink coat.

Never argue with a woman. You might win — and then you'll really be in trouble.

One thing a man learns from an argument with a woman is how to be a good loser.

A woman has the last word in any argument. Anything a man says after that is the beginning of a new argument.

Never start an argument with a woman when she's tired — or when she's rested!

When a wise man argues with a woman, he says nothing!

Automation is man's effort to make work so easy that women can do it.

A bachelor in Denver advertised for a wife in a newspaper: "Bachelor with waterbed desires to meet a nice, hard-working girl with short toenails."

Chivalry is a man's inclination to defend a woman against every man but himself.

Chivalry is opening the door and standing aside so some female can rush in and get the job you're after.

A woman's hat tells you something about her, including whether her husband was along when she bought it.

The clothes that make a woman break a man.

College never hurts a young man — unless, of course, he meets his future wife there.

Nothing confuses a man more than to drive behind a woman who does everything right.

The average dinner conversation is a series of cold cuts — her spiced tongue and his baloney.

The woman who constantly interrupts a man's conversation is either already married or never will be.

Cosmetics are a woman's hope of keeping men from reading between the lines.

A man gave a woman his seat on the bus; she fainted. When she revived, she thanked him; then he fainted.

He took his defeat like a man; he blamed it on his wife.

It's always embarrassing for a man to run unexpectedly into a girl he was once engaged to.

Behind every famous man there's a woman — telling him he's not so hot.

Sign in a florist's window: "Send flowers to the one you love. While you're at it, don't forget your wife."

You've never heard of a woman making a fool out of a man without a lot of cooperation.

If a man tells a woman she's beautiful, she'll overlook most of his other lies.

A man doesn't know the value of a woman's love until he starts paying alimony.

He loved a girl so much he worshiped the very ground her father discovered oil on.

A girl may love you from the bottom of her heart, but there's always room for some other fellow at the top.

A woman feels a man's love should be like a toothbrush. It shouldn't be shared.

One nice thing about being a man is that you don't have to kiss somebody who hasn't shaved in three days.

By the time a man understands women, he's no longer interested.

A timid man said to his wife, "We're not going out tonight and that's semi-final."

Man can control everything except a woman and a hurricane.

A practical man is one who looks for a wife who already has a fur coat and her appendix out.

The man who owes it all to his wife seldom pays her back.

A man's heart is like a sponge — soaked with emotion and sentiment. He can squeeze out a little bit for every pretty woman he meets.

A woman's ideal man is one clever enough to make money and foolish enough to spend it.

A man is a peculiar animal. For instance, his head will turn when a woman's hip moves.

A woman always remembers where and when she got married; a man sometimes forgets why!

About the only time some men ever look up to a woman is from their seat in a bus.

Most men have a way with women, but it's seldom their own.

Men often congregate in the kitchen because it's one of the few places thay can get away from women.

You can tell who handles the money in families nowadays — they're making women's handbags bigger and men's wallets smaller.

A newspaper is a portable screen, behind which a man hides from the woman who is standing up in a bus.

An optimist is a young man who hurries because he thinks his date is ready and waiting for him.

A coed concluded her prayer with a modest appeal, "Lord, I don't want to be selfish about it, but I would appreciate it very much if you would send my mother a son-in-law."

The modern woman has a lot of problems, and she seems to think she can solve most of them by yelling at her husband.

Psychiatrists say big men make docile husbands — so do big women!

A traveling salesman explained why he was fired, "The accountants found a blond hair on my expense account."

A successful man is one who can get a woman to listen to reason — or anything else for that matter!

Behind every successful man is a woman who keeps reminding him that she knows men who would have done even better.

A man is never as weak as when some woman is telling him how strong he is.

No woman has to twist a man's arm when she can wrap him around her finger.

It does not take a very bright woman to dazzle some men.

A woman likes a man best who has a will of his own — made out in her name.

Even if a man could understand women, he still wouldn't believe it.

Anybody who says this is a man's world is probably not too bright about other things either.

If this is a man's world it's because women don't want it.

Middle Age

Youth looks ahead, old age looks back, and middle age looks tired.

The least likely way for a middle-aged woman to celebrate her birthday is annually.

At the age of fifty, one settles down into certain well-defined convictions — most of which are wrong.

Cosmetics were used in the Middle Ages; in fact, they're still used in the middle ages.

"Girls" is what women over forty-five call each other.

Life not only begins at forty — that's when it really begins to show.

They tell us that life begins at forty, but they don't say what kind of life.

In this life the old believe everything, the middle-aged suspect everything, and the young know everything.

Life may begin at forty, but so does rheumatism.

Middle age is when your legs buckle — and your belt doesn't.

You've reached middle age when, instead of sensations, you have symptoms.

Middle age is that time of life when a woman won't tell her age, and a man won't act his.

You are slightly passed middle age if, before you step off the curb, you look down once more to make sure the street is still there.

About the only way a middle-aged woman can hold her school girl figure is in fond memory.

Middle age is when you go all out and end up all in.

You've reached middle age when you can't kick up your heels without finding that your conscience isn't the only thing that hurts.

Middle age is the time of life when everything starts to wear out, fall out, or spread out.

You know you've reached middle age when your weightlifting consists solely of standing up.

Middle age is when you can do just as much as ever — but don't.

The big shock in reaching middle age is that you discover you keep on growing older even after you're old enough.

Middle age is actually the prime of life — it just takes a little longer to get primed.

By the time we're ready to admit we've reached middle age, we're beyond it.

Middle age is when all you want for your birthday is not to be reminded of it.

The five B's of middle age are: baldness, bridgework, bifocals, bay windows, and bunions.

Middle age is that time in life when physical fitness gives way to aches, arthritis, and acid indigestion.

Our vigor wanes with middle age, we find our footsteps lagging, our backbones creak, our sight grows dim, and yet our tongues keep wagging.

Middle age is when you've given up all your bad habits and still don't feel good.

You've reached middle age when all you exercise is caution.

Middle age is the awkward period when Father Time starts catching up with Mother Nature.

Middle age is that time of life when you finally know your way around but don't feel like going.

When a middle-aged man says he's worried about fallout, he probably means hair, not atoms.

One symptom of middle age is when the "morning after" lasts all day.

Middle age is that time of life when you convince yourself it's only a vitamin deficiency.

Every young man starts out in life expecting to find a pot of gold at the end of the rainbow. By the time they reach middle age, most of them have at least found the pot.

Middle age is when your memory is shorter, your experience longer, your stamina lower, and your forehead higher.

There are two ways to determine middle age — one is by the calendar, and the other by the waistline.

Middle age is when a man's favorite nightspot is in front of a TV set.

When a middle-aged woman still has her schoolgirl figure, it probably wasn't much to begin with.

One thing is certain about middle age — you wonder how you got there so fast.

Middle age is when you realize that your get-up-and-go has got up and went.

There was a middle-aged man in Ohio who married an eighteen-year-old girl. He didn't know whether to take her on a honeymoon or send her to camp.

A woman is at middle-age when she takes her high school annual out of the bookcase and hides it where the children can't find it.

In middle age it's difficult to decide what there's most of — middle or age.

Middle age is when a man finds he's taking his teeth out more than he takes his wife out.

When you begin to smile at things that once caused you to laugh, middle age is approaching.

Middle age is when a man chases a girl only if she's going downhill.

You've reached middle age when your wife tells you to pull in your stomach, and you already have.

When a man turns off the light for economical reasons rather than for romantic reasons, he has definitely reached middle age.

Middle age is when your clothes no longer fit, and it's not the clothes that need the alterations.

Modern medicine still hasn't decided whether it's harder on a middle-aged man to mow the lawn himself or argue to get his teen-age son to do it.

Middle age has set in when a man is more interested in what his wife's clothes cost than in how they fit her.

You're definitely at middle age when the telephone rings and you hope it's not for you.

Middle age is when you start eating what's good for you instead of what you like.

Middle age is the time of life when the fellow who always acted like a human dynamo starts showing signs of ignition trouble.

A middle-aged woman is one too young for Medicare and too old for men to care.

Youth is that period when we're looking for greener fields. Middle age is when we can hardly mow what we've got.

Mind

The fellow who boasts of his open mind may only have a vacant one.

A college boy in Ohio reported to his parents that he was about to flunk out — because he found out he had a klinker in his thinker.

It isn't easy for an idea to squeeze itself into a mind that is filled with prejudice.

Quite often when a man thinks his mind is getting broader, it is only his conscience stretching.

Most things that broaden the mind also narrow the conscience.

Conversation is an exercise of the mind, but gossiping is merely an exercise of the tongue.

Crime begins in the mind. A man has to think wrong before he acts wrong.

Small minds are the first to criticize large ideas.

Have you ever noticed how extremely difficult it is for a person to keep his mind open and his mouth shut at the same time?

The most difficult thing to open is a closed mind.

It has been said that dignity is the ability to hold back from the tongue that which never should have been on the mind in the first place.

Education means developing the mind, not stuffing the memory.

Fanaticism is the false fire of an overheated mind.

Girls are creatures who can make up their faces more easily than their minds.

Hate is the most inefficient use a person can make of his mind.

Hatred is cancer of the intellect.

Hate pollutes the mind.

The head never begins to swell until the mind stops growing.

If you want to be the picture of health, you'd better have a happy frame of mind.

Your brain becomes a mind when it's fortified with knowledge.

A man's language is an index of his mind.

Language is the dress of thought; every time you talk your mind is on parade.

Most of us are lazier in mind than in body.

No constitution, no court, no law can save liberty when it dies in the hearts and minds of men and women.

Love is a condition of the mind at a time when the mind is out of condition.

A mature mind is not always found in a mature body.

To have an open mind doesn't mean you must always have an open mouth.

Many a man thinks he has an open mind when, in reality, it's merely vacant.

If a cluttered desk is a sign of a cluttered mind, just what does an empty desk mean?

Before you give somebody a piece of your mind, be sure you can get by with what you have left.

At a certain age some people's minds close up — they live on their intellectual fat.

People with a one-track mind often have a derailed train of thought.

An open mind is wonderful if a matching mouth doesn't go with it.

It would not be so bad to let one's mind go blank — if one always remembered to turn off the sound.

You can't go around giving folks a piece of your mind without eventually being called empty-headed.

A person with a closed mind can get by nicely — if he keeps his mouth closed too.

Quite often when a man thinks his mind is getting broader, it's just his conscience stretching.

Only hungry minds can become educated.

A human mind is a terrible thing to waste.

Some people have open minds; others just don't have anything between their ears.

Folks who never change their minds usually have no minds to change.

A lot of people work but their minds are unemployed.

The person who doesn't know his own mind probably hasn't missed much.

Too many of us are broad-minded about the wrong things.

Some minds are like concrete — thoroughly mixed and permanently set.

Great minds discuss ideas, average minds discuss events, small minds discuss people.

Some minds should be cultivated; others should be plowed under.

The human mind was intended to be a storehouse, not a wastebasket.

The most difficult thing to open is a closed mind.

Some people seem to think a fertile mind requires a lot of dirt.

Great minds have purposes; others have wishes.

You're never quite sure what kind of mind a person has until he gives you a piece of it.

One way to have a clean mind is to change it now and then.

Small minds are the first to condemn great ideas.

The mind is like the stomach. It's not how much you put into it that counts, but how much it digests.

In the mass mind there is no mind — just mass.

Your mind is a sacred enclosure into which nothing harmful can enter except by your permission.

Instead of great minds being in the same channel, sometimes it's a matter of little minds being in the same rut.

The minds of some people are like water — always seeking the lowest level.

An open mind is sometimes too porous to hold a conviction.

Minds are like parachutes; they only function when they're open.

A boy's mind is a wonderful thing. It starts working the minute he gets up, and never stops until he gets to school.

Too many people aren't equipped to attend a meeting of minds.

Human minds are like wagons. When they have a light load to carry, they're much noisier than when the load is heavy.

A person's mind may be so broad that it's shallow.

The fellow with the smallest mind is the one usually most willing to give someone a piece of it.

A woman's mind is like the moon. No matter how often she changes it, there's always a man in it.

The value of an open mind depends on what comes in and makes itself at home.

If you keep your mind too open, people will throw a lot of rubbish into it.

The one thing worse than a vacant mind is one filled with spiteful thoughts.

An open mind, like an open window, should be equipped with a screen to keep the bugs out.

Many people have a photographic mind — too bad they never had it developed!

If you have nothing on your mind, it shows.

Many a person's mind has been closed for years, but not for repairs or alterations.

Like swift water an active mind never stagnates.

Nine out of ten people who change their minds are wrong the second time too.

An open mind tolerates an empty one.

The narrower the mind, the broader the statement.

A great deal of laziness of mind is called liberty of opinion.

The mind of a liberal politician is open at both ends.

Sometimes when a politician changes his mind, it doesn't work any better than the old one.

Never before has the world had so many big problems and so many little minds.

Temptation seldom breaks your door down; it quietly and cunningly enters the open portals of your mind.

A sharp tongue and a dull mind are usually found in the same head.

The student of truth keeps an open Bible, an open dictionary, and an open mind.

Truth is something which must be known with the mind, accepted with the heart, and enacted in life.

Mistakes

Alimony is a system in which one pays for the mistakes of two.

The quickest way to get a lot of individual attention is to make a big mistake.

Character is made by many acts; it may be lost by a single act.

Character is like glass — even a little crack shows.

The computer is a great invention. There are as many mistakes as ever, but now they're nobody's fault.

Computers will never replace human beings entirely. Someone has to complain about the errors.

Some computers are almost human. When they make a mistake they put the blame on another computer.

A person can save himself from many hard falls by refraining from jumping to conclusions.

The fellow who is always jumping to conclusions isn't always sure of a happy landing.

The chief hazard of jumping to conclusions is the high percentage of misses.

The least expensive education is to profit from the mistakes of others — and ourselves.

An error doesn't become a mistake until you refuse to correct it.

It's true that to err is human — but it can be overdone.

Plaque on the desk of an executive: "Once I thought I was wrong — but I was mistaken."

An executive reports that his secretary is making two hundred a week. Not dollars — mistakes!

Experience is what helps you make an old mistake in a new way.

Experience is what you have left after you've pulled the boner.

Experience is what makes your mistakes so familiar.

Those who fear the future are likely to fumble the present.

The biggest fool of all is the person who refuses to profit by his mistakes.

Freedom is not worth having if it does not include the freedom to make mistakes.

The man who boasts that he never made a mistake has a wife who did.

An income-tax return is like a girdle. If you put the wrong figure in it, you're apt to get pinched.

There's a new invention on the market — a pencil with an eraser on both ends. It's for people who do nothing but make mistakes.

Getting married is one mistake every man should make.

Everybody makes mistakes. That's why we keep having political elections.

It's a lot easier to make a mistake than to undo one.

The man who never makes a mistake must get awfully tired doing nothing.

Mistakes aren't so bad. Columbus found America by mistake!

An inexcusable mistake is always made by the other fellow.

If people learn from their mistakes, many are getting a fantastic education.

He who makes the same mistake over and over again learns to do at least one thing well.

We seldom admit mistakes that have not caught up with us.

Making mistakes isn't stupid; disregarding them is.

Don't worry about your mistakes. Some of the dullest people don't make any.

The only thing most of us learn from our mistakes is how to blame them on somebody else.

Do it tomorrow — you've made enough mistakes today!

Anyone who corrects all his mistakes is probably writing his memoirs.

A fellow's mistakes always bother him, especially when he realizes he's too old to repeat them.

Often our mistakes serve a useful purpose. Our friends find great satisfaction in pointing them out to us.

Do you realize how many mistakes you'd make if you didn't sleep a third of your day?

Why do some people make the same mistake time after time when there are so many new ones they could be making?

Here's a good way to reduce the number of mistakes you make at work — get there late and leave early.

It's tough when you make an embarrassing mistake. It's even tougher when you discover that you're so unimportant that no one noticed it.

It's not so bad making mistakes so long as you don't make a habit of it.

The greatest mistake you can make in this life is to be constantly fearful you will make one.

Anybody who tells you he never made a mistake in his life is probably relying on a poor memory — his or yours.

One skill that most of us seem to be born with is that of making mistakes.

When a friend makes a mistake, don't rub it in. Rub it out.

A hundred mistakes are a liberal education — if you learn something from each one.

Few things in life are more difficult for some of us than admitting a mistake.

Stupid mistakes are made by others — we only make "unavoidable errors."

The man who never makes an error never plays ball.

Some people never make a mistake, nor do they ever make anything else.

Everybody is liable to make mistakes, but fools practice them.

A person who never makes a mistake is pretty boring.

More people would learn from their mistakes if they weren't so busy denying they made them.

If you don't make mistakes you might live and die without ever hearing your name mentioned.

A mistake is proof that someone was at least trying to accomplish something.

It is easier to hide mistakes than to prevent their consequences.

Learn from the mistakes made by others. You won't live long enough to make them all yourself.

Most people make the mistake of looking too far ahead for things close by.

The man who invented the eraser had the human race pretty well sized up.

When it comes to profiting from your mistakes, you can be sure that the IRS will.

A man must be big enough to admit his mistakes, smart enough to profit from them, and strong enough to correct them.

It would be wonderful if mistakes could be sold for as much as they cost.

Architects cover their mistakes with ivy, doctors with sod, and brides with mayonnaise.

All men make mistakes — husbands just find out about them sooner.

The main difference between a wise man and a fool is that a fool's mistakes never teach him anything.

When a fellow makes the same mistake twice, he's got to own up to carelessness or cussedness.

If some people had their lives to live over, they could make the same mistakes much more easily.

To get maximum attention, it's hard to beat a big mistake.

A man who has made a mistake and doesn't correct it is committing another mistake.

If we all profited by our mistakes, millionaires would be commonplace.

There's nothing wrong with making a mistake; just don't respond with an encore.

A mistake proves somebody stopped talking long enough to do something.

If you don't learn from your mistakes, there's no sense in making them.

Our mistake is loving things and using people, when we should use things and love people.

Man is inclined to exaggerate almost everything — except his own mistakes.

It is the highest form of self-respect to admit mistakes and make amends for them.

The man who takes time to explain his mistakes has little time left for anything else.

A first-class mistake is to treat anyone as a second-class person.

One of life's major mistakes is being the last member in the family to get the flu — after all the sympathy has run out.

It's easier to profit from mistakes you don't make.

Being perfect requires a knack for shoving your mistakes off on someone else.

It is good to pray for the repair of mistakes, but praying earlier would likely keep us from making so many.

Do it tomorrow — you've made enough mistakes for today!

You are making progress if each mistake you make is a new one.

Modern science is simply wonderful. It would take fifty people twenty years to make the same mistake a computer can make in only two seconds.

Silence never makes any blunders.

A window sign in Chicago: "Tax Returns Prepared — Honest Mistakes Are Our Specialty."

The three most difficult words to speak are, "I was mistaken."

Modesty

Those who have a right to boast don't need to.

The hen that laid the biggest egg usually does the least cackling about it.

In summer mosquitoes put more clothes on people than modesty.

A style expert can make a woman feel modest when she doesn't look it.

Can you remember when a girl's charms were hidden?

The more a man knows, the more modest he is inclined to be.

The greater the man's talent, the more becoming his modesty.

Do all you can and make no fuss about it.

Modesty is the art of enhancing your charm by pretending not to be aware of it.

A person shouldn't be too modest. A light hidden under a bushel is seldom seen and less often appreciated.

Modesty is the triumph of mind over flatter.

A modest person hardly ever blows his "knows" in public.

Modesty is the art of encouraging people to find out for themselves how modest you are.

A modest man is generally admired — if people ever hear of him.

Some people are just too modest to tell the naked truth.

The more a man knows, the more he is inclined to be modest.

Nothing makes a man so modest about his income as a tax return.

A style expert can make a woman feel modest when she doesn't look it.

Money

One day an American worries about going to the poorhouse, and the next day he buys a new automobile.

There are a lot of hot arguments over "cold cash."

What do atheists do with their money? Surely they wouldn't carry around anything that says, "In God We Trust."

Perhaps the most necessary automobile accessory is a wallet.

By the time a man can afford to buy one of those little sports cars, he's too fat to get into it.

It is generally agreed that the first thing a new car runs into is money.

A new car isn't a barometer of how much money a fellow has, but it's a pretty good indication of how much he owes.

Some auto mechanics can estimate the cost of repairs very closely. They can usually get within a dollar or two of what you have in your pocket.

Having a big car doesn't always mean you have money; it may mean you once *had* money.

Married men can't understand why every bachelor isn't a millionaire.

A bachelor may have no buttons on his shirt, but a married man often has no shirt.

Many banks have a new kind of Christmas club in operation. The new club helps you save money to pay for last year's gifts.

The only difference between a "hair stylist" and a regular barber is the price.

The one book that always has a sad ending is a checkbook.

The thing a little boy outgrows fastest is his allowance.

A family budget is a device to make you worry about money before you spend it.

A balanced budget is when the month and the money run out together.

Many people hate any change that doesn't jingle in their pockets.

A person's character is put to a severe test when he suddenly acquires or quickly loses a considerable amount of money.

A kid who learns the value of a dollar these days is certain to grow up cynical.

Christmas is a race to see which gives out first — your money or your feet.

The average couple splits the Christmas chores. She signs the cards and he signs the checks.

There are many nerves in the human body, but the most sensitive is the one that goes from the brain to the pocketbook.

At Christmas most parents spend more money on their children than they did on the honeymoon that started it all.

A family in San Francisco is reliving its Christmas holidays — the man of the house is showing colored slides of his cancelled checks.

On Christmas Eve Santa carries the bag. After Christmas dad is holding it.

Separation of church and state could hardly be more complete. The church teaches that money isn't everything, and the government keeps telling us it is.

Some are late for church service because they have to change a tire; others, because they have to change a dollar.

New shoes hurt the most when you have to buy them for the whole family.

Nothing makes a woman's clothes go out of style faster than her husband's raise in salary.

Many college students can write home for money in four or five languages.

Nothing irks the college boy more than shaking out the envelope from home and finding nothing but news and love.

A survey shows that college students prefer ties with dots, suits with stripes, and letters with checks.

The poor complain about the money they can't get, and the rich complain about the money they can't keep.

Contentment is when your earning power equals your yearning power.

Crime may cost billions of dollars each year, but you've got to admit we're getting plenty for our money.

He who dances must pay the fiddler — also the waiter, the florist, the hatcheck girl, the doorman, and the parking attendant.

Debts are about the only thing we can acquire without money.

A Georgia woman got a divorce because of religious differences. She worshiped money, and he didn't have a dime.

We could get along better with fewer economists and more economizers.

An economist can tell you what to do with your money after you've done something else with it.

An economist in Los Angeles recently completed writing a book titled *The Short Story of Money*. The book contains only seven words, "Here it is and there it goes."

Economists say we must devalue the dollar. What do they think Congress has been doing the past twenty years?

The exercise that wears most people out is *running* out of cash.

About the only exercise some young fellows get is running out of money and after women.

Extravagance is anything you buy that you can't put on a credit card.

A man is a failure who goes through life earning nothing but money.

Nowadays the family that buys together cries together.

The trouble with some American families is that they have Cadillac tastes and compact incomes.

It really doesn't matter who wears the pants in the family, just so there's money in the pockets.

Growing families have a way of outgrowing everything — especially their incomes.

A fool and his money are soon parted. The rest of us wait until we reach the supermarket.

There was a time when a fool and his money were soon parted. Now it happens to everybody.

Fools sometimes make money, but money also sometimes makes fools.

We know that a fool and his money are soon parted, but how did they ever get together?

With money you can buy all the friends you want, but they are never worth the price.

Having money and friends is easy. Having friends and no money is an accomplishment.

A friend is like a dollar — hard to get and easy to throw away.

Time separates the best of friends, and so does money — and marriage!

A friend you can buy can be bought from you.

There are three faithful friends: an old wife, an old dog, and ready cash.

Sensible folks would rather have friends than money — especially friends with money.

Friendship is like money — easier made than kept.

Some people will gamble on anything. Now they're saving money with the hope that it'll be worth something someday.

People who can afford to gamble don't need money, and those who need money can't afford to gamble.

The gift people appreciate most is something you made youself — such as money.

Many a girl is looking for a man with a strong will — made out to her!

There are many nerves in the human body, but the most sensitive is the one that goes from the brain to the pocketbook.

Support the church with your money. You can't take it with you, but you can send it on ahead.

In the Book of Revelation we read of a book which no man could open. Some believe this was the pocketbook.

Even if money could buy happiness, just think what a luxury tax there'd be!

They tell us that money doesn't bring happiness, but it would be nice to find that out for yourself.

Money, achievement, fame, and success are important, but they are bought too dearly when acquired at the cost of health.

Money can build a house, but it takes love to make it a home.

There is no place like home if you haven't got the money to go out.

Most men would be willing to earn their money honestly if it didn't take so long.

The average man has more money than sense; the trouble is that he doesn't know it.

Imagination is what makes you think you're having a wonderful time when you are only spending money.

If you live within your income you'll live without worry — and without a lot of other things.

When it comes to income tax, most of us would be willing to pay as we go if we could only catch up on where we've been.

Inflation is when petty cash is the only kind there is.

Inflation is a state of affairs in which you never had it so good or parted with it so fast.

Intelligence is very much like money — if you don't reveal how little you've got people will treat you as though you have a lot.

The guy who invented the boomerang was probably the same one who invented the credit card.

Money will buy a fine dog, but only kindness will make him wag his tail.

Laziness is like money — the more a man has of it, the more he seems to want.

If George Washington never told a lie, what's his picture doing on a dollar bill that's worth about forty-three cents?

Life is an eternal struggle to keep money coming in and teeth, hair, and vital organs from coming out.

A woman knowns the value of love, but a man knows its cost.

Love is oceans of emotions surrounded by expanses of expenses.

A woman's ideal man is one clever enough to make money and foolish enough to spend it.

The person who marries for money usually earns every penny of it.

Some wives believe the secret of a happy marriage is doing things together — like opening a joint checking account.

Many people who suddenly realize that they can't afford to get married already are.

An Oklahoma woman refused to marry her boyfriend for religious reasons. He was broke, and she worshipped money.

Girls expect money with marriage because they have difficulty finding anything else worthwhile in a man.

A typical marriage is where the husband keeps his mouth shut and his checkbook open.

A model marriage is one in which the wife is the treasure and the husband the treasury.

There are a lot more counterfeit men than money in this country.

The only way to make a dollar go far these days is to mail it overseas.

About all you can do with a nickel these days is flip it.

Nowadays a lucky coin is any coin you still have in your possession.

Money not only changes hands — it changes people.

This year about the only thing not enriched, fortified, or reinforced is money.

One of the things a dollar can't buy today is a dollar's worth of anything.

A fool and his money are soon parted — especially with the government to expedite matters.

If the dollar bill shrinks much more, George Washington will be forced to get a haircut.

About all you can get for a penny nowadays is your incorrect weight.

It might help if we were all paid in Confederate money. It would be harder to get rid of.

Dough is the wrong term for money. Dough sticks to your hands.

Money can't buy health, but it can keep doctor's wives in mink.

Always remember that money isn't everything — but also remember to make a lot of it before talking such nonsense!

Money still talks, of course, but it has to stop and catch its breath more often.

Saving money these days is harder than playing a trumpet from the wrong end.

The value of a dollar will never drop as low as some people will stoop to get it.

The real trouble with money is that we can't use it more than once.

About the only thing we get more of for our money these days is requests.

Every year it takes less time and more money to get where we didn't really want to go anyway.

The average man has quit dreaming of having enough money to last him the rest of his life. He'd settle for enough to last him the rest of the month.

We're told that money isn't everything. The way things are going, it soon won't be anything.

Some people have more money than brains — but not for long.

Even with inflation money still talks, but it carries on a quieter conversation.

Money never did buy happiness, and credit cards aren't doing much better.

Anybody who thinks money is everything has never been sick.

American money talks in just about every foreign country.

Many seem more concerned about *making* money than about *earning* it.

Today's dollar goes as far as it ever did — just beyond reach.

About the only thing you can get with a nickel today is heads or tails.

It's funny how a dollar can look so big when you take it to church and so small when you take it to the supermarket.

Nowadays everybody is putting their money where their mouth is — to kiss it goodby.

The nice thing about money is that it never clashes with anything you're wearing.

Money may not be everything, but it's a pretty good cure for poverty.

Wouldn't it be wonderful if there were as many new ways of making money as there are of spending it?

Money is a thing you'd get along without beautifully if only other people weren't so crazy about it.

The more money is inflated, the less it can be stretched.

You can tell who handles the money in families nowadays — they're making women's handbags bigger and men's wallets smaller.

If we could use the money political candidates spend on their campaigns, we could cure a lot of the ills they complain about.

Anybody who thinks there's a shortage of coins hasn't been to church lately.

Finance is the art of passing currency from hand to hand until it finally disappears.

Once upon a time it was hard to save money. Now it's difficult just to stay broke without going into debt.

Have you found a penny in the street lately? It was probably a dime when someone dropped it.

About the only way to get as much as ever for a dollar is to have it changed.

Money is an ideal gift — everything else is too expensive!

Eagles on dollars are proper and right because they symbolize swiftness of flight.

Money isn't everything, but it does quiet the nerves a little.

Nothing gets out of hand quicker these days than money.

Of course you can't take it with you, and with high taxes, lawyer's fees, and funeral expenses you can't leave it behind either.

The most expensive way to make money is to spend your entire lifetime doing nothing else.

Nothing makes money so useful as being yours.

We spend our lives trying to accumulate money, then look back to the times when we had none and call them the "good old days."

Money doesn't really talk; it just makes a sonic boom as it goes by.

The reason it is called "cold cash" is because of the way the temperature drops when you try to borrow some.

Money is something a man saves so he can get married — and then be broke the rest of his life.

Taking your money with you when you die isn't important. The real problem is making it last until you're ready to go.

Money can't buy happiness, but it helps you to be unhappy in comfort.

All our money these days is tied up in the market — the supermarket.

One thing you can still get for a quarter is five nickels.

Money won't buy real friends, but it does help you if you want to lease a few nice acquaintances.

Making money is getting to be like bees making honey. You can make it, but they won't let you keep it.

One sure way to get more for your money than you expect is to stand on a penny scale.

The man who overestimates the value of money will never be happy by amassing more of it.

With many folks money comes first, but they can't make it last.

Money won't buy happiness, but it will keep you from being more than moderately sullen and depressed.

Money may be a curse, but you can always find someone to take the curse away from you.

Using money is the only advantage of having it.

In the "good old days" the man who saved money was a miser. Now he's a wonder.

The love of money, and the lack of it, is the root of all kinds of evil.

It's so difficult to save money when your neighbors keep buying things you can't afford!

Money can't buy love, health, happiness, or what it did last year.

Some people get the idea they're worth a lot of money just because they have it.

When a man is broke he can count his friends on his thumb.

Appearances can be very deceptive. For instance, the dollar looks just like it did thirty years ago.

Money is a good servant but a poor master.

We are told that money isn't everything. This may be true, but it's way ahead of whatever is in second place.

Most people's financial problems are simple. They're short of money.

The only time a nickel goes as far as it once did is when it rolls under the bed.

Money brings happiness to those who find happiness earning it.

Another reason you can't take it with you — it goes before you do.

Friendless indeed is the man who has friends only because he has money.

It's true that money talks, but nowadays you can't hold on to it long enough to start a conversation.

If you want to know the value of money, try and borrow it.

A dime is not entirely useless. It still makes a good screwdriver.

It's sad to see people squandering money and know you can't help them!

A nickel isn't supposed to be as good as a dollar, but it goes to church more often.

Money is circulating so fast these days that the germs on it are suffering from air sickness.

No one knows whether or not a person would be happy if he had all the money he wanted. There isn't that much money.

A financier says that currency should be more elastic. How about making it a little more adhesive at the same time?

Money may be used as a universal passport to everywhere except heaven and as a universal provider for everything except happiness.

Our money talks today as if it were exhausted.

Benjamin Franklin had an axiom, "A penny saved is a penny earned." But that was before the sales tax was invented.

The darkest hour in any man's life is when he sits down to plan how to get money without earning it.

It takes a raft of money to keep the family afloat these days.

Money alone will not bring happiness, but it will attract interesting companions.

People are funny. They spend money they don't have to buy things they don't need to impress people they don't like.

Those anxious to invest their money in a "going" concern should make sure which way it's going.

The average man already has more money than he has sense; the trouble is that he doesn't know it.

We do not need more money in our pockets as much as we need more grace in our hearts.

A dime is a dollar with all the various taxes deducted.

The younger generation will learn the value of a dollar when it begins paying off our debts.

It is good to have money and the things money will buy, but it is also good to occasionally make sure we haven't lost some of the things that money can't buy.

The reward for saving money is being able to pay our taxes without borrowing.

A dollar will not go as far as it once did, but it will go much faster.

Money talks these days, but its list of speaking acquaintances is growing narrower and more exclusive.

There has been much argument in recent years about a fitting motto for our coins. How about "Abide with me"?

No drunken sailor ever spent money as fast as a sober congressman.

Money is something that merely passes through our hands on its way to Washington.

Money can't go to heaven, but it can do something heavenly here on earth.

One thing you can still get for a dime these days is a sneer.

The value of money lies altogether in the uses to which it is put.

Try to save money. Someday it may be valuable again.

Not only is Washington's face on our money, but now Washington's hands are on it.

Before borrowing money from a friend, decide which you need more.

Money will do more *to* you than it will do *for* you.

Hush money talks — and it also stops talk.

The fellow who really understands the value of cold cash is the one whose salary is not so hot.

It's all right to save money, but too many are trying to save it from people they owe it to.

A lot of people still have the first dollar they ever made — Uncle Sam has all the others.

Money no longer talks — it just gasps. Many people can hear its death rattle!

Your money goes farther these days. In fact, a lot of it winds up in outer space.

Money separates more friends than it unites.

In the field of finance a dividend is a certain per centum, per annum, perhaps.

It's easy to borrow money from the government. All you have to do is pretend you're a foreign power.

Money is like knowledge — the more you have, the less you need to brag.

About all you can do with money nowadays is owe it.

Some people's finances are in such a mess they must be getting advice from the government.

Money is often used as a bleach to take stains out of reputations.

Of all the valuable things that money can't buy, the most valuable is a man who can't be bought.

If money is all you want, money is all you'll get.

Twenty dollar bills have become terribly fragile. It seems we break one every time we go into a grocery store.

Money often unmakes the man who makes it.

The principal export of the United States is money.

Money may not make a person happy, but it keeps his creditors in a better frame of mind.

It's not surprising that dollar bills wear out so quickly. Americans keep passing the buck.

Yes, there are bigger things in life than money — bills, for instance.

The dollar doesn't go very far these days, but what it lacks in distance, it makes up in speed.

Money cannot buy one necessity of the soul.

Economists tell us that we may have to devalue the dollar. What do they think Congress has been doing for the past twenty-five or thirty years?

Everybody is willing to lend a helping hand to the fellow who has trouble opening his pocketbook.

The love of money is the root of all evil, except now it isn't around long enough for even a fleeting romance.

In the old days a woman married a man for his money, but now she divorces him for it.

The only way to earn an honest dollar these days is to earn five.

If germs cling to money, as we are told, let's learn how they do it.

The man who gets his money the hard way is the one who has to ask his wife for it.

George Washington set a poor precedent when he threw that dollar across the Potomac. Since then our government has felt impelled to throw billions of them across the oceans.

The fellow who has no money is poor; the fellow who has nothing but money is poorer still.

There is one thing you can get without money — sick!

There's nothing wrong with money that having a lot of it won't cure.

"In God We Trust" is inscribed on a dollar we can't trust.

Many names in the social register got there by way of the cash register.

You're getting old when you're on vacation and your energy runs out before your money does.

Many people seem to think that opportunity means a chance to get money without earning it.

The best thing that parents can spend on their children is time — not money.

A surgeon in Kansas doesn't believe in unnecessary surgery. He refuses to operate unless he desperately needs the money.

Politicians are poor tippers — they're not as careless with their own money as they are with ours.

Some politicians campaign for the funds of it.

Another thing money can't buy is an honest politician.

If campaign money talks, it is careful not to tell where it came from.

How about appointing a plumber to Secretary of the Treasury? We've got to do something about all the money going down the drain.

If a man can see both sides of a problem, you know that none of his money is tied up in it.

One of the problems of modern life is for a husband to teach his wife that even bargains cost money.

An example of progress is the fact that every year it takes less time and more money to get where you want to go.

The price of progress is change, and it is taking just about all we have.

Some men's religion runs up against a stone wall when it reaches the location of their pocketbooks.

A man may be able to trade his reputation for money, but he can't trade back.

Retirement can be a great joy if you can figure out how to spend time without spending money.

Next Christmas Santa Claus won't be the only one in the red.

If your youngster asks how Santa Claus gets into your house, tell him he comes in through a hole in daddy's wallet.

A secret is the only thing that circulates more rapidly than money.

If it's true that we're approaching a moneyless society, some of us are ahead of our time.

It seems that some women would rather be out of money than out of style.

Success measured merely by money is too cheap.

Even if money could bring happiness, think what the luxury tax would be!

A tax-dodger is a man who does not love his country less, but loves his money more.

Most of us have enough money to pay our taxes. What we need is something to live on!

It isn't what you have in your pocket that makes you thankful, but what you have in your heart.

There was a time when you saved up for your old age; now you save up for April 15th.

Time separates the best of friends, and so does money — and don't forget marriage!

Time may be money, but it's much easier to persuade a man to give you his time than to lend you his money.

Travel not only broadens the mind, but it also flattens the finances.

Men's troubles are largely due to three things: women, money — and both.

Everybody shuns trouble unless it comes to him disguised as money.

A vacation makes you feel good enough to return to work — and so poor you have to.

The fellow who first said, "Spend your vacation..." never realized how right he was.

Change is what a person wants on a vacation — and a lot of currency too.

Washington is recalling all the one dollar bills. There's a defect in the value.

Sometimes a man gets a reputation for wisdom simply because he doesn't have enough money to make a fool of himself.

The two most beautiful words in the English language are, "Check Enclosed."

Mothers

We are now told that automation is a process that gets all the work done while you just stand there. When we were younger, this process was called MOTHER.

The most terrible thing about a divorce is that somewhere, maybe miles apart, two mothers are nodding their heads and saying, "See? I told you so."

Mother love is dangerous when it becomes *smother* love.

A man is seldom as smart as his mother thinks, or as dumb as his mother-in-law says he is.

A mother who makes a match for her daughter usually intends to referee it as well.

A mother may hope that her daughter will get a better husband than she did, but she knows her son will never get as good a wife as his father did.

Another reason for unhappy marriages is that men can't fool their wives like they could their mothers.

All mothers are physically handicapped. They have only two hands.

A mother should be like a quilt — keep the children warm but don't smother them.

The old-fashioned mother who used to have prunes every morning now has a granddaughter who has dates every night.

Most mothers aren't really interested in taking their weight off — they just want to rearrange it.

The mother of the bride gushed, "I hope she'll make *her* husband as happy as she's making *my* husband."

Simply having children does not necessarily make a woman a mother.

The joys of motherhood are never fully experienced until all the children are in bed.

What a mother should save for a rainy day is patience.

A mother in Colorado is so ashamed of her unruly kids that she attends the PTA under an assumed name.

Have you ever wondered what some mothers would find to talk about if their children weren't allergic to something?

You can be sure it's her firstborn if a mother cries when Junior starts school.

The quickest way for a mother to get her children's attention is to sit down and look comfortable.

A typical mother, seeing there are only four pieces of pie for five people, promptly announces she never did care for pie.

A modern mother is one who can hold a safety pin and a cigarette in her mouth at the same time.

It sure would be wonderful for mother if she could collect time-and-a-half for overtime.

Mothers can have a few minutes to themselves at the end of the day by doing the dishes.

The young mother gets along beautifully with her mother-in-law because she probably can't afford a baby sitter.

A Mississippi mother said to her children, "Mind your manners, they may come back in style someday."

It took the old-time mother less than a minute to dress for dinner. All she had to do was take off her apron.

Many mothers had their daughters vaccinated in places they wrongly thought would never show.

Mothers who scold their sons for carrying useless things in their pockets should take a look in their handbags!

On the matrimonial sea, the hand that rocks the cradle seldom rocks the boat.

Throughout the ages no nation has ever had a better friend than the mother who taught her children to pray.

Why does a mother do all she can to help her daughter catch a man — and then cry at her wedding?

A mother takes twenty-one years to make a man of her boy, and another woman can make a fool of him in twenty minutes.

There are still a few old-fashioned mothers who would like to tuck their children in bed, but they can't stay awake that late.

The most difficult thing for a mother to remember is that other people have perfect children too.

A mother is a woman who decorates her life with babies.

It has been rightly said that a mother is not a person to lean on, but a person to make leaning unnecessary.

A modern mother is one who worries only when her daughter gets home from a date at a decent hour.

A mother's patience is like a tube of toothpaste — it's never quite all gone.

There's only one perfect child in the world and every mother has it.

Rejecting things because they are old-fashioned would rule out the sun and the moon — and a mother's love.

Many a man met his wife through a dating service — her mother!

Mothers-in-law

The penalty for bigamy is two mothers-in-law.

The wife isn't always boss in the American home. Sometimes it's her mother.

The most terrible thing about a divorce is that somewhere, maybe miles apart, two mothers are nodding their heads and saying, "See? I told you so."

To the average husband, the "blessed event" is when his mother-in-law goes home.

English law prohibits a man from marrying his mother-in-law. This is the epitome of useless legislation.

A man is seldom as smart as his mother thinks, or as dumb as his mother-in-law says he is.

When it comes to broken marriages most husbands will split the blame — half his wife's fault, and half her mother's.

Listen men: Maybe you'll never be as big a hero as your son thinks you are but you'll never be as big a fool as your mother-in-law thinks your are either!

The young mother gets along beautifully with her mother-in-law because she probably can't afford a baby sitter.

No man is really successful until his mother-in-law admits it.

"Double trouble" is a mother-in-law with a twin sister.

Movies

History does repeat itself, but not as often as old movies.

Can you remember when movies used to boast of being in technicolor instead of off-color?

The couple who used to walk out of a movie because it was off-color now has a grandson who walks out because it isn't.

You can tell it's an old movie when the doctor tells the patient, "You're as sound as a dollar."

Just about the only people who still cry at the movies are theater owners.

Once upon a time movies were rated on how good they were, not on who was allowed to see them.

In today's movies the theme is a dirty story, and the admission price is a dirty shame.

Why can't we occasionally have a movie rated "E" for entertainment?

About the only thing that modern movies leave to the imagination is the plot.

A producer in Hollywood plans a film entitled "Marriage, Hollywood Style." It will be short.

Maybe these movies with so much violence should be shown in black and blue.

You're getting old if you can remember when movies were made for the smart set — not the smut set.

Today's movies are either comedies or traumas.

The best way to stop kids from seeing dirty movies is to label them "Educational."

Sometimes a movie is so bad you're sorry you asked the lady in front of you to remove her hat.

Movies shown on TV are getting shorter. Any day now we'll be seeing "The Five Commandments."

Terror films are coming back in vogue, and sometimes the prices are more terrifying than the films.

Ad for an x-rated move: "For people over XXI."

The happiest ending in the movies is when the guy behind you finishes eating his popcorn.

Sometimes a movie hero is one who sits through it.

Not all the dummies in the movies get thrown over the cliffs.

Some of the movies of today should be pitied rather than censored.

The reformers need not worry. The movies are never as wicked and vulgar as the advertisements promise.

A man misses silent films. It was so good in those days to see a woman open her mouth and have no sound come out.

Can you remember way back when the saltiest thing you got in a movie was popcorn?

Many people still cry at the movies — especially when they pay four dollars to see a dull one.

They're producing a sequel to *Roots* but on a higher plane. It's called *Trees.*

There's nothing wrong with the motion picture market that a lot of nonattendance won't cure.

One good thing about radio — it never shows old movies.

Music

Is there any music as sweet as that of a car starting on a cold morning?

The reason some parents want their children to play the piano instead of the violin is that it's harder to lose a piano.

The first thing a child learns when he gets a drum is that he's never going to get another one.

No one can whistle a symphony. It takes an orchestra to play it.

The dentist's favorite marching song is "The Yanks Are Coming."

Happiness is learning that your daughter's boyfriend has had his electric guitar repossessed by the finance company.

Laughter is the sweetest music that ever greeted the human ear.

Take time to laugh — it is the music of the soul.

A certain man in Texas has such a big mouth he can sing a duet by himself.

These days it's better to face the music than to have to listen to it.

There is one good thing about today's popular music. If the acoustics are bad you don't know it.

A scientist claims that rock music is beneficial in some cases of deafness. But, then, deafness is also beneficial in some cases of rock music.

Marriage brings music into a man's life — he learns to play second fiddle.

Music has been called medicine, and some of it is hard to take.

Learning to play a musical instrument isn't difficult. Anybody who can fold a road map can quickly learn to play an accordion.

The kind of music people should have in their homes is domestic harmony.

A harp is a piano after taxes.

Popular music just has to come from the brain of the composer. Nothing else has stuff like that in it.

Two songs, "The Star-Spangled Banner" and "Melancholy Baby," need to be rewritten. The first, because very few can sing it; the second, because everybody can.

Everytime we hear a disc jockey play the top ten tunes, we really get the shakes wondering what the bottom ten will be.

A true music lover is a woman who applauds when her husband comes home singing at four in the morning.

We need to change our National Anthem to "Deep in the Heart of Taxes."

When it comes to music lessons, most kids make it a practice not to practice.

The rock music field is uncertain. A singing group can be only ordinary one day and retired millionaires the next day.

What this country needs is more shorthaired music.

An unsung hero is a guy who knows he can't sing and doesn't.

Classical music threatens to develop a tune with every other bar and then disappoints you.

Many musical groups don't play rock music because, if they did, they'd have to listen to it.

A person is in a tough predicament when he has to face the music with his nose to the grindstone and his back to the wall.

They tell us that jazz music is dying. It always did sound that way.

Music is certainly a wonderful thing. If it weren't for music a lot of people could be put in jail for what they do on a dance floor.

It isn't facing the music that hurts these days; it's listening to it.

There is plenty of heavenly music for those who are tuned in.

Now for a brief lesson in music: B-sharp, never B-flat, always B-natural.

If today's music is a thing of beauty which will endure forever, the prospects of immortality is a dismal one.

Music is an attempt to express emotions that are beyond speech.

Jazz music is an appeal to the emotions by an attack on the nerves.

The proper pitch for most electrical guitars is right out the window, followed by the player.

Canaries have to demonstrate their ability to sing before they can be imported. What a pity that this doesn't also aply to imported opera singers!

The trouble with country music is that it doesn't stay there.

A lot of singers on TV are worth watching. Too bad they're not worth listening to.

There's one advantage to the music the younger generation is crazy about — nobody can whistle it.

A folk singer is a guy who sings through his nose by ear.

Practicing the saxophone should either improve the execution of the player or hasten it.

It seems that songs making the most money make the least sense.

There should be music in every home — except the one next door.

Nowadays what is not worth saying is sung.

Even if rock 'n' roll music died tomorrow, it would take several weeks for the sound to fade away.

Opera is where a guy gets stabbed in the back, and instead of bleeding he sings.

If you can write a song that's crazy enough your fortune is made.

There's one thing to be said for modern music — you can't tell the difference when the record wears out.

Music is much more enjoyable if you listen with your eyes shut. It is also more enjoyable if the people sitting near you would listen with their mouths shut.

The saxophone was invented a century ago, thus proving that "the evil which men do lives after them."

There would be a lot fewer folk singers if they had to know anything about either folks or singing.

Many a violin sounds as though its strings were still in the cat.

Many rock singers have the kind of voice that belongs in silent films.

The ukelele is the missing link between music and noise.

A concert is where people's conversations are constantly being interrupted by music.

To write a hit song, just take something composed by one of the old masters and decompose it.

A violinist is always up to his chin in music.

Jazz will endure just as long as people hear it through their feet instead of their brains.

The only music that is typically American is that of the mockingbird, the saxophone, and the cash register.

An opera is a place where anything that is too dumb to be spoken is sung.

Much of modern music is so fast and loud you can't tell what the band is playing, much less what song it was stolen from.

Too many rock groups seem to be composed of a hot guitar, a cool organ, and a drummer who doesn't like music.

Much of our modern music makes you feel like clapping your hands — over your ears!

Even in its exteme form modern jazz will never replace the old-fashioned earache.

The sweetest music to a woman's ear is another woman playing second fiddle.

Rock singers are usually long on hair and short on talent.

Rock music is confusing. Just when you figure out what they're playing, they stop.

A folk singer is someone who sings constantly about the joys of the simple life — using a five-thousand-dollar sound system.

You're an old-timer if you can remember when rock was something you did in a chair.

Politics and music are much alike. The person who is off-key always seems to have the loudest voice.

Musicians

A rock and roll singer had a bad accident recently. His partner slammed the car door on his hair.

Newspaper ad in New Orleans: "Retired trombone player will sell one dozen sport jackets with one arm longer than the other."

A music magazine recently took a poll to name the best-dressed rock star — and nobody won.

Never poke fun at someone who misuses and abuses the English language. He may be in training to write tomorrow's hit songs.

You don't have to be much of a musician to toot your own horn.

Musicians who play by ear should remember that people listen the same way.

Many a musician who plays Beethoven should play bridge.

The musician who invented "swing" ought to.

Did you hear about the drummer who attended a rock school and graduated *Magna Cum Louder?*

The piano is usually in good condition, but the musician needs tuning.

Most of the rock 'n' roll musicians should be plucking chickens instead of guitars.

A concert pianist in Chicago claims he's doing his part to conserve energy. He's now playing the piano with only one hand.

The reason some of these rock groups sound the way they do is that they rehearse separately.

A veteran musician in New Orleans claims rock music isn't new. "We played it twenty-five years ago — when the lights were too dim to read the music."

Some of today's musicians carry a tune as if it were too heavy for them.

You don't have to be an accomplished musician to play on your neighbor's nerves.

One thing we learn from television these days is that the country is full of people who can't sing.

N

Names
Narrow-Mindedness
National Anthem
Nature
Necessities
Needs

Neighbors
Nervousness
Newlyweds
News
Newspapers

New Year
Night Clubs
Noise
Nostalgia
Nudists

Names

An elderly gentleman in Nevada calls his car Abe. It's a Lincoln.

When a girl starts calling a man by his first name, she may have her eye on his last name.

Why shouldn't a woman take her husband's name? She takes everything else!

A man has three names: the name he inherits, the name his parents gave him, and the name he makes for himself.

If civilized people won't take advantage of the weak and helpless, how do you explain some of the names given to little babies?

Carve your name on hearts — not on marble.

A good name, like good will, is attained by many actions and may be lost by one.

Never has a man who lived a life of ease left a name worth remembering.

Many names in the social register got there by way of the cash register.

If you can't remember names, a pretty safe greeting to anyone over fifty is, "I hear you've been sick."

A good name is to be chosen over great riches. It's tax free!

The best inheritance parents can leave a child is a good name.

In politics a guy who is out to make a name for himself gets called many names.

Narrow-Mindedness
see also Prejudice

A bigot is a person who slams his mind in your face.

The mind of the bigot is like the pupil of the eye; the more light you shine into it, the more it will contract.

Education will broaden a narrow mind, but there is no known cure for a big head.

It isn't easy for an idea to squeeze itself into a head that is filled with prejudice.

Nothing dies quicker than a new idea in a closed mind.

The most difficult thing to open is a closed mind.

There is no one so narrow as the fellow who disagrees with you.

Narrow-minded people are like narrow-necked bottles — the less they have in them, the more noise they make pouring it out.

A narrow mind and an open mouth usually go together.

It's a pity more people can't travel the straight and narrow path without becoming strait-laced and narrow-minded.

The narrower the mind, the broader the statement.

Don't be so narrow-minded that your ears rub together.

There are some people so narrow-minded they have to stack their prejudices vertically.

Did you ever notice how often a narrow mind and a wide mouth go together?

A lot of trouble is caused by combining a narrow mind with a wide mouth.

National Anthem

A well-informed American knows the lineup of baseball teams and about half the words of the "Star-Spangled Banner."

Two songs, "The Star-Spangled Banner" and "Melancholy Baby," need to be rewritten. The first, because very few can sing it; the second, because everybody can.

We need to change our National Anthem to "Deep in the Heart of Taxes."

People stand up when they hear our National Anthem — and fall down when they start to sing it.

A political platform is like the second stanza of our National Anthem. Everybody knows it's there, but very few know the words.

Nature

As a man gets older he suspects that nature is plotting against him for the benefit of doctors and dentists.

If Mother Nature could have foreseen Bermuda shorts, she surely would have done a better job on the male knee.

When nature made great men she made critics out of the chips that were left over.

An echo is nature's instant replay.

By nature all men are much alike, but by education they become different.

Nature couldn't make us perfect, so she did the next best thing: she made us blind to our faults.

Nature never makes any blunders; when she makes a fool, she means it.

No matter how hard you try to improve on Mother Nature, you're not kidding Father Time.

What Mother Nature giveth, Father Time taketh away.

We're approaching spring when Mother Nature begins to liquidate her frozen assets.

Man has conquered almost every dangerous thing in nature except human nature.

Nature didn't make us perfect, so she did the next best thing. She made us blind to our faults.

People who say that you can't fool nature have never watched a beautician at work.

Nature often makes up for a nugget-size brain with a bucket-size mouth.

Nature must have a sense of humor to let spring fever and house cleaning come at the same time.

Nature never intended for us to pat ourselves on the back. If she had, our hinges would be different.

Nature may have known what she was doing, but sometimes it looks like she deliberately constructed mankind for the benefit of doctors and dentists.

Mother Nature gets the blame for a lot of things you can't explain any other way without implicating yourself.

Take a tip from nature — your ears aren't made to shut, but your mouth is!

Nature gave men two ends — one to sit on and one to think with. Man's success or failure is dependent on the one he uses most.

Nature makes blunders too — she often gives the biggest mouths to those who have the least to say.

Necessities

There, little luxury, don't you cry — you'll be a necessity by and by.

The difference between a luxury and a necessity depends on whether your neighbor has it and you don't.

Nowadays we spend so much on luxuries we can't afford to buy the necessities.

The necessities of life are food, clothing, shelter, and credit cards.

A necessity is almost any luxury you see in the home of a neighbor.

Needs

What this country needs is a good five-cent anything.

Our greatest need is someone smart enough to foretell the future, and then change it before it happens.

One thing this country needs is fewer needs.

What America needs is a credit card for wives that self-destructs after fifty dollars.

The world's greatest need is an assurance of tomorrow.

America needs a car that can't go any faster than a driver can think.

We are sorely in need of a voting machine with a space for "Remarks."

Our greatest need at the present time is a cheap substitute for food.

We need more watchdogs at the United States Treasury and fewer bloodhounds at the Internal Revenue Service.

What we need in this country is a car that eats oats.

America needs more free speech that is worth listening to.

What this country needs most is more people who smile even when they're not on "Candid Camera."

Our greatest need is an investigating committee to investigate investigating committees.

The people of the United States do not need more judges but more judgment.

What this country needs most is a SPCTT — The Society for the Prevention of Cruelty to Taxpayers.

Our beloved country needs another holiday — a day set aside to celebrate having survived all the others.

Oh, how this world needs a computer that can figure out all the things in life that don't add up!

Our greatest need in the United States is a shortage of shortages.

We are sorely in need of a special encyclopedia with blank pages for the fellow who knows everything.

We all need a ballpoint pen that starts writing when the writer does.

Our most pressing need in America today is more slow readers and fewer fast talkers.

Man's greatest need is something to feel important about.

Oh, how we need more free speech that doesn't cost so much to listen to!

Above all, we need tranquility without tranquilizers.

This country needs a man who can be right and president at the same time.

Another great need of this country is guns of smaller caliber and men of larger.

What America needs is a return to Saturday night baths and Sunday morning churchgoing.

Our country's most basic needs can be summed up in four words: bread, brains, beliefs, and brotherhood.

There is a growing need for fewer busybodies and more homebodies.

Most men need a vitamin pill that can make them enjoy raking leaves more than playing golf.

The United States needs more tractors and fewer detractors.

One thing all of us need is a grocery cart with four wheels that all go in the same direction.

Our country needs more soil conservation and not so much soiled conversation.

What we need is less government in business and more business in government.

What this world needs is fewer rules and more good examples.

What the world needs is peace that passes all misunderstanding.

What the nations of the world need is a peace conference with the "Prince of Peace."

What the world needs is an amplifier for the still, small voice.

Neighbors

Americans sink millions of dollars in unsound financial schemes, one of which is trying to keep up with the neighbors.

The only people who really listen to an argument are the neighbors.

Nothing depreciates a car faster than having a neighbor buy a new one.

Folks would enjoy us more if we gave as much thought to our own behavior as we do to our neighbor's.

Nothing helps to stabilize the family budget like an economy drive by the closest neighbors.

A "brat" is a child who acts like your own but belongs to your neighbor.

Church is where you go to find out what your neighbors should do to lead better lives.

A contented neighborhood is one in which each man thinks he is doing just a little better than the man next door.

A contented person is one who has all the things his neighbor has.

Most of us would be better off financially if it weren't for the extravagance of our neighbors.

You can shut your eyes to your own faults, but the neighbors always refuse to cooperate.

A hypocrite prays on his knees on Sunday — and on his neighbors the rest of the week.

Everybody is for justice, thinking it will bring them rewards and give the neighbors what they have coming to them.

It's easier to love humanity as a whole than to love one's neighbor.

357

The Bible admonishes us to love our neighbors, and also to love our enemies — probably because they are generally the same people.

It's much wiser to love thy neighbor than his wife.

A good memory test is to recall all the kind things you have said about your neighbor.

It's so difficult to save money when your neighbors keep buying things you can't afford!

There should be music in every home — except the one next door.

You don't have to be an accomplished musician to play on your neighbor's nerves.

A necessity is almost any luxury you see in the home of a neighbor.

A good neighbor is one who doesn't expect you to return the things you borrow.

There's nothing quite so annoying as a neighbor who keeps the noise up and the shades down.

It used to be when we saw our neighbor's light on late at night we wondered if there was sickness. Now we wonder if there is a party we didn't get invited to.

The best neighbor is one who has everything you're out of.

If you have an unpleasant neighbor, the odds are that he does too.

A cooperative neighbor is one who advises you on what to buy, so he can borrow it later.

Why is it that the best neighbors in the world are always the ones who just moved away?

Your neighbor will seem like a better man when you judge him as you judge yourself.

Borrowing neighbors will take anything but a hint.

A good neighbor is a fellow who smiles at you over the back fence but doesn't climb it.

It's hard to keep up with the neighbors without falling behind with the creditors.

A neighbor is always doing something you can't afford.

One record we are anxious to break is the one our neighbor plays at one o'clock in the morning.

Neighbors resent hearing a married couple have words — especially when half of them can't be understood.

A man cannot touch his neighbor's heart with anything less than his own.

Nothing makes you more tolerant of a neighbor's noisy party than being invited to it.

A neighbor likes to borrow your equipment and loan you his troubles.

The neighbor we really like is the one who doesn't care what goes on at our house.

"Love thy neighbor," but first be sure she isn't married!

When the new neighbors move in, it's only friendly to keep a close check on what they have that's worth borrowing.

The ideal neighbor is the one who makes noise at the same time we do.

How much you love your neighbor can be measured by whether you feel the same when he borrows from you as you borrow from him.

It may be tough to keep up with the neighbors, but just think how tough it must be for the neighbors to stay ahead!

He thought his new neighbor had three daughters, until he found out they had one daughter with three wigs.

The easiest way to keep up with your neighbors is to pick ones who don't have any more than you have.

A good neighbor is one who, when he wants to borrow your corkscrew, asks you to bring it over.

Poverty is often a state of mind induced by a neighbor buying a new car.

An honest prayer: "Stop my neighbors, O Lord, from buying things I can't afford."

A good reputation may merely be proof that you don't have inquisitive neighbors.

One thing that helped Rip Van Winkle sleep for twenty years was the fact that none of his neighbors owned a lawn mower.

Fast transportation has made us all neighbors — but, unfortunately, not brothers.

Wealth is usually a curse — especially when the neighbors have it.

Nervousness

Then there was the woman who was cured of her nervousness in one treatment. The doctor told her it was a sign of old age.

Nervousness is when you feel in a hurry all over and can't get started.

The difference between psychoneurosis and plain old-fashioned nervousness is approximately seven hundred dollars.

Don't call a restless man nervous; he may be wearing scratchy underwear.

Anybody who's relaxed these days is probably nervous about it.

Nervous prostration was unknown when people worked more and worried less.

Unless world tension abates, soon we'll all be as nervous and jittery as school bus drivers and den mothers.

Today's news makes us so nervous we have to take a tranquilizer to steady our nerves long enough to open a bottle of sleeping pills.

Newlyweds

Description of a newlywed couple: His aim is to save money. Her ambition is to spoil his aim.

You can always recognize the newlywed in the supermarket. She's the one who squeezes the can of soup to see if it's fresh.

Most modern-day brides have the makings of a good wife, but they haven't been "kitchen-tested."

It's hard for some of these new wives to get used to being whistled for instead of at.

News

What a scarcity of news there would be if everybody obeyed the Ten Commandments!

Current events are so grim that we can't decide whether to watch the six o'clock news and not be able to eat, or the ten o'clock news and not be able to sleep.

How did dogs learn to bark their loudest during a television news bulletin?

It's true that an echo is quite accurate, but it doesn't contribute much that's new.

Bad news travels fast. In many instances, it concerns people who did the same.

The difference between gossip and news is whether you hear it or tell it.

Isn't it discouraging to contemplate that tomorrow's history will consist of today's current events?

Today's news makes us so nervous we have to take a tranquilizer to steady our nerves long enough to open a bottle of sleeping pills.

Nothing is as dead as yesterday's news — except yesterday's prices.

Current events are so grim that we often can't decide whether or not we dare watch the six o'clock news.

These are the days when we wish newscasters would cast their news somewhere else.

Most of today's news is too true to be good.

The way some people sound off about news, you'd think the daily paper printed only one copy — and they had it!

Not all the news that's fit to print is fit to read.

Lately the news has been so bad that people are tuning in on soap operas, trying to find something that will cheer them up.

News is the same old thing — only happening to different people.

When everybody attends to his own business, news is scarce.

If your wife waits until you've eaten a well-prepared meal to tell you about a dented fender — that's "managed news."

What a scarcity of news there would be if everybody obeyed the Ten Commandments!

The news makes the world very confusing. Sometimes it seems the Near East is too far, and the Far East is too near.

Have you noticed that on TV the good guys win out every time — except on the six o'clock news?

It was thoughtful of the television people to put the aspirin commercials right after the six o'clock news.

There are TV anchormen who receive twice as much money to read the news as the President gets to make the news.

Would you enjoy a horror show on TV? If so, take a look at the six o'clock news.

There is now some talk of eliminating violence from TV. Well, there goes the eleven o'clock news.

Anyone who doesn't worry about the world situation these days must be getting lousy reception on his television set.

Newspapers

A small town newspaper in Texas advertised, "Read your Bible to know what people ought to do. Read this paper to know what they actually do."

Nothing improves a man's appearance as much as the photograph the newspapers use with his obituary.

One way to deflate your ego is to read the want ads in the newspapers and discover all the jobs you're not equipped to handle.

Some men's names appear in the paper only three times: when they're too young to read, when they're too dazed to read, and when they're too dead to read.

Newspapers have reporters to write the news, columnists to misrepresent it, and delivery boys to throw it into your rosebushes.

A good way to get your name in the newspaper is to cross the street reading one.

A newspaper editor's business is to separate the wheat from the chaff and see to it that the chaff is printed.

Not all the dope this country swallows is narcotic!

Another thing about a newspaper is that you never have to ask someone to turn down the volume.

Newspapers are owned by individuals and corporations, but freedom of the press belongs to the people.

A newspaper is a portable screen, behind which a man hides from the woman who is standing up in a bus.

A newspaper reporter says it's dangerous for a young man to propose to a girl while he's driving a car. It's dangerous anywhere, son!

Most newspapers condemn gambling on the editorial page and print racing tips on the sports page.

A newspaper is a circulating library with high blood pressure.

Do you realize we're living in a time when almost everybody reads a newspaper, and the only thing they believe are the ads?

Newspaper ad: "Lady with trailer wants to meet man with car. Object: to get hitched."

The trouble with being optimistic is that some people will think you're illiterate.

It's not a bad idea for a politician to remember that no newspaper can misquote silence.

The radio will never take the place of the newspaper, because you can't swat flies with it.

Two newspaper editors had been feuding for years and one of them died. The other saw an opportunity for final revenge. He printed the obituary under "Public Improvements."

It's not a bad idea for a politician to remember that no newspaper can misquote his silence.

One of the main differences in newspapers and television is that editors report violence, while TV producers create it.

The first thing every morning when we get out of bed we look in the newspaper to see if the world is still here.

New Year

Many Americans no longer celebrate the arrival of the New Year — they celebrate the survival of the old year.

There's only one good thing that can be said for bad habits. If it weren't for them we couldn't make New Year's resolutions.

Many people look forward to the new year for a new start on old habits.

The New Year gives people a fresh start on their old habits.

The New Year is when some people drop in for a call and others call in for a drop.

The New Year is like a new baby — many changes will be necessary, some of which may be neglected.

What the New Year brings us will depend a great deal on what we bring to the New Year.

New Year's Eve is when you take your wife out, and she takes you back home.

A New Year's resolution is a promise to stop doing everything you enjoy most.

Serious trouble comes when the New Year's resolutions collide with the old year's habits.

Why not be sure by having your New Year's resolutions notorized?

Most of the leaves we turned over in January have already started to fall.

A New Year's resolution is something that goes in one year and out the other.

May your troubles in the coming New Year be as short-lived as your resolutions.

Night Clubs

Naturalists who claim America's wildlife is disappearing don't stay up very late at night.

America has some fine old ruins. Many of them can be seen in our nightclubs.

The best way to avoid the flu is to visit a night club. No flu bug can live in that environment.

America has may fine old ruins. A lot of them may be seen in our taverns and nightclubs.

At today's nightclub prices it's harder than ever for a comedian to make people laugh.

A cocktail lounge is a half-lit room full of half-lit people.

All the tables are reserved in a first-class nightclub, but the guests aren't.

A nightclub is a place where people who have nothing to remember go to forget.

Nightclub business is so slow these days that even the waiters are insulting each other.

A nightclub is a unique place on a rainy night. You can stay outside and get wet or go inside and get soaked.

The modern nightclub is a place where they check people's hats and coats — but not their drinking.

Noise

Many an argument is sound — and only sound!

Present-day cars are so quiet that the only noise you hear is from the finance company.

Nothing lowers the level of conversation more than raising the voice.

Home is a man's refuge, a place of quiet and rest, says a certain writer. That's true except for the telephone, the children, the vacuum cleaner, and the salesman at the door.

Intelligence is like a river — the deeper it is, the less noise it makes.

It's a mistake to try to judge a man's horse-power by the size of his exhaust.

It's when a man gets tight as a drum that he makes the most noise.

The ukelele is the missing link between music and noise.

Narrow-minded people are like narrow-necked bottles — the less they have in them, the more noise they make pouring it out.

The loudest noise in the world is the first rattle in a new car.

Oratory is the fine art of making deep noises from the chest sound like important messages from the brain.

You would be surprised to know how many people are like a brass drum — with plenty of noise, but nothing on the inside.

Tennis is a game that can't be played without raising a racket.

Nostalgia

It was more fun driving a car in the old days when the crank was in front of the engine.

It isn't the "good old days" a bachelor fears he'll miss if he marries — it's the good old nights.

Today's kids call it "finding themselves." In the "good old days" it was called loafing.

In the "good old days" men stood up for women — but there were no buses then.

Many a parent sighs for the "good old days" when a stocking could hold what a child wanted for Christmas.

The people who talk most about the "good old days" are the first to complain when their TV set goes on the blink.

If life is worth what it's costing now, people were getting a bargain in grandpa's day.

The best thing about the "good old days" is that they are forever gone.

Enjoy yourself. These are the "good old days" you're going to miss in the years ahead.

It's disheartening to think that sometime in the future we may look back on these as the "good old days."

In the "good old days" we were told to think about the future; but if a fellow stops to think these days, the future is already here.

Don't you long for the "good old days" when Uncle Sam lived within his income and without most of yours?

In 1913 Uncle Sam collected only 13 million dollars in income taxes. That's why they were called the "good old days."

The "good old days" were when inflation was something you did to a balloon.

In the days when a woodshed stood behind the American home, a great deal of what passes as juvenile delinquency was settled out of court.

Do you remember the "good old days" when a juvenile delinquent was a boy who played the saxophone too loud?

Can you remember way back when a juvenile delinquent was a kid with an overdue library book?

Living in the past has one thing in its favor — it's cheaper.

In the "good old days" life was what we made it, but now it's a case of *if* we make it.

The "good old days" date back to the time when marriage produced more triangles on the clothesline than in the courtroom.

The reason people can remember the "good old days" is that there were so few of them.

Nothing is more responsible for the "good old days" than a poor memory.

We spend our lives trying to accumulate money, then look back to the times when we had none and call them the "good old days."

In the "good old days" the man who saved money was a miser. Now he's a wonder.

Once upon a time movies were rated on how good they were, not on who was allowed to see them.

Can you remember way back when the saltiest thing you got in a movie was popcorn?

If you can't remember names, a pretty safe greeting to anyone over fifty is, "I hear you've been sick."

Everything is changing so fast these days that even nostalgia isn't what it used to be.

Nostalgia is the desire to repossess what you never had.

Formula for nostalgia: The "good old days" multiplied by a bad memory.

Nostalgia has really caught on in show business. Some Hollywood actors are remarrying their ex-wives.

Nostalgia is remembering the pleasures of sitting in front of a big fireplace — without remembering you had to cut the wood for it.

Most people like the old days best — they were younger then.

In the "good old days" there were fewer pleasures but we had more time to enjoy those we had.

In the "good old days" problems could be solved without raising taxes.

Can you remember "way back" when radios plugged in and toothbrushes didn't?

In the "good old days" the biggest grab for a man's salary took place after he got home.

Nudists

People who quit smoking cigarettes have the same problem as newcomers to nudist camps — they don't know what to do with their hands.

The only clothing permitted in a nudist camp is a coat — of tan.

A nudist is a person who goes shirtless, coatless, vestless, and wears trousers to match.

One thing about nudists — you can't pin anything on them.

No respectable person is in favor of nudity, but after paying taxes, some of us may not have any other choice.

Did you hear about the female nudist who was voted one of the "Ten Best Undressed Women"?

The fastest thing in the world is a nudist on whom a waiter has just spilled hot coffee!

You can't blame nudists for being the way they are. They were born that way!

O

Obedience

Who said kids aren't obedient? They'll obey any TV commercial about buying a new toy.

The time to teach obedience to authority is in the playpen instead of the State pen.

It is our duty to obey God's commands, not to direct His counsels.

Delayed obedience is the brother of disobedience.

Every great person first learned how to obey, whom to obey, and when to obey.

Christ was one child who knew more than His parents — yet He obeyed them.

A patient cannot accept the physician and, at the same time, reject his remedy.

You have to give American parents credit — they know how to obey their children.

Obesity

Americans are getting bigger and broader, a fact which has filtered through to everybody except the people who mark off the seats in football stadiums.

By the time a man can afford to buy one of those little sports cars, he's too fat to get into it.

The trouble with bucket seats in automobiles is that not everyone has the same size bucket.

Many fat people have cut down to five cigarettes a day — one after each meal.

When some women show up in stretch pants, they sure do.

Always trust a fat man. He'll never stoop to anything low.

Most of our faults can be hidden, except overeating.

The trouble with square meals is that they make you round.

There is now a margarine on the market for people over forty. It's called the "Middleage Spread."

The Agriculture Department says the average American eats 1,148 pounds of food a year. Of course, a lot of it goes to *waist*.

A fat man is no good at golf because if he tees the ball where he can hit it, he can't see it; and if he tees the ball where he can see it, he can't hit it.

No woman is ever fat. She is just short for her weight.

You've put on too much weight when you try to loosen your belt — and can't find it.

Like charity, obesity begins at home.

Overweight people don't like to hear four-letter words — such as diet.

A fat man is no good in war; he can neither fight nor run away.

Some folks go *starch* raving mad when they see food.

Overweight doesn't happen overnight. It snacks up on you.

You're overweight when you begin living beyond your seams.

Don't get too round around the middle or you won't be around very long.

Some people are so fat they'd have a "wide load" sign on them if they were a truck.

The reason some husbands are overweight is that the only time they get to open their mouths is when they're eating.

An overweight woman was told by her doctor, "Under my new diet you can eat anything you like. Now, here's a list of what you're going to like."

He who indulges bulges.

The weight of a man's years invariably settles around his waistline.

Overweight people usually watch what they eat very closely — all the way from plate to mouth.

A great many people have a soldier's stomach — everything they eat goes to the front.

Fat people have the kind of inflation that even the government can't keep down.

Did you hear about the woman in North Carolina who got fat from the sugar coating on the reducing pills she was taking?

A fat man finds it difficult to stoop to anything low.

Said a weight watcher, "I'm fat because I have a hand-to-mouth disease."

Some people put on weight in certain places — soda fountains, for instance.

Fat people are usually good-natured because it takes them so long to get mad clear through.

Everybody loves a fat man, but not when he has the other half of the seat on the bus.

There are many people who seem to be broad-shouldered across the hips.

A woman is never overweight until she has run out of places to hide it.

Obesity is surplus gone to waist.

Excess weight is like sugar in iced coffee — after a while it settles to the bottom.

A fat man knows where his cigar ashes are going to land.

Many people are like the famous Liberty Bell — old, heavy, and slightly cracked.

Some people grow up and spread cheer; others just grow up and spread.

Old Age

By the time a man finds greener pastures, he's too old to climb the fence.

To be seventy years young is sometimes more cheerful and hopeful than to be forty years old.

By all means go ahead and mellow with age. Just be wary of getting rotten.

Years make all of us old and very few of us wise.

Many of us are at the "metallic age" — gold in our teeth, silver in our hair, and lead in our pants.

The three ages of man are youth, middle age and, "My, but you are looking well."

By the time most folks learn to behave themselves they're too old to do anything else.

At the birthday party of a prominent spinster, many of the guests were overcome by the heat of the candles.

Children are a comfort to us in our old age, and they help us to reach it a lot sooner.

In youth we run into difficulties. In old age difficulties run into us.

Years wrinkle the skin, but lack of enthusiasm wrinkles the soul.

Experience is what you've got when you're too old to get a job.

By the time you learn all the lessons of life, you're too old and weak to walk to the head of the class.

The trouble with the Golden Rule is that before men are ready to live by it they have lead in their legs and silver in their hair.

Some of our modern grandmothers are so young and spry they help the Boy Scouts across the street.

Gray hair usually comes along about twenty years after you thought it would make you look distinguished.

We don't stop laughing because we grow old; we grow old because we stop laughing.

In this life the old believe everything, the middle-aged suspect everything, and the young know everything.

Old age is when most of the names in your little black book are doctors.

A senior citizen's "swinging party" is where they spike the punch with Geritol.

It's old age when each day makes you feel two days older.

The trouble with growing old is that there's not much future in it.

Old age has overtaken a man when he has to run to go as fast as he used to walk.

You can recognize the golden years by all the silver in your hair.

Old age is the time of life when one learns what the statute of limitation is all about.

You can tell when you're getting old. Your feet hurt even before you get out of bed.

One nice thing about being old — as the noise level goes up, your hearing goes down.

Old age is when it takes you longer to get over a good time than to have it.

It's wonderful to grow old, if you can remember to stay young while you're doing it.

She wasn't old, but when she lit the candles on her birthday cake, six people passed out from heat exhaustion.

You can tell you're getting old when you sit in a rocking chair and can't get it going.

A senior citizen in Indiana reports, "I'm getting old. I took my first airplane flight yesterday and the stewardess asked if I wanted coffee, tea, or Geritol."

The reason old folks enjoy living in the past is because it's larger than their future.

Old age is when you're willing to get up and give your seat to a lady — and can't.

A sure-fire formula for living to be one hundred — *keep breathing!*

Most women not only respect old age — they approach it with caution.

A Missouri husband said sadly, "It's terrible to grow old alone. My wife hasn't had a birthday for many years."

Old age is when you get enough exercise just trying to stay out of the way.

Growing old is only a state of mind — brought on by gray hairs, false teeth, wrinkles, a pot belly, and an overall feeling of being totally pooped.

The best way to grow old is not to be in a hurry about it.

You have arrived at old age when all you can put your teeth into is a glass.

The best thing about old age is that a person only has to go through it once.

Most old people enjoy living in the past. It's cheaper.

You're getting old when you're on vacation and your energy runs out before your money does.

Old age is unpredictable. You just wake up one morning and you've got it!

One of the nice things about growing old is that, with all the emphasis on youth, you can go pretty much unnoticed.

Old age is when your idea of getting ahead is just to stay even.

Regardless of how many birthdays you've had, you are old if it takes longer to rest than it does to get tired.

Old age is something everybody else reaches before you do.

The worst thing about growing old is having to listen to a lot of advice from one's children.

When saving for old age be sure to lay up a few pleasant memories.

Growing old is no cause for hysteria. The rosebush does not scream when the petals begin to fall.

Some people will never live to be as old as they look.

It's funny how we never get too old to learn some new ways to be foolish.

By the time old people decide it's wise to watch their step, they aren't going anywhere.

Don't resent growing old — many are denied the privilege.

The only way to keep from growing old is to die young.

Old age is that time of life when you don't care where your wife goes, just so you don't have to go with her.

One of the privileges of old age is to relate experiences that nobody will believe and give advice that nobody will follow.

Three things indicate we are getting old. First, the loss of memory — and we can't remember the other two.

One of the nice things about old age is that you can whistle while you brush your teeth.

To make success of old age a fellow sure has to start young.

The trouble with life is that by the time a fellow gets to be an old hand at the game, he starts to lose his grip.

If you can't grow old gracefully, do it any way you can.

All some people do is grow old.

The man who says he's too old to learn new things probably always was.

You are quite old if you can remember when children were strong enough to walk to school.

Old age is when the gleam in your eyes is just the sun shining on your bifocals.

You can't win. When you get too old for pimples, you go right into wrinkles.

The older a man gets, the less room he has in his medicine cabinet.

369

You're getting old when almost everything hurts, and what doesn't hurt doesn't work.

By the time we get old enough not to care what anybody says about us, nobody says anything.

The older we get, the fewer things seem worth waiting in line for.

Old age is the only thing that comes to us without effort.

The best time for a man's ship to come in is before he's too old to navigate.

Grandchildren don't make a man feel old — it's knowing that he's married to a grandmother.

A man is really old when he watches the food instead of the waitress.

To keep young, stay around young people. To get old, try to keep up with them.

The best thing about getting old is that all those things you couldn't have when you were younger, you no longer want.

A sure sign of old age is when you feel your corns more than your oats.

Everybody wants to live a long time, but nobody wants to get old.

Nothing is more disgraceful than that an old man should leave nothing to prove that he has lived a long time, except his years.

The most telling sign of old age is not caring any more.

To avoid old age keep taking on new thoughts and throwing off old habits.

A man is not old as long as he is seeking something worthwhile.

As you grow older you find it takes just about half as long to get tired and twice as long to get rested. The iron in your blood has turned to lead in the seat of your pants.

A man is getting old when he's warned to slow down by his doctor instead of the police.

The one great advantage of growing old is that you can stand for more and fall for less.

Old age is that period when a man is too old to take advice but young enough to give it.

One of the greatest pleasures of growing old is the freedom we enjoy from life insurance salesmen.

We grow old not so much by living, but by losing interest in living.

Why do folks make such a fuss about growing old? All it takes is a little time!

If you're a senior citizen, don't try to keep up with the freshman class.

A woman is getting old when she feels insulted, rather than flattered, by a whistle.

Old age is that time of life when you spend more time talking to your druggist than anyone else.

The only thing worse than growing old is to be denied the privilege.

Old age is a birthday cake where the candle power can't be overcome by wind velocity.

People may grow old gracefully, but seldom gratefully.

The best thing about growing old is that it takes such a long time.

Things would be a lot nicer if antique people were valued as highly as antique furniture.

Many people are like the famous Liberty Bell — old, heavy, and slightly cracked.

About the only thing that comes to him who waits is old age.

Responsibility is like old age in that it is not possible to escape from either of them.

Most of our old folks are against sin. In fact, they're against just about everything they're too old to enjoy.

You're getting old when the girl you smile at thinks you're one of her father's old friends.

Not only are teen-agers a comfort in old age — they help bring it on.

An Idaho man sighed, "At my age, by the time I find temptation, I'm too tired to give in to it."

There was a time when you saved up for your old age; now you save up for April 15th.

What a married couple should save for their old age is each other.

Why is it that wisdom arrives with old age — too late to do us much good?

Old-timers

An old bachelor in Kentucky finally fell in love. He got a cortisone shot so he could propose on bended knees.

Some of those old codgers who keep complaining that things are not what they used to be always forget to include themselves.

An old gentleman in the hospital refused to eat a bowl of quivering jello. Pressed for an explanation by the nurse, he replied, "I'm not going to eat anything that's more nervous than I am."

Old golfers never die. They just tee off and putt away.

According to a number of old-timers, the only thing wrong with government today is the same thing that's always been wrong with it.

Did you hear about the old-timer in Kentucky who drank more than a quart of whiskey a day for sixty years? When he passed away at the age of ninety-seven they tried to cremate him, but he blew up and wrecked the place!

Old-timers can remember when the wonder drugs of the day were quinine and castor oil.

A senior citizen in Nebraska says his memory is so poor he can't even remember all the words to Happy Birthday!

A senior citizen in Indiana reports, "I'm getting old. I took my first airplane flight yesterday and the stewardess asked if I wanted coffee, tea, or Geritol."

On his one hundredth birthday, a salty gentleman in Florida said, "If I'd known I was going to live this long, I'd have taken better care of myself."

An old-timer is one who can remember when a girl with hidden charms hid them.

When old-timers were kids they were lucky to have wall-to-wall floors.

When old-timers were kids they thought a film was obscene if the horse wasn't wearing a saddle.

You can qualify as an old-timer if you can remember when people didn't need any more than a day to do a day's work.

An old-timer is someone who once believed that whatever went up must come down.

You're an old-timer if you can remember when rock was something you did in a chair.

Old-timers well remember when a family that couldn't afford to own a car didn't.

An old-timer is the married man who can remember when the only guided missiles were small vases and rolling pins.

You're an old-timer if you can remember when just about the only laborsaving device was Sunday.

An old-timer is one who can remember when going to the eternal rest didn't mean landing a job with the government.

The old-timer can remember when the only thing bad on TV was the reception.

Old-timers used to say that anyone could become president, and sometimes it looks like they were right.

Grandpa is living in the past. He's three generations behind in his cussin'.

Opinions

Most people, when they come to you for advice, want their opinions strengthened, not corrected.

Have you ever noticed that the most conceited person is one whose opinions differ from your own?

People generally have too many opinions and not enough convictions.

Every man has a right to his opinion, but no man has a right to be wrong about the facts.

Fact is fact and feeling is feeling; never does the second change the first.

Facts do not change; feelings do.

A fanatic is one who can't change his opinions and won't change the subject.

There are two kinds of fools: those who can't change their opinions, and those who won't.

One of the marks of a gentleman is his refusal to make an issue out of every difference of opinion.

A hick town is usually a place that is divided by a railroad, a main street, two churches, and a lot of opinions.

You will make a mistake if you judge a man by his opinion of himself.

Many people think they are broad-minded just because they are too lazy to form an opinion.

A fellow can't keep people from having a bad opinion of him, but he can keep them from being right about it.

Man is never as hard of hearing as when his opinions are being challenged.

A foolish opinion shared by thousands is still a foolish opinion.

Only the foolish and the dead never change their opinions.

A man is getting along on the road to wisdom when he begins to realize that his opinion is just an opinion.

Always listen to the opinions of others. It may not do you much good but it will them.

Public opinion is what folks think folks think.

It's a lot easier to form an opinion when you have only a few of the facts.

Some people never change their opinions because they've been in the family for generations.

Every man has a right to his opinion — if it parallels ours!

Many opinions which are expressed should have gone by slow freight.

We may ask for information, but we are usually only interested in what confirms our opinions.

It is a sign of mediocrity to have settled opinions on unsettled subjects.

Public opinion is private gossip which has reached epidemic proportions.

An obstinate man does not hold opinions — they hold him.

About the only opinions that do not eventually change are the ones we have about ourselves.

The man who has strong opinions and always says what he thinks is courageous — and friendless.

An opinion is usually a prejudice with a few unrelated facts.

The quickest way to kindle a fire is to rub two opposing opinions together.

Everyone has the right to express an opinion; however, no one has the right to expect everyone to listen.

A wise man gives other people's opinions as much weight as he does his own.

Public opinion is the greatest force for good — when it happens to be on that side.

Risk little on the opinion of a man who has nothing to lose.

A great deal of laziness of mind is called liberty of opinion.

An opinion is often a minimum of facts combined with prejudice and emotion.

Our present generation is so smart it can form an opinion without consulting any of the facts.

The man who has a good opinion of himself is usually a poor judge.

Public opinion is just private opinion that makes enough noise to be heard.

Prejudice is a great timesaver. It enables you to form opinions without bothering to get the facts.

You're prejudiced when you weigh the facts with your thumb on the scales.

Your reputation can be damaged by the opinions of others. Only you yourself can damage your character.

One of the most difficult secrets for a man to keep is his opinion of himself.

Opportunity

There is far more opportunity than there is ability.

A small town newspaper in Texas advertised, "Read your Bible to know what people ought to do. Read this paper to know what they actually do."

America is a land of opportunity. Everybody can become a taxpayer.

Good behavior gets a lot of credit that really belongs to a lack of opportunity.

Be grateful for the doors of opportunity — and for friends who oil the hinges.

When opportunity knocks a grumbler complains about the noise.

Sometimes it's difficult to know who's knocking — opportunity or temptation.

This would be a better world if we'd let opportunity do all the knocking.

Opportunity never knocks at the door of a knocker.

It might not be opportunity you hear knocking — it could be one of your relatives!

Life is full of golden opportunities for doing what we don't want to do.

Luck is what happens when preparation meets opportunity.

Of course this is the land of opportunity. Where else do you have the chance to buy so many things you can't pay for?

Opportunity usually knocks but once, and that may be the reason it has a better reputation than other knockers.

It's easier to open the door of opportunity after you have a key position.

If opportunity came in the form of a temptation, knocking once would be sufficient.

A wise man will make more opportunities than he finds.

An opportunist hears opportunity at the door before it knocks.

No business opportunity is ever lost. If you fumble it your competitor will find it.

Did you ever notice how many "once-in-a-lifetime opportunities" you can do without?

You probably won't hear opportunity knock if the television set is always on.

Many of us have heard opportunity knocking at our door, but by the time we unhooked the chain, pushed back the bolt, turned two locks, and shut off the burglar alarm — it was gone!

God makes opportunities, but He expects us to hunt for them.

Why don't we jump at opportunities as quickly as we jump to conclusions?

This is still the land of opportunity. Where else could you earn enough to pay the interest on what you owe?

Life is full of hard knocks, but answer them all. One might be opportunity.

When you have a chance to embrace an opportunity, give it a big hug.

A great opportunity will only make you look ridiculous unless you are prepared to meet it.

Opportunities are often missed because we are broadcasting when we should be listening.

The reason a lot of people can't find opportunity is that it is often disguised as hard work.

Never neglect the opportunity of keeping your mouth shut.

Even when opportunity knocks, a man still has to get off his seat and open the door.

Great opportunities come to those who make the most of small ones.

Opportunity is a good deal more conspicuous on the way out than on the way in.

You don't have to be in a key position to open the door of opportunity.

Many a man creates his own lack of opportunities.

Many people seem to think that opportunity means a chance to get money without earning it.

The gates of opportunity swing on four hinges: initiative, insight, industry, and integrity.

Those who wait for opportunities to turn up usually find themselves turned down.

For the modern girl, opportunity doesn't knock. It parks in front of her home and honks the horn.

Never waste time reflecting on opportunities you have missed. While thus reflecting you might miss some more.

Opportunity has the uncanny habit of favoring those who have paid the price of years of preparation.

Between tomorrow's dream and yesterday's regret is today's opportunity.

Weak men wait for opportunities; strong men make them.

Opportunity does not batter the door off its hinges when it knocks.

In the orchard of opportunity, it is better to pick the fruit than to wait for it to fall.

Opportunity does not send letters of introduction.

There is no point in going back to look for lost opportunities — someone else has found them.

If you create the circumstances, opportunity will knock more than once upon your door.

Once an opportunity has passed, it cannot be caught.

The door of opportunity is opened by pushing.

Opportunity does knock sometimes, but most of the time it's just a salesman.

Too many men are out in the backyard looking for four-leaf clover when opportunity knocks at their front door.

Opportunities drop in your lap if you have your lap where opportunities drop.

We are seldom able to see an opportunity until it has ceased to be one.

Opportunity has been described as a baldheaded man with a lock of hair in front. If you don't grab it as it approaches, you can't grab it at all.

Many a man has turned and left the dock just before his ship came in.

For some reason a pessimist always complains about the noise when opportunity knocks.

Procrastination is the grave in which opportunity is buried.

If the knock at the door is loud and long, it isn't opportunity. It's relatives.

The reason some men don't go very far in life is that they sidestep opportunity and shake hands with temptation.

Opportunity has to knock, but it is enough for temptation to stand outside and whistle.

Temptations, unlike opportunities, will always give you a second chance.

Every child comes into the world endowed with liberty, opportunity, and a share of the war debt.

Optimists

Better a bald head than none at all.

A good business manager hires optimists as salesmen and pessimists to run the credit department.

Keep your face to the sunshine and you will never see the shadows.

Remember the steam kettle! Though up to its neck in hot water, it continues to sing.

Few cases of eyestrain have been developed by looking on the bright side of things.

The typical fisherman is long on optimism and short on memory.

You can't have rosy thoughts about the future when your mind is full of the blues about the past.

We all hope for the best, but an optimist actually expects to get it.

Nowadays an optimist is any supermarket customer who holds out his hand for the change.

An optimist is a fisherman who takes along a camera.

Optimism is man's passport to a better tomorrow.

The trouble with being optimistic is that some people will think you're illiterate.

If you see good in everything, you may be an optimist. On the other hand, you may be nuts.

A real optimist is the husband who goes to the marriage bureau to see if his license has expired.

Have you noticed that an optimist is always able to see the bright side of other people's troubles?

An optimist is a young man who hurries because he thinks his date is ready and waiting for him.

The greatest of all optimists is the man who proclaims we live in the best of worlds. The pessimist fears that such is true.

Don't try to be too optimistic; it's impossible to smile and whistle at the same time.

The optimist says his glass is half full; the pessimist says his glass is half empty.

An optimist tells you to cheer up — especially when things are going his way.

The trouble with being an optimist is that people think you don't know what's going on.

An optimist is often as wrong as the pessimist, but he has a lot more fun.

Optimism is often the determination to see more in something than is there.

An optimist looks at an oyster and expects a pearl; the pessimist expects ptomaine poison.

Optimists count their blessings; pessimists discount theirs.

An optimist is a fellow who's happy thinking how unhappy he would be if he weren't optimistic.

The woman who starts putting on her shoes when the preacher says, "And now in conclusion," is a real optimist.

An optimist thinks the woman in the phone booth will be right out because he heard her say goodby.

A typical optimist knows it's bound to happen — but doesn't think it will happen soon.

An optimist is a person who's cheerful about other people's worries.

To the optimist, a fireplace is a center of warmth and beauty. To the pessimist, it is a source of smoke and ashes.

A pessimist has no motor; an optimist has no brakes.

A successful man is one who has the horsepower of an optimist and the emergency brakes of a pessimist.

Orators

An orator tries to see how long he can talk without saying anything.

To be a successful orator one must be able to cover indefinite facts with infinite words.

A soapbox orator is a speaker who enjoys the advantage of being unhampered by any knowledge of the subject.

What orators lack in depth they make up in length.

The first mistake that some orators make is opening their mouth.

Political orators have no chance of becoming endangered species.

When the commencement orator tells the graduating class that the world is their oyster, he should also explain the difficulty of cracking the shell.

Oratory

Political oratory is an art in which nothing you say reveals the fact that you're saying nothing.

If oratory is a lost art, let's keep it that way.

Speech is silver, silence is golden, and oratory, at the moment, is mainly brass.

God gave eloquence to some, brains to others.

Oratory is the fine art of making deep noises from the chest sound like important messages from the brain.

Trying to settle a problem with oratory is like attempting to unsnarl a traffic jam by blowing horns.

The object of oratory is not truth but persuasion.

Too much oratory is quite "boratory."

P

Parents
Parking
Parties
Patience
Patriotism
Peace
Pedestrians
People
Perfection
Perseverance
Personality
Perspective
Pessimists
Philanthropists
Philosophy
Physicians

Pleasure
Poise
Politeness
Political Platforms
Politicians
Politics
Pollution
Popularity
Popular Songs
Postal Service
Poverty
Power
Praise
Prayer
Preachers

Preaching
Prejudice
Preparation
Pride
Principles
Problems
Procrastination
Profanity
Progress
Promises
Prosperity
Psychiatrists
Psychology
Public Speakers
Punctuality

Parents

Adolescence is when children start bringing up their parents.

Adolescence is the period when children are certain they will never be as stupid as their parents.

Adolescence is a period of rapid change. Between the ages of twelve and seventeen, for example, a child may see his parents age twenty years.

When a child pays attention to his parents, they're probably whispering.

Most of us want other people's children to behave the way ours should.

A father is usually more pleased to have his child look like him than act like him.

The behavior of some children suggests that their parents embarked on the sea of matrimony without a paddle.

More boys would follow in their father's footsteps if they weren't afraid of being caught.

Having your boy follow in your footsteps can be very disconcerting, especially when you *think* you've covered your tracks — but aren't absolutely certain.

The footsteps a boy follows are apt to be those his father thought he'd covered up.

Too often an abandoned child is one who is still living with his parents.

An unusual child is one who asks his parents questions they can answer.

The only thing that children wear out faster than shoes are parents and teachers.

Next year 3 1/2 million kids will turn sixteen, and 7 million parents will turn pale.

Children will be children — even after they are fifty years old.

Some children are running everything around the house except errands.

Infant prodigies are young people with highly imaginative parents.

There are no illegitimate children — only illegitimate parents.

One reason so many children are seen on the streets at night is because they're afraid to stay home alone.

Modern parents think children should be seen, not heard; children think parents should be neither seen nor heard.

What most children learn by doing is how to drive their parents almost crazy.

Many children would take after their parents if they knew where they went.

Children always know when company is in the living room — they can hear their mother laughing at their father's jokes.

To train children at home, it's necessary for both the children and the parents to spend some time there.

Christmas shopping should include buying toys for the children that their father would enjoy playing with.

It's possible that a college education doesn't always pay off, but that doesn't release dad from his financial obligation.

A college education is very educational. It teaches the parents of the student how to do without a lot of things.

A college boy in Ohio reported to his parents that he was about to flunk out — because he found out he had a klinker in his thinker.

Advice to college students: Be kind to your parents. After sending you through college, you're all they have left.

College debts are obligations that with diligence, economy, and stern self-denial, father will be able to pay.

A diplomat is a parent with two boys on different Little League teams.

With as many divorces as we have nowadays, it seems that more parents are running away from home than children.

Education is something you get when your father sends you to college, but it isn't complete until you send your own son.

The extravagant girl usually makes a poor mother and a bankrupt father.

The parents gave their daughter a new car as a birthday present. On the windshield was a card signed, "With all our love. Mama and Pauper."

Some girls are so homely they could sue their parents for damages.

Having teen-agers is often what undermines a parent's belief in heredity.

The law of heredity is that all undesirable traits come from the other parent.

One reason for juvenile delinquency is that many parents are raising their children by remote control.

One of the problems of juvenile delinquency is children running away from home. It is entirely possible they may be looking for their parents.

Juvenile delinquency is now defined as a situation where the youngsters stop asking their parents where they came from and start telling them where to go.

One way to curb juvenile delinquency is to take the parents off the streets at night.

If juvenile delinquency gets any worse, parents will have to post a five thousand dollar bail bond everytime a child is born.

The trouble with the average juvenile delinquent is not always apparent — sometimes it's two parents!

Juvenile delinquency is no mystery. Mama is so busy keeping up with the Joneses and Papa is so busy keeping up with Mama that neither of them has any time left for keeping up with John and Mary.

We need tougher child abuse laws — parents have taken enough abuse from their children.

The reason parents don't lead their children in the right direction is because the parents aren't going that way themselves.

The most important thing a father can do for his children is to love their mother.

A real family man is one who looks at his new child as an addition rather than a deduction.

Christ was one child who knew more than His parents — yet He obeyed them.

When all the kids have grown up, married, and moved away, many parents experience a strange new emotion; it's called ecstacy.

Nowadays a parent can remember his son's first haircut — but not his last.

Parents of the long ago were extremely permissive — they permitted their children to work.

Sending children to college educates parents. It teaches them how to do without a lot of things.

Some people make you wish their parents had never met.

Parents are always embarrassed when their children tell lies, but sometimes it's even worse when they tell the truth.

A father who encourages his boy to follow in his footsteps has probably forgotten a few.

Just about the time some parents get their daughters off their hands, they have to start putting their sons-in-law on their feet.

A really good parent is a provider, a counselor, an adviser, and when necessary, a disciplinarian.

Parents of college students get poorer by degrees.

A Kentucky father of a teen-age boy says his hardest job is getting his son to realize that "No" is a complete sentence.

The experienced parent is one who has learned to sleep when the baby isn't looking.

Too many parents tie up their dogs and allow their children to run loose.

All a parent has to do to make a child thirsty is to fall asleep.

It's beginning to look like America has too many parttime parents.

The ability to say no is perhaps the greatest gift a parent has.

The modern father wants his son to have all the things he never had — such as straight A's on his report card.

Parents are people who bear infants, bore teen-agers, and board newlyweds.

Some parents begin with giving in and end with giving up.

Parents would not have to worry so much about how a kid turns out if they worried more about when he turns in.

The accent may be on youth these days, but the stress is still on the parents.

Parenthood is a gamble. You never know how far you're going to be driven out of your mind.

You have to give American parents credit — they know how to obey their children.

Did you hear about the father who fainted when his son asked for the keys to the garage and came out with the lawn mower?

The best thing that parents can spend on their children is time — not money.

Nothing worries a parent more than the uneasy feeling that his children are relying more on his example than his advice.

The frightening thing about heredity and environment is that parents provide both.

Parents of the modern generation talk as if they had nothing to do with it.

Some parents could do more for their children by not doing so much for them.

Nothing discourages parenthood more than driving a school bus.

Parents who have fine children usually have children who have fine parents.

Parents of children studying the "new math" not only don't know the answers, they can't even understand the questions.

The best time for parents to put their children to bed is while they still have the strength.

The best inheritance parents can leave a child is a good name.

A father expects his son to be as good as he meant to be.

There was a time when parents taught their children the value of a dollar. Today they try to keep the bad news from the kids as long as possible.

The average father is one who wears out a pair of shoes while the rest of the family wears out a set of tires.

Among those things which are so simple that even a child can operate them are parents.

Parents these days don't bring up their children — they finance them.

Most parents of teen-agers seem to agree that one "hang-up" their kids don't have is when on the telephone.

Probably the most cruel thing a parent can do these days is to push a bright child through school too fast. What if he arrives in college too young to grow a beard?

Mother to father about their rebellious son, "And to think we planned him."

A father is often a man who is working his son's way through college.

This electronic age has its drawbacks. Parents who once showed you their kids' pictures now bore you with their tape recordings.

Psychologists tell us today's parents have trouble communicating with their children. For a starter, how about turning down the stereo?

The psychiatrist who urges parents to spend more time with their children may just be trying to drum up more business!

It's incredible when we think how little our parents knew about child psychology and how wonderful we turned out to be!

Child psychology is what children manage their parents with.

It seems that Satan first makes friends with the parents to make it easier to get their boys and girls.

School days can be the happiest days of your life — if your kids are old enough to attend.

The creatures that sleep standing up are horses and fathers of month old babies.

A problem teen-ager is one who refuses to let his parents use the car.

The main problem with teen-agers is that they're just like their parents were at their age.

The average teen-ager still has all the faults his parents outgrew.

Before dealing too harshly with our teen-agers, let's remember who reared them.

Nothing seems to make a wedding so expensive as being the father of the bride.

A father in Georgia called his local IRS office to ask if he could deduct the cost of his daughter's wedding as a "total loss"?

After paying for the wedding, about the only thing a father has left to give away is the bride.

This country would be much better off if more parents stopped sowing wild oats and started cultivating their children.

Father must work for two reasons: Christmas and vacation.

Many modern dads worry more about their golf swing than they do their offspring.

381

At a certain period in the life of every youth, he wonders how such dull parents produced such a bright child.

Parking

Once it was ambition that kept people on the move. Now it's no parking signs.

America has drive-in theaters, drive-in supermarkets, drive-in restaurants, and drive-in banks. What it needs now are more drive-in parking places.

Most Americans are vitally interested in space problems — especially parking and closet.

The nicest looking car is the one pulling out of a parking space you want.

Don't get discouraged and sell your car. Any day now you may find a place to park it.

There was a time when you could rent a car for a week for what it now costs to park it for a day.

It's reported that some of last year's cars haven't yet found parking places.

The used car business is on the boom. Old cars that no longer run are rented to young couples who just want to park.

There are still a few people who can remember when it cost more to operate a car than to park it.

Always look at the brighter side of things — whenever a car is stolen, it creates another parking place.

One of the best bargains you can get these days is parking on what's left of the other fellow's dime.

A teen-age boy is at that awkward age. He likes to park but he doesn't know exactly why.

The children of today think they have it rough in school if they have to walk more than a block to park their cars.

Nothing destroys the Christmas spirit faster than looking for a place to park.

If Congress really wants to help the auto industry sell more cars, it should start building more parking lots.

A smart girl knows all the hazards of parking.

A hick town is where you can park as long as you want to, but don't want to.

The course of true love never runs — it stops and parks!

Nowadays when a motorist goes looking for a parking place, it's a good idea to have someone go along to share the driving.

Do you remember the politician who promised two cars in every garage? We've come close to that now — we have two cars for every parking space.

What most people pray for when they arrive at church on Sunday is a parking place.

Despite the promises of politicians, we'll never achieve an equal and satisfactory distribution of wealth, rainfall, or parking space.

A rumor is afloat that we have a new trade agreement with Russia. We will send them 10,000 automobiles from Detroit, and they will send us 20,000 parking spaces from Siberia.

We have more cars in the United States, but Russia has more vacant parking places.

Few things in life are more satisfying than parking on what's left of the other person's dime.

Driving schools no longer teach their students how to park. They consider it a waste of time.

Science says the world's population will have doubled in twenty years — which means one thing, you'd better find a parking place fast.

The thing that most teen-age drivers dislike about parking is the noisy crash.

The way traffic is today, instead of getting a ticket for parking you ought to get a medal.

The woman driver wouldn't have so much trouble squeezing into a parking place if she'd just imagine it was a girdle or a pair of shoes.

The thing that most women dislike about parking is the noisy crash.

A woman learning to drive a car is making progress when she can park the front end of the car.

Parties

Naturalists who claim America's wildlife is disappearing don't stay up very late at night.

Sign in a liquor store: "Preserve wild life — throw a party."

A cocktail party is an excuse to drink for people who don't need any excuse.

It used to be when we saw our neighbor's light on late at night we wondered if there was sickness. Now we wonder if there is a party we didn't get invited to.

Nothing makes you more tolerant of a neighbor's noisy party than being invited to it.

A senior citizen's "swinging party" is where they spike the punch with Geritol.

It's what the guests say after they leave the party that counts.

Some parties are formal; at others you wear your own clothes.

The success of a big party is usually measured by the money that is wasted.

The life of the average party is usually the fellow who is full of sex-temporaneous stories.

The three major parties in the United States are the Democratic party, the Republican party, and the cocktail party.

The life of the party is the person who can talk louder and longer than the radio or television.

Patience

Better be patient on the road than a patient in the hospital.

Patience, forbearance, and understanding are companions to contentment.

You have to have patience on a diet — especially if it's your wife who's on it.

Be patient with the faults of others; they may have to be patient with yours.

God makes a promise — faith believes it, hope anticipates it, patience quietly awaits it.

Happy homes are built with blocks of patience.

Some people who get credit for being patient are just too lazy to start anything.

The true measure of a man is the height of his ideals, the breadth of his sympathy, the depth of his convictions, and the length of his patience.

What a mother should save for a rainy day is patience.

If folks had more patience the hospitals wouldn't have so many patients.

Sign in a Texas country store: "Be patient. None of us am perfect."

You never realize how patient you can be until the fellow who is arguing with you is your boss.

Job was a man of great patience, but he never had to wait for a Social Security check.

Lack of pep is often mistaken for patience.

Even a waiter finally comes to him who waits.

Wait patiently and sooner or later something will turn up — your nose, your toes, or both.

The trouble with people today is that they want to get to the promised land without going through the wilderness.

Many a man has turned and left the dock just before his ship came in.

Patience is when you listen silently to someone tell about the same operation you had.

This would be a wonderful world if men showed as much patience in all things as they do in waiting for a fish to bite.

Patience is a quality that is most needed when it is exhausted.

The trouble with patience is the more a fellow has, the more folks want to use it.

Patience is the art of concealing your impatience.

You should bear with people because they have to bear with you.

Patience is the ability to throttle your motor when you feel like stripping the gears.

It's easy finding reasons why other folks should be patient.

A mother's patience is like a tube of toothpaste — it's never quite all gone.

Sometimes a handful of patience is worth more than a bucket full of brains.

Patience is often bitter, but its fruit is sweet.

Nothing worthwhile ever happens in a hurry — so be patient!

Patience is the ability to remain silent and hungry while everybody else in the restaurant gets served.

A patient man is one who can put up with himself.

Have patience. If you pluck the blossoms, you must do without the fruit.

You can accomplish almost anything if you have patience. You can even carry water in a sieve if you wait until it freezes.

Patience is the ability to count down before blasting off.

Nothing worthwhile is achieved without patience, labor, and disappointment.

Patience strengthens the spirit, sweetens the temper, stifles anger, subdues pride, and bridles the tongue.

Like farmers we need to learn that we can't sow and reap the same day.

Patience is the greatest of all shock absorbers. About the only thing you can get in a hurry is trouble.

About the only thing you can get without patience is impatient.

Patience may be simply the inability to make decisions.

True patience means waiting without worrying.

Be patient. You get the chicken by hatching the egg — not by smashing it open.

It just may be that our hospitals would have fewer pedestrian patients if there were more patient pedestrians.

Everything we have is taxed — even our patience.

In the near future Congress is expected to raise the legal limit on the taxpayer's patience.

It's getting to where even the taxpayer's patience is being taxed.

Patriotism

The way to get ahead of Russia is to get behind America.

Americans are endowed with certain inalienable rights, but if we don't stick up for them somebody will come along and un-endow them.

A patriotic American likes to discuss the Constitution of the United States despite the fact he has never taken the time to read it.

A patriotic American never orders anything from a menu that he can't spell.

Many Americans love their country for the same reason a farmer loves his cow — because they can milk it.

Patriotism is the willingness to make any sacrifice as long as it won't hurt business.

Asking your boss for a raise is really a patriotic duty since the government needs that additional tax on your salary.

When patriotism becomes a dirty word, a nation is ready to be taken to the cleaners.

True patriotism is your conviction that this country is superior to all others because you were born in it!

Patriotism will probably never develop to the point of parading in honor of the "unknown taxpayer."

Some people *wave* the American flag but *waive* what it stands for.

A wit in Nebraska says patriotism is that pain you feel in your neck when a foreigner wins a championship.

A man's country is not just a certain area of land. It is a principle, and patriotism is loyalty to that principle.

True patriotism should make the heart beat faster and the tongue wag slower.

A dyed-in-the-wool patriot is one who says he's sorry he has only one income to give to his country.

A patriot is the fellow who is always ready and willing to lay down your life for his country.

A patriot is a man working for his country's future instead of boasting of its past.

The real patriot is a person who saves enough of his salary each week to pay his income tax.

An appeal to patriotism seems to be the last refuge of a politician who doesn't know what else to say.

Peace

Christmas carolers sing about peace on earth, but they don't tell us where.

Some members of Congress would best promote the country's peace by holding their own.

Diplomacy couldn't prevent the last war, but it usually does a good job of preventing the peace.

One good hearty laugh together could be the greatest insurance of lasting peace that men of all nations could contrive.

The amazing thing about a man being arrested for disturbing the peace these days is that he found any.

In spite of all the plans for world peace, there will probably be the usual number of June weddings.

It seems that perfect peace can be found only in the cemetery.

Peace may cost as much as war, but it's a better buy.

What the world needs is peace that passes all misunderstanding.

Peace is a period of international truce when haggling and cheating replace fighting.

When a man finds no peace within himself, it is useless to seek it elsewhere.

Keeping peace in the family requires patience, love, understanding, and at least two television sets.

There's just one sure way to find *peace* — in the dictionary.

The dove of peace still finds the world covered with the waters of hate and jealousy.

Peace is not made in documents, but in the hearts of men.

There can be no peace in the world until the caliber of its statesmen is equal to the caliber of its guns.

Even peace may be purchased at too high a price.

Another argument in favor of lasting peace is that it would give us time to finish paying for the last war.

Thousands of Americans are trying to find peace in a pill.

Peace is a period of confusion and unrest between two wars.

Perpetual peace seems as far removed as perpetual motion.

Peace won by the compromise of principles is a short-lived achievement.

There will be no peace as long as God remains unseated at the conference table.

Peace is a thing you can't achieve by throwing rocks at a hornet's nest.

It's hard to find lasting peace as long as there are more dogs than bones.

The highest honor that could be paid to the "Unknown Soldier" would be to not have any more of them in the future.

What the nations of the world need is a peace conference with the "Prince of Peace."

About all we see of the dove of peace these days is the bill.

The new era of peace will begin when somebody invents a way to get all the axes on the grindstone at the same time.

Before the next peace conference it might be advisable to hold a few rehearsals.

General Sherman defined war as hell, but the definition of a modern peace is unprintable.

Peace can be achieved by the substitution of reason for force, right for might, law for war.

A means to a permanent peace is for all nations to agree not to start another war until the last one is paid for.

Domestic peace is the luxury you enjoy between the children's bedtime and your own.

There are always two sides to a peace conference — but no end.

The key to lasting peace is to rely less on arms and more on heads.

As we bargain for peace let us remember there will be no refunds on lives given toward the same purpose.

The best place to hold productive peace conferences is a few hundred yards behind the lines of battle.

The world will never be the dwelling place of peace until peace has found a home in the heart of each and every man.

The aim of some men is to have peace in the world, but others would settle just to have peace in the family.

A "peace rally" is as much of a misnomer as a "slumber party."

The greater the philosopher, the more difficult it is for him to answer the questions of the average man.

If nations began telling each other nothing but the truth, peace would immediately vanish from the earth.

History has seen wars which used up less ammunition than a cease-fire does today.

Washington has a large assortment of peace monuments. They build one after every war.

Pedestrians

Some accidents are caused by two motorists aiming at the same pedestrian.

The automobile has certainly discouraged walking, particularly among pedestrians.

Automobiles did away with horses and now they're working on people.

The springs of the late-model cars are of such high quality that you can hardly feel the bump when you run over a pedestrian.

There are few Americans who have never seen an automobile, but plenty who have not seen one soon enough.

It is estimated that by 1985 there will be more than 190 million automobiles in the United States. If you want to cross the street, you'd better do it now.

An automobile has been described as a four-wheeled vehicle that runs up hills and down pedestrians.

Driver! Please give the pedestrian a break instead of a fracture.

We had complete confidence in reaching the moon. Now if we could only feel the same way about getting to the other side of the street.

Walking is good exercise if you can dodge those who aren't.

Golf is a good game. It gives a fellow a chance to be a pedestrian without the danger of being run over.

The value of horse sense is shown by the fact that the horse was afraid of the automobile at the time the pedestrian laughed at it.

American motorists take the best possible care of their cars — and they keep pedestrians in good running condition too.

The only reason some motorists slow down for pedestrians is because they're afraid they'll damage their cars.

Quite often a motorist will knock a pedestrian down because his windshield is obscured by safety stickers.

An expert has predicted that in twenty years every motorist will be flying. And by that time every pedestrian will be playing a harp.

A motorist recently admitted running over the same man twice. The time evidently has come when there aren't enough pedestrians to go around.

It's strange that a motorist never remembers he was once a pedestrian.

A good way to get your name in the newspaper is to cross the street reading one.

A pedestrian may be wrong but he doesn't deserve the death penalty.

In certain parts of the world the people pray in the streets. In this country they are known as pedestrians.

Don't run over a pedestrian. He may be on his way to take his car out of a parking space.

The pedestrian may soon be added to the list of endangered species.

Another good way to learn to think fast on your feet is to be a pedestrian.

Anyone who tries to be a rugged individualist and a pedestrian at the same time has a limited future.

For most of us life is what we make it, but for the pedestrian it's *if* he makes it.

Recent figures show more accidents but fewer fatalities. The drivers are no more careful than usual, but pedestrians are getting tougher.

Automobile dealers say that motorists are demanding lighter cars. So are the pedestrians.

The law gives the pedestrian the right-of-way but makes no provision for flowers.

What pedestrians need more than just traffic rules are wings — and sometimes they get them.

The pedestrian who allows the grass to grow under his feet soon finds it growing over his head.

One reason why so many pedestrians don't look where they're going is because they're in an ambulance.

All that pedestrians ask is a little more cooperation between horsepower and horse sense.

About all the pedestrian can hope for nowadays is to be only slightly injured.

The only person who genuinely and sincerely believes in safe driving is the pedestrian.

One traffic hazard that drivers seem determined to eliminate is the pedestrian.

It just may be that our hospitals would have fewer pedestrian patients if there were more patient pedestrians.

Give a pedestrian an inch and he'll take a chance.

In the old days a man who "died with his boots on" was known as a bad man. Now he's a pedestrian.

The wise thing for a pedestrian to do is to get a suit of armor, insure his life, and then stay at home.

If evolution works, nature will eventually produce a pedestrian who can jump three ways at once.

One nice thing about being a pedestrian is that it's easy to find a parking place.

A pedestrian is someone on his way from where he had to park to where he has to go.

Scientists show us how to sail under the North Pole, and fly over the moon, but you're on your own when you cross the street.

Another good way to learn to think fast on your feet is to be a pedestrian.

Traffic is so slow in some large cities that if a driver wants to hit a pedestrian he has to get out of his car to do it.

People

No matter what you do, someone always knew you would.

There are two kinds of people in your church: those who agree with you and the bigots.

A college professor in Michigan says he has found five different kinds of dumbness. It seems incredible that an educated man like that should have met so few people.

A committee is composed of five persons — one does the work, three give him moral support, and the fifth gives the story to the newspapers.

A committee usually consists of three persons, each of whom thinks the others talk a lot of nonsense.

There are only two kinds of egotists — those who admit it and the rest of us.

God cares for people through people.

The person who looks up to God rarely looks down on people.

There is a mad scramble to improve just about everything in the world except people.

Laugh with people — not at them.

When you laugh, be sure to laugh at what people do and not at what people are.

Laws are no stronger than the devotion to them by the people who live under them.

When you come right down to it, the problem isn't alcohol — it's the people who drink it.

A first-class mistake is to treat anyone as a second-class person.

Money not only changes hands — it changes people.

People are funny. They spend money they don't have to buy things they don't need to impress people they don't like.

You can't tell if some people are the strong silent type or just plain dumb.

The trouble with many people is they stop faster than they start.

Quiet people aren't the only ones who don't say much.

A lot of people consider themselves ahead of the times when they aren't even going in the same direction.

There are some people who can't tell a lie, some who can't tell the truth, and a few others who can't tell the difference.

Many people are flexible. They can put either foot in their mouth.

People with a lot of brass are seldom polished.

When you give some people an even break they feel cheated.

The only time some people don't interrupt is when you're praising them.

Some people never get interested in anything unless it's none of their business.

Have you noticed that certain people have gear trouble? They talk in high and think in low.

Many people don't get ulcers — they're only carriers.

It's not difficult to pick out the best people. They'll help you do it.

All some people want is their fair share — and yours too.

There are two kinds of people: those who think there are two kinds of people, and those who think it's not that simple.

People who are carried away by their own importance seldom have far to walk back.

No two people are alike — and both of them are glad of it.

People who say they don't get all they deserve probably don't know how lucky they are.

Things would be a lot nicer if antique people were valued as highly as antique furniture.

Many people would like to be respected without having to be respectable.

There must be a lot of good in some people because very little of it ever comes out.

Have you noticed that many people have flat feet — and heads to match?

Many people never learn to relax. Others never learn anything else.

It's useless to try to hold some people to anything they say while they're madly in love, drunk, or running for office.

Most people are willing to change, not because they see the light, but because they feel the heat.

People who talk about things they can't afford often forget to include pride, envy, and malice.

There are two kinds of people — the "haves" and the "have nots." Or to put it more simply — wives and husbands.

All many people want out of life is a little unfair advantage.

Isn't it strange that so many folks have no sense of direction? They even get lost going up an escalator.

Nothing is something many people are good for.

People who do the most for the world's advancement are the ones who demand the least.

There are a few people among us who are like boats — they toot the loudest when in a fog.

People will fight for everything that's coming to them — whether they want it or not.

There are more self-marred people in the world than self-made.

Many people look ahead, some look back, but most look confused.

It's too bad that more people are thoughtless than speechless.

About the only things impossible these days are some people.

In looking over people, you find there are many you would rather overlook.

There are two types of people who'll tell you there are better places to be than where you are — real-estate salesmen and preachers.

A lot of people would pull their weight if some weren't so busy dragging their feet.

People should not forget the mama whale's advice to the baby whale, "Remember, it's only when you spout that you get harpooned."

People are great manufacturers. Some make good, others make trouble, and some just make excuses.

Many people don't do anything on time, except buy.

There are two types of people who say very little: the quiet ones and the gabby ones.

The trouble with some people is that during trying times they stop trying.

It is generally agreed that some people are wise and some otherwise.

Those who think they are dreamers are usually just sleepers.

People are certainly funny — they want to be in the front of the bus, in the back of the church, and in the middle of the road.

The people who think they're bearing a cross are only putting up with themselves as best they can.

It's so sad that people are like plants — some go to seed with age and others go to pot.

People generally look too high for things close by.

Everything people want to do is either illegal, immoral, or fattening.

People who say they sleep like a baby haven't got one.

A radical person is one who insists on convincing us instead of letting us convince him.

With some people you spend an evening; with others you invest it.

The most reliable thing about some people is the assurance they will be unreliable.

You can't fool all the people all the time, but that doesn't keep some people from trying.

The human race seems to be improving everything except people.

Many people are like wheelbarrows, trailers, or canoes. They need to be pushed, pulled, or paddled.

The distance between some people's ears is one block.

Some people can stay longer in an hour than others can in a week.

If you wish to get along with people, pretend not to know whatever they tell you.

You would be surprised to know how many people are like a brass drum — with plenty of noise, but nothing on the inside.

It's sad when a person has a head like a doorknob — anybody can turn it.

It takes too long for some people to start to begin to commence to get ready.

There are still a few people who believe in gittin' up and gittin', while a great many prefer sittin' down and sittin'.

People who look back know where they've been but not where they're going.

While some people rise to the pinnacle of fame, others reach the height of folly.

A move is under way to abolish the exclamation point. People aren't surprised at anything any more.

There is very little difference between people, but the little difference there is makes all the difference in the world.

Most people like the old days best — they were younger then.

It would be interesting to know the number of people who pride themselves on the ability to find corruption. So does the vulture.

People are the main thing wrong with the world.

Many people who try to use the weekend to unwind simply unravel.

People differ. Some object to the fan dancer, and others to the fan.

The world is full of people making a good living but poor lives.

It's not the difference between people that's the difficulty. It's the indifference.

It's quite obvious that what makes some people tick needs winding.

People who are always walking on clouds leave too many things up in the air.

A lot of people use mighty thin thread when mending their ways.

The only people you should want to get even with are those who have helped you.

More people are flattered into virtue than bullied out of vice.

It's funny thing about some people. They don't want to be treated like everybody else — they want to be treated better.

We all agree that the nicest people in the world are those who minimize our faults and magnify our virtues.

Have you noticed that people who have stopped smoking and drinking haven't stopped talking about it?

Some people don't have enough push to go through a revolving door.

A lot of people do nothing in particular but they do it well.

It's rather strange how so many people go into a summer slump that lasts all winter.

Some people are so ingenious they can complicate simplicity.

It must be a problem for two-faced people to put their best face forward.

There is no perfect solution to any problem with human beings mixed up in it.

The only thing wrong with the world is the people.

The world isn't getting smaller — just some of the people who inhabit it.

If it takes all kinds of people to make a world, it seems as if there are still some we haven't got.

The world is divided into people who do things and people who get the credit.

Perfection

If the church were perfect, you could not belong.

You will never have a friend if you must have one without a fault.

The husband who boasts that he never made a mistake has a wife who did.

None of us is perfect, but the worst of it is that many of us are impossible.

There's only one perfect child in the world and every mother has it.

The only way a man can attain perfection is to follow the advice he gives to others.

A man who knows his imperfections is just about as perfect as anyone can be.

The nearest to perfection that most people ever come is when filling out a job application.

We all know it isn't human to be perfect, and too many of us take advantage of it.

A perfectionist is a person who takes enough pains to give everybody else one.

If biologists are right in their assertion that there is not a perfect man on earth today, a lot of personal opinions will have to be altered.

The person who tells you how perfect he thinks you are will lie to others too.

Being perfect requires a knack for shoving your mistakes off on someone else.

If you insist on perfection, make the first demand on yourself.

Perseverance

There are four steps to accomplishment: Plan purposefully. Prepare prayerfully. Proceed positively. Pursue persistently.

The thing to try when all else fails is again.

Just over the hill is a beautiful valley, but you must climb the hill to see it.

Giving it another try is better than an alibi.

It pays to keep your feet on the ground, but keep them moving.

The man who gets ahead is the man who does more than is necessary — and keeps on doing it.

When things get rough, remember: It's the rubbing that brings out the shine.

Character, like embroidery, is made stitch by stitch.

The best way out of difficulty is through it.

The man who really wants to do something finds a way; the other man finds an excuse.

Many of life's failures are men who did not realize how close they were to success when they gave up.

Stopping at third base adds no more to the score than striking out.

If you have tried your hand at something and failed, the next best thing is to try your head.

Falling down doesn't make you a failure, but staying down does.

Many a man has failed because he has a wishbone where his backbone ought to have been.

The last time you failed, did you stop trying because you failed — or did you fail because you stopped trying?

Failure is the path of least persistence.

Faith either moves mountains or tunnels through.

Often GENIUS is just another way of spelling perseverance.

God often tries us with a little to see what we would do with a lot.

The secret of happiness is to learn to accept the impossible, to do without the indispensable, and to bear the intolerable.

If you can't think up a new idea, try finding a way to make better use of an old one.

The trouble with some people is that during trying times they stop trying.

Stick to your job until one of you is through.

Better the shoulder to the wheel than the back to the wall.

Any man can see farther than he can reach, but this doesn't mean he should quit reaching.

If you get up one time more than you fall, you will make it through.

Perseverance has been defined as sticking to something you're not stuck on.

It is often the last key on the ring that opens the door.

Keep trying. It's only from the valley that the mountain seems high.

Perseverance is the result of a strong will. Obstinacy is the result of a strong "won't."

The man of the hour spent many days and nights getting there.

The road to success runs uphill, so don't expect to break any speed records.

Some men may succeed because they are destined to, but most men succeed because they are determined to.

The basic rules for success may be defined as follows: Know what you want. Find out what it takes to get it. Act on it and persevere.

The secret of success is to start fom scratch and keep on scratching.

If at first you don't succeed, try, try again. Then quit. There's no point in making a fool of yourself.

To succeed — do the best you can, where you are, with what you have.

Working hard means going all out until you're all in.

Personality

Did you hear about the Hollywood actor with so little personality that he appeared on a color TV show and it came out in black and white?

Personality is the art of making people admire in you those qualities which you don't possess.

It's easy to spot a person with a lot of personality — he always reminds you so much of yourself.

Personality is the name we give to our little collection of funny ways.

It's easy to have a balanced personality. Just forget your troubles as easily as you do your blessings.

Personal magnetism is that indefinable something that enables us to get by without ability.

Some people think they have dynamic personalities because they're always exploding.

Perspective

Be big enough to admit and admire the abilities of people who are better than you are.

Just over the hill is a beautiful valley, but you must climb the hill to see it.

If you don't climb the mountain, you can't see the view.

To some young actresses the difference between fame and farm is form.

Advice is never appreciated. If it turns out well, the recipient thinks it was his own idea; and if it turns out badly, he eternally blames the giver.

The greatest danger for most of us is not that our aim is too high and we miss it, but that our aim is too low and we reach it.

An alcoholic is not one who drinks too much, but one who can't drink enough.

The kind of ancestors we have is not as important as the kind of descendents our ancestors have.

The size of a man is measured by the size of the thing that makes him angry.

The difference between antiques and junk depends on who's selling what to whom.

The choice is simple — you can either stand up and be counted, or lie down and be counted out.

No one appreciates the value of constructive criticism more thoroughly than the one who's giving it.

Constructive criticism is when I criticize you. Destructive criticism is when you criticize me.

When a man praises discipline, nine times out of ten this means he is prepared to administer it rather than submit to it.

Think of doubt as an invitation to think.

Duty is a task we look forward to with distaste, perform with reluctance, and brag about afterwards.

An egotist is a man who thinks he's smarter than you are — though you know very well he isn't.

Experience is what tells you to watch your step, and it is also what you get if you don't.

The faults of others are like headlights on a passing car. They seem more glaring than our own.

There is no fool like an old fool. Ask any young fool.

The freedom of slaves is measured by the length of their chains.

If freedom is important when we don't have it, why shouldn't it be just as important when we do have it?

The girl in Mississippi explained the breakup with her boyfriend, "Once he was all the world to me — but I've learned a lot of geography since.

The difference between gossip and news is whether you hear it or tell it.

It isn't your position that makes you happy or unhappy. It's your *disposition.*

Happiness does not come from what you have, but from what you are.

Hatred is a boomerang which is sure to hit you harder than the one at whom you throw it.

The relative values of health and wealth depend on which you have left.

The distance from earth to heaven is not so much a matter of altitude as it is attitude.

A genuine sense of.humor is the pole that adds balance to our steps as we walk the tightrope of life.

Getting a husband is like buying a house. You don't see it the way it is, but the way you think it's going to be when you get it remodeled.

A husband is never as good as his wife thought he was before marriage, and never as bad as she thinks him to be after marriage.

The mind stretched by a new idea never returns to its original dimensions.

It's too bad that the only men who can solve the world's problems are too busy sitting on the front porch whittling.

Improvement is what you see a need for in other people, but can't see the same need in yourself.

There are few people who are fast enough to keep up with their good intentions.

Anybody who thinks a joke about a plumber is funny hasn't had a faucet replaced lately.

Judge each day, not by the harvest, but by the seeds you plant.

In judging others it's always wise to see with the heart as well as with the eyes.

A psychologist says kissing is where two people get so close together they can't see anything wrong with each other.

Knowing what's none of your business is just as important as knowing what is.

When you laugh at something that happens to somebody else, that's a sense of humor. If it happens to you, that's an outrage.

Many people believe in law and order as long as they can lay down the law and give the orders.

The man who is able to distinguish between tiredness and laziness in himself will go far.

We can't lead someone else to the light while we are standing in the dark.

Love makes a man think almost as much of a woman as he thinks of himself.

The true measure of a man is the height of his ideals, the breadth of his sympathy, the depth of his convictions, and the length of his patience.

Marriage is the difference between painting the town and painting the back porch.

When you have to swallow your own medicine, the spoon seems very large.

An inexcusable mistake is always made by the other fellow.

Stupid mistakes are made by others — we only make "unavoidable errors."

A person shouldn't be too modest. A light hidden under a bushel is seldom seen and less often appreciated.

The fellow who really understands the value of cold cash is the one whose salary is not so hot.

The most difficult thing for a mother to remember is that other people have perfect children too.

A person is in a tough predicament when he has to face the music with his nose to the grindstone and his back to the wall.

There is no one so narrow as the fellow who disagrees with you.

The best thing about old age is that a person only has to go through it once.

We grow old not so much by living, but by losing interest in living.

We are seldom able to see an opportunity until it has ceased to be one.

Have you noticed that an optimist is always able to see the bright side of other people's troubles?

You never realize how patient you can be until the fellow who is arguing with you is your boss.

Patriotism is the willingness to make any sacrifice as long as it won't hurt business.

There's only one perfect child in the world and every mother has it.

It's easy to spot a person with a lot of personality — he always reminds you so much of yourself.

Many a politician who considers himself far-sighted is a poor judge of distance.

Popularity is a form of success that's seldom worth the things we have to do in order to attain it.

Popularity is a matter of whether people like you wherever you go or like it whenever you leave.

There are two sides to almost every question, and if you wish to be popular you must take both.

Poverty of purpose is worse than poverty of purse.

Prejudice is being down on something you're not up on.

Pride is something we have; vanity is something others have!

A man without principle never draws much interest.

Answers are what we have for other people's problems.

If a man can see both sides of a problem, you know that none of his money is tied up in it.

The trouble with some speakers is that you can't hear what they're saying. The trouble with others is that you can.

Most of us are broad-minded enough to admit there are two sides to every question — our own side, and the side that no intelligent, informed, sane, and self-respecting person could possibly hold.

If your religion leaves your life unchanged, you'd better change your religion.

Reputation is a personal possession, frequently not discovered until lost.

Have you noticed how today's restaurant prices seem to make home cooking taste a lot better?

Revenge may be sweet, but not when you are on the receiving end.

God never alters the robe of righteousness to fit the man, but the man to fit the robe.

It's invariably the little devil in your neighborhood who starts the fight with your little angel.

Silence is what you can't say without breaking it.

If at first you don't succeed, try trying.

The secret of success is to never let down and never let up.

The road to success is dotted with many tempting parking spaces.

Success is a matter of luck and pluck — mostly pluck.

Nowadays a "disaster area" is the supermarket checkout counter.

Tact is the ability to describe others as they see themselves.

A lot of people who talk constantly about capital and labor never had any capital and never did any labor.

Another thing that seems to improve the longer you keep it is your temper.

Nothing makes it easier to resist temptation than a proper upbringing, a sound set of values, and witnesses.

Isn't it aggravating how little value other people put on your time?

Tolerance gets a lot of credit that belongs to apathy.

We admire the truth, provided it agrees with our views.

Many people have ulcers these days — caused by mountain climbing over molehills.

If this age is to be saved, it will be saved by the recovery of the sense of discrimination between what is passing and what is eternal.

The real measure of a man's wealth is how much he would be worth if he lost all his money.

It is better to become bent from hard work than to become crooked without it.

The Lord didn't burden us with work. He blessed us with it.

Look on the world as a big fruit cake. It wouldn't be complete without a few nuts in it.

The world isn't getting smaller — just some of the people who inhabit it.

If you think the world is all wrong, remember that it contains people like you.

Worry often gives a small thing a big shadow.

Let's stop criticizing the younger generation. If we can't keep up with them we can at least get behind them.

You are only young once. After that you merely think you are.

Pessimists

A good business manager hires optimists as salesmen and pessimists to run the credit department.

Current events are so grim that we can't decide whether to watch the six o'clock news and not be able to eat, or the ten o'clock news and not be able to sleep.

The greatest of all optimists is the man who proclaims we live in the best of worlds. The pessimist fears that such is true.

The optimist says his glass is half full; the pessimist says his glass is half empty.

An optimist looks at an oyster and expects a pearl; the pessimist expects ptomaine poison.

Optimists count their blessings; pessimists discount theirs.

Many people aren't pessimists — they're merely discontented optimists.

Pessimism is contagious — you can get it by listening attentively to the six o'clock news.

A pessimist expects nothing on a silver platter except tarnish.

One reason a pessimist isn't very well-liked is that he so often has the opportunity to say, "I told you so."

A California pessimist carries a card in his wallet that reads, "In case of an accident — I'm not surprised."

A pessimist burns his bridges before he gets to them.

Most pessimists are seasick during the entire voyage of their lives.

A pessimist thinks the world is against him — and it is.

It it weren't for the optimist, the pessimist would never know how happy he isn't.

A pessimist can hardly wait for the future so he can look back with regret.

For some reason a pessimist always complains about the noise when opportunity knocks.

With a choice of two evils, the pessimist takes both.

The pessimist is a person who absorbs sunshine and radiates gloom.

When he smells flowers, a pessimist looks around for the funeral.

To the optimist, a fireplace is a center of warmth and beauty. To the pessimist, it is a source of smoke and ashes.

A pessimist actually thinks the chief purpose of sunshine is to cast shadows.

Nothing worries the pessimist like the optimist who says there's nothing to worry about.

With riots, demonstrations, and high taxes, if the pessimists aren't satisfied today they never will be.

To the pessimistic patient, "consultation" means that his doctor has decided to call in an accomplice.

A pessimist has no motor; an optimist has no brakes.

It is impossible to be prayerful and pessimistic at the same time.

A successful man is one who has the horsepower of an optimist and the emergency brakes of a pessimist.

Philanthropists

A philanthropist is a wealthy man whose vanity has temporarily gotten the better of his greed.

An honest philanthropist always atones openly for the wrongs he has done secretly.

If only philanthropists would give it back to the same people they took it from!

Philanthropy is giving your money to people who will appreciate it, rather than leaving it to your relatives.

A philanthropist is one who returns to the people publicly a small amount of the wealth he has stolen from them privately.

Philosophers/Philosophy

If you have to borrow, always borrow from a pessimist. He doesn't expect to be paid anyway.

A philosopher always knows what to do until it happens to him.

The average philosopher is ahead of his time with ideas and behind time with his payments.

A philosopher thinks in order to believe. He formulates his prejudices and systematizes his ignorance.

If you can see yourself as others see you and not get mad, you're a philosopher.

Philosophy is a study which enables men to be unhappy more intelligently.

Philosophy is an orderly way of discussing subjects we don't know anything about.

Philosophy is nothing but common sense in a dress suit.

Philosophy is a science that enables us to view misfortune more calmly, thereby enabling us to be miserable with the greatest possible degree of intelligence.

Philosophy is something rich people use to convince the rest of use that it's no disgrace to be poor.

"Poverty is a state of mind," says the philosopher with a full stomach.

Physicians

Doctors and lawyers are always giving *fee* advice.

As a man gets older he suspects that nature is plotting against him for the benefit of doctors and dentists.

Never argue with your doctor; he has inside information.

On his examination paper a boy wrote, "A natural death is where you die by yourself without a doctor's help."

Nobody likes to criticize the medical profession, *but* — it has failed to conquer the common cold and babies continue to be born at the most outlandish hours.

In these modern times a man is considered out of debt when he owes no more but the doctor and dad.

Human diseases are the same as they were a thousand years ago, but doctors have selected more expensive names for them.

It seems that almost everybody you meet has a cure for the common cold — except your doctor.

You have a very common disease, if you're sick of high doctor fees.

If all men are born free, why doesn't somebody tell the hospitals and doctors about it?

Few of us are proud of our bad habits, but without them there wouldn't be anything for the doctor to tell us to give up when we aren't feeling well.

Specialization has reached such a state today that patients have to learn to diagnose themselves before they know which specialist to call.

Medical doctors measure physical health by how the tongue looks. The Great Physician measures spiritual health by how the tongue acts.

One good place to study ancient history is in a doctor's waiting room.

A real hypochondriac is one who wants to be buried next to a doctor.

A prominent physician says that in fifty years kissing will be unheard of — but in fifty years, who cares?

The lawyer agrees with the doctor that the best things in life are fees.

A group of doctors is trying to develop a cure for laziness. Somebody is always trying to take the joy out of life!

There is entirely too much specialization in medicine. When your head cold moves down to your chest you have to change doctors.

Penicillin is called a "wonder drug" because any time your doctor wonders what you've got, that's what you get.

Money can't buy health, but it can keep doctor's wives in mink.

Nature may have known what she was doing, but sometimes it looks like she deliberately constructed mankind for the benefit of doctors and dentists.

Old age is when most of the names in your little black book are doctors.

To the pessimistic patient, "consultation" means that his doctor has decided to call in an accomplice.

There's a shortage of doctors everywhere except on TV.

Some doctors tell their patients the bad news man-to-man; others prefer to send the bill by mail.

A physician in San Francisco is doing so well financially that he can occasionally tell a patient there's nothing wrong with him.

There aren't many old-fashioned family doctors around these days largely because there aren't many old-fashioned families.

A doctor is a guy who tells you if you don't cut out something he'll cut something out of you.

It seems that a doctor is the only person you'll meet who doesn't have a guaranteed cure for a cold.

A doctor in Chicago turned kidnapper but was not very successful. Nobody could read the ransom notes.

If you don't rest as much as your doctor tells you, he says you're uncooperative. If you rest more than he advises, he says you're lazy.

Doctors have noted that women's feet are getting larger. Presumably that's because they're trying to fill men's shoes.

There's no doubt that we need all the doctors we can get. If we didn't have them what would happen to all the old magazines?

You may not be able to read your doctor's handwriting on a prescription, but you'll notice that his bills are neatly typewritten.

There's a doctor in a small town in Oklahoma so old-fashioned he still calls a cold a cold.

When a physician doesn't know what's wrong with you he calls it a virus. When he does know and can't cure you, he calls it an allergy.

About the only way you can get a doctor these days is to grow your own.

A Michigan doctor warned one of his patients to avoid all excitement such as tennis, baseball, football, and supermarkets.

Doctors always tell you to give up smoking and drinking. It won't make you live longer but you'll die healthier.

The majority of American doctors don't believe in acupuncture. They'd rather stick us with their bill.

One doctor in Washington, D.C., treats only Senate members — he refuses to make "House" calls.

The only way you can get a doctor to come to your home these days is to give a party.

A plastic surgeon increases your face value.

Did you hear about the Colorado doctor who was in such bad financial condition that he tried to rob a bank, but nobody could read his holdup note?

Most doctors specialize today — and the specialty of some is banking.

A physician is the only man who keeps right on getting paid whether his work is satisfactory or not.

A consulting doctor is one who is called in at the last moment to share the blame.

The surgeon wears a mask while performing an operation so that if he makes a mess of it the patient won't know who did it.

A practicing physician is a doctor who says, "If this doesn't cure you, I'll give you something that will."

A surgeon in Kansas doesn't believe in unnecessary surgery. He refuses to operate unless he desperately needs the money.

A specialist in the medical field is a physician who has his patients trained to become ill only during office hours.

A doctor recently said to one of his patients, "Let me know if this prescription works. I'm having the same trouble myself."

In a doctor's office you find the newest in medicine and the oldest in reading material.

The appendix may be useless to man, but just think of what it has done for the medical profession!

His doctor advised a complete change — so he changed doctors.

Much of the sickness people experience in this life is located immediately north of the neck.

A doctor in New Orleans examined a patient and said somberly, "I'm afraid you're beyond medical help — you have a cold."

Locating a doctor these days is a matter of course — the golf course.

Human diseases are the same as they were five thousand years ago, but doctors have selected more expensive names for them.

The quickest way to get a doctor is to turn on the TV set.

A surgeon is a doctor who knows people inside out.

An Oklahoma doctor was recently put under psychiatric observation. The American Medical Association caught him making a house call.

A skin specialist is nothing more than an itch doctor.

Sign in a doctor's waiting room: "Patients in the waiting room are asked not to exchange symptoms. It will get the doctor hopelessly mixed up."

A doctor recently gave one of his male patients only six months to live. When the guy didn't pay his bill, the doctor gave him another six months.

Is there any significance in the fact that doctors are generally described as "practicing"?

The more successful the doctor, the less legible his handwriting.

A Georgia man recently submitted to a medical examination, and reports, "My doctor placed his hand on my wallet and said, 'Cough.'"

Give a quack enough rope and he'll hang up a shingle.

Doctors say Americans are living too fast, and the traffic statistics indicate they are dying the same way.

A fitting revenge is paying your doctor bill with a check signed illegibly.

The man who treats himself when he is sick has a fool for a physician — but at least he doesn't have to wait for an appointment.

If you think time heals everything, try sitting in a doctor's office.

When a worried, haggard patient enters the doctor's office, the doctor hardly knows whether to prescribe a vacation or treat the patient for the one he has just had.

Pleasure

The trouble with mixing business and pleasure is that pleasure usually comes out on top.

There is more pleasure in building castles in the air than on the ground.

Two vastly underrated pleasures are scratching and sneezing.

Many people who are pleasure-bent tonight will end up pleasure-broke tomorrow morning.

In diving to the bottom of pleasures, we often bring up more rocks of sorrow than pearls of joy.

Some people seem to get an awful lot of pleasure being shocked by other people's sins.

The greatest pleasure in life is doing what other people say can't be done.

We tire of those pleasures we take, but never of those we give.

In the "good old days" there were fewer pleasures but we had more time to enjoy those we had.

The greatest and noblest pleasure men can have in this world is to discover new truths, and the next is to shake off old prejudices.

A toast: MAY ALL YOUR PLEASURES BECOME HABITS.

Work is the meat of life; pleasure, the dessert.

Poise

Perfect poise is not looking self-conscious in the front pew.

Poise is often being too stupid to know you should be embarrassed.

One woman's poise is another woman's poison.

Poise is the difference between flipping your lid and raising your eyebrows.

You have poise when you buy a new pair of shoes without seeming conscious of the hole in your sock.

Poise is the ability to continue talking while the other fellow picks up the check.

Poise is the ability to be ill at ease inconspicuously.

It is generally agreed that poise is the art of raising your eyebrows instead of the roof.

Politeness

Anybody who thinks crime doesn't pay probably doesn't realize what a good living politicians make.

White House employees are no longer permitted to use the polite expression "Pardon me."

Frequently he who laughs last didn't get the point at all but is just being polite.

A polite driver is one who honks his horn before he forces you off the road.

Occasionally you meet one of those strange people who is polite and isn't trying to sell you anything.

Politeness is to human nature what warmth is to wax.

The height of politeness is to listen with interest to things you know about, and from someone who doesn't.

Politeness is offering a lady your seat when you get off the bus.

Being polite to your wife only makes her wonder what you've been up to.

Politeness is like an air cushion — there may be nothing to it, but it eases our jolts wonderfully.

A polite person seldom yawns in the presence of others — and another polite person never notices it when he does.

Political Platforms

Some political platforms that look so good in August start to warp in October.

Slippery elm seems to be the wood most extensively used in building political platforms.

A political platform is like the second stanza of our National Anthem. Everybody knows it's there, but very few know the words.

A political platform is what a candidate stands on until he takes his seat.

Political platforms are for one party to stand on, and the other to jump on.

It is generally agreed that there are over ten thousand useless words in the English language, but a great many of them come in handy in framing a political platform.

If a politician had to stand on the planks of his party platform, it would be better constructed.

A political platform is like the one on a streetcar — not actually meant to stand on, but just to get in on.

Politicians

Never in the history of America have so few loused up so much for so many.

According to recent reports, America produces 92 percent of the world's natural gas — not counting the speeches of our senators and congressmen.

In America today there is a surplus of food, a surplus of manufactured goods, and a surplus of people who think they know how to run the government.

Isn't it remarkable how our pioneering ancestors built up a great nation without asking Congress for help?

A hat is something the average man covers his head with, the beggar passes around, and the politician talks through.

The latest new dance craze is called, "The Politician." It's two steps forward, one step backward, and then a sidestep.

Democracy is a wonderful system. It permits you to vote for a politician, and then sit on the jury that tries him.

Democracy is a word all politicians use, and very few seem to understand.

A diplomat is usually an old worn-out politician who, when he's being run out of town, can make it look like he's leading a parade.

The occupational disease of politicians is SPENDICITIS.

How can political candidates discuss the economy when there isn't any?

The trick is to get education out of politics — and get it into politicians.

Not everybody has been affected by inflation. We still have two-bit politicians.

People are not against political jokes — they just wonder how they get elected.

Politicians should watch their language — they use so much of it.

It's beginning to look like we need a law so we can sue successful candidates for breach of promise.

Strict enforcement of the law against polluting the air should result in fewer, shorter, and better political speeches.

If we could use the money political candidates spend on their campaigns, we could cure a lot of the ills they complain about.

One thing about politicians — it's nice to know they can't all be elected.

Politicians should take up skiing. Then they could go downhill with the rest of the country.

Some of our politicians who act foolish aren't acting.

A politician is a man who never met a tax he didn't try to hike.

Politicians admit the two-party system consists of the appointed and the disappointed.

All politicians fear high unemployment — they fear they may be next.

The smart politician keeps envy out of his voice when he accuses his oppponents of fooling the public.

You can't fool all the people all the time, but politicians figure that once every four years is good enough.

A Michigan politician reports that he concluded a very pleasant and profitable campaign. He only kissed the babies who were old enough to vote.

Political bumper stickers usually last longer than the politicians.

A politician is a man who gets sworn in and then cussed out.

It's a good thing that politicians don't live up to their promises. If they did, the country would be ruined.

Politicians are poor tippers — they're not as careless with their own money as they are with ours.

Most politicians periodically mend their fences so it will be more comfortable when they straddle them.

A politician is a man who says, "Glad to meet you again," although he's never seen you before.

Many politicians refuse to answer all your questions on the grounds that it might eliminate them.

Politicians do more funny things naturally than most of us can do purposely.

The politician who tells you the office should seek the man is apt to be busy meeting it at least halfway.

Many politicians seem to support ecology, judging by the way they recycle their speeches.

In a recent TV appearance two politicians almost got to talking about the issues — but caught themselves in time to avoid it.

The cheaper the politician, the more he costs the country.

A good politician has prejudices enough to meet the demands of all his constituents.

Politicians must be able to foretell what will happen tomorrow, next month, or next year — and then explain why it didn't happen.

No two issues are so far apart that a politician can't straddle them.

Once upon a time there was a politician so honest that he was never investigated — and a group got together to investigate that.

No wonder politicians pass the buck — it's now worth only forty-three cents.

To be a successful politician, find out where the public is going, take a short cut across the field, get out in front, and make the people think you're leading the way.

Some politicians campaign for the funds of it.

Deceased politicians go to heaven and play harps. They're good at pulling strings.

Too many politicians are more concerned about running for office than running the country.

An honest politician stands out like a do-it-yourself haircut.

Politicians are all vegetarians — they are always interested in straw votes and grass roots.

An Oklahoma politician announced that he perfectly understood the questions of the day. The trouble was he didn't know the answers.

A politician isn't likely to throw his hat in the ring until he knows which way the wind is blowing.

If a bomb wiped out the entire population except two politicians, they'd form a committee.

Wouldn't it be grand if politicians would fight poverty with something besides taxes?

Some politicians are elected because of their gift of gab, and then defeated because of their gift of grab.

Nothing makes a politician's statement harder to understand than his clarification.

Everytime a politician expresses a growing concern for something the price goes up.

If some politicians said what they thought, they'd be speechless.

The task of a politician is to keep ahead of several crowds, each going in a different direction.

These are difficult days for politicians. With the population explosion, they can't even declare themselves in favor of motherhood without losing a lot of votes.

Give a politician some facts and he'll draw his own confusions.

After all is said and done, the politicians say it and the taxpayers do it.

A skillful politician is one who can stand up and rock the boat, then make you believe he's the only one who can save you from the storm.

Politicians are the same all over the country. They promise to build bridges where there are no rivers.

If it weren't for their offices being bugged, a lot of politicians would have no listeners at all.

Politicians should be good in geometry. They know all the angles and talk in circles.

Some politicians have trouble deciding whether they were born in a log cabin or in a manger.

A politician who says he won't accept an appointive office from the president is like a woman who says she won't get married. They are both just waiting to be asked.

Voters distrust politicans too much in general and too little in particular. There's a politician in Atlanta, who can throw his hat in the ring and talk through it at the same time.

Many a politician who considers himself farsighted is a poor judge of distance.

A politician approaches every subject with an open mouth.

All politicians will stand for what they think the voters will fall for.

If the statements of opposing political candidates are true, none of them is fit to hold public office.

The election isn't very far away when a candidate can recognize you across the street.

A typical politician is usually shortsighted and longwinded.

The mind of a liberal politician is open at both ends.

Wasn't it too bad about the politician in Ohio who ran for reelection unopposed — and lost?

Another thing money can't buy is an honest politician.

Our politicians have thought of just about everything to help the farmer but to leave him alone so he can operate his own business.

It is reported that a certain politician in Louisiana is so windy that he can give mouth-to-mouth resuscitation by telephone.

There were never as many log cabins in this country as politicians claiming they were born in one.

Most politicians spend half their time making promises and the other half making excuses.

It never occurs to some politicians that Lincoln is worth imitating as well as quoting.

A lot of politicians have been attending so many dinners that they spend more time fighting indigestion than inflation.

Just think how speechless some politicians would be if they didn't say nasty things about each other!

A politician should phrase his promises in such a way that nobody could remember them after the election.

We like to see politicians pray with uplifted hands. It keeps their hands where we can see them.

A politician was describing himself as the backbone of the legislature, but others said they wouldn't go quite that high.

Old politicians never die — they just run once too often.

No politician is ever as bad as he is painted by his enemies, or as good as he is whitewashed by his friends.

Politicians who try to please everybody at once are like a puppy trying to follow four kids at the same time.

The only time a politician can't demand a recount is when his wife gives birth to triplets.

A politician leads a terrible life. When he isn't straddling an issue he's dodging one.

An old-time politician is one who, when he comes to the parting of the ways, goes both ways.

Give a politician a free hand and he'll put it in your pocket.

George Washington could broadjump twenty-three feet, which was a record in those days. Today we have politicians who can sidestep farther than that.

It's not a bad idea for a politician to remember that no newspaper can misquote silence.

Some politicians repair their fences by hedging.

The ideal politician votes for all appropriations and against all taxes.

Politicians take the simplest way out when they're in the dark — they simply cloud the issue.

We are not so much interested in where a politician stands as we are in *what* or *who* is holding him up!

When a politician discusses the great moral issues involved, it's because he hasn't had time to look up the facts.

The successful politician keeps on his toes all the time but never steps on the other fellow's.

When a politician says the nation is due for a reawakening, it means he is running for office.

A politician needs three hats: one to cover his head with, one to toss into the ring, and one to talk through.

It's beginning to look like some of our politicians have more solutions than we have problems.

The mockingbird can change its tune eighty-seven times in seven minutes. Politicians regard this interesting fact with envy.

A mayor is a politician who gives you the key to the city after he's taken everything worth having.

A politician is a fellow who's got what it takes to take what you've got.

A wit has said that a politician is the only acrobat who can open his mouth and put his foot in it while straddling a fence.

The honest politician never takes anything that's nailed down while he's being watched.

An election year is when a lot of politicians get free speech mixed up with cheap talk.

Most politicians are continually running for office or for cover.

If politicians don't stop calling each other crooks, cranks, liars, idiots, and morons, folks will begin to believe them.

It is reported that the politicians in Washington are thinking of abolishing the income tax — and taking the income.

History tells us about presidential candidates splitting rails, but modern politicians keep busy splitting hairs.

The trouble with many politicians is that too many of them received an honorary degree from an elementary school.

No politician can ever fly higher in office than he flew while getting there.

A politician is willing to do anything on earth for the workers except become one.

Most politicians have four speeches: what they have written down, what they actually say, what they wish they had said, and what they are quoted as saying the next day.

A politician hopes his platform will serve as a springboard to throw him into office.

An appeal to patriotism seems to be the last refuge of a politician who doesn't know what else to say.

A lot of politicians can stump the country without ever leaving Washington.

Nothing irks a politician as much as the discovery that other politicians are playing politics.

And then there was the candidate who took his defeat like a man. He blamed his wife!

Most politicians are both conservative and liberal — conservative with their own money, and liberal with ours.

Politicians fear that the young voters will vote intelligently.

The reason so many politicians are always so anxious to be reelected is that they'd hate to try and make a living under the laws they helped to pass.

Sometimes when a politician changes his mind, it doesn't work any better than the old one.

Politicians wonder how the Lord can run the world without appointing committees.

Running for president is like asking a girl to marry you — you may say a lot of things you later wish you hadn't.

Politicians who refer to themselves as "we" should remember that the only people entitled to use "we" are monarchs, editorial writers, and pregnant women.

The honesty of many politicians has never been questioned. In fact, it's never been mentioned.

Today's most pitiful case is the politician who's so unimportant that nobody bothers to misquote him.

A politician has a good memory, but hopes other people haven't.

Politicians make headlines running *for* something or running *from* something.

A successful politician is one who can stay in the public eye without irritating it.

The reason a politician puts his best foot forward is because it keeps it out of his mouth.

Some politicians are so good at double talk they could easily get a job as a weather forecaster.

Politicians soon learn that many things done in the public interest don't interest the public.

A Virginia politician recently said, "Half of my friends stand for this, and half of them stand for that, and I stand with my friends."

Do you remember the politician who promised two cars in every garage? We've come close to that now — we have two cars for every parking space.

Any politician will tell you the trick is to hit the taxpayer without hitting the voter.

Any political candidate will tell you that what this country needs is him.

A defeated candidate is another person who doesn't believe that the majority is always right.

In a presidential campaign the party platform is first planned, then panned, and finally canned.

A man's fitness for public office can be judged by the means he uses to get in.

The presidential candidates usually try to sweep the country with each other.

Many governors should beg pardons instead of granting them.

Politics is too important to be left to the politicians.

Our beloved country has made remarkable progress. Now politicians have arranged to spend taxes before they collect them.

Despite the promises of politicians, we'll never achieve an equal and satisfactory distribution of wealth, rainfall, or parking space.

Nothing makes it harder to remember campaign promises than getting elected.

A candidate's promises aren't really extravagant when you compare them to a bridegroom's.

Prosperity is something that businessmen create for politicians to take the credit for.

There are two sides to every question, and a politician usually takes both.

Most folks were satisfied with their lot in life until the politicians started giving them free rides.

You'd think that science, which has come up with a quackless duck and a stingless bee, would start working on a wordless politician.

In spite of its great accomplishments of the past years, science has not yet discovered adequate controls for a number of natural phenomena, including tornadoes, hurricanes, and politicians.

Most women keep secrets like politicians keep promises.

It's not a bad idea for a politician to remember that no newspaper can misquote his silence.

Why not slap a tax on political gas?

A politician will consider every way of reducing taxes except cutting expenses.

Take a look at your tax bills and you'll quit calling them "cheap politicians."

Taxes and politicians are closely related. Once we get stuck with a tax, the only thing politicians know how to do is to raise it.

When all is said and done, it's the politicians who say it and the taxpayers who do it.

The American taxpayers wouldn't object to free transportation for certain government officials if they'd go where we wish they would.

Like its politicians and its wars, society has the teen-agers it deserves.

Political commercials on TV prove one thing — some candidates can tell you all their good points and qualifications in thirty seconds.

If one political candidate gets free time on TV, his opponent demands equal time to deny everything.

Most politicians don't lie on TV any more than the average sponsor.

Too many of us spend our time the way politicians spend our money.

It's a weird world. The strong take away from the weak, the clever take away from the strong, and the government takes away from everybody.

The capitol building in Washington has a rotunda because politicians like to go around in circles.

The way things are going in Washington, some politicians who planned to run for office will be running for cover.

Every man who takes office in Washington either grows or swells.

Washington seems to be filled with two kinds of politicians — those trying to get an investigation started, and those trying to get one stopped.

The world's work must be done by some of us. We can't all be politicians and efficiency experts.

Politics

Politically speaking, the ideal accident would be a collision between the man seeking the office and the office seeking the man.

It's reported that half of all accidents occur at home. Apparently the rest happen in voting booths.

America is always a land of promise in an election year.

We are sorely in need of a voting machine with a space for "Remarks."

Americans have come to learn that it's easier to vote for something they want than to work for it.

Nothing makes a man faster on his feet than politics, unless it's bigamy.

Congress is confronted with the unsolved problem of how to get the people to pay taxes they can't afford for services they don't need.

We'll never stop crime until we get over the idea that we can hire or elect people to stop it.

If you want economy, never let an economic question get into politics.

The trick is to get education out of politics — and get it into politicians.

Darwin's theory of evolution suggests that first came the baboon and then man. Politics is proving that it can go either way.

The cheapest way to have your family tree traced is to run for public office.

A good place to keep your friends is out of politics.

Golf was invented so that even the man who isn't in politics would have something to lie about.

If you lie to people to get their money, that's fraud. If you lie to them to get their votes, that's politics.

George Washington never told a lie — but then he entered politics when the country was very young.

Everybody makes mistakes. That's why we keep having political elections.

Political orators have no chance of becoming endangered species.

Political oratory is an art in which nothing you say reveals the fact that you're saying nothing.

Politics is like inflation. The more we have of it, the more things cost.

Nowadays a man goes into politics with a bright future and comes out with a horrible past.

There'll never be a woman president. No woman will admit to being over thirty-five.

The time is coming when the American people will elect two presidents — one for the White House and one for the road.

Politics is the science of who gets what, when, and why!

The object of a political primary is to choose a promiser who'll outpromise the other party's promiser.

We are all ready to vote a straight ticket next election — as soon as we can find out which party is straight.

There seems to be too much political jam on the relief rolls.

A political candidate once remarked that he would rather be right than to be president. Is there something in the Constitution that says he can't be both?

Don't vote a straight ticket unless it's filled with straight men.

Politics is like milking a cow. You can accomplish a lot if you have a little pull.

Republicans think Santa Claus is a Democrat — so do Democrats!

The trouble with pulling the wool over the voter's eyes is that they soon recognize the yarn.

In national politics it's not so much how you play the game as it is who's keeping the score.

A political straw vote shows which way the hot air is blowing.

Two Texas political candidates were having a heated debate. One shouted, "What about the powerful interests that control you?" The other screamed back, "You leave my wife out of this."

It's time for both political parties to come to the aid of their country.

We should hold elections every year because there never seem to be tax increases in an election year.

The only thing dirtier and harder to clean up than a small boy is politics.

Now we know why they call politics the most promising of all careers.

The vice-presidency is like the last cookie in the jar. Everybody says he won't take it, but somebody always does.

Nothing stretches quite as far as a campaign promise.

The bedfellows politics makes are never strange. It only seems that way to those who have not watched the courtship.

Foreign dictators are difficult to figure out. You can never tell whether they are smart men bluffing or imbeciles who mean it.

Regardless of who wins the election they have to raise taxes to pay for the damage.

Casting one's vote is commendable. Throwing it away is another matter.

The United Nations has just about as much influence as the average husband.

Any day now the primary campaign will reach the violent stage — the candidates will start telling the truth about each other.

Our foreign policy is "speak softly and carry a big wallet."

A political spellbinder is someone who can talk for hours without having to stop to think.

Why not move the political conventions to one of the winter months so all that hot air won't go to waste?

Adding insult to injury is interrupting a political speech on TV to show a baloney commercial.

Fortunately for the country, neither political party can possibly be as bad as the other insists it is.

Politics and music are much alike. The person who is off-key always seems to have the loudest voice.

Some people are still thinking about the last election, trying to figure out if they lost because they lied too much or not enough.

Political economy are two words that should be divorced on the grounds of incompatibility.

Political speeches are usually just baloney disguised as food for thought.

When the political pot boils, it gives off the odor of applesauce.

International politics seems to be as shifty as an armful of coat hangers.

There's one good thing about politics — it beats working!

Some nations have a dynamic two-party system; while one party is in power, the other stays in jail.

It's unfortunate that contestants in political campaigns don't behave with as much dignity as the contestants in livestock shows.

Political conventions remind us that the White House is a little like heaven — not everybody who talks about it is going there.

Nothing makes your past so wicked as running for a political office.

Political differences are wholesome. It's political indifference that hurts.

When you listen to a political speech it's like shooting at a target — you must allow for the wind.

What's needed during a presidential campaign is an epidemic of lockjaw.

People don't necessarily vote for the best man these days. They vote for the one they think will give them the most or cost them the least.

A convention keynote address is a combination of oratory, grand opera, and hog calling.

It takes two things to conduct a successful political campaign: hot issues and cold cash.

Our legislators would practice more economy if they weren't so out of practice.

The most important thing in politics is sincerity, whether you mean it or not.

Politics has gotten to be so expensive that it takes a lot of money even to get beat.

During an election year the political races get rough, and many candidates develop straddle sores.

The handshaking of presidential candidates provides enough energy to milk the taxpayers for four more years.

There's one thing the Democrats and Republicans have in common — our money!

Political candidates aren't very exciting. Their delivery is about as ineffective as that of the post office.

The guy who never votes is the first to tell you what's wrong with the government.

Political conventions consist of a donkey, an elephant, and a lot of bull.

Don't let campaign literature fool you. For instance, one candidate is using a picture showing him with his hands in his own pockets.

It shouldn't be difficult to make an honest living in politics — there doesn't seem to be too much competition.

The whole purpose of any political campaign is to stay calm, cool, and elected.

A third party seems to be about as unpopular in politics as in love.

In political matters much may be said on both sides, and it always is.

Politics is the only well-oiled machine that develops friction.

We've now switched from the New Deal, Fair Deal, and Square Deal to the Ordeal.

In this country only half of the voters vote and generally it's the wrong half.

The farm bloc in Congress does more blocking than farming.

In a presidential campaign the party platform is first planned, then panned, and finally canned.

It seems a bit premature to talk about a third political party until we find out if we have enough good candidates for two.

Millions of Americans don't vote. They figure they can't earn their keep under Republicans and can't keep what they earn under Democrats.

Political science is the art of knowing how to point with pride to the same thing we viewed with alarm when your opponent held the office.

When any issue becomes a political football there are always lots of fumbles.

A man's fitness for public office can be judged by the means he uses to get in.

A totalitarian state is a place where the people in jail are better than the people who put them there.

An independent voter is one who hasn't made up his mind which "truth" he likes best.

A lot of presidential timber is bark.

Nothing is politically right when it is morally wrong.

It is the secret ambition of every loyal American to discover the stream in which a president should never be changed in the middle of.

The presidential candidates usually try to sweep the country with each other.

A mugwump is a man sitting on a political fence with his mug on one side and his wump on the other.

The three major parties in the United States are the Democratic party, the Republican party, and the cocktail party.

Occasionally an innocent man is sent to the legislature.

The United States Constitution is a great document with one defect. It does not require intelligence tests for congressional candidates.

Politics is the art of obtaining money from the rich and votes from the poor on the pretext of protecting each from the other.

The "voice of the people" is sorely in need of a megaphone.

A political landslide buries almost everything except the hatchet.

In politics a radical is a man with both feet firmly planted — in the air!

There are two kinds of voters: those who vote for your candidate, and a lot of ignorant prejudiced fools.

The most dangerous vote in America is the vote that is not used.

The toughest part of politics is to satisfy the voter without giving him what he wants.

Socialism is communism without the firing squad.

The tricky thing about dispensing political patronage is that for every person who gets a plum, several others wind up with nothing but sour grapes.

The chief weakness of our political system is that the man who has sense enough to handle government business usually has a business of his own that he can't afford to quit.

If campaign money talks, it is careful not to tell where it came from.

Political plums don't grow from seeds. They come from grafting.

In some parts of Africa a man can't hold a public office until he has a shot at a rhinocerous. In America voters consider a man qualified if he can shoot the bull.

There are always more candidates running for something than there are those who stand for something.

A bipartisan issue is a problem neither party knows what to do about.

At any moment the United States Supreme Court is expected to declare all of us unconstitutional.

The donkey and the elephant play important roles in American politics. The bull plays a major role too.

The "radical left" says it will work within the system. So do termites.

Nothing stretches quite as far as a campaign promise.

Americans have never expected the best from their elected representatives. They've only hoped for the best.

If you are able to express yourself clearly you should be especially careful not to enter politics.

Remember that when a man runs for Congress, you are his friend; when he is elected, you are a constituent; and when he's in office, you're just a taxpayer.

An ambitious young man in Oklahoma is determined to enter politics. He says he's looking for something where he won't get punished for lying.

In politics a guy who is out to make a name for himself gets called many names.

International politics sometimes looks like a square dance. Just about when everything is going smoothly, everybody changes partners.

Modern political theory seems to hold that the best way to keep the economy in the pink is to run the government in the red.

During political elections all political parties campaign for better education. When we take a close look at some of the men elected, we have to admit it's needed.

A political forum is where the spectators are seated in chairs while the candidates straddle fences.

A dictator would have a pretty tough time in a country where people want to kill the umpire for making just one bad decision.

A bloc is usually a minority group led by a blockhead.

The Supreme Court is a group of judges who correct the errors of the lower courts and perpetuate their own.

Old-timers used to say that anyone could become president, and sometimes it looks like they were right.

Listening to political speeches is a lot like listening to your wife — you know something is going on even though you're not paying much attention to it.

The time may come when the national political conventions will be assigned to certain cities as punishment.

Politics is the only profession in which a man can make a living solely by bragging.

Politics and tennis have much in common. In tennis you have two sides and a net; in politics you have two sides and a fence.

How about appointing a plumber to Secretary of the Treasury? We've got to do something about all the money going down the drain.

Putting a man in the White House is almost as expensive as putting a man on the moon.

Democrats and Republicans finally agreed on one thing — to cut out nonessential spending. Now they're fighting again — about what's nonessential.

A good political candidate needs three things — the patient understanding of a bartender, the political knowledge of a barber, and the assurance of a cab driver.

Politics isn't a bad profession. If you succeed there are many rewards, and if you disgrace yourself, you can always write a book.

The President has asked us to cut down on our power. Some people are asking the President to do likewise.

The chaplains who pray for the United States Senate and the House of Representatives might speak a word now and then on behalf of the taxpayers.

There is no permanent solution to our international problems. All we can hope for is relief from the last solution.

A political promise today means another tax tomorrow.

Before you undertake to change a man's religion or politics, be sure you've got something better to offer him.

The Russians accuse us of being a warlike people because they have been reading what the Democrats and Republicans are saying about each other.

A prominent Russian newspaper announces that it plans to run a contest for the best political joke. First prize is twenty years.

Russian girls are more interested in boys than in politics. They obviously figure it's better to be wed than Red.

Baseball is different from politics. You're always out in baseball when you get caught stealing.

Patrick Henry ought to come back and see what taxation *with* representation is like.

Anybody who thinks the United States isn't still the land of promise just hasn't been listening to political speeches lately.

A political war is one in which everybody shoots from the lip.

Pollution

One quarter of America is covered with forests and the rest with beer cans.

America leads the world in the highway distribution of beer cans.

If you want to really appreciate what an enormous job it is to clean up the environment, start cleaning out your garage.

It's a soul-stirring experience to hear Yule carolers standing in a Los Angeles smog singing, "It Came upon a Midnight Clear."

Why worry about the future? Between the bomb and pollution, there may not be any.

Gossip is what might be called "ear pollution."

Highway billboards must go — we need the room for roadsigns, garbage dumps, and junkyards.

If they really want to beautify our highways, they might start by removing those toll booths.

Strict enforcement of the law against polluting the air should result in fewer, shorter, and better political speeches.

In some American cities the water supply is so polluted the water is lumpy.

Blowing your stack adds to air pollution.

If air pollution increases much more, some wise guy will try to package it.

Fifty years ago the only water pollution people knew anything about was the Saturday night bath.

Thanks to the air pollution, the breath of spring has halitosis.

There's so much air pollution that people are coughing even when they're not in church or watching a movie.

Water pollution is getting worse each passing day. If George Washington were alive today he could roll that dollar across the Potomac.

Many people will never be bothered by air pollution because they don't stop talking long enough to take a deep breath.

If water pollution gets any worse, walking on it will be a cinch.

Every way we look somebody is doing something about pollution — like contributing to it.

Pollution is so bad in Omaha that when a drum majorette threw her baton in the air it stuck!

Concerning water pollution: If Moses wanted to part the Red Sea today, he'd have to use a shovel.

With all the pollution in our streams today, all the bridges are over troubled waters.

Detroit has finally come up with a 100 percent effective anti-pollution device. It's an ignition key that doesn't fit.

Air pollution is something we'll have to pay for through the nose.

Popularity

Popularity is a do-it-yourself job.

It may be easy to become the most popular citizen in town — if you can only find a town small enough.

Your popularity will depend on *how* you treat your friends — and how often!

The man of the hour spent many days and nights getting there.

Popularity is a form of success that's seldom worth the things we have to do in order to attain it.

One way to be popular is to listen attentively to a lot of things you already know.

Popularity is a matter of whether people like you wherever you go or like it whenever you leave.

A good way for your daughter to be popular is for you to be rich.

It doesn't always pay to be popular. Look what the popularity of horsepower did to the horse!

To be extremely popular, one must be more tactful than truthful.

There are two sides to almost every question, and if you wish to be popular you must take both.

When a person sells principles for popularity, he is soon bankrupt.

Tact will make you popular, provided you endure being taught many things you already know.

Popular Songs

If popular songs indicate national character, we're in bad shape.

The old popular songs are best because no one sings them now.

Popular songs should be sung only in the hearing of those with whom they are popular.

Whatever isn't worth saying is certain to be made into a popular song.

We are gradually reducing the number of illiterates in this country — which makes it harder and harder on the popular song writers.

Several million people in this country cannot read or write. They devote themselves to composing our popular songs.

It seems that the popular songs which make the most money make the least sense.

A popular song is the licensed medium for bawling things in public too silly to be uttered in ordinary speech.

The most wonderful thing about a popular song is that it can't last very long.

The most comforting thing about the ten top hits is that next week they won't be.

It's not surprising that popular songs don't last long. Look how many people murder them!

The most popular song in Washington nowadays is titled, "Here Comes the Bribe."

Postal Service

Wouldn't it be nice if Congress would divert some of that foreign aid to the Postal Service!

The economy is moving so slow these days that the Postal Service is getting jealous.

They tell us they are going to do something about junk mail, but they continue to send out income-tax forms.

There is only one sure way to slow down inflation — turn it over to the Post Office.

More marriages will be inevitable if postage continues to increase. It'll be cheaper to marry the girl than to write to her.

There's now a Geritol for postmen — when they've lost their zip.

Memory is the faculty that enables you to give someone most of your zip code.

Political candidates aren't very exciting. Their delivery is about as ineffective as that of the post office.

If the service rendered by the Postal Service ever gets worse — how will we know it?

Our mail service is very discouraging and disappointing. The fifteen-cent stamp includes nine cents for transportation of the letter and six cents for storage.

Did you know that if your letters aren't delivered on time you can sue the Postal Service for malpractice?

Old postmen never die. They just lose their zip.

One advantage of today's high postal rates is that when you write a girl a love letter, she knows you mean it.

For fifteen cents Americans deserve a postage stamp that tastes better.

Our mail service seems to be improving. The letter you mailed yesterday will be delivered to the wrong address today.

The only good thing about increased postal rates is that we don't hear from some of our relatives as often.

If it isn't rain, hail, sleet, or snow that's holding up the mail service, what is?

The next postal increase will be easy on the public — they plan to use some kind of tranquilizer in the glue.

If you want to speed a package through the mail, try stamping it "Fresh Fish."

Considering what's in it, what difference does it make if the mail takes two extra days to reach you?

If the price of postage goes up again, receiving junk mail may become a status symbol.

The United States Postal Service is almost two hundred years old. If you were that old you'd move slowly too.

There is one good thing about the Postal Service. A lot of letters we wish we hadn't written are delivered long after anyone cares.

From the personal ads in the *Tulsa World*: "Due to the increase in postal rates, I would like all my friends to come by my home and pick up their Christmas cards this year."

Can you imagine how much more stamps would cost if the Postal Service went to the expense of putting glue on them?

It now costs $1.08 to mail a letter from Boston to Chicago — fifteen cents for postage, and ninety-three cents for a phone call to see if it got there.

It seems like they ought to have put a picture of Jesse James or Bonnie and Clyde on those fifteen-cent stamps.

A man in New Hampshire complained about slow mail delivery, "Today, I received an invitation to the wedding of a couple who are already divorced."

With postal rates so high, there'll soon be another vanishing species — pen pals.

One sure way to speed up postal delivery — send all postal employees their paychecks by mail.

Why do bills always arrive on time when everything else the Postal Service delivers comes late?

If the cost of mailing a letter continues to increase, pretty soon it'll be cheaper to go yourself.

If Moses had sent the Ten Commandments by mail, three would have arrived late, four would have been broken, and the other three wouldn't have gotten there at all.

Postal rates have gone up again — which means we are getting more of a licking than the stamps do.

If postal rates get any higher, college kids won't be financially able to write home for money.

We shudder to think what would happen if Russia broke our zip code.

The fellow who said "What goes up must come down" must have lived before they invented taxes and postal rates.

If it's true the world is getting smaller, why do they continue to raise the price of postage?

Poverty

America is rapidly achieving a high standard of poverty.

Sign in an automobile showroom in Little Rock, Arkansas: "Let's all fight poverty together. Buy a new car.

The two great tests of character are wealth and poverty.

Children who are reared in homes of poverty have only two mealtime choices — take it or leave it.

No person is so poor that he cannot give a compliment.

Friends are like a priceless treasure; he who has none is a social pauper.

It's pretty hard to tell what brings happiness; poverty and wealth have both failed.

The chief reward for idleness is poverty.

Idleness travels so slowly that poverty soon overtakes it.

A man is truly poor, not when he *has* nothing, but when he *does* nothing.

Poverty is no disgrace, but ignorance is.

The reason they say the income tax is the fairest tax of all is that it gives every individual an even chance at poverty.

It is generally agreed that the income tax is the government's idea of instant poverty.

A man isn't really poor if he can still laugh.

Poverty never drives a man to drink unless he wants to go, but drink will drive a man to poverty whether he wants to go or not.

Love conquers all things except poverty and toothaches.

Money may not be everything, but it's a pretty good cure for poverty.

The fellow who has no money is poor; the fellow who has nothing but money is poorer still.

Wouldn't it be grand if politicians would fight poverty with something besides taxes?

Poverty is contagious. You can get it from your wife.

Being poor is no sin, but what good is it?

America is achieving a high standard of poverty.

Poverty is often a state of mind induced by a neighbor buying a new car.

The quickest way to win the war against poverty is to stop pretending we're rich.

Apparently the government has abandoned the idea of abolishing poverty. Investigation has shown it was the only thing within reach of everybody.

Children who are reared in homes of poverty have only two mealtime choices — take it or leave it.

We are determined to conquer poverty in this country, even if it bankrupts us.

Poverty of purpose is worse than poverty of purse.

For many the idea of poverty is a black-and-white television.

Even the price of being poor today has gone up at least 20 percent.

Poverty is no disgrace — provided no one knows it.

Another advantage of being poor is that it doesn't cost much.

With today's extensive poverty program, the fastest way to get rich is to be poor.

It would be extremely helpful if the poor were to get half the money that is spent studying them.

Quite a number of people are beginning to develop combat fatigue in their private war on poverty.

"Poverty is a state of mind," says the philosopher with a full stomach.

There is one thing about poverty — it sticks to a fellow even after most of his friends leave him.

It's no shame to be poor, and, besides, the salesmen leave you alone.

With just a little more help from the government, there'll be a fortune made in poverty.

It's easy to pick out the poor in America — they wash their own cars.

A man can stand his own poverty better than he can the other fellow's prosperity.

Poverty has its drawbacks, but it has enabled many a man to have a good reputation, which he wouldn't have had if he'd been wealthy.

Poverty isn't dishonorable in itself — but it is dishonorable when it comes from idleness, intemperance, extravagance, and folly.

If it's a crime to be poor, there must be a lot of people who have broken out of jail.

Poverty is often the sidekick of laziness.

Not only are the poor always with us, but currently they're in the midst of a population explosion.

The best way to wage war on poverty is to abolish credit cards.

The poorest of all men is not the one without a cent. It's the man without a dream.

One sure-fire poverty program is to continually try to spend more than you can possibly earn.

Poverty is no disgrace, but that's about all you can say in its favor.

When you hear a man say that poverty builds character, chances are you're listening to a millionaire.

Poverty is a state of existence which deprives a person of many things he is better off without.

The real tragedy of the poor is that they can't afford anything but self-denial.

If our President wants to abolish poverty, he can do it by abolishing the IRS.

The poorest people in this world are those who think only in terms of profit.

Poverty is what you experience the day after you pay your income tax.

The best ammunition to fight poverty is a load of ambition fired with effort toward a definite goal.

Being poor has its advantages — the car keys are never in your other pants.

During the depression the shortage of butter was not very noticeable, because no one had anything to spread it on.

Separate the greedy from the needy and any poverty program will work.

It seems the poverty level is rapidly gaining on us.

If you want a definition of poverty, ask parents with three or four teen-agers in the family.

It's no disgrace to be poor, but it might as well be.

A father recently advised his son to go into poverty, since that's where the money is nowadays.

When a person sells principles for popularity, he is soon bankrupt.

If the responsibility for all poverty is placed on the wealthy, why not blame all sickness on the healthy?

Mandatory retirement is another form of compulsory poverty.

Taxpayers are the casualties of the War on Poverty.

Power

Men of genius are admired; men of wealth are envied; men of power are feared; but only men of character are trusted.

Nearly all men can stand adversity, but if you want to test a man's character, give him power.

You can kill men and cripple nations, but you cannot kill a good idea.

There is nothing in the world more powerful than an idea. No weapon can destroy it; no power can conquer it, except the power of another idea.

An idea is the only lever which really moves the world.

Knowledge is power only when it is turned on.

Power will either burn a man out or light him up.

The greatest power for good is the power of example.

Enough spiritual power is going to waste to put Niagara Falls to shame.

There is more power in the open hand than in the clenched fist.

The power of man has grown in every sphere except over himself.

Power is dangerous unless you have humility.

The President has asked us to cut down on our power. Some people are asking the President to do likewise.

Many a promising young man has been ruined, or reduced to mediocrity, by getting his hands on too much power before he was able to handle it.

A man with compassion wields more power than a man with muscle.

The less power a man has, the more he brags of what he'd do if he had it.

Prayer provides power, poise, peace, and purpose.

This will be a better world when the power of love replaces the love of power.

Praise

It's easy to keep from being a bore. Just praise the person to whom you're talking.

It is all right to be always looking for compliments — to give to somebody else.

If you're not mature enough to take criticism, you're too immature for praise.

The trouble with most of us is that we'd rather be ruined by praise than saved by criticism.

The more praise a man is willing to take, the less he deserves it.

Insincere praise is worse than no praise at all.

It is not he who searches for praise who finds it.

The man who sings his own praises may have the right tune but the wrong words.

Remember, whenever you're praised to the sky, it's best to keep your feet on the ground.

Praise is like garlic in a good salad — a little goes a long way.

It is usually best to be generous with praise, but cautious with criticism.

When you see a fellow turn his back on praise, he's doing it to make it easier to pat.

A song that never gets an encore is when you sing your own praises.

Be the first to praise and the first to deserve praise.

The test of any man's character is how he takes praise.

Encouragement is like premium gasoline. It helps to take the knock out of living.

An overdose of praise is like ten lumps of sugar in coffee; only a few people can swallow it.

Praise does wonders for a person's hearing.

Try praising your wife occasionally. It may surprise her at first, but she'll appreciate it. On the other hand, she may burst out crying — thinking you're drunk again.

Probably a man's most profitable words are those spent praising his wife.

Prayer

America was better off when folks opened meals with a prayer instead of a can opener.

The trouble with being an atheist is you have nobody to talk to when you're alone.

The Bible is a book of prayers. Out of 667 recorded prayers, there are 454 recorded answers.

A small boy said to his best friend, "It may be unconstitutional, but I always pray before an exam."

Let us pray, not for lighter burdens, but for stronger backs.

A Christian must get on his knees before he can get on his feet.

A Christian is like ripening corn: the riper he grows, the lower he bows his head.

Sign outside a Dallas church: "Last chance to pray before entering the freeway."

413

If the church is ever to get on its feet, it must get on its knees.

Congress is a legislative body whose members make the laws and whose chaplain prays for the country.

No one can live in doubt when he has prayed in faith.

Families that pray together stay together, and families that work together — eat.

A real friend warms you by his presence, trusts you with his secrets, and remembers you in his prayers.

God honors no drafts where there are no deposits.

God is never more than a prayer away.

He who would be great must be fervent in his prayers, fearless in his principles, firm in his purposes, and faithful in his promises.

To grow tall spiritually, a man must first learn to kneel.

When you get the daily bread you've been praying for, don't grumble because it's not cake.

The big question is: Where can we put our hatred while we say our prayers?

Some people talk about heaven being so far away. It is within speaking distance of those who belong there.

A hypocrite prays on his knees on Sunday — and on his neighbors the rest of the week.

Throughout the ages no nation has ever had a better friend than the mother who taught her children to pray.

Prayers can't be answered unless they are prayed.

What most people pray for when they arrive at church on Sunday is a parking place.

Let's all bow our heads and pray as follows: "Lord, help me to admit it when I am wrong, and make me easier to live with when I am right."

Most of us would be in more trouble than we are if all our prayers had been answered.

Someone said to a man who led in public prayer, "You should speak louder. I didn't hear a word you said." His reply was, "I wasn't talking to you."

Most of us pray for more things than we are willing to work for.

People who do a lot of kneeling don't do much lying.

A suggested prayer: "Oh God, give the world a lot more common sense, beginning with me."

It's not the body's posture, but the heart's attitude, that counts when we pray.

Sign in a Nebraska high school building: "In the event of an earthquake or tornado, the Supreme Court ruling against prayer in school will be temporarily suspended."

Prayer provides power, poise, peace, and purpose.

Life is fragile — handle with prayer.

Strength in prayer is better than length in prayer.

The prayers a man lives on his feet are just as important as those he says on his knees.

Prayer is a little bit like eating salted peanuts; the more you do it, the more you want to do it.

When life knocks you to your knees, you're in position to pray.

It is good to pray for the repair of mistakes, but praying earlier would likely keep us from making so many.

Live prayerfully — the life you save may be your own.

After we bow our heads seeking divine guidance, we often bow our necks in resistance to His divine will.

If you would have God hear you when you pray, you must hear Him when He speaks.

A lot of little prayers as we go along through life would save a lot of long ones in case of emergencies.

You can't possibly stumble if you're on your knees.

A lot of kneeling keeps you in good standing with God.

Nothing lies outside the reach of prayer except that which is outside the will of God.

Too many of us are like the old deacon who prayed, "Use me, O Lord, in thy work — especially in an advisory capacity."

Sooner or later we all need some foreign aid — the kind we get from praying.

Prayer must mean something to us if it is to mean anything to God.

A short prayer will reach the throne of grace — if you don't live too far away.

Prayer must not be taken out of the public schools. That's the way, the only way, many of us got through.

Some people feel we don't need prayer any more since we now have penicillin!

An honest prayer: "Stop my neighbors, O Lord, from buying things I can't afford."

Prayer will either make a man leave off sinning, or sin will make him leave off prayer.

A young Christian once prayed, "Lord, fill me to overflowing. I can't hold much, but I can overflow a great deal."

Prayer does not need proof, it needs practice.

If you are too busy to pray, you are too busy.

Prayer by people in the pew will give preachers power in the pulpit.

Hem in both ends of the day with prayer, and then it won't be so likely to unravel in the middle.

Prayer lubricates the machinery of life.

The person who gets down on his knees occasionally is better able to stand up to the problems of life when he has to face them.

Some people pray for a bushel, but carry a cup.

The following is the revised edition of an American prayer: "Forgive us our debts, O Lord, as we forgive our international debtors."

Prayer is more than asking God to run errands for us.

If your prayer isn't of sufficient importance for you to try to answer it, why expect the Lord to answer it?

He stands best who kneels most.

Practical prayer is harder on the soles of your shoes than on the knees of your trousers.

An unreasonable prayer: "Lord, give us this day our daily bread — with butter."

Keep your chin up and your knees down.

It is strange that in our prayers we seldom ask for a change in character, but always a change in circumstances.

When leading a public prayer, speak loudly enough to be heard of men and sincerely enough to be heard of God.

The mistake a lot of people make when they pray is putting in too many commercials.

After saying our prayers we ought to do something to make them come true.

Do not expect a thousand-dollar answer to a ten-cent prayer.

Those who pray only when in trouble at least know where to turn for help.

Prayer is talking something over with God, rather than trying to talk God out of something.

A person's most fervent prayers are not said when he is on his knees, but when he is flat on his back.

Prayer is the prelude to peace, the prologue to power, the preface to purpose, and the pathway to perfection.

He who does not pray when the sun shines will not know how to pray when the clouds come.

Don't pray for an easy life; pray to be a stronger person.

"Help me, O God! My boat is so small and the ocean so wide."

A coed concluded her prayer with a modest appeal, "Lord, I don't want to be selfish about it, but I would appreciate it very much if you would send my mother a son-in-law."

Prayer can *keep* us out of trouble a lot easier than it can *get* us out of trouble.

When the outlook is bad, try the "uplook."

The religion of some people consists principally in praying that the Lord will provide.

Prayer ought not to mean that we stop trying to help ourselves.

The secret of prayer is prayer in secret.

Fobidding prayers in school won't hurt our country half as much as forgetting prayers at home.

The tragedy of our day is not unanswered prayer — but unoffered prayer.

When your knees are knocking, it might help to kneel on them.

A small boy prayed, "Lord, if you can't make me a better boy, don't worry about it. I'm having a good time as it is."

God never tires of hearing us in prayer.

Prayer is not a gadget we use when nothing else works.

Are we as enthusiastic in our prayers as we are in all other areas of our lives?

The chaplains who pray for the United States Senate and the House of Representatives might speak a word now and then on behalf of the taxpayers.

Please don't pray for rain if you're going to complain about the mud.

When the road of life is steep and slippery, prayer in action gives us traction.

As long as there are final examinations, there will be at least *secret* prayers in our schools.

Bending our knees in prayer keeps us from breaking under the load of cares.

Prayer gives strength to the weak, faith to the fainthearted, and courage to the fearful.

Wonderful things happen to us when we live expectantly, believe confidently, and pray affirmatively.

Satan hinders prayer, but prayer also hinders Satan.

It is impossible to be prayerful and pessimistic at the same time.

Regardless of your position in life, getting on your knees will help to keep you on your toes.

The soul without prayer is like lungs without air.

Some preachers seem to use big words to conceal the smallness of their thoughts.

A suggested prayer for all preachers: "O Lord, fill my heart with worthwhile stuff and nudge me when I've said enough."

A problem not worth praying about is not worth worrying about.

In times of prosperity men ask too little of God. In times of adversity, they ask too much.

Nations and men are much alike. They seldom appeal to God unless they're getting licked.

"Kneeology" will do more for the world than theology.

Selfishness short-circuits prayer.

A sermon should never be preached until it is soaked in prayer.

The best cure for a short temper is a lengthy prayer.

The prayer of modern youth seems to be, "Lord, lead us not into temptation. Just tell us where it is and we'll find it."

Most of modern man's troubles come from the fact that he has too much time on his hands and not enough on his knees.

If your troubles are deep-seated and long-standing, try kneeling.

Preachers
see also Sermons

Preachers who formerly gave lectures on women's clothes have been compelled to turn to other subjects. There just wasn't enough material.

Those who are so perturbed over the present divorce rate evidently do not understand the law of supply and demand. There are more lawyers in this country than there are preachers.

If you need some kind of an excuse, see your preacher; he has heard more than anybody else.

Preachers and lawyers are paid for zeal, but fools dish it out for nothing.

All forms of gambling are frowned upon by preachers — except marriage.

It's difficult to tell who gives some couples the most happiness, the preacher who married them or the judge who divorced them.

It's difficult to tell who gets the most pleasure out of marriage, the preacher who ties the knot, or the lawyer who severs it.

There are two types of people who'll tell you there are better places to be than where you are — real-estate salesmen and preachers.

The most interesting point some preachers make is the stopping point.

A preacher who will not try to practice what he preaches is not fit to listen to.

Parting words of a Louisiana preacher to a departing friend at the airport: "May God and your luggage go with you."

The work of the preacher and the policeman is similar. The policeman usually gets the preacher's dropouts.

It seems that some young men enter the ministry because it's easier to stand up and yell than to sit down and listen.

A group of preachers in Phoenix recently formed a bowling league. They call themselves "Holy Rollers."

Most preachers have all the Christian virtues except resignation.

If there is no hell, many preachers are obtaining money under false pretense.

The world looks at preachers out of the pulpit to know that they mean in it.

Some preachers fish for compliments, while others fish for men.

When a famous preacher is willing to preach in a small church, he's got religion.

The preacher who cannot broaden and deepen his sermons usually lengthens them.

Preachers prefer holding service *with* you, not *over* you.

Far too many preachers, when they get in the pulpit, are dealers in dry goods and notions.

A preacher's pious look will not cover a poorly prepared sermon.

Preachers are determined — if they don't step on your toes, they get in your hair.

Preacher at wedding: "If this check for one dollar clears, I now pronounce you husband and wife."

It is a good idea for a preacher to quit preaching before the audience quits listening.

Too few preachers know the difference between a sermon and a lecture.

A preacher usually takes a text and preaches from it — sometimes very far from it.

When some preachers get up, their thoughts sit down.

A popular preacher is one who knows where to draw the line between preaching and meddling.

Some preachers are so sad of voice and countenance that they should apply for membership in the enbalmer's union.

Preachers find more sleeping sickness than does the physician.

The preacher's business is to comfort the afflicted and afflict the comfortable.

If the preacher aims at nothing in his sermon, he usually hits it.

Jonah learned more at the bottom of the sea than some preachers learn at a theological seminary.

Second wind is what some preachers get when they say, "And now in conclusion."

All preachers should be sure of what they are saying. Someone in the audience might be listening.

A preacher in Richmond, Virginia, reports that he has four hundred active members in his church — two hundred active for him, and two hundred active against him.

The preacher who wants to make a big noise should get a job in a boiler factory.

There are two kinds of preachers: one kind has something to say, the other has to say something.

When people go to sleep in church, somebody should wake up the preacher.

If a preacher can't strike oil in thirty minutes, it shows he's either using a dull auger or he's boring in the wrong place.

Preachers should remember that the capacity of the mind to absorb is limited to what the seat can endure.

Preachers don't talk in their sleep; they talk in other people's sleep.

A suggested prayer for all preachers: "O Lord, fill my heart with worthwhile stuff and nudge me when I've said enough."

There's a preacher in Texas so religious he has stained glass windows in his car.

It is difficult for a preacher to break a hard heart and mend a broken one at the same time.

The preacher is called to be a shepherd, not a sheep dog.

A churchman in Florida reports that his minister recently preached on the subject of gossip, followed by the hymn, "I Love to Tell the Story."

"Deep" preachers are not actually deep. They just muddy the water enough so that you can't see the bottom.

The preacher's business is to preach God's will. He is an executor, not a legislator.

Some preachers manipulate the people; others teach them.

A preacher's audience will lose confidence in the well if every visit to the pump exhausts the water.

A preacher in Alabama was recently fired for two reasons. First, he had a poor delivery. Second, he never had very much to deliver.

Glancing over the audience as he spoke, the preacher thought he spotted an old friend. On second glance, he discovered it was only a "nodding" acquaintance.

It is futile for a preacher to drum up trade during the week unless he is prepared to deliver the goods on Sunday.

The misleading thing about some preachers is that they carry their sermons around in a *brief* case.

He who practices what he preaches may have to put in some overtime.

If people generally cared as much for their souls as they do their looks, the preachers would soon be out of a job.

Nowadays we have sermonettes by preacherettes for Christianettes.

In preparing their sermons, many preachers prepare no place to stop.

The best way to compliment the sermon delivered by your minister is to bring a friend to hear the next one.

Many sermons are dull because preachers often try to answer questions that nobody is asking.

How can a preacher expect to fill heaven with people when his sermons won't even fill the church building where he preaches?

Preachers should learn that for a sermon to be immortal it need not be eternal.

Preaching

Every Christian occupies some kind of a pulpit and preaches some kind of a sermon every day.

A nodding congregation may or may not mean assent to what the preacher is saying.

Perhaps you can improve your preacher's preaching by being a better listener.

We need more *candid* preaching and less *candied* preaching.

If some of us practiced what we preached, we'd work ourselves to death.

He preaches well who lives well.

It is impossible to preach with one eye on the conscience and the other on the collection.

Some of the best preaching is done by holding the tongue.

One reason for poor preaching in our pulpits is that there is poor praying in the pew.

When a woman preaches a sermon to her husband, she usually ends it by taking up a collection.

Softsoap in the pulpit will not cleanse the sinners in the pew.

Those who don't practice what they preach don't have anything worthwhile to preach about.

To get something across to a congregation by preaching is like trying to fill a longnecked bottle by throwing a bucket of water over it.

Preaching dogmas is fighting the devil with the scabbard instead of the sword.

The spirit in which a man preaches is as vital as what he says.

The theological preaching we hear nowadays settles a lot of problems people never heard of, and answers a lot of questions nobody ever asks.

It isn't very difficult for some people to practice what they preach, because they don't do much preaching.

If some people preached what they practice, it would have to be censored.

It takes great listening, as well as great preaching, to make a great sermon.

You can preach a better sermon with your life than with your lips.

Prejudice
see also Narrow-Mindedness

The bigot agrees there are two sides to every question — his side and the wrong one.

The person who boasts of having no religious prejudice quite often has no religion.

No Christian is strong enough to carry a cross and a prejudice at the same time.

If there is anything stronger than your convictions, it's the heat of your prejudices.

The difference between a prejudice and a conviction is that you can explain a conviction without getting angry.

What some people call a conviction may be just a prejudice.

It isn't easy for an idea to squeeze itself into a head that is filled with prejudice.

Two people can't hate each other if they both love God.

We spend half our time crying for leaders, and the other half nailing them to the cross of prejudice.

Don't be so narrow-minded that your ears rub together.

There are some people so narrow-minded they have to stack their prejudices vertically.

We may ask for information, but we are usually only interested in what confirms our opinions.

An opinion is usually a prejudice with a few unrelated facts.

A philosopher thinks in order to believe. He formulates his prejudices and systematizes his ignorance.

The greatest and noblest pleasure men can have in this world is to discover new truths, and the next is to shake off old prejudices.

A good politician has prejudices enough to meet the demands of all his constituents.

The trouble with not having prejudices is that people are apt to think you don't understand our social system.

Prejudice is being down on something you're not up on.

There is nothing so easy to acquire and so difficult to drop as prejudice.

Prejudice is a lazy man's substitute for thinking.

Don't air your prejudices — smother them.

Prejudice is a great timesaver. It enables you to form opinions without bothering to get the facts.

No prejudice has ever been able to prove its case in the court of reason.

A prejudiced person is someone who's too stubborn to admit you're right!

The judgment of a man on a subject on which he is prejudiced isn't really worth much.

Prejudice is when you decide a fellow is a stinker before you even meet him.

If there is anything stronger than your convictions, it's the heat of your prejudices.

Prejudice squints when it looks and lies when it talks.

Many people think they're thinking when they're merely rearranging their prejudices.

Prejudice is a wall of fear built on the sands of suspicion surrounding the city of insecurity.

You're prejudiced when you weigh the facts with your thumb on the scales.

Prejudice is an unwillingness to be confused with facts.

Instead of uprooting his prejudices, the average person whitewashes them and presents them as principles.

Prejudice is essentially an outgrowth of ignorance.

Prejudice cannot see things that are, because it is always looking for things that aren't.

Prejudice, which sees what it pleases, cannot see what is plain.

Prejudice runs so deep in some people they won't even listen to both sides of a phonograph record.

It is always easier to see both sides of a question if your prejudices are not involved.

Many people tailor their religion to fit the pattern of their prejudice.

Very often a person who boasts of having no religious prejudice has no religion either.

Maybe our teen-agers aren't maturing too fast, but it's a little frightening to find that a lot of them already have as many prejudices as they'll ever need.

Few people seek to discover truth; most of us seek to confirm our errors and perpetuate our prejudices.

It takes a wise man to know when he is fighting for a principle, or merely defending a prejudice.

Preparation

There are four steps to accomplishment: Plan purposefully. Prepare prayerfully. Proceed positively. Pursue persistently.

Today's preparation determines tomorrow's achievement.

A lot of people who are worrying about the future ought to be preparing for it.

Luck is what happens when preparation meets opportunity.

Opportunity has the uncanny habit of favoring those who have paid the price of years of preparation.

Prepare and prevent instead of repair and repent.

When you're thirsty it's too late to think about digging a well.

Get ready for eternity. You're going to spend a lot of time there.

Some folks prepare for an emergency before it emerges.

The price of mastery in any field is thorough preparation.

With a birth certificate and a burial policy, a fellow is prepared to live or die.

Hope for the best, and be ready for the worst.

Pride

Some folks are as proud of their ancestors as if they were responsible for them.

The fellow who gets on a high horse is riding for a fall.

Nothing intoxicates some people like a sip of authority.

Nothing pleases a little man more than an opportunity to crack a big whip.

If there's anything small, shallow, or ugly about a person, giving him a little authority will bring it out.

Many a bee has been drowned in his own honey.

Always hold your head up, but be careful to keep your nose at a friendly level.

Lots of people get credit for being cheerful when they are just proud of their teeth.

If some children are as bright as their parents think they are, they should be looked at through sunglasses.

Some proud folks are always letting off esteem.

As the chest swells, the brain and the heart shrink.

Some folks are so proud of themselves they can strut sitting down.

Nature never intended for us to pat ourselves on the back. If she had, our hinges would be different.

Patience strengthens the spirit, sweetens the temper, stifles anger, subdues pride, and bridles the tongue.

People who talk about things they can't afford often forget to include pride, envy, and malice.

A little pride is a small thing to lose when compared with losing honor.

Pride is something we have; vanity is something others have!

Don't let your pride become inflated — you may have to swallow it someday.

You can't give a man pride, but you can rob him of it.

Some of our greatest bounces result from the fall that pride went before.

There are some people who would rather be the head of nothing than the tail of something.

Temper gets people into trouble, but pride keeps them there.

Swallow your pride occasionally — you'll find it's nonfattening.

Pride hides a man's faults to himself and magnifies them to everyone else.

The remarkable thing about family pride is that so many people can be so proud of so little.

Sometimes it takes a large throat to swallow your pride.

The best kind of pride is that which compels a man to do his best work — even when no one is looking.

Success that goes to a man's head usually pays a very short visit.

Isn't it too bad that when success turns a fellow's head, it doesn't wring his neck?

When success turns a man's head, it leaves him looking in the wrong direction.

People who talk about things they can't afford sometimes forget that the list should include pride, envy, and malice.

What makes eating your words so difficult is swallowing your pride at the same time.

Principles

Compromise is always wrong when it means sacrificing a principle.

He who would be great must be fervent in his prayers, fearless in his principles, firm in his purposes, and faithful in his promises.

A man's country is not just a certain area of land. It is a principle, and patriotism is loyalty to that principle.

Instead of uprooting his prejudices, the average person whitewashes them and presents them as principles.

When a person sells principles for popularity, he is soon bankrupt.

A man without principle never draws much interest.

No man is better than his principles.

Most people are blind to principles, the rest of us are blinded by them.

It's easier to fight for principles than to live up to them.

Great principles do not need men and women as much as men and women need great principles.

What this world needs is fewer rules and more good examples.

It takes a wise man to know when he is fighting for a principle, or merely defending a prejudice.

Problems

A satisfying class reunion is one where you discover all your former classmates have bigger problems than yours.

Congress has figured out the right system. When the members encounter a problem they can't solve, they subsidize it.

Congress is unpredictable. You never know what urgent problem they're not going to do anything about.

A harried housewife in Nebraska sighed, "I have so many problems that if something terrible happened to me it would be at least two weeks before I could get around to worrying about it."

Laughter is like changing a baby's diaper — it doesn't permanently solve any problems, but it makes things more acceptable for a while.

Everything is much simpler today. Instead of solving problems, we just subsidize them.

International problems are becoming so complex that even taxi drivers and teen-agers don't have the solutions.

A major problem facing housewives is that ovens are self-cleaning but kids aren't.

Answers are what we have for other prople's problems.

School teachers have to face their problems every day, whereas bus drivers have all their problems behind them.

The problem is that the key to success doesn't always fit your ignition.

If a man can see both sides of a problem, you know that none of his money is tied up in it.

The modern woman has a lot of problems, and she seems to think she can solve most of them by yelling at her husband.

Sign in a Cleveland bar: "Feel free to discuss your problems here, but be sure you don't create any."

The problem that baffles Washington is how to dig the country out of the hole without making the hole any bigger.

Part of the problem today is that we have a surplus of simple answers, and a shortage of simple questions.

The biggest problem that a wife has is the one sitting across from her at the breakfast table.

Some people find their cholesterol problem nearly solved by the high cost of meat, eggs, and butter.

There is no permanent solution to our international problems. All we can hope for is relief from the last solution.

It must be a problem for two-faced people to put their best face forward.

One of the major problems we face each summer is how to get the watermelon into the refrigerator without taking the beer cans out.

The biggest problem today is that everybody's fixing the blame and nobody's fixing the trouble.

One solution to the energy problem is to bale up all the government red tape and use it for fuel.

Many men are able to solve big problems at the office, but are unable to settle little ones at home.

In the "good old days" problems could be solved without raising taxes.

Never before has the world had so many big problems and so many little minds.

The reason some people know the solution is because they created the problem.

A problem not worth praying about is not worth worrying about.

Man's biggest problem is not "outer space" but "inner space."

Instead of counting their blessings many people magnify their problems.

It's better to put your finger on a problem before sticking your nose into it.

We once settled our problems over coffee and cigarettes — now, they're our problems.

He who makes the most noise about his problems usually does the least about them.

Our national and international problems would soon fade away if we could find a key to fit the deadlock.

If you can't state your problem in ten minutes or less, you don't understand it yourself.

Psychiatrists tell us that talking helps solve our problems — it often causes them too.

Problems shouldn't be faced; they should be attacked.

The trouble with today's problems is that we can't turn to the back of the book for the answers.

Having problems may not be so bad after all. There's a special place for folks who have none — it's called a cemetery.

A young man's toughest problem is to find a girl attractive enough to please him and dumb enough to like him.

With all the world's problems, it's nice to read the etiquette columns and learn there are still a few people whose chief worry is using the wrong fork.

With man's great ability to think, reason, and compute, we can now pinpoint most of our current problems. The trouble is that we can't solve them.

If you could kick the fellow responsible for most of your problems, you couldn't sit down for three weeks!

Why can't life's problems hit us when we're eighteen and know everything?

There is no perfect solution to any problem with human beings mixed up in it.

The problems of the world are changing so fast that some of them become obsolete before they can cause any serious trouble.

Heads, hearts, and hands could settle the world's problems better than arms.

The best time to tackle a minor problem is before it grows up.

You've got a problem when your dentist tells you that you need a bridge, and you can't pay his toll.

We must live with people to know their problems and live with God to solve them.

Life's most difficult problem is to keep clean of debt, dirt, and the devil all at the same time.

One of the most important things in life is to know how to keep problems from tackling you first.

We should exchange problems. Everybody seems to know how to solve the other fellow's.

Most people spend more time and energy in going around problems than in trying to solve them.

The problem the average housewife faces is that she has too much month left over at the end of the money.

Do you help to solve problems, or are you one of them?

To work out our problems we need to add love, subtract hate, multiply good, and divide between truth and error.

The world has so many problems that if Moses had come down from Mount Sinai today — the two tablets he carried would be aspirin.

If only men took the nation's problems as seriously as they do its sports!

The main problem with liquor is that it makes you see double and feel single.

Many a problem will solve itself if we forget it and go fishing.

The right angle to approach a difficult problem is the "try-angle."

One of the problems of modern life is for a husband to teach his wife that even bargains cost money.

Maybe the reason we have traffic problems is because the traffic has become as dense as the drivers.

Problems would lessen if people would listen.

If we continue to solve problems by sweeping them under the rug, we may end up in the dustpan of civilization.

International problems are simple compared to the difficulties in a home with three teen-agers and one phone.

One reason for the world's problems is that we know more ways to get into trouble than to get out of it.

A major drinking problem is the unwillingness of some to drink at the fountain of knowledge.

The easiest way to solve a problem is to pick an easy one!

We all might as well face our problems. We can't run fast or far enough to get away from them all.

World problems are so confusing that even computers are asking questions.

Our problems are very much alike, except that I don't worry about yours.

A straight line is the shortest in moral problems as well as in geometry.

Most of us enjoy TV soap operas. The folks on those shows are the only ones we know who have more problems than we do.

A fellow could get rich by opening a tailor shop in Washington — there are so many pressing problems there that need to be ironed out.

Procrastination

The best time to do something worthwhile is between yesterday and tomorrow.

You can never get much of anything done unless you go ahead and do it before you are ready.

It's easier to get folks to agree to do better tomorrow than to get then to do their best today.

Anybody who brags about what he's going to do tomorrow probably did the same thing yesterday.

A conference is a meeting at which people talk about things they should be doing.

Congress seems to favor a stable government, judging from the amount of stalling it does.

One thing you can be sure of — there will always be more people going on a diet tomorrow than those on a diet today.

A diet is something you went off yesterday — or expect to start tomorrow.

A diet is what you keep putting off while you keep putting on.

No farmer ever plowed a field by turning it over in his mind.

The future is the time when folks will be wishing they'd done all the things they ain't doin' now!

One can conquer a bad habit easier today than tomorrow.

One of the greatest laborsaving inventions of all time is tomorrow.

The kindness planned for tomorrow doesn't count today.

You cannot do a kindness too soon, because you never know how soon it will be too late.

The kindness we resolve to show tomorrow cures no headaches today.

No one is ever too old to learn, but many people keep putting it off anyway.

The lazier a man is, the more he is going to do tomorrow.

When a man says he is going to do this or that tomorrow, ask him what he did yesterday.

In the orchard of opportunity, it is better to pick the fruit than to wait for it to fall.

Procrastination is the thief of time. So are a lot of other big words.

Some people seem to be afflicted with acute procrastination.

Never put off until tomorrow what you can order someone else to do today.

Some put off procrastination as long as they can.

Procrastination is the greatest laborsaving invention of all time.

Some tasks have to be put off dozens of times before they completely slip your mind.

Procrastination is the fertilizer that makes difficulties grow.

What you put off today, you'll probably put off tomorrow too.

It is always wise to put off until tomorrow what we ought not to do at all.

Most people who sit around waiting for their ship to come in often find it is a hardship.

Sometimes it is better to put off until tomorrow what you are likely to mess up today.

Too many things we wait for are not worth the delay.

The main thing that comes to a man who waits is regret for having waited.

Procrastination is the grave in which opportunity is buried.

Ten percent of what we intend to do tomorrow will be a good day's work today.

Don't put off until tomorrow what you can do today; by tomorrow there may be a law against it.

All things may come to him who waits, but they are apt to be shopworn.

A lot of folks postpone until tomorrow those things they should have done several days ago.

A procrastinator is one who puts off until tomorrow the things he has already put off until today.

Don't postpone reading the handwriting on the wall until you have your back to it.

Those things that come to a man who waits seldom turn out to be the things he's waited for.

A preacher in New Mexico reports that about five years ago he decided to procrastinate — but never got around to it.

Do it tomorrow — you've made enough mistakes for today!

About the only thing that comes to him who waits is old age.

No one can build a reputation on what he's going to do tomorrow.

You cannot escape the responsibilities of tomorrow by evading them today.

Some tasks have to be put off dozens of times before they completely slip our minds.

The hardest work in the world is that which should have been done yesterday.

Hard work is usually an accumulation of easy things that should have been done last week.

Profanity

If swearin' and cussin' and cheatin' are crimes, then golf should be outlawed.

The kid who used to get spanked for writing obscenities in restrooms is now cleaning up as a writer in Hollywood.

About the time a man is cured of swearing, another income tax is due.

A certain IRS office has two signs over the door. The one going in says, "Watch your step." The one going out says, "Watch your language."

People who spout filthy language in public are trespassing on our eardrums, and we don't like it.

Language, like linen, looks best when it's clean.

Thousands of Americans can speak at least two languages — English and profanity.

Language is the apparel in which our thoughts parade before the public. Let's never clothe them in vulgar or shoddy attire.

There are no curse words in the Indian language. They don't need any because they don't pay taxes.

Profanity is an evidence of the lack of a sufficient vocabulary — and brains.

When a man uses profanity to support an argument, it indicates that either the man or the argument is weak — probably both.

Profanity is a means of escape for the person who runs out of ideas.

Grandpa is living in the past. He's three generations behind in his cussin'.

Profanity is the use of strong words by weak people.

He knew not what to say, so he swore!

Profanity is the mark of a conversational cripple.

Progress

Begin where you are. But don't stay where you are.

Bees can't make honey and sting at the same time.

There are some Christians who can't be called "pilgrims" because they never make any progress.

There are a few church members who may be described as the farmer described his mule: "Awfully backward about going forward."

A conceited person never gets anywhere because he thinks he is already there.

If everyone were perfectly contented there would be no progress.

A farmer once said his mule was awfully backward about going forward — and this is also true of a lot of people today.

A mule makes no headway while he's kicking; neither does a man.

What we want is progress, if we can have it without change.

Unquestionably, there is progress everywhere. The average American now pays out as much in taxes as he formerly received in wages.

Keeping things the same as they've always been is the kind of progress many people like to see.

An example of progress is the fact that every year it takes less time and more money to get where you want to go.

It is generally agreed that progress is what most inactive committees report.

Progress is wonderful. Forty years ago only hobos cooked their meals outside.

All forward motion isn't necessarily progress. Did your brakes ever go out as you were driving down a hill?

While progress in laborsaving devices has been phenomenal in the last several years, there's still a lot to be said for staying single.

Our country has made great progress. George Washington couldn't tell a lie. Now, just about everybody tells them.

Progress is seldom made without leaving somebody behind.

It is not enough to make progress; we must make it in the right direction.

The price of progress is change, and it is taking just about all we have.

All progress is due to those who were not satisfied to let well enough alone.

If everybody were perfectly contented, there would be no progress.

What a wonderful world this would be if we could have made as much progress in the last fifty years with people as we have with things.

The wheels of progress are not turned by cranks.

Everybody is in favor of progress. It's the change they don't like.

There have been many changes for the better in recent years, and some people have been against all of them.

What we call progress is often the exchange of one nuisance for another.

The best way to slow progress is to form a committee to do something about it.

Progress is going around in the same circle — but faster.

Our beloved country has made remarkable progress. Now politicians have arranged to spend taxes before they collect them.

It's our desire to get ahead of each other that creates progress — and friction!

Progress always involves a certain amount of risk. After all, you can't steal second base with one foot on first.

You are making progress if each mistake you make is a new one.

Progress is largely a matter of discarding old worries and taking on new ones.

Some men keep up with the Joneses by wearing last year's suits and driving this year's car on next year's salary. This is real progress.

Progress is the development of more machines to provide more people with more leisure time in which to be bored.

Progress has little to do with speed, but much to do with direction.

True progress consists not so much in increasing our needs as in diminishing our wants.

Progress comes from making people sit up when they want to sit down.

Progress may have been all right for a while, but it sure seems like it has gone on too long.

No one has ever backed into prosperity.

Coming together is a beginning, keeping together is progress, working together is success.

The right train of thought can take you to a better station in life.

Promises

America is always a land of promise in an election year.

What's wrong with this country is that you can't sue a congressman for breach of promise.

Promises may get friends, but it is performance that keeps them.

The promises of God are certain, but they don't all mature in ninety days.

God makes a promise — faith believes it, hope anticipates it, patience quietly awaits it.

He who would be great must be fervent in his prayers, fearless in his principles, firm in his purposes, and faithful in his promises.

It's beginning to look like we need a law so we can sue successful candidates for breach of promise.

Lawyers would have a hard time making a living if people behaved themselves and kept their promises.

It's useless to try to hold some people to anything they say while they're madly in love, drunk, or running for office.

Most politicians spend half their time making promises and the other half making excuses.

A politician should phrase his promises in such a way that nobody could remember them after the election.

The object of a political primary is to choose a promiser who'll outpromise the other party's promiser.

Now we know why they call politics the most promising of all careers.

When liquor talks in a business deal, don't pin your faith on what it says.

Nothing stretches quite as far as a campaign promise.

Promises are like money — easier made than kept.

A political promise today means another tax tomorrow.

Some people stand on the promises; others just sit on the premises.

Your promise to God should be as binding as those you make at the bank.

It is better to refuse a request with firmness and courtesy than to make a promise you can't keep.

A promise cannot be made more binding by using a lot of red tape.

Promises are only as dependable as the individuals who make them.

Despite the promises of politicians, we'll never achieve an equal and satisfactory distribution of wealth, rainfall, or parking space.

God's promises are like life preservers. They keep the soul from sinking in the sea of trouble.

A broken promise is one thing the best glue can't fix.

Nothing makes it harder to remember campaign promises than getting elected.

It is well to remember that the more you are promised the less you should expect.

Promises are like crying babies in church — they should be carried out immediately.

A candidate's promises aren't really extravagant when you compare them to a bridegroom's.

If you kept every resolution you made last year, you'd probably be skinny, smart, healthy, rich — and bored.

A resolution is always stronger at its birth than at any subsequent period.

One thing you can give and still keep is your word.

When you break your word, you break something that cannot be mended.

Prosperity

We learn some things from prosperity, but we learn many more from adversity.

The average man can stand adversity better than prosperity.

He who swells in prosperity will shrink in adversity.

Americans have two chickens in every pot, two cars in every garage, and two headaches for every aspirin.

If you get a good education, you can become prosperous — if you marry a rich widow.

Education is an ornament in prosperity and a refuge in adversity.

The friends you make in prosperity are those you lose in adversity.

A real friend will tell you your faults and follies in times of prosperity, and assist you with his hand and heart in times of adversity.

Prosperity makes friends; adversity tries them.

Only big government could advocate spending our way to prosperity while being broke.

The people who look to government to bring them security and prosperity ought to remember what happened to the American Indians.

Modern prosperity means two cars in the garage, a boat in the driveway, and a note due at the bank.

Prosperity is only an instrument to be used, not a deity to be worshipped.

Being prosperous means your credit is good enough to borrow money at the bank.

We are living in an unprecedented era of prosperity. Never before have people acquired so many unpaid for things.

We are told that prosperity has ruined many men. If we're going to be ruined, we'd prefer to have prosperity do it.

People become well-to-do by doing what they do well.

Prosperity is something you fold and forward to Washington.

We have reached an era of such prosperity in this country that living within our means is considered to be almost unpatriotic.

Let's all work toward having an affordable prosperity.

As a general rule, prosperity is what keeps us in debt.

Until he becomes prosperous, a man doesn't realize how many old friends he has.

Prosperous times are when we pay installments on ten things instead of one.

Few of us can stand prosperity — especially the other fellow's.

No one has ever backed into prosperity.

In times of prosperity men ask too little of God. In times of adversity, they ask too much.

Prosperity is that short period of time between the final installment and the next purchase.

Prosperity is something that businessmen create for politicians to take the credit for.

We won't continue having a horn of plenty if we keep blowing it.

Prosperity is just a matter of not being quite as broke this month as last month.

Sometimes virtue and prosperity have trouble living together.

Only Americans have mastered the art of being prosperous and broke at the same time.

You can always tell when an American is prosperous. He fills his home with old furniture and new whiskey.

It may be true that most people can't stand prosperity. But it's also true that most people don't have to.

When prosperity comes your way, don't use all of it.

Prosperity has arrived when a man begins to bag at the pockets instead of the knees.

All that a wave of prosperity means to many of us is the privilege of watching others buy new cars.

Prosperity is that wonderful time when we can always get enough credit to live beyond our means.

At no time is self-control more difficult than in time of success.

Psychiatrists

In the old days a father didn't have to take his kid to a psychiatrist to find out that he was a little stinker.

The difference between psychoneurosis and plain old-fashioned nervousness is approximately seven hundred dollars.

An Oklahoma doctor was recently put under psychiatric observation. The American Medical Association caught him making a house call.

Psychiatrists tell us that talking helps solve our problems — it often causes them too.

The role of a psychiatrist is to find out what makes you tick before you blow up.

Some people go to a psychiatrist slightly cracked and leave completely broke.

Psychiatrists don't fare too well in Texas — no inferiority complexes!

A psychiatrist's couch is where you land when you're off your rocker.

Maybe it takes a psychiatrist to find it, but everyone has a streak of sanity in him somewhere.

In this ulcerated, frustrated age in which we live, psychiatrists themselves are so nervous they're going to each other for help.

Psychiatrists get paid for asking a man the same questions his wife asks him for nothing.

A psychiatrist adds to your mental balance while reducing your bank balance.

A Chicago psychiatrist received the following card from a patient who was vacationing in Las Vegas, "Having a wonderful time. Wish you were here to tell me why."

Psychiatrists tell us the best way to prevent a nervous breakdown is to work hard every day. We'd like to ask — what's the next best way?

Is a psychiatrist called a "shrink" because that's what he does to your wallet?

Psychiatrists don't have to worry as long as other people do.

A Louisiana wit says that a psychiatrist is nothing more than a talent scout for a mental institution.

Psychiatrists say big men make docile husbands — so do big women!

A new branch of psychiatry has been started: Psycho-Ceramics, the study of crackpots.

The psychiatrist who urges parents to spend more time with their children may just be trying to drum up more business!

Psychiatry is just common sense clothed in a language no one can understand.

Practicing psychiatry without faith in God is like meeting a hungry man and giving him a toothpick.

Psychiatry has certainly changed things. The kid who used to be just a chatterbox is now a "compulsive talker."

Psychiatry is the only business where the customer is always wrong.

Anybody who thinks there's free speech everywhere in this country has never been on a psychiatrist's couch.

Psychiatrists tell us that girls tend to marry men who are like their fathers. Now we know why mothers cry at weddings.

When the world starts making sense to you, it's time to consult your psychiatrist.

Psychology

Psychologists say that no one should try to keep too much to himself. The IRS is of the same opinion.

Does the IRS permit a double exemption for a split personality?

A psychologist says kissing is where two people get so close together they can't see anything wrong with each other.

Although psychologists tell us that man is afraid of the unknown — it is what we *know* that really scares us.

It's incredible when we think how little our parents knew about child psychology and how wonderful we turned out to be!

Those who are well-versed in psychology tell us no one should keep too much to himself. As long as the IRS is around, nobody is likely to do so.

Child psychology is what children manage their parents with.

Applied child psychology was more effective when the applicator was a small razor strap.

Once a sin was called a sin; now it's called some kind of complex.

The man who claims he understands women is a psychologist — or needs one.

Public Speakers

At most banquets you'll find more after-dinner speakers than after-dinner listeners.

The banquet's honored guest was introduced as follows: "We're very pleased to have as our guest speaker a man who has to catch a plane in twenty minutes."

A banquet is an affair where you eat a lot of food you don't want before talking about something you don't understand to a crowd of people who don't want to hear what you have to say.

Education is a wonderful thing but it doesn't go far enough. It merely teaches a man *how* to speak, not *when* or *how long.* And neither does it teach him exactly when to shut up.

Some of the driest speeches are made by people who are all wet.

Many public speakers can talk for hours without any notes — or knowledge!

Public speaking is like eating salted peanuts. You have to know when to stop.

The trouble with after-dinner speakers is that after you've eaten the chicken they start dishing out the baloney.

Some public speakers are guilty of podium pollution.

A speaker who doesn't strike oil in twenty-five minutes should stop boring.

The trouble with some speakers is that you can't hear what they're saying. The trouble with others is that you can.

Commencement speaker in Michigan: "My advice to young people who are going out in the world today — don't go!"

Why do so many speakers who want to be breezy end up windy!

Many a speaker exhausts his audience before he exhausts his subject.

When a speaker says, "Well, to make a long story short" — it's too late.

There are two kinds of public speakers: one needs no introduction, the other deserves none.

It's all right for public speakers to have a train of thought if they also have a terminal.

The three secrets of success in public speaking are: be sincere, be brief, be seated.

A speaker ought to be the first person to know when he's through.

The difficulty with amplifiers is that they amplify the speaker's voice but not his ideas.

Sometimes when a speaker has his audience on the edge of their seats, they're trying to muster the nerve to get up and go home.

Some speakers who don't know what to do with their hands should try clamping them over their mouths.

There are two rules every speaker should observe — never drink on an empty stomach, and never speak on an empty head.

If the speaker won't boil it down, the audience must sweat it out.

You can't tell whether a man is a finished speaker until he sits down.

Nature makes blunders too — she often gives the biggest mouths to those who have the least to say.

The most important thing an after-dinner speaker has to learn is not to nod approval while the toastmaster is praising him.

A guest speaker said, "As I understand it, my job is to speak to you. Your job is to listen. I hope we finish together."

Attention public speakers: Nothing can be said after thirty minutes that amounts to anything.

Too many speakers have diarrhea of words and constipation of ideas.

When you make a speech, never tell all you know. Some nut in the audience might wake up and demand an encore.

Why don't speakers leave their audience before it leaves them?

An after-dinner speaker talks in other people's sleep.

It often takes a speaker twice as long to tell what he thinks as to tell what he knows.

Free advice to public speakers: When you're done pumping, let loose of the handle.

Far too many speakers try to impress rather than express.

A few public speakers never seem to learn the difference between an address and a filibuster.

Public speakers should speak up so they can be heard, stand up so they can be seen, and shut up so they can be enjoyed.

Public speaking is like drinking liquor. A few men can do it in moderation, but the majority don't know when to stop.

A good speaker usually turns out to be someone who says exactly what you wanted him to say.

An after-dinner speaker told his audience, "We have something in common. You don't know what I'm going to say — and neither do I."

Many a public speaker who rises to the occasion stands too long.

Some after-dinner speakers are like the horns of a steer; a point here, a point there, and a lot of bull in between.

A long-winded speaker should realize that, while the Constitution guarantees free speech, it doesn't guarantee listeners.

A noted guest speaker addressed his audience, "Now before I start I want to say something."

To be a good speaker in public, you must be a good thinker in private.

Most dull speeches are delivered by people who have nothing to say but are anxious to say it.

When both the speaker and the audience are confused, a speech is considered profound.

Punctuality

Sign at the New Orleans airport: "Start kissing goodby early, so the plane can leave on time."

Some folks are very punctual in always being late.

The drawback of being punctual is that there's nobody there to appreciate it.

A great man once said that punctuality is the art of wasting only your own time.

Punctuality assures loneliness.

Punctuality is like having bad manners. You're sure of having lots of time to yourself.

One way a person can lose a lot of time is to always be on time for appointments.

Some folks never do anything on time but buy.

The trouble with getting to work on time is that it makes the day so long.

Q

Quarrels   Questions

Quarrels

Quarrels would not last very long if the faults were only on one side.

Some husbands quarrel with their wives, and others have learned to say, "Yes, dear."

Two things would prevent many quarrels: first, to make sure we are not disputing about terms rather than facts. Second, to examine if the difference of opinion is worth contending about.

Too many people pick a quarrel before it's ripe.

When one will not, two cannot quarrel.

It takes two to make a quarrel, but one gets the blame.

A quarrel is like buttermilk. The longer it stands, the more sour it becomes.

It takes two to make a quarrel and three to make it interesting.

Perhaps the only way to avoid quarreling with your wife is to let her go her way and you go hers.

What a great world this would be if people would spend as much energy practicing their religion as they spend quarreling about it.

When one word leads to another, it generally ends up in a quarrel, a speech, or a dictionary.

Questions

An argument is a question with two sides — and no end.

An unusual child is one who asks his parents questions they can answer.

Commencement is when the college students who learned all the answers discover that there are a new set of questions.

A dentist expects you to answer his questions after he fills your mouth with everything but the kitchen sink!

An educated man is one who has finally discovered that there are some questions to which nobody has the answer.

It seems that when a fellow claims to know all the answers some fool comes along and asks the wrong questions.

An expert knows all the answers — if you ask the right questions.

The friend we admire most is the one who asks us important questions that we are able to answer.

You may not know all the answers, but you probably won't be asked all the questions either.

Women are to blame for men telling lies. They keep asking questions!

Life has more questions than answers.

The greater the philosopher, the more difficult it is for him to answer the questions of the average man.

Many politicians refuse to answer all your questions on the grounds that it might eliminate them.

An Oklahoma politician announced that he perfectly understood the questions of the day. The trouble was he didn't know the answers.

Part of the problem today is that we have a surplus of simple answers, and a shortage of simple questions.

There are two sides to every question, and a politician usually takes both.

Where do kids get all those questions parents can't answer?

A good question to ask ourselves: What kind of a world would this world be if everybody were just like me?

Don't be afraid to ask dumb questions. They're easier to handle than dumb mistakes.

Anybody who thinks he knows all the answers just isn't up to date on the questions.

Surveys have become so popular there are more people asking questions than answering them.

Things get more complicated each passing day. Can you remember when every question had only two sides?

The question we all must face sooner or later is how to fit a long vacation into a short bankroll.

You can usually dodge a question with a long-winded answer.

435

It's frustrating when you know all the answers — and nobody bothers to ask you the questions.

You don't need to know all the answers. No one is smart enough yet to ask you all the questions.

It is not every question that deserves an answer.

The paramount question before the country today is, "How much is the down-payment?"

What is worse than to ask a thirty cent question and have to listen to a sixty-four dollar answer?

It is always easier to see both sides of a question if your prejudices are not involved.

Beware of the man who knows the answer before he understands the question!

If there are two sides to every question, why is there only one answer?

Just about the time we finally learn all the answers, they change all the questions.

When somebody says, "That's a good question," you can be pretty sure it's a lot better than the answer you're going to get.

There are two sides to every quesion, except when it happens to be a love triangle.

Most of us are broad-minded enough to admit there are two sides to every question — our own side, and the side that no intelligent, informed, sane, and self-respecting person could possibly hold.

Many sermons are dull because preachers often try to answer questions that nobody is asking.

The reason that teen-agers know all the answers is that they haven't heard all the questions yet.

One sure way to test your will power is to see a friend with a black eye and not ask any questions.

Modern youth is looking for new answers so they can question them.

R

Radio

Rain

Reckless Driving

Reform

Reformers

Regret

Relatives

Religion

Repentance

Reputation

Resolutions

Responsibility

Restaurants

Retirement

Revenge

Rheumatism

Riches

Righteousness

Romance

Rumors

Russia

Radio

In the old days a comedian took a dirty joke and cleaned it up for radio. Today he hears a clean joke and dirties it up for television.

Can you remember "way back" when radios plugged in and toothbrushes didn't?

One thing about those CB radios — people with nothing to say now have some place to say it.

Today what isn't worth saying is usually sung in a radio commercial.

Rip Van Winkle slept for twenty years, but, of course, his neighbors didn't have a radio.

One good thing about radio — it never shows old movies.

The radio will never take the place of the newspaper, because you can't swat flies with it.

There's one thing radio and soap operas do for mankind. They temporarily silence women.

The radio has added thousands of words to our vocabulary, not counting those used when it's out of order.

A radio announcer is a person on the ether who should be under it.

Scientists now can tell us that the moon throws back the radio waves from the earth. We certainly don't blame it.

There's a small town in Nevada where so little ever changes that the local radio station is still running last year's weather forecasts.

The radio remains popular for the simple reason that it can't show you what your headache looks like.

A certain radio station phoned one thousand men, asking to whom they were listening. Ninety-seven percent said they were listening to their wives.

Radio is a miraculous device which enables people who have nothing to say to talk to people who aren't listening.

A radio announcer talks until you have a headache and then tries to sell you something to relieve it.

Another nice thing about radio sermons is that people don't turn and stare at you when the preacher denounces your pet sin.

Television has been a great teacher — it taught a lot of folks to turn to radio.

Rain

Don't pray for rain if you're going to complain about the mud.

Despite the promises of politicians, we'll never achieve an equal and satisfactory distribution of wealth, rainfall, or parking space.

Rain is what makes flowers grow and taxis disappear.

It's a shame that a shower of rain can't freshen people like it does flowers and grass.

Rain is something that, when you carry an umbrella, it doesn't.

Modern man has the genius to make rain, but often lacks enough common sense to come in out of it.

Reckless Driving

Auto accident statistics prove that telephone poles are getting more careless all the time.

Most accidents are caused by motorists who drive in high while their minds are in neutral.

It's the nut *behind* the wheel and not the nut *on* the wheel that causes traffic accidents.

Americans are a religious people. You can tell they trust in God by the way they drive.

There may be fewer cars on the road nowadays, but the number of nuts driving them hasn't diminished.

Automobiles continue to be driven at two speeds — lawful and awful.

There are too many middle-of-the-roaders in America, and they all drive cars.

There are a lot of nuts rattling around inside automobiles that the manufacturers didn't put there.

It's not the used cars that are a menace on the highways — it's the mis-used cars.

Bumper sticker on the back of a car in Guthrie, Oklahoma: "Watch out for the driver in the car following me."

In these days of high speed and crowded highways, it doesn't take much of a car to last a lifetime.

Even the best running cars have some jerks in them.

The most dangerous thing about an automobile is one nut — the one behind the steering wheel.

The biggest need in auto safety is the recall of a few million defective drivers.

The careful driver stops at a railroad crossing for a minute; the careless one, forever.

A motorist offered a new excuse when he was arrested for speeding, "This highway is so dangerous I was speeding to get off it."

A reckless driver is seldom reckless for very long.

Many people drive like tomorrow isn't worth waiting for.

If you don't care how soon you're dead, keep driving through the red.

Day dreams at the steering wheel lead to nightmares in the hospital.

The safest way to follow a reckless driver is with long-range binoculars.

Reckless drivers may find they have plenty of HEARSE-POWER!

The trouble with reckless drivers is that their cars are too heavy and their sentences too light.

Trying to beat the red light is a gamble. You never know how much the hospital bill will be.

Drive like lightning and you may crash like thunder.

Many drivers don't need seat belts as much as they need straight jackets.

When you race, you may beat the other fellow — to the hospital!

Better step on the brakes and be laughed at than step on the gas and be cried over.

The easiest way to commit suicide is to take gas or step on it.

"All the world is a stage," and railroad crossings furnish some of the exits.

A sure way to lose the pursuit of happiness is to chase it at a hundred miles an hour.

Some of our speeding motorists might do well to remember that it's better to be a little late down here than too early up there.

Many people drive their automobile as if they were rehearsing for an accident.

It's extremely dangerous to drive in a fog, especially if it's mental.

Nowadays drivers seldom sound their horns. The angel Gabriel does it for them.

Doctors say Americans are living too fast, and the traffic statistics indicate they are dying the same way.

If you are determined to drive with your head in the clouds, you are almost certain to find a permanent home there.

There's a line on the ocean where you can lose a day by crossing it. There's one on the highway where you can do even better than that.

Take one natural-born fool and one high-powered automobile. Soak fool in liquor, place in car, and turn loose. After due time, remove fool from wreckage, place in a satin-lined box, and garnish with flowers.

Don't race trains to the crossing. If you tie, you lose.

A reckless driver is one who passes you on the highway in spite of all you can do!

Every year thousands of American motorists discover that their car lasted them a lifetime.

It takes a thousand nuts to hold an automobile together, but just one to spread it all over the landscape.

You can tell Americans trust in God by the way they drive.

Don't drive as if you owned the road — drive as if you owned the car.

What some people don't know about driving would fill a hospital.

Take chances and the chances are you won't have many chances left.

Just because you see its tracks is no sign that a train has just passed.

The right-of-way is not worth dying for.

People who drive fast usually get where they're going ahead of time — sometimes forty or fifty years ahead of time.

What has not happened to you in ten years of driving may happen to you in the next ten minutes.

The advisability of passing a car on a curve depends on whether your widow thinks the loss will be covered by insurance.

A middle-of-the-road policy may succeed in politics, but it gets you into a lot of trouble on a highway.

It appears that the horsepower explosion on our highways may cancel out the population explosion we hear so much about.

If you aspire to a ripe old age, never drive your car while in a rage.

Motorists might feel a lot safer if some of the roadhogs were in the pen.

You may out-distance, outmaneuver, and outbrag the other driver, but the question is, will you outlive him?

High speed may get you somewhere quicker, but it can also keep you from going anyplace else.

Reckless drivers drive like living is going out of style.

A telephone pole never hit an automobile except in self-defense.

Statistics show that an average of 39,000 people are killed by gas annually. Sixty inhale it, forty light matches in it, and 38,900 step on it.

Sleeping at the wheel is a good way to keep from growing old.

The lighter the motorist's head, the heavier his foot.

In a car a tight nut is more dangerous than a loose bolt.

The only wheel that man has not thoroughly mastered is the steering wheel.

A good way to give your car a lasting finish is to try and beat a train to the crossing.

A lot of friction on the highway is caused by half the drivers trying to go fast enough to thrill their girl friends, and the other half trying to go slow enough to placate their wives.

A roadhog is a person who speeds up every time you speed up to get in front of him.

People who haven't the time to stop at a railroad crossing somehow have the time to be present at the funeral.

The driver who sticks his elbow out too far may find it going home in another car.

When two cars try to get into a place meant for one, there's often room for a third — the ambulance.

People who drive at breakneck speed are liable to do it.

Keeping up with the Joneses is bad enough, but passing them on a hill is worse.

The way motorists drive, it pays to look both ways when you cross a one-way street.

In the long ago Lot's wife, who looked back, turned into a pillar of salt. In the United States, many people who look back while driving their cars turn into a telephone pole.

A young man was arrested while necking with his girl friend on a freeway. He was charged with driving while "infatuated."

Drivers who weave in traffic often wind up in stitches.

Your children may not be angels, but bad driving habits could change that.

If all the cars in the United States were placed end to end, some idiot would try to pass them.

A road sign in Texas: "Drive like hell, and you'll get there."

Famous last words: "Go right ahead, don't let that big truck crowd you off the road."

The eminent scientist who once said we all behave like human beings obviously never drove a car.

The only safe place to fall asleep behind the wheel is at a drive-in theater.

If you sleep in a chair, you have nothing to lose, but a nap at the wheel is often a permanent snooze.

Frequent naps will keep you from getting old — especially if taken while driving.

Reform

A lot of people use mighty thin thread when mending their ways.

How easy it would be for governments to reform if there were nothing to grab.

We may need tax reform, but it seems we need a lot of spending reform too.

It is always easy to reform the city — especially if you live in the country.

There'll never be much prison reform until we send a better class of people there.

The only sweeping reform that has ever succeeded is the vacuum cleaner.

We reform others unconsciously when we walk uprightly.

Reformers

The best reformers the world has ever known were those who began with themselves.

Most reformers insist that their conscience be your guide.

Many men would do a great deal more good if they would quit trying to reform the whole world.

A reformer is often so eager to do good that he tries to right the wrongs that do not exist.

When a man begins to realize the truth about himself, it frequently retards his program of reforming his neighbor.

A reformer sees his duty and overdoes it.

There's so much good in the worst of us, and so much bad in the best of us, that it's difficult to tell just which of us ought to reform the rest of us.

The law of supply and demand doesn't always hold true. Look how many reformers we have and how little reform!

Reformers waste their time trying to clean up the horse races; it's the human race that needs cleaning up.

The reformer who says that all scandals should be made public probably doesn't know the present price of paper.

Regret

It is a great deal better to do all the things you should do than to spend the rest of your life wishing you had.

Speak when you are angry and you will make the best speech you will ever regret.

Anger is a state that starts with madness and ends with regret.

When you can think of yesterday without regret and tomorrow without fear, you are near real contentment.

The nearer the time comes for our departure from this life, the greater our regret for wasting so much of it.

You can't have rosy thoughts about the future when your mind is full of the blues about the past.

You can't have a better tomorrow if you are thinking about yesterday all day today.

Be grateful for what you have, not regretful for what you haven't.

A kindness put off until tomorrow may become only a bitter regret.

Between tomorrow's dream and yesterday's regret is today's opportunity.

The main thing that comes to a man who waits is regret for having waited.

When you can think of yesterday without regret, and of tomorrow without fear, you are well on the road to success.

No matter how limited your vocabulary is, it's big enough to let you say something you'll later regret.

Relatives

Anybody who has to ask for advice probably doesn't have any close relatives.

If a man's character is to be abused, there's nobody like a relative to get the job done.

Don't complain if your brother-in-law comes to visit you from Christmas to New Year's — he might stay with you from New Year's to Christmas.

A survey shows that slender executives make more money than fat ones. The chunky son of the president is apt to be an exception.

After a good meal one can forgive anybody, even one's relatives.

God gives us our relatives, but thank heaven we can choose our friends.

Some people want to go to heaven for the same reason they want to go to California — they have relatives there.

Never judge a man by his relatives; he did not choose them.

It might not be opportunity you hear knocking — it could be one of your relatives!

Of all the laws we have to contend with, the most troublesome are usually the in-laws.

Philanthropy is giving your money to people who will appreciate it, rather than leaving it to your relatives.

The only good thing about increased postal rates is that we don't hear from some of our relatives as often.

In locating lost relatives, nothing succeeds like getting rich.

If the knock at the door is loud and long, it isn't opportunity. It's relatives.

The easiest way to make relatives feel at home is to visit them there.

A recent survey proved that the people who live longest are rich relatives.

With today's jet travel, there's no such thing as a distant relative.

It's real nice to see out-of-town relatives — out of town!

Relatives are persons who come to visit us when the weather is too uncomfortable for them to do their own cooking at home.

A relative thinks a lot of you — but only if you make a fortune and drop dead!

The man whose ship comes in usually finds most of his relatives at the dock.

A distant relative is not quite distant enough.

If a man's character is to be smeared, there's nobody like a relative to do the job.

The hardest thing to disguise is your true feelings when you put a lot of relatives on the plane for home.

We call our rich relatives 'the kin we love to touch.'

Remember, your relatives had no choice in the matter either.

Folks bragging about their relatives usually forget to mention the one who started on a shoestring and wound up at the end of a rope.

Everybody can use a rich and generous relative — and those who have usually do.

Many people seem to think that distant relatives are the best kind to have.

When relatives visit your hideaway, they usually take everything but the road home.

It is only after a man gets rich that he discovers how many poor relatives he has.

Success is relative — the more success, the more relatives.

When you finally save enough for a rainy day, some of your relatives start sending in bad weather reports.

Among the many things a wealthy man finds coming to him are poor relatives.

Religion

Americans are a religious people. You can tell they trust in God by the way they drive.

It is never worthwhile to argue about the religion you haven't got.

The person who boasts of having no religious prejudice quite often has no religion.

The Christmas season reminds us that a demonstration of religion is often better than a definition of it.

The less religion a church has, the more ice cream and cake it takes to keep it going.

When the churches discover they can't successfully compete with the theater, perhaps they will try religion again.

A man may attend church services regularly, but this does not necessarily mean he attends religiously.

Cleanliness may be next to godliness, but it is not a substitute.

The family altar would alter many a family.

A Sunday golfer is a person who is more interested in a hole-in-one than the Holy One.

A really good golfer is one who goes to church on Sunday first.

The man who expects to go to heaven must take the time to study the route that will get him there.

A critically-ill lawyer was found frantically leafing through the Bible in his hospital room. When asked the reason, he replied, "Looking for loopholes."

There is plenty of heavenly music for those who are tuned in.

The religion of some people consists principally in praying that the Lord will provide.

Still water and still religion freeze the quickest.

A man in Louisiana is so religious he wears stained glass contact lenses.

You have to do more than just examine religion. It won't satisfy your thirst unless you drink it.

If your religion leaves your life unchanged, you'd better change your religion.

Many people tailor their religion to fit the pattern of their prejudice.

Heathens are about the only folks who don't argue about religion.

People are won to your religious beliefs less by description than by demonstration.

True religion is keeping one's heart clean and hands dirty — in human service.

Religion costs, but irreligion costs more.

There's a growing suspicion that what the world needs now is a religion that will cover the other six days of the week.

Religion should be the motor of life, the central heating plant of personality, the faith that gives joy to activity, hope to struggle, dignity to humility, and zest to living.

In our generation the popular religion is CONFUSIONISM.

People seldom lose their religion by a blowout; usually it's just a slow leak.

Men will wrangle for religion, write for it, die for it — anything but live for it.

Why expect men to unite on religion when they can't on anything else?

You cannot prove your religion by its noise.

A religion that does nothing, costs nothing, suffers nothing — is worth nothing.

Religion is like music — it does not need defense, but rendition.

God wants spiritual fruit, not religious nuts.

A man has no more religion than he acts out in his life.

We are more comfortable with Christ in print than in practice.

A religion that is not worth exporting is not worth keeping at home.

True religion is the life we live, not the creeds we profess.

Some folks seem to think religion is like a parachute — something to grab when an emergency occurs.

The person who argues most about religion usually has the least of it.

What a great world this would be if people would spend as much energy practicing their religion as they spend quarreling about it.

The world does not need a definition of religion as much as it needs a demonstration.

Some men's religion runs up against a stone wall when it reaches the location of their pocketbooks.

The gospel of Jesus Christ breaks hard hearts and heals broken hearts.

The hardest job that people have is to move their religion from their throats to their muscles.

Isn't it strange how some people insist on having expensive clothes, yet are perfectly satisfied with a shoddy religion?

People don't really pay much attention to what we say about our religion, because they'd rather watch what we do about it.

It's time for us to stop putting more saints in stained glass and start putting more in shoe leather.

Religion is a cloak used by some people in this world who will be warm enough without one in the next.

Arguing about religion is much easier than practicing it.

Some people really enjoy their religion; others just endure it.

A bitter world cannot be sweetened by a sour religion.

There are still a few people who think that religion is like a faucet — to be turned on and off as the need arises.

Most people have some sort of religion; at least they know what church they're staying away from.

Very often a person who boasts of having no religious prejudice has no religion either.

Some folks think that all the equipment you need to discuss religion is a mouth.

If people were as religious as statistics show them to be, we could get along with fewer police.

Religion is no different from other things. The less you invest in it, the poorer the quality.

Too many folks use their religion as they do a bus — they ride it only when it's going their way.

It is never wise to argue about the religion you don't have.

A lot of people are interested in a religion that makes them look good without having to act that way.

Religion is meant to be bread for daily use, not cake for special occasions.

There are too many people practicing religion today, and not enough people who are good at it.

Why don't those who hate the church move to where there are none?

Thousands of people are experts on religion but never practice it.

It has always been easier to oppose a religious effort than to work and sacrifice on behalf of it.

Religion is life. Faith is the only fuse.

When folks clamor for a new religion, what they really want is a religion that isn't too religious.

The most uncomfortable person on earth is one who has just enough religion to make him uneasy and not enough to make him happy.

Some people carry their religion like a burden on their backs, when they should carry it like a song in their hearts.

Amusement will help you forget things; religion will help you surmount them.

To avoid the risk of losing their religion, a lot of people don't take it to work with them.

Before you undertake to change a man's religion or politics, be sure you've got something better to offer him.

A man without religion is like a horse without a bridle.

The religion of some folks is like the merry-go-round — it doesn't get them anywhere.

It's extremely difficult to sell anyone a product you've never used — or a religion you've never lived.

Religion at its best is a lift and not a load.

Your religion doesn't amount to very much unless it causes you to come out of the grandstand onto the playing field.

The religion of some is well-developed at the mouth but lame in the hands and feet.

Some folks have too much religion to be happy at a dance, but too little to be happy at a prayer meeting.

Religion is not a way of looking at certain things. It is a certain way of looking at everything.

It is a sad religion that is never strong except when the owner is sick.

Religion furnishes education with a true sense of values. It shows what is worthwhile.

Some people think religion, like aspirin, should be taken only to relieve pain.

A religion that is small enough for us to understand would not be large enough for our needs.

True religion can be both steering wheel and brakes; it can guide you along the right road and stop you at the wrong one.

If your religion is the kind that can easily be hidden, it can easily be lost.

The weekend religion of some Christians is weak at both ends, and unreliable between the two ends.

Religion is the best armor a person can wear, but it is the worst cloak.

The religious indifference of the masses is to be accounted for partly by the differences in the churches.

445

One reason why some people don't talk about their religion is that they don't have much to talk about.

If your religion means much to you, live so it will mean much to others.

It is generally in summer that religion is snowed under.

Your religion will do more for you if you do more for it.

To really enjoy religion, one must first have it and then use it.

When your religion gets into past tense, it becomes pretense.

Quite often religion is like soap — those who need it most use it least.

The sword of the Spirit never becomes dull from use.

Nations and men are much alike. They seldom appeal to God unless they're getting licked.

Religion is like a bank — neither one pays dividends unless we make deposits.

Religion is like a wheelbarrow — you have to push it.

The main object of religion is not to get a man into heaven, but to get heaven into him.

Religion doesn't fail. It's the people who fail religion.

If a man has any religion at all, he must either give it away or give it up.

"Kneeology" will do more for the world than theology.

We talk a great deal of religion in this country, but we need to stop long enough to let our feet catch up with our mouths.

To the truly religious person, every day is Sunday.

Some people's religion is like a wooden leg. There is neither life nor warmth in it; although it helps them to hobble along, it never becomes a part of them, but has to be strapped on every morning.

If you hold your religion lightly you are sure to let it slip.

Why expect men to unite on religion when they can't unite on anything else?

A great many men still like to think of their wives as they do their religion — neglected, but always there.

A bitter world cannot be sweetened by a sour religion.

Repentance

It takes more courage to repent than to keep on sinning.

True repentence has a double aspect. It looks upon things past with a weeping eye, and upon the future with a watchful eye.

It is much easier to repent of sins that we have already committed than to repent of those we intend to commit.

Some people repent of their sins by thanking the Lord they aren't half as bad as some of their neighbors.

Did you ever suspect that folks who repent loud and long are really just bragging?

To grieve over sin is one thing; to repent is another.

You can't repent too soon, because you don't know how soon it may be too late.

It seems that more people repent of their sins from fear of punishment than from a change of heart.

Reputation

Reputation is precious, but character is priceless.

Reputation is what you need to get a job; character is what you need to keep it.

A good past is the best thing a man can use for a future reference.

Take care of your character and your reputation will take care of itself.

There are two very difficult things in this world. One is to make a good name for one's self, and the other is to keep it.

An open confession is good for the soul, but bad for the reputation.

Everyone should fear death until he has something that will live on after his death.

White lies are likely to leave black marks on a man's reputation.

A man has three names: the name he inherits, the name his parents gave him, and the name he makes for himself.

A good name, like good will, is attained by many actions and may be lost by one.

The best inheritance parents can leave a child is a good name.

If some folks lost their reputation, they should consider themselves very lucky.

No one can build a reputation on what he's going to do tomorrow.

Reputation is character with whatever you've been caught doing subtracted.

No human being is rich enough to buy back his past.

Many a man gets a reputation for being energetic when in truth he is merely fidgety.

Nothing deflates as fast as a punctured reputation.

You can trust any number of people with your money, but very few with your reputation.

It is easier to acquire a good reputation than to lose a bad one.

One way to cover up a bad past is to build a big future over it.

Reputation is one of the few things that looks worse when you try to decorate it.

A good reputation may merely be proof that you don't have inquisitive neighbors.

A man's reputation is a blend of what his friends, enemies, and acquaintances say behind his back.

So live that when death comes the mourners will outnumber the cheering section.

When a man has a reputation for telling the truth, he doesn't have to prove everything he says.

Reputation is a large bubble which bursts when you try to blow it up yourself.

A reputation once broken may possibly be repaired, but the world will always keep an eye on the spot where the crack was.

Many a man's reputation would not recognize his character if they met in the dark.

The easiest thing to get, but the most difficult thing to get rid of, is a bad reputation.

You have to be quite a juggler if you have a reputation to keep up and one to live down.

A man may be able to trade his reputation for money, but he can't trade back.

It takes a very short time to lose a good reputation but a long, long time to regain it.

What people say to your back is your standing in the community.

Reputation is a personal possession, frequently not discovered until lost.

The best way to suppress a bad past is to start in on it while it is present.

Reputation is something to live up to in your youth and to live down in your old age.

The only time you realize you have a reputation is when you're not living up to it.

It is generally agreed that a man is known by the company he keeps — out of!

The easiest way to live up to your reputation is by having a poor one.

A man can tell how good his reputation is by how hard it is for him to live up to it.

A good reputation is what usually makes people wonder what you're hiding.

Your reputation can be damaged by the opinions of others. Only you yourself can damage your character.

Nobody raises his own reputation by lowering others.

No man is rich enough to buy back his past.

Many men would turn over a new leaf if they could tear out some of the old pages.

The slanderer differs from the assassin only in that he murders the reputation instead of the body.

Resolutions

The only thing most of us learn from our mistakes is how to blame them on somebody else.

A New Year's resolution is a promise to stop doing everything you enjoy most.

Every year many American girls resolve that they're going to give up rich foods and poor boyfriends.

If you kept every resolution you made last year, you'd probably be skinny, smart, healthy, rich — and bored.

A resolution is always stronger at its birth than at any subsequent period.

Serious trouble comes when the New Year's resolutions collide with the old year's habits.

Why not be sure by having your New Year's resolutions notorized?

We should keep all our resolutions secret. That way nobody will know when we break them.

The fragments of broken resolutions can be cemented together, but the cracks will show.

Most of the leaves we turned over in January have already started to fall.

A New Year's resolution is something that goes in one year and out the other.

Most good resolutions start too late and end too soon.

May your troubles in the coming New Year be as short-lived as your resolutions.

Responsibility

Man blames most accidents on fate — but feels a more personal responsibility when he makes a hole-in-one on the golf course.

We increase our ability, stability, and responsibility when we increase our sense of accountability to God.

We cannot do everything we want to do, but we should do everything God wants us to do.

Our actions are our own; their consequences are not.

You can do everything you ought to do.

None of us is responsible for all the things that happen to us, but we are responsible for the way we act when they do happen.

It's a terrible responsibility to own a Bible.

A real man is one who finds excuses for others, but never for himself.

Freedom is a package deal — with it comes responsibilities and consequences.

Life is one dodge after another — cars, taxes, and responsibilities.

No individual raindrop ever considered itself responsbile for the flood.

Responsibility makes just as many cowards out of men as it makes successes.

A worker in Illinois says he has a very responsible job — when anything goes wrong, he's responsible.

It is easy to dodge our responsibilities, but we cannot dodge the consequences of dodging our responsibilities.

We may not be responsible for many of the things that happen to us, but we are responsible for the way we react when they do happen.

Responsibility develops some men and ruins others.

Those who shrink from responsibilities keep on shrinking in other ways too.

If the responsibility for all poverty is placed on the wealthy, why not blame all sickness on the healthy?

Some people grow under responsibility, while others only swell.

When you take responsibility on your shoulders there is not much room left for chips.

Some people recognize their responsibilities in time to dodge them.

You cannot escape the responsibilities of tomorrow by evading them today.

God holds us responsible, not for what we have, but for what we could have; not for what we are, but for what we might be.

If you would like to keep your feet on the ground, carry some responsibilities on your shoulders.

Man is responsible to God for becoming what God has made possible for him to become.

Responsibility is like old age in that it is not possible to escape from either of them.

A man's work is a portrait of himself.

Restaurants

A customer in a cafeteria complained that everything there was terrible, including the self-service.

Most of us can't afford to eat out any more, but sometimes we park near a restaurant and inhale.

Pie isn't fattening — not the way some restaurants slice it.

Doctors who tell us never to eat when we're unhappy should revise restaurant prices.

Many restaurants are now listing hash on the menu as "Today's Conglomerate."

Even a waiter finally comes to him who waits.

Restaurant owners talk about their "service with a smile." Actually their service is a laugh!

You get fed up in a restaurant these days by just looking at the menu.

Sign in a small restaurant in Oklahoma: "Don't complain about our waitress. She has an energy crisis."

Prices in some restaurants are now so high that you'd be wiser to watch your steak than your hat and topcoat.

Have you noticed how today's restaurant prices seem to make home cooking taste a lot better?

A restaurant owner said to his waitresses, "Girls, put on a big smile today. The meat's tough."

Remember that when you eat out in a swanky restaurant the food may be plain, but the prices will be fancy.

It's strange how restaurant owners whose menus are printed in French are smart enough to make up the bills in English!

A French restaurant is where they consider ketchup a dangerous food additive.

Some restaurants are now saving energy — drink two or three of their cocktails and the lights go out.

In some plush restaurants you can see executives having twenty-five dollar lunches while they discuss how to cut expenses.

Sign in a Milwaukee restaurant: "Come in and eat before we both starve."

Have you noticed that in many restaurants the food is frozen and the waiters are fresh?

In San Francisco there's a Chinese restaurant that serves all you can eat for one dollar — but they give you only one chopstick.

In some restaurants you'll notice three shakers on every table — salt, pepper, and Alka-Seltzer.

A restaurant in Little Rock, Arkansas, is so unsanitary the waitresses usually ask, "Coffee, tea, or Lysol?"

The modern restaurant is a place where the public pays the proprietor for the privilege of tipping the waiters for something to eat.

When ordering a dinner in a swank restaurant, if you can't pronounce it, you probably can't afford it.

In some restaurants the music makes you feel like dancing; in others it's the food.

A restaurant owner in a southern state grumbled about poor business, "If I could drop dead right now I'd be the happiest man alive."

In restaurants where the service is slow, the best waiters are the customers.

Sign in a South Carolina restaurant: "Don't make fun of our coffee. You may be old and weak yourself someday."

One nice thing about restaurant coffee — in most places they make it too weak to stain your necktie.

Retirement

Sixty-five is the age when one acquires sufficient experience to lose his job.

There are a lot of books telling you how to manage when you retire. What most people want is one that'll tell them how to manage in the meantime.

Inflation is making the green pastures of retirement look parched.

Retirement can be a great joy if you can figure out how to spend time without spending money.

Forty years ago when a fellow said something about retiring, he was talking about going to bed.

Before deciding to retire from your job, stay home a week and watch daytime television.

Retirement is when your wife realizes she never gave your secretary enough sympathy.

"Retirement security" is making sure all the doors are locked before you go to bed.

The best time to start thinking about retirement is before your boss does.

Retirement is when you sit around and watch the sunset — if you can stay up that late.

The key to a happy retirement is to have enough money to live on, but not enough to worry about.

When some people retire it's going to be mighty hard to tell the difference.

We have reached the point where too many folks want to retire before they go to work.

A male retiree says he's been playing golf occasionally — but only on days ending with y.

He who laughs last at the boss's jokes probably isn't very far from retirement.

A recent retiree writes that he's tired of retirement already, "I wake up in the morning with nothing to do, and by bedtime I have it only half done."

The worst thing about retirement is having to drink coffee on your own time.

Retirement is when the living is easy and the payments are hard.

One wife's definition of retirement: "Twice as much husband, and half as much income."

Retirement is when a man who figured he'd go fishing seven times a week finds himself washing the dishes three times a day.

Mandatory retirement is another form of compulsory poverty.

Many a retired husband becomes his wife's full-time job.

The hardest people to convince that they're ready to retire are children at bedtime.

Retirement has cured many a businessman's ulcers — and given his wife one!

A Kansas father said his teen-age son took an aptitude test and was found to be well-suited for retirement.

Retirement is wonderful if you have two essentials — much to live on and much to live for.

Retirement is the time of life when you stop lying about your age and start lying about the house.

One of the problems of retirement is that it gives you more time to read about the problems of retirement.

Nothing is impossible in Russia but reform.

Revenge

Have you noticed that it's much easier to forgive an enemy after you get even with him?

It's extremely difficult to endure hatred without resentment and a desire to reciprocate.

Las Vegas is where you go the first time for fun — and the second time for revenge.

A fitting revenge is paying your doctor bill with a check signed illegibly.

Revenge is the poorest victory in all the world. To kill a hornet after it has stung you was never known to make the wound heal any faster.

If revenge is sweet, why does it leave such a bitter taste?

There is no passion of the human heart that promises so much and pays so little as that of revenge.

Two newspaper editors had been feuding for years and one of them died. The other saw an opportunity for final revenge. He printed the obituary under "Public Improvements."

Revenge may be sweet, but not when you are on the receiving end.

The longest odds in the world are those against getting even with someone.

Revenge is like biting a dog because the dog bites you.

You will never get ahead of anyone as long as you're trying to get even with him.

Revenge is the sword that wounds the one who wields it.

The world has always acted on the principle that one good kick deserves another.

Rheumatism

With some people it's rheumatism more than conscience that keeps them on the right path.

The best medicine for rheumatism is being thankful it isn't gout.

Rheumatism was nature's first primitive effort to establish a weather bureau.

While we're ridding the country of radicalism, communism, socialism, and fascism, why not include rheumatism?

Riches

A limousine is a car with a glass partition to shut out stupid remarks from the backseat.

How-to-get-rich books are now filed under FICTION.

Most of us secretly wish we were so rich that we wouldn't have to pay an income tax.

Be kind to people until you make your first million. After that, people will be kind to you.

He loved a girl so much he worshiped the very ground her father discovered oil on.

Philosophy is something rich people use to convince the rest of use that it's no disgrace to be poor.

Being poor is a problem, but being rich isn't always the answer.

What's all this talk about getting rich the hard way? Is there any other way?

The trouble with the road to riches these days is there are too many toll booths along the way.

It's not a sin to be rich — it's a miracle!

There's nothing wrong with men possessing riches. The wrong comes when riches possess men.

The rich may not live longer, but it certainly seems like it to their poor relatives.

It's about as hard for a rich man to enter heaven as it is for a poor man to remain on earth.

It is usually the rich who say to the poor, "Be of good cheer."

There are two ways of being rich. One is to have all you want, and the other is to be satisfied with what you have.

It's better to live richly than to die rich.

No man is rich enough to buy back his past.

Plenty in the purse cannot prevent starvation in the soul.

If you would like to get rich, earn a little more than you spend — and keep on doing it.

It's extremely difficult for a rich man to enter the kingdom of heaven, but it's not difficult for him to get on the church board of stewards.

Once people wanted to be rich, but now they seem satisfied just to live as if they were.

Riches are often harder to manage than to acquire.

Whatever it is that keeps people from getting rich — most of us have it!

The futility of riches is stated very plainly in two places: the Bible and the income-tax form.

It is only after a man gets rich that he discovers how many poor relatives he has.

The richest man in the old hometown at the turn of the century would be classified with the underprivileged now.

Fewer folks nowadays are suffering from the embarrassment of riches.

No amount of riches can atone for poverty of character.

Riches are a golden key that opens every door, save that of heaven.

In your search for riches, don't lose the things that money can't buy.

Anybody could get rich if he could guess the exact moment at which a piece of junk becomes an antique.

It is not what we *take up*, but what we *give up*, that makes us rich.

Riches are a burden to those who have them and a greater burden to those who don't have them.

It is what we value, not what we have, that makes us rich.

Many girls are very romantic. They expect a declaration of love to have a ring in it.

Righteousness

Even the hypocrite admires righteousness. That is why he imitates it.

You can always tell when you are on the road of righteousness — it's uphill.

Garments of righteousness never go out of style.

There are only two classes of people: the righteous and the unrighteous. The classifying is always done by the righteous.

Where there is no thirst for righteousness, the sermon is always "dry."

Righteousness does not consist in being just a little less bad than our neighbors.

God never alters the robe of righteousness to fit the man, but the man to fit the robe.

Most people favor righteousness — or so many of them wouldn't pretend to have it.

Romance

Fishing is like romance; the next best thing to experiencing it is talking about it.

Romance goes out the window when she stops knitting and starts needling.

There's nothing like a marriage to break up a beautiful romance.

Sudden romances usually end the same way.

Romance often begins by a splashing waterfall and ends over a leaky sink.

There is nothing so unromantic as a seasick bride.

Nothing chills a romance like a cold shoulder.

A romantic fire is often kindled by a little spark in the park.

Romance is like a game of chess — one false move and you're mated.

A romance sometimes begins by deceiving one's self and ends by deceiving others.

Rumors

There is nothing as effective as a bunch of facts to spoil a good rumor.

There's a new margarine on the market named RUMOR — because is spreads so easily and quickly.

It's easier to float a rumor than to sink one.

A lot of people seem to have RUMORTISM.

There is nothing busier than a so-called idle rumor.

Some people will believe anything if you tell them it's a rumor.

We still can't understand how rumors without a leg to stand on get around so fast.

A rumor is like a check — never endorse it till you're sure it's genuine.

All rumors should be fitted with girdles to keep them from spreading.

There are no idle rumors. They are all busy.

Whenever we fan the flames of a rumor, we're likely to get burned ourselves.

All women don't repeat rumors. Some originate them.

Did you ever know of an idle rumor that remained idle?

Unfortunately, an unfounded rumor isn't one that is lost.

A groundless rumor often covers a lot of ground.

Slander, like coffee, is usually handed to you without grounds.

The slanderer differs from the assassin only in that he murders the reputation instead of the body.

A tongue four inches long can kill a man six feet tall.

Everybody likes to hear the truth — especially about somebody else.

Russia

The way to get ahead of Russia is to get behind America.

Communism is freedom — Russian style!

All that communism in Russia lacks for success is something for the people to eat, something to wear, and something constructive for the people to do.

One reason why the Russian Communists are increasingly adopting free-market practices in their economy is that they'd rather be fed than "red."

A Communist in the United States is a person who says everything is perfect in Russia but stays in this country because he likes to rough it.

In Russia it doesn't take a fellow very long to talk his head off.

It is reported that someone recently broke into the Kremlin and stole next year's election.

There are two political parties in Russia — the one that's in power and the one that's in jail.

Russia conceals her gold, but she is never backward about displaying her brass.

One of Moscow's finest hotels proudly boasts that there is a television set in every room — only it watches you!

The main difference between Russia and the United States is that in Russia the state owns everything and in the United States the finance companies do.

Russia is just about the only country in the world where nobody sits up all night to see how the elections come out.

Freedom of speech is still guaranteed in Russia. You can say anything you want — at least once.

We shudder to think what would happen if Russia broke our zip code.

In Russia the people have only what the government gives them; in America the people have only what the government does not take away from them in taxes.

A rumor is afloat that we have a new trade agreement with Russia. We will send them 10,000 automobiles from Detroit, and they will send us 20,000 parking spaces from Siberia.

Nothing is impossible in Russia but reform.

The Reds won't have to bury us if we keep going deeper in the hole.

Russia reports that life under the communistic system is longer than under capitalism. On the other hand it may just *seem* longer.

How often do you hear of a protest march in Russia?

We have more cars in the United States, but Russia has more vacant parking places.

Russia has abolished God, but so far God has been more tolerant of Russia.

Russia is a gambler's paradise; you'd never lose an election bet.

Have you ever thought that Adam and Eve were Russians? They had nothing to wear, nothing to eat but an apple — and yet they were told they were living in paradise!

The Russians accuse us of being a warlike people because they have been reading what the Democrats and Republicans are saying about each other.

Maybe one reason the Russians are so confident is they've watched our TV programs and figure all Americans have tired blood, indigestion, bad breath, and a nagging backache.

A prominent Russian newspaper announces that it plans to run a contest for the best political joke. First prize is twenty years.

Russian girls are more interested in boys than in politics. They obviously figure it's better to be wed than Red.

The Russians have one big advantage over us. They don't have to spend half their time and money fighting communism.

S

Safety
Salesmanship
Salesmen
Santa Claus
Satan
Satisfaction
Scandals
Schools
Science
Scientists
Secrets
Self-control

Selfishness
Senators
Sermons
Service
Sickness
Silence
Sin
Sincerity
Slander
Sleep
Smiles

Snoring
Society
Speech
Sports
Statistics
Stinginess
Strength
Success
Supermarkets
Suspicion
Sympathy

Safety

The biggest need in auto safety is the recall of a few million defective drivers.

The most effective auto-safety measure is accidentally locking the keys inside the car.

All the safety devices on a car can be replaced by one careful driver.

If disarmament doesn't make us love one another, it will at least make it safer to hate one another.

Personal liberty ends where public safety begins.

Any safety campaign that does not throttle booze overlooks the main cause of accidents and crime.

Quite often a motorist will knock a pedestrian down because his windshield is obscured by safety stickers.

The safest way to spend a holiday is to sit at home and yawn.

In case of an air raid, go to the nearest slot machine. It hasn't been hit in years.

To avoid trouble and insure safety, breathe through your nose. It keeps the mouth shut.

The only safe place to fall asleep behind the wheel is at a drive-in theater.

The best safety device ever invented for automobiles is a careful driver.

Salesmanship

When selling yourself don't misrepresent the goods.

Selling is a little like hog calling. It isn't what you say, it's the appeal in your voice.

Salesmanship is transferring a conviction from a seller to the buyer.

Selling is quite easy if you work hard enough at it.

Successful salesmanship is 10 percent preparation and 90 percent presentation.

More sales have been started when the salesman's mouth was closed than when it was open.

He who has the habit of smiling at the cash register instead of the customer won't be smiling long.

Salesmen

Sign on the front door of a Georgia home: "We shoot every third salesman, and the second one just left."

Home is a man's refuge, a place of quiet and rest, says a certain writer. That's true except for the telephone, the children, the vacuum cleaner, and the salesman at the door.

It's not the land that lies, it's the real-estate agent.

One of the greatest pleasures of growing old is the freedom we enjoy from life insurance salesmen.

Opportunity does knock sometimes, but most of the time it's just a salesman.

There are two types of people who'll tell you there are better places to be than where you are — real-estate salesmen and preachers.

Occasionally you meet one of those strange people who is polite and isn't trying to sell you anything.

It's no shame to be poor, and, besides, the salesmen leave you alone.

Too many salesmen know how to say nothing. Too few know when.

A traveling salesman explained why he was fired, "The accountants found a blond hair on my expense account."

A super salesman is a husband who can convince his wife that she's too young for a mink coat.

As a general rule, a green salesman is a better producer than a blue one.

A certain high-pressure salesman in California is so convincing that he's now making a fortune selling burial suits with two pairs of trousers.

Salesmen who keep passing the buck never seem to make any of them.

The object of a salesman is not to make sales, but to make customers.

Good salesmen, like good cooks, create an appetite when the buyer doesn't seem to be hungry.

The world's best salesman is probably the guy who sold two milking machines to a farmer who had only one cow — and took the cow as the down-payment.

Some salesmen electrify their prospects; others merely gas them.

The typical salesman is a man with a smile on his face, a shine on his shoes, and a lousy territory.

A salesman need never be ashamed of his calling. He should only be ashamed of his not calling.

Salesmen are frequently employed to say things their employer would not dare to put on paper.

On his first day out as a salesman he received two orders, "Get out" and "Stay out."

Salesmen are people with both feet on the ground, who take orders from people with both feet on the desk.

The traveling salesman is a man who wishes he had as much fun on the road as his wife thinks he does.

Old salesmen never die — they just get out of commission.

A good salesman can talk you to debt.

Musically speaking, a super salesman is one with a perfect pitch.

Santa Claus

It's always charming to see little children lined up waiting to talk to the department store Santa Claus — some with parents, some with lists, and some with chicken pox.

Can you remember when Christmas was so simple that one Santa Claus could work an entire town?

Last year a big store in Milwaukee started its Christmas sale so early that Santa Claus wore Bermuda shorts.

Christmas is the time of the year when Santa Claus comes down the chimney and your savings go down the drain.

There have always been some Christmas stockings that provided Santa with a few problems, but one wonders about his reaction to panty hose!

A father's biggest difficulty at Christmas time is convincing the children that he is Santa Claus and his wife that he is not.

Next Christmas Santa Claus won't be the only one in the red.

If your youngster asks how Santa Claus gets into your house, tell him he comes in through a hole in daddy's wallet.

Some men refuse to believe in Santa Claus until they get married and have to be him.

By the time most fellows are in shape to play Santa Claus, the kids no longer believe in him.

A man goes through three stages: he believes in Santa Claus; he doesn't believe in Santa Claus — then he is Santa Claus.

In some sections of the country Christmas shopping starts so early that Santa Claus wears Bermuda shorts.

When Santa Claus comes down the chimney, your money goes down the drain.

Last Christmas a stingy father told his little children that Santa Claus had been drafted into the army.

Satan

Satan can quote Scripture for his purpose.

Read your Bible. A chapter a day keeps Satan away.

Satan is not afraid of a Bible with dust on it.

Satan is perfectly willing to have a person confess Christianity as long as he does not practice it.

Satan is never too busy to rock the cradle of a sleeping Christian.

Too many Christian soldiers fraternize with the enemy.

For every sin Satan is ready to provide an excuse.

The devil also loves a cheerful giver — providing he is the receiver.

The only way to be good is to obey God, love your fellowman, and hate the devil.

The devil is the father of lies, but he forgot to patent the idea.

Satan hinders prayer, but prayer also hinders Satan.

Judging by the way some church members live, they need fire insurance.

Satan is not as black as he is painted. In fact, he is more like us than we care to admit.

Old Satan has no unemployment problems.

Satan is never too busy to rock the cradle of a sleeping Christian.

It seems that Satan first makes friends with the parents to make it easier to get their boys and girls.

Satan is perfectly willing for a person to confess Christianity as long as he does not practice it.

It's invariably the little devil in your neighborhood who starts the fight with your little angel.

Satan uses a vacant mind as a dumping ground.

A tongue was intended to be a divine organ, but Satan often plays upon it.

Satan doesn't care what we worship, as long as we don't worship God.

Satisfaction

Character grows in the soil of experience, with the fertilization of example, the moisture of desire, and the sunshine of satisfaction.

The strange thing is that man is satisfied with so little in himself but demands so much in others.

It's remarkable how large a part ignorance plays in making a man satisfied with himself.

Among the things that enable a man to be self-satisfied is a poor memory.

Few men are ever satisfied when they get what they deserve.

There are two ways of being rich. One is to have all you want, and the other is to be satisfied with what you have.

Almost anything can be bought at a reduced price except lasting satisfaction.

About the only satisfaction that comes from being broke is that it enables you to deal decisively with investment salesmen.

Satisfaction is the best kind of internal revenue.

Few things in life are more satisfying than parking on what's left of the other person's dime.

Life's greatest satisfactions include getting the last laugh, having the last word, and paying the last installment.

Most folks were satisfied with their lot in life until the politicians started giving them free rides.

Satisfaction is the state of mind produced when you witness the discomfort of someone you don't like.

If you are satisfied with yourself, you had better change your ideals.

The greatest reward for serving others is the satisfaction found in your own heart.

Scandals

A scandal is a breeze whipped by two or more windbags.

A scandal-monger is one who pours social sewage into people's ears.

Usually the half of a scandal that has not been told is the better half.

The trouble with a skeleton in the closet is that it doesn't have sense enough to stay there.

A scandal is one thing that has to be bad to be good.

When folks get to talking to one another, instead of about, you can always expect a better community.

A scandal is what half the world takes pleasure in inventing and the other half in believing.

A breath of scandal makes conversation breezy for some people.

The reformer who says that all scandals should be made public probably doesn't know the present price of paper.

Why is it that a scandal runs, while truth must crawl?

Schools

The school kids in some towns are getting so tough that teachers are playing hooky.

Nothing grieves a child more than to study the wrong lesson and learn something he wasn't supposed to.

One thing that keeps a lot of people from going to college is high school.

Since the advent of sex education, the old fellow who drives the local school bus can't tell whether the kids are talking dirty or discussing their lesson assignment!

"Class hatred" is what makes kids want to stay out of school.

Sign on a high school bulletin board in Dallas: "Free every Monday through Friday — knowledge. Bring your own containers."

It is poor economy to cut down on schools and use the money later on jails and reformatories.

One-fifth of the population of the United States is in the schools, and the other four-fifths are in the school of experience.

School and education should not be confused; it is only school that can be made easy.

At reform school, he was voted the student most likely to return.

The trouble with school dropouts is not that they see the handwriting on the wall, but they can't read it.

School is the mouse race that equips you for the rat race.

The most difficult school is the school of hard knocks. One never graduates.

The toughest school in America is located in Georgia. It has the only school paper with an obituary column.

A school is a place where children go to catch a cold from other children so they can stay home.

Many dropouts go from school to night court.

Some of our schools have gone modern. The kids who once cleaned the erasers now dust the computers.

Driving schools no longer teach their students how to park. They consider it a waste of time.

All a youngster wants out of school is himself.

A young man in Chicago played hooky from a correspondence school. He mailed in empty envelopes.

School days can be the happiest days of your life — if your kids are old enough to attend.

Science

If science says nothing is impossible, how about a mechanical taxpayer?

While science has made giant strides in communication in recent years, there's still a lot to be said for paying attention.

You'd think that science, which has come up with a quackless duck and a stingless bee, would start working on a wordless politician.

Modern science is simply wonderful. It would take fifty people twenty years to make the same mistake a computer can make in only two seconds.

If medical science has done so much to add years to our lives, how come you never meet a woman who's past thirty-five?

Why doesn't science come up with a pain-killer for medical and hospital bills?

Science has increased our life span considerably. Now we can look forward to paying our taxes at least ten years longer.

Despite all our ingenuity and know-how, science still hasn't found a better way to get firemen downstairs than by sliding down a pole.

Will medical science ever find a cure for foot-in-mouth disease?

Science says the world's population will have doubled in twenty years — which means one thing, you'd better find a parking place fast.

Science will never discover a way to make a man live long enough to do all the things his wife wants him to do.

If medical science has made so much progress, why do we feel so much worse than we did twenty years ago?

Science has not yet discovered how the birds know exactly when we've washed our car.

There are two sciences which every man ought to learn: the science of speech and the more difficult one of silence.

Science has found a tranquilizer to combat car sickness. You take it just before the car payment is due.

In spite of its great accomplishments of the past years, science has not yet discovered adequate controls for a number of natural phenomena, including tornadoes, hurricanes, and politicians.

Science tells us that nothing is impossible. That's nonsense. Did you ever try getting a plumber to come to your home on Sunday?

The only thing left for science to control are women and the weather.

Science is proving that man can live in outer space and at the bottom of the sea. It's the area in between that's causing all the trouble.

Science is progressing so rapidly that it is discovering cures for diseases that don't exist.

Science is only a tool. The harm or good it does depends on how men use it.

Medical science says that whiskey can't cure a cold. But neither can medical science.

Science has never come up with a better office communication system than the coffee break.

The most humiliating thing about science is that it keeps filling our homes with gadgets smarter than we are.

Science has done some great things, but it hasn't yet discovered why a woman's slip sags down and a man's shirt creeps up.

Someone has described science as an orderly arrangement of what, at the moment, seems to be facts.

A major scientific advancement would be the development of cigarette ashes that would match the color of the rug.

Medical science is adding years to our lives, but it's up to us to add life to our years.

Science has been producing so many substitutes lately that it's hard to remember what it was we needed in the first place.

A cynic in New Jersey asks, "If science is so smart, why doesn't it discover an ailment that can be cured only by smoking and drinking?"

Science has put several men on the moon; now let it try getting pigeons down from public buildings.

Why doesn't science figure some way to make our ailments as interesting to others as they are to us?

Science had better not free the minds of people too much before it has tamed their instincts.

Science is nothing but trained and organized common sense.

Science can tell us how to do many things, but it cannot tell us what ought to be done.

Science can predict an eclipse of the sun many years in advance but cannot accurately predict the weather over the weekend.

Scientists

Scientists tell us that our universe is made up of protons, electrons, and neutrons. They forgot to mention morons.

An eminent scientist has announced that, in his opinion, intelligent life is possible on several of our planets — including the earth!

Certain scientists are working on a new scheme to abolish sleep. The new baby has beaten them to it.

Scientists tell us that the most devastating thing in the world is the A-bomb; the second most devastating thing is coming home with lipstick on your collar.

Space scientists have made an analysis of the lunar soil. It shows that corn can't be raised on the moon, but it's great for raising taxes.

If the space scientists keep it up, there'll be so many satellites circling the earth that the flying saucers can't get through.

Scientists have predicted the earth will explode in five billion years, and some are already using that as an excuse for not looking for a job.

A scientist recently crossed a carrier pigeon with a woodpecker. The bird not only carries messages, but he knocks on the door.

A scientist is a person who can solve problems, not just a person crammed with information.

Scientists have found a petrified man sitting with his feet elevated. He was probably a primitive bureaucrat.

Look at cows and remember that the greatest scientists on earth have never discovered how to convert grass into milk.

The eminent scientist who once said we all behave like human beings obviously never drove a car.

A scientist recently revealed that it took millions of years to carve out the Grand Canyon — a government job, no doubt.

Scientists show us how to sail under the North Pole, and fly over the moon, but you're on your own when you cross the street.

Secrets

What this country needs is more people raising beans and fewer people spilling them.

Spilling the salt might be bad luck, but spilling the beans is much more dangerous.

The trouble with having outspoken children is that you're frequently left holding the bag they let the cat out of.

Egotism is the world's most poorly-kept secret.

A real friend warms you by his presence, trusts you with his secrets, and remembers you in his prayers.

If there's anything harder than breaking a bad habit, it's trying not to tell how you did it.

The idea some people have of keeping a secret is lowering their voices when they tell it.

Most women keep secrets like politicians keep promises.

It's a great kindness to entrust people with a secret. They feel so important while telling it to their friends.

Men don't usually give secrets away. They trade them.

If you think a woman can't keep a secret, ask one her age!

A secret is the only thing that circulates more rapidly than money.

Nothing is more annoying than to find everyone knows the secret you promised to keep to yourself.

If you want a secret kept — keep it.

Secrets are a burden. That's the reason we are so anxious to have somebody help us carry them.

One of the most difficult secrets for a man to keep is his opinion of himself.

Three people can keep a secret if two of them are dead.

If it folly to believe that the bosom of a friend can hold a secret your own could not contain.

A secret is usually something that is told to only one person at a time.

Some folk's idea of keeping a secret is merely refusing to tell who told it to them.

Sign on a desk in the Pentagon. "The secrecy of my job does not permit me to know what I am doing."

The only way to keep a secret is not to tell it.

A woman has two ideas about keeping secrets. They are either not worth keeping, or they are too good to keep.

A secret is like an aching tooth — it keeps you uneasy till it comes out.

Keeping a secret requires the ability to remember to forget what was told you.

The "little bird" that is always giving away secrets must be a stool pigeon.

Can you imagine anyone being as unhappy as a woman with a live secret and a dead telephone?

Secrets are things we give to others to keep for us.

Most people can keep a secret; it's the folks they tell it to who can't.

It's true that a woman can keep a secret — in circulation!

The secret of success is seldom well-kept.

Any man who has no secrets from his wife either has no secrets or no wife.

Secret sins won't stay secret for very long.

The secret of success is still a secret to the average American.

Self-control

He is a fool who cannot get angry, but he is a wise man who will not.

Never strike a child! You might miss and hurt yourself.

Hot words never resulted in cool judgment.

When angry count ten before speaking. When very angry count one hundred and then don't speak.

Striking while the iron is hot may be all right, but don't strike while the head is hot.

You are not a dynamic person simply because you blow your top.

Be strong enough to control your anger instead of letting it control you.

No matter whether you are on the road or in an argument, when you begin to see red, STOP!

The emptier the pot, the quicker the boil — watch your temper!

The man who loses his head is usually the last one to miss it.

We have found that it's much easier to restrain our wrath when the other fellow is bigger than we are.

When a person strikes in anger, he usually misses the mark.

Form the habit of closing your mouth firmly when angry.

As a general rule, the angriest person in a controversy is the one who is wrong.

In an argument the best weapon to hold is your tongue.

Character does not reach its best until it is controlled, harnessed, and disciplined.

If you can pat a guy on the head when you feel like bashing it in, you're a diplomat.

If a diplomat says yes, he means perhaps; when he says perhaps, he means no; and when he says no, he is no diplomat.

A diplomat can keep his shirt on while getting something off his chest.

The best executive is the one who has sense enough to pick good people to do what he wants done, and self-restraint enough to keep from meddling with them while they do it.

We first make our habits, and then our habits make us.

At no time is self-control more difficult than in time of success.

Self-control is giving up smoking cigarettes; extreme self-control is not telling anybody about it.

What chance can a man have to control his destiny when he can't control himself?

Have you ever noticed that self-control comes in mighty handy when you're eating salted peanuts?

Self-expression is good; self-control is better.

Self-control might be defined as the ability to carry a credit card and not abuse it.

Women in supermarkets should exercise shelf-control!

If you lose your head, how do you expect to be able to use it?

If you would like to control your temper, be like a kettle — sing when you boil.

The best time to keep your shirt on is when you're hot under the collar.

When a man loses his temper, his reason goes on a vacation.

It is always a good idea to be selfish with your temper — so always keep it.

Whether you're on the road or in an argument, when you see red it's time to stop.

Selfishness

The person who is all wrapped up in himself is overdressed.

Some of us veer to the left and some of us swing to the right, but most of us are self-centered.

Staring up to admire your halo usually creates a pain in the neck.

A man who is self-centered is off-centered.

Egotism is the glue with which you get stuck on yourself.

A selfish fool is a man who says it's nobody's business what he does.

The person who lives for self alone usually dies the same way.

It's give and take in this world, with too many people trying to take.

Selfishness short-circuits prayer.

The man who lives only for himself runs a very small business.

Selfishness tarnishes everything it touches.

He who lives for himself does not have very much to live for.

Ninety-nine out of every one hundred people are still more interested in the honey than they are in the bees that produced it.

Too many people conduct their lives on the cafeteria plan — self-service only!

The selfish man, like a ball of twine, is wrapped up in himself.

Master selfishness or it will master you.

A man is a selfish fool who says it's nobody's business what he does.

Selfish individuals have a very easy time of it — if they can get along without friends.

The trouble with most people is that every time they think, they think only of themselves.

Senators

According to recent reports, America produces 92 percent of the world's natural gas — not counting the speeches of our senators and congressmen.

Have you ever noticed how extremely difficult it is for a person to keep his mind open and his mouth shut at the same time?

One of the large drug companies has been asked to compound a pill to inhibit spending — by senators.

One doctor in Washington, D.C., treats only Senate members — he refuses to make "House" calls.

A filibuster is when a senator talks a long time without saying anything — as usual.

The United States Senate opens with prayer, and closes with an investigation.

The chaplains who pray for the United States Senate and the House of Representatives might speak a word now and then on behalf of the taxpayers.

A senator is usually a man who has risen from obscurity to something worse.

The best way to entertain a senator is to just sit down and listen.

Bull-throwers in Spain are called Senors, while in this country they are called senators.

There's only one person who can speak louder than a senator, and that's another senator.

A senator should return home after a term in office and try to make a living under the laws he helped to pass.

The world was created in six days — no Senate confirmation being necessary.

Sermons
see also Preachers

A Christian is a living sermon, whether or not he preaches a word.

A nodding congregation may or may not mean assent to what the preacher is saying.

Sign outside a church building in Shreveport, Louisiana: "All new sermons — no reruns."

Church members who need defrosting should hear a few "red-hot" sermons.

A good example is the best sermon you can preach.

Too few preachers know the difference between a sermon and a lecture.

A preacher in Alabama was recently fired for two reasons. First, he had a poor delivery. Second, he never had very much to deliver.

The misleading thing about some preachers is that they carry their sermons around in a *brief* case.

When a woman preaches a sermon to her husband, she usually ends it by taking up a collection.

Nowadays we have sermonettes by preacherettes for Christianettes.

Sermons and biscuits are improved by shortening.

It is easier to preach ten sermons than it is to live one.

The sermon will be better if you listen to it as a Christian rather than a critic.

A sermon should never be preached until it is soaked in prayer.

Very few people find a sermon too long if it is helpful.

It takes great listening, as well as great preaching, to make a great sermon.

The sermon you enjoy most is not likely to be the one that will do you the most good.

If some sermons were for sale, they would be labeled: "Dry Goods and Notions."

All sermons should have handles on them so people could pick them up and carry them home.

No baldheaded man was ever converted by a sermon during the fly season.

Before criticizing the sermon, why not consider how much it actually cost you? You might conclude that you got your money's worth.

Every sermon should change the person in the pew, or it should be changed by the preacher in the pulpit.

In preparing their sermons, many preachers prepare no place to stop.

The best way to compliment the sermon delivered by your minister is to bring a friend to hear the next one.

Many sermons are dull because preachers often try to answer questions that nobody is asking.

You can preach a better sermon with your life than with your lips.

One of the best things about sermons is the ease with which we can listen to them while thinking about something entirely different.

The most striking sermon is usually the one that hits the man who is not there.

Another nice thing about radio sermons is that people don't turn and stare at you when the preacher denounces your pet sin.

Too many people would rather hear a sermon on Sunday than live one through the week.

How can a preacher expect to fill heaven with people when his sermons won't even fill the church building where he preaches?

If a sermon pricks the conscience, it must have good points.

The feast of the sermon is always followed by spiritual indigestion unless followed by religious exercise.

Preachers should learn that for a sermon to be immortal it need not be eternal.

Everybody should listen to a sermon occasionally, including those who go to church.

The old-fashioned sermons on hell were not so different from the ones we hear today on current events.

If some sermons don't reach down to posterity, it won't be due to the fact that they aren't long enough.

The eternal gospel does not require an everlasting sermon.

A man usually considers it a good sermon when he feels the preacher didn't refer directly to him.

You can find the world's shortest sermon on a traffic sign, "Keep Right."

It's easy to appreciate the points of a sermon that prod the other fellow.

A good sermon helps in two ways. Some rise from it greatly strengthened. Others wake from it refreshed.

The half-baked sermon causes spiritual indigestion.

Before passing judgment on a sermon, be sure to try it out in practice.

A great many sermons are of the cotton candy variety: colorful, sweet, harmless, and a bit short on content.

In preaching a funeral sermon, a preacher made the following remarks, "We have here before us only the shell — the nut is gone."

A poor listener seldom hears a good sermon.

What we customarily call a "good sermon" is one that we smugly feel applies to all the people who didn't attend the service that day.

Service

An advisory capacity is the only capacity in which some people are willing to serve.

Our aim should be service, not success.

Greatness is not found in possessions, power, position, or prestige. It is discovered in goodness, humility, service, and character.

There are not great men except those who have rendered service to mankind.

The measure of a man's greatness is not the number of servants he has, but the number of people he serves.

The roots of happiness grow deepest in the soil of service.

Service is nothing but love in work clothes.

The man who serves — deserves.

The greatest reward for serving others is the satisfaction found in your own heart.

Don't beg men to serve — stimulate them.

The greatest of all arts is the art of losing ourselves in the service of others.

Service is the rent we pay for the space we occupy in this world.

Some people are willing to serve God, but only as His consultant.

It is not always the talented people who serve the Lord best — it is the consecrated ones.

The measure of a man is not the number of servants he has but the number of people he serves.

The unpaid service you render humanity is exalting only as long as you don't mention it.

Sickness

It doesn't take very long to save enough cigarette coupons to get a radio to listen to while you're propped up in bed with emphysema.

Worrying about smoking cigarettes can be beneficial — it takes your mind off lung cancer.

What this country needs is more men in Congress with throat trouble.

A man and his wife were divorced because of illness — they got sick of each other.

When you have broken ribs, a hiccup is a crisis, a cough is a calamity, a sneeze is a disaster, and a slap on the back is the meanest thing one human being can do to another.

Some think God is like medicine; you don't need Him when you're feeling well.

A cynic in New Jersey asks, "If science is so smart, why doesn't it discover an ailment that can be cured only by smoking and drinking?"

Get-well cards have become so humorous that if you don't get sick you're missing a lot of fun.

Nobody is sicker than the man who is sick on his day off.

The people of this nation are sick of the high cost of being sick.

The man who treats himself when he is sick has a fool for a physician — but at least he doesn't have to wait for an appointment.

Nothing will drive a sick man back to his job like knowing how much work his wife has lined up for him if he stays home.

All some people do for a cold is sneeze.

Much of the sickness people experience in this life is located immediately north of the neck.

An eminent doctor in Chicago denies that spring fever is incurable. The trouble he says is that it's impossible to find a patient who wants to get well.

An illness is like a TV commercial — even a short one is too long.

The mental cases most difficult to cure are the persons who are crazy about themselves.

Ordinary people have sore throats. Broadway stars have laryngitis.

Why is the virus that causes the common cold so hard to find, when it's so easy to catch?

Silence

A bit of advice: Say nothing often.

It's surprising how often people will agree with you if you just keep your mouth shut.

It's a lot easier to nod as if you agree with someone than it is to explain why you don't.

When angry count ten before speaking. When very angry count one hundred and then don't speak.

Form the habit of closing your mouth firmly when angry.

You must speak up to be heard, but sometimes you have to shut up to be appreciated.

In an argument the best weapon to hold is your tongue.

When an argument flares up, the wise man quenches it with silence.

When a wise man argues with a woman, he says nothing!

Nothing makes a barber suffer in silence as much as not talking.

It's easy to save face. Just keep the lower half of it tightly closed.

So many books are now being written on how to speak that there ought to be a market for one on how to shut up.

If there is a substitute for brains it has to be silence.

The Christian should learn two things about his tongue — how to hold it and how to use it.

Another nice thing about being quiet and dumb is that you won't be picked to head a committee.

Some members of Congress would best promote the country's peace by holding their own.

The secret of polite conversation is never to open your mouth unless you have something to say.

The real art of conversation is not only saying the right thing in the right place, but to leave unsaid the wrong thing at the tempting moment.

Have you ever noticed how extremely difficult it is for a person to keep his mind open and his mouth shut at the same time?

Discretion is putting two and two together and keeping your mouth shut.

Some people speak from experience; others, from experience don't speak.

Wise men think without talking; fools reverse the order.

A wise man reflects before he speaks; a fool speaks and then reflects on what he has uttered.

The quickest way to stop gossip is for everybody to shut up.

One of the best ways for some people to make others happy is to shut up and go home.

When it comes to income these days, about all you can keep is quiet.

We often show command of language when we say nothing.

A person with a closed mind can get by nicely — if he keeps his mouth closed too.

A man misses silent films. It was so good in those days to see a woman open her mouth and have no sound come out.

Never neglect the opportunity of keeping your mouth shut.

Speech is silver, silence is golden, and oratory, at the moment, is mainly brass.

More sales have been started when the salesman's mouth was closed than when it was open.

There are two sciences which every man ought to learn: the science of speech and the more difficult one of silence.

Try to understand silence — it's worth listening to.

Silence is what you can't say without breaking it.

Another thing marriage brings out in a lot of men is silence.

If silence is golden, not many people can be arrested for hoarding.

Some folks suffer in silence louder than others.

At no time is it easier to keep your mouth shut than during an audit of your income-tax return.

An ounce of keep your mouth shut is worth a ton of explanation.

Often people who think before they speak don't speak.

There isn't anything more becoming for a fool than a closed mouth.

Some people suffer in such silence it can almost deafen you.

Silence never makes any blunders.

There is a time when silence is the best way to yell at the top of your voice.

One way to get silence at a woman's bridge club is to ask who is the oldest.

Silence is one of the most beautiful, impressive, and inspiring things known to man. Don't break it unless you can improve on it.

Most people don't mind suffering in silence — if they're sure everybody knows they're doing it.

The best way to say a thing is to say it, unless remaining silent will say it better.

It's better to be silent like a fool than to talk like one.

When a man suffers in silence, it's most likely his wife's.

To be thought wise, keep your mouth shut.

Silence is often the most perfect expression of scorn.

We would like to see some folks take a few lessons in domestic silence.

A marriage counselor says a man should make his wife a silent partner in all his business affairs. It would be a great trick if he could do it.

Silence is the best and surest way to hide ignorance.

You never have to take a dose of your own medicine if you know when to keep your mouth shut.

Don't repeat anything you will not sign your name to.

Most of us know how to say nothing, but few of us know when.

If men talked only about what they understand, the silence would be unbearable.

Another nice thing about silence is that it can't be repeated.

You can learn a lot about a man by how much he doesn't say.

To avoid trouble and insure safety, breathe through your nose. It keeps the mouth shut.

Very seldom can you improve on saying nothing.

The art of silence is as great as that of speech.

If you don't say anything, you won't be called on to repeat it.

No flies ever got into a shut mouth.

He who will not understand your silence will probably not understand your words.

People who can hold their tongues rarely have any trouble holding their friends.

If a thing will go without saying — let it.

The hardest thing to keep is quiet!

Silence is a wife's best weapon. It upsets her husband.

Man's ears are not made to shut — but his mouth is.

It's funny how people on a diet are never reduced to silence.

You don't have to explain something you haven't said.

About all that's worth listening to these days is silence.

It is better to remain silent and be thought stupid than to speak and remove all doubt.

You may not be very wise, but if you manage to keep your mouth shut you can fool a lot of people.

When a woman suffers in silence, she really does.

One can easily recognize a wise man by the things he doesn't say.

The best way to save face is to keep the lower half of it closed.

It's no fun to suffer in silence unless you first make enough noise to attract attention — and sympathizers!

Blessed is the man who does not speak until he knows what he is talking about.

A wise man, even when he is silent, says more than a fool when he talks.

Wise men are not always silent, but they know when to be.

Keeping one's mouth shut keeps a lot of ignorance from leaking out.

When at a loss for the right word to say — try silence.

If you keep your mouth shut, you will never put your foot in it.

It's not a bad idea for a politician to remember that no newspaper can misquote his silence.

An open mind and a closed mouth make a happy combination.

Spending half of the time keeping quiet and the other half saying nothing is one way to keep out of trouble.

Might as well keep your mouth shut. If you talk about yourself you're a bore, and if you talk about others you're a gossip.

It often shows a fine command of language to say nothing.

Some men boast of their ability to speak in five different languages; others are proud of their ability to keep silent in one.

Silence has never yet betrayed anyone.

Women can do almost everything men can — except listen.

There is a time for everything. The best time for you to hold your tongue is the time when you feel you must say something or bust.

There is no real substitute for brains, but silence does pretty well.

Nothing so excites a man's curiosity as a woman's complete silence.

A still tongue makes no enemies.

Some people wouldn't have a thing to say if they were forbidden to speak well of themselves and evil of others.

Nobody ever listens themselves out of a job.

When a woman suffers in silence, the phone is probably out of order.

If you don't say it, you won't have to unsay it.

Let's keep our mouths shut and our pens dry until we know the facts.

One way to keep people from jumping down your throat is to keep your mouth tightly closed.

There's no harm in having nothing to say. Just try not to say it out loud.

If some people would keep their mouths shut, all the ignorance wouldn't keep falling out.

Silence is at its golden best when you keep it long enough to get all the facts.

If you keep your mouth shut and look natural, a lot of people will think you're smarter than you are.

Some of us learned many years ago that the only substitute for intelligence is to keep your mouth shut.

Some who have a habit of thinking out loud make others appreciate how golden silence really is.

You can think better if you close your eyes — and mouth.

When men hold their tongues you can't tell a fool from a sage.

There are two types of people who say very little: the quiet ones and the gabby ones.

Truth is often violated by falsehood, but can be equally outraged by silence.

There is no substitute for wisdom, but the next best thing is silence.

A wise man is one who has an open mind and a closed mouth.

You can always tell a wise man by the smart things he does not say.

Half of wisdom is being silent when you have nothing to say.

Sin

A Christian has not lost the power to sin, but the desire to sin.

A real Christian is as horrified by his own sins as he is by his neighbor's.

Announcement on the bulletin board of a church in Ohio: "This is a segregated church — for sinners only. All welcome."

The most difficult thing imaginable is to keep clean of debt, dirt, and the devil all at the same time.

Confess your sins to the Lord, and you will be forgiven; confess them to men, and you will be laughed at.

Confessing your sins is no substitute for forsaking them.

For every sin Satan is ready to provide an excuse.

Friendships cemented together with sin do not hold.

Sin has many tools, but a lie is a handle that fits them all.

Love covers a multitude of sins — temporarily.

Love does not keep a ledger of the sins and failures of others.

Prayer will either make a man leave off sinning, or sin will make him leave off prayer.

A preacher recently announced over the radio that there were 572 different sins mentioned in the Bible. He received numerous requests for the list from people who thought they might be missing something.

To grieve over sin is one thing; to repent is another.

There are no new sins — we just keep rerunning the old ones.

We are told the wages of sin is death — shouldn't you quit before payday?

Our courts and legislatures have just about put sin out of business. They've made it legal.

Most of our old folks are against sin. In fact, they're against just about everything they're too old to enjoy.

An innovative priest in San Francisco has a fast confession line for those with three sins or less.

Sins are expensive — why not behave yourself and save the difference?

No matter how many new translations of the Bible are made, the people still sin the same way.

Confess your sins, not your neighbor's.

The way of the transgressor is hard — especially on other people.

Making a sin legal does not make it harmless.

Sin deceives, then defiles, then deadens.

One cannot be isolated from sin, but he can become insulated against it.

Sin always starts out as fun.

Unless sin is confessed it will fester.

No power on earth can make a man sin without his consent.

There is always more sin when folks can afford it.

God may forgive your sin, but your nervous system won't.

A sin takes on new and real terrors when there's a chance that it's going to be found out.

If you would not fall into sin, keep away from the brink of temptation.

The wages of sin are the only wages not subject to the income tax.

Some people seem willing to do anything to become a Christian except to give up their sins.

The three greatest sins of today are indifference to, neglect of, and disrespect for the Word of God.

Original sin is a misnomer because every kind of sin has been practiced before.

Some think they are saints because they are selective in their sins.

Our government could raise unlimited revenue simply by taxing sin.

Secret sins won't stay secret for very long.

There may be some new sinners today, but there are no new sins.

Inflation has affected everything except the wages of sin.

Some people think the sins of omission are the sins we ought to commit but don't.

No man ever found the pleasure of sin equal to the picture of sin.

Once a sin was called a sin; now it's called some kind of complex.

Sin causes the cup of joy to spring a leak.

One reason why the way of the transgressor is hard is because it's so crowded.

Sin would have very few takers if its consequences occurred immediately.

The wages of sin are always paid on time.

When the wages of sin are paid, a lot of people are going to get time-and-a-half for overtime.

The other fellow's sins, like the other fellow's car lights, always seem more glaring than our own.

Sin is mothered by ignorance.

We are not punished for our sins, but by them.

The way of the transgressor may be hard — but it isn't lonely.

Sin is a short word and it often makes short work of its victim.

The ability to sin differs between people. A short-armed fisherman is not as big a liar as a long-armed one.

Fear of getting caught sometimes keeps a fellow from sinning until the opportunity has passed.

You simply can't put your sins behind you until you face them.

To some men sins are like old neckties. The longer they have them, the dearer they become.

You don't have to institute a lawsuit to collect the wages of sin.

It is the sin we try to excuse that finally gets us down.

Often the wages of sin are unreported.

Temptation is not sin, but playing with temptation invites sin.

The wages of sin are apt to include a lot of overtime.

The wages of sin are never frozen.

Sincerity

A blush is one thing that can't be counterfeited.

Be sincere with your compliments. Most people can tell the difference between sugar and saccharine.

A hypocrite never intends to be what he pretends to be.

The most important thing in politics is sincerity, whether you mean it or not.

Insincere praise is worse than no praise at all.

Prayer must mean something to us if it is to mean anything to God.

When leading a public prayer, speak loudly enough to be heard of men and sincerely enough to be heard of God.

The sincere man suspects that he, too, is sometimes guilty of the faults he sees in others.

A fellow ought to be sincere whether he means it or not!

The trouble with being sincere is that people will be inclined to think you're just putting on an act.

The sincerity of a person does not make false doctrine right just because he believes it.

Slander
see also Gossip

Rare is the person who can weigh the faults of others without putting his thumb on the scales.

Slander, like coffee, is usually handed to you without grounds.

The slanderer differs from the assassin only in that he murders the reputation instead of the body.

You'll never move up if you're continually running somebody down.

Sleep

The trouble with alarm clocks is that they always go off when you're asleep.

When the alarm clock rings the best part of the day is over.

It's extremely difficult for a baby sitter to wake up five or ten minutes before the parents return home.

It's disconcerting to fall asleep in church and have a fly buzz into one's open mouth.

Many churches are now serving coffee after the sermon. Presumably this is to get the people thoroughly awake before they start to drive home.

A real surprise is when the college boy comes home and discovers people sleep at night rather than in the daytime.

Conscience is like a baby. It has to go to sleep before you can.

The best tranquilizer is a good conscience.

Nothing goes to sleep as easy as one's conscience.

Next to debt, the hardest thing to get out of is a warm bed on a cold morning.

It doesn't do any harm to dream, providing you get up and hustle when the alarm goes off.

If you want your dreams to come true, don't oversleep.

Boasting and sleeping are the forerunners of failure.

It's hard to raise a family — especially in the morning.

You need to start worrying about health if you can't sleep when it's time to get up.

Do you realize how many mistakes you'd make if you didn't sleep a third of your day?

The experienced parent is one who has learned to sleep when the baby isn't looking.

Those who think they are dreamers are usually just sleepers.

People who say they sleep like a baby haven't got one.

Rip Van Winkle slept for twenty years, but, of course, his neighbors didn't have a radio.

Certain scientists are working on a new scheme to abolish sleep. The new baby has beaten them to it.

One thing that helped Rip Van Winkle sleep for twenty years was the fact that none of his neighbors owned a lawn mower.

If you count sheep two at a time you'll fall asleep twice as fast.

Sleep is something that always seems more important the morning after than the night before.

The amount of sleep required by the average person is usually thirty minutes more.

There seems to be a catch to almost everything. For instance, it's wonderful to sleep till noon, but it sure ruins your afternoon nap.

Oversleeping is a mighty poor way to make your dreams come true.

A man's conscience, and not his mattress, has most to do with his sleep.

The trouble with sleep is the going to and the coming from.

Sleep is something that science cannot abolish — but babies can.

The best bridge between despair and hope is a good night's sleep.

If plenty of sleep is an aid to good looks, it seems that a considerable number of people are suffering from insomnia.

Those who say sleep is nature's greatest gift to man have not priced very many motels lately.

The only safe place to fall asleep behind the wheel is at a drive-in theater.

If you want your wife to listen to what you have to say, talk in your sleep.

Sound sleep is the sleep you're in when it's time to get up.

The only person entitled to be asleep at the switch is the owner of an electric blanket.

When a man walks in his sleep, he leaves his wife; when he talks in his sleep, his wife leaves him.

A good way to have the world beat a path to your door is to try to take a nap.

Many folks contend that sleeping out of doors makes one beautiful. That explains the charming appearance of the town drunk.

Sleep is a condition in which some people talk, some walk, and others snore.

The creatures that sleep standing up are horses and fathers of month old babies.

If you sleep in a chair, you have nothing to lose, but a nap at the wheel is often a permanent snooze.

Most of us spend a lifetime going to sleep when we're not sleepy and getting up when we are.

A sleepwalker is the only person who gets his rest and his exercise at the same time.

Frequent naps will keep you from getting old — especially if taken while driving.

The most dangerous position in which to sleep is with your feet on your office desk.

Smiles

Your day goes the way the corners of your mouth turn.

Perhaps the best Yuletide decoration is being wreathed in smiles.

Life is like a mirror. If we frown at it, it frowns back. If we smile, it returns the greeting.

What this country needs most is more people who smile even when they're not on "Candid Camera."

Why not wear a smile? It's just about the only thing you can wear that isn't taxed.

One thing is certain — smiles never go up in price or down in value.

Sometimes a smile happens in a flash, but the memory of it can last a lifetime.

It's easy to smile when someone cares.

There's a face-lift you can perform yourself that is guaranteed to improve your appearance. It is called a smile.

The thing that costs the least and does the most is a pleasant smile.

You're never fully dressed in the morning until you put on a smile.

If you can't crown yourself with laurels, you can wreathe your face in smiles.

A smile is a powerful weapon; you can even break ice with it.

Most smiles are started by another smile.

Smile now — you may not feel like it later.

The nice thing about wearing a smile is that one size fits everybody.

If you can look in the mirror and smile at what you see, there's hope for you.

A smile is the lighting system of the face and the heating system of the heart.

The ultimate in shapely curves is found within a smile.

If you would like to spoil the day for a grouch, give him a smile.

Smile often and give your frown a rest.

When you meet a man without a smile, give him one of yours.

If you can't smile, imitate one who can.

You know a woman is in love with her husband if she smiles at him the way she does at a traffic cop.

There are two things that everybody must face sooner or later: a camera and reality. A smile will help greatly in both instances.

The world looks brighter from behind a smile.

One smile in public is worth ten before your mirror.

A smile is the same in all languages.

All of us like to see people smile and hear them laugh, but not when we're chasing our best hat down the street on a windy day.

If there is a smile in your heart, your face will show it.

Another smile does not make the giver poorer, but it does enrich the receiver.

You don't have to know a person's name to greet him with a friendly smile.

A smile is the light in the window of your face that tells people you're at home.

People seldom notice old clothes if you wear a big smile.

The man who smiles in the face of trouble is either brave or covered by insurance.

If you want pleasant things to turn up, keep the corners of your mouth that way.

The smile that lights the face will also warm the heart.

Something of a person's character may be discovered by observing how he smiles.

A smile goes a long way, but you're the one who must start it on its journey.

Smiles is the longest word in the world. There's a "mile" between the first and the last letters in the word.

A pleasant smile brings the largest return on the smallest investment.

It takes twenty-six muscles to smile and sixty-two muscles to frown. Why not make it easy on yourself?

A smile is mightier than a grin!

It is almost impossible to smile on the outside without feeling better on the inside.

A smile is a curve that can set a lot of things straight.

The only thing you can wear that's never out of style is a smile.

A smile is the shortest distance between two people.

473

While enormous strides have been made in communication in recent years, there's still a lot to be said for the smile.

You're getting old when the girl you smile at thinks you're one of her father's old friends.

If you didn't start out the day with a smile, it's not too late to start practicing for tomorrow.

We are admonished to "Keep Smiling," but if we do we're going to look mighty silly at a funeral.

A smile is the magic language of diplomacy that even a baby understands.

No matter how hard you try, you can't get rid of a smile by giving it away; it always comes back to you.

A smile is a curve that you throw at another, and it always results in a hit.

He who has the habit of smiling at the cash register instead of the customer won't be smiling long.

The world always looks brighter from behind a smile.

Snoring

Every businessman ought to sit back, close his eyes, and meditate for a while every day — and try not to snore.

How come it's always the loudest snorer who falls asleep first?

It's a rare husband who tells everybody that his wife snores — but not so with the wife.

Women can cure their husband's snoring by kindness, patience — or stuffing a old sock in his mouth.

Society

Let's all sympathize with the poor girl who spent four years learning how to behave in polite society and the rest of her life trying to locate it.

The money saved this year on education will be spent later on jails and reformatories.

Education has produced a vast population able to read but unable to distinguish what is worth reading.

A good family tree is a useful object to climb into society with.

Friends are like a priceless treasure; he who has none is a social pauper.

If we all said to people's faces what we say behind their backs, society would be impossible.

Kindness is the golden chain by which society is bound together.

What this country needs is more of the milk of human kindness in the cream of society.

The trouble with not having prejudices is that people are apt to think you don't understand our social system.

High society is that which some people are born in, others are taken in, but most folks pay to get in.

It's said that society will achieve the kind of education it deserves. Heaven help us if this is true!

Society is always taken by surprise by any new example of common sense.

In today's society you have to be a little crazy to keep from going insane.

If it's true that we're approaching a money-less society, some of us are ahead of our time.

If the good Lord had intended for us to live in a permissive society, wouldn't the Ten Commandments have been called the Ten Suggestions?

Society judges you not by what you stand for, but by what you fall for.

Some wit said that society invites the crime, and criminals accept the invitation.

"Polite society" is a group which says to your face the reverse of what it says behind your back.

In a materialistic society your problem is to get your share of the material.

Like its politicians and its wars, society has the teen-agers it deserves.

We are only young once. This is all society can stand.

Speech

Strict enforcement of the law against polluting the air should result in fewer, shorter, and better political speeches.

Liberty doesn't work as well in practice as it does in speeches.

An orator tries to see how long he can talk without saying anything.

Speech is silver, silence is golden, and oratory, at the moment, is mainly brass.

America needs more free speech that is worth listening to.

Oh, how we need more free speech that doesn't cost so much to listen to!

It's too bad that more people are thoughtless than speechless.

Most politicians have four speeches: what they have written down, what they actually say, what they wish they had said, and what they are quoted as saying the next day.

Adding insult to injury is interrupting a political speech on TV to show a baloney commercial.

Political speeches are usually just baloney disguised as food for thought.

When you listen to a political speech it's like shooting at a target — you must allow for the wind.

Second wind is what some preachers get when they say, "And now in conclusion."

Some of the driest speeches are made by people who are all wet.

There are two sciences which every man ought to learn: the science of speech and the more difficult one of silence.

Some speeches are like broiled lobster. You have to pick through an awful lot to find any meat.

The recipe for a good speech includes quite a bit of shortening.

After-dinner speeches can make you feel dumb at one end and numb at the other.

The best time to end your speech is when you feel the listening is lessening.

Almost nobody listens to a commencement address, except a few parents in one last effort to get something for their money.

To make his speeches bear fruit, the smart political candidate will prune them to a considerable degree.

Boiling down a speech is one way of keeping it from being dry.

An after-dinner speech is like a headache — always too long, never too short.

The best after-dinner speech is when the guy with you says, "Waiter, bring me the check."

The easiest way to stay awake during an after-dinner speech is to deliver it.

What is in the well of your heart will show up in the bucket of your speech.

A congressional speech is one printed by the government without profit and read the same way.

A good speech is one with a good beginning and a good ending, which are kept very close together.

When both the speaker and the audience are confused, a speech is considered profound.

A speech should be like a woman's skirt — long enough to cover the subject, but short enough to be interesting.

Some people are so intelligent they can speak on any subject — others don't seem to need a subject.

A speech is like a love affair — any fool can start one, but it requires considerable skill to end one.

No speech is entirely bad if it's short enough.

An Arizona husband says his wife is an after-dinner speaker — also before and during.

Wisdom is knowing when to speak your mind and when to mind your speech.

When one word leads to another, it generally ends up in a quarrel, a speech, or a dictionary.

Sports

Americans are getting bigger and broader, a fact which has filtered through to everybody except the people who mark off the seats in football stadiums.

A well-informed American knows the lineup of baseball teams and about half the words of the "Star Spangled Banner."

The head of a Mississippi college says he is trying to develop an educational institution the football team can be proud of.

Abraham Lincoln had great difficulty getting an education — but what can you expect from a guy who didn't play football or basketball?

We'll be in trouble as long as we pay the best professors less than the worst football coach.

Things could be worse. Suppose your errors were counted and published everyday like those of a baseball player!

If exercise is so good for us, why do so many athletes retire at thirty-five?

A religious family has been described as one where the father says grace before every meal, and the mother says "Amen" when the football game is over.

Golf is a sport in which a small white ball is chased by men who are too old to chase anything else.

A Michigan doctor warned one of his patients to avoid all excitement such as tennis, baseball, football, and supermarkets.

If only men took the nation's problems as seriously as they do its sports!

Tennis is a game that can't be played without raising a racket.

A major difference between football and baseball is that in football it's the spectators, not the bases, that get loaded.

An umpire is like a woman. He makes snap decisions and never reverses them.

Baseball is a business that can't thrive without strikes.

No matter where they seat you at a baseball game, you're always located between the hotdog peddler and his best customer.

A Colorado woman took skiing lessons last winter and reports, "By the time I learned to stand up, I couldn't sit down."

There are times when one gets the impression that football games should be called the "Battle of the Wounded Knees."

Old quarterbacks never die; they just fade back and pass away.

Cab drivers in Chicago have organized a football team. They call themselves the "Taxi Squad."

Any sports fan can tell you the most brutal thing about professional football is the price of the tickets.

The quietest sport of all must be bowling — you can hear a pin drop.

A seven foot basketball player in Alabama is majoring in astronomy. He felt it would be nice to be near his work.

Skiing is one major sport where success involves starting at the top and working your way down.

The true sports fan is a guy who'll do anything to get to the game — even taking his wife along with him.

A coach is a fellow who will gladly lay down your life for his college or university.

Pro football is like nuclear warfare. There are really no winners, only survivors.

Talk to your wife now — the baseball season starts soon.

Winter sports are characterized by settings of ice, snow, and bones.

Baseball is almost the only place where a sacrifice is really appreciated.

The only time where ends meet nowadays is on a football field.

Sometimes we get so worked up over football we almost wish it was only a game.

What's needed for skiing is a lot of snow — and Blue Cross!

Football isn't as violent as it appears. It's nothing like trying to get to the rest rooms at half time.

To many football fans the pint after the touchdown is the most important part of the game.

Nothing bothers grid coaches more than defensive linebackers and offensive alumni.

Football is popular with girls. They like to see men making passes.

Once there was a cross-eyed discus thrower in the Olympics. He didn't set any records, but he sure kept the crowd alert.

Football stadiums are usually filled to capacity — and so are some of the fans.

There are only two groups of football coaches: those who have been fired and those who will be.

A great football coach knows how to spot weaknesses in his opponent's line and loopholes in his contract.

In college football the real triple threat is one who can run, kick, and pass all his exams!

During the baseball season a domestic triangle is a husband, a wife, and a TV set.

Football builds self-discipline. What else would induce a spectator to sit out in the open in sub-freezing weather?

Many fans rush to the football stadium to get good seats — then stand up to watch the game.

Skiing may be a winter activity, but some think of it as a fall sport.

Baseball is different from politics. You're always out in baseball when you get caught stealing.

Notice on a new TV set: "Warning — extended watching of basketball and baseball games may be harmful to your marriage."

Statistics

Statistics show that in 1940 each car on the road had an average of 2.2 persons; in 1950 it was 1.4. At this rate, by 1985 every third car on the road will be empty.

Statistics show there are three ages when men misbehave: young, old, and middle.

Doctors tell us that Americans are living too fast. Traffic statistics show they are dying the same way.

Statistics show that men who kiss their wives goodby in the morning live five years longer than those who don't. Some of you men had better pucker-up before you tucker-out.

According to sales reports, automobile manufacturers had a bang-up year. According to accident reports, so did their customers.

Statistics show that an average of 39,000 people are killed by gas annually. Sixty inhale it, forty light matches in it, and 38,900 step on it.

If people were as religious as statistics show them to be, we could get along with fewer police.

Statistics are like witnesses — they will testify for either side.

Some people use statistics like a drunken man uses a lamp post — for support rather than for illumination.

Facts are stubborn, but statistics are more pliable.

Statistics are like a bikini. What they reveal is suggestive, but what they conceal is vital.

According to the latest statistics, there are five million Americans who aren't working. And there are even more if you count those with jobs.

Statistics can be used to support just about everything — including statisticians.

Statisticians collect facts, then draw their own confusions.

We have statistics to prove that locomotives aren't the least afraid of automobiles.

Stinginess

Beware of a Christian with an open mouth and a closed pocketbook.

Many church members could appropriately begin all church services by singing, "Nothing in my hand I bring."

Generosity will always leave a more pleasant memory than stinginess.

Some folks give according to their means, and some give according to their meanness.

Everybody is ready to lend a helping hand to the fellow who has trouble opening his pocketbook.

A miser might be pretty tough to live with, but he often makes a nice ancestor.

In the "good old days" the man who saved money was a miser. Now he's a wonder.

Penny-pinchers are tight even when money isn't.

Many people are not exactly stingy — they're just economical in a very obnoxious way.

It is reported that a man in Nevada is so stingy he won't even give his cold to Contac!

Beware of the church member with an open mouth and a closed pocketbook.

The only time a miser puts his hand in his pocket is during cold weather.

477

Last Christmas a stingy father told his little children that Santa Claus had been drafted into the army.

Some folks are so tight they squeak when they walk.

There are thousands of people in this country whose hearts bleed for the poor — but their pocketbooks don't.

Stingy people squeeze pennies so hard the Indians get Excedrin headaches.

Some men are so stingy they'd rather pinch pennies than a girl.

Strength

To be angry with a weak man is proof that you are not very strong yourself.

Be strong enough to control your anger instead of letting it control you.

Let us pray, not for lighter burdens, but for stronger backs.

Children need strength to lean on, a shoulder to cry on, and an example to learn from.

Some Christians have will power; others have *won't* power.

The strength that comes from confidence can be quickly lost in conceit.

Many with the strength to diet lack the strength to keep it quiet.

Many a man has failed because he has a wishbone where his backbone ought to have been.

A friend will strengthen you with his prayers, bless you with his love, and encourage you with his hope.

Greatness lies not in being strong, but in the right use of strength.

The business of a leader is to turn weakness into strength, obstacles into stepping stones, and disaster into triumph.

A leader is anyone who has two characteristics: first, he is going somewhere; second, he is able to persuade other people to go with him.

The weakness of man is the thing to be feared, not his strength.

Weak men wait for opportunities; strong men make them.

Strength in prayer is better than length in prayer.

Don't pray for an easy life; pray to be a stronger person.

Prayer gives strength to the weak, faith to the fainthearted, and courage to the fearful.

Pound for pound the American taxpayer is the strongest creature on earth. For many years he has been carrying Washington and a considerable portion of the world on his shoulders.

Trouble is what gives a fellow a chance to discover his strengh — or lack of it.

The weakness of man is the thing to be feared, not his strength.

Success

If you're going to climb, you've got to grab the branches, not the blossoms.

The man who gets ahead is the man who does more than is necessary — and keeps on doing it.

The fellow who does things that count doesn't usually stop to count them.

Our ship would come in much sooner if we'd only swim out to meet it.

The lines actors like best are the ones in front of the box office.

Successful men follow the same advice they prescribe for others.

Our aim should be service, not success.

One guy who always goes to the top is a barber.

If you want to go far in business, you'll have to stay close to it.

It isn't the number of people employed in a business that makes it successful. It's the number working.

Business is made good by yearning, learning, and earning.

A successful executive in business is the one who can delegate all the responsibility, shift all the blame, and appropriate all the credit.

Ability will enable a man to get to the top, but it takes character to keep him there.

Every church has all the success it prays for and pays for.

Some complain that the stepping stones to success bruise their feet.

Conceit in a man is a sure sign that he still hopes to become successful someday.

If your head sticks up above the crowd, expect more criticism than bouquets.

The kind of success that turns a man's head always leaves him facing the wrong direction.

Enthusiasm is the propelling force necessary for climbing the ladder of success.

Envy provides the mud that failure throws at success.

Many of life's failures are men who did not realize how close they were to success when they gave up.

Failure is a better teacher than success, but she seldom finds an apple on her desk.

There are a great many more trapdoors to failure than there are shortcuts to success.

Sometimes a noble failure serves the world as faithfully as a distinguished success.

The difference between failure and success is doing a thing almost right and doing it exactly right.

Failure always catches up with those who sit down and wait for success.

The fact that a man can do as he pleases often accounts for his lack of success.

If you're not afraid to face the music, you may someday lead the band.

God doesn't call us to be successful. He calls us to be faithful.

Money, achievement, fame, and success are important, but they are bought too dearly when acquired at the cost of health.

Success in Hollywood consists in having your name in the gossip columns and out of the phonebook.

A man hopes that his lean years are behind him; a woman, that hers are ahead.

The man with a new idea is often considered a crank until the idea succeeds.

The reason many successful men are so lonely is because they sacrificed too many friends on the way up.

Good luck is a lazy man's estimate of a worker's success.

Luck is that mysterious something that enables others to succeed at something we have failed to accomplish.

The average man doesn't usually increase his average.

A wise man will not walk down the road of success with you. He'll simply point you in the right direction.

The man who tried his hand at something and failed might try using his head for a change.

An upright man can never be a downright failure.

There is not much difference between one man and another, but that small difference is very important.

Success in marriage is more than finding the right person. It's also a matter of being the right person.

Nature gave men two ends — one to sit on and one to think with. Man's success or failure is dependent on the one he uses most.

To make success of old age a fellow sure has to start young.

The best time for a man's ship to come in is before he's too old to navigate.

The success of a big party is usually measured by the money that is wasted.

The trouble with people today is that they want to get to the promised land without going through the wilderness.

To be a successful politician, find out where the public is going, take a short cut across the field, get out in front, and make the people think you're leading the way.

The problem is that the key to success doesn't always fit your ignition.

The man whose ship comes in usually finds most of his relatives at the dock.

Responsibility makes just as many cowards out of men as it makes successes.

Go straight. Every crooked turn delays your arrival at success.

The secret of success is seldom well-kept.

At no time is self-control more difficult than in time of success.

Skiing is one major sport where success involves starting at the top and working your way down.

Success doesn't always go to the head; sometimes it goes to the mouth.

No man is really successful until his mother-in-law admits it.

There are two elements of success: aspiration and perspiration.

Success measured merely by money is too cheap.

To succeed — keep your head up and your overhead down.

A successful man continues to look for work after he has found a job.

Don't forget the folks who are holding the ladder while you're climbing to success.

Success is relative — the more success, the more relatives.

Behind every successful man there are usually a lot of unsuccessful years.

Being a success today means the government takes away in taxes what you used to dream of earning.

The hardest thing about climbing the ladder of success is getting through the crowd at the bottom.

You're not successful till someone brags they sat beside you in grade school.

If at first you don't succeed, try trying.

It's easy to climb the ladder of success if your daddy made the ladder.

Many people carefully avoid discovering the secret of success because deep down they suspect the secret may be hard work.

A successful man is one who can get a woman to listen to reason — or anything else for that matter!

You don't have to lie awake nights to succeed; just stay awake days.

Behind every successful man stands a proud but surprised wife.

When a man has climbed high on the ladder of success, quite often some of his friends begin to shake the ladder.

Success is a matter of luck. Ask any failure.

The secret of success is to never let down and never let up.

Any man who is honest, fair, tolerant, charitable of others, and well-behaved is a success no matter what his station in life might be.

You can be 100 percent certain of being a success if you decide to go into faultfinding.

Success that goes to a man's head usually pays a very short visit.

It is impossible to gain a foothold on success by acting like a heel.

Most of us aren't prepared to accept success — especially somebody else's.

Success isn't necessarily permanent — but neither is failure.

Behind every successful man is a woman who keeps reminding him that she knows men who would have done even better.

Many people would have been a tremendous success long ago if they had used the advice they gave to others.

All men want to succeed, but some men want to succeed so much they're willing to work to achieve it.

For success, try aspiration, inspiration, and perspiration.

Men who are afraid of being ruined by success should get a job with the weather bureau.

Success is like underwear. We should have it without showing it off.

If at first you don't succeed, try, try again — to get somebody else to do it.

Success depends on your industry or on the ignorance of others.

Forget the past; no man has yet backed into success.

Those who try to float to success will wind up at sea.

The shortest route to success is the straight road.

A person interrupts and endangers his climb up the ladder of success when he stops to pat himself on the back.

Formula for success: When you start a thing, finish it.

Success is the only thing some people cannot forgive in a friend.

The dictionary is the only place where success comes before work.

If at first you don't succeed, you're running about average.

There isn't any map on the road to success. You have to find your own way.

Success is sweet, but its secret is sweat.

No one has yet climbed the ladder of success with his hands in his pockets.

Success is like falling off a log — you can't always explain exactly how it happened.

God gave to man five senses: touch, taste, smell, sight, and hearing. The successful man has two more — horse and common.

He has achieved success who has lived long, laughed often, and loved much.

The secret of success is still a secret to the average American.

If you itch for success, keep on scratching.

Most people do only what they are required to do, but successful people do a little more.

You won't find many rules for success that will work unless you do.

The road to success is dotted with many tempting parking spaces.

Isn't it too bad that when success turns a fellow's head, it doesn't wring his neck?

Success is the ability to hitch your wagon to a star while keeping your feet on the ground.

To succeed you must be easy to start and hard to stop.

One of the biggest troubles with success is that its recipe is often the same as that of a nervous breakdown.

There may be splinters in the ladder of success, but you don't notice them until you start sliding down.

Some people succeed because they find greener pastures; others, because they find greener people.

The successful man has a wife who tells him what to do, and a secretary who does it.

You certainly want to make good somewhere, so why not make good where you are?

When success turns a man's head, it leaves him looking in the wrong direction.

Everybody has two chances to succeed in life — either through his own endeavors or through the foolishness of others.

When a man becomes a success, his wife takes most of the credit and the government takes most of the cash.

If at first you don't succeed, find out why before you try again.

The measure of success is not whether you have a tough problem to deal with, but whether it's the same problem you had last year.

A formula for success in bureaucracy: shoot the bull, pass the buck, and make seven copies of everything.

The worst use that can be made of success is to boast of it.

Success always comes as a conquest — not as a bequest.

If the truth were known, most successes are built on a multitude of failures.

A man owes it to himself to become successful. Once successful, he owes it to the IRS.

The law of success: More bone in the back and less in the head.

Coming together is a beginning, keeping together is progress, working together is success.

Men sometimes credit themselves for their successes, and God for their failures.

Those who never succeed themselves are always first to tell you how.

Some men succeed by what they know, some by what they do, and a few by what they are.

A man's success depends on his knowledge of what is his business, and what is none of his business.

The secret of success and happiness lies not in doing what you like, but in liking what you do.

Success consists of doing the common things of life uncommonly well.

The man who wins may have been counted out several times, but he didn't hear the referee.

The secret of success is making hay with the grass that grows under other people's feet.

One reason why people who mind their own business are successful is that they have so little competition.

Any person who looks happy when he isn't is well on the road to success.

One secret of success is to be able to put your best foot forward without stepping on anybody's toes.

An American can consider himself a success when it costs him more to support the government than to support a wife and children.

When you can think of yesterday without regret, and of tomorrow without fear, you are well on the road to success.

Even the woodpecker has discovered that the only way to succeed is to use one's head.

The successful man is one who does what he has to do at the time he hates to do it most.

Formula for success: Hitch your wagon to a star, put your shoulder to the wheel, keep an ear to the ground, and watch the handwriting on the wall.

If success made the heart swell like it does the head, this world would be a far better world.

Inventions are coming so fast that the ladder of success may soon be replaced by an escalator.

One thing that keeps a lot of people from being a success is work.

Success depends partly on whether people like you *wherever* you go or *whenever* you go.

The only way to succeed in life is to work hard, stay clean, walk with your back to the wall, and keep your Bible handy.

You can't carve your way to success with cutting remarks.

The man who fails while trying to do good has more honor than he who succeeds by accident.

It is doubtful if anyone ever made a success of anything who waited around until all the conditions were "just right" before starting.

Success in life ought to be determined, not by accumulations, but by contributions.

The man who wakes up and finds himself successful really hasn't been asleep.

There are no shade trees on the road to success.

Most people find they can scale the ladder of success quicker when they're debt-propelled.

Men usually get somewhere when they develop a brake for the tongue and an accelerator for the brain.

If you want to succeed, wear out two pairs of shoes to every suit.

There are many keys to success, but they keep changing the lock.

Few people travel the road to success without a puncture or two.

Successful folks don't just entertain thoughts — they put them to work.

Most of us measure our success by what others haven't done.

If at first you don't succeed, you'll get a lot of unsolicited advice.

Industry is the mother of success — luck, a distant relative.

To reach the front many a man has to be kicked in the rear.

The road to success runs uphill, so don't expect to break any speed records.

Some men may succeed because they are destined to, but most men succeed because they are determined to.

Be careful where you inquire for directions along the road of success.

It sometimes takes years for a fellow to become an overnight success.

If at first you don't succeed, try looking in the wastebasket for the directions.

Sometimes the people who succeed have neither gold nor silver — but lots of brass.

No one has ever traveled the road to success on a pass.

If you look forward to Monday with more enthusiasm than you did to Friday, you're in danger of becoming successful.

Every outstanding success is built on the ability to do better than good enough.

Success is when you make both ends meet — and overlap.

The road to success is filled with women pushing their husbands along.

The basic rules for success may be defined as follows: Know what you want. Find out what it takes to get it. Act on it and persevere.

A successful man is one who can lay a firm foundation with the bricks that others throw at him.

The secret of success is to start from scratch and keep on scratching.

Unless you can look interested when you're bored, you'll never become a social success.

Success comes from having the proper aim as well as the right ammunition.

If at first you don't succeed, try, try again. Then quit. There's no point in making a fool of yourself.

Success is a matter of luck and pluck — mostly pluck.

A successful man is one who thinks up ways of making money faster than the government can take it away from him.

You are not obligated to succeed. You are obligated only to do your best.

There is really no such thing as the "ladder of success." It's a greased pole.

Success makes failures out of too many people.

A successful man is one who has the horsepower of an optimist and the emergency brakes of a pessimist.

It's amazing how some fellows managed to climb the ladder of success — with one foot constantly in their mouth.

Behind every successful man there's a woman — competing for his job.

If at first you don't succeed, try doing it the way your wife told you.

To succeed — do the best you can, where you are, with what you have.

Success is the result of backbone, not wishbone.

Wisdom is learned more from failure than from success.

Right is a bigger word than either success or failure.

If hard work is the key to success, most people would rather pick the lock.

Supermarkets

Anybody who thinks hit-and-run accidents aren't on the increase hasn't been in a supermarket lately.

If you think your automobile is expensive to operate, try operating a shopping cart in a supermarket.

Now that Congress has made it possible for Americans to buy gold, somebody should suggest they make it possible for us to buy groceries.

The cost of operating a car is high, but it's not at all bad in comparison with the low mileage-per-dollar when you push a grocery cart.

At today's prices the shopper is left holding the bag — and there's very little left in it.

The economy is as confusing as a cross-eyed Ping-Pong player. The stock market keeps going down and the supermarket keeps going up.

To market, to market/ my groceries to buy/ home again, home again/ to sit down and cry.

Grocer checking a ten dollar grocery order: "Is this take-out, or will you eat it here?"

Visit the frozen-food department in any supermarket and you'll find everything is frozen except the prices.

A fool and his money are soon parted. The rest of us wait until we reach the supermarket.

With today's inflation, it's a question of which is more costly — investing in the stock market or shopping in a supermarket.

It's funny how a dollar can look so big when you take it to church and so small when you take it to the supermarket.

All our money these days is tied up in the market — the supermarket.

Twenty-dollar bills have become terribly fragile. It seems we break one every time we go into a grocery store.

Nowadays an optimist is any supermarket customer who holds out his hand for the change.

One thing all of us need is a grocery cart with four wheels that all go in the same direction.

A Michigan doctor warned one of his patients to avoid all excitement such as tennis, baseball, football, and supermarkets.

Once upon a time when you felt the need for a good cry, you went to the movies; later soap operas did the trick; now it's the supermarket.

A typical visit to the supermarket begins with an empty shopping cart and ends with an empty wallet.

Nowadays a "disaster area" is the supermarket checkout counter.

Supermarkets are like churches. People walk down the aisles saying, "Lord, help us."

You can always recognize the newlywed in the supermarket. She's the one who squeezes the can of soup to see if it's fresh.

Supermarkets are very convenient. They permit a shopper to go broke in one store.

Always get in the shortest line at the supermarket. That way you stand a chance to get to the cashier before the prices go up.

When you hear about somebody who took a financial beating in the market, they might be talking about the supermarket.

When two women used to get together, they talked about another woman; now they talk about supermarket prices.

Have you noticed that most supermarket shopping carts are just the right size — big enough to kill one paycheck?

A supermarket used to be a place where people came out with a bundle. Now it's where they go in with a bundle — of money!

The newest and most popular game these days is called "Supermarket Roulette," which consists of trying to get all the groceries in your basket before the prices go up.

Maybe the reason supermarkets now sell underwear, magazines, and cosmetics is that many people can't afford to buy groceries.

Women in supermarkets should exercise shelf-control!

Sign at a checkout counter in a Chicago supermarket: "English and Spanish are spoken here. Tears understood."

Today millions of Americans are suffering from respiratory problems. It comes from standing at supermarket check-out counters holding their breath.

One thing can be said about values in the United States — they're not to be found in the supermarkets.

Suspicion

If it were as easy to arouse enthusiasm as it is suspicion, just think what could be accomplished!

When a man brings flowers to his wife, she figures it's because of something he did or something he forgot to do.

Nothing makes the average wife so suspicious of her husband as an unexpected gift.

A disgruntled housewife suspects her butcher of using phony scales, "Just recently I didn't buy anything and it weighed three pounds."

That so-called female intuition is just the old habit of being suspicious.

Suspicion is like a pair of dark glasses — it makes all the world look dark.

Most of our suspicion of others is aroused by a knowledge of ourselves.

The easiest thing in the world to cultivate is suspicion.

If the world could disarm suspicion, the rest would be easy.

Suspicion is a mental picture seen through an imaginary keyhole.

Television sets are three dimensional. They give you height, width, and *debt*.

When your wife hangs on every word you say, she probably wants to see if your story will hold together.

Candy and flowers may serve one of two purposes — they make a wife happy or suspicious.

Some wives are so concerned about their husband's happiness that they hire private detectives to find out the cause of it.

Not all wives are suspicious — they know!

Sympathy

Children need strength to lean on, a shoulder to cry on, and an example to learn from.

Friendship is a living thing that lasts only as long as it is nourished with kindness, sympathy, and understanding.

A heart enlarged by sympathy has never yet killed anyone.

The true measure of a man is the height of his ideals, the breadth of his sympathy, the depth of his convictions, and the length of his patience.

One of life's major mistakes is being the last member in the family to get the flu — after all the sympathy has run out.

It's no fun to suffer in silence unless you first make enough noise to attract attention — and sympathizers!

Some folks who have a sympathetic disposition sure waste a lot of it on themselves.

Sympathy is two hearts tugging at the same load.

It takes a big man to sympathize — a little man can criticize, and usually does.

A person who is not sympathetic is simply pathetic.

Sympathy is the result of thinking with your heart.

A sympathizer is a fellow who's for you as long as it doesn't cost anything.

The only time sympathy is ever wasted is when you give it to yourself.

Sympathy is what you give to a man when you don't want to lend him money.

One manifestation of genuine sympathy is worth more than any amount of advice.

Sympathy is the golden key that unlocks the hearts of others.

Be sympathetic — you know it could happen to you!

T

Tact

Talking

Tasks

Taxes

Teachers

Tears

Teen-agers

Telephones

Television

Television Commercials

Temper

Temptation

Ten Commandments

Thankfulness

Theft

Thinking

Thoughts

Thrift

Time

Tobacco

Tolerance

Tongue (the)

Tourists

Traffic

Transportation

Travel

Truth

Tact

The real art of conversation is not only saying the right thing in the right place, but to leave unsaid the wrong thing at the tempting moment.

People with tact have less to retract.

Tact is the rare talent for not quite telling the truth.

A foolish man tells a woman to stop talking so much, but a tactful man tells her that her mouth is extremely beautiful when her lips are closed.

Tact is the ability to describe others as they see themselves.

Tact is the ability not to say what you really think.

Social tact is making your company feel at home even though you wish they were.

Tact is the art of saying whatever is required — including nothing.

Making people around you think they know something is real tact.

Tact is the art of removing the stinger from the bee without getting stung.

Some people have tact, others tell the truth.

Tact is the ability to make a person see the lightning without letting him feel the bolt.

Tact is the rare ability to keep silent while two friends are arguing and you know both of them are wrong.

Tact is the ability to stay in the middle of the road without being caught there.

Formula for tact: Be brief, politely; be aggressive, smilingly; be emphatic, pleasantly; be positive, diplomatically; be right, graciously.

Tact is the knack of getting your way without stirring up a fuss.

Tact is considered to be the pause that refreshes.

Tact will make you popular, provided you endure being taught many things you already know.

Tact fails the moment it is noticed.

Tact is the art of saying nothing when there is nothing to say.

Tact is the unsaid part of what you think.

Tact is something that if it is there, nobody notices it. But if it is not there, everybody notices it.

Tact is not saying what everybody is thinking.

Tact is the art of complimenting your host for a wonderful dinner that has left you with a bad case of indigestion.

Tact is to lie to others as you would have them lie to you.

Tact is the art of treating everyone as if he knew what he was talking about.

Tact is changing the subject without changing your mind.

Blunt words often have the sharpest edge.

Talking

It isn't so much *what* we say as the number of times we say it that makes us a bore.

Most folks would benefit themselves and others if they would synchronize their tongues with their brains.

What the church needs is more men who talk less and work more.

An Arizona man complained, "My wife always has the last word — and all the words before it."

There is now a female computer on the market. You don't ask it anything, but it tells you anyway.

When all is said and nothing done, it's time for the conference to adjourn.

What this country needs is more men in Congress with throat trouble.

Congress is proof that women don't do all the talking.

Congress will not know what a real filibuster is until women members are in the majority.

With telephone rates due to go up again, we begin to wonder if what we have to say is still worth saying.

The dictionary must be wrong. It says the dumb can't talk.

You can't reduce by talking about it. You must keep your mouth shut.

Many with the strength to diet lack the strength to keep it quiet.

If dogs could talk, perhaps we'd find it just as hard to get along with them as we do with people.

A dog is smarter than some people. It wags its tail and not its tongue.

There's something to be said for the egotist, and he's usually saying it.

We make more enemies by what we say than friends by what we do.

About the only part of the body that is over-exercised is the lower jaw.

Fishing is like romance; the next best thing to experiencing it is talking about it.

Wise men think without talking; fools reverse the order.

A fool empties his head just about every time he opens his mouth.

A fool may have a knowing look — until he opens his mouth.

Among the most expensive gifts on earth is the gift of gab.

The most difficult part of golf is learning not to talk about it.

A South Carolina husband grumbles that his wife has an annoying speech impediment — she won't shut up!

Too many people run out of ideas long before they run out of words.

Many a man is not suspected of being ignorant till he starts to talk.

Intelligence is like a river — the deeper it is, the less noise it makes.

If you can't remember a joke — don't dismember it.

Kindness has influenced more people than eloquence.

What frightens most men about marriage is not another mouth to feed — but another one to listen to!

To have an open mind doesn't mean you must always have an open mouth.

It would not be so bad to let one's mind go blank — if one always remembered to turn off the sound.

A person with a closed mind can get by nicely — if he keeps his mouth closed too.

A mistake proves somebody stopped talking long enough to do something.

Nature often makes up for a nugget-size brain with a bucket-size mouth.

Take a tip from nature — your ears aren't made to shut, but your mouth is!

Opportunities are often missed because we are broadcasting when we should be listening.

An orator tries to see how long he can talk without saying anything.

There are two types of people who say very little: the quiet ones and the gabby ones.

Have you noticed that people who have stopped smoking and drinking haven't stopped talking about it?

It is reported that a certain politician in Louisiana is so windy that he can give mouth-to-mouth resuscitation by telephone.

What's needed during a presidential campaign is an epidemic of lockjaw.

A convention keynote address is a combination of oratory, grand opera, and hog calling.

In some parts of Africa a man can't hold a public office until he has a shot at a rhinocerous. In America voters consider a man qualified if he can shoot the bull.

Many people will never be bothered by air pollution because they don't stop talking long enough to take a deep breath.

Why do so many speakers who want to be breezy end up windy!

Too many salesmen know how to say nothing. Too few know when.

Some people are so intelligent they can speak on any subject — others don't seem to need a subject.

Many a mouth is working overtime while their brain is on vacation.

If folks wouldn't talk too much about people who talk too much there wouldn't be too much talking.

Usually the first screw that gets loose in a person's head is the one that controls the tongue.

The trouble with this country is that there are too many wide open spaces entirely surrounded by teeth.

What a wonderful world this would be if we all would think as much as we talk.

Instead of broadcasting so much, why not try tuning in at intervals?

Some people are such talkers that you can't get a word in edgewise even if you folded it.

Talk is cheap because the supply always exceeds the demand.

It isn't the people who tell all they know that cause most of the trouble in this world — it's the ones who tell more.

Some talk wouldn't be so irritating if it weren't handed out in such large quantities.

It seems that some people turn their tongues on and leave them running.

Everybody wants to talk, few want to think, and nobody wants to listen.

A lot of people who talk constantly about capital and labor never had any capital and never did any labor.

Did you ever notice how often a narrow mind and a wide mouth go together?

Talking too much usually follows thinking too little.

Listen carefully to some talkers and you will know that practice does not make perfect.

The unhappiest man is the one whose expenditure of speech is too great for his income of ideas.

The mouths of many people seem to have the habit of going on active duty while their brains are on furlough.

Big mouths do not advertise big brains.

Some women talk so much that others actually get hoarse listening to them.

Open air, open doors, open shop, open covenants, and open minds are all desirable, but this country is still suffering from open mouths.

Too many people are like buttons — always popping off at the wrong time.

If God had intended that we should talk more than we hear, He would have given us two mouths and one ear.

The life of the party is the person who can talk louder and longer than the radio or television.

A lot of people have the gift of gab; others have the gift of grab.

Too many folks have a breaking out right under their nose.

If a woman could talk out of the two corners of her mouth at the same time, there would be a great deal said on both sides.

The best way to save face is to stop shooting it off.

Eyes that are set too close together may indicate a mean disposition, but lips that are too far apart indicate a blabber mouth!

Waiting for some people to stop talking is like looking for the end of a roller towel.

Some women work their tongues so fast they say things they haven't even thought of yet.

Many people who have the gift of gab don't seem to know how to wrap it up.

If Alexander Graham Bell had had a daughter, he would have never had a chance to test the telephone.

They think too little who talk too much.

Some people have eyes that see not and ears that hear not, but there are very few people who have tongues that talk not.

Many people these days are jumping into trouble mouth first.

A lot of trouble is caused by combining a narrow mind with a wide mouth.

Most of our troubles arise from loafing when we should be working, and talking when we should be listening.

A lot of people get unlimited mileage out of a limited vocabulary.

Hot air is the most common method of heating in Washington.

Windmills in Washington could ease the energy crisis. Washington has an abundance of wind and hot air.

A fellow wearily described his gabby wife, "She doesn't even keep her mouth shut when she's listening."

Speaking of his wife, a weather forecaster said, "She speaks about 150 words per minute, with gusts up to 190."

491

Wisdom is divided into two parts — having a great deal to say, and not saying it.

As a man grows older and wiser, he talks less and says more.

No man is so full of wisdom that he has to use his mouth as a safety valve.

Why is it that when a woman tells a doctor she's all tired out, he immediately looks at her tongue?

No one objects to what you say that's worthwhile — if you say it in few words.

A multiplicity of words indicates poverty of thought.

Tasks

Before proceeding with a difficult task, stop and think. Then remember to start again.

Some tasks have to be put off dozens of times before they completely slip our minds.

People who say that a task is just as easy as taking candy from a baby have obviously never tried it.

Taxes
see also Internal Revenue Service

Ambition in America is still rewarded — with high taxes.

America is a land of opportunity. Everybody can become a taxpayer.

America is the only country in the world where it takes more brains to make out the income tax return than it does to make the income.

There are two things in America that are growing bigger together — garbage cans and taxes.

It's hard to believe that America was founded to avoid high taxation.

Americans everywhere are now in a daze from INTAXICATION.

We often wonder if automation will ever replace the taxpayer!

There was a time when $200 was the down-payment on a car; now it's the sales tax.

There's no tax on brains; the take would be too small.

The tax collectors take up so much of your earnings to balance the budget that you just can't budget the balance.

Business is tough these days. If a man does something wrong he gets fined; if he does something right he gets taxed.

An Oklahoma businessman reports that if his business gets any worse he won't have to lie on his next income-tax return.

Capital punishment is when Washington comes up with a new tax.

Capital punishment is when the government taxes you to get capital so that it can go into business in competition with you, and then taxes the profit on your business in order to pay its losses.

Drive carefully. Uncle Sam needs every taxpayer he can get.

Children may be deductible, but they're still taxing.

There's no child so bad that he can't be used as an income-tax deduction.

The tobacco industry would really be doing something if it could come up with a cigarette that eliminated tar, nicotine, and taxes.

The path of civilization is paved with tax receipts.

If Congress can pay farmers not to raise crops, why can't we pay Congress not to raise taxes?

It appears that Congress has found it's a lot easier to trim the taxpayers than expenses.

Congress does some strange things — it puts a high tax on liquor, and raises the other taxes that drive people to drink.

The biggest job Congress has is how to get money from the taxpayers without disturbing the voters.

The attitude of Congress toward hidden taxes is not to do away with them, but to hide them better.

It seems that everytime Congress sets out to trim the budget, the knife slips and trims the taxpayers instead.

Congress is confronted with the unsolved problem of how to get the people to pay taxes they can't afford for services they don't need.

We don't seem to be able to check crime, so why not legalize it and then tax it out of business?

Every year around April 15 Americans have a rendezvous with debt.

One of the great blessings about living in a democracy is that we have complete control over how we pay our taxes — cash, check, or money order.

Ours is a democracy where the rich and the poor are alike — both complain about taxes.

The next disarmament conference might be a great success if the delegates were representative taxpayers.

The wealth of experience is one possession that has not yet been taxed.

A fool and his money are soon parted. The rest of us wait until income-tax time.

This country is as free today as it ever was — unless you happen to be a taxpayer.

Golf is a lot like taxes — you drive hard to get to the green and then wind up in the hole.

It's a mistake to believe that government can give things to some people without first taking it away from others.

Some folks feel the government owes them a living. The rest of us would gladly settle for a small tax refund.

One great thing about our form of government is that everybody gets something out of it, even if it's only free income-tax forms.

The government should supply a slide rule, prayerbook, and a Ouija Board with each income-tax form.

President Herbert Hoover was the first President to give his salary back to the government. Now the government would like everybody to do it.

Everybody works for the government, either on the payroll or the taxroll.

In the old days it was two chickens in every pot; now it's two government employees for every taxpayer.

Any government big enough to give you everything you want is big enough to take everything you've got.

Even if money could buy happiness, just think what a luxury tax there'd be!

A man's home is his castle. At least that's how it seems when he pays taxes on it.

The honeymoon is over when the bride begins to suspect that she was never anything to him but a tax deduction.

Don't you long for the "good old days" when Uncle Sam lived within his income and without most of yours?

Nothing makes a man so modest about his income as a tax form to fill out.

Pity the guy in the middle-income bracket — earning too much to avoid paying taxes, and not enough to afford paying taxes.

Our income-tax forms this year have been simplified beyond all understanding.

Most of us secretly wish we were so rich that we wouldn't have to pay an income tax.

In preparing his income-tax return, the average American man resembles a girl getting ready to go to the beach. They both take off as much as the law allows.

Wouldn't it be great if we could force the recall of all Form 1040s?

It's strange how a man with no sense of humor can come up with such funny answers on his income-tax returns!

The reason they say the income tax is the fairest tax of all is that it gives every individual an even chance at poverty.

When making out your income-tax returns, 'it's better to give than to deceive.'

They tell us they are going to do something about junk mail, but they continue to send out income-tax forms.

When it comes to income tax, most of us would be willing to pay as we go if we could only catch up on where we've been.

An income-tax return is like a girdle. If you put the wrong figure in it, you're apt to get pinched.

The new income-tax form is printed in red, white, and blue. When you've filled in the white, you're left in the red, and that makes you blue.

Income tax is Uncle Sam's version of "Truth or Consequences."

After a man pays his income tax, he knows how a cow feels after she's been milked.

The latest income-tax form has been greatly simplified. It consists of only three parts: (1) How much did you make last year? (2) How much have you got left? (3) Send amount listed in part 2.

It is generally agreed that the income tax is the government's idea of instant poverty.

Next to being shot at and missed, nothing is quite as satisfactory as an income-tax refund.

An income-tax form is like a laundry list — either way you lose your shirt.

About the time a man is cured of swearing, another income tax is due.

When they consider candidates for the next Pulitzer Prize for the best definitive biography, many a man would be delighted to submit his last income-tax report.

Loafing is the only way to beat the income tax.

Nothing has done more to stimulate the writing of fiction than the itemized deduction section of the income-tax forms.

The income tax has made more liars out of the American people than golf.

People who squawk about their income tax can be divided into two classes: men and women.

If you want to get even with the income-tax people, get Junior to work out your tax return using the new math.

The average man knows as much about the atomic bomb as he does about his income-tax form.

Income taxes are not so bad and certainly could be worse. Suppose we had to pay on what we think we are worth?

George Washington never told a lie, but then he never had to file a Form 1040.

What the present income-tax form needs is a section which would explain the explanations.

When making out your income-tax report, be sure you don't overlook your most expensive dependent — the government.

It has almost reached the point where, if a person takes a day off, he falls behind in his income-tax payments.

Income-tax forms are nothing more than the government's quiz program.

Some of us can recall the day when a person who had to pay income tax was considered to be wealthy.

No stretch of the imagination is as complete as the one used in filling out income-tax forms.

Income tax is the fine you pay for thriving so fast.

It is difficult to predict the future of an economy in which it takes more brains to figure out the tax on our income than it does to earn it.

Income-tax forms should be printed on Kleenex because so many of us have to pay through the nose.

We wouldn't mind paying income tax if we could know which country it's going to.

Income-tax forms should be more realistic by allowing the taxpayer to list Uncle Sam as a dependent.

Paying your income tax is for a good cause — such as keeping you out of the penitentiary.

In 1913 Uncle Sam collected only 13 million dollars in income taxes. That's why they were called the "good old days."

The guy who said that truth never hurts never had to fill out a Form 1040.

Come to think of it, these income-tax forms leave little to the imagination and even less to the taxpayer.

Just thinking about income taxes often taxes the mind — which is something people once said the IRS couldn't do.

Making out your own income-tax return is something like a do-it-yourself mugging.

Trying to curb inflation by raising taxes is like giving a drunk another drink to sober him up.

If you think you can keep everything to yourself, the IRS doesn't.

If the IRS gave green stamps, thousands of Americans would look forward to paying their income tax.

Behind every successful man stands a woman and the IRS. One takes the credit, and the other takes the cash.

With a billion dollar budget, it ought to be possible to set aside enough money to teach the IRS the basic English necessary to write a readable income-tax form.

Another American invention is the permanent temporary tax.

There are no curse words in the Indian language. They don't need any because they don't pay taxes.

The best tax law is the one that gets the most feathers with the least squawking.

Which has made the biggest liars out of Americans — golf or the income tax?

A man in Oklahoma admitted he lied on his income-tax return — he listed himself as the head of the household!

Life is one dodge after another — cars, taxes, and responsibilities.

The best things in life are free — plus tax, of course.

The way the cost of living and taxes are today, you might as well marry for love.

The average man now lives thirty-one years longer than he did in 1850. He has to in order to get his taxes paid.

A serious impediment to a successful marriage these days is the difficulty of supporting both the government and a wife on one small income.

Blessed are the meek for they shall inherit the earth — less 40 percent inheritance tax.

When the time comes for the meek to inherit the earth, taxes will most likely be so high that they won't want it.

The meek may inherit the earth just in time to see it sold for taxes.

Of course you can't take it with you, and with high taxes, lawyer's fees, and funeral expenses you can't leave it behind either.

Benjamin Franklin had an axiom, "A penny saved is a penny earned." But that was before the sales tax was invented.

A dime is a dollar with all the various taxes deducted.

The reward for saving money is being able to pay our taxes without borrowing.

A lot of people still have the first dollar they ever made — Uncle Sam has all the others.

A harp is a piano after taxes.

We need to change our National Anthem to "Deep in the Heart of Taxes."

A good name is to be chosen over great riches. It's tax free!

No respectable person is in favor of nudity, but after paying taxes, some of us may not have any other choice.

What this country needs most is a SPCTT — The Society for the Prevention of Cruelty to Taxpayers.

Patriotism will probably never develop to the point of parading in honor of the "unknown taxpayer."

A dyed-in-the-wool patriot is one who says he's sorry he has only one income to give to his country.

The real patriot is a person who saves enough of his salary each week to pay his income tax.

A politician is a man who never met a tax he didn't try to hike.

Wouldn't it be grand if politicians would fight poverty with something besides taxes?

After all is said and done, the politicians say it and the taxpayers do it.

It is reported that the politicians in Washington are thinking of abolishing the income tax — and taking the income.

Regardless of who wins the election they have to raise taxes to pay for the damage.

If our President wants to abolish poverty, he can do it by abolishing the IRS.

Poverty is what you experience the day after you pay your income tax.

One of the biggest advantages of being poor is that you'll never have to undergo the trauma of a tax audit.

The chaplains who pray for the United States Senate and the House of Representatives might speak a word now and then on behalf of the taxpayers.

Unquestionably, there is progress everywhere. The average American now pays out as much in taxes as he formerly received in wages.

Our beloved country has made remarkable progress. Now politicians have arranged to spend taxes before they collect them.

A political promise today means another tax tomorrow.

We may need tax reform, but it seems we need a lot of spending reform too.

The futility of riches is stated very plainly in two places: the Bible and the income-tax form.

In Russia the people have only what the government gives them; in America the people have only what the government does not take away from them in taxes.

If science says nothing is impossible, how about a mechanical taxpayer?

Science has increased our life span considerably. Now we can look forward to paying our taxes at least ten years longer.

Space scientists have made an analysis of the lunar soil. It shows that corn can't be raised on the moon, but it's great for raising taxes.

At no time is it easier to keep your mouth shut than during an audit of your income-tax return.

Our government could raise unlimited revenue simply by taxing sin.

Being a success today means the government takes away in taxes what you used to dream of earning.

An American can consider himself a success when it costs him more to support the government than to support a wife and children.

Patrick Henry ought to come back and see what taxation *with* representation is like.

Taxation, like a lot of other things, is based on supply and demand. The government demands, we supply.

The greatest general to emerge from any war is general taxation.

Taxation is the gentle art of picking the goose in such a way as to secure the greatest amount of feathers with the least amount of squawking.

The ideal form of taxation is the kind that will be paid by somebody else.

Our forefathers should have fought for representation without taxation!

The fourth of July, 1776 — that's when we declared our freedom from unfair British taxation. Then, in 1777, we started our own system of unfair taxation.

It's extremely difficult to believe that America was founded to avoid excessive taxation.

Taxation is a lot like sheep shearing. As long as you shear a sheep it will continue to produce a new crop of wool. But you can skin the animal only once.

In two hundred years we've gone from taxation with representation to taxation without relaxation.

If something new has been added, it's probably another tax.

The man who said taxes would keep us halfway broke was a lousy judge of distance.

The only thing left to tax is the wolf at the door.

Why don't high taxes and high prices marry and settle down?

Is there any human activity that isn't taxed, licensed, regulated, or restricted?

It looks like we all will eventually make our living collecting taxes from one another.

Stay on your job and pay your taxes promptly. Thousands of workers in the government bureaus are counting on you.

A penny saved is a penny taxed.

There is nothing more permanent than a temporary tax.

When it comes to a tax reduction, never has so little been waited for by so many for so long.

Why not slap a tax on political gas?

After paying all our taxes we're tempted to call Washington and try to get ourselves declared a disaster area.

Another difference between death and taxes is that death is frequently painless.

Tax forms are entirely too complicated and get worse every year. All they have to do is "simplify" them one more time and nobody will be able to understand them.

You really can't beat the game. If you win anything, it's minus taxes. If you buy anything, it's plus taxes.

One hopeful note on hidden taxes is that there can't be many more places to hide them.

We wonder why they call them "tax returns" when so little of it does.

The best things in life are still free, but the tax experts are working overtime on the problem.

We all get excited these days about paying taxes because we never know which country our money is going to.

It will be real nice if taxes get down to where we can afford to make a living.

What's all this howling about hidden taxes? We wish they would hide all of them.

Next year will be the year they lower taxes — it always is.

Breathing seems to be about the only activity in this country that isn't taxed.

It's about time that somebody invents a tax that can't be hiked.

There's a "tax cocktail" on the market — two drinks and you withhold nothing.

A gentleman in Maryland says he's going to invest his money in taxes — the only sure thing to go up.

Old taxes never die — they just change their names.

A window sign in Chicago: "Tax Returns Prepared — Honest Mistakes Are Our Specialty."

Nowadays anybody who puts two and two together also has to add in the sales tax.

About the only thing about those withholding taxes is that a fellow doesn't get so mad all at once.

Increasing taxes to stop inflation makes about as much sense as fanning a fire to cool its heat.

A "slight tax increase" costs you about $300, while a "substantial tax cut" lowers your taxes by about $30.

In view of the inheritance tax, the meek and humble will get nothing when they inherit the earth.

Some tax loopholes become nooses.

Death and taxes are inevitable, but death is not a repeater.

When Congress tries to decide between two new taxes, it's like a woman deciding between two dresses — she usually decides to take both.

If you don't hear some people murmuring about taxes these days, it's probably because so many others are screaming.

Nobody jumps on taxes when they're down.

By the time you finish paying all your taxes, about all you have left is a receipt.

If Congress would repeal the nuisance tax, we wouldn't have any taxes to pay.

They keep telling us about a tax-freeze plan. How about a tax-free plan?

One can be born free and then be taxed to death.

The attitude of Congress toward hidden taxes is not to do away with them, but to hide them better.

When the average man looks at what he has left after his taxes are paid, he begins to realize that Social Security may have real meaning for him.

No matter how staggering the taxes, they never fall down.

When the time comes for the meek to inherit the earth, taxes will be so high they won't want it.

Save your pennies and the sales tax will take care of them.

Whenever one tax goes down, another goes up.

A certain Senator recently informed us that the average American is not "tax conscious," and this is doubtless true. If he shows signs of coming to, he is immediately struck down with another tax.

There's one consolation about life and taxes — when you finish the former, you're through with the latter.

We have been anesthetized by hidden taxes, hypnotized by indirect taxes, and pulverized by camouflaged taxes.

A politician will consider every way of reducing taxes except cutting expenses.

One thing about death — it doesn't get worse every time Congress meets.

Even if money could bring happiness, think what the luxury tax would be!

The reward for saving your money is being able to pay your taxes without borrowing.

A tax-dodger is a man who does not love his country less, but loves his money more.

Everything we have is taxed — even our patience.

Thinking is one thing that no one has ever been able to tax — but the IRS is getting jealous about the situation.

"What you don't know doesn't hurt you" doesn't apply to the hidden taxes in the things you buy.

A man pays a luxury tax on a leather billfold, an income tax on the stuff he puts into it, and a sales tax when he takes the stuffing out of it.

Take a look at your tax bills and you'll quit calling them "cheap politicians."

It's a mistake to believe that Uncle Sam can open his pocketbook and let you keep yours closed.

No enemy nation could risk invading the United States. It couldn't afford the high taxes.

A tax cut is like motherhood, apple pie, and the Star-Spangled Banner — everybody is for it.

We wouldn't mind this "pay-as-you-go" tax so much if we knew what we were paying for and where it was going.

If taxes climb any higher, they may go into orbit.

A man listed the government as a dependent on his income-tax return. The claim was disallowed because he wasn't contributing more than one half of his income toward its support.

There doesn't seem to be any justice. If you fill out an income-tax return correctly, you go to the poorhouse. If you don't, you go to jail.

More than two hundred years ago our forefathers declared that we should be able to tax ourselves. We have proved we could, and how!

What Americans need most is "Taxicare" to help us pay our taxes.

A tax refund is the next best thing to being shot at and missed.

Have you noticed that everytime something terrible happens any place in the world, someone in Washington tries to use it as an excuse to raise taxes?

Let's be thankful we don't have to pay taxes on our debts.

A tax cut is the 'kindest cut of all.'

New taxes are like mustard plasters — easy to put on but almost impossible to remove.

Most of us have enough money to pay our taxes. What we need is something to live on!

The fellow who said "What goes up must come down" must have lived before they invented taxes and postal rates.

There's no tax on brains — the take would be too small.

With taxes what they are today, a fellow has to be unemployed to make a living.

The tax-eaters are destroying the tax-earners.

Taxes and politicians are closely related. Once we get stuck with a tax, the only thing politicians know how to do is to raise it.

Some tax refunds are slower than a helicopter over a nudist colony.

The thing raised most abundantly in the United States is taxes.

Those who think their tax dollars don't go very far should glance at the moon occasionally.

Actually we wouldn't mind Uncle Sam's tax bite — if he didn't come back for dessert.

Only two kinds of people complain about excessive taxes — men and women.

Three cases where supply exceeds demand are: taxes, trouble, and advice.

As we pay our taxes, most of us are not worried about Congress letting us down — but we often wonder if it will ever let us up.

One of the great things about living in a democracy is that we have complete say over how we pay our taxes — by cash, check, or money order.

The trouble with today's taxes is that they keep your take-home pay from ever getting there.

Nothing has done more to stimulate the writing of fiction than the itemized deduction on the income-tax form.

The income tax, the property tax, and the sales tax are an unbeatable combination. They get you coming and going. Add the inheritance tax and they get you after you've gone.

With estate taxes what they are, the happiest mourner at a rich man's funeral is Uncle Sam.

People who grumble about taxes have one consolation — they don't have to pay on what they think they're worth.

The way taxes are now, you seldom hear any more about a girl getting married for money.

Tax collectors are funny folks. They expect a fellow to give them the money he's already spent for something better.

With another tax hike pants pockets will become unnecessary.

It's getting so your annual property tax is more than you paid for your home in the first place.

Regardless of who wins the election they'll raise your taxes to pay for the damage.

What about welfare for the taxpayer? He isn't faring so well these days either!

There should be a special watch for the taxpayer — it wouldn't tick, just wring its hands.

A California taxpayer recently moaned, "I owe the government so much money it doesn't know whether to throw me out or recognize me as a foreign power."

Taxpayers are always hoping for a break in the levy.

The only thing easier to skin than a banana is a taxpayer.

Regardless of where a shot is fired in the world today, the American taxpayer is the one who is invariably hit.

When taxpayers go broke or crazy, or both, they are taken care of by those who haven't gone yet.

The shorter the time to April 15, the longer the face of the taxpayer.

With all the hidden taxes, what about a place where the taxpayer can hide?

Pound for pound the American taxpayer is the strongest creature on earth. For many years he has been carrying Washington and a considerable portion of the world on his shoulders.

A taxpayer recently sent the IRS twenty-five cents with a note saying he understood that he could pay his taxes by the quarter.

The trouble with our foreign policy is that the enemy nations are living beyond our means.

The only people who don't have to pass the Civil Service exams to work for the government are taxpayers.

If the folks in Washington are so disturbed about human suffering, they ought to take a look at the American taxpayer.

It has been suggested that we have a new postage stamp bearing the picture of a weeping taxpayer.

The president has the next to the hardest job in the United States. The taxpayer has the hardest.

It's a lot easier to trim the taxpayer than to trim the budget.

The elephant and the donkey were probably chosen as political party emblems because they are beasts of burden. If a new political party is started, a taxpayer might suitably be used as an emblem.

When all is said and done, it's the politicians who say it and the taxpayers who do it.

The taxpayer who thinks his money doesn't go very far should brush up on his geography.

It takes the wool of twenty sheep and the hides of ten taxpayers to clothe one United States soldier.

The American taxpayers wouldn't object to free transportation for certain government officials if they'd go where we wish they would.

A deputy income-tax collector in Washington was recently the victim of a holdup man who took all his money and stripped him to his underwear. Now he knows how we taxpayers feel.

A taxpayer resents the fact that death and taxes don't come in that order!

Trimming expenses in government operations is the last resort when the taxpayers can stand no more trimming.

A taxpayer might be referred to as a government worker with no vacations, no sick leaves, and no holidays.

It seems that almost every group of workers now has a union except taxpayers.

Flying saucers are nothing but taxpayers blowing their tops.

Instead of taking the pants off the taxpayer it might be better to take the vest off the vested interests.

After the government takes enough to balance the budget, the taxpayer has the job of budgeting the balance.

Any company that manufactures a mechanical taxpayer will make a fortune in a hurry!

Taxpayers are the casualties of the War on Poverty.

It might be well to bear in mind that when Uncle Sam plays Santa Claus, it's the taxpayer who holds the bag.

We should not become too enthusiastic until some statesman comes along with a scheme to make the world perfect without soaking the taxpayer.

In the near future Congress is expected to raise the legal limit on the taxpayer's patience.

We've had the New Deal and the Fair Deal. Some taxpayers are calling what we have now the Ordeal.

They say politics makes strange bedfellows, but it's the taxpayer who has the nightmare.

It seems like a lot of taxpayers are suffering from "shell-out shock."

Those income-tax forms leave little to the imagination, and less to the poor taxpayer.

Nowadays many taxpayers are writing letters of protest to their congressmen — and some are so hot they're steaming themselves open.

If Washington D. C. is the seat of government, then the taxpayer is the pants pocket.

Most American taxpayers gladly support their own government by paying their taxes promptly, but they resent having to support the government of several other countries.

Nothing spurs a taxpayer into filing an income-tax return like the expectation of a refund.

The American taxpayer is the unforgotten man.

This talk about a "new source of revenue" simply means tapping the same old taxpayer in a brand new place.

It's getting to where even the taxpayer's patience is being taxed.

Pity the poor taxpayer who has the whole government on his payroll.

There's nothing wrong with teen-agers that becoming taxpayers won't cure.

A person doesn't realize how much he has to be thankful for until he has to pay taxes on it.

There was a time when you saved up for your old age; now you save up for April 15th.

Responsibility for a considerable portion of the world's troubles rests upon two people of the past. One of them invented credit; the other, taxes.

It was easier to tell the truth in George Washington's day. There were no income-tax forms to fill out.

We often wondered why Uncle Sam wears such a tall hat, until he started passing it around for taxes.

It often seems like the United States is building up its enemies and flattening its taxpayers.

Advice to vacationers: Don't overtax yourself. The government will do it for you.

The two agencies now being used to redistribute wealth are taxation and offspring.

Untold wealth is the wealth which does not appear on income-tax returns.

A father in Georgia called his local IRS office to ask if he could deduct the cost of his daughter's wedding as a "total loss"?

The sneakiest two words in the English language are "plus tax."

Nowadays when you miss a day's work the government loses as much as you do.

Nothing is certain in this world except death, taxes, and teen-agers.

Nowadays the world revolves on its taxes.

It's a weird world. The strong take away from the weak, the clever take away from the strong, and the government takes away from everybody.

The American people should worry less about the population explosion and more about the tax explosion.

We expect youth to be strong, courageous, and prepared to pay even more taxes than their fathers did.

This is the day of youth, and they can have it. They'll age rapidly when taxpaying time starts.

Teachers

Teachers in the lower grades needn't worry about automation until someone invents a machine that can blow noses and remove snowsuits and boots.

The school kids in some towns are getting so tough that teachers are playing hooky.

The only thing that children wear out faster than shoes are parents and teachers.

Education pays less when you are an educator.

Education helps you earn more. But not many school teachers can prove it.

We'll be in trouble as long as we pay the best professors less than the worst football coach.

Experience is the best teacher, and considering what it costs, it should be.

Experience may be a thorough teacher, but no man lives long enough to graduate.

One reason experience is such a good teacher is that she doesn't allow any dropouts.

Another reason why experience is the best teacher — she is always on the job.

School teachers have to face their problems every day, whereas bus drivers have all their problems behind them.

School teachers are given too much credit and too little cash.

Efficient school teachers may cost more, but poor school teachers cost the most.

As a general rule, teachers teach more by what they are than by what they say.

School teachers are not fully appreciated by parents until it rains all day Saturday.

It's not so much what is poured into the student, but what is planted, that really counts.

A teacher's constant task is to take a roomful of live wires and see to it that they're grounded.

The mediocre teacher tells. The good teacher explains. The superior teacher demonstrates. The great teacher inspires.

Did you hear about the two unemployed school teachers? One had no principle; the other, no class!

The world seldom notices who the teachers are; but civilization depends on what they do and what they say.

Tears

Laugh and the world laughs with you; cry and the other guy has an even better sob story.

Sometimes we get the feeling we laugh by the inch and cry by the yard.

Marriage is like horseradish — men praise it with tears in their eyes.

There are many tears in the heart that never reach the eye.

Nothing dries quicker than a tear.

A woman's tears are the greatest waterpower known to man.

Tears are the safety valves of the heart when too much pressure is put upon them.

When a woman resorts to tears, she's either trying to get something out of her system or out of her husband.

Keep your teen-age daughter out of hot water — put dirty dishes in it!

Teen-agers

A baby sitter is a teen-ager who behaves like an adult, while the adults are out behaving like teen-agers.

Teen-age boys will drive anything — except a lawn mower.

A teen-age boy is at that awkward age. He likes to park but he doesn't know exactly why.

It never occurs to a boy of sixteen that someday he will be as dumb as his father is now.

Next year 3 1/2 million kids will turn sixteen, and 7 million parents will turn pale.

Adult education got its start in a household with teen-age children.

Sometimes an adult education begins with a teen-age marriage.

You're not going to get anywhere telling your teen-age son his hair looks like a mop. He probably doesn't know what a mop is.

Did you hear about the teen-age boy who let his hair down — and smothered?

Having teen-agers is often what undermines a parent's belief in heredity.

Home is a place where teen-agers go to refuel.

It's nice to kiss the kids goodnight — if you don't mind waiting up for them.

Modern medicine still hasn't decided whether it's harder on a middle-aged man to mow the lawn himself or argue to get his teen-age son to do it.

A Kentucky father of a teen-age boy says his hardest job is getting his son to realize that "No" is a complete sentence.

Most parents of teen-agers seem to agree that one "hang-up" their kids don't have is when on the telephone.

If you want a definition of poverty, ask parents with three or four teen-agers in the family.

International problems are becoming so complex that even taxi drivers and teen-agers don't have the solutions.

Why can't life's problems hit us when we're eighteen and know everything?

International problems are simple compared to the difficulties in a home with three teen-agers and one phone.

A Kansas father said his teen-age son took an aptitude test and was found to be well-suited for retirement.

The teen-ager of today thinks he's underprivileged if he has to play a guitar without electricity.

A problem teen-ager is one who refuses to let his parents use the car.

Teen-age boys who whistle at girls are just going through a stage which will probably last fifty years.

Nowadays when you tell a teen-ager he must shift for himself, he thinks you're going to buy him a new sports car.

Nothing seems to sharpen a teen-ager's appetite more than eating.

'Blessed are the teen-agers, for they shall inherit the national debt.'

The best way to keep teen-agers home is to make their surroundings pleasant — and let the air out of the tires.

Today's teen-agers will listen to records, radio, TV — they'll listen to anything but reason.

Maybe our teen-agers aren't maturing too fast, but it's a little frightening to find that a lot of them already have as many prejudices as they'll ever need.

The main problem with teen-agers is that they're just like their parents were at their age.

According to a recent survey, today's teen-agers are alike in many disrespects.

A stage is what a teen-ager thinks she should be on, when actually it's something she's going through.

The reason that teen-agers know all the answers is that they haven't heard all the questions yet.

Nothing makes it more difficult to understand teen-agers than listening to what they say.

It will be interesting to hear the teen-agers of today tell their children what they had to do without when they were young.

The thing that most teen-age drivers dislike about parking is the noisy crash.

Some teen-agers never make outgoing telephone calls for fear they'll miss an incoming one.

The easiest way to get a teen-age boy to be quiet is to ask him where he's been when he gets home.

Anyone who doesn't believe the younger generation is creative should watch a teen-ager construct a sandwich.

Teen-agers haven't changed very much. They still grow up, leave home, and get married. The big difference is that today they don't always do it in that order.

No one could possibly know as much as a teen-ager thinks he knows, or as little as he thinks his father knows.

Not only are teen-agers a comfort in old age — they help bring it on.

The average teen-ager still has all the faults his parents outgrew.

Too many teen-agers don't pay any more attention to their conscience than they do their parents.

Little wonder that our present-day teen-ager is all mixed up. Half the adults are telling him to "find himself" and the other half are telling him to get lost.

Like its politicians and its wars, society has the teen-agers it deserves.

Teen-agers aren't interested in putting their shoulders to the wheel these days — all they want to do is get their hands on it.

Once a teen-ager passes his driving test, he can pass almost anything except his school subjects.

Teen-age is the interval between pigtails and cocktails.

The modern teen-ager doesn't leave any footprints on the sands of time — just tire tracks.

It's difficult to decide whether growing pains are something teen-agers have — or are!

There's nothing wrong with teen-agers that becoming taxpayers won't cure.

Before dealing too harshly with our teen-agers, let's remember who reared them.

A teen-age girl does her homework in the same length of time it takes her mother to do the dishes.

A few teen-agers think they know all about driving a car once they learn where the horn is located.

Teen-agers are the only people who can slam a revolving door.

A teen-age girl reports that she's been trying to run away from home for several months — but everytime she gets to the front door the phone rings.

About the only time teen-agers get homesick these days is when they're at home.

To a teen-ager, liquid assets consist of a refrigerator filled with soft drinks.

If Alexander Graham Bell had had a daughter, he would have never had a chance to test the telephone.

Any mother can tell you a teen-agers hangup doesn't include clothes.

Teen-agers are young people who get too much of everything, including criticism.

A distressed father said to his teen-age daughter, "Young lady, either that dress is too short or you're not in it far enough."

Some teen-agers used to spin the bottle at parties. Now they give the pot a whirl.

It seems that many teen-agers still have faults we older people have outgrown.

A teen-age girl usually makes up her face easier than her mind.

The current generation of teen-agers is more affluent than any in history — thanks to their "funding fathers."

Alexander Graham Bell gave us the telephone, but teen-agers took us one step further — they gave us the busy signal.

The telephone is a remarkable instrument. It enables teen-agers to go steady without holding hands.

Wild oats is a juvenile's favorite cereal.

Nothing is certain in this world except death, taxes, and teen-agers.

Getting the baby to sleep is most difficult when she is eighteen years old.

Telephones

With telephone rates due to go up again, we begin to wonder if what we have to say is still worth saying.

The only place in America where you don't have free speech is in a telephone booth.

An old grouch in Alabama had a telephone installed — just so he could hang up on people.

You're definitely at middle age when the telephone rings and you hope it's not for you.

An optimist thinks the woman in the phone booth will be right out because he heard her say goodby.

International problems are simple compared to the difficulties in a home with three teen-agers and one phone.

Can you imagine anyone being as unhappy as a woman with a live secret and a dead telephone?

When a woman suffers in silence, the phone is probably out of order.

Some teen-agers never make outgoing telephone calls for fear they'll miss an incoming one.

A teen-age girl reports that she's been trying to run away from home for several months — but everytime she gets to the front door the phone rings.

If Alexander Graham Bell had had a daughter, he would have never had a chance to test the telephone.

When a man answers the phone he reaches for a pencil; when a woman answers she reaches for a chair.

The telephone service is getting worse. Now it takes twice as long to get a wrong number.

To make a long story short, try long distance.

Alexander Graham Bell gave us the telephone, but teen-agers took us one step further — they gave us the busy signal.

The first telephones had cranks on them. Some still do.

If they raise the telephone rates any higher, we'll soon be a part of the silent majority.

Women and telephones repeat what they hear, but the telephone repeats it exactly.

Before the telephone was invented, people thought it was impossible — it still is!

The telephone is a remarkable instrument. It enables teen-agers to go steady without holding hands.

When thou art in the bathtub, ask not for whom the phone ringeth, for thou knowest it ringeth for thee.

There's an advantage to having an unlisted number — if you get an obscene call at least you know it's from a friend.

Many years ago we blamed phone operators for wrong numbers. Today, thanks to science, we can dial wrong numbers all by ourselves.

A telephone booth is now called a GABRATORY.

A man answers the telephone by saying, "Hello." A woman answers with, "Wait a minute till I turn out the burner under the potatoes."

There's a service, similar to Dial-A-Prayer, called Dial-A-Doubt. It's for atheists who aren't sure.

We have been watching more TV dramas lately. It's such a pleasure to see someone pick up the phone and get the right number immediately.

Some women can talk their way out of anything except a phone booth.

Television

Did you hear about the Hollywood actor with so little personality that he appeared on a color TV show and it came out in black and white?

On TV talk shows the Hollywood actresses always seem to mention either their last picture or their next husband.

A gorilla in a Dallas zoo watches a TV set near his cage. He appears to be almost human — except that he seems to enjoy the commercials.

The easiest way to get a kid's attention is to stand in front of the TV set.

Small children start to school these days with a big advantage. They already know two letters of the alphabet — TV.

Modern kids are so TV-oriented they think there are two kinds of rainbows. One in color and the other in black and white.

A child's definition of a torture chamber is a living room or den without a TV set.

The people who talk most about the "good old days" are the first to complain when their TV set goes on the blink.

Out west corn is measured by the foot; down south, by the gallon; and on TV, by the hour.

The rising crime rate would be slowed down considerably if we'd put as many cops on the streets as there are on television.

Many Americans are in favor of disarmament — especially if it starts with those noisy "Westerns" on TV.

How did dogs learn to bark their loudest during a television news bulletin?

Shakespeare said that the evil men do lives after them. On TV this is called a rerun.

A woman in Montana recently complained that the only exercise her husband gets is changing the dial on their TV set.

Your neighbor friend will continue to talk to you over the back fence even though he knows he's missing his favorite TV program.

We are told that history always repeats itself. But, then, so does television.

A typical home is where the TV set is better adjusted than the kids.

Writing TV humor isn't as hard as listening to it.

The world might be improved with less television and more vision.

In the old days a comedian took a dirty joke and cleaned it up for radio. Today he hears a clean joke and dirties it up for television.

Many married couples never go out. The husband sits in front of the TV set and smokes. The wife sits in front of the TV set and fumes.

You know that your memory is failing when you watch TV reruns and they seem new to you.

Middle age is when a man's favorite nightspot is in front of a TV set.

Movies shown on TV are getting shorter. Any day now we'll be seeing "The Five Commandments.

A lot of singers on TV are worth watching. Too bad they're not worth listening to.

Another thing about a newspaper is that you never have to ask someone to turn down the volume.

The old-timer can remember when the only thing bad on TV was the reception.

You probably won't hear opportunity knock if the television set is always on.

There's a shortage of doctors everywhere except on TV.

The quickest way to get a doctor is to turn on the TV set.

Before deciding to retire from your job, stay home a week and watch daytime television.

During the baseball season a domestic triangle is a husband, a wife, and a TV set.

Have you noticed that on TV the good guys win out every time — except on the six o'-clock news?

Television has added a new dimension to boredom — eyestrain!

Those detective stories on TV always end at precisely the right moment — after the criminal is arrested and before the court turns him loose.

Before television we could only hear static. Now it is possible for us to see it.

If you think television has killed conversation, you've never heard people trying to decide which program to watch.

Sometimes the television hero is the one who sits through the program.

Daytime TV isn't a total loss — six states are now using it to replace capital punishment.

A television announcer is another person who should be seen and not heard.

To some people television is just a sleeping pill plugged in.

Television is still in its infancy, though a lot of its jokes aren't.

The world could certainly use more vision and less television.

One thing we learn from television these days is that the country is full of people who can't sing.

If TV doesn't start getting better, husbands may go back to listening to their wives.

A television set is a device that changes a child from an irresistible force to an immovable object.

There are TV anchormen who receive twice as much money to read the news as the President gets to make the news.

Sometimes the most imaginative thing about TV is the repairman's bill.

Television is changing our language. In some homes what used to be called leftovers is now known as "Instant Replay."

Most of us have been watching TV on and off for many years — and between the two we prefer it off.

Thanks to TV today's kids are smarter than previous generations. Just mention a detergent and they'll tell you the secret ingredients in it.

Some TV comics are like crackerjacks — half nuts and lots of corn.

Notice on a new TV set: "Warning — extended watching of basketball and baseball games may be harmful to your marriage."

Educational TV has proved quite successful. Just having a set repaired is a good lesson in economics.

The trouble with TV is that we sit watching a twenty-five inch screen so much that we develop a thirty inch bottom.

Television is a great blessing — you can sit at home any evening, relax, and watch your wife's favorite program.

As an educational device, TV rates above everything else. No nation in history has ever known as much as we do about detergents and deodorants.

Television is with us to stay — if we can keep up the payments.

The TV reruns always begin when summer begins — including weather forecasts.

Television is what gives you nothing to do when you aren't doing anything.

If one political candidate gets free time on TV, his opponent demands equal time to deny everything.

Television brings us a strange kind of progress — you can twist a dial and see exactly what you saw five years ago.

What's so bad about the new TV shows? The worst they can do is drive you to drink.

The easiest way to find more time to do all the things you want to do is to turn off the television.

Television is simply great. We should all be proud and happy to go blind watching it.

Pay television has been with us for years. It's called the installment plan.

Daytime television is the punishment inflicted on people who stay home from work when they're really not sick.

Nothing improves a television program as much as getting the children to bed.

It's important to watch the new season's shows, so you'll know which ones to miss when they show up in summer reruns.

Television has opened many doors — mostly on refrigerators.

Would you enjoy a horror show on TV? If so, take a look at the six o'clock news.

Many people are in favor of pay television, that is, they believe they should be paid for watching some of the TV shows that are now being aired.

Nothing promotes better television reception than being childless.

An efficient TV repairman can fix anything that's wrong with your TV set except the lousy programs.

Most of us enjoy TV soap operas. The folks on those shows are the only ones we know who have more problems than we do.

Next season more and more leading actors on TV programs will get married. It helps the ratings if a little violence is shown occasionally.

We are told that television is still in its infancy — which explains why you have to get up so often and change it.

Maybe there's nothing new under the sun, but if you watch the late shows on TV, you'll learn there's nothing new under the moon either.

Everything about a TV mystery story is easy to understand — except the commercials.

There are so many medical shows on TV these days that you can't get your set repaired without a prescription.

We doubt that those TV soap operas are true to life. Did you ever experience a crisis that was interrupted for a commercial?

Television is a device which permits people who haven't anything to do to watch people who can't do anything.

There is now some talk of eliminating violence from TV. Well, there goes the eleven o'clock news.

Television may not be as violent as it once was — but with all the bad breath, deodorant, and detergent commercials, it certainly is smelly and dirty!

In many respects television is true to life. You can seldom get what you want when you want it.

Children who watch television every night will go down in history — not to mention arithmetic, geography, and science.

It is generally agreed that television is the proof that you can't talk without a voice, but that you can sing without one.

Television is that remarkable invention that makes it necessary for you to wake up before you can go to bed.

One of the main differences in newspapers and television is that editors report violence, while TV producers create it.

What stops most people from buying a color TV set is seeing the black and white price tag.

Some of our TV shows are getting so dull that most of the kids have gone back to doing their homework.

A grandmother is a baby sitter who watches the kids instead of the television.

The only tools that TV repairmen carry at all times are a screwdriver and an adding machine.

When the Roman Empire was falling apart, the people were kept reasonably happy with circuses. Now we have television.

A recent medical TV show was so dramatic the surgeon got nervous and cut out the commercial.

TV repairmen can estimate costs very closely — they can get within a dollar of what you have in your pocket.

Nowadays, "Early to bed and early to rise" probably mean the TV is busted.

An Ohio man reports he can't stand TV, but anything that keeps his wife quiet can't be all bad.

We have been watching more TV dramas lately. It's such a pleasure to see someone pick up the phone and get the right number immediately.

Most of us have seen TV grow from infancy to adultery.

Television has been a great teacher — it taught a lot of folks to turn to radio.

One of the recent TV game shows offered a male contestant a week in Paris as first prize. Second prize was two weeks in Paris — with his wife!

We've been seeing a lot of TV shows this season about crime and doctors. Half the actors were holding up banks and the other half were holding up x-rays.

There must be a studio somewhere that makes nothing but reruns.

It seems that the main idea of TV is to provide, as cheaply as possible, something to fill in the time between those expensive commercials.

Late night TV is educational. It usually teaches you that you should have gone to bed earlier.

Prisoners watch daytime TV programs. They think it's part of the punishment.

Television isn't so bad if you don't turn it on.

TV has turned the family circle into a half circle.

Medical programs aren't realistic. You never see a doctor collecting a fee.

Some people's idea of roughing it is to spend their vacation in a small town where they can get only one channel on TV.

Anyone who doesn't worry about the world situation these days must be getting lousy reception on his television set.

Television Commercials

A gorilla in a Dallas zoo watches a TV set near his cage. He appears to be almost human — except that he seems to enjoy the commercials.

Nowadays it's easy for a bachelor to remain single. Every time he turns his TV set on he hears that most women have stringy hair, rough red hands, bad breath, and are overweight.

There is one good thing you can say for a book. It does not interrupt at the most interesting part for a word from the sponsor.

A bore is like a TV commercial — often loud and dull.

Do you know what happens to little boys who continually interrupt? They grow up and make a fortune doing TV commercials.

At last one of the tobacco companies has found a way to make its cigarettes less irritating; it filters the commercials.

A "miracle drug" is any drug that'll do about half what the TV commercial promises it'll do.

Many men are doing well on TV today. They have great faces for acid indigestion commercials.

Who said kids aren't obedient? They'll obey any TV commercial about buying a new toy.

The radio remains popular for the simple reason that it can't show you what your headache looks like.

Maybe one reason the Russians are so confident is they've watched our TV programs and figure all Americans have tired blood, indigestion, bad breath, and a nagging backache.

An illness is like a TV commercial — even a short one is too long.

Television commercials are educational. They teach us how much we can take before we become nauseated.

If TV hadn't come along many of us would have never seen the picture of a common cold.

A sponsor makes television possible and impossible at the same time.

To find what your doctor recommends, watch television.

Television is a wonderful medium. It enables someone in New York City to see someone in Los Angeles suffering from acid indigestion.

It was thoughtful of the television people to put the aspirin commercials right after the six o'clock news.

There's one thing about TV commercials — they won't be interrupted.

One trouble with television commercials is too much "tell" and not enough "vision."

The country is finally getting back to normal. Television is once again devoting more time to detergents than to politicians.

It's nice to know that in this world there are still a few things you can count on — such as a happy ending in TV commercials.

As we view all the aches and pains shown on TV, it seems that all the cures have provided only temporary relief.

Political commercials on TV prove one thing — some candidates can tell you all their good points and qualifications in thirty seconds.

Everybody knows how a TV mystery will end — with a long commercial.

TV commercials are educational. They teach you how stupid advertisers think you are.

About the only clean, non-violent things on TV nowadays are the detergent commercials.

On those TV medical shows you see a surgeon cut out an appendix or tonsils, but they never cut out the commercials.

After hearing all the headache and backache remedies on TV, many have decided the best painkiller is turning off the set.

Television is a well-balanced medium. You get new commercials with old movies.

If you see something on TV with a good cast, bright plot, and clever dialogue — it's probably a commercial.

What used to be a station break is now more like a compound fracture.

Television may not be as violent as it once was — but with all the bad breath, deodorant, and detergent commercials, it certainly is smelly and dirty!

If the products advertised on TV are really "mild," "soothing," and "refreshing," why can't they make the commercials less irritating?

Did you hear the TV announcer when he said, "And now a word from our sponsor, who makes this program impossible."?

A recent medical TV show was so dramatic the surgeon got nervous and cut out the commercial.

Most politicians don't lie on TV any more than the average sponsor.

With all the interruptions for commercials, it takes longer to watch an old movie than it did to make it.

What annoys the TV sponsors is having people remember the tune of the commercial but forgetting what brand it's advertising.

It seems that the main idea of TV is to provide, as cheaply as possible, something to fill in the time between those expensive commercials.

Commercials on the TV late shows are like labor pains — toward the end they're longer and closer together.

Temper

The world needs more warm hearts and fewer hot heads.

People who fly into a rage always make a bad landing.

The emptier the pot, the quicker the boil — watch your temper!

Every time you give someone a piece of your mind you make your head a little emptier.

About the time a man gets his temper under control, he goes out and plays golf again.

Before you give somebody a piece of your mind, be sure you can get by with what you have left.

You can't go around giving folks a piece of your mind without eventually being called empty-headed.

Some people think they have dynamic personalities because they're always exploding.

Poise is the difference between flipping your lid and raising your eyebrows.

Blowing your stack adds to air pollution.

Temper gets people into trouble, but pride keeps them there.

If you aspire to a ripe old age, never drive your car while in a rage.

You never know what a hothead will do — and neither does he.

If you lose your head, how do you expect to be able to use it?

When you're right you can afford to keep your temper; when you're wrong you can't afford to lose it.

You'll never get to the top if you keep blowing yours.

If you would like to control your temper, be like a kettle — sing when you boil.

Today's temper tantrum is tomorrow's anti-establishment demonstration.

People who have an ax to grind often fly off the handle.

Smart people lose their temper permanently.

The best cure for a short temper is a lengthy prayer.

People who fly into a rage usually make a bumpy landing.

Nothing can "cook your goose" quicker than a boiling temper.

The best time to keep your shirt on is when you're hot under the collar.

Better watch your temper. Remember, the emptier the pot the quicker the boil.

The most important time to hold your temper is when the other person has lost his.

A hothead seldom sets the world on fire.

Your temper is a funny thing. You can't get rid of it by losing it.

He who "blows his stack" adds to the world's pollution.

Striking while the iron is hot is all right, but don't strike while the head is hot.

When a man loses his temper, his reason goes on a vacation.

A temper displayed in public is indecent exposure.

Men are like steel. When they lose their tempers they're worthless.

It is always a good idea to be selfish with your temper — so always keep it.

Hitting the ceiling is the wrong way to get up in the world.

A show of temper is often a testimonial of indecision, weakness, inadequacy, defeat, and frustration.

When tempers grow hot, Christianity grows cold.

509

Some people are like firecrackers — they explode when the heat is applied.

It is extremely difficult for a man who loses his temper to hold his friends.

Keep your temper. Nobody else wants it.

The person who loses his head probably doesn't miss it.

Temper is a funny thing. It spoils children, ruins men, and strengthens steel.

Folks who are constantly blowing a fuse are generally left in the dark.

Hot tempers will mean cool friends.

Another thing that seems to improve the longer you keep it is your temper.

Keep your temper to yourself. It's useless to others.

Your temper improves the more you don't use it.

Whether you're on the road or in an argument, when you see red it's time to stop.

When your temper boils over you are usually in hot water.

What a wonderful thing it would be if all those who lost their tempers could find them again.

Beware of using sharp words. You may have to eat them later on down the line.

Temptation

You can't see the flaw in a bridge until it falls down, or the flaw in a man's character until he meets with temptation.

All men are honest — until they are faced with a situation tempting enough to make them dishonest.

Sometimes it's difficult to know who's knocking — opportunity or temptation.

If opportunity came in the form of a temptation, knocking once would be sufficient.

If you would not fall into sin, keep away from the brink of temptation.

Most people can resist everything but temptation.

When temptation calls you, just drop the receiver.

Temptation often comes through a door that has been deliberately left open.

It's not that you can resist temptation any easier in a small town — you just can't find it.

What we miss most as we grow older is temptation.

The whisper of temptation can be heard farther than the loudest call of duty.

Resisting temptation is a lot easier when we think we'll probably get another chance on down the line.

Nothing makes it easier to resist temptation than a proper upbringing, a sound set of values, and witnesses.

It's rather odd how temptation always seems to get action quicker than good intentions.

Temptation seldom breaks your door down; it quietly and cunningly enters the open portals of your mind.

By yielding to temptation one may lose in a moment what it took a lifetime to gain.

Few speed records are broken when people run away from temptation.

Watch out for temptation — the more you see it, the better it looks.

Temptation bothers some folks most when they can't find any.

When you meet temptation — turn to the right!

Many people who flee from temptation leave a forwarding address.

Temptations from without have no power unless there is a corresponding desire within.

Most people don't need to be led into temptation — they usually find their own way.

Temptations are certain to ring your doorbell; but it's your own fault if you ask them in to stay for dinner.

Temptation is something which, if resisted, may never come your way again.

Temptations are like tramps. Treat them kindly and they will return bringing others with them.

Don't worry about avoiding temptation after you pass sixty. That's when it starts avoiding you.

The man who is suddenly overpowered by temptation has probably been dreaming about it for a long time.

Nothing makes temptation so easy to resist as being broke.

There are several good protections against temptation, but the surest one is cowardice.

The reason some men don't go very far in life is that they sidestep opportunity and shake hands with temptation.

Temptation is not sin, but playing with temptation invites sin.

A person falls into temptation because he is unwilling to stand up against it.

All you need to be introduced to a big temptation is to give in to a little one.

Opportunity has to knock, but it is enough for temptation to stand outside and whistle.

The prayer of modern youth seems to be, "Lord, lead us not into temptation. Just tell us where it is and we'll find it."

When a fellow shuts his eyes to temptation, he ought to be sure he ain't winkin'.

Temptations, unlike opportunities, will always give you a second chance.

The temptation to say an unkind word should be first rehearsed to see how it sounds to you.

Temptation can cause us to succumb, sink, sin — or stand.

An Idaho man sighed, "At my age, by the time I find temptation, I'm too tired to give in to it."

Some folks flee from temptation, then wait around the corner for it to catch up with them.

Most people can resist the temptation to do right.

Temptations are easiest to resist with your eyes closed.

Ten Commandments

What a scarcity of news there would be if everybody obeyed the Ten Commandments!

God's laws last longer than those who break them.

If the good Lord had intended for us to live in a permissive society, wouldn't the Ten Commandments have been called the Ten Suggestions?

Many a man has followed the Ten Commandments all his life but never quite managed to catch up with them.

Moses was a great law giver. The way he was satisfied to keep the Ten Commandments short and to the point shows clearly that he was not an ordinary lawyer.

It's a good thing Moses didn't have to submit the Ten Commandments to a council of foreign ministers for approval.

The United States Supreme Court has handed down the eleventh commandment, "Thou shalt not, in any classroom, read the first ten."

One reason why the Ten Commandments are so short and to the point is the fact they did not come out of a committee.

The Ten Commandments were given to men in tablet form, and by following their directions, we could save a lot of other tablets from being used.

A successful criminal lawyer in Montana reports that he has found several loopholes in the Ten Commandments.

The most pleasant fact about the Ten Commandments is that there are only ten of them.

We often wonder what the Ten Commandments would look like today if Moses had been compelled to submit them to a hostile legislature!

When the Lord gave us the Ten Commandments, He didn't mention amendments.

Thankfulness
see also Gratitude

There's one thing for which you should be abundantly thankful — only you and God have all the facts about yourself.

Thankfulness could well be the finest sentiment of man — and also the rarest.

It isn't what you have in your pocket that makes you thankful, but what you have in your heart.

There's always something to be thankful for. If you can't pay your bills, you can be thankful you're not one of your creditors.

If you have nothing for which to be thankful, make up your mind that there's something wrong with you.

Be thankful if your job is a little harder than you like. A razor can't be sharpened on a piece of velvet.

We should be thankful for the good things that we have and, also, for the bad things we don't have.

A person doesn't realize how much he has to be thankful for until he has to pay taxes on it.

Even though we can't have all we want, we ought to be thankful we don't get what we deserve.

Let us give thanks — if only for all the bad things that are never going to happen.

We ought to be thankful that we are living in a country where folks can say what they think without thinking.

If you think you haven't much to be thankful for, why not be thankful for some of the things you *don't* have?

Theft

He who buys what he doesn't need steals from himself.

Some people have the habit of finding things before they are lost.

An embezzler is one who keeps too much to himself.

If Robin Hood were alive today, he'd steal from the poor because the rich carry only credit cards.

The employee who will steal *for* his boss will steal *from* his boss.

In Washington they're either tapping the phones or tapping the till.

Thinking

America has the highest standard of living in the world. Now let's raise our standard of thinking.

Always remember that a man is not rewarded for having brains, but for using them.

The human brain is the apparatus with which we think we think.

Nowadays most brains are suffering from chronic unemployment.

Think right, act right; it is what you think and do that makes you what you are.

With computers doing our thinking, all we need now is a worrying machine.

A cheap but top-rate computer is the one between your ears.

Nature abhors a vacuum. When a head lacks brains, nature fills it with conceit.

You can lead a horse to water, but you can't make him drink. You can send a man to Congress, but you can't make him think.

Crime begins in the mind. A man has to think wrong before he acts wrong.

Think of doubt as an invitation to think.

The true object of education should be to train one to think clearly and act rightly.

If a person has no education he is forced to use his brains.

Some big executives have computers to do all their thinking for them. Some just have wives.

People don't accidentally stumble into failure. They think their way into it.

If you have tried your hand at something and failed, the next best thing is to try your head.

Thinking will get us to the foot of the mountain; faith will get us to the top.

While fear slows down our thinking process, it greatly improves our footwork.

When it comes to food for thought, some folks are on a hunger strike most of the time.

Many people seem to be allergic to food for thought.

A wise man reflects before he speaks; a fool speaks and then reflects on what he has uttered.

So few people think. When we find one who really does, we call him a genius.

Women's intuition is the result of thousands of years of not thinking.

If a man is too lazy to think for himself, he should get married!

Prejudice is a lazy man's substitute for thinking.

Many people think they're thinking when they're merely rearranging their prejudices.

With man's great ability to think, reason, and compute, we can now pinpoint most of our current problems. The trouble is that we can't solve them.

To be a good speaker in public, you must be a good thinker in private.

Straight living cannot come out of crooked thinking.

Often people who think before they speak don't speak.

Even the woodpecker has discovered that the only way to succeed is to use one's head.

Talking too much usually follows thinking too little.

Before proceeding with a difficult task, stop and think. Then remember to start again.

Thinking is one thing that no one has ever been able to tax — but the IRS is getting jealous about the situation.

Thinking is like living and dying. Each of us must do it for himself.

We don't all think alike. In fact, we don't all think.

Think! It might be a new experience.

People who say what they think would not be so bad if they thought.

Think small and you'll remain small.

The trouble with most people is that every time they think, they think only of themselves.

When you stop to think, don't forget to start again.

There is entirely too much thinking these days by those who aren't really qualified.

Which needs to be raised more — our standard of living or our standard of thinking?

Thinking is only a process of talking to yourself intelligently.

It's about time for folks to carry this do-it-yourself craze to thinking.

Some who have a habit of thinking out loud make others appreciate how golden silence really is.

There is a lingering suspicion on the part of some that the trouble with this country is that too many people are trying to think without having had any previous experience.

If it's true that people think best on their feet, there must be a lot of folks sitting around these days.

Acting without thinking is a lot like shooting without aiming.

You can think better if you close your eyes — and mouth.

Five percent of the people really think, ten percent think they think, and the remainder would rather die than think. It's the five percent who change things.

Serious thinking is the kind of thinking to which most people resort only when they're broke, in jail, in the hospital, or in some other disaster.

Some people can't think and the rest don't.

The reason it's later than some folks think is that they can't think as fast as time passes by.

The reason some people get lost in thought is that it is such unfamiliar territory.

The trouble with some folks who stop to think is that they stay parked.

Too many folks get through thinking before they get through thinking things through.

A man can never get so confused in his thinking that he cannot see the other fellow's duty.

The Lord gave us two ends — one for sitting and the other for thinking.

Laugh and the world will laugh with you; think and you will almost die of loneliness.

The man who thinks he knows it all has merely stopped thinking.

Man can live without air for a few minutes, without water for two weeks, without food for six weeks — and without a new thought for a lifetime.

You can lead a man to Congress but you can't make him think.

A shallow thinker never leaves a deep impression.

Some people don't think before they speak — nor afterwards.

A person who thinks too much of himself isn't thinking enough.

Do you think, or do you just think you think?

Another good way to learn to think fast on your feet is to be a pedestrian.

They think too little who talk too much.

To know what not to think about is a major intellectual virtue.

When you're up to your ears in trouble, try using the part that isn't submerged.

A lot of trouble arises from workers who don't think, and from thinkers who don't work.

Those who think they are dreamers are usually just sleepers.

Thoughts
see also Ideas

Kind actions begin with kind thoughts.

Do it now! Today will be yesterday tomorrow.

The actions of men are the best interpreters of their thoughts.

More and more food is coming canned or prepackaged — including food for thought.

If your would attain greatness, think no little thoughts.

Language is the dress of thought; every time you talk your mind is on parade.

Language is the apparel in which our thoughts parade before the public. Let's never clothe them in vulgar or shoddy attire.

People with a one-track mind often have a derailed train of thought.

The one thing worse than a vacant mind is one filled with spiteful thoughts.

To avoid old age keep taking on new thoughts and throwing off old habits.

It's too bad that more people are thoughtless than speechless.

If some politicians said what they thought, they'd be speechless.

Some preachers seem to use big words to conceal the smallness of their thoughts.

When some preachers get up, their thoughts sit down.

Satan uses a vacant mind as a dumping ground.

The reason some people get lost in thought is that it is such unfamiliar territory.

Man can live without air for a few minutes, without water for two weeks, without food for six weeks — and without a new thought for a lifetime.

This country would be in a sorry mess if everybody thought alike, but it would be better if everybody thought.

Be careful of your thoughts. They may break out into words at any time.

Despite inflation a penny for the thoughts of many people is still a fair price.

It's bad for a fellow to be left alone with his thoughts, but it's a lot worse to be left alone without any thoughts.

He is never alone who is in the company of noble thoughts.

The right train of thought can take you to a better station in life.

Test the value of your thoughts by deciding whether you'd want them said out loud.

See that you have a supply of worthy thoughts before you begin to talk.

One of the least popular items on the menu today seems to be food for thought.

Thoughts rule the world.

If thoughts could be read, faces might be redder.

You cannot escape the results of your own thoughts.

Human thought is like a pendulum — it keeps swinging from one extreme to another.

Why use a tub of words to express a spoonful of thought?

A multiplicity of words indicates poverty of thought.

Our words may hide our thoughts, but our actions will reveal them.

Thrift

Saving money these days is harder than playing a trumpet from the wrong end.

In the "good old days" the man who saved money was a miser. Now he's a wonder.

Try to save money. Someday it may be valuable again.

Is thrift becoming unfashionable or just impossible?

Some people are saving their money for a rainy day. But, for most of us, a light mist could wipe us out.

There was a time when you saved up for your old age; now you save up for April 15th.

In North Dakota there's a man who is noted for his thrift. He never goes hunting because he can't find a store that sells used bullets.

What a married couple should save for their old age is each other.

The person who works and saves will someday have enough wealth to divide with those who don't.

When you finally save enough for a rainy day, some of your relatives start sending in bad weather reports.

Everybody thinks thrift is a wonderful virtue, especially in our ancestors.

People who save pennies today probably tried dollars first.

It's easier to admire the other fellow's thrift than to practice it yourself.

About the only thing you can save out of your paycheck these days is the envelope.

A saver is a farsighted person who lays money away for the government's rainy day.

Folks who saved for a rainy day are deluged by annoying drips who didn't.

Save your money, and when you have silver in your hair, you'll have gold in your purse.

Wisdom enables one to be thrifty without being stingy, and generous without being wasteful.

Time

A man ordinarily has time to do all the things he really wants to do.

Americans have more time-saving devices and less time than any other people in the world.

Have you noticed that a bore always takes his time taking your time?

Few things are more dangerous to a person's character than having nothing to do and plenty of time in which to do it.

The best thing to spend on children is your time.

A committee usually keeps minutes and wastes hours.

Time wasted thinking up excuses would be better spent avoiding the need for them.

Time separates the best of friends, and so does money — and marriage!

Americans will pay a big price for an invention that will help them save time they don't know what to do with.

No matter how hard you try to improve on Mother Nature, you're not kidding Father Time.

What Mother Nature giveth, Father Time taketh away.

The best thing that parents can spend on their children is time — not money.

The easiest way to find more time to do all the things you want to do is to turn off the television.

Too many of us spend our time the way politicians spend our money.

Time separates the best of friends, and so does money — and don't forget marriage!

No wonder time flies. Have you ever noticed how many people are out to kill it?

One way a person can lose a lot of time is to always be on time for appointments.

If you think time heals everything, try sitting in a doctor's office.

Time changes things. Nowadays the couple has the honeymoon first, and if it's a success, they have the engagement, and if that works out all right, they *may* have a wedding.

Killing time is not murder, it's suicide.

If you gave the same amount of time to your work as you do your church, how long would you hold your job?

Daylight Saving's Time just makes some people tired an hour earlier.

Time is so powerful it is given to us only in small quantities.

When you kill time, just remember it has no resurrection.

Nothing makes time pass faster than vacations and short-term loans.

Many people have time on their hands — also on their faces.

Time is what we want the most, and what we use the worst.

Isn't it aggravating how little value other people put on your time?

Counting time is not nearly as important as making time count.

The busy man seems to have time for everything. The man who just thinks he's busy hasn't time for anything.

Whenever we waste time, we should remember that Father Time never makes a round trip.

Time may be a great healer, but it's no beauty specialist.

The real problem with leisure time is how to keep other people from using it.

If you want to kill time, why not try working it to death?

Today is the tomorrow you worried about yesterday.

Time waits for no man — but it stands still for a woman of thirty-five!

Hours and flowers soon fade away.

Time is that which the average American never seems to have quite enough of and is almost always behind.

Daylight Saving's Time is founded on the old Indian idea of cutting off one end of the blanket and sewing it onto the other end to make the blanket longer.

Some folks never do anything on time but buy.

Time is like money — you can only spend it once.

Why is there seldom enough time to do a thing right, but always enough time to do it over?

Those who make the worst use of their time are usually the ones who complain of its shortness.

Time may be money, but it's much easier to persuade a man to give you his time than to lend you his money.

Saving time is well and good, but it is deplorable that time can't be placed in storage for future use.

It is difficult to live in the present, ridiculous to try to live in the future, and impossible to live in the past. Nothing is as far away as one minute ago.

Nothing makes time go faster than buying on it.

If time is money, it can't be worth very much these days.

Lost time is never found again.

Time is what passes rapidly between the "easy monthly payments."

You can't beat old Father Time — but some women manage to drive a mighty close bargain with him.

Time can be wasted but never recycled.

The only person who saves time is the one who spends it wisely.

Time invested in improving ourselves cuts down on time wasted in disapproving of others.

Father Time grants no rebate for wasted hours.

One realizes the importance of time only when there is little of it left.

Time is nature's way of preventing everything from happening at once.

The person who kills time hasn't learned the value of life.

Time marches on but seldom to a brass band.

Father Time is the only man who has never waited on a woman.

Most of modern man's troubles come from the fact that he has too much time on his hands and not enough on his knees.

Tobacco

The first health hazard in smoking a pipe is high blood pressure caused by trying to keep the thing lit.

A Colorado highway sign: "Help prevent forest fires. *Chew tobacco.*"

Love may make the world go 'round, but so will a big swallow of tobacco juice.

A tobacco chewer in North Carolina has agreed that if smokers won't blow smoke in his face he won't spit on them.

One of the nice things about smoking a pipe is that you can't light the wrong end.

Tobacco is a nauseating plant consumed by only two creatures: a large green worm and man. The worm doesn't know any better.

Never slap a man who is chewing tobacco.

Some things are better eschewed than chewed; tobacco is one of them.

In Texas there was an old man who was the sloppiest tobacco chewer that ever lived. He died of cancer of the vest.

Pipe smokers are almost invariably solid, reliable, upright citizens. They spend so much time cleaning, filling, and fooling with their pipes they don't have time to get into mischief.

The first hazard in smoking a pipe is high blood pressure from trying to keep it lit.

One argument in defense of chewing tobacco is that it never started any forest fires.

Tolerance

The chief evil of many people consists not so much in doing evil, but in permitting it.

A sense of humor can help you overlook the unattractive, tolerate the unpleasant, cope with the unexpected, and smile through the unbearable.

Good manners is being able to put up with bad ones.

An open mind tolerates an empty one.

The peacemaker's most difficult task is to persuade the intolerant to tolerate the intolerable.

Tolerance gets a lot of credit that belongs to apathy.

Proof that Americans are a tolerant people lies partly in the fact that the inventor of the juke box died a natural death.

The most impressive evidence of tolerance is a golden wedding anniversary.

To allow others to be happy in their own way is tolerance at a high level.

Tolerance is really nothing but putting the Golden Rule into practice.

In people, as in machines, tolerance permits a maximum of efficiency with a minimum of friction.

Tolerance is seeing things with your heart instead of your eyes.

Tolerance is getting a lot of credit that belongs to tranquilizers.

How to be tolerant: Learn to accept yourself, then you can accept anybody!

It is extremely difficult for the tolerant to tolerate the intolerant.

Always be tolerant with a person who disagrees with you. After all, he has a right to his ridiculous opinions.

Tolerance is the spirit of a man who knows — and who patiently listens to a fool who doesn't.

When some folks yell for tolerance, what they really want is special privileges.

Tolerance is the ability to smile when somebody else's children behave as badly as your own.

The average fellow seems to think more of tolerance than he does of truth.

Tolerance starts when you practice it, not when you just talk about it.

The test of courage comes when you are in the minority; the test of tolerance comes when you are in the majority.

Tolerance is the ability to listen to a fish story and pretend that you believe it.

Condescension is the counterfeit coin that often passes for tolerance.

Tolerance is something that enables you to laugh when someone steps on your mental corns.

Men argue for tolerance but will not listen to reason.

Tolerance often gets the credit that belongs to indifference.

The trouble with being tolerant is that people think you don't understand the problem.

Tolerance is the ability to be kind to dumb animals, especially when they're human beings.

Most people are willing to practice tolerance — that is, tolerance with themselves.

Tolerance is the patience shown by a wise man when he listens to an ignoramus.

Tolerance is the positive and cordial effort to understand another's beliefs, practices, and habits without necessarily sharing or accepting them.

It's surprising how easy it is to tolerate people when you don't really have to.

Tongue (the)

He who has a sharp tongue soon cuts his own throat.

Anger makes your mouth work faster than your mind.

In an argument the best weapon to hold is your tongue.

Be sure your brain is engaged before putting your mouth in gear.

The Christian should learn two things about his tongue — how to hold it and how to use it.

Conversation is an exercise of the mind, but gossiping is merely an exercise of the tongue.

Good deeds speak for themselves. The tongue only interprets their eloquence.

It has been said that dignity is the ability to hold back from the tongue that which never should have been on the mind in the first place.

A dog is smarter than some people. It wags its tail and not its tongue.

The only exercise some people get in the morning is brushing their teeth and sharpening their tongues.

Happiness is often punctured by a sharp tongue.

Medical doctors measure physical health by how the tongue looks. The Great Physician measures spiritual health by how the tongue acts.

Liquor makes a man tight, and his tongue loose.

Our vigor wanes with middle age, we find our footsteps lagging, our backbones creak, our sight grows dim, and yet our tongues keep wagging.

Patience strengthens the spirit, sweetens the temper, stifles anger, subdues pride, and bridles the tongue.

Some of the best preaching is done by holding the tongue.

People who can hold their tongues rarely have any trouble holding their friends.

A still tongue makes no enemies.

Usually the first screw that gets loose in a person's head is the one that controls the tongue.

Everybody agrees that a loose tongue can lead to a few loose teeth.

A sharp tongue is the only tool with an edge that grows keener with constant use.

A tongue was intended to be a divine organ, but Satan often plays upon it.

A sharp tongue and a dull mind are usually found in the same head.

Some people have eyes that see not and ears that hear not, but there are very few people who have tongues that talk not.

Cats are not the only creatures that can lick themselves with their tongues.

The tongue is a deadly weapon, whether it is sharp or blunt.

Long tongues will mean short friends.

The human tongue is only a few inches from the brain, but when you listen to some people talk, they seem miles apart.

518

A tongue doesn't weigh much, but many people still have trouble holding it.

The tongues of some folks are like a friendly dog's tail — always wagging.

No matter which screw in the head is loose, it is the tongue that rattles.

People who can hold their tongues rarely have any trouble holding their friends.

The tongue runs fastest when the brain is in neutral.

The most untameable thing in the world has its den just behind the teeth.

The critical tongue gets its wrapping orders from an untrained eye, an unthoughtful mind, and an ungrateful heart.

A tongue four inches long can kill a man six feet tall.

Some people have learned that a sharp tongue often invites a split lip.

When the tongue is making 1200 revolutions per minute, it's a safe bet that the brain is in neutral.

When men hold their tongues you can't tell a fool from a sage.

Tourists

Some resort ads don't always tell the truth. One place that promised "miles of uncrowded beaches" turned out to be a naval gunnery range.

The first thing that strikes a visitor in New York City is a big car.

Heaven is a place many Americans wouldn't want to go if they couldn't send back picture postcards.

Never judge a summer resort by its post cards.

The one crop that is always harvested green is the tourist crop.

Why is it that a tourist will travel thousands of miles to get away form people — just so he can send cards saying, "Wish you were here"?

People in other countries are not really rude; they are just trying to imitate some of our American tourists.

A tourist is a person who travels a few thousand miles just to get a snapshot of himself standing beside his car.

The American tourist will go to any length to get back to nature — provided he can make the trip in an air-conditioned car.

An Alabama man who recently returned from overseas says it's good to be back home where people give you a hard time in a language you can understand.

A returning tourist said his trip would have been more pleasant without two things — billboards and board bills.

Tourists visit Washington, D. C., as if it were a zoo, and it's no wonder. That's where they shoot the bull, the buck is passed, and you get a bum steer.

Traffic

Fewer accidents are caused by traffic jams than by pickled drivers.

Those who complain that Americans are going too fast haven't been caught in a traffic jam lately.

One thing we've learned about compact cars is that it takes twice as many of them to make a traffic jam.

Whoever called them "pleasure cars" never drove them in traffic.

Doctors tell us that Americans are living too fast. Traffic statistics show they are dying the same way.

Never gamble in heavy traffic. The cars may be stacked against you.

Recently a hick town in Idaho decided to go big time and install a traffic light, but the authorities didn't know whether to make it red or green.

Maybe the reason we have traffic problems is because the traffic has become as dense as the drivers.

The straight and narrow road has not yet developed enough traffic to require a four-lane highway.

You can find the world's shortest sermon on a traffic sign, "Keep Right."

A traffic light is a device for trapping you in the middle of the intersection.

Freeway traffic moves at two speeds — so fast you can't get on and so slow you can't get off.

The straight and narrow path is the only one that has no traffic problems.

There are three kinds of traffic; urban, suburban, and bourbon.

Traffic tickets are like wives. No one complains about them until he gets one of his own.

Five o'clock traffic is better described as "a site for sore guys."

People seem to have thought up every solution to the traffic problem except staying at home.

The way traffic is today, instead of getting a ticket for parking you ought to get a medal.

Traffic warning on entering Plover, Wisconsin; "Go slow. This is a one-hearse town."

If it's true that misery loves company, how come we don't enjoy getting caught in a traffic jam!

It took the early settlers months to cross the country. With today's traffic, that's still pretty good time.

Traffic is so slow in some large cities that if a driver wants to hit a pedestrian he has to get out of his car to do it.

The way traffic is today, it's easier to star on Broadway than it is to cross it.

A traffic expert predicts that the motorcar will eventually drive people underground. If often does that now if it hits a person hard enough.

Traffic lights are what give pedestrians so much confidence that they never see who or what hits them.

The most you can say about midtown traffic is that it lets you meet a cross section of humanity.

The way traffic is in some cities, we'll soon have no-way streets.

The rush hour is when the traffic is almost at a standstill.

The best rule in driving through five o'clock traffic is to try and avoid being a part of the six o'clock news.

The way traffic is nowadays, a Sunday driver is someone who doesn't have to be back at work until the following Tuesday.

Many a traffic jam is caused by a woman driver who signals to make a turn — and does!

Transportation

America has more transportation facilities than any other nation, but they're so crowded we can't use them.

The American taxpayers wouldn't object to free transportation for certain government officials if they'd go where we wish they would.

Fast transportation has made us all neighbors — but, unfortunately, not brothers.

In Washington the favorite form of transportation is riding the President.

Travel

Some resort ads don't always tell the truth. One place that promised "miles of uncrowded beaches" turned out to be a naval gunnery range.

We had complete confidence in reaching the moon. Now if we could only feel the same way about getting to the other side of the street.

If you go to the beach just remember that the family that bakes together aches together.

Never judge a summer resort by its post cards.

Travel is educational. It teaches you that enough luggage is too much.

Air travel is wonderful. It allows you to pass motorists at a safe distance.

If a man has anything in him, travel will bring it out — especially ocean travel.

Travel not only broadens the mind, but it also flattens the finances.

It's true that travel broadens a person — but so does sitting at home in a rocking chair.

Travel is an experience that enlarges the minds of some people but swells the heads of others.

The world is full of cheap vacation spots. The trouble is that it costs a lot of money to get there.

Truth

Autobiography is an excellent medium for revealing *some* of the truth about yourself.

Parents are embarrassed when their children tell lies, but sometimes it's even worse when they tell the truth.

When in doubt, tell the truth.

Blessed are our enemies, for they tell us the truth when our friends flatter us.

It is one thing to show a man he is in error, and quite another thing to put him in possession of the truth.

Fishing is a sport that makes men and truth strangers.

There is not true greatness where simplicity, goodness, and truth are absent.

If you don't know, simply say so.

There's nothing so kingly as kindness, and nothing so royal as truth.

As a general rule, a liar is not believed even when he speaks the truth.

A pathological liar is a person so addicted to falsehood that he can't tell the truth without lying.

There are many people who are not actually liars, but they keep a respectful distance from the truth.

The truth may hurt but a lie is agony.

A lie is the deliberate withholding of any part of the truth from someone who has the right to know.

Truth often hurts, but it's the lie that leaves the scars.

Many people don't actually lie; they merely present the truth in such a way that nobody recognizes it.

A lie will go twice around the world while the truth is getting its boots on.

The most dangerous lies are those that most resemble the truth.

Lies don't live nearly so long as the truth does, but their birthrate is much higher.

Lying about people annoys them very much, but sometimes telling the truth annoys them a lot more.

It's extremely difficult to believe that a man is telling the truth when you know that you would lie if you were in his place.

The trouble with man is twofold. He cannot, or will not, learn truths which are too complicated, and he forgets truths which are too simple.

Some people remember a lie for ten years but forget the truth in ten minutes.

The first thing you'll notice in the glove compartment of your new car is a little booklet telling you how to lie about your gas mileage.

There are some people who can't tell a lie, some who can't tell the truth, and a few others who can't tell the difference.

The greatest and noblest pleasure men can have in this world is to discover new truths, and the next is to shake off old prejudices.

An independent voter is one who hasn't made up his mind which "truth" he likes best.

To be extremely popular, one must be more tactful than truthful.

Why is it that a scandal runs, while truth must crawl?

Tact is the rare talent for not quite telling the truth.

Some people have tact, others tell the truth.

The average fellow seems to think more of tolerance than he does of truth.

Of course truth hurts. You would too if you got stretched so much.

Truth is so valuable many people economize when using it.

Nothing is harder for some folks to see than the naked truth.

It was easier to tell the truth in George Washington's day. There were no income-tax forms to fill out.

You can't stetch the truth without making your story look pretty thin.

Truth is often violated by falsehood, but can be equally outraged by silence.

The man who requests truth instead of flattery should be careful or he might get it.

Truth crushed to earth will rise again, but a rubber check will do even better — it rebounds.

The student of truth keeps an open Bible, an open dictionary, and an open mind.

Nothing can relieve the pain of truth.

Many men seek the truth — not because it is lost, but because they are.

If nations began telling each other nothing but the truth, peace would immediately vanish from the earth.

Some people seem to think truth is not where you find it, but where you hide it.

The truth hurts—especially on the bathroom scales.

Truth is as clear as a bell, but it isn't always tolled.

Why is it that everytime a witness offers to tell all the truth, some lawyer objects?

Nothing makes a wife more skeptical than when her husband tells the exact truth.

Truth can be stretched, but it cannot be broken.

Truth is stranger than fiction — cleaner, too!

The surest way to be lonesome is to always tell the truth.

We admire the truth, provided it agrees with our views.

There must be a shortage of truth the way so many folks are stretching it these days.

Let's all work together in an effort to stop "truth decay."

In this world, truth can wait; she's used to it.

The truth does not hurt unless it ought to.

Truth never dies, but it is often paralyzed by man's indifference.

The temple of truth has never suffered so much from woodpeckers on the outside as from termites from within.

Not many people get weak eyes from searching for the truth.

Stretching may be an aid to health, but it doesn't seem to help the truth.

Two half-truths do not necessarily constitute the whole truth.

All truths are equally true but not equally important.

Some people stretch the truth; others mutilate it.

Truth crushed to earth will rise again — but so will a lie.

When truth stands in your way, it's time to change directions.

Truth is so precious some people use it sparingly.

The greatest homage you can pay the truth is to use it.

Some people do not lie — they merely present the truth in such a way that nobody recognizes it.

The truth is one thing for which there are no known substitutes.

It is seldom as hard to tell the truth as it is to hide a lie.

Truth fears nothing but concealment.

Beware of the half-truth. You might get hold of the wrong half.

Some agile people got that way from dodging the truth.

Truth is something which must be known with the mind, accepted with the heart, and enacted in life.

Some practice economy only with the truth.

Truth does not need a defender — only an investigator.

Most women want to hear the truth, no matter how flattering it is.

As scarce as the truth is, the supply has always been in excess of the demand.

Truth needs no crutches. If it limps it's a lie.

Few people seek to discover truth; most of us seek to confirm our errors and perpetuate our prejudices.

Another good thing about telling the truth — you don't have to remember what you said.

Some people seem to have a reverence for the truth. They always keep a respectable distance from it.

Truth, like iodine, helps when it hurts.

To hear truth and not accept it does not nullify it.

Truth is so stubborn it doesn't apologize to anybody.

It is difficult to believe that a man is telling the truth when you know that you would lie if you were in his place.

The truth is something hard to get people to listen to and harder to get them to believe.

Truth is like a burr in a cow's tail. The more she tries to shake it off, the closer it sticks.

A half-truth and a whole lie are congenial companions.

Truth uttered before its time is often dangerous.

The trouble with man is twofold: He cannot or will not learn truths that are too complicated; he forgets truths which are too simple.

Truth will win every argument if you stick with it long enough.

When a fellow tells you, "I'm going to tell you the truth," you wonder what he has been telling you since the conversation began.

The real truth cannot be distorted, though it is very often misused.

Truth angers those whom it does not fully convince.

One thing you can say for the truth is that it doesn't seem to be habit-forming.

Truth is not always popular, but it is always right.

Know the truth and it will make you free. Speak the truth and you may get a punch in the nose.

The truth hurts — especially when someone's telling it about you.

The fact that nobody wants to believe something doesn't keep it from being true.

Some things cannot be measured. We do not think of a ton of truth, a bushel of beauty, or an inspiration a mile long.

In time of war the first casualty is truth.

Words sometimes serve as a smoke screen to obscure the truth, rather than as a searchlight to reveal it.

U

Ulcers   Uncle Sam   Unemployment
Unbelief

Ulcers

The trouble with the business world is that there are too many one-ulcer men holding down two-ulcer jobs.

What many a store clerk gets for Christmas is an ulcer.

Slogan of a new executive: "If you haven't developed ulcers, you're not carrying your share of the load."

There are only two classes of people — those who have ulcers, and those who give them.

Many people don't get ulcers — they're only carriers.

Retirement has cured many a businessman's ulcers — and given his wife one!

Some ulcers are caused by the inflammation of the wishbone.

Ulcers are contagious. You can get them from your boss.

Your ulcers can't grow while you're laughing.

Ulcer victims are members of the "fret set."

Many people have ulcers these days — caused by mountain climbing over molehills.

Some people get ulcers, others give them.

An ulcer sometimes indicates that the owner is in the big money — either making it or owing it.

A man can acquire an ordinary size ucler at the office, but the larger ones are usually home grown.

Unbelief
see also Atheists

There are two things that no one will believe — how a man got a black eye, and how a girl got a mink coat.

The fact that nobody wants to believe something doesn't keep it from being true.

Few women believe what their mirrors and bathroom scales tell them.

Seeing ourselves as others see us wouldn't do much good, because most of us wouldn't believe what we saw.

Uncle Sam

Drive carefully. Uncle Sam needs every taxpayer he can get.

Don't you long for the "good old days" when Uncle Sam lived within his income and without most of yours?

Income tax is Uncle Sam's version of "Truth or Consequences."

Income-tax forms should be more realistic by allowing the taxpayer to list Uncle Sam as a dependent.

In 1913 Uncle Sam collected only 13 million dollars in income taxes. That's why they were called the "good old days."

A lot of people still have the first dollar they ever made — Uncle Sam has all the others.

It's a mistake to believe that Uncle Sam can open his pocketbook and let you keep yours closed.

Actually we wouldn't mind Uncle Sam's tax bite — if he didn't come back for dessert.

With estate taxes what they are, the happiest mourner at a rich man's funeral is Uncle Sam.

It might be well to bear in mind that when Uncle Sam plays Santa Claus, it's the taxpayer who holds the bag.

Despite what the cartoonists make him look like, Uncle Sam is a gentleman with a very large "waste."

It seems that life these days has gotten to be a matter of give and take; what you don't give Uncle Sam takes.

We often wondered why Uncle Sam wears such a tall hat, until he started passing it around for taxes.

It's hard for Uncle Sam to keep his balance with so many hands in his pockets.

Whenever Uncle Sam arrives at an international convention, he is invited to draw up a check and be seated.

Uncle Sam has the whole world eating out of his hand.

Unemployment

Automation has opened up a whole new field of unemployment.

If some folks aren't careful, they'll stretch their coffee break to the unemployment office.

An employee in Chicago stretched his coffee break all the way to the unemployment office.

A business executive in Denver gave his employees long vacations to find out which ones he could do without.

Any girl who wants to be sure she will never be unemployed should marry a farmer.

It's always hard to find a job for the fellow who doesn't want one.

It was recently revealed that there are many volunteers in the army of the unemployed.

All politicians fear high unemployment — they fear they may be next.

Old Satan has no unemployment problems.

Scientists have predicted the earth will explode in five billion years, and some are already using that as an excuse for not looking for a job.

With taxes what they are today, a fellow has to be unemployed to make a living.

Did you hear about the two unemployed school teachers? One had no principle; the other, no class!

The greatest area of unemployment in the United States is just above the shoulders.

The army of the unemployed seems to have a lot of volunteers.

One disadvantage of being unemployed is that a person has no payday to borrow money until.

Unemployment takes the worry out of being late for work.

V

Vacations   Vices   Vision

Values   Virtue   Vocabulary

Vacations

A business executive in Denver gave his employees long vacations to find out which ones he could do without.

A girl certainly has a wide choice of vacations. She can go to the mountains and see the scenery, or go to the beach and be the scenery.

The ideal summer resort is where the fish bite and the mosquitoes don't.

Most people could live within their incomes if they were as economical all year round as they are right after their vacations.

You're getting old when you're on vacation and your energy runs out before your money does.

The question we all must face sooner or later is how to fit a long vacation into a short bankroll.

Nothing makes time pass faster than vacations and short-term loans.

Why is it that a tourist will travel thousands of miles to get away from people — just so he can send cards saying, "Wish you were here"?

A vacation makes you feel good enough to return to work — and so poor you have to.

The fellow who first said, "Spend your vacation..." never realized how right he was.

Why not spend your vacation in Las Vegas? You can't beat the sunshine, the climate, or the slot machines.

Next summer one-third of the nation will be ill-housed and ill-fed — but they'll call it a vacation.

The only thing that goes faster than vacation time is vacation cash.

Some people's idea of roughing it is to spend their vacation in a small town where they can get only one channel on TV.

People usually go on a vacation to forget — and when they open their luggage they learn what is was they forgot.

Vacation is a system whereby people who are merely tired become exhausted.

At today's prices people don't take vacations — vacations take people.

Thousands of people will not be going on vacation this year. In fact, many of us can't even afford to stay at home.

You can enjoy a glorious vacation and stay within your budget — but not both in the same summer.

A Kansas couple couldn't afford a winter vacation last year. However, they did save enough money to turn up their thermostat for one weekend.

There's nothing so dull as going on the kind of vacation we can afford.

Let's hope we can take our vacation before postcards go up again.

Vacations are a little like love — anticipated with relish, experienced with inconvenience, and remembered with nostalgia.

Note to summer vacationers: When you're advised to travel light, they mean luggage, not your wallet.

Summer vacations get kids tan, mothers in the pink, and fathers in the red.

Any guy who looks completely exhausted should take a vacation — or has!

The trouble with vacations is that it takes such a long time paying for such a short time playing.

Some of the best vacations this past summer were spent at home, where you don't have to tip for lousy service, and the insolence is free.

A vacation is a holiday from everything except expenses.

It's pretty hard to take a vacation from doing nothing.

A Texan, just back home from a Nevada vacation, says he underwent a bit of "Las Vegas Surgery." He had his bankroll painlessly removed.

Don't tell the tired-looking person he needs a vacation — the chances are he just had one.

A vacation is a two week's experience where money and time race each other until both are exhausted.

If you want a successful vacation, take half the clothes you figured on and twice the money.

A vacation consists of equal parts of sunburn, sore muscles, and discomfort.

The best place to spend your vacation is just inside your income.

Vacations are easy to plan — the boss tells you when, and the wife tells you where.

If you can't get away for a vacation, you can get the same feeling by staying home and tipping every third person you see.

Frankly, no one needs a vacation as much as the person who just had one.

Spend your vacation next year in your own backyard and your friends will know what you are — sensible, home-loving, and broke.

Your vacation is over when your money is spent, and so are you.

The one book that really tells you where you can go on your vacation is your pocketbook.

When a worried, haggard patient enters the doctor's office, the doctor hardly knows whether to prescribe a vacation or treat the patient for the one he has just had.

The ideal summer resort is where the fish bite and the mosquitoes don't.

A vacation is a success if we manage to change the color of the circles under our eyes from black to tan.

Vacation is a brief period of recreation, preceded by a period of anticipation, and followed by a period of recuperation.

A vacation is something you need by the time you finish paying for one.

One reason many of us can't afford a European vacation is because our dollars made the trip without us.

Even if your vacation isn't long, you'll come back short.

The biggest obstacles to planning this year's vacation are the payments still due on last year's.

Change is what a person wants on a vacation — and a lot of currency too.

If you have not taken a vacation by now, you can at least figure what you've saved by listening to friends who have just returned.

One of the most common disruptions of marital bliss is the choice of where to spend a vacation. What this country needs is an ocean in the mountains.

A vacation is what you take if you can't take what you've been taking.

The world is full of cheap vacation spots. The trouble is that it costs a lot of money to get there.

The question we all must face sooner or later is how to fit a long vacation into a short bankroll.

The trouble with most vacation spots is they don't have the same girls you saw in their ads.

Vacation means two weeks on the sand and the rest of the year on the rocks.

Advice to vacationers: Don't overtax yourself. The government will do it for you.

Those who say you can't take it with you have never seen a family car packed for a vacation.

Vacation time is when the highway department closes all the roads and opens up all the detours.

Wouldn't it be nice if two weeks on vacation seemed to last as long as two weeks on a diet?

For a vacation some will go to the mountains, while others go to the seashore, but most of us will go in the hole.

Some people take everything on a vacation except their manners.

Vacation is a time when you get away from the people and places you love best, so you can put up with them when you get back.

A Mississippi couple couldn't decide whether to use their vacation money for a trip abroad or a steak at home.

Some people who went on a vacation last summer made the usual mistake — they took along more clothing than they used and less money than they needed.

A vacation is usually nothing but a sunburn at premium prices.

You don't have to vacation at the seashore to get soaked.

A vacation is two weeks of fun followed by weeks of short funds.

Values

It is extremely easy for us to give our major attention to minor matters.

A Bible stored in the mind is worth a dozen stored in the bottom of a trunk.

A good deed gets about as much attention these days as a homely face.

Don't call it education unless it has taught you life's true values.

We may rest assured that freedom is worth whatever it costs.

With money you can buy all the friends you want, but they are never worth the price.

Be slow in choosing friends, slower in changing them.

Friendships will last if they are put first.

Friendship that is bought will not stay bought; sooner or later there will be a higher bidder.

Money can build a house, but it takes love to make it a home.

No constitution, no court, no law can save liberty when it dies in the hearts and minds of men and women.

The things in life that count most are the things that can't be counted.

A man doesn't know the value of a woman's love until he starts paying alimony.

Things would be a lot nicer if antique people were valued as highly as antique furniture.

A little pride is a small thing to lose when compared with losing honor.

Religion furnishes education with a true sense of values. It shows what is worthwhile.

There's nothing wrong with men possessing riches. The wrong comes when riches possess men.

Plenty in the purse cannot prevent starvation in the soul.

In your search for riches, don't lose the things that money can't buy.

One thing can be said about values in the United States — they're not to be found in the supermarkets.

The relative value of health and wealth depends on which you have left.

Don't buy it for a song — unless you're sure you know what the pitch is.

The highest values are priceless.

Some things cannot be measured. We do not think of a ton of truth, a bushel of beauty, or an inspiration a mile long.

Rejecting things because they are old-fashioned would rule out the sun and the moon — and a mother's love.

The value of all things, even our lives, depends on the use we make of them.

Most folks pay too much for the things they get for nothing.

The most valuable thing a man can have up his sleeve is a good strong arm.

People who talk about things they can't afford sometimes forget that the list should include pride, envy, and malice.

We rearrange our furniture, our flowers, and our finances — but how about our values?

When we look at the price tag on some articles, we don't know whether they represent value or nerve.

The things of greatest value in life are those things that multiply when divided.

If this age is to be saved, it will be saved by the recovery of the sense of discrimination between what is passing and what is eternal.

A sense of values is the most important single element in human personality.

The child who knows the value of a dollar these days must be terribly discouraged.

Spiritual bankruptcy is inevitable when a man is no longer able to keep the interest paid on his moral obligations.

It is what we value, not what we have, that makes us rich.

The trouble with teaching a child the value of a dollar is you have to do it almost every week.

Vices

It is the business of a censor to acquaint us with vices we didn't know we had.

More people are flattered into virtue than bullied out of vice.

Vice of any kind must become respectable before it is dangerous.

Vices are to be condemned and eradicated, not condoned and taxed for revenue.

Man's greatest vices are the misuses of his virtues.

Cultivate vices when you are young, and when you are old they will not forsake you.

All vices are of personal origin. Playing cards do not make the gambler, nor a bottle of liquor the drunkard.

Vice of any kind has to become respectable before it becomes dangerous.

Virtues are usually learned at mother's knee, and vices are learned at some other joint.

Virtue

Maybe we were better off when charity was a virtue instead of a deduction.

In the old days charity was a virtue instead of an industry.

Sometimes we learn more from a man's errors than from his virtues.

A fault which humbles a man is of more use to him than a virtue which puffs him up.

Folks who are friends usually have the same virtues, the same enemies, or the same faults.

Gratitude is the rarest of all virtues, and yet we invariably expect it.

Gratitude is not only the greatest of virtues, but the parent of all the others.

More people are flattered into virtue than bullied out of vice.

We all agree that the nicest people in the world are those who minimize our faults and magnify our virtues.

Sometimes virtue and prosperity have trouble living together.

To know what not to think about is a major intellectual virtue.

Everybody thinks thrift is a wonderful virtue, especially in our ancestors.

Man's greatest vices are the misuses of his virtues.

To know what not to think about is a major intellectual virtue.

When one robs another of virtue, he loses his own.

Rarely do we admire the virtues we do not possess.

While virtue is its own reward, most people are looking for a better offer.

Virtues are usually learned at mother's knee, and vices are learned at some other joint.

If our good deeds were immediately and invariably rewarded, then virtue would become a racket.

Virtue has more admirers than followers.

He who parades his virtues seldom leads the parade.

Vision

It's better to look where you're going than to see where you've been.

An eye specialist in Chicago is a trifle conceited. Instead of an eye chart, he makes you read his diploma.

Conceit is a form of "I" strain that doctors can't cure.

Some folks who do their duty as they see it need to consult an eye specialist.

Faith is the daring of the soul to go farther than it can see.

When it comes to spotting the faults of others, everybody seems to have 20-20 vision.

Few people have good enough sight to see their own faults.

Carrots are definitely good for the eyes. Have you ever seen a rabbit with glasses?

The world might be improved with less television and more vision.

We usually see things, not as they are, but as we are.

Man is like a tack; he can go only as far as his head will let him.

Any man can see farther than he can reach, but this doesn't mean he should quit reaching.

The world could certainly use more vision and less television.

Vision is definitely affected by glasses, especially after they've been filled and emptied several times.

The world would be happier if its leaders had more vision and fewer nightmares.

Vocabulary

No matter how limited your vocabulary is, it's big enough to let you say something you'll later regret.

A lot of people get unlimited mileage out of a limited vocabulary.

If you add five new words a month to your vocabulary, in a year your friends will wonder just who you think you are.

W

Wages

War

Washington, D.C.

Weakness

Wealth

Weathermen

Weddings

Weight

Wife

Wild Oats

Wisdom

Women

Women and their Age

Women Drivers

Words

Work

World

Worry

Worship

Wages

The average man's modest ambition is to make his weekly paycheck last a week.

If your boss doesn't pay you what you deserve, be thankful!

A factory worker in Akron complained, "If there's one more deduction from my take-home pay, I won't have any home to take my pay to."

A democracy is a form of government that believes at least part of what you earn belongs to you.

Our present economy is terrible. We're making more and more dollars and less and less money.

Economy is defined as a reduction in some other fellow's salary.

Education helps you earn more. But not many school teachers can prove it.

An efficiency expert's idea of lowering costs is to cut the other fellow's salary.

When a distillery employee works overtime, does he get time and a *fifth?*

If things don't change for the better, the day is not far off when employees will demand the deductions instead of the pay.

A survey shows that slender executives make more money than fat ones. The chunky son of the president is apt to be an exception.

An executive refused an employee's request for a raise, adding, "I know you can't get married on what I pay you — and someday you'll thank me."

Nothing makes it harder to live within your income than being paid what you're really worth.

We make a living by what we get, but we make a life by what we give.

The most wonderful thing ever made by man is a living for his family.

The fellow who really understands the value of cold cash is the one whose salary is not so hot.

Asking your boss for a raise is really a patriotic duty since the government needs that additional tax on your salary.

The world is full of people making a good living but poor lives.

Too many Model-T congressmen are drawing Cadillac salaries.

Unquestionably, there is progress everywhere. The average American now pays out as much in taxes as he formerly received in wages.

We are told the wages of sin is death — shouldn't you quit before payday?

The wages of sin are the only wages not subject to the income tax.

The wages of sin are always paid on time.

When the wages of sin are paid, a lot of people are going to get time-and-a-half for overtime.

You don't have to institute a lawsuit to collect the wages of sin.

Often the wages of sin are unreported.

The trouble with today's taxes is that they keep your take-home pay from ever getting there.

School teachers are given too much credit and too little cash.

There are TV anchormen who receive twice as much money to read the news as the President gets to make the news.

About the only thing you can save out of your paycheck these days is the envelope.

One disadvantage of being unemployed is that a person has no payday to borrow money until.

The definition of a minimum wage varies, depending on whether you're getting it or paying it.

Most people are interested in the higher things in life these days — such as wages.

The wages of sin are apt to include a lot of overtime.

It's getting harder for some fellows to get back some of their take-home pay after taking it home.

The minimum wage has gone up considerably. Wouldn't it be wonderful if we could just do something about the minimum effort?

It is not the employer who pays wages — he only handles the money. It is the product that pays wages.

The salary with the fringe on top is taking industry for a ride.

It's getting so that take-home pay can hardly survive the trip.

Most folks need higher wages to pay the higher prices caused by higher wages.

The trouble with take-home pay is that it won't stay there.

Wages can't meet higher prices if they're both going in the same direction.

You cannot lift the wage earner by pulling down the wage payer.

It's easy to figure out a living wage for the other fellow to live on.

In the "good old days" the biggest grab for a man's salary took place after he got home.

Increased earnings nearly always lead to increased yearnings.

A raise is an increase in pay which you get just before going a little more into debt.

The salary we used to dream of is the one we can't live on today.

About the only way to keep some of your take-home pay is not to go home.

Somehow a living wage has suddenly become twice what anyone makes.

The wages of sin are never frozen.

Do what you are told to do and then some. It's the "then some" that gets your salary raised.

The world owes you a living, but only when you have earned it.

War

Why worry about the future? Between the bomb and pollution, there may not be any.

History shows that war is better at abolishing nations than nations are at abolishing war.

Another war worth waging is one against the poverty of ideas.

If we can't win the war against inflation — how about a cease-fire?

The world needs a new law that would prevent any country from waging war unless it pays for it in advance.

A fat man is no good in war; he can neither fight nor run away.

Another great need of this country is guns of smaller caliber and men of larger.

Another argument in favor of lasting peace is that it would give us time to finish paying for the last war.

Peace is a thing you can't achieve by throwing rocks at a hornet's nest.

General Sherman defined war as hell, but the definition of a modern peace is unprintable.

A means to a permanent peace is for all nations to agree not to start another war until the last one is paid for.

The best place to hold productive peace conferences is a few hundred yards behind the lines of battle.

No enemy nation could risk invading the United States. It couldn't afford the high taxes.

Like its politicians and its wars, society has the teen-agers it deserves.

The next war will be like a fight with your wife — impossible to win it or end it.

If push-button warfare is anything like push-button elevators, we'll wait a long time for it to arrive.

A political war is one in which everybody shoots from the lip.

The world would be a much happier place if it was as hard to start a war as it is to stop one.

In time of war the first casualty is truth.

Old men declare wars, but it is youth that must fight them.

War does not, and cannot, prove which side is right, but only which side is stronger.

The tragedy of war is that it uses man's best to do man's worst.

There will be no more wars when nations learn how to completely bankrupt themselves without fighting.

Machinery and electricity now do almost everything in wars — except the walking on crutches.

In time of war the rich get the shekels and the poor get the shackles.

Those at war with others are seldom at peace with themselves.

A military inductee, when asked if he had any physical defects, replied, "No guts."

History has seen wars which used up less ammunition than a cease-fire does today.

Every child comes into the world endowed with liberty, opportunity, and a share of the war debt.

The biggest farce of man's history has been the argument that wars are fought to save civilization.

It is almost impossible to tell what wars make the world safe for!

The best thing about war is the end of it.

Every war causes soldiers to change nearly all their ideas, except their opinion of officers.

War is a condition where youngsters get caught in the draft and oldsters get caught in the graft.

History reveals that wars create more problems than they solve.

The terrible thing about war is that it usually kills the wrong people.

Will we ever see the last of war, or will war see the last of us?

War would be virtually impossible if everything were on a cash basis.

Cold wars call for too much cold cash.

The greatest paradox of them all is to speak of "civilized warfare."

Every cloud has a silver lining except a war cloud.

Guerrilla warfare isn't new. It's as old as tenants and landlords.

In an atomic war all men will be cremated equal.

A great war leaves the country with three armies: an army of cripples, an army of widows, and an army of thieves.

The nations of the world are so sick of war that, to avoid it, they are willing to do anything except to be reasonable.

War does not determine who is right — only who is left. Next time it won't even do that.

The entire civil war was covered with fewer photographs than are taken at the average wedding today.

We've had wars to end all wars — why not have one to end all debts?

War may not pay, but it must be paid for.

Some of the big guns are silenced when a war ends; others begin work on their memoirs.

It's extremely comforting to know that wars fought in the eleventh and twelfth centuries are now paid for.

The United States is determined that there shall be no more wars and is equally determined to be ready for the next one.

Wars are never caused by the little men, just fought by them.

In the war of right and wrong, we can't afford to be neutral.

Washington, D.C.

Confession is not only good for the soul; in Washington it can be turned into a bestseller.

A veteran congressman told a freshman colleague, "In Washington, if you're not confused, you haven't heard all the facts.

White House employees are no longer permitted to use the polite expression "Pardon me."

The typical inferiority complex in Washington results from not having a telephone worth tapping.

About the only way Washington will ever be able to stop inflation is to stop inflating.

Not only is Washington's face on our money, but now Washington's hands are on it.

One doctor in Washington, D.C., treats only Senate members — he refuses to make "House" calls.

The problem that baffles Washington is how to dig the country out of the hole without making the hole any bigger.

After paying all our taxes we're tempted to call Washington and try to get ourselves declared a disaster area.

If the folks in Washington are so disturbed about human suffering, they ought to take a look at the American taxpayer.

If Washington D. C. is the seat of government, then the taxpayer is the pants pocket.

In Washington they're either tapping the phones or tapping the till.

The most popular song in Washington nowadays is titled, "Here Comes the Bribe."

With all due respect to Chicago, isn't Washington, D. C., the "windy city"?

It would be a great blessing if Washington would solve our money problems like we continue to solve theirs!

The boys in Washington seem to think our foreign policy is a endowment policy.

The only things that seem to be on the up and up in Washington are the Washington Monument and the Capitol Dome.

Things are now more relaxed in Washington. If you visit Lincoln's Monument you'll see Abe sitting in a rocker.

The capitol building in Washington has a rotunda because politicians like to go around in circles.

Washington is not going to get rid of any bureaucrats and bureaus — there has to be some place to put the shirts they are taking off our backs.

Trial balloons from Capitol Hill are invariably filled with hot air.

Sign on an elevator in Washington, "Button for eighth floor is out of order. Push five and three."

Washington's delay in reducing prices is puzzling. Why don't they just call in the stock market people and find out how it's done?

The way things are going in Washington, some politicians who planned to run for office will be running for cover.

Hot air is the most common method of heating in Washington.

Windmills in Washington could ease the energy crisis. Washington has an abundance of wind and hot air.

Nothing in our nation's capitol seems to be on the level anymore. Even the Washington Monument is slightly tilted.

Tourists visit Washington, D. C., as if it were a zoo, and it's no wonder. That's where they shoot the bull, the buck is passed, and you get a bum steer.

A lot of folks are flocking to Washington to ask what they can do for their country — and what the salary will be!

In Washington the favorite form of transportation is riding the President.

The boys in Washington seem to be trying to control everything except their spending.

What we need in Washington are not hot lines but firm lines.

The mess in Washington shouldn't be blamed on one man. It took real teamwork.

Washington is a city where half the people wait to be discovered and the other half are afraid they will be.

Washington is recalling all the one dollar bills. There's a defect in the value.

Every man who takes office in Washington either grows or swells.

It's beginning to look like a lot of things being aired in Washington really need to be fumigated.

These are interesting days in Washington. Some are getting posts, while others are getting the gate.

The city of Washington is divided into two parts: "Who's Who" and "Who's Through."

Some Americans refer to Washington as the city of protocol, alcohol, and Geritol.

Washington has a large assortment of peace monuments. They build one after every war.

Can you remember when it was only Washington's face that was on our money? Now Washington's hands are on it.

Needed in Washington, D. C.: Fewer hawks and doves, and more wise owls.

A fellow could get rich by opening a tailor shop in Washington — there are so many pressing problems there that need to be ironed out.

In Washington nowadays even the "yes men" aren't too sure.

Washington is a city where a 74-year-old man can be referred to as a "Junior Senator."

In Washington they figure that if you're not confused you haven't heard all the facts yet.

Washington seems to be filled with two kinds of politicians — those trying to get an investigation started, and those trying to get one stopped.

Weakness

To be angry with a weak man is proof that you are not very strong yourself.

You can't see the flaw in a bridge until it falls down, or the flaw in a man's character until he meets with temptation.

Show how strong you are by not noticing how weak the other fellow is.

There are always excuses available if you are weak enough to use them.

The weakness of man is the thing to be feared, not his strength.

Weak men wait for opportunities; strong men make them.

Profanity is the use of strong words by weak people.

Some people's weakness is the strongest thing about them.

When we do what we can, God will do what we can't.

A man is never as weak as when some woman is telling him how strong he is.

We all have weaknesses, and some of us have some mighty strong ones.

Wealth

One of the secret ambitions of many people is to be able to enjoy some of the evils which go with having too much money.

As the IRS sees it, America is a land of untold wealth.

Fewer Americans are drunk with wealth nowadays. It's just the price of everything that causes them to stagger.

It is not by a man's purse, but by his character, that he is rich or poor.

A person's character is put to a severe test when he suddenly acquires or quickly loses a considerable amount of money.

Men of genius are admired; men of wealth are envied; men of power are feared; but only men of character are trusted.

The two great tests of character are wealth and poverty.

The latest class of underprivileged children are those whose parents own two cars — but no speedboat.

The poor complain about the money they can't get, and the rich complain about the money they can't keep.

The greatest wealth is contentment with a little.

Contentment in life consists not in great wealth, but in simple wants.

A lot of American families are so poor they have only one automobile and one boat.

Wealthy people don't get enough roughage in their food, and poor people don't get enough food in their roughage.

A man never gets so rich that he can afford to lose a friend.

Our Lord is needed on the avenue as much as in the alley.

It's pretty hard to tell what brings happiness; poverty and wealth have both failed.

If health is wealth, how come it's tax-free?

A lot of people lose their health trying to become wealthy, and then lose their wealth trying to get back their health.

The relative values of health and wealth depend on which you have left.

Those who ignore health in the pursuit of wealth usually wind up losing both.

The easiest way to live within your income is to have a big one.

Most of us secretly wish we were so rich that we wouldn't have to pay an income tax.

Some of us can recall the day when a person who had to pay income tax was considered to be wealthy.

Let's stop inflation. It's hazardous to our wealth.

Be kind to people until you make your first million. After that, people will be kind to you.

If you want to know how to handle a big fortune, ask the man who hasn't any.

Despite the promises of politicians, we'll never achieve an equal and satisfactory distribution of wealth, rainfall, or parking space.

The person who works and saves will someday have enough wealth to divide with those who don't.

The relative value of health and wealth depends on which you have left.

A good wife and good health are a man's best wealth.

Whatever is it that keeps people from becoming wealthy — most of us have it.

The quickest way to become wealthy is to come up with something that's low-priced, nonhabit forming, and tax deductible.

Sixty percent of the country's wealth is in the hands of women. They're allowing men to hold the other forty percent because their handbags are full.

The two agencies now being used to redistribute wealth are taxation and offspring.

Wealth is a worry if you have it, and a worry if you don't have it.

Among the many things a wealthy man finds coming to him are poor relatives.

Wealth may not bring happiness, but it seems to bring a pleasant kind of misery.

Most of us have two chances of becoming wealthy — slim and none.

It is not wealth, but the arrogance of wealth, that offends the poor.

Untold wealth is the wealth which does not appear on income-tax returns.

The real measure of a man's wealth is how much he would be worth if he lost all his money.

Wealth makes people admire qualities in you that you don't possess.

Some people may still have their first dollar, but the man who is really wealthy is the fellow who still has his first friend.

Wealth is usually a curse — especially when the neighbors have it.

There are two ways to become wealthy: spend less and earn more.

Wealth doesn't change a man. His rudeness becomes just an eccentricity and his vulgarity becomes wit.

The kind of wealth most of us need isn't dollars as much as sense.

Wealthy people miss one of the greatest thrills of life — paying the last installment.

Hard work never hurt anybody who happened to be wealthy enough to hire somebody else to do it.

Weathermen

Science can predict an eclipse of the sun many years in advance but cannot accurately predict the weather over the weekend.

Men who are afraid of being ruined by success should get a job with the weather bureau.

Little boys who don't always tell the truth will probably grow up and become weather forecasters.

The only person who's constantly wrong and still keeps his job is the weatherman.

Weather forecasting is still a few hours behind arthritis.

What the weatherman saves for a rainy day is probably an alibi.

A weather forecaster in a certain southern city recently reported, "For tonight, I predict darkness."

The sophisticated equipment of today's weatherman is what enables him to explain in greater detail why he was wrong.

A weather forecast is a program in which it takes fifteen minutes to say something that should be covered in forty words.

Weather forecasters are so unpredictable we never know how wrong they're going to be.

A meteorologist is one who has more scientific aids than you have, in guessing wrong about the weather.

The son of a weather forecaster told his teacher, "Two and two are four — probably."

Weathermen are never wrong — it's the weather that's wrong!

A weatherman in Ohio had so much trouble with his forecasts that when he tried to get a jukebox to play "Blue Skies" it came up with "Stormy Weather."

Weddings

To the bachelor, horror films are pictures of a wedding.

The best and surest way to save a marriage from divorce is not to show up for the wedding.

There's nothing like a little exercise to change a man's life — especially if it's a walk down a church aisle.

A wedding cake is the only cake that can give you indigestion for the rest of your life.

Give a girl enough rope and she'll ring the wedding bell.

Most girls seem to marry men like their fathers. Maybe that's the reason so many mothers cry at weddings.

Then there was the good little girl who had been saying no so long that she almost loused up her wedding ceremony.

A young Georgia husband is mad at the minister who performed his marriage ceremony. The minister asked his bride, "Do you take this man for better, or probably worse?"

A recent wedding between two hypochondriacs was very touching. They exchanged vows and symptoms.

The most difficult years of marriage are those following the wedding.

In spite of all the plans for world peace, there will probably be the usual number of June weddings.

Preacher at wedding: "If this check for one dollar clears, I now pronounce you husband and wife."

A candidate's promises aren't really extravagant when you compare them to a bridegroom's.

There is nothing so unromantic as a seasick bride.

Time changes things. Nowadays the couple has the honeymoon first, and if it's a success, they have the engagement, and if that works out all right, they *may* have a wedding.

The entire civil war was covered with fewer photographs than are taken at the average wedding today.

Nothing seems to make a wedding so expensive as being the father of the bride.

Not all weddings planned for June will end in divorce. Some won't even get past making out the guest list.

At an Alabama wedding the bride was so homely everybody kissed the groom.

Some people never go to a wedding. They can't stand to see a man deprived of his human rights.

A father in Georgia called his local IRS office to ask if he could deduct the cost of his daughter's wedding as a "total loss"?

In Hollywood the bride tossing the bouquet is just as likely to be the next one to get married as the girl who catches it.

A tenth wedding anniversary is difficult to celebrate. It's too soon to brag and too late to complain.

It's unlucky to postpone a wedding, but not if you keep on doing it.

A Hollywood wedding is one where they take each other for better or worse — but not for long.

Weddings have become so costly that it's now the father of the bride who breaks down and weeps.

The man leads the woman to the altar at a wedding ceremony — after which his leadership ends.

The wedding is a ceremony where the bridegroom starts kissing the bride and the other fellows stop.

Have you heard about those computer arranged weddings? The couple promises not to fold, spindle, or mutilate?

A young woman in Missouri reports she had an economical wedding last year. The invitations were not engraved — they were xeroxed.

People cry at weddings because they have been through it and know it's no laughing matter.

After paying for the wedding, about the only thing a father has left to give away is the bride.

A wedding is a ceremony at which a man loses complete control of himself.

Psychiatrists tell us that girls tend to marry men who are like their fathers. Now we know why mothers cry at weddings.

It takes only a few words mumbled in church and you're married. It takes only a few words mumbled in your sleep and you're divorced.

Weight

Someone described an aging film beauty, "Her figure was legendary — but now the legend is beginning to spread."

A Hollywood actress once had an hourglass figure, but the sands of time have shifted.

To some young actresses the difference between fame and farm is form.

Too many Americans go in for weightlifting with the wrong equipment — a knife and fork.

Childhood is that wonderful period when all you need to do to lose weight is take a bath.

There's a new diet that will reduce weight like nothing else. It's called the high price of food.

The best way to lose weight is to eat all you want of everything you don't like.

People who can't stay on a diet do the next best thing — they stay off the scales.

Among life's mysteries is how a two pound box of candy can make a woman gain five pounds.

We'd better go easy on "stick to the ribs" food, because that's not where it usually sticks.

The Agriculture Department says the average American eats 1,148 pounds of food a year. Of course, a lot of it goes to *waist.*

If only our minds instead of our waistlines would grow with the passing of the year.

Some people grow up and spread cheer. Others just grow up and spread.

To feel "fit as a fiddle" you must tone down your middle.

It would be better if the overstuffed things in the home were confined to furniture.

A husband who still calls his wife the "little woman" very likely hasn't looked lately.

Indigestion is the failure to adjust a square meal to a round stomach.

A great invention for dieters would be a refrigerator that weighs you every time you open the door.

Life has become a struggle to keep our weight down and our spirits up.

It may be true that life begins at forty, but everything else starts to wear out, fall out, or spread out.

To many people living life to the fullest simply means overeating.

Middle age is when your legs buckle — and your belt doesn't.

You know you've reached middle age when your weightlifting consists solely of standing up.

There are two ways to determine middle age — one is by the calendar, and the other by the waistline.

You've reached middle age when your wife tells you to pull in your stomach, and you already have.

One sure way to get more for your money than you expect is to stand on a penny scale.

Most mothers aren't really interested in taking their weight off — they just want to rearrange it.

No woman is ever fat. She is just short for her weight.

The truth hurts — espcially on the bathroom scales.

Few women believe what their mirrors and bathroom scales tell them.

A woman will go to almost any length to change her width.

A lot of folks who are worrying about fat around the waist ought to be worrying about fat between the ears.

Wives

Some men achieve distinction by the kind of car they drive — others by the kind of wife that is driving them.

The best time to do the dishes is right after your wife tells you to.

A man whose actions leave his wife speechless has really done something!

Advertising can be very expensive, especially if your wife can read.

Some wives appreciate their husbands the most while they are away at work.

Married couples who claim they've never had an argument in forty years either have poor memories or a very dull life to recall.

When you're arguing with your wife, make absolutely sure you're right — and them let the matter drop.

The argument you just won with your wife isn't over yet.

Arguing with your wife is as useless as trying to blow out a lightbulb.

After winning an argument with his wife, the wisest thing a man can do is apologize.

Nothing is so apt to start an argument with your wife as winning one.

If you would like to get your wife's attention — just look comfortable!

Some men who speak with authority at work know enough to bow to a higher authority at home.

The best way to remember your wife's birthday is to forget it once!

Brains are what a man looks for in a wife, after not using any in selecting one.

No wife objects to being put on a budget as long as she isn't expected to stay within it.

Not too long ago business got so bad that some men went bankrupt, and some went back to their wives.

The average couple splits the Christmas chores. She signs the cards and he signs the checks.

A man promised his wife five hundred dollars if she'd stop smoking cigarettes — and she did. Now he's offering her one thousand dollars if she'll stop talking about it.

Sometimes a woman gets a mink coat the hard way — by being nice to her husband.

Trousers are more important to a man than his wife is because there are lots of places he can go without his wife.

A man hates to see a woman in cheap clothes, unless, of course, it's his wife.

Most husbands wouldn't object to their wives wearing their skirts a little shorter if they would wear them a little longer.

Nothing makes a woman's clothes go out of style faster than her husband's raise in salary.

A Nevada husband complains that there are two reasons why his wife won't wear last year's dresses — she doesn't want to, and she can't.

An Arizona man complained, "My wife always has the last word — and all the words before it."

The best way to compliment your wife is frequently.

Attending a convention in your home city is like kissing your own wife.

When a man takes his wife to a convention, he has twice the expense — and half as much fun.

You have to have patience on a diet — especially if it's your wife who's on it.

A diplomat is a man who can make his wife believe she would look fat in a fur coat.

The safest way to disagree with your wife is very quietly.

The most foolhardy way to disagree with your wife is out loud.

A man likes his wife to be just clever enough to comprehend his cleverness and just stupid enough to admire it.

A flimsy excuse is one that your wife can see through.

Some big executives have computers to do all their thinking for them. Some just have wives.

The trouble with some wives is that their idea of exercise is making bank withdrawals.

Extravagance is buying whatever is of no earthly value to your wife.

Faith is better company than imagination for the wife whose husband fails to come home on time.

A family consists of a husband who gets an idea, the kids who say it can't be done, and the wife who does it.

Some women have what it takes to wear the latest fashions — rich husbands.

A man who has faults he doesn't know about probably doesn't listen to his wife.

Note from a fisherman's wife: "Wouldn't it be great if all men showed as much patience with their wives as they do with fish?"

When a man brings his wife flowers for no reason — he'd better have one.

When a man brings flowers to his wife, she figures it's because of something he did or something he forgot to do.

Sign in a Florida flower shop: "Bring flowers home to your wife. She must be mad at you for something."

When a man is generous, the last one to find it out is usually his wife.

A genius is any man who can adjust the thermostat to please his wife.

Nothing makes the average wife so suspicious of her husband as an unexpected gift.

An Oklahoma husband says the only thing his wife ever got secondhand was gossip.

Genuine happiness is when a wife sees a double chin on her husband's old girl friend.

A married couple in Montana is so concerned with their health that whenever they have an argument, she jogs to her mother's.

The honeymoon is over when you realize that everything she says or cooks disagrees with you.

Horse sense is what keeps a woman from being a nag.

Most housewives are very careful about money. They're afraid their husbands might lose it, so they spend it as soon as possible.

An angry Texas wife said to her husband, "You are being deliberately calm."

Did you hear about the wife who lamented, "My husband once showered me with gifts, but lately there's been a long dry-spell."

God gave women a sense of humor — so they could understand the jokes they married.

A Wyoming husband reports that his wife thinks swimming is good for his health. She's always telling him to go jump in the river.

Many a husband comes home from work and hopes the kitchen stove is as warm as the TV set.

When a husband says he can't do something due to circumstances beyond his control, he means his wife won't let him.

Many husbands go broke on the money their wives save at sales.

There are two reasons why husbands leave home — wives who can cook and won't, and wives who can't cook and do.

A South Carolina husband grumbles that his wife has an annoying speech impediment — she won't shut up!

Imagination is something that sits up with a wife when her husband comes home late.

Intuition is what tells a wife her husband has done something wrong before he even thinks of doing it.

The man who says his wife can't take a joke forgets that she took him.

A good wife laughs at her husband's jokes, not because they are clever, but because she is.

Don't judge your wife too harshly for her weaknesses. If she didn't have them, chances are she wouldn't have married you.

If you must go against your better judgment, do it when *she's* not around!

Don't trust your wife's judgment — look at whom she married!

When a woman laughs at her husband's jokes, either they're good jokes or she's a good wife.

Husbands lay down the law, but wives usually repeal it.

Most women don't buy life insurance — they marry it.

A man may be drinking because his wife walked out on him — or because she walked in on him.

Many men give up drinking on account of the wife and bad kidneys.

A husband knows his wife loves him when she returns a dress he can't afford.

To see through a man it takes an x-ray or an ex-wife.

A practical man is one who looks for a wife who already has a fur coat and her appendix out.

The man who owes it all to his wife seldom pays her back.

There would be a lot more happy marriages if husbands tried to understand their wives and wives tried to understand football.

Some men who say they're not interested in marriage have wives sitting home alone to prove it.

Some wives have such good memories that they can even remember things that never happened.

Another reason men don't live as long as women is that they suffer so much waiting around in hospitals for their wives to have babies.

The man who gets his money the hard way is the one who has to ask his wife for it.

When his wife nags the civilized man goes to a club instead of reaching for one.

What America needs is a credit card for wives that self-destructs after fifty dollars.

There are two kinds of people — the "haves" and the "have nots." Or to put it more simply — wives and husbands.

Being polite to your wife only makes her wonder what you've been up to.

Listening to political speeches is a lot like listening to your wife — you know something is going on even though you're not paying much attention to it.

Poverty is contagious. You can get it from your wife.

Try praising your wife occasionally. It may surprise her at first, but she'll appreciate it.

The biggest problem that a wife has is the one sitting across from her at the breakfast table.

One of the problems of modern life is for a husband to teach his wife that even bargains cost money.

Psychiatrists get paid for asking a man the same questions his wife asks him for nothing.

Some husbands quarrel with their wives, and other have learned to say, "Yes, dear."

Perhaps the only way to avoid quarreling with your wife is to let her go her way and you go hers.

Many a retired husband becomes his wife's full-time job.

A super salesman is a husband who can convince his wife that she's too young for a mink coat.

The traveling salesman is a man who wishes he had as much fun on the road as his wife thinks he does.

Science will never discover a way to make a man live long enough to do all the things his wife wants him to do.

Any man who has no secrets from his wife either has no secrets or no wife.

Nothing will drive a sick man back to his job like knowing how much work his wife has lined up for him if he stays home.

If you want your wife to listen to what you have to say, talk in your sleep.

It's a rare husband who tells everybody that his wife snores — but not so with the wife.

Talk to your wife now — the baseball season starts soon.

Behind every successful man stands a proud but surprised wife.

The successful man has a wife who tells him what to do, and a secretary who does it.

When a man becomes a success, his wife takes most of the credit and the government takes most of the cash.

The road to success is filled with women pushing their husbands along.

If at first you don't succeed, try doing it the way your wife told you.

When a woman resorts to tears, she's either trying to get something out of her system or out of her husband.

An Ohio man reports he can't stand TV, but anything that keeps his wife quiet can't be all bad.

If you think you have trouble supporting a wife, just try not supporting her!

Vacations are easy to plan — the boss tells you when, and the wife tells you where.

It's getting harder for some fellows to get back some of their take-home pay after taking it home.

About the only way to keep some of your take-home pay is not to go home.

The next war will be like a fight with your wife — impossible to win it or end it.

A good wife and good health are a man's best wealth.

A wife was the first person to find another use for the rolling pin.

An exhaustive study of police records shows that no wife ever shot her husband while he was doing the dishes.

Treat your wife like a thoroughbred and you won't have an old nag on your hands.

A good wife is one who will wash up when asked and dry up when told.

The handiest thing a wife can have at her fingertips is a good husband.

There's only one thing more expensive than a wife — an exwife!

Why is it that the average wife seldom talks to her husband except when he's reading the daily paper?

A wife will always forgive and forget — but she'll never let you forget that she forgave and forgot.

When a wife gets up in the air, she usually comes down on her husband.

Wife to husband, "I'm going shopping and will be home in about fifty dollars."

It must be wonderful to be a wife. Just imagine knowing that every time there's an argument you are going to win.

A wife doesn't usually check up on her husband. Unless, of course, she doesn't know what he's doing.

Just because a wife is often up in the air and harping about something doesn't necessarily make her an angel.

When your wife hangs on every word you say, she probably wants to see if your story will hold together.

The best thing about some men is their wives.

A wife in Mississippi sighed, "Oh, how I wish I could have my husband recycled."

A wife is absolutely unpredictable. You never know what she's going to ask you to do — once you sit down.

An Arkansas husband thought his wife wore too much makeup — until he saw her without any.

Don't forget that your wife still likes candy and flowers. Show her you remember by mentioning them occasionally.

A good wife is one who believes her husband, who does all the work, should get at least half the credit.

If your wife doesn't treat you as she should, be grateful!

The average wife remembers when and where she got married. What escapes her is *why*.

Wife to henpecked husband: "And if you have anything to say — shut up."

Most husbands want a wife they can love, honor, and display.

Never contradict your wife. Just wait awhile and she will contradict herself.

If you want your wife to pay attention to what you say, address your remarks to another woman.

If a man's wife is his better half, and he marries twice, what then becomes of him?

A wife usually asks for something she knows her husband can't afford so she can compromise on what she really wants.

The best way to surprise your wife is frequently.

Of all the home remedies, a good wife is the best.

There is only one thing more exasperating than a wife who can cook and won't, and that's a wife who can't cook and will.

A wife can often surprise her husband on their wedding anniversary by merely mentioning it.

The wife of a pilot is the only woman who is glad to see her husband down and out.

When a wife chooses her husband's hats and ties for him, it is more than likely that she was the one who chose his wife for him.

A recent draftee claimed exemption on the grounds that he had poor eyesight, and brought his wife along as evidence.

The easiest way to support a wife in the manner to which she's accustomed is to let her keep her job.

All the average wife wants is a roof over her head and the right to raise it occasionally.

The ideal wife is one who sits up with you when you're sick, and puts up with you when you're not.

A man may be able to read his wife like a book, but he can't shut her up like one.

Every man needs a wife because many things go wrong that he can't blame on the government.

A model wife is one who, when she spades the garden, picks up the fish worms for her husband.

The wife who once complained about dishpan hands is now suffering from push-button fingers.

The wife of a prominent businessman took up gardening, but all she grew was tired.

Try praising your wife occasionally. It may surprise her at first, but she'll appreciate it. On the other hand, she may burst out crying — thinking you're drunk again.

The average wife is very talented, since she is endowed with three different voices — a company voice, a telephone voice, and the voice she uses on her husband.

The one thing that proves you can't afford to support a wife is having one.

A smart wife sees through her husband. A good wife sees him through.

Many a wife leads a double life — hers and his.

Most modern-day brides have the makings of a good wife, but they haven't been "kitchen-tested."

When your wife looks appealing, defensive, and beguiling, she's probably bought something awfully expensive.

An Arizona husband says his wife is an after-dinner speaker — also before and during.

How can a husband break even working a four-day week when his wife shops six days a week?

A fellow wearily described his gabby wife, "She doesn't even keep her mouth shut when she's listening."

The economical wife is one who uses only thirty candles on her fortieth birthday cake.

Candy and flowers may serve one of two purposes — they make a wife happy or suspicious.

A husband needs a nagging wife about like a baldheaded man needs a hair dryer.

Many a man met his wife through a dating service — her mother!

Distressed wife to her attorney: "My husband always said everything he has is mine, and now I want it."

A wife is a great comfort to a husband during the distressing times a bachelor never has.

The perfect wife is one who doesn't expect a perfect husband.

Many a wife finds it as hard to find a husband after marriage as before.

Speaking of his wife, a weather forecaster said, "She speaks about 150 words per minute, with gusts up to 190."

Only two things are necessary to keep a wife happy. First, let her think she's having her way. Second, let her have it.

No man should tell his wife any more than he wants to be reminded of later.

A word to the wife is never sufficient.

Most men would like to have a wife who's beautiful, understanding, economical, and a good cook. Unfortunately, the law allows a man only one wife!

The average wife can talk much faster than the average husband can listen.

It's amazing how easy it is for a man to understand a wife — when she isn't his.

A wife cannot make her husband do anything — but she can make him wish he had.

Any man who doesn't know what his wife is thinking hasn't been listening.

No man admires a wife who is constantly pushing the furniture around — with him in it.

A man's wife is his best character witness.

The old-fashioned wife is one who can stay on a budget and a diet.

They now have a lie detector without wires; it's called a wife!

An Alabama husband says his wife is a human dynamo — she charges everything.

Many wives have a wonderful way to make a long story short — they interrupt.

There's a new organization called Wives Anonymous. You phone them and they will send someone over to talk your husband out of watching football on Sunday afternoons.

Some American wives have found a way to blackmail their husbands into taking them out to dinner. They threaten to cook!

It's hard for some of these new wives to get used to being whistled for instead of at.

Wives are like baseball umpires. They don't think you're safe when you're out.

Some wives leave their husbands and take everything; others take everything and don't leave.

The reason a great many men don't bring their boss home for dinner is because she is already there.

Some wives are so concerned about their husband's happiness that they hire private detectives to find out the cause of it.

The trouble with modern wives is that they'd rather mend your ways than your socks.

It's wonderful what some wives can do with an old house — or a new husband.

A great many men still like to think of their wives as they do their religion — neglected, but always there.

Husbands never know what their wives are worth until a judge sets the alimony payments.

Not all wives are suspicious — they know!

Some wives do wonderful things with leftovers — they throw them out.

When a woman listens to what her husband has to say, she's probably on the extension.

A woman spends her life straightening out her two most priceless possessions — her handbag and her husband.

When a woman says she loves the simple things of life, why does she always look at her husband?

A woman in Maryland recently gave birth to her tenth child and has run out of names — to call her husband.

The old-fashioned woman of today is one who tries to make one husband last a lifetime.

A woman's work is never done, especially if she asks her husband to do it.

Just about the time a woman's work is done for the day, her husband asks her to help him with the dishes.

How long a woman works after her marriage is often determined by the number of payments still due on her husband's car.

It's foolish to worry about something beyond your control — such as your wife.

A yawn is nature's provision for making it possible for husbands to open their mouths.

A young man spends at least twelve years in school learning the English language, then becomes a husband and never gets a chance to use it.

Wild Oats

When a boy begins to "feel his oats," he should strongly resist the urge to sow a few wild ones.

A Chicago gangster was recently converted to Christianity. He confessed that he had sown enough wild oats to make a grain deal with Russia.

"Wild oats" take something out of the soil of one's life that no system of crop rotation can restore.

Farmers are so closely inspected by the federal government that the country teen-agers hesitate to sow any wild oats.

The favorite cereal of juvenile delinquents is "Wild Oats."

When a youth begins to sow wild oats it's time for father to start the threshing machine.

A juvenile delinquent sows his wild oats and his parents pray for a crop failure.

"Wild Oats" and "Old Rye" grow in the same field.

Another trouble with juvenile delinquency is that it's harder to say than "just plain cussedness."

The trouble with sowing wild oats is that sometimes the crop has to be "thrashed" out in court.

Perhaps the only real guarantee against crop failure is sowing wild oats.

The price of wheat, wool, and corn goes up and down, but the price of wild oats stays the same.

Wild oats is a juvenile's favorite cereal.

One thing about wild oats — sowing them is not confined to any one season of the year.

Juvenile delinquency is a modern term for what we did when we were kids.

Wild oats need no fertilizer.

If you want a sure crop and a big yield, sow wild oats.

Wild oats take something out of the soil of a man's life that no system of crop rotation can restore.

Many people spend the first six days of each week sowing wild oats — then go to church on Sunday and pray for a crop failure.

If you sow wild oats you must be prepared to take the consequences.

Wisdom

Action is what you don't take when the other guy is bigger than you are.

To profit from good advice requires more wisdom than to give it.

We can give advice but we can't give the wisdom to profit by it.

Advice is that which the wise don't need and fools won't take.

People sensible enough to give good advice are also sensible enough not to.

Years make all of us old and very few of us wise.

Age doesn't always bring wisdom. Sometimes age comes alone.

He is a fool who cannot get angry, but he is a wise man who will not.

When an argument flares up, the wise man quenches it with silence.

When a wise man argues with a woman, he says nothing!

An unusual amount of common sense is sometimes called wisdom.

Heads that are filled with knowledge and wisdom have little space left for conceit.

The courage to speak must be matched by the wisdom to listen.

A person should have enough education so he doesn't have to look up to anyone. He should also have enough to be wise enough not to look down on anyone.

You can buy education, but wisdom is a gift from God.

A wise man learns by the experience of others. An ordinary man learns by his own experience. A fool learns by nobody's experience.

Experience increases our wisdom but doesn't seem to reduce our follies.

A fool tells you what he will do; a boaster, what he has done. The wise man does it and says nothing.

Wise men think without talking; fools reverse the order.

Wise people sometimes change their minds — fools, never.

A wise man can sometimes learn from a fool — as soon as it can be detemined which is which.

A wise man reflects before he speaks; a fool speaks and then reflects on what he has uttered.

There is only one way to acquire wisdom. But when it comes to making a fool of yourself, you have your choice of thousands of different ways.

Wise is the man who fortifies his life with friendships.

It's a wise husband who puts his foot down only to shift positions.

The most effective way to conceal ignorance is to listen and shake your head when asked for an opinion.

A wise man once said that intuition is something that women have in place of common sense.

Knowledge becomes wisdom only after it has been put to practical use.

The fellow who knows more than his boss should be careful to conceal it.

The wise carry their knowledge as they do their watches — not for display but for their own use.

Knowledge comes by taking things apart, but wisdom comes by putting things together.

A little knowledge properly applied is more important than a tremendous number of facts accumulated and not utilized.

Knowledge is knowing a fact. Wisdom is knowing what to do with that fact.

Knowledge is like dynamite — dangerous unless handled wisely.

Not all the teeth put into our laws these days are wisdom teeth.

A wise man will not walk down the road of success with you. He'll simply point you in the right direction.

A wise man never enjoys himself so much, or a fool so little, as when he is alone.

A man is getting along on the road to wisdom when he begins to realize that his opinion is just an opinion.

A wise man gives other people's opinions as much weight as he does his own.

A wise man will make more opportunities than he finds.

It is generally agreed that some people are wise and some otherwise.

It is always wise to put off until tomorrow what we ought not to do at all.

To be thought wise, keep your mouth shut.

You may not be very wise, but if you manage to keep your mouth shut you can fool a lot of people.

One can easily recognize a wise man by the things he doesn't say.

A wise man, even when he is silent, says more than a fool when he talks.

Wise men are not always silent, but they know when to be.

Smart people lose their temper permanently.

Tolerance is the patience shown by a wise man when he listens to an ignoramus.

A person becomes wise by observing what happens when he isn't.

Our wisdom usually comes from our experience, and our experience comes largely from our foolishness.

Why is it that wisdom arrives with old age — too late to do us much good?

Wisdom enables one to be thrifty without being stingy, and generous without being wasteful.

Sometimes a man gets a reputation for wisdom simply because he doesn't have enough money to make a fool of himself.

Wisdom is knowing when and how to appear ignorant.

There's no point in saving wisdom for a rainy day.

You can't pay cash for wisdom. It comes to you on the installment plan.

Wisdom might be defined as having the means to make a fool of yourself and not doing it.

Wisdom is the right use of knowledge.

It is impossible to make wisdom hereditary.

Many a man pursues wisdom, but he doesn't always catch up with it.

An unusual amount of common sense is sometimes called wisdom.

It takes a wise man to know when he is fighting for a principle, or merely defending a prejudice.

Most men wish they were as wise as they think their wives think they are.

To know what to do with what you know is the essence of wisdom.

Knowledge is knowing a fact. Wisdom is knowing what to do with that fact.

If you don't claim too much wisdom, people will give you credit for more than you have.

Knowledge comes by taking things apart, but wisdom comes by putting things together.

Wise men always know more than they tell, but fools tell more than they know.

It is wise to act wise, unless you're otherwise.

Wisdom is divided into two parts — having a great deal to say, and not saying it.

A wise man never plants more garden than his wife can hoe.

Wisdom is nothing more than common sense refined by learning and experience.

A wise man is not as certain of anything as a fool is of everything.

If wisdom were on sale in the open market, the stupid wouldn't even ask the price.

Wisdom is knowing when to speak your mind and when to mind your speech.

Many people might have attained wisdom had they not assumed that they already had it.

As a man grows older and wiser, he talks less and says more.

A wise man will desire no more than he can get honestly, use wisely, and leave cheerfully.

Wisdom is knowledge in action.

In the process of acquiring wisdom, one occasionally makes a fool of himself.

Wisdom never pretends to be wise; foolishness often does.

There is no substitute for wisdom, but the next best thing is silence.

No man is so wise that he knows everything, nor is any man so stupid that he knows nothing.

Knowledge can be memorized. Wisdom must think things through.

A wise man is one who has an open mind and a closed mouth.

Wisdom is learned more from failure than from success.

A wise man is never confused by what he doesn't understand, but a fool is sure to be.

Some folks are wise, and some are otherwise.

The wise man uses his mouth less, eyes more, ears more — and knows more.

No man is so full of wisdom that he has to use his mouth as a safety valve.

You can always tell a wise man by the smart things he does not say.

Half of wisdom is being silent when you have nothing to say.

The door to wisdom swings on hinges of common sense and uncommon thoughts.

It is frightening to consider how little wisdom governs the world.

The word that is sufficient to the wise is usually enough for the rest of us too.

Zeal is fit only for wise men, but is found mostly in fools.

Women
see also Men and Women, Wives

Alimony probably works out right after all. The less a woman deserves it, the more it's worth to be rid of her.

Nowadays it's easy for a bachelor to remain single. Every time he turns his TV set on he hears that most women have stringy hair, rough red hands, bad breath, and are overweight.

A bargain sale is where women fight for merchandise that's reduced in price because nobody wanted it in the first place.

It is well for a girl with a future to avoid the man with a past.

One reason it's often difficult to coax men to go to church is that men aren't interested in what other men are wearing.

The best way to stop smoking cigarettes is to marry a woman who objects to it.

If you don't think smoking cigarettes makes a woman's voice harsh, try dropping cigarette ashes on her rug.

The nicest things in men's clothing are women.

Many women suffer discomfort because they often buy shoes to fit the occasion instead of the feet.

Women buy their husbands loafer shoes and leisure slacks — and then call them lazy when they play the part they're dressed for.

Sign in a women's clothing shop in Laramie, Wyoming: "We have everything for tall women — except tall men."

What the well-dressed woman is wearing this year is less.

Fabulous wealth and fame awaits the man who designs a woman's shoe that's bigger on the inside than it is on the outside.

Men no longer hide behind women's skirts; neither do women.

A girdle is a garment to hold a woman in when she goes out.

Some women say they have nothing to wear — others demonstrate it.

When some women show up in stretch pants, they sure do.

A woman with a new mink coat can't wait to show it to the man she likes most and the woman she likes least.

Nowadays when a girl says her new evening gown is nothing, she means it.

By the time a husband is in shape to buy his wife beautiful clothes, she isn't.

There is now a female computer on the market. You don't ask it anything, but it tells you anyway.

Congress is proof that women don't do all the talking.

Congress will not know what a real filibuster is until women members are in the majority.

The man who said the art of conversation is dead never stood outside a telephone booth waiting for a woman to finish talking.

Women have one main topic of conversation — how thin they used to be, or how thin they're gonna be.

Cosmetics are used by teen-age girls to make them look older sooner, and by their mothers to make them look younger longer.

Cosmetics were used in the Middle Ages; in fact, they're still used in the middle ages.

Cosmetics are a woman's hope of keeping men from reading between the lines.

Courtship is that period during which the female decides whether or not she can do any better.

Many a woman's final decision is not the last one she makes.

Members of the dental profession are the only men on earth who can tell a woman to open or close her mouth and get away with it.

Generally, women don't like the dictionary, because it has the first and the last word.

Some women diet to keep their girlish figure; others, to keep their boyish husbands.

There would be fewer divorces if women hunted for husbands with as much thought as they hunt for bargains.

The efficiency expert is a man whose work, if it were done by a woman, would be called nagging.

The real efficiency expert is the woman who finds what she wants in her handbag at the first swoop.

Real embarrassment is when you tell a girl her stockings are wrinkled when she's not wearing any.

The head of the American family should speak in a loud, firm voice — and she does!

Most women despise flattery, especially when it's directed toward other women.

For every woman who makes a fool out of a man, there's another woman who makes a man out of a fool.

A gentleman is a man who makes it a cinch for a woman to remain a lady.

The man who wants a girl who is good, clever, and beautiful doesn't want one; he wants three.

Girls have an unfair advantage over men. If they can't get what they want by being smart, they get it by being dumb.

Just about the time a woman thinks her work is done, she becomes a grandmother.

Behind every successful man stands a woman and the IRS. One takes the credit, and the other takes the cash.

If women's intuition is so good, how come they ask so many questions?

It is intuition that enables a woman to put two and two together and come up with any answer that suits her.

Intuition is the strange power a woman has that enables her to guess right — and wrong!

The only time a woman's intuition doesn't work is when trying to decide which way to turn at the street intersection.

That so-called female intuition is just the old habit of being suspicious.

Woman's intuition often gets the credit that belongs to eavesdropping.

A woman's intuition is merely a guess that made good.

Of all the laborsaving devices invented for women, none has ever been as popular as a devoted man.

If you think the average American woman can't take a joke, take a look at the average American husband.

If you believe that a woman hasn't a mind of her own, you've never served on a jury.

Any man who laughs at women's clothes has never paid the bill for them.

Women are to blame for men telling lies. They keep asking questions!

A truthful woman is one who does not lie about anything but her age, her weight, and her husband's salary.

Most women don't buy life insurance — they marry it.

There are three things most men love but never understand: females, girls, and women.

A woman cherishes the memory of her first love affair with the same zeal with which a man forgets his.

A woman feels a man's love should be like a toothbrush. It shouldn't be shared.

Every man has three secret wishes — to outsmart racehorses, women, and fish.

Some women have a terrible memory — they remember everything!

Middle age is that time of life when a woman won't tell her age, and a man won't act his.

A woman's mind is like the moon. No matter how often she changes it, there's always a man in it.

The main difference between a wise man and a fool is that a fool's mistakes never teach him anything.

Most mothers aren't really interested in taking their weight off — they just want to rearrange it.

The sweetest music to a woman's ear is another woman playing second fiddle.

All women don't nag. Some aren't married.

The woman who starts putting on her shoes when the preacher says, "And now in conclusion," is a real optimist.

An optimist thinks the woman in the phone booth will be right out because he heard her say goodby.

Doctors have noted that women's feet are getting larger. Presumably that's because they're trying to fill men's shoes.

One woman's poise is another woman's poison.

There's one thing radio and soap operas do for mankind. They temporarily silence women.

All women don't repeat rumors. Some originate them.

The only thing left for science to control are women and the weather.

Most women keep secrets like politicians keep promises.

It's true that a woman can keep a secret — in circulation!

When a woman suffers in silence, she really does.

Women can do almost everything men can — except listen.

When a woman suffers in silence, the phone is probably out of order.

An umpire is like a woman. He makes snap decisions and never reverses them.

It seems that some women would rather be out of money than out of style.

A woman's dress usually stays in style until the next time she goes shopping.

There are some things that never go out of style. A feminine woman is one of them.

Behind every successful man there's a woman — competing for his job.

Some women talk so much that others actually get hoarse listening to them.

If a woman could talk out of the two corners of her mouth at the same time, there would be a great deal said on both sides.

When a man answers the phone he reaches for a pencil; when a woman answers she reaches for a chair.

Women and telephones repeat what they hear, but the telephone repeats it exactly.

557

You can't beat old Father Time — but some women manage to drive a mighty close bargain with him.

Men's troubles are largely due to three things: women, money — and both.

Most women want to hear the truth, no matter how flattering it is.

Sixty percent of the country's wealth is in the hands of women. They're allowing men to hold the other forty percent because their handbags are full.

A woman will usually buy anything she thinks the store is losing money on.

If you think a woman doesn't have a mind of her own, you've never served on a jury.

A woman will go to almost any length to change her width.

It isn't a woman's will that makes her diet — it's her ego.

A San Francisco woman says she's allergic to furs. Every time she sees a friend wearing a new mink coat she gets sick.

If a woman can be a sweetheart, valet, audience, cook, and nurse, she is qualified for marriage.

It matters more what's *in* a woman's face than what's *on* it.

The time isn't far off when a woman won't know any more than a man!

Time and tide waits for no man — but a woman will.

A woman marries the first time for love, the second time for companionship, the third time for support, and the rest of the time from habit.

Why is it that when a woman tells a doctor she's all tired out, he immediately looks at her tongue?

The modern woman seems to go through three stages — her first crush, her first divorce, and her first diet.

It does not take a very bright woman to dazzle some men.

No woman will wear a hat or a dress identical to another woman's — but all rules are off when it comes to mink coats.

A middle-aged woman is one too young for Medicare and too old for men to care.

The smart woman knows how to play tennis, golf, the piano, and dumb.

If you want to make a woman nervous, just put her in a room with a hundred hats and no mirror.

There are very few certainties in this world, but one of them is that no woman is wearing shoes that are too large for her.

By the time a woman is wise enough to select a husband, she has been married for years.

A woman makes up her face and her mind several times a day, and is seldom satisfied with the results of either.

The old-fashioned woman of today is one who tries to make one husband last a lifetime.

A woman likes a man best who has a will of his own — made out in her name.

In many cases when a woman throws herself at a man, she's aiming at his pocketbook.

A woman in Ohio says she's wearing her wedding ring on the wrong finger because she married the wrong man.

If a woman lowers her voice, it means she wants something. If she raises it, it means she didn't get it.

A woman usually underestimates two things — her age and how long it'll take her to get ready to go out.

It's obvious that on some women stretch pants have no other choice.

The best thing about women is that there are so many of them.

It's sad to realize that twenty years from now all of today's beautiful women will be five years older.

It's a toss up whether more married or single women spend their evenings alone.

Women like silent men. They think they're listening.

Some women can talk their way out of anything except a phone booth.

Women distrust men too much in general and not enough in particular.

The man who claims he understands women is a psychologist — or needs one.

Most women won't admit anything over fifty-five — whether it's age or speed.

All women should learn to defend themselves. Most of them will marry someday.

Some women have very little regard for husbands, especially if they already have one.

Some women take a man for better or worse; others for all he has.

Women not only keep a man's nose to the grindstone, but what's worse, they make him turn it.

One of the most difficult tasks in the world is to convince women that even a bargain costs money.

Even if a man could understand women, he still wouldn't believe it.

Some women grow old gracefully — others wear stretch pants.

Some women grow old before their time trying to look young after their time.

Most men need two women in their lives — a secretary to take everything down, and a wife to pick everything up.

Some women are like watches. They may have pretty hands and shining faces, but they're hard to regulate once they're wound up.

Most women have great difficulty finding good husbands — both before and after marriage.

Many married women who waited for the right man to come along will tell you they didn't wait long enough.

Women and their Age

The age of an actress is like the speedometer on a used car — you know it's been set back but you can't tell how far.

It's easy to find out how old a woman is — ask her sister-in-law.

Nothing makes a woman feel older than meeting a baldheaded man who was two grades behind her in school.

The best way to tell a woman's age is in a whisper.

It's not true that women change their minds frequently. Ask a woman her age and she'll give you the same answer for several years.

A man who correctly guesses a woman's age may be smart, but he's not very bright.

A woman rarely realizes her age until her birthday cake begins to look like a small forest fire.

Twenty-nine is a wonderful age for a man to be — and for a woman to stay.

The best place for a woman to hide her age is in the nearest beauty salon.

No matter how clever a woman may be mathematically, it is impossible to make her realize that she is ten years older than she was ten years ago.

Many women won't tell their age, but their age tells on them.

Forty is the most difficult age for a woman to pass. Sometimes it takes her ten years or more!

Any woman who tells the truth about her age is probably applying for Social Security.

When the census-taker asked how old she was, she couldn't remember whether she was thirty-eight or thirty-nine, so she said twenty-five.

Women are usually very secretive about their age, but they'll gladly tell their husbands how old their fur coats are.

Few women admit their age. Few men act theirs.

The average woman of thirty-five — isn't!

One out of every two Americans is under twenty-five, and all women are under thirty.

The least likely way for a middle-aged woman to celebrate her birthday is annually.

The design on a woman's birthday cake is often very beautiful, but the arithmetic is terrible.

When a man has a birthday he may take a day off. When a woman has a birthday she may take as much as five years off.

A woman bakes a child's birthday cake big enough to hold all the candles — and her own small enough not to.

Your wife will drive more carefully if you tell her that in accident reports they always give the driver's age.

There are only two things children will share willingly — communicable diseases and their mother's age.

Courage is what it takes for a woman to show friends the old Family Bible containing the date of her birth.

No one can find as many detours as a woman approaching middle age!

A diplomat remembers a lady's birthday but forgets her age.

A woman usually starts lying about her age when her face begins telling the truth about it.

About the only thing a woman is sure to remember is another woman's age.

A woman is at middle-age when she takes her high school annual out of the bookcase and hides it where the children can't find it.

The least likely way for a middle-aged woman to celebrate her birthday is annually.

Then there was the woman who was cured of her nervousness in one treatment. The doctor told her it was a sign of old age.

She wasn't old, but when she lit the candles on her birthday cake, six people passed out from heat exhaustion.

Most elderly women were born in the year of our Lord only knows.

There'll never be a woman president. No woman will admit to being over thirty-five.

If medical science has done so much to add years to our lives, how come you never meet a woman who's past thirty-five?

If you think a woman can't keep a secret, ask one her age!

One way to get silence at a woman's bridge club is to ask who is the oldest.

Time waits for no man — but it stands still for a woman of thirty-five!

The economical wife is one who uses only thirty candles on her fortieth birthday cake.

A woman likes to be reminded about her birthday — but not which one it is.

A woman usually underestimates two things — her age and how long it'll take her to get ready to go out.

Most women won't admit anything over fifty-five — whether it's age or speed.

Some women grow old before their time trying to look young after their time.

Women Drivers

Nothing confuses a man more than to drive behind a woman who does everything right.

Most women drivers have only two problems — starting and stopping.

"Double jeopardy" is when a woman teaches another woman how to drive.

When a woman driver puts on her directional signal, it probably means she's going to turn one way or the other.

A woman driver in Kansas City told her passenger: "Fasten your seatbelt. I'm getting ready to park."

Always give a woman driver half the road, that is, if you can tell which half she wants.

The safest time to pass a woman driver is when she's parked.

Most of the people who get into trouble every time they turn around are women drivers.

A husband can't figure out which is more dangerous — allowing his wife to drive the new car, or refusing to let her.

Many a traffic jam is caused by a woman driver who signals to make a turn — and does!

Here's to the woman driver. Like charity her left hand "knoweth not what her right hand doeth."

The woman driver wouldn't have so much trouble squeezing into a parking place if she'd just imagine it was a girdle or a pair of shoes.

Once upon a time a man got out of the way of a woman driver because of chivalry. Now, it's sheer panic.

Women can drive as well as men, says a traffic expert. When you think about it, that isn't such a great achievement.

A tree is something that stands still for more than one hundred years, and then suddenly jumps out in front of a woman driver.

A woman driver is known by the fenders she keeps.

Few things are as touching as a woman trying unsuccessfully to drive a car into a garage.

Nothing confuses a man more than to drive behind a woman who does everything right.

The thing that most women dislike about parking is the noisy crash.

A woman driver in Ohio hit a guy and knocked him six feet in the air. Then she sued him for leaving the scene of the accident.

Women not only drive as well as men, but they can do it on either side of the road.

When a woman driver holds out her hand, you can be certain she's either going to turn left, turn right, back up, or stop.

A woman learning to drive a car is making progress when she can park the front end of the car.

Words

Actions speak louder than words — and speak fewer lies.

People may doubt what you say, but they will always believe what you do.

Kind words can never die, but without kind deeds they can sound mighty sick.

Action speaks louder than words but not nearly as often.

Actions speak louder than words — and are just as apt to be misquoted or misinterpreted.

Antique is a magic word that makes something worthless suddenly priceless.

An argument is where two people are trying to get in the last word first.

Most children seldom misquote you; they repeat what you shouldn't have said word for word.

It is much wiser to choose what you say than to say what you choose.

Some people can talk Christianity by the yard but they can't, or won't, walk it by the inch.

The Christian's walk and talk must go together.

A country boy was afraid to go to college because he was told he would be compelled to matriculate.

There are more than 200,000 useless words in the English language, and at some committee meetings you hear all of them.

Superior to a kind thought is a kind word; better than both is a kind deed.

A dictionary is a guide to the spelling of words — provided you know how to spell them.

Virus is a Latin word used by doctors, meaning, "Your guess is as good as mine."

Many a good idea has been smothered to death by words.

Have you ever noticed that the smaller the idea, the bigger the words used to express it?

The soundness of your ideas is more important than the sound of your words.

A lot of indigestion is caused by people having to eat their own words.

Let all your words be kind, and you will always hear kind echoes.

Remember, there has never been an overproduction of kind words.

Learn to speak kind words — nobody resents them.

Never part without loving words. They might be your last.

Always speak kindly to your enemy and maybe he'll come close enough for you to box his ears!

When all the affairs of life are said and done, there is more said than done.

Works, not words, are the proof of love.

There's a new medicine on the market called ZIP. It doesn't cure anything, but at least it's easy to spell.

It is generally agreed that there are over ten thousand useless words in the English language, but a great many of them come in handy in framing a political platform.

Smiles is the longest word in the world. There's a "mile" between the first and the last letters in the word.

Beware of using sharp words. You may have to eat them later on down the line.

The two most beautiful words in the English language are, "Check Enclosed."

No one objects to what you say that's worthwhile — if you say it in few words.

Why use a tub of words to express a spoonful of thought?

The written word can be erased — not so with the spoken word.

Kind words are short to speak, but their echoes are endless.

Blunt words often have the sharpest edge.

It takes only a few words mumbled in church and you're married. It takes only a few words mumbled in your sleep and you're divorced.

The man who has to eat his own words never asks for another serving.

Kind words do not wear out the tongue –– so speak them.

The trouble with some men of few words is they use them over and over.

The sneakiest two words in the English language are "plus tax."

What makes eating your words so difficult is swallowing your pride at the same time.

Words can make a deeper scar than silence can ever heal.

A kind word picks up a man when trouble weighs him down.

It is vain to use words when deeds are expected.

Words and feathers are easily scattered, but not easily gathered up.

The three most difficult words to speak are, "I was mistaken."

Right is a bigger word than either success or failure.

A spoken word and a thrown stone cannot be recalled.

The word that is sufficient to the wise is usually enough for the rest of us too.

When one word leads to another, it generally ends up in a quarrel, a speech, or a dictionary.

Another form of wastefulness is the expenditure of words beyond the income of ideas.

The man of few words doesn't have to take many of them back.

Probably a man's most profitable words are those spent praising his wife.

Many wise words are spoken in jest, but they don't compare with the number of foolish words spoken in earnest.

Words sometimes serve as a smoke screen to obscure the truth, rather than as a searchlight to reveal it.

There has never been an overproduction of kind words.

In the use of words, quality is more important than quantity.

One thing you can give and still keep is your word.

Those who have the most to say usually say it with the fewest words.

A multiplicity of words indicates poverty of thought.

Fire is the word that empties buildings, and *sale* is the word that fills them.

Strong and bitter words indicate a weak cause.

Of all the one hundred thousand useless words in the English language, you hear almost all of them at some committee meetings.

The word you're forced to get in edgewise is apt to be sharp.

Etc. is a perfect word — when you can't think of the right one.

People who are forced to eat their own words should find it a good diet to reduce their big mouths.

Our words may hide our thoughts, but our actions will reveal them.

A new word is "smearsay," meaning heresay with a smear.

Words should be used as tools of communication and not as a substitute for action.

Words are seductive and dangerous material and should be used with caution.

The four most important words in the English language are: I, me, mine, and money.

When you break your word, you break something that cannot be mended.

Work

Some fellows dream of worthy accomplishments, while others stay awake and do them.

If you want a place in the sun, you will have to expect some blisters.

Just over the hill is a beautiful valley, but you must climb the hill to see it.

God gives us the ingredients for our daily bread, but He expects us to do the baking.

Our ship would come in much sooner if we'd only swim out to meet it.

You can often gauge a man's ambition by whether he hates his alarm clock or considers it his dear friend.

Ambition never gets anywhere until it forms a partnership with work.

Watch out for ambition! It can get you into a lot of hard work.

America's number one energy crisis is Monday morning.

If you want to go far in business, you'll have to stay close to it.

You can tell a man's character by what he turns up when offered a job — his nose or his sleeves.

Christianity is a roll-up-your-sleeves religion.

Christianity, like a watch, needs to be wound regularly if it is to be kept running.

What the church needs is more men who talk less and work more.

What the church needs today is more calloused hands and fewer calloused hearts.

It seems that our modern churches are full of willing people; some are willing to work, and others are willing to let them.

There are two periods when Congress does no business: one is before the holidays; and the other, after.

The dentist is one guy who's always ready to get back to the old grind.

If you burn the candle at both ends you are not as bright as you think.

Lots of people don't have to look at the world through rose-colored glasses — their eyes are already bloodshot.

No dream comes true until you wake up and go to work.

A drunkard can't make both ends meet because he's too busy making one end drink.

Economists predict the year ahead will reward hard workers. What a frightening outlook for many!

We won't go far without enthusiasm, but neither will we go far if that's all we have.

Enthusiasm for hard work is most sincerely expressed by the person who is paying for it.

Don't envy anybody. Every person has something no other person has. Develop that one thing and make it outstanding.

An executive is one who hires others to do the work he's supposed to do.

Often an expert is the fellow you employ to do what you'd rather not.

Families that pray together stay together, and families that work together — eat.

The farmer doesn't go to work. He wakes up every morning surrounded by it.

The American farmer prefers getting bent from hard work rather than getting crooked from trying to avoid it.

Mankind's worst enemy is fear — of work!

Most modern girls detest four-letter words such as wash, iron, cook, and dust.

The modern girl's hair may look like a mop, but that doesn't seem to worry her — she doesn't know what a mop looks like.

For some girls the idea of housework is to sweep the floor with a glance.

God created the world in six days — which probably never could have happened if there had been labor unions.

Happiness is the result of being too busy to be miserable.

A man has happiness in the palm of his hands if he can fill his days with real work and his nights with real rest.

The happiest people are those who are too busy to notice whether they are happy or not.

The plain fact is that human beings are happy only when they are striving for something worthwhile.

A great deal of poor health in this country may be attributed to heavy meals and light work.

Sign at highway construction site: "Men working — we hope."

The ideal of some men is to marry a rich girl who is too proud to have her husband work.

Many people think life would be so much more enjoyable if we didn't have to work our way through it.

Life is like a poker game — if you don't put anything in the pot, there won't be anything to take out.

We get out of life what we put into it — that's the trouble!

To love and to labor is the sum of life; and, yet, how many think they are living when they neither love nor labor?

A task worth doing and friends worth having make life worthwhile.

Luck is a wonderful thing. The harder a person works, the more of it he seems to have.

Good luck is a lazy man's estimate of a worker's success.

Good luck often has the odor of perspiration about it.

It's hard to recognize good luck. It looks so much like something you've earned!

The best medicine in the world is to love your work and your enemies.

There are a lot of men in this world who started at the bottom — and stayed there.

Most men can't tell the difference between working up steam and generating fog.

Nervous prostration was unknown when people worked more and worried less.

You can qualify as an old-timer if you can remember when people didn't need any more than a day to do a day's work.

The reason a lot of people can't find opportunity is that it is often disguised as hard work.

Even when opportunity knocks, a man still has to get off his seat and open the door.

Opportunity has the uncanny habit of favoring those who have paid the price of years of preparation.

Nothing worthwhile is achieved without patience, labor, and disappointment.

The man of the hour spent many days and nights getting there.

Most of us would be in more trouble than we are if all our prayers had been answered.

Most of us pray for more things than we are willing to work for.

The best kind of pride is that which compels a man to do his best work — even when no one is looking.

Heads, hearts, and hands could settle the world's problems better than arms.

Religion is like a wheelbarrow — you have to push it.

What's all this talk about getting rich the hard way? Is there any other way?

The trouble with the road to riches these days is there are too many toll booths along the way.

Selling is quite easy if you work hard enough at it.

A successful man continues to look for work after he has found a job.

Behind every successful man there are usually a lot of unsuccessful years.

Many people carefully avoid discovering the secret of success because deep down they suspect the secret may be hard work.

You don't have to lie awake nights to succeed; just stay awake days.

All men want to succeed, but some men want to succeed so much they're willing to work to achieve it.

The dictionary is the only place where success comes before work.

Success is sweet, but its secret is sweat.

No one has yet climbed the ladder of success with his hands in his pockets.

Most people do only what they are required to do, but successful people do a little more.

You won't find many rules for success that will work unless you do.

One thing that keeps a lot of people from being a success is work.

If you want to succeed, wear out two pairs of shoes to every suit.

Industry is the mother of success — luck, a distant relative.

Success is the result of backbone, not wishbone.

If you gave the same amount of time to your work as you do your church, how long would you hold your job?

The minimum wage has gone up considerably. Wouldn't it be wonderful if we could just do something about the minimum effort?

The hardest work in the world is that which should have been done yesterday.

A woman's work is never done, especially if she asks her husband to do it.

People who do a good day's work won't have much competition.

The only thing you can get without work is debt.

When you see some people work you wonder what they'll do when they retire.

The hardest work some people do is describing the work they do.

The trouble with a lot of folks these days is they want to have their work cut out for them — completely!

Hard work never killed anybody, but some of us sure don't want to take the chance of being the first victim.

Sign in a supermarket in Springfield, Illinois: "Wanted — clerk to work eight hours a day to replace one who didn't."

Work, of course, is the cure for unrest, but there are lots of people who think the remedy is worse than the disease.

July is the time of year when the fellow who worked so hard to graduate wonders what the hurry was.

If you think you work harder than the average worker, you're an average worker.

The reason why so many men can't work any harder in the office is because they wear leisure suits.

Work is one of the greatest things in the world. So don't you think we should save some of it for tomorrow?

Unless we all work for the common good there won't be any.

Everybody has to work for the government — but only the bureaucrats get paid for it.

If you do all the work and somebody else gets the credit — he's probably your boss.

It is better to become bent from hard work than to become crooked without it.

It's predicted that in twenty years people will work two days a week and relax five. Some employers think that's happening now.

The thing most of us don't like about work is that it's so daily.

Folks keep saying that hard work never killed anybody. Come to think of it, we never heard of anybody resting themselves to death either.

The trouble with getting to work on time is that it makes the day so long.

A lot of people are already working a four day week, though it takes them five or six days to do it.

Committee work is like a soft chair — easy to get into but hard to get out of.

Hard work is usually an accumulation of easy things that should have been done last week.

Just about the time a woman's work is done for the day, her husband asks her to help him with the dishes.

Hard work never hurts people who don't do any.

The world's work must be done by some of us. We can't all be politicians and efficiency experts.

Most people like hard work. This is particularly true when they're paying for it.

Organized labor is all right until it becomes organized loafing.

A few people are enthusiastic about work, but most of the time they're the bosses.

The Lord didn't burden us with work. He blessed us with it.

Working hard means going all out until you're all in.

565

About the only way work can kill a fellow is to scare him to death.

Work isn't work if you like it.

Never buy anything with a handle on it. It might mean work!

Hard work is the yeast that raises the dough.

Two things deprive people of their peace of mind: work unfinished, and work not yet begun.

Many people don't mind going to work — it's the long wait until quitting time that irritates them.

Fortunately, in our work there is always a choice. We can do it willingly or unwillingly.

The advantage of working day and night is that you can probably earn enough to pay the doctor when you have a nervous breakdown.

Work is a tonic that contains no habit-forming drugs.

Men who dream of hitching their wagon to a star would be better off to hitch up their pants and go to work.

Work hard. The job you save may be your own.

Some will give an honest day's work even if it takes them all week to do it.

There seems to be no cure for those who are allergic to work.

It's simply fantastic the amount of work you can get done if you don't do anything else.

Housework is something you do that nobody notices unless you don't do it.

Some people are so superstitious they won't work any week that has a Friday in it.

One blessing in being poor, honest, and hardworking is that nobody envies you.

It will be a great day when everybody who has a job is working.

Hard work rarely kills because so few give it a chance.

Work is the meat of life; pleasure, the dessert.

One of the hardest ways to make a living is to work for it.

Almost any system will work if the people behind it will.

Nothing is hard work unless there's something else you'd rather do.

All things come to him who goes after what the other fellow waits for.

Speaking of tranquilizers, even back in grandpa's day there was something to make a fellow sleep — they called it work.

A man should work eight hours and sleep eight hours, but not the same eight hours.

Nowadays when you miss a day's work the government loses as much as you do.

About the only folks who work like a horse these days have a boss riding them.

One way to boost production in this country would be to put the labor bosses to work.

A man's work is a portrait of himself.

Many people are willing to do any kind of work which does not require standing, sitting, bending, or lying down.

It's extremely difficult for men of different nations to work together when they carry a rifle on one shoulder and a chip on the other.

The young man who is able to work his way through college is a pretty good bet to be able to work his way through life.

The man who doesn't do more than he's paid for isn't worth what he gets.

Father must work for two reasons: Christmas and vacation.

Human beings, like chickens, thrive best when they have to scratch for what they get.

Some people are too heavy for light work, and others are too light for heavy work.

If we take care of our work, the results of our work will take care of us.

Hard work won't kill a fellow if he can stay far enough away from it.

There's a difference between working every day and having a perfect attendance record.

The more steam you put behind your work, the louder you can whistle when it's done.

Dodging work is the hardest work of all and yields the poorest returns.

The best way to criticize the other fellow's work is to do yours better.

566

With so many parking difficulties, household errands, and golf, it's almost impossible for a man to find any time for his work.

Most people like work. It fascinates them. They can sit and look at it for hours.

The only state that permits a woman to work more than eight hours a day is the state of matrimony.

It may be that hard work is respectable, but that doesn't make it popular.

Do what you are told to do and then some. It's the "then some" that gets your salary raised.

If hard work is the key to success, most people would rather pick the lock.

Faith may move mountains, but only hard work can put a tunnel through.

The thing that makes it so tough to find fault with some people's work is that they never do any.

Hard work never hurt anybody who happened to be wealthy enough to hire somebody else to do it.

Work is the annoyance people have to endure between coffee breaks.

How long a woman works after her marriage is often determined by the number of payments still due on her husband's car.

Many years ago they didn't put up signs reading, "Men Working," but back then you could tell what they were doing.

It is especially hard to work for money you've already spent for something you didn't need.

Hard work and devotion to duty will surely get you a promotion — unless, of course, the boss has a relative who wants the job.

We can't remember seeing a man get bent over from hard work, but we've seen a lot of them go broke without it.

If you think hard work never hurt anybody, you've never paid for any.

Keeping on top of your work is better than letting your work get on top of you.

Work is the best thing ever invented for killing time.

Worry kills more people than work. Some people play it safe by doing neither.

The reason worry kills more people than work is that people worry more than they work.

Grandpa and grandma were too busy scratching for a living to need books on how to stop worrying.

Two good openings for a young man are the legs in a pair of overalls.

World

The world has finally achieved perpetual commotion.

You need the church, the church needs you, the world needs both.

When you consider the shape it's in, it's no longer a compliment to be told someone thinks the world of you.

The cemeteries are full of people who thought the world couldn't get along without them.

After a man makes his mark in the world, a lot of people will come around with an eraser.

It's difficult to contend that man hasn't descended from some sort of an animal as long as one half of the world goosesteps and the other half pussyfoots.

The world is round so that friendship may encircle it.

Friendship is the only cement that will hold the world together.

A lot of people are worrying about the future of the world, as though it had one.

A grouch thinks the world is against him — and it is.

In a world where death is, we should have no time to hate.

Judging from the general behavior we see in this world, hell must be experiencing a population explosion.

An idea is the only lever which really moves the world.

By improving yourself the world is made better.

If the world laughs at you, laugh right back — it's as funny as you are.

The world needs a new law that would prevent any country from waging war unless it pays for it in advance.

It it weren't for the optimist, the pessimist would never know how happy he isn't.

Foreign dictators are difficult to figure out. You can never tell whether they are smart men bluffing or imbeciles who mean it.

The biggest problem in the world could have been settled when it was small.

Never before has the world had so many big problems and so many little minds.

Our national and international problems would soon fade away if we could find a key to fit the deadlock.

With all the world's problems, it's nice to read the etiquette columns and learn there are still a few people whose chief worry is using the wrong fork.

The problems of the world are changing so fast that some of them become obsolete before they can cause any serious trouble.

The world has so many problems that if Moses had come down from Mount Sinai today — the two tablets he carried would be aspirin.

World problems are so confusing that even computers are asking questions.

The world could certainly use more vision and less television.

Thoughts rule the world.

If nations began telling each other nothing but the truth, peace would immediately vanish from the earth.

While it takes all kinds of people to make a world, you can't blame everything on that.

The way the world is going, every day will soon be the anniversary of something awful.

Look on the world as a big fruit cake. It wouldn't be complete without a few nuts in it.

In Columbus's day few believed the world was round. These days the question is: How long will it be around?

Why not take the world as it is, not as it should be?

Nothing is certain in this world except death, taxes, and teen-agers.

The world is a rat race, and the rats seem to be winning.

Anybody who says this is a man's world is probably not too bright about other things either.

Isn't it wonderful to have such a beautiful world to suffer in?

Too many people want to build a better world by acting only in a foreman's capacity.

If all the world's a stage, it's about time for a new plot.

What a nice world this world would be if we loved others as we love ourselves.

The world doesn't owe anybody anything — it was here first.

You can't clean up this old world with soft soap; it takes grit.

Once we thought the world was flat, then round. Now we know a lot of it is crooked.

It's a small world, once you've made the long trip to the airport.

Columbus proved the world was round, but that has nothing to do with the shape the world is in these days.

If it's true the world is getting smaller, why do they continue to raise the price of postage?

How different the world would be if we did as well today as we expect to do tomorrow.

"All the world is a stage" and some of us are getting stage fright.

The only thing wrong with the world is the people.

Wouldn't it be ironic if the world ended before man can destroy it?

The world isn't getting smaller — just some of the people who inhabit it.

Maybe one of the things wrong with the world is that there are not enough leaders of men and too many chasers of women.

If this is a man's world it's because women don't want it.

What a different world this would be if people would only magnify their blessings the way they do their troubles.

If you think the world is all wrong, remember that it contains people like you.

Nowadays the world revolves on its taxes.

This isn't such a bad world after all — once you get used to being nervous about everything.

What the world needs is an amplifier for the still, small voice.

If the creation of the world had been a federal project it probably would have taken six years instead of six days.

When the world starts making sense to you, it's time to consult your psychiatrist.

The world has too many cranks and not enough self-starters.

We can only change the world by changing men.

The trouble with the world is that so many people who stand up for their rights fall down miserably on their duties.

If we wish to make a new world we have the material ready. The first one was also made out of chaos.

All the world lives in two tents: content and discontent.

The world is composed of givers and takers. The takers may eat better, but the givers sleep better.

Things are pretty well evened up in this world. Other people's troubles are not as bad as ours, but their children are a lot worse.

The world owes you a living, but only when you have earned it.

If it takes all kinds of people to make a world, it seems as if there are still some we haven't got.

It's a weird world. The strong take away from the weak, the clever take away from the strong, and the government takes away from everybody.

The world at its worst needs the church at its best.

If it's such a small world, why does it cost so much to run it?

The world changes so fast that a man couldn't be wrong all the time even if he tried.

"All the world is a stage," and most of us are underrehearsed.

It's difficult to tell *What* and *When* the world is coming to.

The world has always acted on the principle that one good kick deserves another.

Considering its age, this is a mighty fast world.

The world doesn't owe you a living or a loving. You must earn both.

How can such a small world get into so much trouble?

The world is not a madhouse as some people claim. The occupants of a madhouse are kept under control.

Everybody agrees that the world is in a state of ferment, but no one can tell whether the results will be champagne or vinegar.

The first thing every morning when we get out of bed we look in the newspaper to see if the world is still here.

Most folks don't know where the world is going and have concluded the only thing they can do is just hang on for the ride.

Nothing makes us wonder if this is really a man's world as much as watching him trying to run it.

The world would be immensely improved if people would do nothing when they have nothing to do.

If the world blew itself up, the last audible voice would be that of an expert saying it couldn't be done.

The world is divided into people who do things and people who get the credit.

If someone offers you the world on a silver platter, take the platter!

The world always looks brighter from behind a smile.

If the world is a stage, it's putting on a mighty poor show.

The world was created in six days — no Senate confirmation being necessary.

The trouble with the world is that there are too many clowns who aren't in the circus.

Some people call the world dirty because they're too lazy to clean their windows, windshields, and glasses.

The world we live in is old-fashioned. It still judges a man by what he does.

Give the world what it needs and it will supply yours.

The world's a stage all right, with husbands playing the supporting role.

A bitter world cannot be sweetened by a sour religion.

The world would be happier if its leaders had more vision and fewer nightmares.

This will be a better world when the power of love replaces the love of power.

A different world cannot be built by indifferent people.

It's a strange world in which you give others some of your lip and wind up with a thicker one than you started with.

If you worry about missing the boat, remember the Titanic!

People who like to worry have a greater and more varied number of things to choose from than ever before.

Many people seem to be worried about the end of the world — others are just worried about the end of the month.

Probably the most powerful head of steam ever created is that of young people trying to set on fire a world that is all wet.

Worry

Doing beats stewing.

There will always be enough for today without taking on yesterday and tomorrow's burdens.

One nice thing about a college education is that it enables us to worry more intelligently about things all over the world.

With computers doing our thinking, all we need now is a worrying machine.

Molehills of debt build mountains of worry.

A good education is important. It enables you to pick out the most important things to worry about.

An educated man will sit up all night and worry over things a fool never dreamed of.

Every tomorrow has two handles. We can take hold of it by the handle of anxiety, or by the handle of faith.

When you become wrinkled with care and worry, it's time to have your *faith* lifted.

A lot of people who are worrying about the future ought to be preparing for it.

Stop fretting about the future — there'll probably be as much of it as you can stand when you get there.

Don't take tomorrow to bed with you.

Why worry about the future? Between the bomb and pollution, there may not be any.

More people worry about the future than prepare for it.

There is no need to nervously pace the deck of the ship of life when the Great Pilot is at the wheel.

Why worry if your hair falls out? Suppose it ached and you had to have it pulled like teeth.

A harried housewife in Nebraska sighed, "I have so many problems that if something terrible happened to me it would be at least two weeks before I could get around to worrying about it."

If you live within your income you'll live without worry — and without a lot of other things.

By the time a fellow is fixed for life during these trying times, he has just about worried himself to death.

The best way to live a long life is to get somebody to do the worrying for you.

The greatest mistake you can make in this life is to be constantly fearful you will make one.

Nervous prostration was unknown when people worked more and worried less.

An optimist is a person who's cheerful about other people's worries.

True patience means waiting without worrying.

A problem not worth praying about is not worth worrying about.

Instead of counting their blessings many people magnify their problems.

Progress is largely a matter of discarding old worries and taking on new ones.

Psychiatrists don't have to worry as long as other people do.

Today is the tomorrow you worried about yesterday.

Many people have ulcers these days — caused by mountain climbing over molehills.

Wealth is a worry if you have it, and a worry if you don't have it.

If you can't help worrying, remember that worrying can't help you either.

Worry kills more people than work. Some people play it safe by doing neither.

Men usually worry more about losing their hair than their heads.

Worry never robs tomorrow of its sorrows; it only saps today of its strength.

Don't worry if your job is small and your rewards few; remember that the mighty oak was once a nut like you.

And there was the poor old man who worried so much about his debts that the hair began to fall out of his wig.

At least these days you don't have to worry about getting more than you bargained for.

The average husband worries about what his wife spends and what the government spends. The difference is he's not afraid to criticize the government.

Medical authorities tell us to get up early every morning so we can have our worrying done before breakfast.

Folks worry — either about having too little or about losing what they have.

Worry is as useless as sawing sawdust.

The American people should worry less about the population explosion and more about the tax explosion.

There's one sure way to make a man worry — tell him not to.

Blessed is the man who is too busy to worry in the daytime and too sleepy to worry at night.

It doesn't make sense to worry about the future. Why open an umbrella before it starts to rain?

Never worry about the tide that is going out. It always comes back.

Anyone who doesn't worry about the world situation these days must be getting lousy reception on his television set.

Worry can't change the past, but it can ruin the present.

"Don't worry" is a better motto if you add the word "others."

Perpetual worry will get you to one place ahead of time — the cemetery.

Worry is interest paid on trouble before it falls due.

Those who live in a worry invite death in a hurry.

People who like to worry have a greater and more varied number of things to choose from than ever before.

Worry is like a good rocking chair — it will give you something to do, but it won't get you anywhere.

There's not a worry in the world worth the worry.

Why worry about the future? The present is more than most of us can handle.

Don't worry about the job you don't like. Someone else will soon have it.

Worry never changes a single thing — except the worrier.

The fellow who never worries may not be smart enough to know what it's all about.

One good reason for not worrying is that you won't feel like a fool when things turn out all right.

It's foolish to worry about something beyond your control — such as your wife.

Worry never accomplishes anything except wrinkles — which gives you another thing to worry about.

Schedule all your worrying for a specific half hour about the middle of the day — then take a nap during that period.

There is no point in worrying about forgetting things as your grow older because you'll soon forget what you forgot.

Many people seem to be worried about the end of the world — others are just worried about the end of the month.

One good rule for living is not to worry about the future until we have learned to manage the present.

The reason worry kills more people than work is that people worry more than they work.

We worry about the things we want to do but can't, instead of doing that which we should — but don't.

People would worry less about what others think of them if they only realized how seldom they do.

When you're robbed by worry, it's always an inside job.

Things are really tough when you have so many worries that a new one has to be kept waiting until you can get around to it.

About the only way a fellow can keep from worrying these days is to keep his mind off his thoughts!

To worry about what we can't help is useless; to wory about what we can help is stupid.

The only person who can afford to worry is the one who doesn't need to.

Don't worry too much about what lies ahead. Go as far as you can see, and when you get there, you can see farther.

Grandpa and grandma were too busy scratching for a living to need books on how to stop worrying.

Worry often gives a small thing a big shadow.

Among the chief worries of today's business executives is the large number of unemployed still on the payrolls.

Many modern dads worry more about their golf swing than they do their offspring.

Things that never happen seem to worry us most.

The man who worries about the condition of the world will never run out of things to worry about.

Half of the things we worry about never happen, and the other half will happen anyway — so why worry?

Don't worry about your station in life; somebody is certain to tell you where to get off.

Worry reminds us of a treadmill — it can wear you to a frazzle and you still don't get anywhere.

Worries are mostly about yesterday and to-morrow.

A lot of folks who are worrying about fat around the waist ought to be worrying about fat between the ears.

When a fellow says there's nothing to worry about, somebody had better start worrying about him.

A scholar will sit up all night worrying over things a fool never dreamed of.

Worship

If God is small enough for us to understand, He isn't big enough for us to worship.

Too many try to get something from worship without putting anything into it.

Most folks seem to want the right to worship and to make others worship the same way.

Satan doesn't care what we worship, as long as we don't worship God.

If we are going to fight for the liberty to worship, we ought to make use of that liberty.

A place of worship should be of such character that it will be easy for men to find God and difficult for them to forget Him.

Y

Yawns   Youth

Yawns

Advertising is what transforms a yawn into a yearn.

There's a small town in Nevada so dull and unexciting that the favorite pastime is yawning.

Home is a place where you don't have to stifle a yawn and try to cover it up with a smile.

The safest way to spend a holiday is to sit at home and yawn.

If you can't think of a snappy retort, a carefully concealed yawn is often as good and much less dangerous.

A yawn is nature's provision for making it possible for husbands to open their mouths.

Yawning is usually the act of a person inadvertently opening his mouth when he wishes others would shut theirs.

If you think nothing is impossible, try yawning with your mouth closed.

A polite person seldom yawns in the presence of others — and another polite person never notices it when he does.

There is one protest sign that is understood the world over — a stifled yawn.

A yawn is sometimes a silent shout.

A yawn may not be polite, but it lets everybody know how you feel.

Youth

Age is the best possible fire extinguisher for flaming youth.

Young men who leave home to set the world on fire usually have to come back home for more matches.

You are young only once. If you act foolish after that you'll have to find some other excuse.

Youth and beauty fade; character endures forever.

In youth we run into difficulties. In old age difficulties run into us.

The worst danger that confronts the younger generation is the example set by the older generation.

There may be no fool like an old fool, but some members of our younger generation seem to be doing a pretty good job.

The young people of the United States squander over ten billion dollars a year on games of chance. This does not include weddings, starting a business, passing cars on a hill, or buying a television set.

In this life the old believe everything, the middle-aged suspect everything, and the young know everything.

One of the nice things about growing old is that, with all the emphasis on youth, you can go pretty much unnoticed.

The accent may be on youth these days, but the stress is still on the parents.

A young man's toughest problem is to find a girl attractive enough to please him and dumb enough to like him.

Reputation is something to live up to in your youth and to live down in your old age.

The prayer of modern youth seems to be, "Lord, lead us not into temptation. Just tell us where it is and we'll find it."

Old men declare wars, but it is youth that must fight them.

Today's youth has very special problems — like the girl who lost one of her contact lenses in her boyfriend's beard.

Today young people start going steady with the opposite sex as soon as they learn there is one.

One of the advantages of being young is that you don't let common sense get in the way of doing things everybody else knows are impossible.

A young man spends at least twelve years in school learning the English language, then becomes a husband and never gets a chance to use it.

Too many youngsters who have passed their driving test think they can pass anything.

Modern youth is looking for new answers so they can question them.

A gypsy youth in Chicago plans to run away from home just as soon as his parents get one.

A misspent youth may result in a tragic old age.

Getting the baby to sleep is most difficult when she is eighteen years old.

A great many young men are like Easter hats — mostly trimmings.

Two good openings for a young man are the legs in a pair of overalls.

Some boys seem to have dentists confused with barbers — they see both twice a year.

Being young comes only once in life. The trick is to make it last as long as you can.

How far a young man goes these days depends on how much gas was left in the car.

What kids need today is plenty of LSD — Love, Security, and Discipline.

Just a glance at this generation makes us realize we're living in hair-raising times.

The typical American youth is always ready to give those who are older than himself the full benefit of his inexperience.

Probably the most powerful head of steam ever created is that of young people trying to set on fire a world that is all wet.

Young man, don't continue to tell your best girl friend that you are unworthy of her. Let it be a surprise!

The young people of today are tomorrow's leaders, but we sometimes wonder whether they're going to be followed or chased.

Youth is like fashion. Both fade quickly.

The real secret of looking young is being young.

About the only way to stay young is to live honestly, eat sensibly, sleep well, work hard, worship regularly, and lie about your age.

People who wonder where this generation is headed will do well to consider where it came from.

The younger generation knows more about everything than the old folks — except making a living.

It seems a lot of young people want an occupation that doesn't keep them occupied.

We expect youth to be strong, courageous, and prepared to pay even more taxes than their fathers did.

Our young people of today seem to be confused. Half of them extol the virtue of "getting it all together," while the other half are busy taking it all apart.

There's not much wrong with the younger generation that becoming a parent and a taxpayer won't cure.

Let's stop criticizing the younger generation. If we can't keep up with them we can at least get behind them.

Some members of the younger generation believe that elbow grease is a petroleum product.

At a certain period in the life of every youth, he wonders how such dull parents produced such a bright child.

Our tastes change as we mature. Little girls like painted dolls; little boys like soldiers. When they grow up, the girls like the soldiers and the boys like the painted dolls.

This is the day of youth, and they can have it. They'll age rapidly when taxpaying time starts.

The worst danger facing the younger generation is the example of the older generation.

A young man is young only once, but he can stay immature indefinitely.

If the younger generation doesn't know where it's going, it must be following in its father's footsteps.

Youth isn't satisfied with a new deal — they want the whole deck.

No high school boy ever expects to grow up and be as "dumb" as his parents.

Did you hear about the young fellow who spent two years trying to find himself? He got a haircut and there he was!

Young people these days find it hard to believe that years ago most people wouldn't buy or do anything they couldn't afford.

The young people of today are no worse than we were; they just have more and different ways of making fools of themselves.

It must be wonderful to be young enough to know everything.

You are only young once. After that you merely think you are.

Modern youth has been tried and found wanting — everything under the sun.

Young folks of today have the disadvantage
of having too many advantages.

Youth is that period when we're looking for
greener fields. Middle age is when we can
hardly mow what we've got.

Z

Zeal

Zeal

The cross is easier to the Christian who takes it up than to the one who drags it along.

There's always a good crop of food for thought. What we need is enough enthusiasm to harvest it.

He who has no fire in himself cannot warm others.

Zeal without knowledge is like heat without light.

There is no zeal so intemperate and cruel as that which is backed by ignorance.

Zeal without knowledge is fanaticism.

Zeal is fit only for wise men, but is found mostly in fools.

If people were more zealous and less jealous, this world would be a much better place in which to live.

Zeal without knowledge is the sister of folly.